ARTHUR HONEGGER

ARTHUR HONEGGER

by
Harry Halbreich

Translated by
Roger Nichols

Reinhard G. Pauly, General Editor

AMADEUS PRESS
Portland, Oregon

Translation of this book into English was made possible by grants from
the French government, the Paul Sacher Foundation,
and the Pro Helvetia Foundation, Arts Council of Switzerland.

Music examples for this edition rendered by Peter Huszagh.
Music examples for the original French edition rendered by Gunnar Cohrs.

ISBN 1-57467-041-7

Printed in Hong Kong

Translation published in 1999 by
Amadeus Press (an imprint of Timber Press, Inc.)
The Haseltine Building
133 S.W. Second Avenue, Suite 450
Portland, Oregon 97204, U.S.A.

Library of Congress Cataloging-in-Publication Data

Halbreich, Harry
[Arthur Honegger, un musicien dans la cité des hommes. English]
Arthur Honegger / by Harry Halbreich; translated by Roger Nichols;
Reinhard G. Pauly, general editor.
    p.   cm.
Translation of: Arthur Honegger, un musicien dans la cité des hommnes.
Discography: p.
Includes bibliographical references and indexes.
ISBN 1-57467-041-7
1. Honegger, Arthur, 1892–1955. 2. Composers—Biography. 3. Honegger,
Arthur, 1892–1955—Bibliography. I. Pauly, Reinhard G. II. Title.
ML410.H79H313 1999
780'.92—dc21
[B]   98-14759
CIP
MN

Contents

Part Three: GATHERING THE THREADS 565

Photographs follow page 176

In te Domine speravi
Non confundar in aeternum

(In Thee, Lord, have I trusted,
Let me never be confounded)

To Paul Sacher • To Pascale Honegger • To Elisabeth Buzzard
To Switzerland, in memory of 6 October 1942

To Paul Sacher, man of vision and action, man of heart and culture, man of enthusiasm and faith in the Spirit, who put his trust in me a second time, more than a quarter of a century after helping me to produce my book on Bohuslav Martinů. Many years ago he expressed his wish to see me write the present volume. The moment I was ready to start work, his generosity allowed me to devote myself to it entirely. He enabled me to pursue my research at the foundation that bears his name, and gave me access to the vast number of letters sent to him by a composer to whom, as he himself admits, he has always felt closer than any other.

To Pascale Honegger, a woman of enthusiasm and strong will, who has also contributed in large measure to this project to which she has given her blessing. She has allowed me full access to the immense treasure store of autograph scores, letters, and personal documents that she administers so capably. Her generosity allowed the major part of this volume to be written in the peaceful retreat of Arolla, in the heart of the Upper Valais, some seven thousand feet up in the mountains, which, taking no account of frontiers, are my real homeland. Her generosity also permitted the publication of this work.

To Elisabeth Buzzard, my faithful and loving companion through good and ill, who day after day attended the sometimes difficult birth of this child. She was stimulating and creative during its conception, patient and understanding during the pangs of labor, and committed to the subject to the point of joining me in identifying with the man and the creative artist who inspired the book. It is dedicated to her from the bottom of my heart, as is everything I have done from the moment she first allowed me the joy of sharing her life.

To Switzerland, finally, toward whom I pay a half-century-old debt of gratitude. It dates from the day in October 1942 on which she saved my life when, as a boy, I was welcomed by her and snatched from the talons of Vichy France—which, in spite of many great individual acts of courage and devotion to others, was incapable of assuring my own safety. My dedication is a sign of profound attachment to a country whose nature I love passionately and whose people have given the world a model of how to live together democratically; and democracy, despite its inevitable faults, remains, to paraphrase Winston Churchill, "the worst possible system apart from all the others." May this country, of which my first two dedicatees are citizens, accept this offering as my personal participation in the celebrations of her seven-hundredth anniversary.

Harry Halbreich, Arolla, 25 July 1991

Preface

In writing this book, I have tried to say the last word on the subject for a number of years. At the same time, I nurse the hope that this will not be the case and that reading it will provoke those who possess works or autographs I have not discovered to reveal their treasures.

Thanks to the support I have mentioned in my dedication, I was able to devote myself to my task without interruption, spending nineteen months in almost exclusive daily contact with a man and his music. From this serious test, both of them emerged enormously enhanced. If I had entertained the slightest doubt about Honegger's stature and his eminent place in the history of music, this study would have dispelled them.

I had no intention, when I began, of writing a true biography, as this was something I had never done before. But the prodigious abundance of documentation I discovered, especially in the collections of Pascale Honegger and Paul Sacher, moved me to expand my project in this direction. This led me into some real detective work, based on the transcribing, even the deciphering, of diaries, not only Honegger's own but also his wife's, as well as on the careful study of passports, visas, and frontier entry and exit stamps, in order to work out the itineraries of journeys. These inquiries often prompted me to discover concerts I would not otherwise have known about. The biographical cloth, then, whose thread I have been weaving, has few holes in it—from the time of Honegger's adulthood, the longest of them is no more than a month or two. I hope that reading this biography will give an idea of the full and frenetically active life the composer led.

The examination of his output is split into categories. All Honegger's works are at least mentioned, and the most important of them are analyzed in detail. The introductions to each section contain a certain number of general remarks. This has allowed me to keep the chapters of Part Three (Gathering the Threads), in which I discuss the composer's language and style, down to a minimum. For the analyses to have any meaning, they inevitably have had to be made at a certain technical level, but I have always explained the "professional" terms I have used as I go along. I have also included as many music examples as possible. They are intended to make the analyses clearer and more concise by removing the need for long descriptive paraphrases, as well as to show the profound unity of style in Honegger's music and, simply, to give examples of the unusual beauty of his melodic invention. In the hope of making them accessible to readers who are not expert musicians, I have, with rare exceptions, quoted them just as an unaccompanied melodic line on a single staff.

The book contains the three indexes of works that might be expected. The first is organized by types of work: this takes up all of the central part of the book (Inventory of Works), each category being preceded by a short synoptical list to facilitate research. The second is the Chronological List of Works, and the third is the alphabetical Index of Works. These three lists are cross-referenced. The chronological list indicates the work's category and, obviously, the date, while the alphabetical index refers both to the analysis (page numbers are given in bold type) and to the position of the work in the biographical section.

Finally, I should mention that this volume forms one part of a trilogy. The other two parts are Honegger's collected writings, the *Écrits* (edited by Huguette Calmel and published by Honoré Champion, Paris, 1992), and another of my books, *L'Oeuvre d'Arthur Honegger, Chronologie, Catalogue raisonné, Analyse complète, Étude du langage et du style, Discographie critique* (The Work of Arthur Honegger, Chronology, Detailed Catalog, Complete Analyses, Study of Language and Style, Critical Discography) (Honoré Champion, Paris, 1994). Clearly, my second book is more technical and specialized, and more at a university level, which also explains the absence of any biography.

The existence of this triptych is not meant to put an end to Honegger studies, but on the contrary, to stimulate them by providing the basic information on which to build. It is to the initiative and efficiency of Pascale Honegger that her father owes a privileged treatment such as few composers of this century have enjoyed.

Acknowledgments

These are so numerous that I am certain to forget some, for which I apologize in advance. The most important of them figure in the dedication, but there are very many others.

First of all, to my friends at Éditions Salabert, Nelly Boufathal, Jeremy Drake, Radu Stan, and Costin Miereanu, who have generously placed at my disposal all the printed and manuscript scores in their possession, who have given me open access to their archives, and lastly who have given my publisher permission to reproduce the numerous music examples from works that they own. The only exceptions to this are the following, for which I also thank the respective owners/publishers. They too have given me all the help I asked for:

Éditions Max Eschig (La Sirène) for Examples 4, 5, 6, 7, 8, 9, 19, 20, and 21; Éditions Foetisch (Lausanne) for Examples 107, 108, 109, 110, 133, 134, and 135; Éditions Heugel (Leduc) for Examples 146, 152, and 153; Éditions Le Chant du Monde for Example 157; Éditions Josette France for example 164; Chester Music (London) for Example 25; Éditions Choudens for Example 105; Universal Edition (Vienna) for Example 147. Examples 154, 155, 157, 158, 165, and 166 are unpublished and belong to Pascale Honegger.

My thanks also go to my principal research centers—beyond the most important of them, the home of Pascale Honegger—for their kindness and efficiency: to the Bibliothèque nationale, its annex the Phonothèque nationale, the Bibliothèque de l'Arsenal, and the Bibliothèque de Radio-France (all in Paris), and the Paul Sacher Foundation in Basel. I cannot, unfortunately, say the same for the National Audiovisual Institute (INA) in Paris, which, though rich in material, imposes such exorbitant conditions, even on those who merely wish to consult it, that they discourage the majority of researchers, as I discovered. I say this in the hope of getting the present state of affairs changed.

On the other hand, I received the most polite and friendly welcome at the Cinémathèque française, at the Service des Archives du Film (Centre national de la cinématographie) in Bois d'Arcy, at the Musée du cinema in Brussels, at the Cinémathèque suisse in Lausanne (where I should also like personally to thank the enthusiastic and dynamic director, Freddy Buache), and, last but not least, at the Fondation Armand Panigel in Saint-Rémy de Provence. There I was able to see all the films for which Honegger wrote music—or at least those that have survived, which is to say four-fifths of them. I am certainly not forgetting my sister, Janine Euvrard, who helped me with my researches in this field and was of great assistance in making contacts and organizing the showing of films.

I wish to thank the Central Library in Solothurn for allowing me to consult the autograph of *Cris du monde* (which it holds), as well as my American friends Shirley Fleming and Ted Libby for getting hold of photocopies for me of the autographs in the Pierpont Morgan Library in New York and in the Library of Congress in Washington, D.C. I thank Frédéric Robert, the most eminent expert in the music of the time of the Popular Front as well as in music for wind band, for most valuable information, which has been mentioned in its due place. My thanks also to Jean-Claude Honegger, thanks to whose information, documents, and personal memories I have been able to give his mother, Claire Croiza, the important place she deserves in this book. He has also enabled me to unravel the complex background to *Judith*.

I should also like to acknowledge an eminent private collector in Switzerland, a man of taste and culture. I respect his wish to remain anonymous, but I trust he will know that I am referring to him in these lines.

To my friend and editor (of the original French edition), Jean Nithart, I offer gratitude for his trust and confidence.

Finally, my warmest thanks go to my friend Wulf Weinmann, who allowed me to finish part of my work in the paradise of Tenerife, and a friendly greeting to the cordial staff of the Hotel Kurhaus in Arolla.

—Harry Halbreich

The translator for his part would like to express his thanks to Amadeus Press for affording the author the opportunity to read through the translation in draft, and to Professor Halbreich for availing himself of this opportunity to amend various details and to update the translation in the light of the most recent Honegger scholarship.

Amadeus Press also would like to extend appreciation to Pascale Honegger for her invaluable assistance with the preparation of the English translation.

Introduction

At the end of 1989, I was present at the premiere of the opera *Romeo and Juliet* by Pascal Dusapin, undoubtedly the most highly gifted French composer of his generation. I told him that in my opinion—and I made it clear my words were intended as a great compliment—this was the most Honeggerian score written since Honegger's death. I saw Dusapin literally change color, as he replied: "That makes me very worried!" And he immediately went on: "I have to say, I know very little of Honegger's music."

This seemed to me to typify the younger generation's ignorance of Honegger. Like many others thirty or forty years ago, Honegger was a victim of the stranglehold of serialism, but also of supporters of doubtful value. He served, in fact, as a standard, a rallying point, against the passing "serial terror," for the most reactionary forces in music—an indefensible role that he would energetically have refused, had he lived. It is high time to re-evaluate his considerable output in the light of objective, modern criteria, and his music deserves to be examined in the context of the era in which he composed it. We shall see then that it represented an approach that was bold and innovative and in no sense backward-looking. We can also see, with the benefit of hindsight, that the positions he took up at the end of his life, which ran the risk then of seeming old-fashioned, were in fact ahead of their time and were mistaken only in being born too soon. Here we have one of those sudden, unexpected turns so often found in history, which should have warned people not to judge matters too hastily.

The "Honegger case" is among the most fascinating one could wish to defend in Honegger's centenary year of 1992. The case needs to be pled, but it is a good, solid case, and shows every likelihood of being won at the bar of history. I take it on with enthusiasm.

Part One
CHRONICLE OF A LIFE

ONE

Turly

Wald is a large village in the mountainous region known as the Zurich *Oberland*, near the borders of the Swiss canton of St. Gallen, not far from Lake Zurich. The Zurich *Oberland* is fairly modest, not to be confused with the Bernese *Oberland*—no peak here reaches four thousand feet. At the beginning of the nineteenth century there lived in Wald a peasant family of the name of Honegger, a widespread patronymic in the canton of Zurich. It comes from the Swiss-German *Hohen-Egg-Herr*, meaning "the man from the place up there."[1]

From Wald, the branch of the Honegger family that concerns us moved to Thalwil, on the shores of the lake, a few miles from the big city and today part of its residential suburbs. It was there that Arthur, the composer's father, was born on 9 October 1851, the son of Caspar Honegger and Rosalie, née Hasler, also a native of the canton of Zurich. Arthur senior left Zurich for Le Havre to join a large Swiss colony, composed mostly of tradesmen and wholesalers, but came back to Zurich to marry, on 11 May 1891, Julie Ulrich, the daughter of Johann Caspar Ulrich and Margaretha Hausheer. She was born in Zurich on 22 June 1859, and so was nearly eight years younger than he. The Ulrichs were one of the oldest Zurich families and when, in 1935, Arthur Honegger had to establish proof of his "Aryanism" to be allowed to collaborate on a film in Germany, he was able to follow the Ulrich family tree back as far as 1535. The wedding on 11 May 1891 was no more than a consolidation of links already uniting the two families, since on 26 April 1888, Arthur's elder brother, Oskar (born 22 February 1850), had married Julie's elder sister Louise (born 2 September 1857). Unlike his brother, Oskar Honegger stayed in Zurich, where he became an important figure, both as a judge and as an amateur musician. One of Arthur Honegger's first published works, the *Toccata and Variations* for piano (1916), was dedicated to the memory of his uncle Oskar, who died in 1920, the year before its publication.

After settling in Le Havre, Arthur and Julie Honegger had four children, of which the composer was the eldest. On 11 March 1892, the happy father went to the town hall to register the birth of a son, born on 10 March at eight o'clock in the morning, whom he named Oscar-Arthur (the first of these names was never used). The house where the boy was born, since destroyed by bombing in the Second World War, was a fine middle-class structure at 86 boulevard François Ier, on the corner of the rue Frédérick Lemaître. The birth certificate shows the father's profession as "shop assistant," indicating that at that period he had not yet set up on his own. But this soon happened, and Arthur Honegger senior found himself at the head of an extremely prosperous business importing coffee, a sector that, in those days, was largely in the hands of the Swiss colony in Le Havre. This business flourished for a long time, but it collapsed totally after the First World War. Honegger's father had left it by then and retired to Zurich in 1913.

The boy—who, at least in the family, was to be called by the typically Alemannic (German-Swiss) diminutive "Turly" even as a young man—did not remain an only child for long. On 14 March 1893 a sister was born: Marguerite-Julie, called "Toto." On 31 August 1922 she married Rudolf-Hermann Stadler, a doctor of medicine from Zurich, and spent the rest of her life in that city. The youngest child, Julie-Rosa, nicknamed "Wantze" (bug) or "Wantzefloh" (fleabug) and later "Tati," was born on 6 February 1902. She was also married in Zurich, on 1 December 1923, to Hugo Laubi from Winterthur, and later she married the actor Emil Hegetschweiler. But there was also a brother, Caspar-Emile, called "Zigo," born 24 August 1896, who seems to have been a whimsical character, a dreamer, a kind of prodigal son. He first of all tried his hand at acting (Arthur did what he could to help him in this), then at painting, neither of them successfully. On 27 December 1921 he married a Bavarian girl named Anna-Elisabeth Happel in Munich, and then moved to Paris until the Second World War. He lived until the end of his life on his share of the family money, but had to be put under guardianship.

The Honegger family, of course, spoke *züridütsch* (the Swiss-German dialect spoken in Zurich) at home, and the composer would become fluent in the Alemannic dialect, as well as speaking perfect literary German. A number of family photos allow us to see inside this comfortable household. The father, wearing pince-nez, prematurely bald and presenting an ample silhouette, appears the incarnation of bourgeois respectability, and his kind, round face, with its mustache, contrasts with the long, sensitive face of his wife and her serene, withdrawn expression. As for the boy of three or four, wearing a skirt in the manner of the times and clutching a prophetic locomotive, he is recognizably the future composer of *Pacific 2.3.1*. Already we can see the small, firm mouth, the look of intensity about the eye, and the dark curls.

This boy of pure Zurich stock was to live in Le Havre until his coming-of-age, apart from two years spent studying in Zurich, from September 1909 to June 1911. (A document in Zurich's town hall, dated 4 March 1919, certifies that Honegger, "domiciled in Zurich," possesses through his family the freedom of the city of Zurich and is a Swiss citizen by birth.) In one of his autobiographical sketches, Honegger also notes that his family were Protestants and that there was talk at one time of making him a priest! But when the time came to go to school, he found himself in a quite different atmosphere from that of his family circle, and very soon he turned into as much of a Normandy lad as his classmates. Before he ever set foot in Paris, he was, therefore, marked by two quite different and complementary cultures (three, if we include the later *romand*, or French-Swiss, influence), and his art blended these into a uniquely original synthesis.

What distinguished the Honegger household from practically all the others in Le Havre was the presence of music, and good music. Both parents played the family piano, and if Honegger's father had a predilection for opera (while not neglecting Mozart and Beethoven), his mother, probably due to her more refined sensibilities, preferred chamber music. The following story shows the uncultured state of a middle-sized French town at the beginning of the twentieth century. Honegger relates how, after he had moved on from his primary school to his secondary one, he mentioned the name of Mozart to his friends, but they only knew the name of Mansart, the inventor of the mansard roof, and tried to correct him.

With his family's encouragement, the boy's taste for music showed itself very early—not that Honegger was a boy prodigy. His father made outlines of various musical instruments for him cut out of cardboard, and the young Arthur, fascinated by an engraving of Mendelssohn composing the overture *Fingal's Cave* in bed, promptly engaged the help of Toto and Zigo in assembling an imaginary orchestra, which he then conducted with enthusiasm.

Mens sana in corpore sano: we should not imagine a delicate boy with ailing health! The future composer of *Rugby* was a tough little lad, athletic and madly keen on games and violent sports, even inventing one of his own, *bécanard-polo*, or bicycle-polo! Living as he did in a large port town, he was fascinated from his earliest years by the sea and the ocean beyond. Although the mountains must have been in his blood, he would always prefer to spend his holidays by the seaside and was an excellent swimmer, never a mountaineer.

When he was nine, Honegger had an experience that was important for his future. His parents took him to the opera for the first time. Like many other French provincial towns, Le Havre then had an opera season in which the regular repertory of the time was performed with whatever resources were at hand, augmented occasionally by a specially imported singer of renown. He underwent first of all the revelation of *Faust*, and shortly after that of *Les Huguenots*, *Carmen*, *Lakmé*, *William Tell*, and more. The idea of a story told through music greatly appealed to him, and he decided that he too would compose operas. At the very same moment, another budding composer, Sergei Prokofiev, was making the same decision several thousand miles away. Arthur barely knew the notes and was not aware of the existence of a bass clef, but this problem was surmounted by writing the bass roles (which one needs for noble fathers, high priests, and principal malefactors) in the treble clef, with a note requesting they be sung two octaves down. Full of self-confidence, the boy wrote his own libretto, and when the score was finished he bound it himself. As he admitted, it was the binding that gave him the most trouble.

Between May and July 1903 (he was eleven) Arthur Honegger wrote *Philippa*, a grand historical drama set in the fourteenth century, which he finished and entitled his "Opus 1." He found the story in *La Jeunesse illustrée* (an illustrated children's newspaper). The score (a vocal score because, of course, he had never seen a full orchestral one) fills the fifty pages of a bound school exercise book and contains no fewer than fourteen numbers, together with an overture and an introduction for each of the three acts. In the same book, carefully preserved by the composer's daughter Pascale, there is also, sewn in separately, an arrangement of the overture "for two violins and pianoforte" (sic), dated 23 August 1907 and designated as Opus 12. But that is another story.

Then, under the influence of *Lohengrin*, he concocted a second opera, *Sigismond*, of which I have found no trace. Its three or four tableaux covered sixty-seven sheets of music. It was his mother who helped him to put these early attempts together by amplifying his still elementary theoretical knowledge. And on this point, Hélène Jourdan-Morhange cites a curious detail: for Honegger as a child, the upbeat did not exist—a syncopation on the first beat did the same job perfectly well. As she justly remarks, "We shall see that his later style of word-setting remained faithful to this principle."[2] We shall return to this point when we look at *Antigone*.

There were other discoveries too. From time to time, Le Havre was visited by well-known virtuosi on tour, and in this way the boy was able to hear Enesco, Sarasate, Ysaÿe, Pugno, the Cortot-Thibaud-Casals Trio, and, as he himself recalled, "the splendid Capet Quartet playing to about thirty people."[3] It was at this time that his lifelong passion for chamber music was born. His passion for opera was later to come up against material obstacles that, in France, were impossible to overcome. Even so, as he confessed at the end of his life, "my ideal would have been to compose nothing but operas"[4]—like Mozart, who also wrote far fewer than he would have liked.

His parents realized that Turly was musically gifted and decided to let him learn seriously, without there being any idea at this stage of his making music a career. They set him to learn the violin under a teacher called Santreuil. This choice of instrument was to be decisive for Honegger's character as a composer. Certainly, he was later to master the piano and was good enough to play occasionally in public. But he was never a keyboard virtuoso, and his musical thinking, melodic and contrapuntal rather than harmonic, remained that of a violinist, like that of another violinist-composer, Bohuslav Martinů.

Nevertheless, at the age of thirteen he began to learn harmony from the man he later considered to have been his earliest teacher: Robert-Charles Martin, the organist of the church of Saint-Michel. Truth to tell, his help does not seem to have been particularly decisive, to judge by the composer's own testimony. While on holiday in Zurich, the young Honegger submitted his two operas to his uncle Oskar, in his dual capacity as president of the city's choirs and as a judge. His uncle's response was, as one may imagine, gently ironic, and the budding composer was encouraged to learn harmony. It was at this time that the boy was amazed to discover at home the Beethoven sonatas. In them he found the principles of modulation, of tonal planning, of sonata form, and of voice-leading. In short, as he later said,

> my harmony lessons taught me what I'd already known for a long time! But if harmony can be learned in a few hours, it is counterpoint that dictates the movement of parts, it is counterpoint that enriches the texture, and thereby creates the harmony and renews its substance.

He was twelve or thirteen years old at the time, and every week he would bring home with him Georges Tobler, one of his classmates, a violinist like himself, and, to judge by his name, also Swiss by birth. With Honegger's mother at the piano, they reveled in the delights of chamber music. The repertory for two violins and piano is small, it is true, but Turly proceeded to address this deficiency, and sonatas began to accumulate, carefully modeled on those of Beethoven (the only ones he knew, but could there have been better ones?). We have been unable to find any trace of these, but apparently they were grouped in sixes. However, as already mentioned, there does exist the transcription of the *Overture* to *Philippa*, as well as that of the *Overture* to *La Esmeralda*, designated as Op. 8, No. 1.

La Esmeralda was a new opera begun by the fifteen-year-old boy using a libretto that had, in Victor Hugo's lifetime, already been used by a now-forgotten female composer, Mlle Bertin. This time (in 1907) Honegger abandoned the work in the middle of the second scene of Act I, after an overture, a chorus, and an unfinished aria for Esmeralda.

It was unthinkable that a Protestant household like the Honeggers' should not contain both a Bible and works by Johann Sebastian Bach. So when André Caplet, a native of Le Havre and a profoundly religious composer, returned to his home city to conduct two Bach cantatas, the young boy was overwhelmed by the experience.[5] It was enough to make him abandon *La Esmeralda* on the spot and to begin, in the same notebook, his *Oratorio du Calvaire* (Calvary Oratorio) in seven sections, including a prelude, an opening chorus ("Jerusalem"), three arias ("A sword shall pierce thy side," "Jesus Christ all-powerful," and "Eli lama sabacthani"), a final chorus ("O terror"), and an epilogue. So, after opera and Beethoven, a new element entered Honegger's compositional world: Johann Sebastian Bach and the oratorio. The *Oratorio du Calvaire* has not survived, but many years later Honegger spoke to his friend Arthur Hoérée about certain of its technical elements (such as the use of only open strings for two of his friends who were beginners on the violin) that already showed the "artisan" side of him, which knew how to get the best out of the resources at his disposal. This prefigures a decisive moment in his career: the seventeen instrumental players in *Le Roi David* (King David) balanced against the mass of a hundred choral singers. "Composing should be like making a chair," he was to say later: which takes us some way from Berlioz's "Fire and thunder!" and brings us, on the contrary, close to the proud and humble ideal of the cantor of Leipzig. Three songs (now lost) date from this same period, on poems by Moréas, Hérold, and Guillard.

It would be wrong, however, to think of Turly as being entirely absorbed in music. He remained a boy of his age and took a passionate interest in the bustling activity of the great port where he was fortunate enough to live. Here, I cannot resist the temptation of quoting Joseph Delteil (a close contemporary of Honegger) who, in a little-known passage, gives a poetic evocation of a city in which, by the way, he may never have set foot.

> Le Havre is a dirty, cheerful city, with ocean-liners, women from the Caux country, and fishing-boat owners. It rains there, and in poky, disreputable

taverns a damp gloom is refined that breeds wide eyes and thick ears. In the streets, a dog, a man from Cancale, and a seaman's wife follow one another constantly in single file. A siren howls and the captain of an ocean-going vessel swears.[6]

The Honegger family had some years before left the house on the boulevard François Ier for the rue de Picpus, much nearer the ships that fascinated the young Arthur. At the end of his life, he related these memories to Bernard Gavoty:

> What do I owe to Le Havre? My childhood and, the thing that lies at the heart of that wonderful area, the sea. I loved the boats, especially the sailing ships. I knew by name the different kinds of ship and the details of their rigging—three-masters with topsails, brigs, schooners. The sea had a very profound influence on my development, it widened the horizons of my childhood.[7]

Even if this love of the sea and ships did not have the effect of turning him into a sailor, as in the case of Albert Roussel, the attraction of foreign countries was still nourished by the reading of numerous adventure stories. One of them, Gustave Aimard's *Le Souriquet*, was to inspire one of his earliest orchestral works, *Le Chant de Nigamon* (The Song of Nigamon), in 1917.

While the *Oratorio du Calvaire* seems to be lost, this is not the case with what may perhaps be considered the most important fruit of the adolescent composer's efforts: a collection of *Six Sonatas for violin and piano*, the first completed on 8 March 1908 and the last on 3 July. Even though they are clumsy and naive, and desperately Beethovenian, to the point of practically ignoring the century-long development that separates them from their model, they bear witness nonetheless to a keen appetite and to a real creative ambition. Two of the sonatas, the first and the third, adopt the Beethovenian key of C minor. The third, the longest of the six, is in four movements and lasts well over twenty minutes, while two of the others, the fourth and the sixth, even end with a fugue—or at least what the apprentice composer thought he could call a fugue: six or seven entries, all in the tonic, and a polyphonic texture never going beyond three voices.

These sonatas are Honegger's last surviving works before his official Opus 1, the *Three Pieces for piano* published in 1910 by Desforges, a minor publisher in Le Havre. But there does survive one further trace of a "pre-Arthur, ante-Honegger" endeavor: a brief page for organ (or harmonium), probably contemporary with the *Oratorio du Calvaire*, that thirty years later was to find a place in the church scene in the film *Marthe Richard au service de la France* (1937).

Obviously, the boy had reached a turning point. His parents could no longer ignore their son's exceptional musical gifts and, although there was still no question in their minds of a professional career, with a truly Swiss realism and straightforwardness they prepared to face the consequences.

Turly spent every summer in Zurich with his uncle Oskar, who was now president of the city tribunal and honorary president of the choral society. He was increasingly struck by his nephew's gifts, and together with Robert-Charles Martin decided to try and persuade his father to let him study for two years at the Zurich Conservatory. So it was that, from the start of the 1909 academic year, Turly settled on the banks of the river Limmat. Shortly before Turly left Le Havre, the poet Henriette Charasson left this portrait of him: "a small youngster, already solidly built, with abundant dark hair, a powerful forehead and black eyes that seemed to be lit up by intelligence and willpower."[8]

In Zurich, the seventeen-year-old found himself for the first time in a large city with a flourishing musical life. Whereas in Le Havre he had no opportunity of getting to know any modern French music (whose riches he would only discover when he went to Paris in 1911), Zurich was alive to the German music of the time. If the memory of Wagner was still strong (half a century earlier he had conceived *Tristan and Isolde* there in the villa belonging to his benefactor, Otto Wesendonck), that of Brahms was no doubt even more so, and more recent. Johannes Brahms had often stayed in Zurich, largely because it was the home of one of his closest friends, Friedrich Hegar (1841–1927). Hegar was the moving spirit behind the city's musical life, being both founder and director of the Conservatory, conductor of the Tonhalle, and director of the men's choir. In the particular context of the German-speaking Switzerland of the period, the activity of choral societies, and especially male choruses, was the most important of all.

When Hegar got to know Turly, he was so struck by the young composer's ability that he wasted no time before giving him private lessons. The name of Friedrich Hegar, totally unknown in French-speaking countries, is still current in German-speaking Switzerland, especially in connection with his excellent male choruses, some of which, like the well-known *In den Alpen*, are almost part of folklore. One cannot insist too strongly on the fundamental importance of choral culture in Swiss musical life, reflecting as it does a communal spirit that has absolutely no equivalent in France. Hegar offered the young Honegger practical teaching that was both lively and effective. Honegger would bring a piece of his own (for example, his *Adagio for violin and piano*, which impressed his teacher greatly and which certainly dates from after the naive sonatas of 1908), and Hegar, while retaining its substance and thematic ideas, would recompose it, correcting mistakes and eliminating weaknesses. Honegger would never forget the beneficial effects of such a practical composition course.

It was possible in Zurich to hear the most recent works not only of Richard Strauss, but of Max Reger, whose music Honegger took to straightaway (as one can tell from his *String Quartet No. 1*). Later he tried to pass on this enthusiasm to his fellow pupils at the Paris Conservatory, but in vain—Reger remains terra incognita in France.

At the Zurich Conservatory, Honegger entered the violin class of Willem de Boer, an excellent musician of Dutch origin, and for harmony, that of Lothar Kempter, an old man (he died in 1911), but thorough and extremely knowledgeable in the spirit of the old school. We shall see that when, in 1915, Honegger was trying to convince his father to let him continue his studies in Paris rather than send him to Germany, he considered that the standard of the

French harmony and counterpoint classes was distinctly above that of their German counterparts, including those of German-speaking Switzerland.

Otherwise, evidence relating to his two years in Zurich is almost nonexistent, since no correspondence has survived. Nor are there any compositions from these years, as the *Adagio* that Hegar liked has disappeared and the aforementioned *Three Pieces for piano* (*Scherzo, Humoresque, Adagio*), although published in 1910, were probably written before Honegger left Le Havre. They are, for one thing, dedicated to Robert-Charles Martin.

According to Honegger's own account, when he came to the end of his time in Zurich at the beginning of the summer of 1911, his father addressed his nineteen-year-old son as follows: "You're going to come into the family business. You won't have much to do—in the morning you'll spend a couple of hours at the exchange, in the afternoon you'll sign letters, and the rest of the time you can spend on music."[9] But this was not the future Honegger saw for himself. He did not want to become an amateur, but rather to devote himself entirely to his art, make a career of it and, if possible, make a living at it. Friedrich Hegar, for his part, was convinced that the young man had exceptional talent and urged the elder Honegger to send his son to the Paris Conservatory.

It was not an easy decision since there were four children in the family. The youngest was only nine, and in principle it was the duty of Arthur, the eldest, to take up the reins of the family business. During the eleven years of life left to him, Honegger's father would have the opportunity to realize that his sacrifice had not been in vain. We shall be quoting extensively from the letters that his son wrote him during this period. They show a lively and touching sense of gratitude on Turly's part, together with a continuing desire (one that was to be fulfilled, what is more) to prove himself in the eyes of such a generous and understanding father. Both his parents, in their pragmatic Swiss fashion, regarded his chosen career as anything but silly. But, realizing how difficult it was, they merely hoped that he could make a living from it and that it would bring him success. Years later, Honegger remarked to his friend Bernard Gavoty: "Almost all the coffee merchants in Le Havre were ruined after the 1914 War. If I'd taken my father's original advice and stayed there, I'd barely have earned a living as second violin in their Folies-Bergère!"[10]

TWO

The Paris Conservatory and Honegger's Earliest Works

For an adolescent from the provinces, thirsty for music and culture, Paris in 1911 was a veritable treasure house. The sun of Serge Diaghilev's Ballets Russes was approaching its zenith, and it was only by a few months that Arthur missed the premiere of *Petrushka* and also of a somewhat scandalous spectacle commissioned and performed by Ida Rubinstein, a dancer who had left Diaghilev's troupe and who was to play a crucial role in Honegger's career. *The Martyrdom of Saint Sebastian* was a neo-medieval mystery play by Gabriele d'Annunzio, with wonderful music by Claude Debussy—one of the Debussy scores that was always closest to Honegger's heart. At the time Honegger entered the Conservatory, Ravel was working on *Daphnis and Chloë*, Dukas was polishing and repolishing *La Péri*, Roussel, in his garden at Bois-le-Roi, was sketching from life the tiny horrors of *Le Festin de l'araignée* (The Spider's Banquet), while Fauré was slowly and patiently weaving the cloth of his opera *Penelope*. Less than two years later, Stravinsky's *The Rite of Spring* was to explode like a bomb, with a violence that would for years blind people to the more insidious but more profound violence of Debussy's *Jeux*, a bomb with a delayed-action fuse.

Outside France, 1911 was the year of *Der Rosenkavalier* and also, further north, of the austere and enigmatic *Fourth Symphony* of Sibelius, which ran clean against all the tendencies of a time Jean Sibelius described as a "circus," and in particular against the luxuriance of *Prometheus (The Poem of Fire)*, at that very moment being produced by that mystagogue and erotomaniac of genius, Alexander Scriabin. Another bomb was taking shape in the subconscious of Arnold Schoenberg, who had been in a musical limbo of atonality for three years: *Pierrot lunaire* was to emerge in 1912.

This undermining of traditional values went ahead on every front. Just as Honegger reached Paris, the famous Room 41 of the 27th Salon des Indépendants revealed analytical cubism to the general public: Georges Braque, Pablo Picasso, Fernand Léger, Marcel Duchamp, closely followed by Juan Gris. Presenting an object from the front and in profile simultaneously is, intellectually, a close parallel with the procedure, found in *Petrushka*, of simultaneously sounding the tonic, dominant, and subdominant of a key (even if that particular score went on to the next stage, of polytonality). In Germany, different techniques and attitudes came to the fore. Schoenberg had abandoned tonality in 1909 and Wassily Kandinsky's first abstract paintings renounced figurative representation. At the end of 1911, the Blaue Reiter exhibition brought together abstract and expressionist pictures, among the latter some hallucinatory self-portraits by Schoenberg, who had temporarily exchanged manuscript paper for canvas.

The creative artist is a seismograph and a prophet who knows things before they happen. Such a list of attacks on tradition (and, in its way, Louis Blériot's flight from Calais to Dover in 1909 was another) were so many symptoms of the end of an epoch and of a state of balance that the world was never to see again. At the premiere of *The Rite of Spring*, a clairvoyant critic wrote: "Music like this written by a Russian means a revolution in Russia within three years." He was off by only a year. In 1911, the Agadir incident increased the tensions between France and Germany and caused them to accelerate their rearmament; the new Balkan states were disputing the remains of European Turkey, the sick man of Europe; the as-yet-unfinished *Titanic* was only a few months away from its destruction; and Europe less than three years away from hers. As in the years leading up to 1789, humanity, with the exception of a tiny handful of Cassandras, was engaged in a headlong pursuit of luxury and beauty, dancing madly on the slopes of the volcano.

This then was the shape of the world when the timid, well-behaved young Arthur Honegger took his place in the violin class of Lucien Capet (the same Capet whose quartet Honegger had heard playing so marvelously in Le Havre a few years earlier). Very soon he met a young man from Strasbourg a few months older than himself who, like him, made the weekly return journey between home and Paris—Charles Münch, who was one day to be Honegger's most faithful interpreter. At the same time, Honegger became a counterpoint pupil of André Gédalge, in a class that was probably unrivaled in the world at that time, and just what he needed now that he had finished his harmony studies in Zurich.

André Gédalge (1856–1926) was a strong-minded and individual personality. He had been a professor of counterpoint and fugue in the old Conservatory on the rue de Madrid since 1905 and was the author of the *Treatise on Fugue*, published four years earlier, which, according to the enthusiastic young Honegger, was unrivaled. Even though Gédalge is remembered as a teacher of genius rather than as a composer, it would be well worth the effort to revive his best work, the *Third Symphony*, with its proud motto "Neither literature nor painting."

In Gédalge's class, Honegger made friends with Jacques Ibert (who had just abandoned a career as a commercial traveler in cuff buttons to devote himself to music) and they remained close friends all their lives. The same was true of his friendship with a dark-haired young man who was to turn prematurely chubby, Darius Milhaud, a native of Aix-en-Provence. He too was a violinist (in Berthelier's class, not Capet's) and was a fellow pupil of Gédalge's. Milhaud was Honegger's junior by some months (born 4 September 1892), but Honegger immediately fell under the influence of this precociously mature student ("the most gifted of us all," as Honegger later described him) who had already written songs, quartets, and sonatas in abundance while working at a grand opera on Francis Jammes's *La Brebis égarée* (The Lost Sheep). With this meeting between Honegger and Milhaud, the nucleus of the future Les Six was formed, uniting its two strongest members. At this time, according to Honegger, Milhaud

> worked, acted, and spoke with an assurance, an inventiveness, and an audacity that dazzled the shy little boy from the provinces, which I then was! He introduced me right and left, introduced me to the works of composers I didn't realize existed—Magnard, Séverac—and, above all, was very fond of me. I certainly returned the compliment![1]

Milhaud, in his turn, had these memories of his meeting with Honegger:

> In 1911, I was allowed to listen in on André Gédalge's counterpoint class. The attention of all the pupils was drawn to an extremely handsome young man, dressed in a black velvet jacket and carrying a violin case under his arm. . . . It was Arthur Honegger, whom we also called "le petit Suisse" [the little Swiss boy]. His universal kindness endeared him to us all and his counterpoint exercises, like his early compositions, made him all the more noticeable. I became his friend at once, and this firm friendship lasted until his death.[2]

Another meeting took place at this time. We find in Honegger's diary, on 14 January 1913, the note "supper with Enesco," and a friendship born of mutual admiration would always unite these two composers who died only a few months apart, even though Georges Enesco was eleven years older.

The Paris Conservatory had been under the flexible but firm direction of Gabriel Fauré since 1905 and, thanks to a number of drastic steps that led to Fauré being nicknamed "Robespierre," it had been restored to a level worthy of its ancient reputation. A scandal like the one caused by the refusal to allow Ravel to compete in the Prix de Rome after he had already written *Jeux d'eau* and the *String Quartet* was no longer imaginable.

Salutary as Gédalge's teaching was for any talented musician, it was particularly appropriate for the young Honegger, being based on a close study of Bach's *Well-Tempered Clavier* and his Chorales. Gédalge encouraged his pupils to compose right away ("Compose! You don't wait to learn grammar before you speak!"[3]), without the technical mastery that always comes "on the job," and his most extreme demand was that they should bring him "a sixteen-measure tune that can be sung unaccompanied." And in a revealing analysis he showed that the essence of the first movement of Beethoven's *Fifth Symphony* was primarily melodic. Gédalge had no time for tricks. Unlike his colleague Georges Caussade, he didn't turn out first-prize winners, but musicians. Honegger, after seven long years of labor, was armed with one of the most formidable contrapuntal techniques of all time, as the flowing counterpoint of the Finale of the *Fourth Symphony* demonstrates, worthy to be mentioned with that in the Finale of Mozart's *"Jupiter" Symphony*. And yet he left the Conservatory with only a second prize in counterpoint to show for his studies! Not that it matters: Debussy never won a harmony prize there, either.

Honegger remained grateful to Gédalge until the end of his life and spoke of him in the following terms:

> He gave us the necessary courage and sense of enjoyment to overcome difficulties. With an often cruel clairvoyance he would put his finger on tricks and short cuts. "There's nothing difficult about that," he'd say with a smile, "but Bach and Mozart . . . look!" "Counterpoint, you know," this thick-set little man would say, "isn't a study, it's a practice. You must do it all the time, like breathing. When you become flexible, when you have the answer to every problem at your fingertips, then you can allow yourself every liberty."[4]

When Honegger and Milhaud, by now inseparable, returned to the Conservatory in the autumn of 1912, they got to know a gentle, studious, blonde girl of their own age (to be exact, nine days younger than Honegger) named Germaine Tailleferre. She was studying counterpoint with Caussade and was already in Charles-Marie Widor's composition class. The future Les Six had now reached three!

There remain from those two years of coming-and-going between Le Havre and Paris no more than a couple of compositions, but both are worth a mention. On 23 October 1912 in Le Havre, Honegger finished the *Sonata for violin and piano in D minor*, the first two movements of which, also written in Le Havre, are dated 12 February and 22 June respectively. It is a serious, passionate, and desperately romantic work that is a long way from the childish sonatinas of 1908. The lessons from Hegar and then from Gédalge had begun to bear fruit. Even if this work does not as yet bear the real stamp of its composer, its three movements, lasting some twenty-five minutes (with the first considerably longer than the other two), already show impressively solid craftsmanship.

The second, more ambitious work is a string quartet, the first movement of which he started and finished in Zurich, where he was spending the summer of 1913. It is the first version (later to be largely rewritten on two separate occasions) of what would later become the opening movement of his *String Quartet No. 1*, his first masterpiece.

In the autumn of 1913, the composer's father gave up his business in Le Havre and retired. In September his parents joined their family in Zurich, while Arthur for his part took up permanent residence in Paris. His diary contains the entry, for 30 September, "Leave Le Havre." The great advantage of this move, from a biographer's point of view, is that it led, especially from the end of 1914, to an abundant and regular exchange of letters that allows us to follow the composer's existence at that period almost step by step.

Honegger's first Paris home was on the rue Say, near the avenue Trudaine, and he stayed there until October 1916. He remained faithful to Montmartre all his life and did not follow the tendency of artists in the 1920s to move down to Montparnasse. For Honegger, Paris was and always would be the Right Bank, and the Pigalle fountain was "the center of the world."

He was now twenty-one—his parents would seem to have waited for him to come of age before letting him live on his own in the big city—and from here on Honegger's destiny would be shaped by two quite distinct influences. He was French and Parisian in culture, in intellectual affinities, and soon, in his career, but profoundly Swiss in his roots, his feeling for the past, and in his inner nature. Not only did he always keep his Swiss passport (with the military obligations that brought with it, which were now pending), but he would never try to benefit from the double nationality that was his by right. He was never a French citizen, which, under the Occupation during the Second World War, made his life a little easier. As we shall see, he often stayed in Switzerland, some-times for long periods, but at no time did he envisage settling there. His artis-tic roots were too firmly grounded in Paris, whose spiritual oxygen was indis-pensable for him.

We know little about that first winter he spent on his own in Paris. Apart from spending Christmas in Switzerland with his family, he led a serious, well-organized life and was soon placed in the care, and from time to time under the tyranny, of Salomé, the housekeeper who saw to his material well-being. As Milhaud lived close by, the two friends generally made the walk to and from the Conservatory together. Milhaud remembered:

> Arthur and I had long conversations about music that were mutually enriching, because if Arthur often had under his arm Richard Strauss's *Die Frau ohne Schatten* or Reger's *Variations on a Theme of Mozart*, my music case would more likely contain scores of *Boris* or *Pelléas*.[5]

(It is worth noting that Milhaud must be referring to Strauss's *Salome* or *Elektra*, since *Die Frau ohne Schatten* was not completed until 1918.)

Unlike Honegger and Milhaud, Germaine Tailleferre was in Caussade's counterpoint class. In the autumn of 1913, she met there a fourteen-year-old boy of extraordinary precociousness and maturity, who was on the brink of making a name for himself in Parisian musical circles thanks to the amazing success, in the salons, of his song *Le Gloxinia*, which had received its first per-formance at the august Société nationale. With the arrival of Georges Auric from his native Languedoc (he was born in Lodève), the future Les Six were now four.

The first letter to Honegger's parents that has survived, dated 7 June 1914, announces Turly's imminent arrival in Zurich, where he would spend the rest of the year, as war broke out in the meantime. But in these seven months he was not idle—far from it. On 3 October (or 5, the writing is unclear) he finished the first movement of a *Trio for violin, cello, and piano in F minor*, which he had begun in August. The other movements have not survived—and perhaps they were never written—but he set enough store by this piece to present it two years later in Widor's class. It remains unpublished, though it would be well worth having in print. From November dates a song, "Sur le basalte," on a poem by the Belgian symbolist writer André Fontainas, which was to be the first of the *Four Poems for Voice and Piano*. He continued to work on them until May 1916 and dedicated them to Jane Bathori.

From here on, thanks principally to the large number of letters that survive, the available information on the composer is sufficiently continuous for us to establish a chronicle year by year.

1915

Arthur Honegger returned to France at the very beginning of 1915 and, after a brief stay in Le Havre, was back in Paris on 10 January. On 25 February he started again at the Conservatory. "I'm working hard on counterpoint and fugue. Gédalge is urging me insistently to compose," he wrote his parents.[6] But at the beginning of March, he warned them that he would not be able to take the Conservatory exam on 23 June because he had been summoned by the Rekrutenschule (the school for Swiss army recruits) to serve in defending the country's frontiers.

Until then he went on working very hard, trying to revise and finish his quartet.[7] In fact, the end of the work was still some way off, but certainly the second (undated) of the three different versions of the first movement comes from this period.

For some time he had been making fewer mentions of his violin studies. Increasingly he came to feel that his future lay elsewhere, and on 28 April 1915 he wrote his parents the decisive letter, deliberately on large paper, in which with some solemnity he confirmed his vocation as a composer:

My dear parents,
   This is a serious letter, which is why I've chosen this imposing format. To judge by Mama's suggestions about returning my books and music, and by what I remember of your remarks, you are thinking of this year as being the last I shall spend in Paris. After my military service I was to have gone to Germany to complete my studies. After much reflection, I have come to the conclusion that it would be far better to let me stay on next year in Paris, and I'll try and explain to you why.
   I have now firmly chosen a career as a composer. I believe I have the natural disposition that is the principal basis for this, and so far all the musicians who have been competent to give an opinion have agreed in recognizing that I have a certain talent, which means that I may have a reasonable chance of getting somewhere. You probably have a vague idea of the difficulty of this career since you know how many great composers have lived in humble obscurity all their lives and have made a success with the public only after their death. So, as the saying goes, my life will be "a time of long patience" and I hope that you will have patience as well, that is to say, that you won't be discouraged if success seems to you to be long in coming.
   Learning to be a composer is a long and time-consuming business. Even so, I believe I shall be able to complete my studies (I'm thinking of my academic studies, naturally, since one goes on learning all one's life), that is to say, that I'll know my craft, and after I leave Gédalge I shan't need any other teachers except the study of the great masters of all the ages. I'm working on fugue now and have practically finished everything

to do with harmony and counterpoint. Next year I expect to finish studying fugue and to have enough knowledge of orchestration and what is called the study of composition to get by, and learn the rest from personal experience.

I think this is the place to say something about Gédalge's importance from the teaching point of view. Gédalge's *Treatise on Fugue* is the most complete work that has ever been written on the subject. It is used in conservatories all over Europe and all musicians agree that it's a masterpiece of clarity and logic. So I couldn't find anyone better than the author of this treatise to teach me fugue.

There are two counterpoint classes at the Conservatory (Gédalge's and Caussade's) and two composition classes (Widor's and Vidal's). Caussade's is the pedantic class par excellence, so most of the prize winners come from among his students. But no musician has ever come out of it, for the simple reason that Caussade is very strong on the technical front but completely empty on the artistic one. The same goes for Vidal's class. Widor's class is less academic, but Widor is the kind of academic musician who can't understand anyone writing music different from his own. My friend Milhaud, who has the gifts of a genius and tends in an ultra-modern direction, had to leave Gédalge's class and go to Widor. He goes to it for appearance's sake but continues having private lessons with Gédalge because he regards him first of all as the best teacher and also the only one who, while teaching technique, doesn't influence a pupil's ideas and personality. At the Conservatory the composition class is effectively the fugue class, since a fugue is part of the exam, so no one has ever understood why it wasn't Gédalge who taught it. As a final proof of what I've been saying, one only has to recall that the most modern-minded composers like Ravel, Florent Schmitt, and Koechlin were Gédalge's pupils.

When I was working with Seidmann this summer, I was amazed to find that a pupil who had completed his studies, passing in succession through classes in counterpoint, fugue, composition, and orchestration at the Vienna Conservatory, was ignorant of the most elementary rules of harmony and absolutely incapable of writing either a correct bass or correct counterpoint. What's more, he had absolutely extraordinary ideas about the basics of music and his head was stuffed with stupid principles that went totally against everything you can find in composers like Palestrina, Bach, Mozart, and others. I expressed my astonishment to Gédalge, and he said: "When Enesco arrived in Paris he brought with him all the first prizes in harmony, counterpoint, and fugue from the Vienna Conservatory, but he was incapable of stringing two triads together. What they call a fugue is a piece that has four successive entries of a theme, and the rest consists simply of a succession of chords. He had to start right back at the beginning. As he was exceptionally gifted, it didn't take long, and now he's very grateful to me that he's turned into the composer we know." If Seidmann came to Paris, I'm convinced they wouldn't let him into a first-year harmony class. And he isn't an exception either, since in Zurich we were doing exactly the same thing and that's how it must be all over Germany. So I think that for me it could only delay the end of my studies, as I would of course have to get used to new ways of working, and especially as they seem to me far less profitable than the ones I'm following here.

From another point of view, when the war is over, it would be difficult for me to stay in Germany. I don't know the language well enough and my general outlook is too French for me to be welcome there. What's more, my musical sympathies with the new French school are growing daily. There's no doubting that, for the first time, France is currently at the head of musical developments. I got to know and love Reger and Strauss while I was in Switzerland, and I continue to love them, but I realized that composers like Debussy, Dukas, d'Indy, Florent Schmitt, and others, were newer and more original, and above all contained more feeling than the modern Germans. Strauss's music, considered on its own and apart from its orchestral clothing that is its principal strength (and a strength of genius in that composer), is infinitely less rich in invention than the music of Debussy, for example, and often contains things that are extremely banal and old-fashioned. Reger's music is admirably written, but it often lacks real imagination or emotion, and for that reason constitutes an abuse of technical procedures.

This, then, was the young composer's clear profession of his musical tastes, and today his opinions seem absolutely right and remarkably penetrating. He finished this important letter by mentioning money matters: he was doing his best to stay within a budget that had been modest right from the start. In particular, he noted that "next year I shan't be having violin lessons, as I've reached a level where it will be enough for me to work on my own, and as I have no intention of becoming a virtuoso, I can play well just by keeping in practice."

The arguments put forward in that letter are certainly highly reasonable and show considerable maturity of outlook in the writer. We should, even so, take off our hats to the composer's parents for accepting its contents without complaint, and not demurring at the prolongation of real financial sacrifices at a time when their son's career was still built more on hopes than on achievement.

Meanwhile, unknown certainly to those involved, the ingredients of the future Les Six continued to come together like pieces in a jig-saw puzzle. In June, Milhaud

> met a young man of sixteen at the house of some friends. Being older, he didn't attach any importance to him. The boy wrote him . . . , he replied with extreme condescension, and matters rested there. Milhaud had let Francis Poulenc cross his path without recognizing him; four years later they both had a good laugh about it.[8]

It was around the same time that Honegger met Erik Satie and Jean Cocteau in the salon of Valentine Gross (soon to become Valentine Hugo).

During June Turly arrived in Zurich, where his military duties were shortly to claim him. In the course of two periods of leave he wrote two new songs. The first, "Prière" (taken from the collection *De l'angélus de l'aube à l'angélus du soir* and written in Zurich in July), was his sole inroad into the poetic world of Francis Jammes, and it later found a place in his collection of *Four Poems for Voice and Piano*. He was later to regard it as containing his most perfect melodic line, in Gédalge's sense. As for "Automne" (written in Zurich in August), which was his first and most highly fruitful contact with the poetry of Guillaume Apollinaire, he later admitted that in his soldier's uniform he had lived this poem, to the extent of identifying himself with the wretched yokel, the stooped peasant plodding slowly next to his ox under a lowering November sky—a vision not far removed from the more tragic, fatalistic one evoked in Mussorgsky's *Bydlo*.

From 30 July to 14 August, he underwent two weeks of intensive weapon training. Arthur Honegger the marksman was not one of the most brilliant: his *Schiessbüchlein*, or firing record, puts him 166th out of a group of 185—the Honegger who, as a composer, was to hit the bull's-eye practically every time! But he also told Hélène Jourdan-Morhange,

> When the officer saw me, he said: "You're the musician? Conduct the choir!" One of my comic memories from that miserable period was the story of the trousers that split in the crucial place, the day I was conducting the choir in front of the colonel. What a scandal! When I raised my arms, you could see my bottom![9]

He was drafted into the 71st Battalion, 2nd Company, 3rd Section, and in September he found himself at Maglio di Colla, in the canton of Ticino on the Italian border. Milhaud remembered Honegger sending him two "highly picturesque letters describing the sentinels on the other side of the frontier who, in the summer heat, mounted guard under sunshades."[10]

After this military intermezzo—in truth more boring than alarming—Honegger got back to Paris on 3 October. He had managed to bring back with him from Switzerland some valuable scores that were unobtainable in France in wartime, and he had his parents send him others. Thanks to him, Milhaud discovered "scores by Bartók and Schoenberg, such as the wonderful *Book of the Hanging Gardens*, which we were very enthusiastic about."[11]

He went back to his studies at the Conservatory, and after a few days the worthy pupil announced to his parents, "Gédalge would like me to go into one of the Conservatory composition classes next year (either Vidal's or Widor's), because he hopes that I'll be at the top of his class by the end of this year."[12]

In the course of November Honegger finished the first version of the Finale of his *String Quartet No. 1*, which still had to undergo serious revision. The slow central movement still had to be written. At the same time he composed his *Hommage à Ravel*, which in 1919 was to be included between a prelude and a dance to form the *Three Pieces for piano*.

On 7 November he again wrote his parents: "My friend Milhaud is urging me strongly to join him in Widor's class. I'll ask Gédalge for his advice." And on the 24th, "Gédalge is going to give me a note allowing me to join Widor's course."

Two weeks later the deed was done. His letter of 15 December is particularly detailed:

> I'm still working with Gédalge and I've also gone into Widor's class, where I made my debut with two little songs, sung by my friend Milhaud. Widor said they were "charming, intelligent, and ingenious," and when Milhaud

claimed that the second one was like a Neapolitan ditty called *Funiculì, funiculà*, Widor exclaimed indignantly, "not at all!" Milhaud and I were splitting our sides with laughter because they were both old pieces (*Barcarolle* and one other). I've gone back to music-making at de Toledo's house[13]: we played my cello sonata together.

The *Barcarolle* mentioned has disappeared completely, and neither is there a trace of a "cello sonata" dating from this period. All this suggests, at the very least, that there must be several Honegger works that have since been lost, and that he wrote more music than might appear to be the case. It is worth noting that according to his diary this sonata was rehearsed on 25 and 26 May 1913 and then played at a Lyre Havraise concert on the 31st.

1916

The year 1916—the year of terrible butchery at Verdun and the longer drawn-out carnage of the Somme—was for Honegger another year of peaceful study like the previous one, but it brought even so some important changes to his life. Before the year was over, Honegger's music had been played several times in public, and notably by a girl he had just met who was to be his lifelong companion; he was separated for a few years from his closest friend Milhaud, who left for Brazil; and, as if to signal these changes, the last letter he wrote his parents that year was also the last to be signed Turly.

Two more songs date from the beginning of this year: in February "Clotilde," destined to become the second of the *Six Poems of Apollinaire*, and in March "La mort passe," on a poem by the Armenian Archag Tchobanian (to whose poetry he would return thirty years later in his *Four Songs for Low Voice*). "La mort passe" was added to the *Four Poems for Voice and Piano* begun two years earlier, but the collection was not published until 1921.

The news he sent his parents in March 1916 was good. "I've just been admitted to the conducting class taught by Vincent d'Indy, which is very interesting. I'm also giving harmony lessons. . . . This month I've written several songs and I'm working on the adagio of my quartet."

Honegger normally approached his large instrumental triptychs by writing the slow central movement first. But this time he left for last the expressive, spiritual heart of this great enterprise of his youth, a work for which the arduous composition extended over more than four years. As for the entry into d'Indy's class, it was an event of signal importance.

Just before the war, Gabriel Fauré, the peacemaker, had buried the hatchet that had for too long been brandished between the Conservatory and the Schola Cantorum. He did so through the excellent idea of appointing Vincent d'Indy to take charge of the Conservatory orchestra and conducting class. The composer of *Fervaal*, then in his sixties but still full of energy, had soon given the class a creative slant by allowing his composing students to try out their own works. In this way the class became a real course in practical orchestration, in which apprentice composers could hear what they had written and correct on the spot any "holes," faults of balance, or blatant banalities. Many years later Honegger remembered his time in this class with gratitude:

> We could in this way work with living material and not merely according to theoretical premises. . . . That was of more use to us in learning our craft than reading all the textbooks. I still feel a sincere gratitude to him. That was the real Vincent d'Indy, far more than the one found in his composition treatise edited by third parties, where inflexibility and unjust prejudice are at the opposite extreme from the encouragement and kindness he showed to us.[14]

D'Indy, for his part, soon recognized Honegger's exceptional character. Several years later he declared, "Some of the young of today will turn into true composers. But Honegger has genius."[15]

The beneficial results of Honegger's attendance at d'Indy's class could soon be seen in his first orchestral score, finished before the end of the year.

We may note at this point that the three teachers with whom he studied most closely were all men of a certain age. In 1916 Gédalge was sixty, d'Indy sixty-five, and Widor seventy-two, a few months older than Fauré, the director. But they were men of tolerant outlook and, up to a point, were willing to accept new ideas, unlike the reactionary wing in the Conservatory, consisting of people like Leroux, Vidal, and Caussade.

Marcel Delannoy, in describing a photograph of d'Indy's class, drew the following portrait of Honegger:

> To the left of d'Indy, very upright and sprightly with his little imperial beard, stands Honegger, already spreading in the middle, with short legs, a childlike smile, and brown curls over his ears. He is no longer the archangel of Zurich, but his eyes sparkle under the long curve of his eyebrows. He stands in a favorite pose, with his left hand on his hip and the right brandishing a tulip-shaped meerschaum pipe, which still has a place of honor in his pipe-rack.[16]

And we shall see that pipes (and pipes by the dozen) played a major role in the composer's life.

In April, he spent the Easter holidays in Le Havre, and from there brought back the completed Adagio for his *String Quartet No. 1* when he returned to Paris on 2 May. Later he asked his parents to send, both for himself and for Milhaud, Schoenberg's *Harmonielehre* (Treatise on Harmony). Honegger had heard it spoken of very highly and was convinced that there existed a French translation. (Schoenberg's *Harmonielehre* would be published in France by Lattès in 1983.) "It is," he wrote his parents, "apparently, an extraordinary work and indispensable for the modern composer."

In May he wrote two new songs: "Petite chapelle," on a poem by Jules Laforgue, finally completing the collection of *Four Poems*, and "À la Santé," which brought the cycle of *Six Poems of Apollinaire* up to three. The three remaining ones would appear at the beginning of 1917.

At the same time he was preparing himself for the final Conservatory counterpoint examination on 25 June. But he warned his parents about his chances of success, saying "Don't have any illusions about a prize I'm unlikely to win. The members of Gédalge's class write a little too freely for the holy men on the jury." This did not prevent him from working steadily. "As well as studying my counterpoint, I'm working at the moment on some variations for piano and a sonata for violin and piano. I'll probably take my quartet into Widor's class. I will let you know what sort of reaction it gets." This reaction came about soon enough and, in a letter of 18 June, Arthur gave his parents a detailed account, after telling them that he would rather give up his idea of going to see them in Zurich (because, in spite of his permanent military leave, he was afraid he might not get permission to return to France):

> I think it is more sensible for me not to come to Switzerland this summer. What a deplorable idea it was of yours to retire there when you would have done so much better in Le Havre or Paris, surrounded by friends who would have made life much more pleasant for you. . . . I hope that after the war we'll be able to see each other more often, and with you in France a good deal more than me in Switzerland.

He went on to say that he was preparing for his history of music examination.

> I'll be glad when it's over because I've got a violin sonata and the variations, which are still only sketched out for the moment. . . . I showed Widor my quartet, but so far he's only been able to take in the first movement, which is much the easiest to understand, being the oldest. He found it extremely extended (at the entry of the second theme he thought he was already in the middle of the development section) and thought the harmony was frighteningly "grimacing." I'm afraid the Adagio, which is much more polyphonic and polyharmonic, will cause him some nasty moments. But he's so nice, and afterward always tells you you have a lot of talent.

The first movement of the *First Violin Sonata* was finished in July, but the whole work was not completed until February 1918. Meanwhile, the *Toccata and Variations* for piano was finished in September 1916.

A letter to his parents, dated 7 July, tells us that, as he expected, he did not win any sort of prize for counterpoint, since the jury was made up for the most part of "harmonic fault-finders." Only one first prize was awarded, to

> a young girl in Caussade's class who is well up in harmony too. Even so, I wouldn't want to change places with her. . . . More interesting for me is the fact that a complete performance took place of my quartet with Yvan Giorod, a first-prize winner for violin, playing second violin, Milhaud on viola, and Delgrange on cello. I'm very happy to find that the overall sound was what I had in mind, which proves that I do at least know something despite the absence of official laurels on my brow.

The "young girl in Caussade's class" was in fact Andrée Vaurabourg, the composer's future wife, mentioned by him here for the first time. As Milhaud recalled, "Arthur and I sat beside each other in Maurice Emmanuel's music history class, and with us always sat Andrée Vaurabourg, the young girl who would later become [Honegger's] wife."[17]

Andrée Vaurabourg was born in Toulouse on 8 September 1894, and so was two and a half years younger than Honegger. She was the daughter of Rodolphe-Séraphin Vaurabourg, commercial traveler (born Auvergny, France, 19 August 1851; died Boulogne-sur-Seine, France, 30 April 1915) and Louise-Adeline Chevallier (born Paris, 11 March 1858; died Mougins, France, 12 February 1935), married at Pontoise, near Paris, 29 April 1889.

The "young girl in Caussade's class" was already an excellent pianist and strong academically, enabling her to snap up the first prizes in the written papers that eluded her newfound friend. She would soon become his favorite interpreter and would from now on always be a part of his life, even though ten years elapsed before they were married. Like so many female musicians who have been the wives or companions of celebrated composers, she gave up the thought of being a composer herself, after showing some considerable gifts in this direction. Instead, she would become for the rest of her life not only a pianist but one of the best harmony and counterpoint teachers of her time. Proof of this would later be given by her most famous counterpoint pupil, the young Pierre Boulez.

For the moment, though, she attended the class of Maurice Emmanuel, for whom teaching, it must be said, was a vocation, masking his output as a first-rate composer. The twenty-two-year-old girl, known then and ever after as "Vaura" (or "Vaurara" to a few close friends), struck her fellow pupils "by the calm, regular beauty of her face, framed by pre-Raphaelite headbands."[18]

In July 1916 Honegger's music was played in public for the very first time. With some of his friends, he founded the CMDI (Centre musical et dramatique indépendant), which gave concerts in the little Salle Oedenkoven at 15 avenue Hoche, just by the Place de l'Étoile. It was there, on 11 July, that Rose Armandie sang the three songs that had then been written of the six that would soon make up the cycle on Apollinaire's *Alcools*. They were, in the order of their future publication, "À la Santé," "Clotilde," and "Automne."

That summer, Honegger stayed in Paris and in August wrote a song on a poem taken from *Complaintes et Dits* by Paul Fort, the so-called Prince of Poets: "Le chasseur perdu en forêt." Two more followed in October ("Cloche du soir") and November ("Chanson de fol"), making up a new little cycle. Honegger's song production was never again so prolific as in his time at the Conservatory. In a letter to his parents of 28 August, he enclosed for the first time a photo of "Vaura," adding,

At the moment I'm making music with the little Pugno pupil whose photo I send you. She's a pianist of the highest caliber and at least as good as any of the first-prize winners I know. . . . I had the opportunity of meeting the famous Claudel at Milhaud's, who is a friend of his, but unfortunately I let it slip.

The meeting between Honegger and Claudel would take place only much later, at the time of *Jeanne d'Arc au bûcher* (Joan of Arc at the Stake), but it would be perhaps the most important meeting of the composer's life. Shortly after this failed meeting, Milhaud left France to serve as secretary for Claudel, who had been appointed ambassador to Brazil. He came back only three years later, infinitely richer in artistic and human experience, just in time to find his place in Les Six, which was then being formed.

In September Honegger finally completed the large piece he had been working on for months and which would remain his most extended enterprise for solo piano. Called *Toccata and Variations*, it was not published until 1921, when it bore a dedication to the memory of his uncle Oskar in Zurich, who had died the previous year.

On 18 October he moved into what he called "the apartment of his dreams" at 21 rue Duperré, where he would remain until the summer of 1931. Three letters to his parents give us a picture of his musical activities at this time.

> During the holidays I finished a fairly important work for piano, *Toccata and Variations*, which has had some success with my colleagues. . . . It's been declared horribly difficult by the pianists. I'm also working on a sonata for piano and violin and on three poems by Paul Fort. I'll get them all performed in Widor's class, also my quartet, which he's asked to hear.[19]

> My little pianist friend, the Pugno pupil, is working at my Variations in order to play them to Widor and Gédalge. . . . I've had a rough ride from Gédalge because of an inoffensive little song that he found incoherent. He claims that as soon as I think up a beautiful melodic idea, I can't wait to spoil it with nasty harmonies.[20]

> Last Thursday, Mlle Vaurabourg played my *Toccata and Variations* to Widor's class. It was nearly a success. Widor almost restrained himself from being rude to me, in spite of the very daring things my music contained, and even the students listened with respect and showered me with praise. I'll be taking other things fairly often, as it makes the class more lively. Everyone is feeling the effects of Milhaud's departure. He won't go to the front. He's involved with the department of photographic propaganda and is already the head of his own office. Perhaps he'll be summoned to Rome as part of a diplomatic mission under Claudel.
>
> By chance I found Schoenberg's treatise at Eschig's. I'm being urged strongly to translate it, but I hesitate to embark on a labor that would be very long and difficult.
>
> I have a lot of work. I've started two large orchestral pieces, I've finished my settings of poems by Paul Fort, and I'm in the middle of my violin sonata. But I'm happy and feeling very fit at the moment.
>
> To help my budget, I'm playing in the orchestra of the Théâtre des Champs-Élysées. An Italian director has taken it over and we play thoroughly awful music on Sunday afternoons, but we get 14 francs for the concert and one rehearsal.
>
> Last Monday Mme Armandie and Andrée Vaurabourg sang for Widor

my settings of poems from Apollinaire's *Alcools*. It wasn't much of a success, but the words took more of a beating than the music. To show that I can also write sensible, classical things, I'm going to arrange a performance of my trio, which will undoubtedly win more friends. After that, we'll see about the quartet and the violin sonata.[21]

Honegger's life as a student was, therefore, almost hermetically sealed, bounded by his studies and by an artistic life that the war restricted only partially. On 15 December Andrée Vaurabourg played the *Toccata and Variations* for the first time in public, in the Salle Oedenkoven. At the same time Honegger was putting the finishing touches to his first orchestral score (there is no further reference to the second piece mentioned above).

I've just completed a prelude for orchestra to Maeterlinck's play *Aglavaine et Sélysette*, which will be played by the Conservatory orchestra on 25 January, first under d'Indy's baton and then mine. At the last concert by the Société du Conservatoire [that is to say, the CMDI, in which the participants were mostly Conservatory pupils] there was another performance of my *Variations*. They first of all amazed and then bored the audience, which was already tired after various long pieces, but they provoked lively discussions among the pupils, which for me is the only real success, because it's rare that one can interest one's colleagues, who are in general rather blasé.... As for the "sensible, classical little trio," Widor had the crust to tell me it was the best thing of mine he'd heard, and he keeps on mentioning it at every class![22]

1917

The year 1917 followed the pattern of the previous one, with the Conservatory remaining the center of an existence devoted increasingly to unremitting hard work. At the same time it also saw Honegger developing his contacts with the outside world, and in particular with the composers who more and more frequently shared with him the concerts devoted to new music and who would soon become Les Six. His friendship with Andrée Vaurabourg also grew closer, and for the first time he would spend his summer holidays with her. But two years passed before he visited his parents in Switzerland.

On New Year's Day 1917 Honegger finished the orchestration of his first orchestral score, the *Prelude* for *Aglavaine et Sélysette*, which Salabert published only in 1956, after the composer's death. The choice of Maeterlinck serves only to confirm that Honegger was then in the middle of his Debussy phase, and the *Rhapsody* written in April was further, almost final proof of this orientation. Debussy was a salutary antidote to the influence of Wagner, Strauss, Reger, and other German Romantics. Honegger later admitted to his biographer Marcel Delannoy, "Debussy has always been one of my greatest musical pleasures and I can see objectively that he was a genius. Impressionism dazzled me as in a flash of rare intensity."[23]

In a letter written at the end of January, Honegger described to his parents the first performance of this orchestral work, which took place on the 25th. He had had to copy out all the orchestral parts himself.

> I had the double satisfaction of finding that my first orchestral work sounded very well and realized my intentions, and the pleasure of hearing my music played by good performers. The strange thing was that, after I'd showed my score to d'Indy, he pointed out two or three places where he said I would probably be disappointed. After the performance, he told me he took back what he'd said and that the piece sounded very good as it was.

Better still, d'Indy got Fauré to agree that the young composer should himself conduct the work at the annual concert given by the student orchestra, and, Honegger wrote, "that is more precious to me than the warmest congratulations."

Honegger did not rest on his laurels. During this same month of January he added another song, "L'adieu," to the collection based on Apollinaire's *Alcools*, and in March completed the collection with "Saltimbanques" and "Les cloches." He wrote another song in February, *Nature morte*, on a poem by the Dutch writer Vanderpyl. This short song was published in July 1919 in the magazine *L'Arbitraire*.

On 28 February he wrote his parents once more:

> I've started translating the main parts of Schoenberg's treatise. It's a fairly long job. I've also written some songs and finished the scherzo of my sonata for violin and piano. . . . I was praised by M. Emmanuel, the professor of music history, who came to hear [*Aglavaine et Sélysette*]. He put his hand on my shoulder and pronounced solemnly "this is a musician." So I shall have to believe it. D'Indy also declared that I was the one who had the most instinctive grasp of orchestration and conducting.

Honegger, then, completed the second movement of his sonata eight months after the first, and it would be almost another year (February 1918) before the work was complete.

In his letter of 17 March, he asked to be sent scores of Schoenberg and of Mahler's *Second Symphony*, which were still impossible to obtain in Paris in wartime. The overriding influence of Debussy had not diminished his interest in the most recent German music.

On 3 April, as planned, Honegger conducted his *Prelude* for *Aglavaine et Sélysette* at the annual concert of the orchestral class. But he was already involved in new projects: ·

> At the moment I'm in the thick of new things. I've started a *Rhapsody for two flutes, clarinet, and piano*, which is going quite well and which I hope to have played at a concert of the Cercle in June. I'm also working on the finale of my violin sonata and on a poem by H. Charasson. He has intro-

duced me to Apollinaire and to a Dutch writer, Vanderpyl, one of whose poems I've set to music. Apollinaire is going to come to the house one evening and hear the settings of his poetry.[24]

In fact, the *Rhapsody* was finished before the end of the month. Its first performance took place not at the Cercle (that is to say, the CMDI), but only toward the end of the year, on 17 November, and for a year or so it would be one of Honegger's most frequently played works. No trace exists of any song on a poem by H. Charasson, and unfortunately Honegger never said anything to his parents about Apollinaire's reaction to his music.

A number of other points, too, remain unclear. Honegger, for example, makes no mention anywhere of his first meeting with Poulenc. Luckily, Poulenc himself had a good deal more to say on the subject, but it could be that his memory was not entirely accurate in placing the meeting in the spring of 1917. A slightly later date seems more likely.

It was at this time that the pianist Ricardo Viñes introduced his favorite eighteen-year-old pupil to the Sunday musical gatherings organized by the singer Jane Bathori in her house. One day André Caplet, a regular visitor there, brought along the *Three Unaccompanied Part Songs for Mixed Chorus* by Ravel, published only the previous year. A sight-reading session promptly began, as Poulenc recalls:

> Naturally, Bathori and some of her pupils took the soprano and mezzo lines, while the bass and baritone parts went to my teacher Charles Koechlin, with his beard like that of some river god, to Honegger, and to myself, among others. It was the first time I saw Honegger, and in the course of singing the Ravel songs I made one or two mistakes. Honegger turned to me and said, "Solfège, young man!" You mustn't forget that he was seven years older than me, which obviously meant that, when it came to it, I should treat him with respect. I was very intimidated and this first contact led to my continuing to be so for a very long time.[25]

On 18 May, Diaghilev's Ballets Russes returned to Paris with the scandalous premiere of Satie's *Parade*. Milhaud could not be there, as he was in Brazil with Claudel, but even so he later referred to it as the real "rallying cry of the younger generation." The cubist decor was by Picasso, while Apollinaire wrote the program notes, in which the word "surrealism" appeared for the first time. But Honegger immediately distanced himself from his future comrades in Les Six. He would never be a fan of Satie, about whose talent he had doubts. Even at the end of his life Honegger had still not changed his mind. Writing to Poulenc on 10 May 1954, he said, "I consider Satie an exceptionally honest spirit, but devoid of all creative ability—'Do what I say, never what I do.'"

The evening was a riotous one. The right-wing reactionaries and chauvinists among the music critics went as far as seeing it as a manifestation of "boche" (a derogatory term for German) attitudes, and it was shortly followed by a highly publicized lawsuit.

In June, Honegger's new *Rhapsody* had a read-through at the Conservatory.

I've had my *Rhapsody* for two flutes and clarinet played in d'Indy and Widor's class. It was a success, and both my teachers thought I treated the wind instruments skillfully. It brought home to me, as did the performances of my quartet and my orchestral prelude, that I can hear very clearly what I'm writing, because I didn't have the slightest disappointment over the sound of any of these pieces, which most young composers do.

I was completely satisfied with all the effects I'd aimed at, even the riskiest ones, and my use of the instruments must have been on the right lines because an hour's rehearsal was enough for a score about thirty pages long. Widor was so complimentary that it even made me a bit cross.

I've also taken the preliminary examination. The result was favorable, but I was the only one out of Gédalge's class to be chosen, and I'll have to compete against thirteen students from Caussade's class, most of whom have been working for this final examination for the last three years. They're careful not to waste their time composing as I do. No, instead they slog away at the same exercise for several hours a day without at any time bothering over music. Naturally, after that sort of training they get a prize, but after that they're musically finished and unable to compose anything whatsoever. You see it in Widor's and Vidal's classes, where only about six or seven of the thirty students compose. The rest grind on till they get their prize for fugue, and then they're completely wiped out forevermore.

The most important thing for me has been my entry into the world of the cubists and futurists.[26]

Honegger's *Six Poems of Apollinaire* were sung at a concert in the rue Huyghens in the middle of an exhibition of paintings.

I had a very good reception. Satie, Apollinaire, Kisling, and the musicians present showed real enthusiasm and made me promise to collaborate in some much more important concerts that they're giving next winter. Satie suggested I join him and ten or so other composers to put on concerts of our own music. An American painter, called Lachman, also asked me to take part in concerts he's organizing this winter. I shall also have a performance soon at a concert organized by Satie and the Simultaneist poet Blaise Cendrars, and finally Apollinaire has arranged a meeting to make me a proposition. I should very much like to send you the event program illustrated by Picasso, but it's rather too large.

Not that it was all praise in my direction. During the performance I was in a corner of the hall next to a group containing the poet Max Jacob, and I overhead myself being dissected as never before in my life. I was really being raked over the coals. The funniest thing was M. Jacob's face when I was introduced to him afterward, and he recognized his neighbor who could have no illusions about what he thought. After the concert I had dinner with a whole group of cubists and spent the evening at the Café de la Rotonde. The most extraordinary collection of people were there, people with long hair and beards. Then we went to Lachman's studio. I've also become a member of a new society called Musique that gives concerts of modern music. I'll probably get some performances there during the winter.

I've also been asked to write the music for a ballet, or rather a "mime-drama," featuring a splendid parrot, who's as fat as a turkey-hen and wonderfully colored.

All these goings-on have left me quite tired and I'm impatient for the moment when I can go and spend a little time in the country. I'm hoping to find a little hideaway near Paris where I can rest, because I really need it.[27]

So it was that a sensible, well-organized young man, still smacking of his bourgeois provincial upbringing, found himself abruptly launched into a totally new and unexpected world, and one that instantly adopted and absorbed him. The result was, for the next year, a curiously double life. Along with all these activities Honegger was, until the summer of 1918, pursuing his studies with his teachers at the Conservatory. He worked hard for them, too, and showed them respect, even if his new friends regarded them all as old codgers. Satie, for instance, used to refer to his "venerable teacher d'Indouille" ("andouille" means "idiot"—Tr.).

The concert Honegger speaks of must have been the one on 6 June about which there is so much contradictory information. The first question is, which of the *Six Poems of Apollinaire* were sung and by whom? We know that the collection had been finished since March, so there is no reason why it should not have been given complete on 6 June—no reason, that is, except that we know the first complete performance was given by Jane Bathori and Andrée Vaurabourg at the Théâtre du Vieux-Colombier on 15 January 1918.

Number 6 rue Huyghens contained the studio of a painter with the prophetic name of Lejeune. Even though Montparnasse, in the middle of which the rue Huyghens lies, would not become the center of Parisian artistic life until after the war, this studio was frequented by all the budding artists of the Left Bank. According to Éveline Hurard-Viltard, it was Cendrars who had the idea of providing exhibitions and *vernissages* (or previews) there with musical accompaniment.[28] He turned first of all to Satie. For his part, the painter Kisling, through his colleague René Durey, brought along Durey's brother Louis, the last name of Les Six to fall into place—though in truth they would only be five until Milhaud came back from Brazil.

It seems that there were small concerts every Saturday, at least from January 1917, in what was called the Salle Huyghens. Jean Cocteau described the place in his book *Carte blanche*:

The Salle Huyghens (a ground-floor studio at the far end of a courtyard at 6 rue Huyghens) is one of those popular places to which the public keeps coming back. You either freeze or suffocate, squashed up against each other, whether you're sitting or standing—it's like being in the Métro.... The contact between artists and audience both helping to move the piano, the petrol lamp that causes arguments, the stove that refuses to catch in winter and gets hot in summer, all that leads to a cantankerous atmosphere, which is why they always come back.[29]

To that we may add the descriptions by the actor Pierre Bertin ("Those garden chairs, that mixture of sweaters and diamonds, that large stove in the middle, that wooden floor") and by Jean Wiéner ("It was a dreadful place, with broken window-panes, but there you rubbed shoulders with the people who fashioned the epoch").[30]

Hélène Jourdan-Morhange took part in these evening gatherings, and she confirms that Blaise Cendrars had been the moving spirit, and that the cellist Félix Delgrange (whom we have already met playing through Honegger's quartet at the Conservatory) now turned impresario and took over the organization and the financial risks, not that these were very great.[31] Later on he would provide the young composers with the more convenient Salle des Agriculteurs, in the rue d'Athènes.

According to Willy Tappolet and Éveline Hurard-Viltard, that famous concert on 6 June contained Satie's *Parade*, Honegger's *Six Poems of Apollinaire* (there were in fact only three at this time, as we have already seen), a trio by Auric, and Louis Durey's *Carillons*.[32] Hurard-Viltard also mentions not only an unspecified work by Germaine Tailleferre, but also a talk given by Satie "announcing that these three young composers and Satie himself had just formed the group of Nouveaux Jeunes." Even so, it is astonishing that Honegger does not breathe a word of this in his letter. He makes no mention of the name until 30 April 1918. It is possible that this talk was instead given at the concert of 1 December 1917, also at the Salle Huyghens, which will be mentioned later. On the other hand, I have found no evidence for Willy Tappolet's claim that the concert of 6 June was given again ten days later.

On 26 July Arthur informed his parents that he had not won any prizes at the Conservatory. He simply would never be an "examination animal"!

> As you can guess, I came away empty-handed, and no one was less surprised by it than I, even though, after all the hard work I've put in, I might have deserved a second, third, or fourth prize. But anyway it doesn't matter in the least. My friend Mlle Vaurabourg, who was so badly treated over her harmony exam, has got the compensation of a second prize, and my chum Marimian was delighted by his fourth prize, which means that his father will receive him with open arms and open wallet.
>
> Musical activity has come to an end for this season. I took my songs to Mme Engel-Bathori and she liked them. She'll probably sing them next season.

On another front, he took part in the highly publicized court case brought by the critic Jean Poueigh, following *Parade*.

> Poueigh, who is among the lower ranks of critics, had poured scorn on Satie's ballet. The composer then made fun of him by sending him a series of open postcards in which he addressed him in fairly direct language. Poueigh was outraged and brought a lawsuit against him. It was hilarious listening to the cards being read out indignantly by Poueigh's lawyer and repeated in the judgment by the president, who looked distinctly cross at

being obliged to read out such epithets. Here, for Toto's [Honegger's sister Marguerite-Julie] amusement, is the third of the cards: "Mr. Jean-Fucker Poueigh, king of the idiots, chief of the nitwits, emperor of the stokers. Asshole. I'm here in Fontainebleau, from where I shit on you with all my might. E. S."

Naturally, Satie was punished, but much more severely than we were expecting. Eight days in prison, a thousand francs in damages and interest, and a one-hundred franc fine. He appealed and it will probably come up in December. According to the newspapers, the public for this consisted of "the whole artistic world of Montparnasse." In fact, there were only the Engel-Bathoris, Cocteau, Auric, Fargue, Viñes, Armandie, and myself.

But hard work still claimed Honegger. "I'm still busy composing and have finished the first movement of a string quartet." This was the third and final version of the first movement of the *String Quartet No. 1*, the first version of which dated from as far back as September 1913 in Zurich. Finally, he announced that he was going to spend the summer at Carantec in Brittany with the Vaurabourgs.

His next letter was dated 7 August, from Carantec where he had been for a week. He described the place, which he found attractive, and added, "I'm also thinking of writing a little trio for flute, violin, and viola." No trace survives of this project. On the other hand, after his return to Paris, he wrote on 3 September: "Since I got back I've been working on my quartet. I've almost finished two preludes for organ and I've started a new orchestral thing to be played at the Conservatory this winter."

He was then putting the Finale of the quartet into its ultimate shape, and the work was nearly finished. The two organ pieces—the only two he wrote for Bach's favorite instrument—are a Fugue, dedicated to his first teacher in Le Havre, Robert-Charles Martin, and a Chorale, dedicated to Andrée Vaurabourg. The "orchestral thing" he had begun was *Le Chant de Nigamon*.

On 5 October he was "still working on the end of the quartet, which is going well." During the same month he put the finishing touches to this fruit of long labor. Despite Honegger's being led to hope for an early performance, nearly two years passed before the public heard this synthesis of all his youthful talents. The work may, from this point of view, be termed his first "masterpiece," marking, as it did, the point at which he ceased to be an apprentice and became a master craftsman. He also started on "a little thing for female voice and piano," which we can no longer identify, and was hoping to enter Widor's class permanently (it seems that up to this point he had merely audited the class).

In a letter he wrote to his parents on 11 November 1917, we learn that he was

just finishing a large work for orchestra that will probably be played at the Conservatory this winter. It's a sort of symphonic poem that I shall call *Le Chant de Nigamon* and which represents an American Indian sacrifice. A jolly subject, as you see, but it's a lot of work and the scoring is for a large orchestra. As I shall have to copy the orchestral parts, that'll be 600 pages to write between now and the beginning of January.

At the same time he was orchestrating an operetta for the Vaudeville Theater to earn some money, as well as having the parts copied for his quartet, which was going to be played at the Théâtre du Vieux-Colombier, where Jane Bathori was also going to sing the *Six Poems of Apollinaire*. Later on, the same theater would see performances of the *Rhapsody* and the *Sonata for violin and piano*, "which people are wanting for different concerts, even though the finale has hardly been begun." He could not think of getting down to it, being so deeply absorbed in composing *Le Chant de Nigamon*. He mentioned a possible performance of his *String Quartet No. 1* in Switzerland, and warned his parents, "I'm not sure you'll like it. It's not very easy on the ear, at least in spots!"

This was the first of his letters to mention Jane Bathori (1877–1970) and the Théâtre du Vieux-Colombier, both of which were to play crucial roles in Honegger's career during the years to come, and in the careers of all his young composing friends. When Jacques Copeau left for the United States, he handed over his theater to Bathori's care, and she immediately set about making it a center for new music. Bathori had a special affection for French song, in which she often accompanied herself on the piano. She was the singer in the first performance of Ravel's *Histoires naturelles* in 1907, which caused such a scandal, and later gave first performances of Debussy's *Le Promenoir des deux amants* (1911) and of Ravel's *Poèmes de Mallarmé* (1914) and *Chansons madécasses* (1926). As well as opening the doors of her theater to the younger composers, she often gave first performances of their works too. She soon did so for Honegger's *Six Poems of Apollinaire*, and she also commissioned him to write *Le Dit des jeux du monde*. Some years later, when she was no longer in charge of the Vieux-Colombier, she organized the first performances in Latin America of *Le Roi David* and *Judith*.

It is impossible to fix precisely the date on which Honegger began to attend the musical soirées that Jane Bathori gave in her flat on the boulevard Péreire. What is certain is that at one of them he met Fernand Ochsé, who, until his tragic death, would remain one of Honegger's closest friends.

One evening Honegger had, as usual, been playing second violin in the quartet formed by Bathori, and afterward he found himself at a table next to a "person you would think had escaped from a nineteenth-century lithograph, with silvery, wavy hair, a rather long, pointed beard like Alfred de Musset's, and something about his clothes too."[33] That is Marcel Delannoy's description of the man Honegger at first took to be the critic Émile Vuillermoz, whom he was dying to meet after the very favorable review the latter had written of the *Rhapsody*. In fact it was Ochsé, who was a painter, theater designer, musician, and writer, an aesthete anyway, with something slightly dandified about him. Ochsé was in the middle of adapting for the Vieux-Colombier the medieval *Game of Robin and Marion*, in which he was going to play the role of one of the two drummers. Honegger agreed to play the other one and this was the beginning of a long friendship. Some weeks later, Ochsé amazed Honegger by sight-reading the *Six Poems of Apollinaire* in his approximate tenor voice. He painted several portraits of Honegger and also introduced him to the conductor Walther Straram.

As a composer, Ochsé was more erratic than professional, but he did compose an operetta called *Choucoune*, which Honegger orchestrated, and in 1930, when Honegger wrote his own operetta, *Les Aventures du roi Pausole* (The Adventures of King Pausolus), he dedicated it "to the composer of *Choucoune*." Between those dates, and indeed later, Honegger often stayed at Ochsé's country house at Montfort l'Amaury. Their friendship came to an end with Ochsé's death. In 1944 he was arrested by the Germans because he was Jewish. Honegger did everything he could, using every influence he could muster, to save his friend. In vain. Ochsé was on the last train from Drancy to Auschwitz a few weeks before the Liberation. Right to the end of Honegger's life, he would always say to himself, when he finished a work, "What would Fernand have thought of it?"[34]

On 17 November the *Rhapsody* received its first public performance. Andrée Vaurabourg was the pianist in the concert, which took place under the auspices of the Université Interalliée du Parthénon, a cultural organization run by the composer Henry Woollett, who had come to Paris from Le Havre. The work, with its seductive, Debussyan overtones, was very well received. It was frequently performed after that, specifically on 1 December at another concert in the Salle Huyghens devoted to music by the Nouveaux Jeunes, which also included a trio by Durey. Ten days later, on 11 December, Francis Poulenc appeared as a composer for the first time, at the Vieux-Colombier, in a performance of his *Negro Rhapsody*, his Opus 1.

For Honegger the year ended with the completion of the orchestral score and the piano reduction of *Le Chant de Nigamon*, which d'Indy found "very interesting and well orchestrated."[35] A first run-through was fixed for 10 January 1918 at the Conservatory. D'Indy and Widor both had a look at the quartet, but Widor found it too complicated: "At one point, he claims, it sounds as though four instrumentalists are each playing a different concerto or as though four pianists are each playing a different piece with each hand."[36] Gédalge too, although he liked it on the whole, found it "too aggressive." But d'Indy wanted to put it on at the Société nationale, together with the *Rhapsody*. He preferred the latter, because the quartet, being so difficult, needed to be played well or not at all. Honegger had come a long way in a year, and now was on the verge of being a young *maître*.

1918

Honegger was, in any case, well on the way to being the most frequently performed of the Nouveaux Jeunes. On 15 January, the poet René Chalupt introduced them in a pre-concert speech. Those represented were Germaine Tailleferre with her *Sonatina for Strings*; Georges Auric, whose *Gaspard and Zoé* was played by the pianist Marcelle Meyer, a fervent champion of the avant-garde; Louis Durey with his *Carillons* for piano duet, in which Mlle Meyer took one of the parts; Francis Poulenc with a repeat of his *Negro Rhapsody*; Arthur Honegger with the first performance of the complete set of the *Six Poems of Apollinaire*, given by Jane Bathori and Andrée Vaurabourg; and finally, a new-comer, an artilleryman on leave named Roland-Manuel, who might, and ought to, were it not for his fortuitous absence a year later, have become the seventh member of Les Six. At the last minute an instrumentalist was missing for the performance of his *Seven Poems of Persia*. As Roland-Manuel recalled,

> The oboist was missing. While I was in despair, a young man with a face straight out of a Raphael painting emerged from the wings, in a black vel-vet suit and with a viola in his hand, and kindly offered to play it as a replacement for the missing oboe. And he did so perfectly, to my surprise and then delight. By way of thanks he received a dedication from the com-poser to M. Honegger, with his Christian name changed inadvertently to André, which, twenty-four years later, fills me with retrospective embar-rassment.[37]

That evening the game of musical chairs continued, with Darius Milhaud being the missing party from the future Les Six. At the concert on 5 February, again at the Théâtre du Vieux-Colombier, Poulenc was the absent member, with Satie taking his place. Before his *Bureaucratic Sonatina* and the song *Daphé-néo*, sung by its dedicatee, Jane Bathori, Satie gave his famous talk *In Praise of Critics*. The program also contained Honegger's *Rhapsody*, Milhaud's *Second Violin Sonata*, Auric's *Poems of Cocteau*, Durey's *Premier concert en trio*, and Tailleferre's *Sonatina*. In her book *Le Groupe des Six, ou le matin d'un jour de fête*, Éveline Hurard-Viltard places these two programs the other way around. She must be mistaken, however, because the 1 February issue of *Le Courrier musi-cal* includes a review, signed Marcel Orban, of the *Six Poems of Apollinaire* ("one is glad to find interesting intentions in the group of songs by Mr. Honegger"). These songs were heard again on 19 January at the Université Interalliée du Parthénon, together with the *Toccata and Variations* and the first two move-ments of the *Violin Sonata* (the Finale had yet to be completed). This occasion was probably the first all-Honegger concert. Honegger himself played the vio-lin, Vaura the piano.[38]

On 17 January Honegger conducted the first read-through of *Le Chant de Nigamon* at the Conservatory. He was congratulated by both d'Indy and Straram, and pronounced himself satisfied with what he had written. In a letter to his parents, he gave a detailed description of the work, complete with story-line and music examples, and finished by saying:

> I conducted so energetically that I've got a blister on my right hand! . . . As for the *Rhapsody*, it's being played frequently and successfully. Leduc wants to publish it. . . . Perhaps I should have sent this to Switzerland instead of the quartet. But it's better I should risk the drubbing I expect the latter will earn me, rather than not have the courage of my convictions.[39]

The Société nationale had, at d'Indy's suggestion, initially accepted the quartet, but now turned it down because Honegger was Swiss. However, the SMI (Société de musique indépendante) put it into their schedule for April. The work aroused controversy. Honegger went on to state in his letter that Ravel thought it was "so aggressive, one doesn't know whether it's beautiful or ugly," and Max d'Ollone told Fernand Ochsé, "Your friend Honegger doesn't mind bumps and blows!" But none of this bothered the composer, who was hard at work.

> At the moment I'm working on the finale of my violin sonata. After that I'd be glad of a short rest. Not that I think it'll happen, because I've already sketched out a trio, a piano piece, and a third prelude for organ. Fernand Ochsé is trying to organize my operatic debut. He wants to have it put on at the Vieux-Colombier with himself as producer.

He did indeed complete the *First Violin Sonata* the following month, but nothing came of the other works he mentions, which were ousted by other ideas.

On 19 March, Hélène Jourdan-Morhange and Andrée Vaurabourg gave the first performance of the finally completed sonata at the Vieux-Colombier. Two days earlier, Honegger had told his parents, "Next Tuesday my violin sonata will be played for the first time. The performers are working hard at it, because apparently it's terribly difficult." But all went well, and in his letter of 26 March he could write, "Last Tuesday the sonata was performed with great success." In addition, the quartet was programmed by the SMI for 15 April.

In Zurich, on the other hand, it was refused by the program committee. The composer and conductor Volkmar Andreae remarked, "He's still got a lot to learn." Honegger was considerably needled by this, and offered a passionate defense of the work, justifying its detail and architecture and insisting that it contained no faults of technique. He quoted the two criticisms that had been leveled against it in France: to Gédalge's objection, that the recapitulation of the first theme comes too near the end of the first movement, he responded for the first time with the principle of the inverted recapitulation, which was to govern practically all his sonata-form movements until the end of his life; and to Milhaud's comment, that the complete reappearance of the second theme in the Adagio was "long and unnecessary," he retorted that he was merely following classical precedent. It is quite clear that the quartet, into which he had put so much of himself, was the work by which the composer set most store.

On the very day he wrote that letter, 26 March 1918, Debussy died after a long and painful illness. On 14 April Arthur told his parents that, as his studies would be coming to an end with that Conservatory year, he would be leaving Gédalge's class. As he would not be able to join Widor's class until the following January, he would therefore not be at the Conservatory in the meantime. He did not then realize that he would never return there.

The final German offensive, including bombardments from "Big Bertha," meant that some concerts, including the SMI program featuring Honegger's *String Quartet No. 1*, had to be postponed. But Honegger conducted *Le Chant de Nigamon* with the Conservatory student orchestra on 25 April (and not on the 18th, as one usually finds in the sources). On 30 April he wrote of the success his work had and, in the same letter, spoke for the first time of the founding of the Nouveaux Jeunes, mentioning Satie, Durey, Auric, Tailleferre, and himself. He also gave a description of the new piece he was working on, *Le Dit des jeux du monde*, which was due to be performed at the end of September.

> The last musical event was the performance of my poem for orchestra at the Conservatory, under my baton. In spite of a slight mishap at the start, it went well and was regarded as a considerable success. I should also say that by general consent my piece went well beyond those of my colleagues, which were classified as correct exercises, written by students who were well-behaved and respectful of tradition.
>
> I'm busy writing a work that's half drama and half ballet, in collaboration with the poet Paul Méral and the painter Fauconnet. This work will be put on at the end of September and will go much further than anything else that's ever been done along these lines. That is to say, by comparison the cubists will look like fuddy-duddy old academics. Which is not to say that it's anything outrageously incomprehensible. Far from it. Our aim is to go back to classical tradition, and the scenario, for example, is constructed like one of Aeschylus's tragedies. The costume designs are sober and linear, and the music will be wholly anti-impressionistic. The performers have been decided. The dramatic side of things will be in the hands of actors from the Comédie-Française, and there'll also be a circus clown (probably Footitt), and the dancing will be done by Raymond Duncan and his school. As you see, it'll be different, and I'd very much like you to be there for this occasion. For me, the score entails ten dance numbers, two intermezzos, and probably a prelude, all of which is a fair number of pages to have to scribble.

This vast, cosmic cycle aimed at nothing less than the representation, through humans, animals, and Nature, of the "three elementary phases of creation: birth, life, and death." In the preface, or rather "foreword," to the work, sumptuously published in three colors on 16 May 1918, Paul Méral expressed the hope that the visual side of the spectacle would be organized by "that subtle genius, Fauconnet," and, as we shall see, this hope was fulfilled. Not without problems, because "the setting is everywhere, or rather nowhere. It is the space in which people and things move. In fact, only space exists." For this reason, lighting plans took the place of scenery.

Work on this absorbed Honegger for more than six months, from May to November. It was the first of the large commissions that were to mark his career. The same letter, of 30 April, tells us that Jane Bathori had also commissioned him to write a stage work for the Vieux-Colombier.

> Albert Roussel, Caplet, and Stravinsky are already working on parallel schemes, and I've been chosen to represent the youngest school of composers. At the moment, everybody is hunting for a text for me, and it's not an easy thing to find. I think I may find something in the dramatic works

of Saint-Pol Roux. If you come across something, send it to me. Or give me some ideas—that would be a help. It's a huge opportunity for me to be able to write a theater work, more or less as a commission, when you think how many composers, even quite well-known ones, only manage to get a work like this on stage after many years of trying. Also, I'm taking this enormous labor on in a spirit of enjoyment and courage, because I hope it won't pass unnoticed and that the result will do my reputation good.

In his letter of 26 May he went into more detail:

I've now got a very interesting text for my stage work: *The Epilogue of the Human Seasons* by Saint-Pol Roux. But it's not definite. The play is too long to be put straight into music, so I'm having to make a sort of résumé, and I don't know whether the author will approve. If he refuses permission, I've already put together a version of an ancient mystery play with Max Jacob, to be written under my direction. [This is Honegger's first allusion to *La Mort de Sainte Alméenne.*] I'm working continuously on my ballet, but I feel a bit squashed.

The orchestral score of my stage work will run to at least 300 pages, and the ballet to around 150, without counting the piano arrangements that are needed for rehearsals. That would make more than three pages of music a day, if I had a year. But I've only got four months. And in addition, I'm being asked to write articles for the review we're going to start, and organ pieces for a collection that's going to be published.

In fact, he had already made progress on *Le Dit des jeux du monde.* He had finished No. 4, "L'homme tournant sur le sol" (Man Revolving on the Ground), and started No. 5 "L'homme fou" (The Madman, or Interlude 1). He began the sixth movement, "Les hommes et le village" (Men and the Village), early in June. In parallel with this energetic activity on the composing front, other, more mundane concerns that seem curiously out of context are mentioned in this letter of 26 May: "Unfortunately I've been allowed through to take the counterpoint examination, and on Sunday I'll be spending a miserable day from six o'clock in the morning to nine at night, and all for what?" This second attempt brought him no more than a fourth prize.

Using the given theme, I wrote a nice little piece that was so like a little sonatina by Mozart, you'd have thought he'd written it. This got me two votes for a first prize, but the other members of the jury were afraid I was pulling their leg, and showed less enthusiasm. So I (and you, come to that) will have to be content with a fourth prize, which doesn't exactly add to my glory. Luckily this news is confined to the Conservatory, and there my exercise has succeeded in arousing a certain curiosity, and people are busy asking themselves whether it's to be taken seriously or not.[40]

Once again, Caussade's class won more prizes than Gédalge's. The first prize went to Andrée Vaurabourg! Honegger's academic ambitions came to an end at that point. Even if his seven years at the Conservatory had led to a slim reward, this was not what mattered; he knew his craft inside-out, and that was what he wanted. His letter of 13 June is angled entirely toward the future. He was thinking of going on vacation to Étel, in the Morbihan department in southern Brittany, with the Strarams and the Vaurabourgs. He was still working on *Le Dit des jeux du monde* and still having discussions with Saint-Pol Roux. On the eve of those summer holidays, a page was turned in the young man's life: Honegger the good pupil, the earnest "little Swiss boy," gave way to a young creative artist full of self-confidence.

THREE

Six or Swiss? From *Le Dit des jeux du monde* to *Le Roi David*

Arthur Honegger came to the conclusion that the orchestra put at his disposal by the Théâtre du Vieux-Colombier was not big enough for the Saint-Pol Roux project, so he spent the time at Étel in August 1918 working on an Easter Mystery for the same theater. He was still mentioning this project in October, but it never came to fruition. What does survive is the *Cantique de Pâques* (Easter Canticle), which he finished in July before leaving Paris, but which he did not orchestrate until November 1922. This single relic of the Ochsé project is a modest work for female chorus and small orchestra, still very much under the influence of Debussy. As his first choral and religious work, it marks an important step along the road leading to *Le Roi David*.

At the same time Honegger was getting on with the long score of *Le Dit des jeux du monde*, which was scheduled for first performance at the end of October. In August he finished Nos. 5 and 6, which had been begun in Paris, and started work on No. 2, "La montagne et les pierres" (The Mountain and the Stones); No. 7, "Les hommes et la terre" (Man and the Earth), initially entitled "Les lances et la terre" (Spears and the Earth); and No. 9 "L'homme qui lutte et conduit" (Man Who Struggles and Leads, or Interlude 2). Movement No. 8, "L'homme et la femme" (Man and Woman), is dated July–August, and Honegger wrote it at Sauzon in Belle-Île. The wild scenery there so inspired the composer, after the more tranquil charms of Étel, that in August and September he also wrote No. 11, "Le rat et la mort" (The Rat and Death). Movement No. 1, "Le soleil et la fleur" (The Sun and the Flower), is undated. That left Nos. 3, 10, 12, and 13 still to write, and he did this in Paris, to which he returned at the beginning of September. That month he completed No. 3, "L'enfant et la mer" (The Child and the Sea); then, in October, No. 10, "L'homme et l'ombre" (Man and the Shadow), and No. 13, the Epilogue; and finally, between the end of October and 6 November, the longest movement, No. 12, "L'homme et la mer" (Man and the Sea). A month earlier, on 6 October, he had sent his father one of the longest of all his letters.

My dear Papa,
    I had intended to get myself organized well in advance, so that this letter would reach you in time for your birthday despite the censor, closed frontiers, and other small delights. The reason it hasn't happened is the 'flu

(from Spain or wherever), which has kept me nailed to my bed for several days. Thanks to the maternal ministrations of Salomé and the superb, cubist-inclined drawings I executed on my stomach with plentiful supplies of tincture of iodine, I'm back to health again and to smoking my pipe, which I haven't been doing much of this last week.

My work was interrupted momentarily, but I've gone back to it with renewed vigor. Shortly after I came back from holiday, the first read-through of the music for *Jeux du monde* took place in front of its creators, Méral, Fauconnet, and various friends, and then in front of Straram and Ochsé. A third performance was given for Mme Lara, Lady Rotherman, and others. I didn't attend because I was in bed with a fever. I have to admit candidly that it was a complete success and that my collaborators are delighted because, after the read-through, the directors of the Vieux-Colombier, instead of merely agreeing to rent the theater to Méral, asked if they could put the work on as part of the theater's season and offered to cover half the expenses, which come to around 15,000 francs. The performances are to begin in December. I can say that the musical side comes off quite well and I feel I've done my best. That aside, I think the novelty and real beauty of the visual aspect will make *Jeux du monde* a huge success. The dancers' costumes, designed by Fauconnet, are something completely new. All the characters wear painted masks. There's no hung scenery, everything's done with lighting and color. The characters are conceived as synthetic entities. For instance, the sun is hoisted up high and dressed in a long white robe and its face is represented by a large round mirror on to which light is projected. The Earth is sometimes a woman crucified on an enormous golden disc, sometimes a figure wrapped in an immense dark cloak on which are presented the riches of the earth: plants, minerals, precious stones. Everyone who has seen the designs and heard about the project has been very struck and they're all counting on a generally amazed reaction.

Obviously, as the war was still going on in October 1918, there were considerable difficulties:

Organizing things is quite hard and there have already been problems. Raymond Duncan can't find the twenty-four men we need for the dances. At the moment men are scarce and we'll have to go out and find them and then rehearse them ourselves. Fauconnet is doing a series of designs for each dance representing movements that are in the spirit of the production, as we don't want anything that looks like the kind of dancing you normally see. You can imagine the enormous labor involved in getting everything straightened out.

This exciting project led Honegger to reflect on the material conditions in which he was working:

I'm not earning any money, it's the only job there is in my life at the moment, and it worries me perhaps more than you can imagine. Every time I receive money from Le Havre, I feel a kind of remorse, thinking that at my age I'm still dependent on my family. And every time I see young composers obliged to earn their daily bread moldering away in cinema or music-hall orchestras, I think of you, dear Papa, with deep love and admiration. Thanks to you, I've been able to work toward a lofty goal without having to worry about the banknote that will allow me to eat on the morrow, and if I've been able to turn into what I am—that is to say, one of the most prominent of the young composers—it's entirely to you that I owe it. I have no wish to be conceited in speaking of myself, but I want you to be able to judge the situation, and at all events to be able to give you the satisfaction of seeing that the sacrifices you have made for me have not been in vain.

This winter I'm going to have a performance of a dramatic work in two scenes, *La Mort de Sainte Alméenne* [The Death of Saint Alméenne], together with *Jeux du monde*. There are less than half a dozen composers in France who, at my age, will have had two works of this importance put on in the same winter. There's no doubt that this has happened thanks to a combination of particularly favorable circumstances, but it must also mean that people in the business have found my music interesting enough for them to risk considerable sums of money on a composer who's totally unknown.

Honegger then described in detail the Saint-Pol Roux project, which he had to abandon because the Vieux-Colombier was not equipped to put it on. He said he had completely finished the first scene of the Easter Mystery, as well as the choral scene at the end, the two no doubt making up the *Cantique de Pâques* we now have, but this suffered the same fate because Fernand Ochsé failed to deliver his text. Following these two abortive attempts, Honegger had, as he explained, gone to see

Max Jacob (the poet who was so rude about me that day, and who has since become a great friend). Two days later he gave me the opening scenes of *La Mort de Sainte Alméenne*. I've started writing it and it's going well. I've promised Straram the score for the end of October (one month and one week from now) but the 'flu has made me lose several days.

Some weeks later, on 14 November, three days after the armistice and three days before the first concert of Harry Pilcer's Jazz Band at the Casino de Paris, *Le Dit des jeux du monde* was "in full rehearsal. There are plans to put it on at the Ambassadors' Theatre in London and in German in Zurich. *Sainte Alméenne* is due to be performed in March." None of these fine plans came to anything. But while, on 30 November in Geneva, Ernest Ansermet, one day to be Honegger's great champion, was conducting the inaugural concert of the Suisse Romande Orchestra, which he had just founded, the great evening was in preparation at the Vieux-Colombier. On 2 December, *Le Dit des jeux du monde*, conducted by Walther Straram, provoked a scandal that was equal in every respect to the ones surrounding *The Rite of Spring* and *Parade*.

Apart from the dress rehearsal, given before the cream of the Parisian artistic world, the performances all led to a fearful uproar. The auditorium was filled with such a din of shouting, screaming, whistling, and clapping that on some evenings you couldn't hear a word of the text or a note of the music. There was even fighting and exchanges of cards.[1]

Among the audience were Count Maurice Maeterlinck, André Gide, André Suarès, Jacques Rouché, Widor, Ravel, Schmitt, Albert Roussel, Picasso, Fernand Léger, and Cocteau. "Roussel and especially Florent Schmitt had a lot of nice things to say about my music." So celebrity had come to the young Honegger, if not perhaps quite in the way he was expecting. Instantly he was asked to write an opera, three ballets, incidental music, songs, operettas, and pieces for the music-hall—and this was a composer who, only a few months earlier, had failed in his counterpoint exam at the Conservatory! Even so, he kept his head and worked on finishing *La Mort de Sainte Alméenne*, which was scheduled for performance in March. Meanwhile, *Le Dit des jeux du monde* reached its twelfth performance on 24 December despite the scandal, or because of it, and there were plans to put it on in London at the end of April or in May, and then in Zurich, Holland, and Belgium.

The year 1918 ended, then, on a note of expectation. New Year's Eve found Turly, the prodigal son, back in Zurich among the family he had not seen for more than three years.

1919

After the year of celebrity and frantic activity came two that consolidated Honegger's position. And if they contained fewer externally notable events, they were nonetheless years of considerable creativity and production. Honegger stayed in Zurich until 15 January and was back there again from 26 February to 20 March. In the meantime (during the second half of January) he wrote to Jane Bathori to thank her for sight-reading the completed fragments of *La Mort de Sainte Alméenne*. As we have seen, it was she who commissioned the work (based on a text by Max Jacob) for the Vieux-Colombier. This allowed only a limited number of characters, a simple production, and a small orchestra of a string quintet, four woodwinds, horn, and trumpet. Even so, the work was never performed nor even completely orchestrated.

The return journey to Paris after Honegger's second stay in Zurich took three days, because travel in eastern France was still difficult several months after the armistice.

As soon as I got back, I began to orchestrate my *Danse macabre*. It was performed yesterday. Next Friday I shall be playing my sonata, and on Saturday they're dancing to my little furniture music to go with *Painting and Music*, scored for string quartet, flute, clarinet, and piano.[2]

La Danse macabre, which now seems to be lost, consisted of two pieces of incidental music, "Dance in the Charnel-Houses" and "Fair on the Market-Square." It was written for a production by Carlos Larronde, with whom

Honegger collaborated again in 1933 in his first score for radio, *Les Douze Coups de minuit* (The Twelve Strokes of Midnight). *La Danse macabre* was given at the Odéon, with costumes by Fauconnet, and it was an enormous success, as we can tell from a letter of 11 April: "*La Danse macabre* was a triumph at the Odéon. In spite of the size of the place, 500 people were turned away. The auditorium was bursting and so were the corridors—they had to leave the doors between them open. It'll be repeated several times."

The "little furniture music" was played in the Salle Huyghens on 5 April in a concert of music by the Nouveaux Jeunes. This consisted of three miniatures of a few bars each, endlessly repeated. Here Honegger, for the one and only time in his life, made a bow in Satie's direction and toward his prefiguring of today's "minimal music" or "muzak," in which the repetitions are organized simply by a tape loop. These were given a second airing on 25 November 1920, as interludes between the scenes of *Vérité? Mensonge?* (Truth? Lies?), when Milhaud reviewed them. It seems likely that these three pieces correspond to a work for piano and small orchestra called *Entrée, Nocturne et Berceuse*, performed in the Salle Huyghens in 1919.[3] In my opinion, these must be the three pieces of *Furniture Music*, as the character of each fits the title of the three movements rather well. The concert in the Salle Huyghens on 5 April, which included the *Furniture Music*, was the subject of a review by Jean Cocteau in *Paris-Midi* in which the names of the future Les Six were linked together exclusively for the first time.

Honegger's letter of 11 April mentions the possibility of another important tour through southern France, but this never came off and Honegger did not get to that part of the country until the following year. The letter ends with a postscript: "Did I leave a pipe in the house? Look after it with respect." Honegger was a famous pipe-smoker and the vast racks in his studio on the boulevard de Clichy would later be the delight of photographers and filmmakers. On 8 May he sent the news that "I've also found my pipe. That brute Salomé had left it in my suitcase." Poor Salomé! She was an unsung sister of those legendary female servants of Beethoven, and of Bruckner's Frau Kathi, and she stayed in Honegger's service until 25 February 1930, long after his marriage.

Honegger stayed in Le Havre from 15 to 21 April. From that and the following month dates the first movement of the *Second Violin Sonata*, whose gestation (and duration) were much shorter than those of its predecessor. Also in May, he wrote two piano pieces: *Prélude* and *Danse*. Together with the *Hommage à Ravel* of 1915 as a central movement, they made up a triptych he published two years later. From this time too comes *Danse de la chèvre* (The Goat Dance) for solo flute, one of his most popular shorter pieces (but see Chapter 10). It was not published until 1932. On 20 June, seven years after Honegger completed it, the *String Quartet No. 1* finally had a public hearing at the hands of the Capelle Quartet. In the letter to his parents in June 1918, announcing this first performance, Honegger also speaks of a projected ballet with Fauconnet—the earliest reference to *Horace victorieux* (Horace Triumphant).

In a letter dated 3 July, Arthur tells his parents that he will be arriving in Zurich in two weeks, adding, "The day peace was signed, the Vieux-Colombier put on a *Dance of Peace*, produced by Fauconnet, with music by me." There is no way of knowing what piece of music this was.

Honegger spent a peaceful vacation composing in Switzerland from 18 July to 30 September (the second movement of the new violin sonata is dated Engelberg, August 1919). Meanwhile, in Paris, Cocteau wrote a second article in *Paris-Midi* on 28 July, referring collectively and exclusively to Les Six. Honegger then had a letter from Fauconnet, dated 23 August, asking "I'm working on the *Horatii*, and I'm sure it'll be good. Are you working on them too?" The letter also contains one happy, prophetic remark: "You're smoking like a train, and from here [Indre-et-Loire] you can, on a clear day, see the clouds rising from your pipe."

On 6 September Vaura, affectionately called "the little crab," came to join him in Zurich. But soon the summer was over and Honegger returned with her to Paris on 30 September. In October he wrote the first of his *Seven Short Pieces*, which was completed in January 1920, while in the London magazine *The Chesterian* there appeared an article by Albert Roussel entitled "Young French Composers." This too drew attention to Les Six. All it needed now was an official baptism, and this was not long in coming.

From 25 to 30 October Honegger went on a short concert tour, going to Toulouse on the 26th and to Pau on the 28th. In November he finished his *Second Violin Sonata* by writing the Finale and wrote the second of the *Seven Short Pieces*, followed in December by the fourth. The letters he wrote to his parents in November and December are full of good news: some of his songs are going to be sung in Brussels on 16 December and there has been a request from The Hague for his *String Quartet No. 1*. *Le Chant de Nigamon* is going to be played at the Pasdeloup Concerts on 3 and 4 January, the *Second Violin Sonata* is due to be given at the SMI, and the string quartet played again at the Concerts d'art et d'action. He has also received contract proposals from Chester in London, while Lucienne Bréval is to sing some of his songs and wants to get together the money to put on *La Mort de Sainte Alméenne* at the Vieux-Colombier. Finally, he is in the middle of composing a viola sonata, the second movement of which will be ready in January, together with the four remaining numbers of the *Seven Short Pieces*. On Christmas Day the Belgian musicologist Paul Collaer, a great defender of new music and the future author of an impressive and indispensable book on Milhaud, published an article in the Brussels newspaper *La Flamme* devoted to Satie and Les Six (as a group and as individuals). Milhaud had indeed returned from Brazil shortly before, the group was complete, and it was in Milhaud's apartment, in the very first days of the following year, that the decisive step was taken.

1920

The next part of the story has often been told and is well known. Milhaud invited to his apartment in the rue Gaillard various critics who were keen to learn about the new music, together with five young composers. If Roland-

Manuel and perhaps Jacques Ibert had been there too, as they could have been, then Les Six would have been seven or eight. Honegger's diary fixes the meeting for 4:30 PM on 8 January, and he and Vaura played Arthur's new *Second Violin Sonata*, which had not been heard in public before. Henri Collet, a critic, composer, and eminent specialist in Spanish music both old and new, was particularly impressed. On 16 January he published in *Comoedia* (for which Honegger would write regularly twenty years later) an influential article entitled "Un ouvrage de Rimsky et un ouvrage de . . . Cocteau: les Cinq Russes, les Six Français," and he returned to the subject on the 23rd in an article entitled "Les Six Français." So it was that, under the dual patronage of Erik Satie, their spiritual father, and of Jean Cocteau, their flamboyant publicist, six wholly different personalities found themselves grouped together. Even so, this grouping was a little less fortuitous than has sometimes been made out, to judge by a letter from Poulenc to Paul Collaer dated 21 January, cited by Éveline Hurard-Viltard.[4] According to this letter, the *Album des Six* for piano had already by this time been prepared for publication. In any case, Honegger's contribution, *Sarabande*, was written that same January.

Jean Cocteau produced various manifestos in violent reaction against the ghosts of impressionism, as well as against the lowering clouds of post-Wagnerism. In these he proposed an aesthetic of clarity, straightforwardness, and simplicity, an art that was "à l'emporte-pièce" (literally, "cut with a puncher"), taking Bach and Satie as his intellectual figureheads. These manifestos, beginning in 1915, culminated in 1918 in the famous pamphlet *Le Coq et l'Arlequin* (Cock and Harlequin), which was followed by the four numbers of the short-lived review *Le Coq* (May to November 1920). The cock, as the symbol of French art, was taken as being opposed to the harlequin's multicolored eclecticism. Cocteau never disguised the fact that, not being a musician himself, he spoke in metaphors, and his intellectual attitude is sometimes ambiguous. For example, in his treatment of Stravinsky, whom he likens paradoxically to Wagner ("Both of them act on our nerves, this is music from the entrails") because of *The Rite of Spring*, while Stravinsky's *The Soldier's Tale*, written in this same year of 1918, is the perfect realization of his ideal. This ideal, more Satie's than Cocteau's, certainly suited the two young "urchins" of the group, Poulenc and Auric, down to the ground. But it sat less comfortably with Milhaud and not at all with Honegger, who had no intention of renouncing his love of Beethoven and Wagner, and who did not find Satie's music at all to his taste.

In his collection of poems *Plain-chant*, Cocteau encapsulated his activity in a famous quatrain—though one often cited in distorted form:

> *Auric, Milhaud, Poulenc, Tailleferre, Honegger,*
> *J'ai mis votre bouquet dans l'eau du même vase*
> *Et vous ai chèrement tortillés par la base,*
> *Tous libres de choisir votre chemin en l'air.*

> (Auric, Milhaud, Poulenc, Tailleferre, Honegger,
> I put your bouquet into the water of the same vase
> And gave the base of your stems a loving twist,
> And you are all free to choose your path in the air.)

The omission of Durey was due not only to the demands of prosody. These lines were written in 1922, and by that time Durey, the most reticent member of the group and the last to arrive, had already left his comrades and retired to the sunlit solitude of Saint-Tropez, because, in 1920, he had refused to subscribe to an anti-Ravel manifesto.

We shall see, when we come to the lengthy interview Honegger gave Paul Landormy in September 1920, how far removed his ideas were from those of the rest of Les Six. In any case, apart from the publication of the little *Album* already mentioned, the group's only other collective activity was the production of *Les Mariés de la tour Eiffel* (The Couple Married on the Eiffel Tower) in June 1921. There was no question of any of them losing their independence and then having to reclaim it. The group would always remain a collection of close and loyal friends, a "mutual admiration society." And then, it would hardly have been sensible not to take full advantage of the exceptional publicity that was being offered them on a plate. What young artist at the start of his career would have refused such a thing? As we shall see, Honegger, despite being the Swiss Romantic, "the least Six of the Six," and their "honorary member," nonetheless subscribed to the group's aesthetic in some of his works and would continue to do so occasionally for many years. In the original version of *Le Roi David*—under the pressure of circumstances, it is true, but he did accept their dictates—he would even realize the ideal described by Cocteau of a "rich band of woodwinds, brass, and percussion." He set Cocteau's poems to music and chose him as librettist for his dramatic masterpiece *Antigone*. The *Sonatina for clarinet and piano*, the *Concertino for piano and orchestra*, and the operetta *Les Aventures du roi Pausole* are all delightfully close to the spirit of the group. We could say, then, that the mountain that is Honegger touches Les Six on at least one of its sides!

The year 1920 opened with the first public performance, at the Cirque d'Hiver on 3 January, of *Le Chant de Nigamon*. It was given by the orchestra of the Pasdeloup Concerts, conducted by Rhené-Baton, and was a great success. But in the letter he wrote to his parents on 11 January, Honegger precedes a description of this with a sad piece of news: "I have just been struck a serious blow by the death of my friend Fauconnet, who died of cold in his bedroom." The young painter, who was barely thirty, had forgotten to take any blankets to his new unheated lodgings. As he had a serious heart condition, congestion carried him off instantly. As a result, *Horace victorieux* would never be produced as originally envisaged, but Honegger turned it into a symphonic masterpiece. It is worth remarking in passing that in general Honegger would never persevere with a project once his collaborator had died. The *Selzach Passion* was abandoned incomplete on the death of Caesar von Arx, as was the project for *Alceste*, a "grand opera in ceremonial style," on that of Jean Giraudoux.

Shortly afterward, Honegger wrote to his parents: "I recently orchestrated a Mussorgsky song for the tenor Koulitzky, who sang it at the Conservatory concerts together with one orchestrated by Milhaud."[5] These two orchestrations seem to have disappeared. The month of February saw the completion of the third movement of the *Viola Sonata* (the first was to follow in March), and the performance of various songs on the 6th (in the series Art et Action at the Salle Gaveau with Rose Armandie and Vaura), on the 7th at the Salle Touche, and on the 14th at the SMI. Then, on the 28th, at the Conservatory, Honegger and the faithful Vaura gave the first public performance of the *Second Violin Sonata*.

Vaura also gave the first performance, at an SMI concert in the Salle Gaveau on 4 March, of the *Seven Short Pieces* for piano. These made something of a stir, as Honegger reported three weeks later: "The sentence that upset Mama in Carraud's article refers to the piano pieces that caused a slight scandal at the Société musicale indépendante. There was whistling and some energetic chair banging. Poor Vaura was very shaken." Not that such a mild event troubled Honegger in the slightest. Having finished the *Viola Sonata* that March, he began a sonatina for two unaccompanied violins and a group of three songs with string quartet accompaniment on Blaise Cendrars's *Pâques à New York* (Easter in New York).

On 11 March another concert, at the Galerie de la Boétie, brought Les Six together once again, and on the 13th Honegger told his parents that he'd soon be leaving with Fernand Ochsé for the south of France, where they hoped to meet Milhaud and perhaps Max Jacob. He added: "The other morning I received back my sonata, which was turned down for the Tonkünstlerfest. No man is a prophet in his own country." The occasion concerned was the annual meeting of the Association of Swiss Composers. But he was discussing with the publishers La Sirène the possibility of their bringing out some of his piano pieces and the *String Quartet No. 1*, which was to appear the following year, and Henri Casadesus was planning to play the *Viola Sonata*.

Arthur was delighted by the thought of his impending journey.

> I'm happy to have a slight change of atmosphere. I'll relax by orchestrating a bit from *Sainte Alméenne*, which is going to be sung by Bréval with the Delgrange orchestra in May. On 1 June they're playing my *Prelude* for *Aglavaine et Sélysette* at the Golschmann Concerts.

This last work was indeed played, but *La Mort de Sainte Alméenne* was passed over yet again. In the following October we come across the final mention of this unlucky piece.

Honegger left Paris on 19 March, and on the 24th he described in a long letter to his parents the friendly atmosphere of his stay near Aix. He and his friends had just arrived and had met with Milhaud:

> Our hotel in Aix is full of old furniture and curious old picture frames. There's a hot spring and a pool and baths, all laid on. The food is less satisfactory but there's Mme Milhaud and some very good confectioners. Recently, the three of us spent 10 francs on cakes at Mme Milhaud's expense, then we went on elsewhere and had two or three more each. I don't know which of us is the greediest—it's quite a competition.
>
> On Sunday afternoon there was a concert given by the quartet from Marseilles. I met Maurech there and he immediately asked me for my

string quartet so that he could put it on next winter. The viola player found out from Milhaud that I'd just written a sonata for his instrument (there are very few such sonatas around) and he really begged me to be kind enough to send it to him, promising he'd play it everywhere.

At this session the Marseilles quartet were supposed to play Milhaud's *First Quartet*, but the committee who were organizing the concert refused to allow it to be played, and one old gentleman even resigned.

The conservatism of the inhabitants of Aix extended, what's more, to painting. There wasn't a Cézanne or a Monticelli in the museum, even though both artists were born there! "We saw the only Cézanne, which is still in the apartment of the painter's sister . . . , an enormous canvas of a landscape, one of the wildest things in all painting." The letter continues in whimsical vein:

> Naturally, Milhaud is quite a celebrity and, as he's gone round everywhere announcing my arrival, I've already had a visit from the editor of a Marseilles review called *Le Feu*, who wants to interview me about Les Six. He admitted that my appearance (bare feet and no hat) had scandalized the locals when they saw me on Sunday afternoon on the cours Mirabeau, which is the fashionable thoroughfare. "How do you expect me to say to them, 'Play Honegger's music instead of your eternal Mozart and Beethoven,' when this same Monsieur Honegger goes around without a hat and with bare feet as if he doesn't give a damn about them?" But then this outfit has given me bronchitis and I've been in bed all day. Ochsé has been looking after me splendidly, applying mustard plasters and bringing me a steady supply of herbal teas. . . . Yesterday Ochsé and Milhaud played my *Viola Sonata*, which sounds quite good. I'm working at the moment on some poems by Cendrars for voice and string quartet and at a sonata for two unaccompanied violins.

An agreement with La Sirène to publish some piano pieces and the *String Quartet No. 1* had more or less been reached, while Chester of London, who had brought out the *First Violin Sonata*, the *Toccata and Variations*, and three early songs, also said they were interested but asked him to be somewhat patient.

As a final echo of his visit, we read the following, from a letter to his parents on 6 April:

> A few days ago we had Jean de Polignac with us. He was on his way back from the wedding of his cousin, who had just married the princess of Monaco and who had thus himself become a prince and a sovereign. The young king, as we call him, is a friend who used to come to our Saturday meetings and dinners. . . . Naturally he'll have to build a theater for Les Six and appoint one of us as Superintendant of Arts in the principality of Monaco.

Honegger spent May in Paris, where he began the third movement of the *Sonatina for two violins* (the first had been finished in Aix and the second would follow in June), as well as the first two songs of the cycle *Six Poems of Jean*

Cocteau. This would not be completed until 1923. The *Album des Six* also appeared that month, at the same time as the first number of *Le Coq*. During June Honegger wrote the third song for the Cocteau collection and, once he'd finished the sonatina, started on the second movement of a sonata for cello and piano. No question but that 1920 was his great year for chamber music.

As he wrote in a letter to his parents on 16 June, Honegger had various projects in mind that he intended to get down to during his forthcoming holiday in Switzerland:

> I'm bringing a bundle of holiday tasks, because I've recently had a number of commissions. I've got to write a Dixtuor for a group consisting of new kinds of string instrument—the commission on this was 500 francs, of which I've already had 250. The painter André Hellé, who collaborated on a ballet called *La Boîte à joujoux* (The Toy Box) with Debussy, also came and asked me to write the music for a pantomine that will be produced next winter. Finally, I've got several manuscripts of plays for which people want incidental music. I'll choose the most interesting of them and the ones most likely to bring in a little money. I've been earning a bit lately and I'm fairly happy with the end-of-season situation.

He goes on to describe in considerable detail the contracts he has just signed. La Sirène paid him 1000, 200, and 500 francs respectively for the *String Quartet No. 1*, the *Seven Short Pieces*, and the *Viola Sonata*, including down-payments of 400 francs on the quartet and 200 on the sonata. For the *Four Poems for Voice and Piano* of 1914–1916, Chester paid him 200 francs ("French, unfortunately, but they're asking for something else"); and Mathot was taking the *Six Poems of Apollinaire* and three piano pieces, and perhaps the *Toccata and Variations* for piano as well. La Sirène even asked him to let them have first refusal for a fixed sum of 150 francs a month, which he was quick to accept.

> Any pieces they don't accept within a fortnight, I can offer to any publisher I like. For the pieces they do take, they'll pay me 150 francs apiece for up to six pages and 25 francs a page above that. The contract is for five years and, if I go a whole year without producing anything or they don't want anything I do produce, then I keep the 1800 francs and the contract is annulled. I think it's a rather good deal for me and now I'm pretty sure of being able to publish everything I want to.

This long letter ends with the news that he has finished the sonatina and two songs for the Cocteau collection, and that the *Cello Sonata* is getting on quite well. Finally, "next Saturday (the 19th) Hewitt, the second violin of the Capet Quartet, is going to play my *Second Violin Sonata*."

How swiftly Honegger's career was taking off can be seen, not only in this letter, but also in the promptness with which his works were now being published (especially by comparison with his colleagues of the same age). The Dixtuor he mentions would become the Hymn for Ten String Instruments (*Hymne pour Dixtuor à cordes*), after some rather complex ramifications that we shall discuss later. The pantomime for André Hellé would be *Vérité? Mensonge?* But his heavy workload meant that he would compose no incidental music for two years.

Before he left Paris, Honegger wrote his mother on 20 June, telling her that he would be arriving on 4 or 5 July.

Milhaud has left for Copenhagen with Claudel in a car, then he'll go to London for the performances of *Le Boeuf sur le toit* [Ox on the Roof]. Today Vaurabourg has been doing her fugue exam since six o'clock this morning, which didn't cheer her up much. . . . I spent yesterday evening with Ravel—we had dinner in a little restaurant and drank till midnight. My *Second Violin Sonata* made a curious impression on him. He detests the first movement, but is very enthusiastic about the other two. On Thursday I have to go to Madame de Clermont-Tonnerre's to meet a lady who wants to commission a ballet from me. That'll mean a lot of work for me these holidays and I hope to make good headway with it.

He left Paris on the morning of 1 July and sent his parents a very amusing sequence of 16 postcards, outlining the stages of his somewhat action-packed journey. This was what car travel was like in 1920:

1 July 1920, 9:00 AM. (Melun) Dear parents, we left at 6:30 this morning and this is our first stop, to have a broken spring repaired. We're planning to spend the night at Avallon. Lovely weather.

1:00. Lunch at Fontainebleau in a large bistro (50 francs for half a chicken). The car caught fire, but luckily we put it out before it got to the gas tank. We're going to have a snooze in the forest.

7:00. Arrived at Sens after three punctures. We'll spend the night here and make up the lost ground tomorrow.

2 July, 9:00 AM. (Auxerre) We left Sens at 5:30, breakfast at Joigny, and then Auxerre. Broken spring, being mended at the garage.

11:30. (Avallon) Good journey from Auxerre. Lunch here. It's raining slightly, which makes it cooler.

3:00. Short stop at Saulieu. The weather is fine and hot again. Leaving for Chalon.

3:45. Stop at Arnay after traveling along a very beautiful route.

4:45. (Cuisery, Saône-et-Loire). A dreadful storm nearly turned the car over. We've had to stop at the little grocery shop, which is on the postcard. We're waiting patiently for it to stop, so we can go on and have dinner at Chalon.

6:00. (Chagny). Very beautiful route as far as here. Rain has stopped.

6:30. Arrived without mishap at Chalon and have decided to go on.

3 July, 5:30 AM. (St. Trivier) It's early and it's cold. We're going on to Bourg-en-Bresse.

8:00. (Bourg) It's still raining but the car's going well. We're having lunch further on.

11:30. (Nantua) Very beautiful journey so far, mountainous and varied. Another storm but no danger. Leaving in an hour for Bellegarde.

3:00. (Annemasse) We've just reached the frontier. Last stop before Thonon. I'll do some shopping in Evian and Geneva and will arrive soon.

5 July. (Thonon) At Thonon since Saturday evening with the Ochsés.

Honegger arrived in Zurich on the 8th and got down to work straightaway. A letter to Milhaud during his stay gives us information about the progress of the compositions he was working on. Apart from the second movement of the *Cello Sonata* and the third of the poems from Cendrars's *Pâques à New York*, he finished two scenes from the André Hellé pantomime, as well as "a long piece for ten instruments, which I'm calling *Poème pastoral*: this is the piece that I'll transcribe for the instruments of Léo Sir, who commissioned it from me."

The piece in question is the *Dixtuor* mentioned in his letter of 16 June. Léo Sir was an instrument maker from Marmande who had invented and built a series of new string instruments, covering a range of seven octaves and filling the gaps left by existing instruments. Milhaud would write the fifth of his *Little Symphonies* for the same unusual combination. But later Honegger changed his mind and during a stay at Wengen, at the foot of the Jungfrau, the piece he mentioned to Milhaud would become the celebrated *Pastorale d'été*. For Léo Sir's dixtuor he wrote a new piece, a Hymn, which he finished in Zurich on 9 October. This remained unpublished until 1984, when it was brought out together with a transcription for conventional string instruments. In this form it is a very fine piece, still unknown, but worthy of revival.

Around the same time, and before returning to Paris on 12 October (he gave another performance of his *Second Violin Sonata* on the 20th), Honegger finished his *Cello Sonata*, writing the first and third movements. He sent Milhaud news of this, adding: "My ballet is still somewhat sketchy, but it won't take long to finish."

In the meantime, on 20 September, the critic Paul Landormy published an extremely important interview in *La Victoire*. In it Honegger defined his aesthetic, which differed considerably from that of his comrades-in-arms:

> I'm not a devotee of the fair and the music hall, but rather of chamber and orchestral music in its most serious and austere manifestations. I attach a great importance to musical architecture and would never willingly sacrifice it to literary or pictorial requirements. I have a tendency, perhaps an exaggerated one, to seek out polyphonic complexity. Unlike some anti-impressionist composers, I don't advocate a return to harmonic simplicity. On the contrary, I feel we should avail ourselves of the harmonic materials created by the school that came before us, but in a different way, as a basis for line and rhythms. As Bach uses elements of tonal harmony, so I should like to use harmonic aggregations of our own time.

There is in fact practically nothing in that paragraph, except an admiration for J. S. Bach, to which the other members of Les Six, Cocteau or Satie, would have subscribed. In the issue of *Le Courrier musical* dated 1 February 1922 Honegger would further refine principles of a lucidly classical approach to composition, the approach not of a revolutionary but of an evolutionary:

> If I subscribe to a process that's on its last legs, that is because it seems to me indispensable, if we're going to progress, that we should be firmly attached to what has gone before us. We must not break the developmental thread of musical tradition. A branch separated from the trunk soon dies. The thing is to be a new player of the same game because, if you change the rules, you destroy the game and take it back to its starting point. Economy of means seems to me often more difficult to achieve but also more effective than extravagant audacity. It is pointless to break down doors that one can open.

His friend Milhaud had in fact just broken down a fairly imposing door with his suite *Protée*, written in a particularly bold and aggressive polytonal language. Gabriel Pierné was brave enough to program it at a Colonne concert on 24 October, and the result was a riot of indescribable proportions in which the police had to intervene, throw out one particularly enraged critic, and physically protect the composer. Pierné was not put out in the least and told the audience he was going to play this controversial work again the following Saturday, 30 October. Honegger described the occasion to his parents in a letter of 27 October:

> Toto will have told you about the scandal during Milhaud's piece. It'll probably happen again on Saturday. We've taken 28 seats in the front row of the gallery. The Saturday gang will be there in force, all ready to make themselves heard.

The program on 30 October also contained a piece by Honegger.

> I've written something for the Colonne Concerts (or at least orchestrated it) and I've got just about a week to write four scenes for the Hellé ballet, which is being put on at the end of November at the Salon d'Automne. I'll soon have it finished and then I think I can have a short breathing space.

The piece was in fact well received, even if it was totally eclipsed by the Milhaud scandal. It was the *Interlude* from his ill-fated *La Mort de Sainte Alméenne*—as it was never staged, he never finished the orchestration. This highly imaginative piece was only recently published and recorded.

It looked like it was going to be a good season for Honegger:

> On 20 November I'm again playing my *Second Violin Sonata*, at the Touche Concerts. The Golschmann Orchestra will probably play a suite from *Jeux du monde*. With that, the Société nationale, the SMI, and the concerts

given by Les Six, I think we'll gain a good hearing. The *Dixtuor* is also due to be played soon and I'm going in for the Verlet [sic] Prize with my *Pastorale* for Orchestra.[6]

All these projects did in fact materialize. As Honegger stated in a letter to his parents at the end of November, new projects announced themselves.

I think La Sirène is going to publish the suite from my *Jeux du monde*. I'm also correcting the proofs of the *Viola Sonata*, which is being played on 2 December at the SMI. On the 29th, Milhaud and I are playing my *Sonatina for two violins* at a concert of Les Six in the Théâtre des Champs-Élysées. I've almost landed a ballet commission for this theater, which would be interesting. The press has been quite well disposed toward *Sainte Alméenne*. I've had a whole heap of articles.

On 25 November *Vérité? Mensonge?* (or at least the four of the ten scenes for which Honegger had composed music) was staged at the Grand Palais as part of the Salon d'Automne, by André Hellé's marionnette ballet. On the same program Madamoiselle Daunt danced "L'homme et l'ombre," No. 10 from *Le Dit des jeux du monde* and, between the scenes of *Vérité? Mensonge?* came the *Furniture Music* of 1919. Milhaud gave an enthusiastic account of the show, which was repeated on the 29th. The sonatina itself was well received but not its performance by our two friends, who were well truly taken to task by Inghelbrecht and Golschmann, both former violinists in their day. As a result they decided to give up playing the violin from then on. Three days later, Honegger in his role of composer took his revenge with the *Viola Sonata*, which had a very successful first performance at the hands of Henri and Robert Casadesus. On 22 December Honegger gave his last performance of the *First Violin Sonata* in a concert of Les Six.[7] Meanwhile, a new project appeared on the horizon.

I've been, not ill, but very low and depressed—probably a touch of nervous exhaustion. But now I've recovered my good humor and have started a major enterprise. Perhaps you recall a ballet project that Fauconnet worked up for me and which is almost completely formulated. I've spoken about it to the director of the Théâtre des Champs-Élysées for the Ballets Suédois and it has a chance of being accepted. That would be for May or thereabouts. I've begun composing the music and, as I want to produce something very special and very different from what is usually done, it's giving me a lot of trouble and taking considerable thought. My score would have to be finished by the end of February so that I could submit it to the Ballets Suédois when they get back from London. I'd be very happy if it came off because I hope you would come and see it. In any case, it would be excellent for me to be played in this theater because this company has 25 million francs capital and has leased the theater for 15 years. One must try to take advantage of this sort of opportunity to do things that are worthwhile. The orchestra is stunning and Inghelbrecht, the conductor, is a very good friend of mine. Milhaud's already succeeded in placing with them a ballet he's done with Claudel.[8]

So, at the beginning of December, Honegger began the boldest of all his works, *Horace victorieux*. The Ballets Suédois did not in fact accept it, preferring to commission *Skating Rink*, while they performed Milhaud's *L'homme et son désir* instead. If Honegger's reputation was increasing daily, even so success did not go to his head. The letter of 11 December continues:

> This evening I'm going to the dress rehearsal of the Ballets Russes. Now-adays they're sending me two seats in the front row of boxes, which proves that I'm becoming more important. . . . I'm even slightly appalled by how easy some things are. I had the chance to meet Schneider, the music critic of *Le Figaro*, who's always been pretty rude about me. After an amiable conversation he asked me for a page of music for his collection of auto-graphs, and in his review of the last SMI concert he suddenly came out with the opinion that the most important work on the program was my *Viola Sonata*. . . . A young lady has asked me if I would agree to undertake a tour of Holland with Bathori and Poulenc, and she's set to work organ-izing it. Perhaps I'll even go and play my music in Frankfurt and Wies-baden. If things go on like this, I dare say that in ten years or so someone will play a piece of mine in Zurich. The impresario Kiesgen has written to say that there have been requests to get to know some of my music in Swit-zerland . . . in Winterthur.

A final letter of 29 December bore an urgent request for large manuscript paper with thirty-six or thirty-eight staffs one centimeter apart, which he needed for *Horace* but couldn't find in Paris. After listing forthcoming per-formances, the letter concludes: "Ansermet, the conductor of the Ballets Russes, may be going to play *Le Chant de Nigamon* in Lausanne and wants to join me in founding the *Groupe des deux Suisses*."

All in all, 1920 was Honegger's most Parisian year, apart from the summer break that saw the composition of the *Pastorale d'été*. In 1921 there would be a startling reorientation in favor of Switzerland. The Winterthur inquiries came from the first of the two great German-speaking artistic patrons of this century, Werner Reinhart. He and Paul Sacher would each, in turn, play a major role in Honegger's life and career. With Ernest Ansermet, French-speaking Switzer-land at last comes into the picture, the final, but not the least important corner of Honegger's cultural triangle. In less than a month a new and central protag-onist, René Morax, would make his entrance. He had already finished a bibli-cal drama for which he needed a young composer: 1921 would be the year of *Le Roi David*.

1921

From the musical point of view, 1921 began under the best auspices. At the Salle Gaveau on 6 January, Vladimir Golschmann gave the first perform-ance of the concert version of *Le Dit des jeux du monde*. Its excellent reception suggested that the staging rather than the music had provoked the scandal in

1918—as had been the case with Stravinsky's *The Rite of Spring*, which was given an ovation at its first concert performance.

Unfortunately, the painful illness Honegger's mother would die of cast a shadow over this period. The following months are full of letters from him to her. On 13 January:

> Dear Mama,
>   I hope your improvement is continuing. . . . The second suite from *Jeux du monde* is probably going to be played at the concert organized by Delgrange. I've given my *Cello Sonata* to the Société nationale. For the moment I'm working at full speed to finish my ballet. Look after yourself.

On the 17th:

> Dear Mama,
>   I'm happy to learn that your health is improving steadily. . . . My *Pastorale* has reached the last four for the Prix Verley and I'm in with a chance of winning. I'm working hard at my score, which is progressing slowly but surely.

On 20 January, again to his mother:

> Milhaud's going to be in Brussels, where they're giving a concert of Les Six. They're playing my *Sonatina for two violins*. As for the proposition from Berlin, thank them, but make it clear that I don't intend to promote my music by paying for performances.

Not only did Honegger's pride forbid his making such payments, he had no need to take this line. The only tiny fly in the ointment was that Zurich, of all places, continued to look askance at him. But not for much longer.

On 4 February he went into more detail about his intense activity. After asking about the still precarious health of both his parents, he goes on:

> I'll be delighted to come and see you for a few days, but that won't be possible for several weeks because I'm up to my ears in work. I wouldn't want to leave Paris before I'd submitted my score of *Horace* to the Ballets Suédois. Despite the enormous amount of work I've been putting into it, it's still not finished, but it could be in a few days' time if all goes well.
>   That will be followed immediately by Loïe Fuller's performances at the Théâtre des Champs-Élysées, with five renditions of *Le Chant de Nigamon* and probably another piece, to which her class will dance. Meanwhile I shall have to . . . start on the music for René Morax's *Le Roi David*. He came to Paris specially to see me and commission this score, which will be performed in June at the Théâtre du Jorat at Mézières in Switzerland. It contains a large number of choruses and several orchestral pieces. They're planning fifteen performances and perhaps another run in September. I don't know whether you know about the Théâtre du Jorat, but that's where they've given works by Gustave Doret and Jacques Dalcroze [sic]. Morax had heard about me from Stravinsky and Ansermet and was look-

ing for a way to put on modern music, while at the same time bringing me to the attention of the Swiss with a major work. . . . Last Monday we had a concert in Brussels, which was a huge success. All the seats had been sold since the Friday and *L'Indépendance belge* claims that my *Sonatina for two violins* is "a real masterpiece." The fiddlers even copied it out so they could play it again. . . . At the moment I also am spending quite some time copying. It's *Pastorale d'été*, the piece for the Prix Verley. Out of some fifty pieces, the jury chose four. Vaurabourg came fifth and so missed getting into the finals. But then I looked at the works that had got through and I realized that one of them had already been played and published in another form. I pointed this out to the jury, and after some deliberation they chose Vaurabourg's piece in its place. Naturally, she's very pleased. So the four that are left are Vaura, Désormière, Jean Cras, and myself. The concert is on 17 February and the public will vote for one of the pieces, which will then win the Prix Verley, worth 1500 francs. It'll be fun because the counting of the votes will take place in public.

I must stop here for today because I have to go to a meeting. It's another reading of a ballet scenario by Cocteau, for which all six of us are going to write music.

The Cocteau ballet in question was *Les Mariés de la tour Eiffel*. For this joint effort Honegger wrote the seventh of the ten pieces, the *Marche funèbre sur la mort du général* (Funeral March on the Death of the General), subtitled *La Noce massacrée* (The Massacred Wedding). But the central work of the year was *Le Roi David*.

The genesis of *Le Roi David* has often been recounted in detail.[9] These versions tell the same overall story but often contradict one another over dates. Only by a close examination of Honegger's correspondence can we arrive at an exact chronology. Before doing this, we should first say something about René Morax, his Théâtre du Jorat, and about the great patron at Winterthur, Werner Reinhart. The poet and playwright René Morax (1873–1963), born in the canton of Vaud in western Switzerland, founded a popular theater in the heart of the countryside in 1903, and regular performances began there in 1907. The site is about eight miles from Lausanne. The road to Bern leaves the city and climbs the steep slope up to the plateau. It reaches the edge of the hill at Chalet-à-Gobet, set about with dark pine trees, and, swerving away from Lake Geneva, the road plunges into the broad, lush countryside of the Jorat, which faces north toward Fribourg and nearby Gruyère. Halfway along to Moudon is the large market-town of Mézières. It was there that René Morax found the setting he had dreamed of, vividly described for us by José Bruyr:

A theater decidedly unlike any other. A sort of vast chalet, a kind of huge barn, smelling of resin, dried hay, fresh fruit, and on days when there was a performance, Sunday clothes, but retaining the rustic dignity of a shrine. A large stage ($10 \times 12 \times 25$ meters [$33 \times 40 \times 83$ feet]) descending in broad steps toward the orchestra pit. A foyer known as "The Deer Park," which is simply an airy meadow in which the snowy blossom of the apple trees in May matches the snow of the Fribourg Alps on the horizon.[10]

This very special setting called for works worthy of it. There René Morax put on various pieces of his own, inspired by popular culture, whether patriotic or legendary, and the music was by local composers. Alexandre Dénéréaz wrote the music for *La Dîme*, which inaugurated the theater, and after that Gustave Doret was for a long time the composer in residence. But Mézières also got to see memorable productions of Gluck's *Orpheus*. Every Saturday and Sunday in summer, a crowd gathered from the city and from the countryside of Vaud and were squashed together under the tall framework of brown wood. The annual performances at the Théâtre du Jorat very soon became an integral part of the cultural and civic life of the people of the area, and even the Federal Council honored premieres with its presence. The outbreak of the war in 1914 put an abrupt end to these activities.

The Théâtre du Jorat could only have been founded in Switzerland, where the popular tradition of the *Festspiel* is part of the social fabric (one thinks of the famous Festival of the Wine Growers in Vevey), and where the community spirit that is particularly a feature of the reformed cantons has favored a spread of amateur choral societies not found anywhere in France. In 1918, René Morax made friends with Werner Reinhart, who from that time on gave him generous financial support for his performances.

The Reinharts were an extraordinary family: extremely rich industrialists from Winterthur and patrons on a scale unknown since the princes of the Renaissance. The father, Théodore Reinhart-Volkart, the founder of the business, was an enthusiastic collector. His four sons would pursue and develop his tastes, splitting the field between them. Georg, the eldest (1877–1955), took over the family business. He too had been an avid collector, and it was not without a certain envious look that he allowed his younger brothers to devote themselves to the arts. The second, Hans (1880–1963), was the literary one of the family, a highly talented writer, poet, and translator. He would later make the German adaptations of Honegger's major works. The youngest, Oskar (1885–1965), the most reticent of the four, was passionate about painting, and his amazing collection constituted without a doubt the most important gift ever made to a Swiss town, in this case Winterthur.

Finally, there was Werner (1884–1951), dubbed by his biographer, Georges Duplain, "the man with the hands of gold."[11] In his imposing residence of the Rychenberg, a veritable castle by the gates of Winterthur, or in the more intimate, country setting of the Fluh at Maur, on the shores of the Greifensee, he entertained poets, painters, and musicians with unlimited generosity, despite his reserved, even cold manner. It was he who installed Rainer Maria Rilke in the manor house of Muzot, above Sierre in the Valais, allowing him to write his final masterpieces, including *Sonnets to Orpheus*. It was Werner who made it possible for Ramuz and Stravinsky to realize their dream of *The Soldier's Tale*. Although he was an enlightened patron of Oskar Kokoschka as well as of René Auberjonois, of René Morax as well as of Alexandre Cingria, his real love was music, and among the composers who benefited from his support Honegger must take pride of place.

From the summer of 1921, Arthur and Vaura were regular guests at the

Rychenberg, and Werner Reinhart would be a true friend and confidant to Vaura, especially when her life went through difficult patches. He was also, as far as time allowed, a musical performer, playing the clarinet well and enthusiastically. (Honegger later wrote for him his sonatina for the instrument and Stravinsky his *Three Pieces*.) Sometimes he would enjoy himself joining the players of the Musikkollegium, an ancient foundation in Winterthur that he helped to survive. Thanks to him it was for at least two decades the most important forum for new music in Switzerland, until Paul Sacher in Basel took up the cause.

This then was the exceptional person who, at the end of the First World War, offered his support to René Morax and his theater. Morax wanted to reopen it in the summer of 1921. To this end he conceived for the first time a drama on a biblical subject, depicting the amazing life of David, the little shepherd boy who became the powerful king of Israel. Peter Sulzer, who has devoted three large volumes to the relationship between Werner Reinhart and "his" composers (*Zehn Komponisten um Werner Reinhart*, Winterthur, 1980), now becomes a particularly useful source of information, both about the correspondence and about the gestation of the works.

On 10 October 1920 René Morax wrote to Werner Reinhart from his house in Morges, near Lausanne (where Stravinsky was then living and where he finished *The Soldier's Tale*): "I'm about to start on my *Le Roi David*, for Mézières next year." And on 14 November:

> I'm going off to spend a fortnight in the Valais . . . most of all to finish *Le Roi David*, which has to be done by 15 December. . . . For my new biblical drama I'm taking some inspiration from Hindu theater. . . . It will be a very rapid succession of short scenes, like a great picture of this Jewish epic.

On 23 December the work was completed:

> I've been meaning to write for a long time, but I've just come back from Palestine and from Louèche-la-Ville, where I finished my *Le Roi David*. . . . I'm to read my play on 9 January at Mézières . . . and I'd like you to be there to give me your impression. It'll be hard work setting these 25 scenes.

Hard work indeed. The poet's brother, the painter Jean Morax, began work on designing costumes and making models of the sets, in collaboration with Alexandre Cingria. The music still had to be written and time was very short. According to some accounts, Gustave Doret refused to compose against such a tight deadline, but it seems that there was never any question of his being involved. As soon as Morax had finished his text, he said to Doret: "For the music of *Le Roi David*, I think it needs a composer younger than you." Doret, who was fifty-four, and a vindictive, jealous man, obviously took this badly. Later he would be a fierce enemy of Ernest Ansermet, and never did anything to support Honegger either at this time or in later years—far from it (to put the matter as politely as possible).

On 31 December Morax announced to Werner Reinhart: "I've asked a young composer from Geneva, Jean Dupérier, to write the music." But on 10 January 1921 Dupérier refused, because time was so short and choral music didn't attract him. The days were passing and a decision had to be made. René Morax decided to consult Ernest Ansermet, who replied categorically: "There's only one man I know who could do that for you, and that's Arthur Honegger."[12] But this young man from Zurich, now living in Paris, was a total unknown in French-speaking Switzerland. The Morax brothers had their doubts and took further advice from Stravinsky; the author of *The Rite of Spring* confirmed Ansermet's choice. Gavoty places this double consultation on 27 January, but he must be wrong. It must have happened immediately after Dupérier's refusal. In fact, René Morax must have written to Honegger around the 15th at the latest, because Honegger replied on 22 January:

> May I say first of all that I take pleasure in agreeing to write the music for *Le Roi David*. I shall be very happy to see you to talk about it, but you mustn't come to Paris specially for that. I think we can reach agreement without your having to make such a journey. . . . I should be glad to get to know the text soon so as to find out how much work exactly it represents. As I'm snowed under at the moment with works in progress, I'd like to sort out in advance how long I should need to write it. You mentioned psalms sung by choirs. I think that is where I should start, to give the singers time to rehearse. The instrumental parts won't be needed so far ahead.

And so Honegger set out on his great adventure without even having read the text. At the end of his life he said to Bernard Gavoty: "I didn't realize the importance of the work I'd been entrusted with, but I accepted with pleasure, because the subject suited my 'Bible-loving' tendencies."[13] The premiere was fixed for 4 June, but because of his current obligations he could not begin for another month, that is to say, until the end of February.

We know from Honegger's letter of 4 February to his parents, from which I have already quoted, that Morax, nevertheless, did go to see the composer in Paris. So Gavoty is once again in error in placing this meeting on 18 February. But the details as told by Honegger himself are doubtless true. Coming back from the cinema late one evening, he found the Morax brothers sitting on the stairs outside his door.

On 18 February he wrote his parents once again:

> I'm still overwhelmed with work. I've finished my score of *Horace* and I'm now starting on *Le Roi David*. . . . I'm also hard at work on rehearsals for the Loïe Fuller rehearsals at the Champs-Élysées. She's dancing to three pieces from *Jeux du monde* and the orchestra's playing *Le Chant de Niga-mon*. Next week I'm getting the Ballets Suédois to listen to *Horace* to see what sort of deal I might get out of them. My *Violin Sonata* is being played at the SMI, my *Viola Sonata* in Brussels, and the one for two violins in Rome in March. The competition for the Prix Verley took place last night

at the Salle Gaveau. The *Pastorale* I wrote last summer was a huge success. I won the prize with 374 votes out of a total of 700. . . . I had to go and take a bow to the audience, who were yelling. Vaurabourg got 51 votes. Her piece was a bit severe for the audience and didn't go down well, except with the musicians. I think she'll get good notices.

It was in fact 25 February when he finally sat down to begin work on *Le Roi David*, starting with the psalm "L'Éternel est ma lumière infinie" (The Eternal is my infinite light) (No. 11 in the score). He immediately found himself facing considerable problems. In two months he had to compose music for twenty-seven different numbers, most of them very short, which meant there was a danger the work would sound bitty. Also, there was no opportunity to change his mind, or even to read through what he'd written, because as soon as each movement was completed it had to be sent to Mézières to be put into rehearsal. How was he to avoid the anecdotal, the irrelevant? How was he to reconcile the demands of a personal, modern musical language with those of a chorus of amateurs and a pick-up instrumental ensemble?

The greatest problem was undoubtedly posed by the opposition of a large group of a hundred choral singers with seventeen instrumentalists. In the Jorat there were a few people who blew things, the odd pianist who played the harmonium in the local parish church, and percussionists who were willing to have a go. Of strings there were none, except for a single double-bass. So Honegger asked that most infallible of musical artisans, Igor Stravinsky, who happened to be in Paris, for his advice. The meeting seems to have taken place on 2 March, and Stravinsky's answer is a model of common sense: "It's very simple. . . . Go ahead as if you had chosen this ensemble, and compose for a hundred singers and seventeen instrumentalists." Honegger would say later, "It seems simple, but that single reply gave me a splendid lesson in composition: never to consider given conditions as something imposed, but on the contrary as a task that I wanted to accomplish, as an inner necessity."[14] This did not, however, prevent him from experiencing a major crisis of confidence at the end of April.

Meanwhile, René Morax wrote to Werner Reinhart on 3 March, asking him for financial support (he did not have to wait long). He added:

> This time I've asked Honegger to write music that is as modern as possible, and his first choruses look very interesting. I was very pleased to get to know him in Paris, and all the musicians spoke of him to me as a composer of talent. But our resources only allow us a very small orchestra of ten players, including woodwinds, brass, and percussion.

On 8 March Reinhart replied: "I am very happy to know that preparations for *Le Roi David* are well in hand and, from all that people tell me about Honegger's music, I am sure you have made an excellent choice in asking this young composer to collaborate in your work." He stated that, in agreement with his brother Hans, he could put at the disposal of the Mézières committee the unconditional sum of 10,000 Swiss francs. Morax immediately expressed his gratitude and then, on 12 March, announced the start of rehearsals for the following week and suggested to Hans Reinhart that he translate *Le Roi David* into German.

From Paris, where he was up to his neck in work, Honegger wrote his parents on 9 March.

> I'm still very busy and am beginning to feel quite disoriented. The Ballets Suédois didn't take *Horace*, but I think I may be able to place it with the Ballets Russes, which would be much better for me. . . . I'm counting on support from Stravinsky and Ansermet. Ansermet came to Paris and asked me if he could program my *Pastorale d'été* for concerts in Geneva and Lausanne on the 19th and 21st of this month. I'm thinking of coming to see you briefly next week. . . . The publisher Sénart has made overtures to me and I'm giving him the *Pastorale*, the *First Violin Sonata*, and the *Rhapsody* for wind instruments. He's offering me a contract as soon as the one I have with La Sirène runs out.

This contract was in fact signed on 5 March and Sénart remained Honegger's principal publisher until 1946, when it was taken over by Salabert. The firm had already been taken over in 1927 by Albert Neuburger, who became its director and one of the composer's friends. In 1941 Neuburger was a victim of the Vichy law canceling the right of Jews to own property, but he continued to look after the catalog at Salabert until 1956. Honegger would never have any luck with the Ballets Russes. Serge Diaghilev, after putting on Satie's *Parade*, went on to work with Milhaud, Poulenc, and Auric, but looked askance at Honegger. The composer therefore turned first to the Ballets Suédois, and then, more particularly, to Ida Rubinstein.

Suddenly, serious news reached him from Zurich about his mother's health, and he went to be with her for two weeks. He took his work, of course, and it must have been in Zurich that he began the outstanding movement in the whole work, "La Danse devant l'Arche" (The Dance Before the Ark).[15] On the 31st he returned to Paris, stopping off at Mézières, where he saw the theater. He also went to Lausanne, where he sold his score to the brothers Foetisch. The Parisian publishers, in their unimaginative way, had shown no interest in a choral work. Their colleague in Lausanne, however, had, for the ridiculous sum of 500 Swiss francs, struck a gold mine, even though they were not yet aware of the fact. Finally, he would also succeed in getting the composer interested in the exploitation of a work that would make his fortune.

Honegger returned from Zurich reassured for the moment about his mother's health. It must have been before this visit that René Morax came once more to Paris to check on the composer's progress. In his presence, in a single afternoon, Honegger wrote the psalm "Ah! Si j'avais des ailes de colombe" (Oh, If I Had the Wings of a Dove!) (No. 7) and the penitential psalm "Miséricorde" (Mercy) (No. 19).

One Friday in April (most likely the 8th), he wrote to Morax to tell him how things were proceeding. He was hoping to finish "The Dance Before the Ark" the following Tuesday, having reached the point where David too begins to dance, and raises an interesting point of prosody. He has put the accent on "dix" in the phrase "dix mille," a typical choice for the composer who, in his opera *Antigone*, would upset the rules of the French language by systematically accenting the first syllable of words, so as to give them greater energy. On the 14th he wrote again to Morax.

> I'm glad to learn that everything is coming along. I sent "The Dance Before the Ark" to Foetisch a few days ago. It's turned into a long movement (thirty-three pages). . . . Now I should like to ask you in confidence if the premiere has been absolutely fixed for 4 June and if it is absolutely impossible to put this date back by just fifteen to twenty days. I'm asking not on my own account, because I'm working with desperate energy and expect to have "my" work finished on time. But the question of the choruses seems to me more difficult. Take for example "The Dance Before the Ark." It won't be possible to have proofs of this movement for about another three weeks. Correcting, posting, and printing them will take at least a week to a fortnight. So the singers won't be able to start rehearsing the movement until 15 or 20 May at the earliest. It seems to me impossible to get it learned in the space of a fortnight, especially as it's not the only one of its kind and other choruses are still to come, including the final Alleluia.

Morax listened to this sensible reasoning, but gave no more than an inch. The premiere was postponed by a week and fixed definitely for 11 June.

On 19 April Honegger wrote his parents:

> I'm working like a slave at the music for *Le Roi David* and it's giving me a lot of trouble. . . . At the moment I'm working on the final Alleluia, which is difficult. After all the choruses are finished, there'll only be five or six short pieces left that will be less problematic. I'm glad the end's in sight because I'm beginning to feel tired. . . . Next Saturday, Vaurabourg and Alexanian are playing my *Cello Sonata* at the Société nationale.

This first performance took place on the 23rd, which enables us to date the above letter. In it we also learn that, contrary to what is claimed by all Honegger's biographers, the composition of *Le Roi David* did not end with the final Alleluia. Honegger finished the work on the 28th (on the same day, Werner Reinhart told Morax that he agreed to lend his precious Hindu drums), but there still remained the enormous, and perplexing, task of the orchestration. It was at this point that an exhausted Honegger suffered a brief lapse in confidence. He wrote to René Morax on 29 April:

> You ask me to come as soon as possible, but first of all I've got to orchestrate my score. There are twenty-eight movements. That comes to nearly a month's work at a movement a day. What's more, the instrumental ensemble I have at my disposal multiplies the difficulty of the work to the point where I don't really know how I'm going to manage. . . . I realize that I was unwise to accept the make-up of the orchestra without thinking about it more carefully. I understood what you were driving at, and that it

was an interesting idea, but I didn't see how difficult it would be to realize. I'll explain.

By having only wind instruments I'm depriving myself of half the orchestral possibilities: 1) I can't have mixed timbres, of wind and strings; 2) because the players get tired, I return all the time to the same colors; 3) there's the constant danger of falling back into an imitation of the organ. In addition, the small number of instruments prevents any use of "pure timbre." Finally, it's almost impossible to achieve a strict balance between a chorus and a group of wind players. And how can I generate any power with one leg turned into a wind instrument?

"The Dance Before the Ark"???

I'm very unhappy. But enough moaning. I accepted the make-up of the orchestra and I must find a way round it. I intend to get down to it energetically and to try and acquit myself honorably. If you want to make my life easier, try and provide me with a second flute, which I need desperately, as the first is often playing piccolo. I'd also like you to make sure who the orchestral musicians are going to be (?), so that you can absolutely rely on them. As soon as my orchestration is finished, and a copy made, I'll come to Mézières, and if there's no one to play the bass drum, I'll do it myself.

In this letter Honegger also brings up the the question of the conductor, which had not been sorted out. Ansermet was not free because of his work with the Ballets Russes and someone called Fouilloux, who was asked next, refused (thanks to Doret, it seems). Two Swiss conductors, Denzler from Zurich and Haug from Vevey, were then considered, but in the end Honegger himself took charge.

While Honegger was slaving away at his orchestration, in Zurich his mother underwent an emergency operation without his knowing really what was wrong with her. It was in fact a cancer of the intestine, from which she would not recover. On 7 May he sent her a postcard (he hopes she's feeling better and will do his best to get to Switzerland soon) and on the next day a letter followed. With just three exceptions (on 4, 8, and 27 October), all his letters to his family were from now on addressed to his mother and no longer to both his parents. He seems to have been very close to her right until the end.

Dear Mama,

I'm writing you this note even though I still haven't had any more news from Toto, and so I don't know what your operation was for. But I'm glad to know that things are going well, and hope it won't be long before you're completely and permanently recovered. I haven't had much time for writing you because I'm having to orchestrate *Le Roi David* at high speed. There are twenty-eight movements and I've been doing as many as four a day. I shall probably have to conduct myself, as Ansermet is busy with the Ballets Russes, and the other conductors who've been asked have been unwilling to shoulder the responsibility.

I hope you can come, even so. It's the thought that you might hear these performances that has supported me through this long and exhausting labor, and it's the only thing that would really make me happy.

As soon as my orchestration is finished, I'll come and spend two or three days in Zurich, then I'll go off to conduct the final rehearsals and the first performances. . . . In London, Loïe Fuller has been giving my dances at the Coliseum for two weeks. Apparently it's caused something of a scandal. Here they've played my *Cello Sonata*, and I enclose some cuttings.[16]

A week later, on 15 May 1921, Honegger was again asking after his mother's health:

I'm very happy to hear that you're feeling better and that you'll be able to get up. The performances at Mézières begin on 11 June and go on until the middle of July. So you'll be able to choose the day you'd like to come and I'll arrange to have it coincide with the performance of *Le Chant de Nigamon* that is to take place in Geneva.

I'm working as hard as I can so that I can come and see you soon, and also so that I can go and lend a hand at Mézières, where I'm needed. The day before yesterday, I wrote forty pages of orchestration in the day.

If my work goes well, I hope to be in Zurich at the end of the week. I'll be glad when it's done, because I'm nervous about the rehearsals.

The score will soon be available from Foetisch. It's beautifully engraved. In Paris, Mme Sheridan will be singing three fragments from *Le Roi David* at the final concert of the SMI in the Salle Gaveau, and the tenor Hubbard will be singing three others in his concert on 7 June.

The same day or the next, Honegger wrote to Morax, telling him about these two small pre-premiere performances and hoping he wasn't disturbed by them. He "is orchestrating madly and the work's coming on," and as soon as he has seen his mother he'll come to Mézières "ready to give all his time to the rehearsals and the production." There follow various technical details.

Honegger must have finished his orchestration on the 20th, because on the 21st he was in Zurich with his parents. (The *Cadenza* for violin for the *Cinéma-Fantaisie*, based on Milhaud's *Le Boeuf sur le toit*, was played by the violinist Benedetti in Paris on the 26th and therefore must have been written the year before.) He arrived in Mézières on the 27th. He stayed with Morax and on the 28th wrote to his mother. Everything was going well. Paul Boepple had prepared most of the choral singers before Honegger's arrival. Simple folk that they were, they were a little nonplused by music that was so novel, and so different from the music by Doret, Lauber, and Jaques-Dalcroze that they were used to. But they were soon showing enthusiasm. "To begin with," said one of them, "we didn't understand this music, but now we like it more every time we sing it." The composer himself wrote:

We're working hard. The choruses are beginning to go quite well. There are singers from Moudon, Carrouge, Mézières, and Lausanne, even from Geneva. The women have bright, clear voices that suit the music well. My choirmasters are driving themselves as hard as they can. The singers are amazed to find that the "composer" is not an old gentleman.

And he adds that the premiere will be splendid, with the whole of the federal council and the thirty members of the SDN (Société des nations). There's a long article in a Lausanne newspaper on the music for *Le Roi David* and the ticket sales are going very well, with the first three performances more or less sold out.

Even so, the dress rehearsal on 10 June was nearly a disaster. It lasted not less than ten hours, words and music together. Several scenes had to be cut (luckily, ones without music), and some of the spectacle had to be eliminated—a large chariot, drawn by horses and driven by a myopic blacksmith, had generated panic in the orchestra pit. On the day itself, 11 June, there was a further hitch. For some hours a short circuit paralyzed the trams from Lausanne, which were the only reliable means of transport in an age when cars were still a rarity.

But once the performance began, it was a triumph, spreading far and wide the fame of a young composer of twenty-nine, soon nicknamed "King Arthur." Late in life, Honegger would remember those heady days:

> Students, peasants, and professional musicians worked happily together. Three painters, Jean Morax, Cingria, and Hugonnet, had designed the sets and costumes. There were twenty-seven scenes, and we had chariots drawn by real horses! Our efforts were crowned with success.[17]

Aloys Mooser, the tough, perspicacious, and respected critic for the Genevan daily *La Suisse*, left us an account of that memorable day in an article that appeared in the 13 June 1921 issue of the paper. His lucid, subtle testimony is all the more valuable because it does not gloss over certain weaknesses—they could certainly be forgiven, but they have tended to be swept away by the general euphoria. He confesses to being slightly embarrassed by a performance that was approximate and inaccurate, containing even "in the absence of a firm guiding hand, several uncertain passages that came near to disaster." But he signals the merits of a score "marked almost throughout by a burning, personal lyricism," in particular in the psalms and canticles for which Honegger has found "tones of a striking conviction and seriousness." In detailing the beauties of the score, he vaunts the monumental grandeur of "The Dance Before the Ark" and of the final apotheosis, as well as the astonishing dramatic intensity of the "Incantation of the Witch of Endor" (No. 12), and he praises "the honesty of this music, which demonstrates disdain in equal measure both for bluff and for the empty eccentricities that are the stock-in-trade of so many contemporary composers." He concludes: "It is the work of a man who is both composer and poet. Do you know of many works of today for which that could be said?"

Le Roi David constituted Honegger's decisive breakthrough in French-speaking Switzerland. Later collaborations with René Morax for the Théâtre du Jorat were *Judith* (1925), *La Belle de Moudon* (1931), and *Charles le Téméraire* (1944). From 1921 Ernest Ansermet also put his new Suisse Romande Orchestra at the service of Honegger's music. Honegger's third collaborator in this area of the country, William Aguet, would not enter the scene until much later, in 1939.

Mézières must have seemed further than ever from Paris, but Honegger returned to the capital on 20 June, leaving the performances of *Le Roi David* to go on without him. The reason for his return was a work of quite a different kind, *Les Mariés de la tour Eiffel*, which had just had its first performance at the Théâtre des Champs-Élysées on the 18th, with the Ballets Suédois and choreography by Jean Borlin, the actors Pierre Bertin and Marcel Herrand, and conducted by Désiré-Émile Inghelbrecht. This piece set the seal on the temporary union of Les Six, even if they were now reduced to five, as Durey had gone off to live in Provence. On 24 June, Honegger wrote to his mother:

On my return I found myself immersed once more in the atmosphere of Paris. On the first evening I saw the ballet for the Swedes, which is fun. My funeral march went very well and even the critics have singled it out. Apparently the first night was a terrific scandal. Yesterday, in honor of the ballet, the whole troupe was invited to lunch on the Eiffel Tower by the director. It was a very nice occasion. . . . Today I've been invited by Marshal Foch himself to lunch with Harvard University [sic] as a representative of French music, together with Ravel, Satie, Milhaud, Auric, and Poulenc. Lastly, I've had a letter from Werner Reinhart asking me to conduct the subscription concert in December for a fee of 400 francs. I think I'll accept.

On 29 June he confirmed that he had accepted Werner Reinhart's proposition for Winterthur and that he would conduct works by, among others, Milhaud, Roland-Manuel, and himself. He was still hoping that his parents would be able to come to Mézières.

Our lunch with the Marshal was very amusing. Both the Institute and Les Six were represented. At the head of my table were Messager, Rabaud, and Wolff, then came Poulenc, Auric, and myself. We signed a pile of menus and the Americans bore them away delightedly.

On 3 July he again wrote his mother:

Dear Mama,
Many thanks for your letter. I'm very happy you're feeling a bit better and that you're getting ready to come to Mézières. I have just had word from Morax that he's found you comfortable rooms and one of the singers has written to say the same. I'm planning to leave Paris on Tuesday or Wednesday so as to be able to meet you when you arrive. Here it's beginning to get hot and heavy. . . . I'm sure the air in Mézières will do you good and I hope you won't be too tired by the journey.

Sadly, things did not turn out as planned. In his letter of 11 July Honegger says how sorry he is to hear that his mother's health will not after all allow her to come to Mézières, and he is going to try and arrange a further run of performances in September as well as German-language ones in Zurich.

After conducting two performances on the 16th and 17th, Honegger went to Zurich. On the 19th he took part in an evening party described the next day by René Morax in a letter to Werner Reinhart:

> In Morges I got together the musicians, the actors and dancers in front of the ark for one last time. We had fun burying King David, who had just had his lovely blond curls cut. And we were all sorry to be splitting up after that tough campaign in Palestine. I have good news of your brother Hans, and Honegger and I are intending to go and see him in August about the translation of *Le Roi David*. We'd be interested in the Zurich project.

Honegger spent August between Zurich and Zug, orchestrating *Horace victorieux*, which he had had to put aside when the commission came in to write *Le Roi David*. He also wrote a little piano piece, which would be the third of the five that make up *Le Cahier romand*, a collection completed in 1923, in which each piece is dedicated to a friend in French-speaking Switzerland. From the Zugerberg he sent his thanks to René Morax, and concluded: "If one day you need me again, you can rely on me being ready to write immense symphonies for flute and cornet."

On 31 August Andrée Vaurabourg came to join Honegger for a private concert given at the Musikkollegium in Winterthur, in which Paul Neuberth and Otto Uhlmann played his *Viola Sonata*. For the first time they were Werner Reinhart's guests at the Rychenberg and then at the Fluh. In the visitors' book at the Fluh, Vaura wrote a few words of thanks dated 6 September, while both their names appear in the Rychenberg book, dated the 12th. Honegger had just found, in Werner Reinhart, one of the most effective and enthusiastic promoters of his art, and also one of the most clear-sighted—he did not always approve Honegger's works, preferring the tougher ones, like *Horace*, to the gentler ones like *Pastorale d'été*. In the weeks that followed Reinhart began to recommend the young composer all over the place, especially to the Schoenberg Verein in Vienna.

After a brief stay in Zurich, where he wrote the first piece of the future *Cahier romand*, Honegger and Vaura returned to Paris. On 20 September, Arthur told his mother that he had just arrived, but a deterioration in her health meant that letters followed each other in swift succession. While expressing his anxiety, they were also full of good news on the professional front.

On 22 September he wrote "it appears that Koussevitzky is very happy with *Horace* and that he's rehearsing it enthusiastically." In the great Russian conductor Honegger had found a valuable ally who would support him throughout his life, first in Paris and then in Boston.

His letter of the 25th sounds a more entertaining note: "Last night I had dinner with Vaura and Milhaud, who has become a sportsman. He's bought a 'cyclo-tractor,' that is to say, a bicycle with a little engine on the front."

The letter of the 27th announces that Rolf de Maré would like a ballet and that he has suggested to the composer a subject (not identified in the letter). This would be for the following May. We know that it was *Skating Rink*, but the time available was much shorter. The first concert of the Comité d'art et d'action was fixed for the beginning of November, and Honegger was conducting his *Dixtuor* there (the Hymn for Léo Sir's instruments). In fact, the first performance took place on 17 October.

Two large projects were now on the horizon. The first of them, the first performance of *Horace victorieux*, took place very soon, but the second never came to anything. Even so, during Honegger's stay in Paris in the middle of the *Le Roi David* performances, Jacques Hébertot had told him that he wanted to put the work on in his Paris theater. In a letter to Morax written in the last days of September (the exact date is missing), Honegger confirmed the fact.

> Hébertot says he's very keen to put on *Le Roi David* if someone can provide scenery and costumes. . . . I think the best thing (if you're interested) would be to get in touch with him yourself, as I'm not sufficiently up in the affairs of the Mézières theater. He would have the choirs and the orchestra.

In a letter to his mother of 29 September, Honegger further confirms all this:

> Koussevitzky is full of enthusiasm for *Horace*, which he's putting on at the Opera in November. I told him Ansermet was playing it in Geneva and he's very happy about it. . . . As for *Le Roi David*, Hébertot is determined to put it on if someone can bring the scenery and costumes from Mézières and if I can conduct the performances. I've written to Morax. . . . I've also had the programs from Winterthur. The concert is on 14 December at eight o'clock. . . . My *Viola Sonata* and the string quartet have been published by La Sirène and I'll send them to you. . . . I'll probably be in Zurich a fortnight from now because I've got to be back with the score of *Horace* as soon as possible after the concert. I'll come back after it, at the end of November, and I'll stay in Zurich until the concert in Winterthur.

The first edition of *Le Roi David* was soon sold out. "In any case, whether it's performed at the Théâtre des Champs-Élysées depends simply on Morax and Cingria and the possibility of transporting the scenery."[18] The ballet for de Maré had to be delivered at the end of February and Raoul Dufy was to be the designer.

Lastly, Honegger had a visit from Rudolph Ganz, an American conductor of Swiss origins who was in charge of the St. Louis and Kansas City Orchestras. He wanted to play *Horace* there in February, followed by *Pastorale d'été*. With him came an American publisher who wanted to bring out anything La Sirène cared to give him. The scores would appear under the imprint of Universal Edition of Vienna for countries in Europe. The scores of *Pastorale d'été* and of *Pacific 2.3.1* would indeed bear the Universal imprint, but as a co-edition with Sénart, and *Pâques à New York* would be the only one of his works published in the United States, by Carl Fischer of New York.

On 26 October René Morax wrote to Hans Reinhart:

> I'm waiting for Honegger to arrive this week. He's bringing me news from Paris, where there's been talk of putting on *Le Roi David* at the Théâtre des Champs-Élysées. Have you gotten any further with the translation? Honegger was very complimentary to me about it.

Two weeks later, on 11 November, Morax returned to the charge and suggested to Hans Reinhart that they might try to combine the Paris performances with the one planned for Zurich. But nothing came of the idea.

However, on 27 October Honegger was in Lausanne for the first concert performance of *Horace victorieux* by Ansermet.

> I've been to see Ansermet. He thinks *Horace* will provoke a fearful scandal. He says he doesn't know anything like it and that Stravinsky's *Nightingale* and Schoenberg's *Five Orchestral Pieces* are pale by comparison. I was at the rehearsal on Wednesday morning. . . . I'm very happy with the way it sounds—it's extremely strange. It's also extremely noisy. I'm curious to know how the people of Geneva will react.[19]

The Geneva audience, which had heard Ansermet's second performance on 2 November, reacted fairly badly, as had the one in Lausanne on 31 October. This was hardly surprising. The rasping, sharp edge of this aggressive work still has not been blunted to this day. But Honegger knew that it was one of his best and took its reception in stride. Some time later, he told Roland-Manuel:

> *Horace victorieux* is, to my way of thinking, the most original and successful thing I've written. But you can't expect the public that enjoys *Le Roi David* to take immediately to such a complex work as *Horace victorieux*. That would be too good to be true![20]

It is still the case that *Horace victorieux* (strangely billed on the posters and programs of that double first performance as *Horace triomphant*) is, together with *Antigone* and *Cris du monde*, one of Honegger's unacknowledged masterpieces.

Honegger returned to Paris on 3 November and expressed his appreciation that it would be Ansermet once more who conducted the work at the Queen's Hall in London on 16 December. But in the meantime he had to take the score and the performing material from him (they were still unpublished) so that Koussevitzky could give the first Paris performance, which took place at the Opera on 1 December. The fact that four performances were given in six weeks of a work that was so difficult and even, as Honegger put it in a letter of 13 November to Ansermet, "slightly rebarbative," speaks volumes for the young composer's fame.

On 10 November Honegger wrote again to his mother: "Have you played my quartet?" Ill as she was, she was still a good enough musician to be able to read this highly complex score.

A more substantial letter followed on 19 November. He was working on *Skating Rink* for the Ballets Suédois, he still had hopes of reaching agreement with Hébertot over *Le Roi David*, and he was writing a small piece of incidental music for a play by Sacha Derek called *La Mauvaise pensée*, which was performed on 2 December at the Nouveau Théatre: "a little dance for the dancer Lysana," whom he saw on the 16th. It could perhaps have been *Danse de la chèvre*, even though the usual sources date this to May 1919. Then he wrote: "I've just sent W. Reinhart my clarinet pieces." These were two pieces for clarinet and piano—one written in October, the other in November—that would become the second and third movements of the *Sonatina for clarinet and piano* dedicated to Reinhart. The first movement was not written until July 1922 in Zurich.

Finally, he mentioned the upcoming first Paris performance of *Horace* under Koussevitzky: "Nearly a dozen critics have already asked to sit in on rehearsals. Everyone seems to be getting ready for it, and it looks as though it may make a certain impact in musical circles." Finally, he thinks he may be able to come to Zurich on 5 or 6 December. The *String Quartet No. 1* was at last played there on 30 November.

Another, equally cheerful letter followed on 26 November. On 3 December he would conduct his *Dixtuor* twice, at three o'clock in the Salle Touche and at five o'clock at the Vieux-Colombier. He was working on his ballet and was pleased with the sketches for the scenery and costumes, which were in the end the work of Fernand Léger. His music was being played in Belgium, Holland, and England. "They even played a bit of *Le Dit des jeux du monde* in a cinema last week. . . . My *Variations* were played in New York too. My work's beginning to spread."

On 30 November, the day before the first Paris performance of *Horace*, he wrote to Ansermet:

> The first session with the orchestra was fairly painful, but things are going well now. . . . I'm very grateful to you for imposing my music on the Londoners. They're afraid of a scandal here as well. Prokofiev's *Suite* has been very badly received by the old regulars of the Opera, and it'll probably be the same with me. I hope you won't have too much trouble with the London orchestra.

But the expected scandal did not materialize. Paris gave *Horace* a warmer welcome than Geneva did, and a warmer welcome too than it had given Prokofiev's brutal *Scythian Suite*.

Suddenly, Rolf de Maré, the director of the Ballets Suédois, decided to bring the date of *Skating Rink* forward. The composer wrote to him on 1 December in considerable alarm:

> I shall do my best to satisfy you and abandon the concerts I had planned so as to be able to work without interruption. That leaves just a month to finish the piece and that's terribly short. I can't write any odd thing and I'm particularly keen to create a work of interest and to do my best. . . . The orchestral score will be about 150 pages long. To help Borlin in his work and save time, I could perhaps send each bit of the ballet as it's finished, so that he can get to know the music and start on the choreography. I'm leaving on 5 December for Switzerland and will be back around 3 or 4 January. I hope to be able to give you the complete score then, but naturally I can't absolutely guarantee it.

In fact, he went to Zurich and then to Winterthur, where he rehearsed for the concert arranged by Werner Reinhart. He conducted it, as planned, on 14 December. The works by Méhul, Saint-Saëns, d'Indy, and Ravel were well received, but not *Le Chant de Nigamon* and still less Milhaud's *Serenade*, having its world premiere. Both the public and the critics were shocked by the aggressive tone and unfamiliar language of these works, and the newspapers were not kind either about the quality of the conducting. But Werner Reinhart was not deterred by such small matters: his confidence in Honegger increased and he continued to recommend him to anyone he had contact with.

In the meantime Honegger himself immediately returned to *Skating Rink*. On 28 December he wrote Rolf de Maré again, from Zurich:

> I'll send you the simplified piano score in three or four days. Around 15 December I sent the beginning of the score, care of the theater. I hope it reached you. The piece is about nineteen or twenty minutes long, that is to say, pretty nearly the length you asked me for.

He then asks for a copyist to be on hand when he gets back around 5 January, so that he can prepare the parts simultaneously with the progress of the orchestral score:

> That way, the music will be absolutely ready around 15 to 20 January. The orchestral score is about 160 pages, so that gives me an average of ten pages of orchestration a day. I don't think I can do more than that, but I think it will leave enough time for rehearsals.

Honegger did not yet know that de Maré had brought the premiere forward to 18 January (in the end it would take place on the 20th). He would learn of this when he returned to Paris on 4 January. And so the years 1921 and 1922 blended into one another without a break and at a hectic pace.

1922

Rehearsals for *Skating Rink* began on 9 January 1922. Honegger found he needed to hire three copyists and to orchestrate flat out. On Sunday 15 January he issued a victory bulletin:

> Dear Mama,
>   We're there at last—I finished the score last night and just as well. I was getting fed up with working until I couldn't think straight any more. The copyists haven't kept up with me and won't finish until Wednesday. Rehearsal in the afternoon, and the premiere is on Friday evening.

He goes on to speak of a polemic unleashed by certain critics, including one called Coller (probably neither Collet nor Collaer),[21] who wrote an article entitled "The Twilight of Les Six," in which he claimed that the other members of the group were nobodies and merely a pedestal for Honegger. "I shall reply in *Le Courrier musical* on 1 February, both to the rumors going round that I'm leaving the group and to Cocteau's tactless letter." His reply did indeed appear under the significant title "Petit historique nécessaire" (A brief, necessary statement of facts):

> I have never dreamed for a moment of breaking away from my colleagues. In any case it seems to me impossible, given that this group is neither an association nor a club, and that a break would mean simply the rupture of our ties of friendship. . . . That's why I don't agree with the "resignation" of our friend Louis Durey, which, in my opinion, remains wholly fictitious. Even if he is no longer one of the "Six," he is an "ex-Six," which comes to the same thing.

Here is a good example of the integrity and complete loyalty that, by common consent, would characterize Honegger throughout his life.

Even though *Skating Rink* did not remain in the repertory, it seems to have been one of the most striking and original productions of the era, to judge by the reviews. "The premiere of *Skating Rink* went well, despite some whistling directed against the scenery." Honegger accepted a commission for some incidental music for André Gide's *Saül* at the Vieux-Colombier in April or May (in fact it was given on 16 June), and he was possibly going to write the music for Abel Gance's film *La Roue* (The Wheel), "which will be an event in the cinema world. It's already grossed two million in America." This is the first allusion in Honegger's letters to the seventh art that would play such a large part in his career. He was introduced to Abel Gance by Ricciotto Canudo, who wrote the scenario for *Skating Rink*.

On Monday 30 January Honegger wrote his last letter to his mother, who was failing fast. Honegger was relaxing a little after the huge effort he had put in:

> Dear Mama,
>   Here's a short note, though I haven't much of interest to tell you. The run of *Skating* ended yesterday and performances begin in Berlin in a few days. . . . I'm dining tomorrow with the Duchess of Clermont-Tonnerre who wants to get me to write a ballet. There's also vague talk of a new commission for the Théâtre des Champs-Élysées. I've got enough work to last me a year and almost every day I get letters offering me ideas and poems. I've had a letter from Mme Thompson, inviting me to a grand lunch in my honor when I'm in Le Havre on the 19th. Poulenc will probably come with me. I've also seen my Brussels friends (Collaer, etc.) who would like me to come to Brussels for a concert of my works. The tenor Hubbard has offered to sing all my songs. Straram is giving several orchestral concerts of modern German, French, and English music. He's going to play *Horace* and the *Pastorale d'été*.
>   Vaura and I are delighted because there's a new wrestling championship at the Apollo.
>   I hope with all my heart that things are going a little better with you. I'll be coming back shortly on a brief tour.

The duchess had been bullying him over a ballet for some time. It would be *Roses de métal*, produced in 1928.

But other flowers would soon be needed, to deck the coffin of Honegger's mother. She died on 16 February at the age of not quite sixty-three, the age at which death would one day take the beloved son whose first steps to glory she had lived to see.

Honegger rushed to Zurich the next day. Obviously, his mother's death was a terrible loss, and all the more so because his father, now seventy, abandoned his will to live. After several months of lassitude he literally died of grief.

When Honegger returned to Paris on 6 March, he found a wonderfully warm, tactful letter of condolence from Max Jacob. The hermit of Saint-Benoît-sur-Loire proved himself on this occasion to be a true friend:

> Monastery of Saint-Benoît-sur-Loire, Loiret.
> 28 February 1922
>
> Dear Arthur,
> Roland-Manuel has told me your sad news. I know a letter is small comfort in real sorrow, and what greater sorrow could you suffer than the disappearance of your whole childhood, of your first experience of love, and of that to which we owe everything. I know nothing about your family, but they say that the caliber of a man depends on that of his mother. The great men of history have had marvelous mothers. This is not the moment to pay you compliments, but I am assuming that you have suffered a very great loss in losing someone worthy of having a son whose character is as fine as his talent.
> No, a letter is of no use when one is in pain, but I do not want you to think that I am a "fair-weather friend" or a "music-lover" who is proud to be close to you from time to time. I want you to know that you have in me a friend who loves and admires you. In these days when your heart is heavy, I want you to recognize my voice as being that of a faithful friend. On another occasion I will give you my news. For the moment, I will merely say that I feel for you, that I shake you by the hand and embrace you. I ask you to try and pray to God as I shall now do, for you and for her who is, alas, no more.

But life went on, and musical projects and events continued to multiply. Honegger's tone in relating news of these to his father is strangely impersonal, as though grief had laid a cold hand on the relations between father and son:

> Tomorrow I shall go to work with Gance in Vincennes, as the score of *Saül* is almost finished. My three Cendrars poems had their first performance in New York on 24 February, given by an American singer and a quartet from New York. . . . Milhaud and Poulenc have brought back two superb Schoenberg scores for me. In July we shall probably go to Salzburg for the international music festival. France will be represented by Ravel and Milhaud, Switzerland by Ernest Bloch and myself (*Viola Sonata* or *Cello Sonata*).[22]

A second and final letter, written shortly afterward, deals almost entirely with money matters. He outlines the excellent terms he has obtained for Abel Gance's film *La Roue* and says that Gance even wants him to appear in his next film, *The End of the World*. It seems as though the young Arthur wants to empha-size once again that the sacrifices made by his parents have not been in vain, and that overall his father has made the best possible investment.

In April he added the last of the five numbers to *Le Cahier romand*. He dedi-cated it to René Morax and wrote him around the same time:

> Perhaps you know that I'm continuing to set the history of the kings of Israel to music, but going further back in time. Gide has asked me for some small pieces of incidental music for his *Saül*, which is to be given shortly at the Vieux-Colombier. After that (if the contracts meet my requirements) I shall write a large score for a film, *La Roue*, which is to last three hours. . . . Since my dear mother died, I've been going to Switzerland quite often to keep my father company. He's very much on his own.

Nothing further is recorded about the *Le Roi David* project with Hébertot. No doubt it foundered for financial reasons, with the transportation of scenery and costumes proving too expensive. Apart from the first performance of *Saül* on 16 June, the second quarter of 1922 was unusually empty. On 14 July, Honegger was again in Paris, and wrote from there to Milhaud, mentioning especially the premiere of Stravinsky's *Mavra* at the Opera on 3 June: "I've got a lot to tell you. *Mavra* is a little like *Parade* and I don't understand it. But it makes Auric and Poulenc weep with emotion. *Saül* was, from the musical point of view, excessively circumcized, even for a king of Israel."

Shortly after that, Honegger left Paris for Zurich with Vaura, and then spent most of the summer with her. While he was there, he finished the *Sonatina for clarinet and piano* meant for Werner Reinhart, which was still with-out a first movement. Arthur and Vaura must have arrived at the Rychenberg around the 20th. Reinhart took them to Salzburg for the festival of contempo-rary chamber music, the first meeting of the ISCM (International Society for Contemporary Music), which was taking place from the 7th to the 10th. This festival became an official one the following year. Thanks to Reinhart's gen-erosity, Arthur and Vaura were able to go on to Vienna and returned to Zurich on the 24th.

On 3 September both of them were with Werner Reinhart at the Fluh. They both rehearsed at Winterthur with the cellist Joachim Stutschevsky, who would play Honegger's sonata with Vaura at a private concert fixed for the 19th. The atmosphere of this stay was extremely cordial. In particular, a very close friendship developed between Vaura and the "man with the hands of gold." Meanwhile, on 5 September, Honegger's father died. A month later, Arthur and Vaura were back in Paris.

With the death in such a short time of both his parents, a chapter in Honegger's life was closed. It is true that he still had his two sisters and his brother in Zurich, and that the latter would settle in Paris after spending some time in Munich, but Arthur's relations with them, although affectionate, did not become close again until after the Second World War and especially during the years that he was ill. For the biographer, the end of Honegger's family correspondence brings with it the disappearance of a crucial source. Arthur's and Vaura's diaries to some extent fill the gaps, when it comes to events and journeys. But one has to wait until the correspondence with Paul Sacher, unbroken from 1936 until the composer's death, to find a source of comparable richness.

FOUR

"King Arthur": Dramas and Triumphs

Back in Paris, life went on as before. Vaura had not been so close to Honegger over the preceding years. She didn't spend the summers of 1920 or 1921 with him and doesn't seem to have been present at the production of *Le Roi David* at Mézières. But now once again she became an important figure in his life, especially with the death of his parents.

His circle of friends was growing. A number of young composers, eager to profit by his advice, began to surround him and some of them became lifelong friends. The first of them was Arthur Hoérée, whom he got to know in November 1922 during a Schoenberg festival at the Vieux-Colombier. Hoérée was a young Belgian, five years Honegger's junior, who would become a very successful film composer (he collaborated with Honegger nine times between 1933 and 1952) and a remarkable musicologist. After him, in 1923, came Marcel Delannoy and Maurice Jaubert.

Honegger remained faithful too to his colleagues in Les Six, especially to Milhaud. According to Henri Hell, around this period Arthur and the singer Claire Croiza used to team up with Auric and Poulenc every week for a game of poker.[1]

On 18 November 1922 Honegger received a letter from Romain Rolland asking him to write incidental music for his play *Liluli*, which would be produced in March. Rolland went into considerable detail and was proposing a fairly enormous score, but Honegger's contribution was restricted finally to two pages of vocal music. In November, he wrote a small piece of chamber music, *Three Counterpoints*, and more importantly, a new orchestral piece called *Chant de joie* (Song of Joy), which he orchestrated in 1923. He also orchestrated his *Cantique de Pâques*, written in July 1918. Meanwhile, on 5 November his *Viola Sonata* was played at the Donaueschingen music days by Paul Hindemith, accompanied by Emma Luebbecke-Job, and on the 9th his friend Bernhard Seidmann (whose musical ignorance Honegger had deplored in his letter to his parents of 28 April 1915!) conducted the Bluethner Orchestra in Berlin in his *Pastorale d'été*. Funds toward this were forthcoming from Werner Reinhart, who also urged him to program *Horace victorieux*, a work he believed, rightly, to be far more important.

In December, Honegger wrote incidental music for Jean Cocteau's *Antigone*, produced at the Théâtre de l'Atelier on the 21st. This slim score was published in January 1923 in the musical supplement to *Feuilles libres*. That same month he also finished a ballet, *Fantasio*, for one of his young American female pupils, on a scenario by the mime Georges Wague. Perhaps the dedicatee took it to the United States, as I have found no trace of a Paris performance. The manuscript score survived and was eventually published in 1992.

The year concluded with a performance of *Horace victorieux* in New York under Pierre Monteux, at the end of December.

1923

The composer's diary tells us that on 11 January 1923, Vladimir Golschmann repeated the suite from *Le Dit des jeux du monde* in the concert version.

On 21 January Honegger was in Lyons for what clearly seems to have been the French premiere of *Le Roi David*, conducted by G. M. Witkowsky. Paris would have to wait another year and more. On 25 January, the *Gazette des 7 arts* published in facsimile a reduction for piano of the Prelude from *La Roue*, which allows us to fix the date of its composition. It contains in embryo some of the ideas for *Pacific 2.3.1*.

February saw the birth of a new orchestral work, the *Prelude* for Shakespeare's *The Tempest*, the first piece in a large collection of incidental music for the performances at the Théâtre de l'Odéon, in the French version by Guy de Pourtalès. The remainder of it was written in stages and was not finished until the beginning of 1930.

On 15 February the *Rhapsody* was played again, in a concert dedicated to André Caplet. And the same day, Honegger had lunch with Gabriel Fauré—he had been an admirer of Fauré's music for many years and later would say that, for him, *Penelope* was a greater work than *Pelléas*. But Fauré in turn had a high opinion of Honegger, and was not alone in considering him to be the dominant talent among the rising generation. This was the beginning of the friendship between the young composer and his illustrious elder, who could have been his grandfather and who had only two years to live, a friendship marked both by respect and by affection from the younger man.

Three days later, on 18 February, Honegger was visited by a young man of twenty who would be one of his first pupils, as well as one of his best biographers: the composer Marcel Delannoy.

> 21 rue Duperré, staircase on the far side of the courtyard, fourth story. A few minutes' wait on the landing. Here, up the stairs, comes Honegger himself, carrying a small parcel done up with blue string. Soft black hat. Soft collar and carefully tied sailor's tie. Watch in the top pocket of his jacket, with the chain attached through the lapel buttonhole. Speech gentle, slightly reticent. Stresses accompanied by a brief nod of the head and a gesture with closed fist on the table, thumb in air. Under curly brown hair, dark eyes of unforgettable intensity, dull complexion. Furnishings very modest, clean, for me rather too austere. His portrait by Fauconnet. Photos one guessed to be of Milhaud, Cocteau, everybody! Behind the piano, a wooden crucifix.

Delannoy continues:

> The cost of lessons was not something to be discussed again. By my fourth
> visit, it was advice from a senior. By the fifth, a free discussion between two
> friends. Often, because of people imposing on his time, he forgot the ap-
> pointment or got the date wrong. A kind of housekeeper, named Salomé,
> mounted guard and dealt more or less capably with visitors.[2]

Later, around the time he was composing *Pacific 2.3.1* and *Rugby*, Honegger abandoned completely this middle-class outfit for a more sporty rig, less
formal and more in tune with the times: round-necked sweaters, leather jacket,
corduroy pants.

Very shortly after his first visit, Marcel Delannoy remarked on someone
with "an Italian face, swarthy complexion, large feverish eyes, warm voice, and
southern accent."[3] It was Maurice Jaubert, who had come up from Nice to
devote himself to music and to ask for Honegger's advice. He would remain
Honegger's friend until his heroic, tragic death in 1940.

On 22 March Paris heard four extracts from *Le Roi David*, conducted by
Victor Brault, and on the 24th, the day he left for Toulouse, Honegger signed
a new, permanent and exclusive contract with Sénart. In Toulouse, he conducted *Le Roi David* on the 27th and the first-ever performance of the forgotten *Cantique de Pâques*. On the 28th he was back in Paris, in time for the first
performance of Romain Rolland's *Liluli* (featuring Honegger's incidental
music, as we have seen) in the Salle des Fêtes de Suresnes.

On 4 April he was in Geneva for the twenty-fourth festival of the AMS
(Association des musiciens suisses), in the course of which Ernest Ansermet
gave the first performance of *Chant de joie* on the 7th. Honegger then went on
to Zurich, before leaving to go back to Paris on the 15th.

On 1 May Walther Straram gave the first performance of the *Prelude* for
The Tempest at the Théâtre des Champs-Élysées. Milhaud wrote an enthusiastic review of the *Prelude* and said that the complete work would be produced at
the Odéon "soon." In fact, this production did not take place until seven years
later, and then first of all in Monte Carlo.

On 3 May Koussevitzky introduced *Chant de joie* to Paris. It was around
this time (certainly in May) that Honegger wrote his *Chanson de Fagus*, not performed until three years later and not published until 1984. This was his first
essay in the lighter vein he would never despise. Indeed, he provided many
examples of it, especially in the 1930s and 1940s, when he was particularly active
in the cinema.

The Franciscan Choir of Saint-Germain-en-Laye gave the Parisian public
their first hearing of the choruses from *Le Roi David* at the Salle du Conservatoire on 28 May. So Paris got to know this masterpiece in bits and pieces,
between the pre-premiere performances of June 1921 and the first complete
performance on 14 March 1924. Meanwhile, on 15, 16, and 25 May, *Skating
Rink* was revived and on the 26th and 27th Honegger traveled to Le Havre for
a concert of his works.

On 1 and 4 June he had his first meeting with Frank Martin, his senior by eighteen months. Martin, who was on his way through Paris, was still completely unknown. His great talent as a composer would not blossom until just before the Second World War.

On 5 June Louis Cahuzac and Jean Wiéner gave the first performance of the *Sonatina for clarinet and piano* in one of the Wiéner Concerts in the Salle Pleyel, and on the 9th Jacques Ibert wrote Honegger a brief note of thanks for the score of the *Rhapsody*. This is the earliest letter that survives from Ibert, who would be one of Honegger's closest friends, especially in the period between 1936, when they collaborated on *L'Aiglon*, and the end of Honegger's life. During May, Honegger wrote the fourth of the five pieces of *Le Cahier romand* and dedicated it to Paul Boepple, the excellent chorus master who had played such a decisive role in the success of *Le Roi David* at Mézières. The collection would finally be completed with the composition in July of the second piece, dedicated to Ernest Ansermet's daughter, Jacqueline. Honegger also finished work on another cycle, completing Nos. 4, 5, and 6 of the *Six Poems of Jean Cocteau*, which he had begun in 1920.

On 17 July Honegger went to stay at Annecy-le-Vieux, a suburb of Annecy in the French province of Savoy, where Fauré was spending the summer with his banker friends the Maillots and working on his *Piano Trio*. Before Honegger left on the 28th, Maillot organized a concert in the little church of Annecy, consisting of Fauré's *Requiem* and portions of *Le Roi David*. Both were given simply with organ and piano for reasons of space. Unknown to the participants, this was a preparation for the first complete Paris performance of *Le Roi David* the following March, with orchestra, when Honegger's oratorio would again be preceded by Fauré's *Requiem*. Fauré would be in the audience.

At Annecy, Honegger worked on his reorchestration of *Le Roi David* for a standard symphony orchestra. No doubt he had already begun this before leaving Paris, and he would finish it in August while staying with Werner Reinhart. Together with him and the violinist Alma Moodie, Honegger and Vaura traveled in the millionaire's "large white automobile" to Salzburg for the first festival of the ISCM. Germain Prévost, the violist of the Pro Arte Quartet, and Vaura played the *Viola Sonata* on 6 August. Ernest Ansermet was also there.

Vaura and Arthur returned to Switzerland on the 10th and stayed at the Fluh until the 20th, in the course of which Arthur finished his reorchestration of *Le Roi David*. At this point Vaura went off to join her mother on holiday in Corsica, while Arthur went back to Paris, then to Montfort-l'Amaury, where he stayed a few weeks with his friend Fernand Ochsé. He left to join Vaura on 11 September, arriving at Cargèse on the 15th. But his stay was a brief one, and on 1 October the two inseparable companions were on their way back to Paris.

Honegger was therefore not present when Hermann Scherchen conducted *Horace victorieux* in Frankfurt at a concert of music by Swiss composers (the program also contained works by Fritz Brun, Hermann Suter, and Friedrich Klose). The poster described Honegger's work as being "based on the play by Racine"!

Back in Paris, Honegger wrote at once to Ernest Ansermet:[4]

I'm at work again on *Pacific 2.3.1* (and not 3.2.1—a bogey in front (2), three powered wheels, coupled (3), a weight-bearing axle (1)). I think I shall finish it on time, and more than that I think you'll like it. . . . I've got back some of the Salzburg photos and you've come out well. Your jacket looks very smart and really puts my yellow overalls to shame. Scherchen has just conducted *Horace* in Frankfurt and Andreae is giving it in Zurich in November. Sénart is publishing it and I hope to send you a copy soon.

This is the first mention of what is perhaps the composer's most famous work. We do not know exactly when he began it, perhaps as early as March or even in January, and it is possible that his work on Gance's *La Roue* gave him the idea for it. In later years, though, he insisted that the initial concept was purely musical and abstract and that the title came afterward. In any case, it was one of the works that gave him the most trouble. The autograph orchestral score, marked at the end "Paris–Winterthur–Zurich," was not finished until December 1923, too late for Ansermet to give the first performance in Geneva on 12 January, as had been planned.

Honegger did not attend either the Zurich performance of *Horace* on 15 November or the first English performance of *Chant de joie* under Ansermet's direction at the Royal Philharmonic Society of London on the 22nd. But he did go to Switzerland on the 24th for the first performance on 2 December of the reorchestrated *Le Roi David*, at the Winterthur Stadthaus under Ernst Wolters. This was the oratorio version current nowadays, with a narrator, given here for the first time in Hans Reinhart's German translation. There were any number of problems in the period leading up to the concert and, when the parts failed to arrive in time, it looked as though the reorchestrated version would have to be abandoned. Werner Reinhart unfortunately missed the occasion, as he was unable to get back from a business trip to India until 5 December. But at least he saw Arthur and Vaura, who stayed at the Rychenberg until the 11th before returning to Paris. It must have been during these few days that Honegger finished *Pacific 2.3.1*.

Finally, Brussels was introduced to *Le Roi David* on the 16th, then again on the 23rd at the Société bruxelloise des concerts spirituels, conducted by Joseph Jongen.

1924

Nineteen twenty-four was the great year of the double triumph of *Le Roi David* and *Pacific 2.3.1* in Paris, setting the final seal on Honegger's popularity and largely eclipsing those of all his young contemporaries. The following year, the clouds began to gather with the partial success of *Judith*, and Honegger would not again enjoy the same unanimous approval until the first performance of *Jeanne d'Arc au bûcher* in 1938. But certainly, before the summer he had already secretly begun to plan the work that would be his favorite, the opera *Antigone* on a libretto by his friend Jean Cocteau, which would take him three years of desperate labor.

The year began with a repeat performance of the *Prelude* for *The Tempest* at the Théâtre Mogador on 5 January. This was followed by Vaura's giving the first performance of *Le Cahier romand* at the SMI in the Salle Érard on the 30th. On the 23rd, Werner Reinhart sent him a letter recommending a young Swiss conductor, Wilhelm Arbenz, who had come to continue his studies in Paris. Arbenz was very impressed by his compatriot and regarded him as

> the leader of the young composers here. Strength fully expressed. I'm very proud of his Swiss nature and fancy I can find it in all his works. Despite some curious wrinkles (*Krausheiten*) his is a healthy, vigorous musicality. And he's full of ideas, which is more than I can say for all these murmuring Frenchmen (*Säuselfranzosen*).[5]

On 24 January, at the Société des Nouvelles Auditions in Geneva, Rose Féart and the Pro Arte Quartet gave the first performance in Europe of *Pâques à New York*. On 4 February, Honegger sent Aloys Mooser the well-known commentary for *Pacific 2.3.1,* and the facetious letter that went with it shows how well they got on. From then on, Honegger would always call Mooser "dear Father Aloys" and sign himself "Your respectful son."

In February, Honegger composed the *Chanson de Ronsard* for the homage offered to the poet by *La Revue musicale* to mark the 400th anniversary of his birth, and it was published and performed in May through the offices of that journal. The same month, Honegger also wrote the Scherzo "Ariel as Hag," intended for *The Tempest.*

But the important event of this period, eagerly awaited by Paris high society, was the delayed first performance of the reorchestrated oratorio version of *Le Roi David*. This took place on 14 March in a Salle Gaveau bursting at the seams, and was preceded by Fauré's *Requiem*. The conductor was Robert Siohan, who would be one of Honegger's most faithful friends and interpreters. The narrator was Jacques Copeau and among the soloists were such illustrious names as Gabrielle Gills and Charles Panzéra. The performance was such a huge success that a repeat had to be given on the 19th. From then on, *Le Roi David* was given so many times in Paris, in France, and in the world at large, that Honegger ended up being annoyed by its popularity, which overshadowed the rest of his output. Marcel Delannoy has left us a description of that unforgettable evening of 14 March:

> I can still see the Salle Gaveau, crammed with an expectant audience. The performance of Fauré's *Requiem* did nothing to soothe their impatience. The interval ended. Behind the soprano, Gabrielle Gills, the narrator, Jacques Copeau, entered, then the baritone, Charles Panzéra, and finally the conductor. The chorus were already in place on their tiers; among the men, if I remember correctly, Fernand Ochsé, Roland-Manuel, and Maurice Jaubert. In the general hubbub I discreetly tried out my voice. Down in the orchestra, Arthur Hoérée was tuning his timpani.
>
> Finally there was silence, broken by the brief, exotic introduction. The score unfolded without a pause, and the audience, which had been pre-

pared to be enthusiastic, gave way to their feelings. After the resounding D-major conclusion, the hall was on its feet. A very special triumph. The young composer was greeted with endless applause and, as he bowed before the storm of acclamation, his handsome face still retained a modicum of gentle, good-natured charm.[6]

Two weeks later, this success was followed by the first performance in France of *Pâques à New York* in the Salle Érard. It had been given in the United States two years earlier, and was performed now by Gabrielle Gills with the Pro Arte Quartet.

On 4 April Honegger was in Geneva to accompany Rose Féart in three of the *Six Poems of Apollinaire* ("À la Santé," "Automne," and "Saltimbanques"). This was as part of a festival of his works given with the help of Paul Boepple and the Klein Quartet, and the program also included the *Rhapsody*, the *Sonatina for two violins*, the *String Quartet No. 1*, and a repeat of *Pâques à New York*.

On 3 May *Le Roi David* was given again at the Théâtre des Champs-Élysées, with Honegger conducting and Jacques Copeau once more taking the role of the narrator. Fauré's *Prometheus* completed the program. René Morax was there and sent word to Werner Reinhart of the immense success of the occasion. Several of the movements were encored and there were requests for an English translation for the United States.

But there was soon to be another triumph. On 8 May, in one of his concerts at the Opera that were patronized by high society, Serge Koussevitzky gave the first performance of *Pacific 2.3.1*. Once again, the success was such that a second hearing was fixed for the 15th. From now on, Honegger would be the "locomotive man," and in an oft-quoted interview he claimed to love trains "as others love horses and women."[7] Numerous photos gave credence to this strange symbiosis. But, with or without a program, *Pacific 2.3.1* remains a masterpiece of pure music and, as such, fully deserves its popularity. Even though harsh words were said about its likeness to Mosolov's *Iron Foundry* of 1927, it escapes both the anecdotal approach and the glorification of noise dear to that composer and to the Italian futurists. It is a granite monolith, as solid as the figured Chorales of Bach, which were its true model.

On 15 May, at the Vieux-Colombier, the concert organized by *La Revue musicale* in honor of Ronsard included the *Chanson de Ronsard*, sung by Claire Croiza. She and Honegger, who had known each other for at least a year or more, would become very close to one another. This was, it would seem, the second occasion on which she sang his music in public. (Croiza had sung *Pâques à New York* on 11 April, two weeks after Gabrielle Gills.)

Croiza's real name was Claire Connolly. She was nearly ten years older than Honegger, born in Paris on 14 September 1882 of an Italian mother and an American father of Irish origin. In 1906, she launched herself on a brilliant career at the Théâtre de la Monnaie in Brussels, singing Dalila, Carmen, Berlioz's Dido, Clytemnestra (in the operas by Gluck and Richard Strauss), and Erda. She made her Paris Opera debut as Dalila in 1908 and went on to sing in the premiere of Pierre de Bréville's opera *Éros vainqueur*. She was later to be an unforgettable Penelope in the opera by Fauré. The above repertory gives a good idea of the quality of her voice, a warm but limpid, crystalline mezzo, ideal for dramatic soprano roles. Paul Valéry called this voice "the most sensitive of our times." The all-too-rare discs that survive also reveal an exemplary style and diction. She was, if anything, more at home in the field of the *mélodie*, and she was unsurpassed in the music of men like Fauré and Duparc. But after the First World War, at the height of her career, she nobly sought to renew her art and put her talents at the disposal of the new music and particularly of Honegger's. He would soon write *Judith* with Croiza in mind. Austerely beautiful, passionate, and moody, she would develop an irresistible attraction toward "King Arthur" and would soon make a dramatic entrance into his life. He returned her feelings, at least for a time, and was in love also with her voice, as Mozart had been with that of Aloysia Weber or Nancy Storace.

On 31 May 1924 *Pacific 2.3.1* was given a triumphant reception at the ISCM festival in Prague. According to Werner Reinhart, it was the high point of the whole festival, even though one member of the audience, who had heard the first performance under Koussevitzky not long before, felt that G. M. Witkowsky's interpretation left the work almost unrecognizable. A few days earlier, on 26 May, Honegger visited his native city of Le Havre for a performance of *Le Roi David*. On 12 June, another festival of his chamber music was given at the Salle Pleyel and three days later he traveled on his own down to Toulouse where, according to José Bruyr, the first performance took place of the *Chanson de Fagus*.

At the beginning of July, Arthur and Vaura had dinner three times with Claire Croiza and, until the drama of the following year, the two women became close friends. Honegger spent the summer in Brittany, at Saint-Jacut-de-la-Mer, with Vaura and her mother, and devoted it to Herculean labors on *Antigone*.

In September, he went to stay with his friend Fernand Ochsé in Montfort-l'Amaury. While he was there, he wrote a short ballet called *Sous-marine*, commissioned by Carina Ari, who had been a leading dancer with the Ballets Suédois, but who now had an independent career and was married to the conductor Inghelbrecht. The ballet was not orchestrated, though, until May 1925.

Next, Honegger turned to writing the *Concertino for piano and orchestra*. He finished it on 17 November and dedicated it to Vaura, who gave it its first performance and innumerable others all over the world. It is among the most likable of his works and one of those closest to the aesthetic of Les Six.

Meanwhile, René Morax had been thinking of another biblical drama to capitalize on the success of *Le Roi David*. On 7 October, he wrote to Werner Reinhart that he had just completed *Judith*, adding: "I'm impatient to see Honegger. I hope he'll like this new play." Their meeting duly took place, in Vaura's presence, on 14 October in Paris. The same day, Volkmar Andreae gave the first Swiss performance of *Pacific 2.3.1* at an ISCM concert in Zurich. The same month, Walter Damrosch introduced the work to New York, and the Arthurian locomotive continued to hurtle through Europe: Manchester, the first English performance with the Hallé Orchestra, conducted by Hamilton

Harty; Paris on 5 and 13 October, under Piero Coppola; Geneva on the 8th, with the faithful Ansermet. On 17 November, Claire Croiza and Honegger performed the last three of the *Six Poems of Jean Cocteau* ("Ex voto," "Une danseuse," and "Madame") at the Salle Pleyel. The concertino was finished the same day, and Honegger then left Paris to conduct *Le Roi David* in The Hague on the 19th and at Antwerp on the 24th.

Antwerp soon became an active center for Honegger's music, thanks to Louis de Vocht and his splendid Coecilia Choir. They would also give, in 1927, the world premiere of Milhaud's *Les Choéphores* 'and the final *Processional* from his *Eumenides*.

Another dinner *à trois* in René Morax's Paris apartment on 1 December shows that work on *Judith* had begun in earnest, even though the lack of family correspondence prevents us from knowing precisely when Honegger began writing the music. It was probably not before the beginning of 1925.

On 16 December the young conductor Wilhelm Arbenz (whose enthusiasm over Honegger early in the year has already been noted) conducted *Pacific 2.3.1* at Winterthur, once again thanks to Werner Reinhart. Reinhart received from Vaura a long, affectionate letter, dated 28 December, in which, after somewhat maternal references to "that great rogue of an Arthur," she wrote:

> In Paris, we've just had a revival of *Penelope*, with Claire Croiza magnificent in the title role. She's an extremely intelligent artist, and a very kind and good friend! . . . Anyway, I expect you'll have the opportunity to see her in *Judith*: I knew that she'd been harboring for a long time the desire to work as a tragic actress; I suggested to Arthur that he put forward the idea, and I think the result will be wonderful.

The year 1924 ended with an important addition to Honegger's circle of friends. On 20 December, the name "Thévenet" appeared for the first time in Honegger's diary, preceded on 23 October by that of "Francis." The Mathelin family had been introduced to Honegger by Abel Gance. They would be inseparable, both at countless happy parties (the famous "Saturday evenings" of Francis Winter) and during the hard times of Honegger's exodus from Paris in 1940.

The eldest of the Mathelin children, Paule, was the wife of the painter Jacques Thévenet, who would paint a number of portraits of Honegger.[8] The second daughter, Andrée, called "Toné," was married to Francis Winter, known as "Cisco," who designed and made jewelry and handbags for the great Parisian couturiers. The youngest, Lucien, or "Lulu," was also a painter. But in fact, Honegger must have got to know this family at least a year earlier, since Jacques Thévenet designed the cover for the piano score of *Pacific 2.3.1*, which was published in 1924.

The following year would be eventful and altogether more dramatic than its predecessors.

1925

The year 1925 began in classic fashion with a triple revival of *Le Roi David* at the Salle Gaveau on 8, 12, and 16 January. Robert Siohan conducted, and for the first time Claire Croiza sang, along with Roland-Manuel as narrator. Then Honegger went with Vaura to Switzerland for the *Pastorale d'été* at Morges on the 18th, and then for another performance of *Le Roi David* the next day in Geneva. The *Pastorale d'été* and the *Prelude* for *The Tempest* were also on the program.

On the 21st Hans Reinhart announced to René Morax that he had finished the complete translation of *Le Roi David*. Honegger and Vaura were then visiting his family in Zurich, where they stayed from the 20th to the 23rd, before attending a performance of *Pacific 2.3.1* in Basel on the 24th. On the same day, in Paris, Régine de Lormoy, the flautist Armand Blanquart, and the Poulet Quartet, conducted by Arthur Hoérée, gave the first performance of the instrumental arrangement of *Chanson de Ronsard*.

On the 25th René Morax wrote to Werner Reinhart from Paris: "I hope you saw Honegger when he came to Zurich. I'm expecting him here in a couple of days and I hope he'll have the time to do some work on *Judith*. We've got a marvelous interpreter in Croiza."

The composer was in the audience on the 29th when *Le Roi David* filled the vast spaces of the Trocadero to bursting point. The same evening, London had its first chance to hear *Pacific 2.3.1* at a Royal Philharmonic Society concert in the Queen's Hall, conducted by Eugene Goossens. On the 30th, the *Viola Sonata* was heard again at the Salle Gaveau, followed by two performances of the *Cello Sonata*, on 2 February at the Salle Pleyel with Pierre Fournier and Yvonne Lefébure, and on the 6th at the Société nationale with Marika Bernard and Suzanne Demarquez.

In February, Arthur left for eastern France, where there were performances of *Le Roi David* at Mulhouse on the 12th, then at Strasbourg on the 15th under the direction of Fritz Münch. Fritz was Charles Münch's brother and a great champion of Honegger's music in Alsace. Honegger returned to Paris on the 16th, in time to hear the first performance of *Three Counterpoints* at an SMI concert in the Salle Érard.[9] On the 18th *Pacific 2.3.1* was recorded on disc, on the 20th Croiza sang *Pâques à New York* and *Chanson de Ronsard* with Honegger conducting, and on the 21st and 22nd more crowds came to the Pasdeloup Concerts to hear *Le Roi David*. One wonders how Honegger found the time to compose. And yet René Morax, back in Morges, wrote to Werner Reinhart on the 23rd: "Honegger has already written the first choruses for *Judith*, which are being published by Sénart in Paris."

From 5 to 7 March, Honegger was in Brussels with Claire Croiza for a "Honegger festival" on the 6th with the Pro Arte Quartet and in the presence of Queen Elisabeth. On the 8th, *Le Roi David* was given in the Salle Gaveau as part of a gala charity concert in aid of tuberculosis sufferers and, on the 11th, he left for Marseilles, where the oratorio was being performed on the 15th.

On the 24th, at the Salle des Agriculteurs, the Casadesus Harp Quartet gave the first performance of *Prelude and Blues for four chromatic harps*. The score of this has disappeared and so have all the copies of the disc made shortly afterward.[10] The piece was a transcription, but I have been unable to identify the original.

A letter from Honegger to Claire Croiza around this time shows him in some embarrassment because "[Firmin] Gémier intends to put on *The Tempest* in April and the music isn't finished yet."

Honegger was then joined once again by René Morax, who had come to work on *Judith* with Croiza. The piece was finished on 7 April and the orchestration was done by the end of the month.

During April, Hermann Scherchen conducted *Pacific 2.3.1* twice in Milan, on the 17th and 18th. He complained to Werner Reinhart about the lack of dynamic indications in the score, which he had had to mark up in its entirety in order to get across what the composer had written. It is true that Honegger was never exactly prodigal in this respect.

In May, Honegger orchestrated his little ballet *Sous-marine*, which he had written the previous September, and which was due to be performed shortly at the Opéra-Comique by its instigator, Carina Ari. This first performance would take place on 27 June, but the composer was not present, being busy at Mézières with *Judith*. He was, however, at the Opera on the evening of 23 May, when Vaura gave the first performance of the concertino, with Koussevitzky conducting. Scriabin's *Poem of Ecstasy* was on the same program. Honegger then left the following day for Le Havre, where there was a repeat of *Le Roi David*. But the first performance of *Judith* was approaching, and on 2 June he set off for Mézières with Claire Croiza.

The atmosphere was nowhere near as favorable as it had been for *Le Roi David*. From the start, the new work seems to have been under the influence of an unlucky star. To René Morax's great surprise, the committee of the Mézières theater was so unenthusiastic about his play that there was even talk of putting the work on in Lausanne. So when they did change their minds, there was not much time left. Honegger's score, too, was much more difficult than that of *Le Roi David* (in four years, his musical language had developed and matured enormously) and, despite Paul Boepple's invaluable help, the amateur forces of the Jorat were not up to the task. As a result, considerable reinforcements had to be brought in from the city and this led to certain tensions.

What is more, this time the two most important soloists were not local, but star performers imported from Paris: Claire Croiza for the title role and the actor Pierre Alcover for the spoken role of Holofernes. An added complication, and one that Morax had not foreseen, was that the more conservative element among the Vaudois audience was troubled by the indelicate, somewhat sensual aspects of the story and began to walk out. Then there were problems with Gustave Doret, who was jealous at being sidelined and was causing difficulties behind the scenes, and finally with the spirit of the rehearsals, as described by Pierre Meylan:

René Morax had, with the best intentions, hired a house to the east of the church for the actors and those working on the production. . . . This new kind of commune had the advantage of bringing interpreters and authors together and of creating a climate of sympathy and camaraderie that helped in putting the work on. Morax had not foreseen that this close interaction might lead to certain complications on the emotional front, and it was in this volatile atmosphere that the performances took place.[11]

Vaura was faced with these emotional complications when she arrived at Mézières on 10 June and they must have come as a profound shock, because her diary is empty until the end of July and makes no mention even of the first performance on 13 June.

So, as Pierre Meylan says, the oratorio was given "under a lowering sky," in the presence not only of the usual authorities but also of Ignace Paderewski, who had settled in Morges some time before. Paul Boepple would take the rostrum for some of the later performances, but that first evening Honegger himself conducted, and "the first thunderclap of a fearful storm rang out at the very moment when Judith emerged from Holofernes's tent, holding in her hands the bloody head of her one-time oppressor."[12] This ultra-Romantic scene was not, perhaps, in the best taste as far as Vaura was concerned.

Pierre Meylan and others have examined at length the reasons for *Judith*'s semi-success, pointing not unreasonably to the dramatic text, of which the level of inspiration is, to say the least, more uneven than that in *Le Roi David*. But it is equally clear that some of the problem lay in Honegger's music. If its quality is beyond doubt (*Judith* is a more mature, accomplished, and profound work than *Le Roi David*, more unified in style, more personal in expression, and more modern in its language), nonetheless it did not conform to the needs of the occasion. In his future collaborations with René Morax and the Théâtre du Jorat, on *La Belle de Moudon* and *Charles le Téméraire* (Charles the Bold), he would confine himself to a language that was simple and popular. What is more, the very fact that the score was so difficult meant that the standard of performance left a lot to be desired.

This time Honegger had scored his music for a fairly large orchestra, including strings. According to Marcel Delannoy, the orchestra at Mézières consisted of only twenty-eight players, which left room for only ten string players. As a result there was a distinct imbalance in the forces. Even though audiences began to stay away quite early on, all the performances had to be given in accordance with the contracts signed with Croiza and Alcover. This led to a large deficit, too large even to be covered by the 10,000 francs held in reserve from the extraordinary success of *Le Roi David*, and a number of subventions had to be called for to meet the shortfall.

In Mézières, during June, Honegger found time to jot down a little piece for trombone and piano, *Hommage du trombone exprimant la tristesse de l'auteur absent* (Homage from the trombone to say how sorry the composer is not to be present). This was commissioned by the magazine *Comoedia* for a tribute to Serge Koussevitzky in its own offices. On 16 July, Honegger had a letter from the writer Saint-George de Bouhélier, who had already written to him once in Paris on 17 May, asking him to collaborate on an important stage work, *L'Impératrice aux rochers* (The Empress of the Rocks), subtitled *Un Miracle de Notre-Dame*. This was a large neo-medieval, pseudo-archaic mystery play, rather on the lines of Debussy's *The Martyrdom of Saint Sebastian*. We can detect in both works the hand of Ida Rubinstein, who commissioned *The Martyrdom* and for whom *L'Impératrice* would in fact be the first of six collaborations with Honegger.

According to René Morax, the final performances of *Judith* were of a far higher quality and seem to have been a great success.

Vaura's diary tells us that Honegger and Croiza left Lausanne for Paris on 31 July or 1 August—she did not know precisely. Vaura herself confided in Werner Reinhart by letter and went to stay at the Fluh from 2 to 5 August.

> When you're a nice elder brother, you're there when Vaurara phones. . . .
> My poor Reinhart, I'm in a rather difficult position where Arthur's con-
> cerned. A run-of-the-mill story, I know, but for me an extremely painful
> one. In front of our mutual friends I have to be cheerful all the time. If I
> have to go on lying to you, my elder brother, that'll be very painful, and I
> don't know that I can. . . . I'd love to see you, Reinhart, but I find the sight
> of Arthur hard to manage, and I'd rather see you without him. . . . Until we
> meet, dear brother.

After finding some solace with her "big brother," Vaura then joined her mother at Mougins. But Reinhart invited both of them to join him up in the mountains, at the Riederfurka, in Upper Valais near the great glacier of Aletsch, where he used to spend the summer. Vaura arrived on her own on the 28th and left on the 31st with Reinhart and the violinist Alma Moodie. They all spent an unforgettable day on 1 September with Rainer Maria Rilke at Muzot, near Sierre, before going down to the Venice Biennale from the 3rd to the 8th. On 5 September, there was a performance of Honegger's *Cello Sonata*.

Meanwhile, Honegger and Croiza had gone back to Paris. On 6 August, he began writing *L'Impératrice aux rochers* and probably spent the rest of the sum-mer in the capital. Contrary to one account,[13] he did not go on any tours around this time either to South or North America. Certainly, *Le Roi David* was per-formed in Buenos Aires on 18 August and in New York on 26 October, but Honegger did not cross the Atlantic until January 1929. In any case, when Vaura returned to Paris on 11 September, she noted: "Arthur and the two Morax brothers were waiting for me at the station."

So relations had not been broken off. The fact that she was met means that she must have announced her arrival. Indeed, shortly afterward she wrote a let-ter, undated, to Werner Reinhart thanking him for the days they had spent together and adding: "Arthur is a wretch, I know he hasn't written to you, but you mustn't be too hard on him. He's working continuously. Four of the five acts of the Bouhélier piece are done and he's orchestrating them, while waiting for Bouhélier to finish his fifth act." The score of *L'Impératrice aux rochers* was completed only on 13 November and it is, in fact, one of Honegger's largest: twenty-six movements and 269 pages of orchestral score.

The handsome Arthur, "with his biblical profile radiating both energy and gentleness,"[14] now found himself being fought over by two women who both loved him passionately. He had already been in Vaura's life for nine years and she was determined to keep him there. For Claire Croiza, ten years older than Vaura, it was no doubt her last chance of finding a loving partnership. It was the classic love triangle.

Vaura wanted to clarify the situation. On 3 October, she traveled, no doubt alone, to Bréthencourt in the Seine-et-Oise department on the outskirts of Paris, where Claire Croiza was staying in the country with her family. On the 4th, she noted: "a curious little scene this evening," and on the 5th: "Left for Paris this morning by car." But with whom? In any case, on the 29th she wrote: "Dinner at Claire's with Arthur and Morax" and a month later, on 29 November: "Dinner with C. C., the two Morax brothers, Fernand, and Arthur." On the 21st, both women even attended a festival of Honegger's chamber music at the Opéra-Comique. From then on, everything seems to have been sorted out, but the two women, who had once been so close, would never meet again on their own, nor as a threesome with Arthur, but only in company, surrounded by friends.

Meanwhile, the musical life of Paris continued and *Le Roi David* went on its triumphant way. Four performances were given at the Pasdeloup Concerts at the Théâtre Mogador, conducted by Rhené-Baton, on 17, 18, and 31 October and 1 November. On 31 October, Claire Croiza sang *Pâques à New York* in Geneva, in a concert by the Suisse Romande Orchestra in which Ansermet also conducted *Le Chant de Nigamon*. On 16 November, Honegger went with Vaura to Strasbourg, where Fritz Münch devoted a whole concert to Honegger's music at the Palais des Fêtes. In addition to the *Cantique de Pâques*, the *Concertino for piano and orchestra*, the *Prelude* for *The Tempest*, and the inevitable *Le Roi David*, the long program contained the first performance of the *Two Songs for Ariel* from the incidental music to *The Tempest*, sung by Joy Demarquette-MacArden and conducted by the composer.

As soon as he had finished *L'Impératrice aux rochers*, Honegger set himself the task of reworking *Judith*, which was, in its original form, hardly more viable outside Mézières than *Le Roi David* had been. Raoul Gunsbourg, the director of the Monte Carlo Opera, suggested that he might turn the work into an opera seria and offered his own services in reworking the libretto. This meant almost doubling the amount of music, and the considerable work involved kept Honegger busy until the end of the year. He finished the second act, which was by far the most thoroughly redone (with Holofernes becoming an important sung role), on Christmas Day, and the first performance of the new version would take place at Monte Carlo on 13 February.[15] But not with Claire Croiza. According to Pierre Meylan, Gunsbourg was not convinced by her acting abilities. She reacted with the ferocity of a wounded lioness and wrote René Morax in Paris on 21 December:

My poor René,
    I find your behavior *unforgivable*, in taking a female singer along to Arthur *without telling me*, for him to hear with regard to *Judith*. Please

come and see me at his apartment at five o'clock today. You must come to
a decision about me. You have wounded me deeply and I certainly did not
deserve it.

Morax responded by admitting his fault in a very long and contrite letter.

The version of *Judith* best-known today, and the only one recorded, is entitled "action musicale" and is in fact an oratorio with narrator, on the model of
Le Roi David. This was prepared just shortly before its first performance in Rotterdam on 16 June 1927, by adding some of the music newly written for the
opera to the original version.

The year 1925 finished with two performances on Christmas Day, *Chant de
joie* at Winterthur, conducted by Paul Boepple, and *Le Roi David* in Bern, with
the St. Cecilia Society under Fritz Brun. As for the storms in Honegger's private life, even if these had still not wholly abated, they would have done so by
the summer of 1926.

1926

From 4 to 8 January 1926, Honegger stayed at the Rychenberg with the
Reinharts as a member of the ISCM jury, replacing Ansermet. His fellow jurors
included Edward Dent, Walther Straram, Karol Szymanowski, and Volkmar
Andreae. But on the 12th, they arrived in Monte Carlo for the rehearsals of the
operatic version of *Judith*. As Ansermet had invited him to conduct a concert in
Geneva on the very day of the premiere, planned for 13 February, Honegger
asked him if it was still possible to change the date, adding: "As a novelty, I've
got *Sous-marine*. It's rather too Debussy-ish, but I think it sounds quite pretty
(I haven't heard it)."[16] The concert finally took place on 1 March. The program consisted of three psalms and the final chorus from *Le Roi David*, the *Concertino for piano and orchestra*, and *Pacific 2.3.1*, this last conducted by the composer. It was not possible to play *Sous-marine*, as Inghelbrecht had gone off to
Scandinavia with the only set of orchestral parts.

More than a year before the premiere of *L'Impératrice aux rochers*, Ida
Rubinstein offered Honegger a second commission: the incidental music for
Gabriele d'Annunzio's *Phaedra*. This extraordinary woman would play an
extremely important role in the composer's career and be the moving force
behind one of his greatest masterpieces, *Jeanne d'Arc au bûcher*. A Russian Jew,
she would be active as dancer, actress, and speaker. Although she would never
reveal the exact date of her birth, she was in fact born in Kharkov on 5 October
1885. She studied recitation and mime, was attracted to dancing by Isadora
Duncan, and studied briefly in private with Michel Fokine. She was a member
of Diaghilev's Ballets Russes from 1909 to 1911 (she danced Schéhérazade in
1910), before going on to form her own company. In 1911 she asked Fokine to
be in charge of the choreography for the Debussy/d'Annunzio spectacle *The
Martyrdom of Saint Sebastian*. This brought both scandal and her first great personal success. She possessed an immense fortune and, in a relentless pursuit of

her ideal of beauty, used it to put on performances of an unheard-of luxury and extravagance. Among the composers she commissioned were Ravel (*La Valse* and *Bolero*), Stravinsky (*The Fairy's Kiss, Persephone*), Jacques Ibert (*Diane de Poitiers*), Florent Schmitt (*Oriane la Sans-Égale*) and Milhaud (*Le Festin de la Sagesse*). But Honegger would always be her favorite.

At the end of January Honegger was back in Paris, and on the 31st Vaura's diary contains a single word, written in capitals and heavy with meaning: "CONFESSION." The abscess was lanced. Arthur admitted to Vaura that Claire Croiza was expecting his child. How long had he known?

He shouldered his responsibilities. A note dated 15 January says: "In case of accident or sudden death, I declare that I am the father of Claire Croiza's child. A. Honegger." Nonetheless, his imperious need for freedom meant that he felt trapped, and he reacted angrily. In February, he wrote to Croiza:

> Naturally, I've done no work on *Phaedra*. I don't know whether I'll be able to write this music. If I do, it will be a miracle. This is sexual vengeance. Women have used me utterly. I didn't realize it, and so much the worse for me.

Vaura remained calm and would soon reap the benefits of so doing. As for Croiza, it is tempting to look back to the "betrayal" she suffered at the hands of Morax and Honegger the previous month. Since she was in fact an admirable actress, Raoul Gunsbourg's doubts about her abilities on stage may simply have referred to her pregnancy, which would have been in its seventh month at the time of the performance.

Whatever the truth, on 2 February, Honegger conducted a program of Bach in the Salle du Conservatoire (*First* and *Fourth Brandenburg Concertos*, the *Violin Concerto in A minor*, and *Geistliche Lieder* with Gabrielle Gills), and the next day left on his own for Monte Carlo. On the 13th, while Claire Croiza was taking the part of the narrator in *Le Roi David* in Geneva, Honegger conducted the premiere of the new *Judith*, with Madame Bonavia in the title role. René Bizet, his future collaborator on *Cris du monde* (Cries of the World), has left us a striking portrait of the composer-cum-conductor in his review for *La Suisse*:

> He is of medium height, with tousled hair and dark eyes. To begin with, that is all you see. His expression is all in the face, like that of a young Beethoven. He doesn't milk the applause. He glances from the gallery to the boxes, then turns on his heel. He raises his hand. The stick describes his will. The orchestra plays. And it is from him alone that there seem to leap these barbarous sounds, these pure melodies, these hymns of energy, these warlike marches. It is from his hands that spring these sheaves of wild or hothouse flowers, it is he that sings, he that plays, he that casts me down or lifts me up. Behind his back, the audience follow him, as, in front, do the singers and instrumentalists. He is the master of the stage and of the auditorium. He has no need to throw himself around to lead these two groups of people who are facing each other. He has only to hold out his fist, to lean

down, to turn his arms into two powerful pistons, driving a formidable machine, to bend like a rider on a galloping horse that he whips with his baton. And we are all bending, leaning, and holding our own with him. . . . You have the feeling that he is a god in a battle and that he is interested only in the clashes; that he is impartial, and that in the fight between audience and orchestra he does not care who wins.

One person who did not share this enthusiasm was René Morax, who no doubt did not relish Raoul Gunsbourg's interference with his text. On 12 February, after the dress rehearsal, he wrote Werner Reinhart:

The interpretation of the music is good, but the production is ridiculous and the plot is now absurd. It's conventional opera with all the boredom that entails. I look back with nostalgia to the Mézières production, which may not have been perfect but which was alive and emotionally moving. This production stifles the tragic element.

After a second performance on the 16th, Honegger went back to Paris ("return of the Toad on the 18th," noted Vaura) and next morning went off to Brussels, where there was a concert that evening, followed by another in Liège on the 22nd. During his stay in Monte Carlo, *Chant de joie* was played at the ISCM in Zurich under Scherchen's direction on the 12th, and *Le Roi David* in Geneva the next day. He heard *Pacific 2.3.1* conducted by Straram on the 25th and attended a concert of his works at the Université des Annales at the Colisée on the 27th. He then left for Geneva with Vaura on the 28th for the concert planned by Ansermet. He returned to Paris on 2 March, traveled immediately to England, and was back in Paris on the 14th.

On 18 March Honegger conducted a concert of his music at the Opera. The program included *Pacific 2.3.1*, the first Paris performance of *Cantique de Pâques*, the *Concertino for piano and orchestra*, *Two Songs for Ariel* (with Gabrielle Gills), and the everlasting *Le Roi David*. On the 21st and 22nd, it was *Le Roi David* again, this time at Angers. On the 24th, there was another concert of his music, under the auspices of *La Revue musicale* at the Salle Gaveau, including the first-ascertained performance of the *Chanson de Fagus* by the faithful Gabrielle Gills.

Honegger wrote to his patron Werner Reinhart on 29 March: "I've still got a lot of work to do but happily I'm coming to the end, and I'll be leaving for Rome on 10 April." The work in question was on the score of *Phaedra*, which, as we have seen, had still not been begun by mid-February. Although the nine movements still came to seventy-eight pages of full score, the work was, luckily for Honegger, not as long as *L'Impératrice aux rochers*, for the premiere was planned for 19 April in Rome, where *Le Roi David* had been given two weeks earlier.

At the end of March, he received an extraordinary letter from Gabriele d'Annunzio, dated the 23rd, in an envelope bearing the escutcheon of Italy's *prima squadriglia navale* (first naval squadron)—the king of Italy had, after all, conferred on him the title of "Prince of the sea." It was addressed simply to "Arthur Honegger, Paris." "You are perhaps aware that I have the most attentive and passionate ear in the world when it comes to listening to beautiful music, and that I owe to this quality, which is rare among writers, the sincere friendship of Claude." After this preamble—it was he who gave Debussy the name "Claude de France"—he goes on: "You may imagine therefore with what anxiety I await the choruses in the third act of *Phaedra*, after the admirable choruses of *Le Roi David*." In fact, the score of *Phaedra* is almost entirely orchestral! D'Annunzio ends by saying: "I should dearly like to talk with you about Palestrina, the equal of Dante and Michelangelo, as we wander past my cypresses and rose-bushes. I send you an aviator's infallible token of good luck. *Cum pennis cor* [My heart comes to you with wings]."

At the time, d'Annunzio was practically under house arrest as being suspect under the Fascist regime. So it appears that he was not in fact able to leave his house, the Vittoriale, to attend the performance on 19 April at the Teatro Costanzi in Rome, which was conducted by Honegger. The composer visited the Vittoriale on 1 May.

On 25 April Arthur and Vaura left Rome for Florence and stayed there until the 28th. On the night of the 26th, Vaura had a strange intuition, noting "bad night." It was on the 26th in Paris that Claire Croiza gave birth to Honegger's son, Jean-Claude.

On 30 April Honegger was at Gardone, where another message from d'Annunzio was waiting for him. The poet sent a car to bring him to the Vittoriale. Marcel Delannoy has described this extraordinary meeting in considerable detail:

> D'Annunzio immediately showed Honegger round his property. He proudly pointed out to him the plinths of ancient marble with roses climbing up them. "A superb setting for open-air chamber music," he commented. He had organized a performance there of Debussy's *String Quartet* for Mussolini, played by a quartet from Verona. But during the andante Mussolini appeared to go to sleep. "That man doesn't like music," he muttered to Honegger, with the air of someone who would have liked to say more on the subject. Their curious walk was resumed. Suddenly, d'Annunzio came dramatically to attention. "And now, to celebrate the visit of the composer to the poet, we are going to send up to the heavens, without number or limit, the seven notes of the scale. . . . Fire!" The peaceful air was rent by a terrifying explosion. Honegger thought he would die of fright. He hadn't noticed the ancient torpedo-boat, a gift from Mussolini in memory of the action at Fiume,[17] whose stern was set in one of the borders of the garden and which seemed to be attended by a single gunner, giving the Roman salute (the Fascist one had yet to be invented). Seven times the cannon sounded. Each time, in front of a flabbergasted composer, d'Annunzio shouted: "do! re! mi! fa! sol! la! ti!" After the seven notes of the scale, the walk continued. They reached the villa. They sat down for lunch, Honegger's naturally healthy appetite sharpened by emotion. The frugal but, of course, exquisite repast was served by a Franciscan monk (d'Annunzio belonged, more or less, to the Franciscan order). Honegger recognized the gunner of Fiume under the rough habit, but managed to keep a straight face.[18]

After this semi-grandiose, semi-ludicrous interlude, Honegger returned to Paris, where on 8 May he met a narrator named Chochana Avivitt, who specialized in reciting passages from the Bible to musical accompaniment. She asked him to provide some music for sections of *Le Cantique des cantiques* (The Song of Songs), and the resulting score, written for chamber orchestra, was first performed by her on 16 June at the Salle Gaveau at one of the Golschmann Concerts.[19]

Vaura's diary for 9 May contains the entry: "Apparently J.-C. C. was born ten days to a fortnight ago." On the 10th another, more laconic, entry: "eleven o'clock. Town hall in the 17th." That was the day Arthur and Vaura were married, but only after he had recognized his son. They had been companions for ten years. From the musical point of view, he had complete confidence in her and took her critical opinions very seriously (unlike him, she had perfect pitch). But their marriage was the fruit of a difficult compromise. While Honegger never took advantage of his liberty and independence, he guarded them fiercely, going as far as to write in his notebook, some time later: "When it comes to it, a woman can never understand that one might prefer solitude to her presence." The fact was that he was incapable of composing unless completely alone. He therefore laid down as a condition of marrying Vaura that they should continue to live apart, he on the rue Duperré, she on the rue Dulong. From Pigalle to Batignolles was a journey of three stops on the Métro, or about twenty minutes by foot. It is true that at the end of 1931 he came nearer to her, moving to square Emmanuel-Chabrier, but after a brief, passing attempt at living together in 1935 and 1936, Honegger would retain his independence until the last year of his life, when he was too ill to live on his own. And in that year he produced not a single note of music.

From now on, unless he was traveling, which he often was, he would work in his apartment all day, and then join his wife, and later their daughter, for supper. They would then generally go out for the evening, before he returned to his solitary existence.

Vaura accepted this sacrifice, but she did not find it easy and was constantly frustrated at not seeing enough of him. As for Claire Croiza, there is no doubt that this marriage hurt her deeply, even if Honegger went to see her and their son every week, as well as supporting her financially. So, despite everything, Jean-Claude Honegger, who would be the living image of his father, had both his parents. But for his mother it was a lonely and bitter life, as she grew older and her career declined. We must emphasize once more that we are not talking here of one of those cheap "eternal triangle" plots you find in popular plays. The three people concerned were all exceptional human beings, and the two women, who had once been so close to one another, would always retain a mutual respect and esteem.

The number of concerts and other professional engagements meant that there was no honeymoon, either now or later. Even so, after a year of great strain, the couple's life adapted now to a less frenetic tempo.

The end of May was marked only by a performance of the *Prelude* for *The Tempest* and the *Two Songs for Ariel*, with Gabrielle Gills at the Salle Gaveau on the 29th and with Honegger conducting. On 1 June, he went to Düsseldorf, where *Le Roi David* was being given on the 2nd and 3rd, then to Frankfurt, where the same work was played on the 11th. On the 15th he joined Vaura in Zurich, where the ISCM Festival ended with *Le Roi David* in its complete stage version, performed for the first time in Hans Reinhart's German translation. With the festival over, they went to spend a few days with Werner Reinhart at the Fluh before returning to Paris. There they found a very friendly letter from Roland-Manuel, dated the 20th, in which he reproached Arthur gently for having kept his marriage such a close secret that he had had to learn of it from a third party, but at the same time congratulating him on his discretion. He went on: "You didn't have a friend, my dear Arthur, who was not also one of Vaura's. . . . I would not have wanted to see either of you married, except to each other."

On 10 July Claire Croiza sang *Pâques à New York* under the composer's direction in the annual concert of the École normale de musique at the Salle des Agriculteurs.

The newlyweds seem to have remained in Paris until the second half of August, but from the 23rd to the 31st we find them briefly in the south of France—Aix-en-Provence, Toulon, and, of course, Mougins. Meanwhile, Ansermet conducted *Le Roi David* in Buenos Aires on the 28th and Honegger directed the work at Évian on the 5th with Roland-Manuel as narrator.

The day before, Honegger met René Morax at Morges and promised him he would write music for Morax's new marionnette story, based on Hans Christian Andersen's *The Little Mermaid*. He kept his word, and the charming *Three Songs of the Little Siren* for voice, flute, and string quartet came from his pen before the end of the year. On 29 September he left for Berlin, where he conducted a concert on 2 October and another on the 18th, at which the Berlin public heard *Pacific 2.3.1* and *Le Roi David* for the first time and Honegger truly "arrived" in Germany. It is likely that he returned to Paris before the 22nd, when Vaura in her turn traveled to Germany, meeting Hindemith in Dresden on the 23rd and arriving in Leipzig on the 24th to play the concertino on the 25th. She then came back to Paris with her husband for the 27th. In their absence, the Pasdeloup Concerts again programmed *Le Roi David* twice, on 23 and 24 October.

From 2 to 5 November, they traveled to Brussels with the Milhauds, "in Darius's Renault," as Vaura records. On the 13th, Arthur left again for Nancy and was soon joined by Vaura. She played the *Concertino for piano and orchestra* there on the 21st and again in Zurich on the 23rd.

On 3 December, in the Salle Gaveau, the SMI put on another all-Honegger concert, including the *Rhapsody*, *Three Counterpoints*, *Le Cahier romand*, the *Second Violin Sonata*, eight songs with Gabrielle Gills, the *Seven Short Pieces* for piano, and the *Sonatina for clarinet and piano*. As usual, Vaura was the pianist, except in the songs, which Honegger accompanied himself. Finally, in distant Vienna, *Le Roi David* on the 15th once again drew a packed audience.

1927

The years that followed were less hectic and less eventful. It is true that Honegger's diaries for 1927 and 1928 have disappeared, but Vaura's are almost empty, and both their passports contain fewer frontier stamps. Even in Paris, Honegger's music seems to have been played less—an imperceptible beginning to the decline that would result in the crisis of 1931–1932.

The year began with a performance of *Judith* in its operatic version in Cologne on 13 January. The Honeggers were there, but not in Düsseldorf on the 21st for the first German performance of the *Pastorale d'été* and the *Chant de joie*.

On 18 January, Vaura noted: "A. came to see us after dinner," and the next day: "A. had dinner with us." Honegger's hermit-like existence was no fiction! With his peace of mind restored, he could again start composing. In February, he finished *Antigone*. Honegger had been working on this for three years, and of all his works it was his favorite, the one into which he knew he had put the best of himself. The work of orchestrating it would be for the summer.

Meanwhile, *Judith* was given twice on the other side of the Atlantic, in Chicago on 27 January and in Boston on 11 February, both times in the operatic version. Serge Koussevitzky wrote Honegger an enthusiastic letter:

> Dear Arthur,
>   I've just heard your opera *Judith*, which the Chicago Opera Company has given here. I can't tell you how much the music has impressed me. A real masterpiece written by a composer of genius. I congratulate you with all my heart.
>   The performance was splendid. The soloists and chorus showed themselves to be excellent artists. The conductor, Polacco, accomplished his task brilliantly, but most of all, Mary Garden created an unforgettable portrait of Judith.
>   The season is coming to an end and I'm already thinking of my concerts in Paris. Might you have something I could give a first performance of? I'd be delighted to have a new piece of yours in one of my programs.

Judith played by the first Mélisande must indeed have been worth seeing! But Honegger had less cause for satisfaction when *L'Impératrice aux rochers* was finally given at the Opera on 18 February (with a dress rehearsal the day before), conducted by Philippe Gaubert. Certainly Ida Rubinstein had not stinted on the sets and production, which were extravagantly opulent, even if Saint-George de Bouhélier complained that the orgy was short on naked women. During rehearsal, the Russian producer Alexandre Sanine exclaimed, in a moment of desperation: "You've heard this tremendous music: it's a disaster, a real disaster!"[20] The "tremendous music" also divided the critics, especially the longer pieces like the orgy mentioned above, or the storm, in which the aggression and boldness of the music recalled the fiercer moments of *Horace victorieux*. Ida Rubinstein defended them with all her might ("They're both splendid. The work is a masterpiece!") But the public was unimpressed and after five further performances, on 23 and 28 February and 2, 7, and 11 March, the work was taken off. It would never be revived, but Honegger rescued the best parts of it in a concert suite.

After being normally so spoiled by success, Honegger took this predominantly hostile reception rather badly. *Phaedra*, it was true, had also been badly received, but that was in Rome. The music had been drowned by shouting young Fascists and the audience had showed its disappointment at the absence of d'Annunzio, who had been expected with full panoply of banners. Was this perhaps another warning shot?

But the operatic version of *Judith* continued to be a success. On 10 March, it was given in Brussels in the composer's presence (it was his thirty-fifth birthday). He missed the umpteenth performance of *Le Roi David* two days earlier in Paris, with Claire Croiza at the Opera. But he did go to England from the 14th to the 18th to hear the performance in London of *Le Roi David* on the 17th. He had the honor of standing on the footplate of a locomotive of the London and North Eastern Railway, which took "King Arthur" and his party from King's Cross to Hitchin in a special coach. A photograph captured the occasion for posterity and would be much publicized, especially in the United States.

Honegger's impressions of the journey were published in *Chantecler* on 2 April 1927:

> It was wonderful, but very hot in the tunnels. Locomotives vibrate with harmonies, they sing. It's a symbol of the mammoth struggle of mankind, who is ever battling against forces greater than himself and triumphing over them. If I were to write *Pacific 2.3.1* again, I would perhaps introduce one or two other elements, because the sensation of speed, which I thought would absorb every other impression, is to some extent dominated by the manifestation of this colossal force, hurled forward with relative ease.

He returned to Paris on 20 March for the performance of the concertino at the Poulet Concerts (an evening organized by the magazine *Comoedia*), which was played this time not by Vaura but by Madame Moreau-Leroy. On the 24th, he presented his newly finished score of *Antigone* to the reading panel of the Opéra-Comique. They, no doubt, had been expecting another *Le Roi David*. They were horrified and instantly rejected this crucial work in Honegger's output. Luckily, other theaters were interested and once again the Théâtre de la Monnaie in Brussels dared to do what Paris did not. The first performance of *Antigone*, which Honegger orchestrated during the summer, took place there right at the end of the year.

Two days after the rebuff from the Opéra-Comique, on 26 March, Honegger conducted the first performance of the *Three Songs of the Little Siren*, written for René Morax's marionnette show. This was at the Salle Pleyel at one of the Durand Concerts, with Régine de Lormoy, the flautist Rémon, and the Roth Quartet.

However, during these months of relative calm, Honegger not only finished *Antigone* but completed a much larger work, the vast score for Abel Gance's monumental *Napoléon*. The showing of this on a triple screen at the Opera on 7 April was a major event. Of the large amount of music Honegger wrote for it, only the eight movements that make up the concert suite seem to have survived intact.

From 9 to 21 April, the Honeggers spent the Easter holidays at Saint-Enogat in Brittany, which would always be one of their favorite places. On Good Friday, Honegger wrote to his friend Koussevitzky in reply to his letter of 14 February, suggesting for their first concert performance the three preludes from *Phaedra*, as well as a revival in concert form of *L'Impératrice aux rochers*, which had been "massacred at the Opera."

An unfortunate misunderstanding prevented Honegger from being in Zurich for the performances of *Judith* given there at the end of May. He wrote to Reinhart on 24 May from Honfleur: "Following your letter, we decided to replace the journey to Switzerland with a little trip to Calvados. Then I had a telegram from Zurich telling me the premiere was on the 28th. Too bad. I hope the plans for Ireland come off." As a result, *Judith* was performed in the absence of both Honegger and René Morax, who had also been misled about the dates. Werner Reinhart reported on how things went. Despite a "production that was at times unimaginative and even clumsy" and "conducting without energy or flair,"

> despite all that, the work's great strength made a strong impression on the audience. As it could only be performed twice because of the season ending, it'll be revived in the autumn and, I hope, in better conditions and above all with a different conductor.[21]

Unfortunately this never came about. But the "plans for Ireland" certainly did. This referred to a relaxing trip organized by Werner Reinhart to include René Morax, Arthur, and Vaura. On 13 June, Morax wrote Reinhart from Paris, thanking him once again for his generosity (Reinhart was paying for everything), and he continued:

> I've just read with great interest J. M. Synge's *The Isles of Arran*, and I'm lending the Honeggers the book to make up their minds for them once and for all. We had dinner last night with Ravel and Roland-Manuel. Arthur's leaving with Vaura for Rotterdam where *Judith* is being done on the 16th in the concert version. They're serious too about the idea of going to Ireland. We'd travel to London together, and meet you there from Ostend.

In Rotterdam, this was the first performance of the oratorio version ("Action musicale") of *Judith*. In the years to come, this version would be given much more frequently than the others, putting the opera-seria version into the shade, even though that version is musically far more complete.

From Amsterdam, the Honeggers sent Werner Reinhart a postcard, dated 21 June: "We're eating up Holland with our 60CV. Arras, Lille, Bruges, Antwerp, Rotterdam, Amsterdam and . . . we're having a good time." Honegger was back in Paris on the 24th and wrote Reinhart the next day:

> We'd like to come to Ireland and will be very happy to spend a few weeks with you and dear René. Common sense obliges me to bring along a little work (the orchestration of *Antigone*) because Schultz Dornburg wants to put it on in Essen as early as November.[22] I think we'll reach London on the 4th around 6 PM, because we have to be at a party of Landowska's on the 3rd with Cortot and a lot of other musicians. Our little trip to Holland went well. We visited Bruges and the Belgian coast, and saw Utrecht and Brussels on the way there and back. On Wednesday Vaura's taking her driving test. She's a bit nervous, but I'm sure she'll sail through it.

On 4 July everybody met up in London as planned, and the trip to Ireland lasted the rest of the month until the 28th, when they disembarked at Calais. A number of charming photos, especially of them in horse-drawn carriages, are the only surviving souvenirs of this trip. Honegger also went on with orchestrating *Antigone*.

On his return, he went on with the work at Montfort-l'Amaury, where he stayed with Fernand Ochsé. The orchestral score of *Antigone* bears the name Perros-Guirec, where the score was completed in September. The house there belonged to one of their friends, Hilda Gélis-Didot, Pascale Honegger's future godmother. They would subsequently often stay in this house, Stereden Vor, which looks out over the sea.

It must have been before his departure from here that Honegger wrote to René Morax, refusing politely his invitation to collaborate on an *Oedipus* that Morax was intending to put on at Mézières the following year.[23] He explained that he still had a lot of work to do on *Antigone*, he had to go to "the Boches" (that is, Germany), then Brussels to attend performances, and then to Copenhagen for a concert. He also had to write an hour-long ballet commissioned by Ida Rubinstein, called *Les Noces d'Amour et de Psyché* (The Wedding of Cupid and Psyche), an orchestration of various movements of J. S. Bach's *English* and *French Suites*. The work would be produced a year later. As for the finally completed score of *Antigone*, it bears the dedication: "To Vaura." She could have asked for no greater homage than this, her husband's favorite among all his works.

Le Roi David was given in Leningrad (now St. Petersburg) on 3 September, then in Copenhagen on 10 November, conducted by the composer. Just before Honegger left for Denmark on the 5th, the work was performed once more at the Salle Pleyel together with the *Concertino for piano and orchestra*, played by Vaura. After that, the only information we have about Honegger comes in a letter from René Morax in Paris to Werner Reinhart, dated 22 November:

> Honegger's back from Copenhagen. In Hamburg he was surprised to hear *Pacific* as the music to a fantasy film. And what he heard was an unpublished arrangement of his work for piano and organ. His publisher will be asking for explanations. On Sunday we spent a jolly evening with Vaura, Arthur, Gance, and Ochsé.

That evening spent at the fair in Montmartre was captured in an entertaining photo showing the composer at the wheel of his convertible, with leather jacket and smoking a pipe, Vaura beside him, her face half hidden by her cloche hat, and his friends round the car, including Abel Gance with his enormous moustache. Shortly after that, on 10 and 11 December in Brussels, Claire Croiza put on to disc excerpts from *Judith* with Louis de Vocht, as well as Milhaud's *Les Choéphores*.

The year was crowned on 28 December by the world premiere of *Antigone* at the Monnaie in Brussels. The bill was shared with Milhaud's *Le Pauvre Matelot*. It was a bold program, in the manner of that great theater director Corneil de Thoran. He was also a remarkable conductor, and he was on the podium for this performance. Faced with the violent tension of these three acts, compressed into a mere forty-five minutes of continuous music, the audience was, as Honegger noted, ill at ease, despite their seriously good intentions. The critics, too, were split.

The reception in the municipal theater at Essen, where the work was given on 11 January in the German version by Leo Melitz, was frankly hostile. Politics were involved, with the sort of accusations of "atonal chaos" that were soon to become so horribly familiar, spiced with chauvinist and anti-Semitic remarks. *Antigone* was preceded by the first staging of *Horace victorieux*, with choreography by Jans Keith. Werner Reinhart was unable to go to any of the performances and would see *Antigone* only at its delayed first performance in Zurich on 8 June 1934. On the other hand, in Brussels the Honeggers were surrounded by a close-knit group of friends, including Morax, Maurice Sénart, Roland-Manuel, Rose Armandie, Hilda Gélis-Didot, and Toto, Honegger's sister.

1928

The controversial Essen production of *Antigone* takes us into the new year of 1928. After a *Le Roi David* performance in Lyons on 22 January and a *Judith* with Croiza in Toulouse on the 30th, the next important event was the Honeggers' first and only visit to the Soviet Union. The numerous stamps on their passports tell us their itinerary through Germany, Poland, and the three Baltic republics. They left Paris on 2 March and on the 7th arrived in Leningrad (where, we may recall, *Le Roi David* had been given on 3 September of the previous year). They stayed there until the 19th, when they went to spend four days in Moscow. The brevity of their stay in the capital confirms the dominant place that Leningrad then occupied in Soviet cultural life as a center of the avant-garde. During the years before Stalin assumed personal power, a number of the most important names in European music would visit the country, either before or after Honegger, including Alban Berg, Ernst Krenek, Paul Hindemith, and Darius Milhaud.

An interview with Honegger gives us various details of the tour. He conducted three concerts with the Leningrad Philharmonic, including *Le Chant de Nigamon, Pastorale d'été, Horace victorieux,* the *Concertino for piano and orchestra* (with Vaura), the Nocturne from *Judith,* and *Pacific 2.3.1.*

> *Pacific* is in the repertory of all the orchestral societies out there. . . . It was because of this piece, which seems to accord totally with the Soviet viewpoint, that permission was given to perform *Le Roi David* (you have to have an official visa to put certain works into a program). It was rebaptized *David the Judge* because of the censor. And since, of course, God doesn't exist any more, they had to take out a number of Jehovahs in favor of less subversive appellations.[24]

It had also been planned that Honegger would take part in various concerts in Moscow, but the numerous societies who laid claim to him—exclusively— could not reach agreement. So he had to content himself with being a tourist. In fact, he seems to have been very enthusiastic about the "country of the Soviets," especially in the cultural sphere, which was flourishing at that period, and he was considering coming back the following year. But circumstances did not permit it, and he could not be present when the Leningrad Academic Theater, the celebrated Maryinsky, produced *Antigone* in the 1928–1929 season, very soon after Brussels and Essen.

From Warsaw, the Honeggers sent a postcard to Werner Reinhart on the 28th:

> Dear Reinhart,
>   After Leningrad and Moscow, here we are in Warsaw. Before we come home, we may go and see Krakow, which is so close. We're very happy with our concerts, slightly less so with the atmosphere of the country we've just left!

As we can see, this opinion differs from the one above given to the journalist. Could it be that the composer was not quoted accurately?

There are not many events to record before the summer, except a concert by the Straram Orchestra in the Salle Pleyel on 18 May, in which Honegger conducted *Judith* (its Paris premiere, with the Dutch singer Berthe Seroen as soloist) and a suite in seven movements taken from *L'Impératrice aux rochers.* This included, as well as the five published movements, two more with choir: "Departure of the Emperor" and "Final Chorus." Three days later, the Honeggers had dinner in Milhaud's apartment with Cocteau and Poulenc. The friendship among Les Six was still holding firm.[25]

On 3 June the premiere took place in the Salle Oedenkoven[26] of the one-act ballet *Roses en métal* (not *Roses de métal,* as it is often called). This was based on a violently anticapitalist scenario by the Countess Élisabeth de Gramont, and produced on Xavier de Courville's "Small Stage." For this incendiary aristocrat, Honegger wrote a score (the first of its kind) combining piano and three "dynaphones Bertrand," the direct forerunner of the ondes Martenot. The music was much talked about at the time, but it has now unfortunately vanished. The summer of 1928 was a quiet one. Vaura's diary tells us that they spent it in Paris and that in August Honegger was working at an important new orchestral work, *Rugby*. He would finish this in September while spending a few days in Montfort-l'Amaury.

As Honegger's 1928 diary is lost, this summer remains something of a mystery, and we cannot pick up the thread of events until 18 October and the inaugural concert of the new Orchestre Symphonique de Paris (OSP), which would be highly active until the Second World War. At that concert, Ansermet gave the first performance of *Rugby*, which, even if it never eclipsed *Pacific 2.3.1*, would still be one of Honegger's most popular orchestral works.

On 3 November Hermann Scherchen conducted the concertino in Winterthur, with Elsa Horber as soloist. But the future American tour was now on the horizon. René Morax wrote Werner Reinhart from Paris on 11 November: "I haven't seen much of the Honeggers, who should have gone off to the Ukraine but have had to cancel at the last moment because they can't get passports. They're leaving for America in December."

Before that, on 22 November (and not in 1930, as is generally stated), Ida Rubinstein and her company gave the premiere at the Opera of *Les Noces d'Amour et de Psyché*. A week before leaving Europe, Honegger conducted a concert of his works in Utrecht, in the Netherlands, including *The Tempest*, *Phaedra*, *Chant de joie*, *Rugby*, the *Concertino for piano and orchestra* (with Vaura), and *Pacific 2.3.1*. They finally embarked from Le Havre on 26 December for a full three months' visit to the United States, just before the catastrophic stock market crash of October 1929.

1929

Arthur and Vaura arrived in New York on 2 January 1929 and settled into the Park Central Hotel. A solid reputation preceded them, thanks to Koussevitzky's efforts as Honegger's champion. On the 6th, they were in Boston, where the composer rehearsed with the famous Boston Symphony Orchestra the extensive program for the concert that would be given three times: on the 10th and 12th in the evening (the one on the 10th was at Cambridge, the site of Harvard University), and on the 11th in the afternoon. The works in question were *Le Chant de Nigamon*, the "Prayer" from *Judith*, the *Three Songs of the Little Siren*, *Pastorale d'été*, *Horace victorieux*, and, after the interval, *Rugby*, the *Concertino for piano and orchestra* with Vaura, and *Pacific 2.3.1*. These concerts were extremely successful, and Vaura's performance, according to one critic, breathed "an inexpressible charm and a pre-Raphaelite grace." The two of them were back in New York on the 13th, with Arthur traveling in the train's locomotive as far as Providence, Rhode Island.

On the 19th and 20th there were further concerts with the New York Philharmonic (*Rugby*, *Concertino for piano and orchestra*, and *Pacific 2.3.1*), but these were the last orchestral ones. The rest of the tour consisted of a long series of chamber music concerts, beginning with two on the 23rd and 24th in Poughkeepsie, New York, the first at Vassar College, the second in the Town Hall.

On both occasions Vaura played the *Hommage à Ravel* and *Toccata and Variations*. On the 26th, the Honeggers were in Detroit where, apart from *Toccata and Variations* and the *Rhapsody*, they played the *Suite for two pianos* arranged (no doubt by Vaura) from the music for *L'Impératrice aux rochers* for them to perform together. The three movements are "Overture," "Intermezzo," and "March." They reached Chicago on the 27th, and then the next day went on to Seattle. Here, on 2 February, they played *Toccata and Variations*, the *Seven Short Pieces*, and the first performance of a new work for two pianos, a transcription of *Three Counterpoints*. Honegger did not consider himself to be a pianist, and only very rarely did he agree to play in public, except as a duo with Vaura.

On 5 February the Seattle program was repeated in Portland, Oregon, and finally, on the 7th, the Honeggers were in San Francisco. All this traveling was done by train and on the way, at the station in Gerber, between Sacramento and San Francisco, Arthur had himself photographed in front of the train wearing a conductor's blue overalls. In San Francisco he had a letter from Koussevitzky: "We played *Rugby* six times during the tour and covered your name with glory all over America!" The concert there on 12 February contained the *Cello Sonata*, the *Seven Short Pieces*, the *Three Pieces for piano* (*Prélude, Hommage à Ravel, Danse*), and the *Suite* for two pianos based on *Three Counterpoints*. The concert in Los Angeles on the 16th repeated the *Seven Short Pieces* and the *Suite* from *Three Counterpoints*, while the Denver performance added to these two the *Toccata and Variations*.

On 21 February they repeated the same program in Kansas City, while in St. Paul, Minnesota, on the 23rd, the *Three Pieces for piano* and the *Suite* from *Three Counterpoints* were joined by the *Sonatina for clarinet and piano*. From there they went back to Chicago and on the 28th repeated the Denver program. After a concert in Cleveland on 1 March and a second one in Chicago, they headed south on the 6th to Houston, Texas, where the concert was preceded by Honegger giving a talk in English at the Rice Institute in the Scottish Cathedral. It was on the very broad subject of "Modern Music" and the printed text has survived.

On the 7th the Honeggers left for New Orleans—purely a sightseeing trip—and then went north again to Chicago on the 10th. After two more concerts there on the 15th and 16th, they moved on to Buffalo and before the concert on the 21st made the obligatory visit to Niagara Falls. Then it was Syracuse, where they gave their last concert on the afternoon of the 23rd, before reaching New York City that evening. On the 26th, Honegger recorded *Pacific 2.3.1* and then, on the 28th, they embarked on the *Rochambeau*. Apparently it was a rough journey (Honegger's diary for the 29th, 30th, and 31st reads simply "vomiting"), so it must have been with some relief that they reached Le Havre on 7 April and were back in Paris that same evening, with more than a handful of dollars to show for the trip.

In Paris they found the Roussel Festival in full swing. It was that composer's sixtieth birthday and, on 12 April in the concert hall of the old Conservatory, the pianist Pierre Maire gave the first performance of the *Hommage à Albert Roussel*, which Honegger had written for a commission from *La Revue musicale* just before leaving for the United States. That journal was currently publishing it with other pieces dedicated to Roussel, for whom Honegger had always had a lively admiration. *Judith* was performed at the Capitole in Toulouse on 16 April, but instead Honegger went to Strasbourg on the 17th to conduct that same work there on the 19th. On 6 May, he conducted *Le Roi David* in Barcelona, preceded by *The Tempest*, the *Pastorale d'été*, and *Pacific 2.3.1.*

In May, Honegger began composing, for him, a surprising piece: an operetta on a libretto by Albert Willemetz (who would soon be a close friend) on Pierre Louÿs's *Les Aventures du roi Pausole*. Honegger would continue to work on it until the end of the following year. Then he left for London (by air, so Vaura informs us) to conduct *Le Roi David* in Cambridge, in the complete stage version. All the preliminary rehearsals had been directed by Cyril Rootham, while Denis Arundell was responsible for the complete translation of Morax's text as well as for the production. Honegger then returned to Paris, where Ida Rubinstein revived *Les Noces d'Amour et de Psyché* on 16 and 21 May.

The entry in the composer's diary for 1 June reads: "Bought the Bugatti." From the 3rd to the 10th, perhaps to run in the vehicle in question, he went on a solo tour through Switzerland, reaching Basel on the 3rd, Zurich on the 5th, Lausanne on the 6th, and Mézières on the 8th. It must have been on this occasion that he first came into contact with a young conductor named Paul Sacher, who would put on *Le Roi David* the very next month and who would play a preeminent role in Honegger's life right up to the end.

Sacher, born in 1906, was now twenty-three years old. Three years earlier he had put his plans before a rich manufacturer of silk ribbons, Otto Senn-Gruner, who had offered him considerable financial support. As a result, Sacher had been able to found his orchestra and choir (with Senn-Gruner as their first president) and decided immediately to put them at the service of music both ancient and modern, in the first place that of Switzerland, then, very soon, that of other countries. His marriage with the heiress of the powerful Hoffmann-La Roche pharmaceutical company made Sacher one of the richest men in Switzerland and enabled him to take over the burden of patronage from the Reinhart brothers. His activities, centered on music, were backed up by a huge body of commissions, as well as by his tireless work as a conductor. Among the composers who have written pieces, and often masterpieces, for Sacher, his Basel Chamber Orchestra, and his choir, as well as for the Collegium Musicum of Zurich, which he also founded and financed,[27] have been Honegger, Frank Martin, Willy Burkhard, Conrad Beck, and, among foreign composers, Richard Strauss, Igor Stravinsky, Paul Hindemith, Béla Bartók, Bohuslav Martinů, Ernst Krenek, and Goffredo Petrassi, as well as, more recently, Henri Dutilleux, Cristobal Halffter, Hans-Werner Henze, and dozens of others. Like Werner Reinhart, indeed more so, Paul Sacher has treated all these composers as friends. They were all guests of his and his wife, Maja, at the Schönenberg, the wonderful house above Pratteln in the suburbs of Basel, with an unparalleled view over the nearby German side of the Rhine and the Black Forest.

Two of these composers, Martinů and Honegger, stayed at Schönenberg often, especially when they were ill, and their hosts looked after them with all possible care. Martinů died in the nearby hospital of Liestal on 28 August 1959; Sacher maintains that he felt closer to Honegger than to any of the others. Even if no record exists of their long conversations, their correspondence is virtually continuous from 1936 on, which was when their friendship really blossomed. Through it we can follow the development of their close relationship, which existed too between their wives. After meeting this exceptional man in 1929, Honegger was glad to have him as a companion on his artistic journey.

A quiet summer gave Honegger the chance to compose. In August he seems to have completed *Amphion*, a large score that he had no doubt begun soon after his return from America. This vast melodrama for female narrator, soloists, chorus, and orchestra, containing some forty minutes of music, was another commission from Ida Rubinstein and also the first of his two collaborations with Paul Valéry. In August he also settled down to compose a lighter, more modest work, the *Cello Concerto*, written for Maurice Maréchal. This work, almost certainly finished in the second half of August, allowed him to go as a tourist through central France, from Cannes to Rocamadour, in his new Bugatti.

Sir Henry Wood gave the first British performance of *Rugby* in a Promenade Concert at the Queen's Hall in London on 7 September. Then Arthur and Vaura spent a week, from 16 to 23 September, in Montfort-l'Amaury, before Honegger went off on his own to Breslau, where *Judith* was performed on 12 October. He was also in Solothurn on the 26th and 27th for *Le Roi David*. In November he worked on the piano reduction of his new *Cello Concerto* for cello and piano, while *Chant de joie* was played again at the Théâtre de la Gaîté-Lyrique on the 30th and Ansermet repeated *Horace victorieux* the next day.

He was not at Winterthur for the performance of *Rugby* conducted by Hermann Scherchen on 4 December, but he did attend the first concert performance of *Sous-marine* on the 7th, in a concert conducted by Robert Siohan at the Gaîté-Lyrique. On the 12th, in a concert of Les Six at the Théâtre des Champs-Élysées, Honegger conducted *Rugby*, "magnificently," according to René Morax in a letter to Werner Reinhart. On the 18th, there was another concert of Les Six, this time at the Salle Gaveau, and the year ended with a revival of *Judith* on the 28th and 29th.

During December, Honegger composed two short occasional pieces that have remained unpublished, *Berceuses for Bobcisco* and *J'avais un fidèle amant*, both written "for Bobcisco," a company founded by two friends, Bob (Robert) de Ribon and Francis Winter, for producing amateur films. They would for a time take over a cinema in Montparnasse (Le Falguière) where they showed experimental and avant-garde films, including Luis Buñuel's famous *Le Chien andalou*.

It was also in December 1929 that the name Montquin appeared for the first time in Honegger's diary. Montquin, in the Morvan, near Château-Chinon, was the house of his friend, the painter Jacques Thévenet, with whom he would often stay from now on.

The long-postponed premiere of *The Tempest* finally took place on 26

December at the Théâtre de Monte-Carlo, to which the personnel of the Odéon moved en bloc. Gémier was the producer and Albert Wolff the conductor. The production was revived in Paris on 2 April 1930, apparently with some extra music.

But the end of the year was especially noteworthy for Honegger's starting work on a very important piece, commissioned by his friend Koussevitzky for the fiftieth anniversary celebrations of the Boston Symphony Orchestra. Beginning with the Finale, Honegger had started on his *First Symphony*.

1930

The new year began, as usual, with numerous performances. On 11 January, Robert Siohan repeated *Le Roi David*. On the 25th, at the Théâtre des Champs-Élysées, in a Pasdeloup concert conducted by the Dutch maestro Albert van Raalte, the soprano Lina Falk sang several of Honegger's early songs ("La mort passe," "Le chasseur perdu en forêt," and the *Six Poems of Apollinaire*, except "Clotilde") in versions with orchestra. On the 29th, at the École normale de musique, Antonia Butler and Vaura played the *Cello Sonata*. Meanwhile, the symphony was coming on well. The Finale was finished during February and, certainly before the 14th, Honegger wrote Koussevitzky the latest news:

> The contracts for the symphony reached me safely and I've now signed them and sent them back. I thank you with all my heart for having thought of me and I'm working at this piece with you in mind. Unless you like it, I shall consider it a failure. I held on to the contracts for some time because I didn't want to send them back until I'd found the basic ideas for the work. Now the three movements are sketched out and I'm working enthusiastically. I'm finding it hard going because I want to do my best and I'm not gifted with the facility I envy in many of my colleagues.
>
> Maréchal is very happy about giving the first performance of my concerto with you, as I am naturally, especially if you weren't so far away and I could be there. I hope you'll like this little work and that it'll sound well on the orchestra. At the time I'll be in Berlin, conducting the Radio Orchestra with Vaura. As for *Sous-marine* (and not *Sous marin*), it's a little thing I wrote some time ago now for Carina Ari. I'll show it to you any time you like.

The Honeggers did indeed leave for Berlin on 15 February. The radio concert was on the 18th, with Vaura playing, of course, the *Concertino for piano and orchestra* under her husband's baton. After spending a day in Frankfurt, they returned to Paris on the 21st and Arthur immediately went back to his symphony. Meanwhile, the first performance of the *Cello Concerto* took place in Boston on the 17th.

On 25 February, Vaura's diary tells us of the departure of Salomé after sixteen years of loyal and devoted service, and some calamities! In 1926, for instance, she lost one of the precious gold cuff links that Honegger had been given by d'Annunzio.

From 6 to 17 March, the Honeggers were in Belgium. They visited Antwerp on the 6th and 7th ("Banquet in Antwerp" Arthur noted on the 6th), then, with a short trip to Liège on the 12th, they stayed in Brussels, where Honegger finished the first movement of the symphony on the 10th. Finally, he appeared as a conductor on the 15th and 16th at the Philharmonic. They traveled again from the 25th to the 30th, first to Vesoul, where *Judith* was performed on the 27th, and then to Épernay.

On the 31st, at the École normale de musique, Pierre Maire and the composer gave the first European performance of the *Suite* for two pianos based on *Three Counterpoints*, which Honegger and Vaura had played frequently on their American tour. On 2 April, at the Odéon, there was a revival of *The Tempest*, which had been premiered at Monte Carlo. Raoul Brunel's review next day in *L'Oeuvre* mentions that the incidental music contained some new pieces "composed quite recently," of which "some had already been used in other works. It seems that M. Albert Wolff, with his profound knowledge of the orchestra, had a hand in putting them into shape." It is no longer possible now to find out what was played in Monte Carlo and what was added in Paris, but it was the final stage in a gestation lasting at least seven years.

We may well ask how, in the middle of all this hectic activity, Honegger could have put the finishing touches to his *First Symphony*, it being one of his densest and most complex works—the first movement above all, which takes atonal polyphony to audacious lengths. But the fact is that, on 3 April, he finished the central slow movement. In later years, this was usually to be his starting point in his three-movement works, whether symphonies or quartets. The symphony then had to be orchestrated, which he did up to the beginning of May, staying with his mother-in-law in the peaceful sunshine of Mougins. On the other side of the Atlantic, *Antigone* was given for the first time in the United States, in English, at the New York Laboratory Theater.

Honegger returned to Paris in time for the first European performance of his *Cello Concerto*, on 16 May at the Salle Pleyel with its dedicatee, Maurice Maréchal, and the Orchestre Symphonique de Paris, conducted by Pierre Monteux.

Other projects were appearing on the horizon. In a letter dated 30 June, René Morax told Werner Reinhart that he had finished a work of a new kind for him: "I had in any case to finish off my *Belle de Moudon*, which I read through the other evening at Mézières. I'll send Honegger a copy soon so he can write us a Vaudois operetta." This third collaboration between the composer and the Théâtre du Jorat would be produced the following year and would indeed be Vaudois to the core!

The Honeggers spent a peaceful, if brief, holiday in July at Villennes, near Passy, in the outer suburbs of Paris, preparing for another important tour, this time in South America. The composer took with him a large new project, a secular oratorio with words by René Bizet, inspired by Keats's "Ode to Solitude." It had been commissioned by the choir of Solothurn and its conductor,

Erich Schild, who had been champions of Honegger's music for years. *Cris du monde*, a crucial work in understanding the composer's views, would meet with an incomprehension that triggered the crisis that had been brewing for so long.

Arthur and Vaura left Paris on 30 July and weighed anchor at Villefranche on the 31st on board the *Giulio Cesare*, bound for Buenos Aires. On 1 August, they stopped off at Barcelona, on the 8th they were on the equator (the Honeggers duly went through the ceremony of "crossing the line"), on the 12th in Rio de Janeiro, on the 13th in Santos, and finally on the 15th in Montevideo and Buenos Aires. They stayed in the Argentinian capital until 7 October, with Honegger conducting some concerts, certainly, but also continuing his work on *Cris du monde*. The complete libretto had reached him when he stopped off at Rio.

Rehearsals for the first concert at the famous Teatro Colon did not begin until 28 August and went on till 1 September. (The delay was caused by a female singer, who was under the protection of President Irigoyen and who wanted to sing in *William Tell*.) The program, which was given on the 2nd and then repeated on the 4th and 6th, consisted of *Pacific 2.3.1*, the *Orchestral Suite* from *Phaedra*, *Rugby*, the *Concertino for piano and orchestra*, and the *Prelude* for *The Tempest*. But on the 6th, a revolution broke out in Buenos Aires and President Irigoyen was deposed. When order was restored, a chamber music concert was organized on the 22nd. The next day, rehearsals began for *Le Roi David* and *Judith*. The first of these was given twice, on 27 September and 1 October, as was the second, on 30 September and 6 October, obviously with Honegger conducting.

Meanwhile, he made a return trip to Montevideo on the 2nd by seaplane. The day after the last *Judith* performance, on 7 October, the two Honeggers boarded the *Massilia* for the long return journey, taking them to Lisbon. They arrived there on the 21st and in Paris the day after. There Honegger found a letter from Eugène Ysaÿe, reminding the composer of his promise to keep the first Brussels performance of his symphony for the Ysaÿe Concerts—a promise that had been made "between two pipes of tobacco." Testimony to the warm friendship between Honegger and the aging virtuoso, who would die the following year, comes from the end of the letter, in which Ysaÿe invokes again "our goddess the pipe."

While, on 29 October, Hermann Scherchen conducted the *Orchestral Suite* from *Phaedra* at Winterthur, Honegger was in Paris working on *Les Aventures du roi Pausole*, which he finished on 18 November. Rehearsals began immediately. On 27 November, more than a dozen years ahead of Paris, the Municipal Theater in Strasbourg produced *Antigone*—the opera's French premiere. On 6 December, Honegger recorded for the Odéon record company the *Prelude* for *The Tempest* and the *Pastorale d'été*. On the 12th, a Honegger concert was given in Brussels, in which Régine de Lormoy sang the *Six Poems of Jean Cocteau* in a transcription for voice and string quartet made by her husband, Arthur Hoérée, who conducted. But the composer did not attend, being in Paris at the time for the premiere that same evening of *Les Aventures du roi Pausole* at the Théâtre des Bouffes-Parisiens. This first experiment in a new genre for him was a triumphant success. The operetta held the stage for some 400 performances, bringing the composer in a small fortune (which he lost, unfortunately, through unwise speculation). The year ended on the crest of this wave, with two more recording sessions with the Odéon company, on 26 and 31 December, devoted to extracts from *Pausole*.

1931

During the first quarter of 1931, Honegger tackled the composition of two works as different in character and importance as could be, even though both were for Switzerland: *Cris du monde*, which he had been working on since the previous fall,[28] and *La Belle de Moudon*. Regarding the latter, René Morax wrote from Morges on 2 February, to Vaura so as not to distract Arthur from his work:

> Everyone is delighted with the music, and the female soloist is thrilled to have a song written for her voice. Great success at the session in Mézières. . . . For the soloists in the fanfare we can count on a good bugle and a saxophone, but it will be easy to get hold of any other instrument of the same family in Lausanne, if the "virtuoso" soloist can't be found in Mézières. I think a little fanfare as an overture would get the play off to a jolly start, since the chorus doesn't come in straightaway. Arthur can follow his fancy over this.

The review *Plans* for January 1931 contains a very important article by Honegger entitled "From Cinema Sounds to Real Music"—a sign of his growing interest in the seventh art.

On 13 February Koussevitzky gave the first performance of the symphony in Boston. Once again Honegger found the audience and the critics divided in the face of an undeniably difficult and demanding work, one of the toughest, most complex, and most "Alemannic" he ever wrote. But Koussevitzky was convinced that it was a masterpiece.

On 1 March Honegger finished *Cris du monde*, which he still had to orchestrate, and then completed *La Belle de Moudon*. Meanwhile, *Pausole* continued to be so successful that there were plans for a German version. On 11 March, Reinhart wrote Conrad Beck to say that Fritz Busch had seen the score of the operetta at his house, wanted to put it on in Dresden, and was looking for a German translator. But he needed to know whether the exclusive rights for a premiere in Germany were still free. Vaura's reply, dated 21 March from Briançon, made it clear that Max Reinhardt had reserved these rights for Berlin. Even so, the first performance of *Pausole* in German did not take place until much later, in Zurich on 30 December 1953.

The Honeggers stayed at Briançon from 14 to 26 March with Vaura's sister Mina and it was there, on the 24th, that Arthur finished the orchestration of *Cris du monde*. According to Pierre Meylan, Honegger also continued work on *La Belle de Moudon*, which he finished in Paris on 31 March. At the end of April, he went to Solothurn for the first performance of *Cris du monde*, the climax of the annual meeting of the Association of Swiss Composers.

None of his works after *Antigone* was so close to his heart, and all through his life he would try and create openings for this awkward child—and awkward *Cris du monde* certainly is. In uncompromisingly stark language it exposes, clearly and bitterly, the great problems facing European society after the 1929 crash, hit hard as it was by an economic crisis that would lead to unemployment, poverty, the rapid rise of totalitarianism (notably of Hitler), and ultimately to the Second World War. But the work goes further. It reaches out far beyond short-term politics to the alienation of mankind, to the loss of his individual liberty, of his quality of life, and to his degradation through machinery and pollution, both industrial, chemical, and aural. As we see the work now, it was prophetic and still has a burning relevance today, but no doubt it came a little early to a human race that has never liked Cassandras or paid much attention to their cries of alarm. Once again, the responsible creative artist played his cruel but necessary role as a seismograph, "which knows things before they happen," in the words of C. F. Ramuz. Switzerland, with its tradition of democracy and its highly developed sense of civic community, in general gave the work a good reception. But there were some dissenting voices who thought they could detect in Honegger some sort of sympathy with the ideas of the extreme left, while René Bizet had never hidden his royalist tendencies. Later Honegger would say ironically: "Some of my friends hinted that I ought to have written the text and left Bizet to write the music."[29]

While Hermann Scherchen conducted a splendid performance of *Antigone* on Munich radio on 19 May (the first time the work had been heard in a concert version), the Théâtre du Jorat was getting ready for the premiere of *La Belle de Moudon*. After his chastening experience over *Judith*, Honegger had turned back to local artists and to the Moudon wind band. The story indeed lent itself to such treatment. As a result, the premiere at Mézières on 30 May went extremely well and cheerfully.

That same evening Honegger returned to Paris by the night train.[30] A new series of concerts was in preparation for which he had to oversee rehearsals and, in the case of the first concert, conduct. On 2 June, after a performance of *Chant de joie*, he gave the first French performance of his symphony with the Straram Orchestra (soon to be disbanded after the early death of its founder and conductor). The reception was mixed, as it had been too often of late, but it was as nothing compared to the frank hostility that greeted *Cris du monde* later that evening, conducted by Erich Schild with his Swiss choir. The frivolous Parisians, already unconsciously making the bed they would have to lie on in 1940, had no way of understanding the cries of warning issued by this spoilsport, even if those cries did not fall entirely on deaf ears among the more perspicacious of his compatriots. For Honegger, this blow, coming after several others, was hard to bear. Suddenly, he was vulnerable, and the news from Scherchen of *Antigone*'s resounding success in Munich, with excellent critical notices, did little to reassure him.

In any case, he was now in the thick of rehearsals for the premiere of

Amphion, which took place at the Opera on 23 June, conducted by Gustave Cloëz, with Ida Rubinstein and Charles Panzéra taking the main roles. Paul Valéry had been mulling over his text for thirty years. It was a grandiose project (nothing less than reinventing the birth of music), and Honegger's fine score matched it. It remains one of his unacknowledged masterpieces. Valéry would claim: "I needed a great composer, I found one," and the critics were almost unanimously in favor of the work. But *Amphion* has been the victim of its hybrid nature—a melodrama involving speaking, singing, and playing—and has hardly survived beyond those first performances. It has only once been revived in its complete form as a stage work, in Zurich in 1934. Much later, in 1948, Honegger would rework the final section for orchestra alone, under the title *Prelude, Fugue, Postlude* from *Amphion*. Its vast double fugue is worthy of comparison with the one in the Finale of Bruckner's *Fifth Symphony*, and altogether this orchestral triptych is one of Honegger's most powerful works. But it too has so far languished in obscurity.

On 30 June Honegger was in Le Havre for a performance of his *Cello Concerto*, and on 4 July, back in Paris, he noted in his diary: "Move piano." This no doubt referred to his impending change of apartments. But then he vanished totally until 6 October. This gap, the longest we shall come across in his adult life, without question marked a pause and a period of reflection. Honegger was in his fortieth year. But was he still "King Arthur"?

FIVE

Reversal of Fortune:
In the Trough of the Wave

Honegger's music was still being played frequently, but less so than in the climactic years of 1920–1926, and his popularity rested essentially on works that were now no longer recent. *Le Roi David*, which continued to fill concert halls, was ten years old. *Judith*, even if performed quite often, had not emulated the success of *Le Roi David*, any more than *Rugby* had that of *Pacific 2.3.1.* The bitterness and doubt that suddenly assailed the hitherto productive and cheerful Honegger were nourished above all by the incomprehension that had greeted his recent large works, ones to which he was particularly attached: *Antigone*, the *First Symphony*, and especially *Cris du monde*. The immense popular success of *Les Aventures du roi Pausole* merely served, in his eyes, to deepen the misunderstanding. Would he be condemned from here on to write light music in order to reach the public?

For him, that was the central problem. He did not doubt the value of his recent large works. He had always been a very lucid judge of his own music, able to evaluate the relative importance of his pieces, but for an artist who had so little of the ivory tower about him, who was so keen to communicate with his contemporaries, it was first and foremost this contact that mattered. So far he had always achieved it, without aesthetic or intellectual compromise of any sort, and in this respect it was impossible for him to change. That was where doubts began to enter and gnaw away at him. It is true that for the next few years he would write less, but the handful of works covered by the present chapter—the *Sonatina for violin and cello*, the *Prelude, Arioso, and Fughetta*, the *Symphonic Movement No. 3*, and *Sémiramis*—show absolutely no reduction in quality. On the contrary, the *Symphonic Movement No. 3* is one of Honegger's finest works, and its only drawback, as he himself knew, was that it did not have a snappy descriptive title like *Pacific 2.3.1* or *Rugby*.

We catch up with the composer on 6 October 1931, thanks to a journey plan in his diary according to which he left Marseilles on that day and reached Paris on the evening of the 9th. On his return he found a letter from Paul Sacher, the first that has survived. Sacher said that he was planning to perform *Cris du monde* with his choir and orchestra on 20 January of the following year. He hoped the composer would be present and would be kind enough to agree to say something about the work to the audience beforehand. He was anxious to know whether, as he'd been told, Honegger at that time would be in China.

An unlikely idea, but it could have been one that Honegger, feeling as he did, had not discouraged in order to get some peace and quiet. His reply, made curiously enough through a secretary and dated 25 October, stated that he would not be in China, that he would come, but that he would rather someone else gave the talk.

On 2 December Honegger's *First Symphony* was performed in Winterthur, conducted by Hermann Scherchen, thanks to the faithful Werner Reinhart. The same day, a letter from Paul Sacher fixed a meeting in Basel on 15 January for the main rehearsal, with the dress rehearsal arranged for the 18th. The musicologist Ernst Mohr (the future biographer of Willy Burkhard) would give the talk. This letter was the first to be addressed to 1 square Emmanuel-Chabrier, in Paris's seventeenth arrondissement (district), where Honegger had moved to shortly before and where he would remain until 1936. And, while *Le Roi David*'s success reached as far as Athens on 5 December, the year finished with a concert by the loyal Jane Bathori at the Vieux-Colombier on the 12th, followed by another in the Salle Chopin-Pleyel in the series of Capelle Concerts, including the *Sonatina for two violins* and various songs, in which the composer accompanied Dolorès de Silvera.

1932

The new year began under better auspices. In a letter of 6 January 1932, Paul Sacher told the composer that after *Le Roi David* in 1929 and the upcoming *Cris du monde*, the Basel Gesangverein intended to perform *Judith* under his direction in December, confirming that Honegger had found in Sacher a new champion who would be the most faithful and effective of them all. Sacher also inquired about an unaccompanied chorus that Honegger had had in mind, but nothing ever came of this.

On 10 January Ernest Ansermet and the Suisse Romande Orchestra gave the first performance of the symphony in Geneva. On 14 January (that same day Louis de Vocht repeated *Le Roi David* in Brussels) *Amphion* was first given in its concert version at the Université des Annales under Robert Siohan, with Ida Rubinstein and Henri Fabert, and this performance was preceded by a long and exceptionally interesting talk by Paul Valéry.

On the 18th Honegger was in Basel where, the following day, Gian Bundi's German adaptation of *Cris du monde* was the high point of the annual session of the Association of Swiss Composers. A few hours before the concert, Arthur sent a victory message to "his dear little Toad" [Vaura]. He was very satisfied with the orchestra, which was much better than the one at Bern that had taken part in the first world performance at Solothurn the previous year. "Little Sacher is a real conductor," he wrote, "and conducts with an authority that many of them don't have" (we may recall that "little Sacher" was only twenty-five years old at the time). Indeed, all the seats were sold and there was talk of a second performance. Meanwhile, Ansermet introduced the difficult symphony to England in a BBC concert on 24 January.

On 1 February Honegger was back in Paris at a repeat performance of *Horace victorieux* by the Orchestre Symphonique de Paris and, on the 7th, the same orchestra played the *Concertino for piano and orchestra*. In Basel, the envisaged second performance of *Cris du monde* did indeed take place on the 3rd, and the work was also performed at Antwerp by de Vocht on the 15th.

Just as this daunting work seemed at last to be making headway, the storm broke in the shape of an article by Honegger, or rather a kind of open letter, with the pregnant title "Pour prendre congé" (Leaving the Ranks), which appeared simultaneously in the journals *Plans*, *Appoggiatures*, and *Dissonances* (the latter published in Geneva).

This was the first outward sign of a profound pessimism, already expressed in *Cris du monde*, that would dominate all his writings and pronouncements at the end of his life. It was without doubt accentuated by illness, but the roots of it go back much further. His frustration is clear right from the opening words: "What is discouraging for a composer is the certainty that his work will not be heard or understood in the way he conceived it and tried to express it."

Fair enough, but the problem was not peculiar to Honegger. He then develops his argument at some length, insisting on the misunderstanding generated by some of his titles (*Pacific 2.3.1*, *Rugby*, and so on), which had seduced public and critics away from a purely musical understanding of his works. Finally, he proclaims: "But still, it is essential that one's music is heard. Artistic expression is essentially the need to communicate these thoughts and emotions, and it follows that it would be better in general if what is heard is what the composer said."

We can but take note of this deeply human and humanistic artistic credo, at the opposite extreme from the purely formalistic one of somebody like Stravinsky, for example. But at what conclusion is Honegger aiming?

He reckons that "opera is finished, its outmoded forms are no longer acceptable or accepted." How sad for someone who would declare on one occasion that, like Mozart, "his ideal would have been to write nothing but operas"! In fact he never wrote any more and, if we leave aside his collaboration with Jacques Ibert on *L'Aiglon*, which had no claims to the same ambition, his contribution to the genre would remain limited to *Antigone* and to the operatic version of *Judith*. But what would be the outcome of this imperious need to express himself for a composer gifted with an exceptional genius for "figurative" music? For the moment, he dreams:

> I dream of a collaboration that would finally be total, in which the librettist would often think as a composer and the composer as a librettist. The result of this union would be, not the fortuitous result of a series of approximations and concessions, but the harmonious synthesis of two aspects of a single thought.

And he goes on later:

> The need is to define and realize this modern operatic method, the forms of which will be adapted to the manifestations of our new world and which

will express the new aspects of man and material objects. Will it be the successive images of the cinema that will provide the composer with these means of renewal? Will it be a new collaboration between music, color and light?

And he concludes:

> For the moment, I retire from the fray. There is a whole new world that wants to understand itself, seek itself, define itself, and celebrate itself in new aesthetic forms. From now on, all my passionate efforts will be channeled in that direction. I prefer to try along these lines and fail, rather than be idly satisfied with hallowed forms and conventional habits.

Temporarily, then, it was an impasse, with Honegger bravely and not unexpectedly refusing all compromise. Indeed, his subconscious had foreseen the future with astonishing accuracy. In any event, Paul Claudel and the cinema would offer him, on two different planes, the solutions he was looking for, and together they would dominate the next phase in his creative life. This is how we should interpret a phrase to be found, much later, in an unpublished autobiographical sketch, in which Honegger says that he wrote a lot for the cinema from 1934 onward "for a number of reasons, from which financial ones were not excluded."[1] Not excluded, but not sole or even primary. For the moment, though, he still had some way to go to reach the end of the tunnel.

The daily routine continued. Still in February, he composed a strange little *Prelude for sub-bass and piano*, once again for the lowest of the new string instruments invented by Léo Sir. In March, he went to Strasbourg, where his followers had remained loyal, for two performances of *Le Roi David* on the afternoon and evening of the 7th, then a chamber music concert on the 9th. From 16 to 24 April, he was in Berlin, where he had a number of meetings with his friend Hindemith. It was probably on that occasion that Wilhelm Furtwängler commissioned him to write a piece for the Berlin Philharmonic Orchestra. This would be the *Symphonic Movement No. 3*. The great German maestro had conducted *Chant de joie* on 7 October 1926 at the Leipzig Gewandhaus, when he was director there, and had been an admirer of Honegger's music for some time.

On 27 April the composer took his car to Spain for one of the tourist trips he used to enjoy. He was obviously very much attracted to this country and, even though two years later another trip would be brutally interrupted by a terrible accident, he would return to Spain to conduct his music.

In June, he was briefly in Zurich, meeting Hindemith on the 10th and the next day attending the production of Othmar Schoeck's *Penthesilea*, which Honegger very much admired.

He then spent the summer in Paris with Vaura, waiting for the great event: the birth, on 11 August at 6:45 PM, of their daughter Pascale, who would remain their only child.

It could be that Pascale's arrival revived inspiration in her doting father. In September he wrote a *Sonatina for violin and cello*, dedicated to his friends Albert and Anna Neuburger—Albert was the director of Sénart, Honegger's exclusive publishers. This work marked a return to chamber music after a gap of nearly ten years. In October he wrote the *Prelude, Arioso, and Fughetta* for the homage to J. S. Bach organized by *La Revue musicale*. This delightful piece, built on the four letters of Bach's last name, would become popular both in its original piano version and in the transcription for string orchestra made four years later by Arthur Hoérée. Honegger suggested the idea and supervised Hoérée's work. Then, on 30 October, Honegger finished the Berlin commission, the *Symphonic Movement No. 3*.

The first performance of the *Prelude, Arioso, and Fughetta on the name BACH* was given by Vaura in the unlikely surroundings of a childrens' concert in the Salle de Géographie. The following month, *La Revue musicale* published the work in the supplement to its special Bach issue. On 16 December, there was the first performance of the *Sonatina for violin and cello* in a Triton concert, given at the École normale de musique. On the 15th, the *Mercure de France* carried a review of a Honegger concert in which, in addition to *Rugby*, the *First Symphony*, the *Cello Concerto*, and *Phaedra*, the composer conducted *J'avais un fidèle amant* (a work that he did not think of as being beneath the dignity of a concert hall). The concert also included extracts from *L'Impératrice aux rochers*, with the Prologue, which had not been heard at the Opera.

1933

Honegger spent the Christmas holidays at Chesières, in the Vaudois Alps, opposite the Muverans and the Dents du Midi. There he worked on the orchestration of the *Symphonic Movement No. 3*, which he finished in Paris shortly after his return on 4 January. During the last week of January he went to Warsaw and conducted the Philharmonic Orchestra there on the 27th. The program consisted of *Le Chant de Nigamon*, the *Cello Concerto*, the *Concertino for piano and orchestra*, *Rugby*, and the *First Symphony*. Among the various Paris concerts in February, we may note the one on the 5th, at the Poulet Concerts, in which Gustave Cloëz conducted the Orchestre Symphonique de Paris in the first concert performance of the *Suite After J. S. Bach*, which Honegger had extracted from *Les Noces d'Amour et de Psyché*. This was only a little more than two months after the first performance of another Bach homage, the *Prelude, Arioso, and Fughetta*.

Meanwhile, the date for the first performances of the *Symphonic Movement No. 3* in Berlin had been fixed for 12 and 13 March. But this did not take account of an event whose importance no one at the time realized. On 30 January, Adolf Hitler became Chancellor of the German Reich and his cultural policy was not slow in bearing its sinister fruits. The performances had to be postponed.

Honegger then left for Switzerland and two concerts of his works, first at Vevey on 6 February, then at Winterthur on the 11th, preceded by a talk. Meanwhile, in Paris the faithful Jane Bathori revived *Pâques à New York* with the Capelle Quartet on the 12th. On his return, Honegger found a letter from Wilhelm Furtwängler, dated 13 March, asking whether he might prefer the first performance of the *Symphonic Movement No. 3* to be postponed until the beginning of the next season, because he was sure that the political climate would by then be more relaxed. This showed the extraordinary blindness of the German intellectual and artistic world, which did not believe that Hitler would last more than a few months. Richard Strauss believed this too.

Some days later, Furtwängler sent a telegram: "Playing as planned but suggest you don't come." As usual, Furtwängler gave the work a preliminary hearing in Hamburg on the 24th, but the Berlin performance the next day got an icy reception and hostile reviews. From this moment, Honegger's music was effectively boycotted in the new Germany. As he was not Jewish (though he would have to prove the fact), he would be allowed to write the music for the UFA film by Andrew Marton and Gunther Oskar Dyhrenfurth called *Der Dämon des Himalayas* (The Demon of the Himalayas) at the beginning of 1935, but the official document authorizing this would state that his music was no longer played in Germany.

This abrupt closing of Germany to his works was a severe blow, both materially and in other senses. Happily, the situation was better in France, and in April there were performances of *Cris du monde* in Strasbourg (rehearsal on the 4th, concert on the 5th), of *Le Roi David* at Évreux on the 9th, and the *Concertino for piano and orchestra* and *Pastorale d'été* in a Cortot concert on the 25th. Honegger continued to compose, too, and in May completed the fifth of Ida Rubinstein's commissions and the second of his collaborations with Paul Valéry: *Sémiramis*—a work totally unappreciated today. On 14 June, he was in Zurich for the first performance of the German version of *Amphion* at the Stadttheater.

Before the summer holidays, two events took place that were to have repercussions on Honegger's future. First, the premiere on 7 May of a production by a group of music students who were enthusiasts of medieval mystery plays. Called the Theophilians, they were directed by Jacques Chailley and were the first link in a chain that would one day lead to the birth of *Jeanne d'Arc au bûcher*. And secondly, Honegger's first meeting, on 3 July, with the cinema director Bertold Bartosch, who was planning an experimental film called *L'Idée* (The Idea), based on wood engravings by Frans Masereel, for which Honegger would write the music. Up to this point, Honegger had only written for those two outstanding classics of the silent cinema, *La Roue* and *Napoléon*, both by Abel Gance. Now he set out on the road he had envisaged in "Pour prendre congé." Between 1933 and 1951, he would compose the music, alone or in collaboration, for no fewer than forty films, often by famous directors, and would become the most prolific of all so-called serious composers writing for the cinema, ahead of Shostakovich who would compose for a mere thirty-five.

SIX

Toward the Summit: Claudel and the Cinema

Arthur Honegger now embarked on a creative regime that was both intense and curiously divided. During the period covered by this chapter (1934–1940), there were on the one hand the large enterprises, stamped with his personality and made to last. These included three oratorios, *Jeanne d'Arc au bûcher*, *La Danse des morts*, and *Nicolas de Flue*; chamber music, in the shape of two string quartets, the *Partita for two pianos*, and the *Three Poems of Claudel*; and the *Nocturne for orchestra*. On the other hand, there were no fewer than twenty-three film scores, popular songs, and occasional pieces, and, between these two extremes, four ballets, the earliest works for radio, contributions to collaborative stage productions, sundry works such as *Les Mille et Une Nuits* (The Thousand and One Nights) and *Radio-Panoramique*, and finally two collaborative efforts with Jacques Ibert, the grand opera *L'Aiglon* and the operetta *Les Petites Cardinal*. In short, Honegger had recovered not only his prolific inspiration, but also his contact with the public, and he was able, thanks to his superhuman energy, to reconcile the demands of art with those of everyday life.

It was during the summer of 1933 that the Honeggers went for the first time to the Bayreuth festival. They would return there in 1936.

On 22 August they left for a holiday at Perros-Guirec and, on 8 October, Arthur had another talk with Bartosch about *L'Idée*. On the 21st, the *Symphonic Movement No. 3* had its first performance in France. The composer who, as we have seen, was not present at the first performance in Berlin, conducted the Pasdeloup Orchestra. On 2 November, Honegger had a meeting over another film project, this time with the producer Raymond Bernard, for whom he would write the substantial score to his huge trilogy on Victor Hugo's *Les Misérables*. On the 10th, he was on the set at Joinville and would return there frequently.

Meanwhile, on the 12th, the faithful Ernest Ansermet, conducting the Suisse Romande Orchestra, introduced the *Symphonic Movement No. 3* to his regular Geneva audience. On the 18th, Honegger found time, in between two periods of composition, to attend another revival of *Le Roi David*, conducted by Robert Siohan. And on 3 December, he left with Vaura for Zurich and two performances of *Cris du monde* on the 4th and 5th, conducted by Volkmar Andreae. From there they went on to Milan, where they took part in a chamber music concert on the 8th, including the *Cello Sonata*, the *Seven Short Pieces*, the *Suite for two pianos*, the *String Quartet No. 1*, three songs, and *Pâques à New York*.

Unlike Nazi Germany, Italy under Mussolini would never boycott Honegger's music.

On their return to Paris Arthur and Vaura met Morax on the 22nd, just before going to have dinner with Ida Rubinstein. The same evening, Adrian Boult gave the first English performance of *Cris du monde* in a BBC concert. The year ended with the first performance, on 27 December, of Honegger's first work for radio, *Les Douze Coups de minuit*, put out by French Colonial Radio and sponsored by the Groupe Art et Action, directed by Madame Autant-Lara. The text and the plot were by Carlos Larronde, for whom Honegger had written the incidental music *La Danse macabre* in 1919.

1934

The year 1934 established a new record for Honegger of no less than six film scores, though he would beat it in 1937! But that did not prevent him making a start on his *Second String Quartet*. The first two movements, which run into one another, are dated 1934–1935. The third would follow in 1936.

In February, he finished the orchestration of *Sémiramis*, including, for the first time in an orchestral work, a part for ondes Martenot, which would be used so often thereafter. He also worked with his friend Arthur Hoérée on another film, Dimitri Kirsanov's *Rapt*, based on Ramuz's *La Séparation des races*.

On 24 February Ida Rubinstein went to a new production by the group called the Theophilians, consisting of *Le Miracle de Théophile*, from which they took their name, followed by *Le Jeu de Robin et Marion*. Paul Claudel was also in the audience. Nothing was said on that occasion, but Rubinstein, as we know, was passionately interested in neo-medieval mystery plays and the idea of a Joan of Arc began to form in her imagination, even if it did not yet involve Claudel.

On 10 March Robert Siohan revived *Judith* in the concert version, but after that there was nothing until the end of April and the rehearsals for *Sémiramis*, which had its premiere at the Opera on 11 May. The success of this fine score was unfortunately compromised to a considerable extent by the dramatic form that, with Paul Valéry's agreement, Rubinstein adopted for the end of the work. Suddenly, music receded into the background, giving way to fifteen long minutes of spoken monologue. Hermann Scherchen was present and described the occasion in a letter to Werner Reinhart. After giving his opinion that *Sémiramis* was one of Honegger's best works and commenting that it was now the fashion in Paris to deny the composer any kind of talent, he went on:

> What a curious place Paris is, a marvelous city chock full of contradictions and yet so transparent. . . . At the end of *Sémiramis* there was practically a scandal. In a spoken apotheosis lasting a good ten minutes, "la Rubinstein" started to meow interminably and unvaryingly on the same plangent, monotonous note. Needless to say, no curtain call for Honegger!

He encouraged Reinhart to come and see the production even so, but Reinhart's commitments did not allow.[1]

It seems that Honegger himself considered *Sémiramis* to have been a failure, but one for which he did not feel he was in any way responsible. After his death, Vaura was opposed to it being revived, but there is nonetheless a strong case for doing so, even though some solution would have to be found for the impossible final monologue (I have suggested one in my analysis of the work in Chapter 12).

During May, Honegger finally wrote the music for the film *L'Idée* and it was recorded on 1 June. A few days later, the Honeggers left again for Zurich, where a double bill of *Antigone* and *Amphion* was given on 8 and 14 June. Between these two evenings, they stayed with Werner Reinhart at the Fluh. But, crazy about racing cars as Honegger was, he had to be back near Paris on the 16th and 17th for the Le Mans Grand Prix.

Honegger's previous biographers have placed the genesis of *Jeanne d'Arc au bûcher* and Claudel's work on the libretto between May and July 1934. Even if the facts have been described correctly, the dates have certainly not. The real chronology, putting events back by about six months, has been established by Pascal Lecroart in his excellent thesis on the work, and obviously these are the dates to which I shall refer.[2]

On 29 June and 2 July the vocal ensemble La Psallette de Notre-Dame gave two concerts in the Sainte Chapelle, which Honegger attended with Ida Rubinstein. A few days later, she organized a candle-lit supper party at which both the Honeggers were present as well as Jacques Chailley. She took the opportunity to explain her project of a *Joan of Arc* for which her friend Jeanne d'Orliac would write the text and Honegger the music. But soon insuperable differences of opinion materialized between the two over the very conception of the work, to which Jeanne d'Orliac reacted by suggesting that Honegger be dropped. Luckily, Rubinstein had no intention of bypassing her favorite composer and the idea got no further. As a result, the project was held in abeyance for the time being.

On 7 August Vaura joined Arthur at the Château de la Fonthaute at Cazoulès, near Souillac, on the edge of the Dordogne. Here, during that month, he wrote his *Petite Suite*, three charming little pieces for an *ad libitum* chamber ensemble.

On 12 September the Honeggers joined their friend Roland-Manuel at Cahors for a driving tour of Spain. The first part of the trip went well, but on 22 September, on a bad stretch of road between Sigüenza and Soria, of the kind that was common in Spain at the time, Honegger was driving his Bugatti at full speed when a tire suddenly burst. He lost control and the automobile crashed into a tree. Roland-Manuel and Arthur, who were thrown onto the tree and into the nearby field, came out of it reasonably well—Honegger merely broke an ankle. But Vaura was wedged into the front passenger seat, so often the most dangerous place to be. She broke both her knees and suffered multiple fractures. She reached Paris by train the following evening ("in separate pieces," as she would later say) and remained in the hospital for months. She only really began to walk again eleven months later, but would never do so as well as she had before. The effects stayed with her to the end of her life and this was doubtless one of the reasons why she never had any more children.

Back in Paris, Arthur began work on various film scores. In addition to two French films (*Cessez le feu* and *Le Roi de la Camargue*, both by Jacques de Baroncelli), he had a commission from Germany for *The Demon of the Himalayas*. In order to work on this, the only German film music of his career, Honegger had to send the authorities a duly authenticated certificate of his Aryan stock, giving him the opportunity to trace the Ulrichs, on his mother's side, back through four centuries. His cinema activities also included an interesting article written in collaboration with Arthur Hoérée, entitled "Particularités sonores du film *Rapt*," published in *La Revue musicale* in December 1934.

Vaura, however, was recovering only slowly from the terrible accident. Her good friend René Morax wrote Werner Reinhart on 29 December with news of her condition:

> I've been going regularly to see poor Vaura. She's still in bed, being very patient. After expecting to be walking by Christmas, she now hopes to be better by Easter. Through her considerable pain she's been calm and courageous, and Arthur has been well and truly knocked by the accident, which could easily have killed her. Their friends are seeing a lot of them.

We now know that the end of 1934 was really when *Jeanne d'Arc au bûcher* was first conceived. Ida Rubinstein was always on the lookout for librettists and, according to Pascal Lecroart, it was during November that she wrote to Paul Claudel, then the French Ambassador in Brussels, asking him to write something. Her idea was for a work that could make up a whole evening with *Le Festin de la Sagesse*, another of her commissions, for which Milhaud would write the music. Honegger's diary contains two cryptic entries: on 21 November, "Joan of Arc—French" and on the 23rd, "Brussels." Did he go there to see Claudel? At any rate, Claudel's diary has the entry, on 3 December: "To Paris. Ida Rubinstein, Honegger, Joan of Arc, Milhaud."

It seems that this meeting, at the Hôtel Crillon, was the very first between Honegger and Claudel. It was also unproductive, since Rubinstein and the composer were met with a blank refusal. The details have often been recounted. "Joan of Arc," said Claudel, "is an official heroine. She spoke, and as her words are in everyone's memories, they cannot be transcribed too freely. It is difficult to accommodate a historical character inside a fictional framework." And he added: "Does one gild gold, or whiten lilies? Let's hear no more on the subject!"

The next day, 4 December, he was on the train going back to Brussels, looking out idly at the monotonous procession of telegraph poles that, because of the speed he was going, seemed to cross one another before vanishing into the distance. Claudel had a sudden vision:

> Immediately, I had an unmistakable shock, the shock of conception. I saw two hands tied together, raised up and making the sign of the Cross. The work was completed, and I had only to write it down, a matter of a few

days. I felt around me the presence of a desire to which I was not allowed to remain indifferent.

Claudel was usually a slow worker but, under the impact of this veritable *raptus*—a tangible incarnation of the creative Spirit—he finished his text in a few days. On 9 December he wrote Milhaud: "Would you tell Ida Rubinstein that I'll come and see her on the 16th at three o'clock. I'll bring her the complete libretto of *Jeanne d'Arc au bûcher*. . . . I trust you and Honegger can both be there so that I can read my work out to you."

The effect this reading had on Honegger was dramatic. As he said later, "I was struck by an emotion that for a time left me speechless, and which also set me wondering anxiously whether I would be up to the task."[3] No doubt his emotions were at work on another front as well, in that in Paul Claudel he had found that "ideal collaborator" he spoke of in "Pour prendre congé."

At this juncture in the story, Pascal Lecroart inadvertently repeats a mistake of earlier biographers, namely that Honegger had already sketched out his score the previous October. There was, after all, no way Honegger could have begun a work for which not a word of text existed and for which there was as yet no librettist. Lecroart is surely right, however, in saying that Honegger was working on the opening pages of *Jeanne d'Arc au bûcher* on 3 January 1935—it is entirely understandable that he should start this oratorio at the beginning. For this, as for the rest of the work, Claudel gave him such detailed instructions that Honegger would consider him almost as a "co-composer." The entire composition of *Jeanne d'Arc au bûcher* belongs, then, to 1935.

The symbiotic collaboration between Honegger and Claudel was one of the cultural miracles of the first half of the twentieth century. After *Jeanne d'Arc*, the collaboration produced two other successful works—*La Danse des morts* (The Dance of the Dead) and the incidental music to *Le Soulier de satin* (The Satin Slipper)—and was a realization of what Wagner had in mind in 1852 when he wrote in crude terms to Liszt about Berlioz, whom he wanted to see at work on a new opera: "He needs a librettist who will penetrate him through and through, who will bring him to ecstasy, who will be to him what man is to woman."[4]

1935

At the beginning of January 1935 Vaura took her very first steps since the accident, but she was still very far from being totally recovered. Arthur left on the 11th for a few days in Berlin to see *The Demon of the Himalayas*, for which he would write the music. That same month he wrote a short orchestral work, commissioned by Radio Geneva for its tenth anniversary. Called *Radio-Panoramique*, it is a witty satire on radio's pollution of the atmosphere. On 19 January, in one of the Siohan Concerts in the Salle Rameau, the first performance took place of the concert suite taken by Honegger from his film music for *Les Misérables*. And from the 22nd to the 27th, Honegger was in Brussels, where he conducted *Sémiramis* on the 26th.

By the beginning of February Vaura was managing to take a short walk twice a day, but on the 12th her mother, who lived with her, died suddenly.

On the 13th Arthur left again for Berlin. Here he set to work furiously on his score for *The Demon of the Himalayas*, one of his most extended film scores. He wrote the whole thing between the 19th and the 26th—speed is the first requisite for a film composer—and left Berlin on 2 March.

On the 4th *Radio-Panoramique* was first performed at the Geneva Conservatory, conducted by Hermann Scherchen. Honegger was not present. He had just received a letter from Ida Rubinstein thanking him for agreeing to write *Jeanne d'Arc au bûcher*, and telling him that the fee for this commission would be 60,000 francs. It was during March that Honegger got down to serious work on the oratorio.

Vaura meanwhile was still seriously handicapped and was also suffering from loneliness. In an attempt to solve this problem, Arthur made what was for him a considerable sacrifice and agreed that they should try and live together. On 21 March, Vaura moved into 1 square Emmanuel-Chabrier. Even though she was back at rue Dulong five days later (Arthur had to leave on the 29th to conduct a concert of his works in Toulouse), she terminated her lease there as of 15 April. Their cohabitation would last less than a year.

On 7 April Scherchen conducted the *Symphonic Movement No. 3* during the annual meeting of the Association of Swiss Composers in Winterthur. Honegger meanwhile was in Paris writing his music for Pierre Chenal's fine film based on Dostoyevsky's *Crime and Punishment*. His equally fine score was soon finished and the recording took place on 16 April. Honegger then left for Marseilles, where he stayed from the 25th to the 28th for a concert of his works.

On 2 May Serge Lifar wrote to the composer with a highly unusual request:

> I've just finished a ballet in which the rhythm derives from the dance. I work in the studio with a pianist: I invent choreographic movements and the pianist immediately notes down the rhythm. This way we've come up with a rhythmic score, but I'm wondering what instrument my rhythms should be entrusted to. . . . I'm appealing to you as you're the only person at this moment who could help me.

Two weeks later, on the 16th (in the meantime, on the 10th, *Les Douze Coups de minuit* had its first public performance at the Conservatory), Honegger replied to Lifar: "Yes, agreed, you can count on me. . . . You could arrange these rhythms for a small percussion ensemble, so as to give the ear a bit of variety."

This was the beginning of one of Honegger's most unusual works, *Icare*, entirely built on rhythms given to him in advance. It would be his only excursion into solo percussion music.

On 4 June there was the first performance at the Cercle Interallié of a tiny piece written for the *Bal des Petits Lits Blancs*. A week after that, Honegger invited Ida Rubinstein, Paul Claudel, and a small group of friends to come to his apartment to hear the completed portions of *Jeanne d'Arc au bûcher*. This took place on the 11th, after a run-through the previous day, and Claudel mentions it in his diary. Ida Rubinstein, who had been told all about *Icare*, chose this opportunity to remonstrate with Honegger about it. *Jeanne d'Arc* was intended for the Opera, and she considered that her commission automatically constituted an exclusive contract for that house.

Honegger was upset, and on 15 June he wrote to Lifar explaining the position. He had worked on *Icare* for several days with J. E. Szyfer, who would conduct it, and the score was now complete. He ended the letter: "[Ida Rubinstein] says she's hurt to see me abandoning such an important work [as *Jeanne d'Arc au bûcher*] to give myself up to irrelevant fantasies. . . . What am I to do?"

Lifar replied on 25 June: "What's all this Rubinstein business? Tell her to go to hell and take no notice of her grumbling! She can't stop a composer putting his name on his work." But this was not how Honegger saw matters, and on the 27th he replied to Lifar with his usual straightforwardness:

> I can see only one way round the problem (not wanting to upset Rubinstein, you understand, as she's always been good to me), and that's to ask Szyfer to put his name on the work. He knows the situation, he even made a few suggestions, and he's going to conduct, so I think that's the best.

The next day, Lifar grudgingly agreed:

> Your news is an absolute catastrophe. But I see there's not a thing I can do. . . . To my intense disappointment, *Icare* will be danced on "rhythms by Serge Lifar, orchestrated by J. E. Szyfer." Szyfer, understandably, insists on it being a total secret—an open secret, no doubt, because people won't have any trouble guessing Honegger's the real composer. It's sad for both of us and for art in general.

So the fate of *Icare* was sealed. It has been revived regularly at the Opera and the score in the Opera library is listed under the name Szyfer. Two years later, Honegger would once again use Lifar's rhythms as the basis for an altogether more important work, *Le Cantique des cantiques*, and on that occasion he was able to put his own name to it.

He did not even attend the premiere of *Icare* at the Opera on 9 July. Three days earlier he and Vaura had left for Zurich, and from the 11th to the 26th they were in the mountains at Rigi-Klösterli, where Honegger went on with *Jeanne d'Arc*. They then traveled to Perros-Guirec, staying there from 9 August until 28 September, and it was there that Honegger finished *Jeanne d'Arc au bûcher* on 30 August. A few days later, he wrote Claudel with the news, but explaining that the orchestration still had to be done.

The first date in the Honeggers' calendar after their return to the French capital was the Paris premiere of *Radio-Panoramique* at the Opéra-Comique on 19 October, with Albert Wolff conducting the Pasdeloup Orchestra.

On 29 October the first complete performance of *Jeanne d'Arc au bûcher* took place in private at Ida Rubinstein's, with Claudel present. The next day, she wrote to Honegger:

Dear friend and Maître,
    I am still utterly overwhelmed by the splendor of what you let us hear yesterday. Joan too now has her own cathedral, and one that rivals in splendor its stone sister of Chartres. I remain yours, with devotion and infinite gratitude.

A second run-through took place on 5 December, again at Rubinstein's with Claudel present. But the endless prevarications, both by Rubinstein and by the personnel of the Opera, meant that the eagerly awaited premiere was continually postponed. This cast something of a shadow over the initial atmosphere of goodwill.
    Honegger's last score of 1935 was for yet another film, *L'Équipage (Celle que j'aime)* (The Crew, or The Girl I Love), based on the well-known novel by Joseph Kessel. This may be the moment to mention that for the last few years Honegger had been trying his hand in a new field, that of the French popular song—perhaps the first of these was *Le Grand Étang*, dated 1932 in his manuscript catalog. Many of these songs, but not all, were intended for films, as was the custom of the time, and some out of the total of forty or so were sung and recorded by well-known stars like Damia, Marianne Oswald, Lys Gauty, and Agnès Capri. They demonstrate Honegger's versatility and the perfectionism he brought even to the most modest endeavors. We may feel that he could have become another Kurt Weill. Indeed, with his usual frankness, he sent Weill a copy of the song *Fièvre jaune* (Yellow Fever) with the inscription: "You see how far your influence is spreading!"
    On 10 November he dined with Darius Milhaud and on the 12th went to a showing of pictures by his friend Jacques Thévenet. But all the time he was concentrating on one thing only: on 24 December 1935, he completed the orchestral score of *Jeanne d'Arc au bûcher*. But more than two years would pass before its first performance.

1936

The first two months of 1936 were given up to work on two film scores: in January, Pierre Chenal's *Les Mutinés de l'Elseneur*, and in February, Anatole Litvak's *Mayerling*. The Viennese ambience of this second film would be a useful preparation for that of *L'Aiglon*, on which Honegger would begin a collaboration with Jacques Ibert in the summer.
    On 23 February the Pasdeloup Concerts gave a concert version of *Sémiramis*. Then, on 7 March, Honegger moved to the large studio at 71 boulevard de Clichy that he would occupy until his death. It was his fourth and final Paris home. Living with his family had not proved compatible with his need for solitude in which to compose. A month later, on 15 April, Vaura and Pascale moved in nearby, at 11 place de Vintimille.
    The day after he moved, Honegger met Werner Reinhart at the Hôtel Meurice and promised to send him the score of *Jeanne d'Arc au bûcher* as soon as possible. A letter from Reinhart dated 16 March explains the reason: "On my

return here, I immediately spoke to Hans, who is very touched that you thought of him in connection with this translation. In principle he is quite ready to take on this task." It seems there were plans for a German performance in Salzburg, but obviously this depended on the premiere at the Paris Opera that had to take place first and which was, apparently, set to do so on 16 June. But when this was postponed (the first of many such delays, which finally left Honegger exasperated), the Salzburg project fell through.

The first work Honegger wrote in his new apartment, that same March, was a short *Nocturne for orchestra*, a good piece and important too as being his only purely orchestral work between the *Symphonic Movement No. 3* of 1932 and the *Symphony for Strings* of 1941. This was a commission from Hermann Scherchen, who had been based in Brussels since the Nazis took over Germany. There he conducted a large number of concerts of new music in his "Soirées de Bruxelles," and even founded a small publishing house, Ars Viva. Even so, it was Universal of Vienna who published this work, before it was taken over by Boosey and Hawkes of London as their only Honegger piece. This is undoubtedly one of the reasons why the *Nocturne*, whose central section is taken from *Sémiramis*, is not better known. Honegger was not present at the first performance, given by Scherchen in Brussels on 30 April.

On 15 and 16 May, after two weeks in the south of France, the two Honeggers were in Brussels for a concert of Swiss music, while on the 23rd *Les Aventures du roi Pausole* was revived at Évreux. In June, Honegger finished the Finale of the *String Quartet No. 2*, completing this work begun in 1934. It is dedicated to the famous Pro Arte Quartet, which was quick to give the first performance.

In June he also finished *La Marche sur la Bastille* (March on the Bastille), a contribution to Romain Rolland's collective production *14 Juillet*, with other offerings from Jacques Ibert, Georges Auric, Darius Milhaud, Albert Roussel, Charles Koechlin, and Daniel Lazarus. This was the first of several large-scale cultural manifestations provoked by the arrival in power of the Popular Front. This was the first truly socialist government in France's history and, during the temporary euphoria that resulted, a number of artists heeded the call of its cultural spokesmen. It is fully understandable that a generous-minded humanist like Honegger, with his desire to communicate to the largest possible audience, should also have responded. He was far from espousing any narrow clique, but his heart was certainly "on the left," whereas Vaura was decidedly more conservative. Honegger's social activity manifested itself in his participation in other collaborative efforts, and in his offering a few small works to the Éditions du Chant du Monde, an overtly communist enterprise, but it found its most striking symbol, in 1937, in *Jeunesse*, a piece written to words by Paul Vaillant-Couturier. This is one of the best crowd songs of those years, written for the Youth Federation and still regarded as the very incarnation of the Popular Front. But this is a far cry from making Honegger a militant Marxist, even momentarily.

On 3 June he attended the inaugural concert of the group Jeune France, consisting of Yves Baudrier, Daniel-Lesur, André Jolivet, and Olivier Messiaen. This group was in some sense taking the succession of Les Six half a generation later. Its spirit was rather on the lines of Honegger's own, as we can judge from its slogan, "Sincerity, Generosity, Conscientiousness," which was a reaction against Les Six's more frivolous side. Later, in his newspaper articles, Honegger would support these young composers passionately, especially Messiaen, in whom he recognized the genius of his generation.

Shortly afterward, Honegger received a letter from Paul Sacher, dated 11 June, asking him to write something for the tenth anniversary celebrations of his orchestra, either an overture (possibly a French overture) for strings, or a piece for string quartet and string orchestra, or a work for strings with no more than four wind instruments. The other works in the program were a piano concerto by Conrad Beck (a Swiss member of the École de Paris who had studied composition with Honegger before going back to Switzerland), a song cycle by Willy Burkhard (another friend of Honegger's: this cycle was the masterly *Das ewige Brausen*, on poems by Knut Hamsun), and a work by Paul Hindemith, the details of which are still unknown. But Honegger was weighed down with work and it would be five years before Sacher's idea came to fruition in the shape of the superb *Symphony for Strings*.

Even so, Sacher returned to the attack on 1 July. Since Hindemith had turned down the commission, he asked Béla Bartók, and the result was the *Music for Strings, Percussion, and Celesta*. But Sacher had not given up getting a string piece from Honegger, and told him at the same time that he wanted to put on *Jeanne d'Arc au bûcher* on 4 and 5 March 1937. Honegger had liked the performance of actor Harry Baur in the film *Les Misérables*, and when he suggested Baur play Brother Dominic in *Jeanne d'Arc*, Sacher asked whether Baur's fee was within "human" limits or whether he was used to being paid in dollars!

On Bastille Day, 14 July, Arthur and Vaura attended the premiere of *14 Juillet* at the Alhambra Theater under the aegis of the Maison de la Culture. The conductor was Roger Désormière, who was deeply engaged in the politics of the Popular Front. Honegger's contribution, *La Marche sur la Bastille*, was used as the overture to the third act.

On 17 July came a complete change of scene, with the Honeggers' departure for Bayreuth. This would be their second and last visit to the festival and they stayed until the 31st. One can imagine the atmosphere, in the same summer as those sinister Olympic Games in Berlin, captured for posterity by Leni Riefenstahl's film. Fortunately, there was always the music, and from that point of view the 1936 Bayreuth was certainly an excellent vintage. Honegger was in touch with Jacques Ibert over their collaboration on *L'Aiglon*, based on the well-known play by Edmond Rostand. For this commission by Raoul Gunsbourg for the Monte Carlo Opera, Ibert would write the first and fifth acts and Honegger the other three. Honegger had in fact already completed the fourth act, the Wagram scene, which he reckoned would last eighteen minutes.

In a letter dated 1 August, Ibert invited him to stay at his summer residence in Houlgate:

It's a large house and we'd be very happy for you to come and stay. We could then have a chat about this tough old *Aiglon*—I'm shamed by your energy in having already started sorting it out! I haven't yet plucked up the courage to go and see our master Raoul. . . . I'm afraid he may ask me "whether I've come racing to the end" of my part in the proceedings!

But the Honeggers preferred to spend the summer at Perros-Guirec, where Arthur worked on *L'Aiglon* until 10 September. We learn from a letter from the composer to Ibert that the second act was nearly done by 14 August. Jacques and Rosette Ibert were friends of Francis and Toné Winter, and the close relations between the Iberts and the Honeggers were made closer still by the two composers' collaborations, first on *L'Aiglon* and then on *Les Petites Cardinal*.

Honegger also had a letter, dated 31 July, from the great American patron Elizabeth Sprague Coolidge. She was particularly interested in supporting chamber music and now asked Honegger to write a new string quartet. The composer was quick to accept the commission and promised her that he would meet the August 1937 deadline. In fact, he would finish this *Third String Quartet* by 5 June. It would, unfortunately, be his last.

Meanwhile, Honegger's correspondence with Sacher took a new lease on life. Sacher wrote, in letters dated 22 and 23 August, that he had received a positive reply from Ida Rubinstein about *Jeanne d'Arc au bûcher*—although she had stipulated that the Basel performance could not precede the world premiere at the Paris Opera—but that he was not certain whether the concert version planned for 4 and 5 March could go ahead. As a result, he was more insistent than ever that he wanted the work for string orchestra.

Honegger did not attend the first performance of his *String Quartet No. 2*, given during September by the Pro Arte Quartet at the Venice Biennale, as he had begun work on the Finale of the *String Quartet No. 3*. On the 19th, he wrote Sacher that he had nothing to say on the subject of Rubinstein and *Jeanne d'Arc*, and that he had too much work on hand to be able to write the string orchestra work by the suggested deadline. He went on: "As proof of my goodwill, I can send you a first movement that you can use as an opening item for the concert (a slow movement lasting about two and a half minutes)."

This piece has survived in manuscript and is, despite its brevity, well worth playing and publishing. There are no musical links, though, with the future *Symphony for Strings*. In letters of 28 September and 8 October, respectively, Sacher told him that he wanted to see it when he next came to Paris, and later asked him to extend it to at least five or seven minutes before Christmas. He was particularly keen on Honegger doing this because he intended to give two concerts with his orchestra in the spring in Paris. The composer's reply was not very promising. *Jeanne d'Arc au bûcher* would not be given at the Opera until May 1937 and this meant that the concerts planned for Basel in March could not now take place. As for the string piece, Honegger could not extend it as he had too much urgent work on hand (films, obviously). Sacher gave in and confirmed that he had abandoned plans for *Jeanne d'Arc*, but he was still hoping that Honegger would finish at least the first movement of the string piece, to bring it up to six or seven minutes' worth.[5]

Among the projects he was working on was another socialist production, *La Construction d'une cité*, on which he would collaborate with Milhaud. The two of them met to discuss it on 4 November, but it did not materialize until a year later.

Werner Reinhart's letter of 7 November is the last of his to Honegger that we possess, but their friendship remained as warm as ever until Reinhart's death.

During the latter part of the year, Honegger again had a heavy workload. First, there were two new film scores, *Nitchevo (L'Agonie du sous-marin)* (Nitchevo, or The Agony of the Submarine) by Jacques de Baroncelli (a score that included two of his best popular songs, "De l'Atlantique au Pacifique" and the sung tango "Triste est mon coeur"), and G. W. Pabst's *Mademoiselle Docteur*, better known as *Salonique, nid d'espions* (Salonica, Nest of Spies). Then Honegger kept up his work on *L'Aiglon*, orchestrating the second act and composing the third. He also wrote a new ballet for Serge Lifar, *Le Cantique des cantiques*, and finally a large score for the open-air celebrations of the Grand Universal Exhibition in Paris during the summer of 1937. He finished the work, called *Les Mille et Une Nuits*, on 3 January 1937. The text and plot were by Dr. Jean-Claude Mardrus, well-known as a translator of Eastern fairy tales, but this attempt at *son et lumière* would be sadly undermined by the rudimentary quality of the sound reproduction at that period.

On 5 December Honegger's music was heard twice. Robert Siohan revived *Chant de joie*, and Jane Évrard's Ladies' Orchestra, to whom Roussel had dedicated his *Sinfonietta*, gave a concert at the Salle Gaveau including the *Six Poems of Jean Cocteau* in the version for strings by Arthur Hoérée, with Hugues Cuénod as soloist, and the first performance of the string orchestra transcription of the *Prelude, Arioso, and Fughetta*.

On 7 December the Honeggers dined with the celebrated author and politician Antoine de Saint-Exupéry. He kept them late and then, in a shocked tone, announced that he had just heard that his aviator friend Jean Mermoz was missing and had to be considered lost. Honegger would one day write one of his best scores to a film about Mermoz's life. This may be the moment to quote part of an undated letter (probably from around 1932) from Saint-Exupéry to Honegger, after the showing of the 1931 film about *Pacific 2.3.1* by the Russian filmmaker Tsekhanuski:

Dear Sir,
    I simply must tell you how excited I was by *Pacific*. That kind of ascension toward the calm finale made me realize, in a way I never had before, the power music can bring to the movement of a film. You may imagine how stirred I was, since I was nursing a slight hope that you would join us if our aviation film came to anything, and I was already eagerly looking forward to this.

This project never materialized, but Honegger did celebrate aviation in several of his scores—in 1937, the ballet *Un Oiseau blanc s'est envolé* (A White

Bird Has Flown Away)—and nowhere more successfully than in his score for *Mermoz*. In 1949, he would also compose a score for radio, *Marche contre la Mort*, to a text by Saint-Exupéry in memory of another great aviator, Henri Guillaumet.

1937

Honegger's creative activity reached a frenetic high point in 1937. For the cinema alone, he produced nine scores, a record he would never surpass. He did not neglect other areas of composition either. In January, he completed *Les Mille et Une Nuits* on the 3rd and *Le Cantique des cantiques* on the 19th. This latter work, we may recall, was a ballet based on rhythms by Serge Lifar, according to the method they had already used for *Icare*. But this score was a much longer one, lasting between forty and forty-five minutes, for soloists, chorus, and orchestra including ondes Martenot, and he did not finish orchestrating it until the autumn. He also completed his contribution to *L'Aiglon*. He finished orchestrating Act III on 27 January, as well as writing what remained to be done of Act IV (the main part, "Wagram," had been composed the previous year).

After attending a performance of *Le Roi David* in Rennes on 4 February, Honegger was back in Paris for the recording of *Mademoiselle Docteur* on the 10th. He finished the overture (for the credit titles) on the 16th. On the 19th, he wrote to Dunoyer de Segonzac to ask him to do the decor and costumes for *Le Cantique des cantiques*. On 1 March, he was at the Joinville studios to work on adding the soundtrack to another film, *Marthe Richard au service de la France*, by Raymond Bernard. For the church organ sequence, Honegger even resurrected a little piece he had written in Le Havre when he was sixteen.

He missed the first French performance on 8 March of his *String Quartet No. 2* by the Calvet Quartet, at a Triton concert at the École normale de musique, because he had left the day before for Monte Carlo where *L'Aiglon* was having its final rehearsals. The first performance on the 11th was a resounding success, and this Honegger/Ibert score, written deliberately in the popular style of traditional grand opera, went on to have a long and brilliant run in French-speaking opera houses.

Honegger then stayed at the Villa Medici in Rome with Ibert, who was the director at the time, from 18 March to the end of the month. On his return to Paris, he received a long letter from his collaborator, dated 18 April, about the Paris premiere, already planned for September at the Opera with Fanny Heldy in the title role. A few small changes had been made to the score after the Monte Carlo premiere, and Ibert made the following suggestions:

> You're right about putting back Rostand's scene at the very end of Act III (after cutting that frightful duet). Do you think we should do the same for the duet in Act I? Could I help you write something to fill out Act III? Tell me honestly. I could—if you give me precise instructions—write two to four minutes of music.

He also thanked Honegger for agreeing to work with him on a new project, an operetta written by the librettist of *Les Aventures du roi Pausole*, Albert Willemetz, based on the story of *Les Petites Cardinal*, an 1880s-style novel by Ludovic Halévy.

On 21 April Paul Sacher, who had been out of contact with Honegger for some months, wrote again to ask whether *Jeanne d'Arc au bûcher* would finally be free for the 1937–1938 season. He hesitated to announce it, if he only had to cancel it again, as in the previous season. Honegger did not reply until 3 May, to say that Ida Rubinstein had definitely postponed *Jeanne d'Arc* until November 1937, so Sacher would be free to perform it at the beginning of 1938. And he insisted that the long delay in replying was not his fault.

Meanwhile, *Cris du monde* was revived at the Salle Gaveau on 23 April. On 2 May the first performance took place at the Théâtre des Champs-Élysées of *Liberté*, a collective work by the socialist group Mai 1936 for the opening of the 1937 Exhibition. Honegger's contribution was *Prélude à la Mort de Jaurès* on a text by the poet Maurice Rostand. The other composers who took part were Milhaud, Roland-Manuel, Tailleferre, Ibert, Marcel Delannoy, the 22-year-old Marcel Landowski, Manuel Rosenthal, Arthur Hoérée, Daniel Lazarus, Robert Siohan, and Maurice Jaubert.[6]

During May, Honegger composed the central slow movement of his *String Quartet No. 3* and finished the first movement on 5 June. The Finale had already been completed in September 1936. When Elizabeth Sprague Coolidge wrote him on 11 June asking about the quartet, he was able to reply on the 20th by sending her the finished work.

Among the many works written for the Universal Exhibition in 1937 was a ballet by Honegger, *Un Oiseau blanc s'est envolé*, on a scenario by Sacha Guitry, taking aviation as its theme. Written for an HEC gala, it was completed on 20 May and performed on the 24th under the composer's direction as part of the Exhibition of Arts and Techniques at the Théâtre des Champs-Élysées. Honegger would reuse the complete score in *Mermoz*. On 7 May, also as part of the Exhibition, the Pro Arte Quartet had given another performance of Honegger's *String Quartet No. 2*, probably the first chance he had to hear it.

On 9 July, opposite the Champ-de-Mars and the Palais de Chaillot, and as part of the Festival of Light and Water organized on the Seine, a large and ineffective bank of loudspeakers relayed *Les Mille et Une Nuits*, which had been pre-recorded under the direction of Gustave Cloëz. This was also the occasion for the first performance of Messiaen's *Fête des belles eaux* for six ondes Martenot. The repeat performance on 13 August was no more satisfactory, and Honegger's piece was not heard properly until the concert performance at the end of the year.

On 10 July Honegger went to Marseilles for a first meeting with Marcel Pagnol over their forthcoming collaboration on the film *Regain*. On the set, down in the heart of Provence, Honegger dressed casually as usual and, when he gave the technicians a hand with their equipment, they took him for a manual worker and called him "tu" (rather than the more formal "vous") and "Arthur." Great was their surprise when they found out who he was.

On his return to Paris, he spent from 24 to 29 July writing the music for another film, Marcel L'Herbier's *La Citadelle du silence*, in collaboration with Milhaud. On 1 September, he told Milhaud that the recording was finished but that some of the mixing had to be done again. He also said that he was extremely busy, having to write the music for *Regain* and *Miarka* and orchestrate his ballet *Le Cantique des cantiques*.

The Paris premiere of *L'Aiglon* at the Opera took place that same evening, conducted by François Ruhlmann. Again, it was a great popular success, although some of the critics grumbled. On the 4th, Honegger left again for Marseilles to work on *Regain*. The score turned out to be one of his best, so much so that he extracted a concert suite from it. Back in Paris on the 24th, Honegger found a letter from Paul Sacher, dated the 21st, and asking urgently for a vocal score of *Jeanne d'Arc au bûcher*. On the 27th and 28th, he recorded the music for *Regain* in the Joinville studios.

On 6 October Louis de Vocht performed *Le Roi David*, and the day before, Milhaud sent Honegger a postcard about *La Construction d'une cité*. Having written "Chanson du Capitaine," he asked Honegger to write "L'Émigrant." In fact, Honegger would also write the "Chanson des quatre," and those two pages are all we possess of his work on this project—it is impossible to say whether he contributed more than this or not. The producer was the communist writer and poet Jean-Richard Bloch; Jean Wiéner also took part, Roger Désormière conducted, and the splendid sets were by Fernand Léger.

During October, Honegger worked at yet another film score, for *Visages de la France*, a short communist film by Paul Nizan, A. Vigneau, and André Wurmser, which was a present to the Soviet Union for the twentieth anniversary of the October Revolution. In the final sequence, Honegger superimposed in counterpoint the *Marseillaise* and the *Internationale*! He remembered his Zurich roots, too, in a cabaret song he wrote on 5 October in *schwyzerdütsch* (Swiss-German dialect), called *Tuet's Weh?* (Did That Hurt?)—the innocent question of a barber to a customer whom he has cut while shaving him. This was for his brother-in-law Emil Hegetschweiler, who ran a cabaret-cinema-theater in Zurich.

But he was also engaged on *Les Petites Cardinal*, and Jacques Ibert brought the project back to his attention in a letter sent from Rome on 10 October. He was sending what he had already written to Albert Willemetz via the diplomatic bag, and gave Honegger an inventory of his progress:

> I got down to work as soon as I arrived the day before yesterday. I'm finishing the tenor aria *C'est la faute à Florence* (a *vomitando* number to make the specialists in this field turn green with jealousy!). After that I've got the young people's quartet and the officers' ensemble to do. I'll also do, as we agreed, the beginning of the Act I finale and of the little revue-finale of Act II. To be fair, I'll even do a bit more . . . as you've got eight numbers to write against my seven! As for the final finale, Willemetz has not yet told me what he intends. I'll wait to hear from you. . . . I'll send you the rest of the numbers as and when they're done.

There follow details and questions about the casting. As their letters crossed, Ibert wrote again two days later in particularly affectionate terms, and his letter shows that, while he enjoyed himself writing this work, he never lost sight of the need for high standards:

> I enclose the tenor aria. . . . As you'll see—and as our good friend Ruhlmann says—it's "distwinguished" music. . . . This is the very best sort of awful music (at least, I hope so). There's even a high B-flat that makes me shudder in anticipation!! Too bad about that brat Yvette: you're absolutely right, it's important that, despite all our concessions, there should be some music in it from time to time. . . . I see you've begun and got on with the Act I finale. In that case, don't you think it'd be better if, instead, I did the little finale? I could also do part of the last one.

On the 16th he sent another colorful little missive:

> My dear Arthur, here's the seventh number (the young people's quartet). As I wasn't sure how high our "ex-virgins" would want to go, I've been extremely cautious about the tessituras of their parts. (What style, my lord . . . for a director, as our friend Will. would put it.) But I've found it darned awkward. I expect you've already received the sixteenth number (parade of the officers). I'm going to get cracking on the little finale. Would you be good enough to write and send me the "captive balloon" . . . and, if you would, the motif for the "marquis . . . who" . . . that you must have included in the first-act finale, and the chorus "Viens Vénus"?

Meanwhile, the first performance of *La Construction d'une cité* took place at the Vélodrome d'Hiver on 18 October. On the 21st Paul Sacher wrote Honegger that in the concert he was conducting at the Triton on 8 November he was including the *Prelude, Arioso, and Fughetta*, "an ideal transition between the *Third Brandenburg* that opens the program and the works by Conrad Beck and Bartók." But he was sorry that Honegger was represented by such a short piece.

The next day, 22 October, the Pro Arte Quartet gave the first performance of the *String Quartet No. 3* in the Salle de la Réformation in Geneva. Honegger could not attend as he was busy in Paris. On the 31st Ibert wrote again, sending the little Finale of *Les Petites Cardinal* and saying that he would be in Paris by 6 November.

On 1 November Honegger wrote a short choral piece called *Armistice* on words by René Kerdyk. Then, after a brief trip to Strasbourg, on the 8th he oversaw the recording of the music for Jean Choux's film *Miarka*, on a story by Jean Richepin, and on the 16th that for *Visages de la France*. Dividing his time in November and December between Paris and Rennes, he worked on his contribution to *Les Petites Cardinal*. Numbers 1, 3, and 10 were finished in November, and Nos. 13 and 14 in December. And during this period he also worked on two other films, René Jayet's *Passeurs d'hommes* (with Arthur Hoérée) and Jean Epstein's documentary *Les Bâtisseurs*, based on the story by Robert Desnos. For the second of these, Honegger merely wrote a couple of songs, leaving the rest to Hoérée.

Through Paul Sacher, Honegger had been put in touch with the German-speaking Swiss poet Caesar von Arx. He had the idea of putting on a large-scale *Passion Game* at Selzach, near Solothurn. The production would be in two halves, lasting an entire day, and Honegger was asked to write the music for it. He was obviously taken with the idea, which was very much the sort of thing he was attracted to, and he wrote to von Arx on 27 November agreeing to take it on. This was the beginning of what Honegger called a "very large job," but one that unfortunately would never be completed.

On the 29th Paul Sacher wrote Honegger that he was worried at having still had no confirmation from Ida Rubinstein that she would take part in *Jeanne d'Arc au bûcher*, which he was planning for Basel on 12 May 1938 (although we now know that this date would be adhered to). On 6 December, Honegger reassured him. She had agreed to do it, even though the premiere at the Paris Opera had been postponed again, from 1 to 15 February.

On 4 December, at the Poulet Concerts, Robert Siohan conducted the first concert performance of *Les Mille et Une Nuits*, and the public could at last form an opinion as to the score's real merits. On the 21st, in the Salle Gaveau, Jacques Chailley conducted the first performance of the *Orchestral Suite* from the film *Regain*, in a concert organized by the French Circle of Foreign Students.

At the end of this hectic year, Arthur and Vaura enjoyed Christmas and New Year at Le Grand Mesnil, near Pontoise, which belonged to their friends Francis and Toné Winter. Here, on 26 December, Honegger completed the Finale of *Les Petites Cardinal*.

1938

January 1938 was a quiet month, starting with a *Le Roi David* performance on the 18th with Croiza and the Conservatory Concert Society, and *Cris du monde* the next day in Geneva. But two first performances of differing kinds were scheduled for February. On the 2nd, the premiere of *Le Cantique des cantiques* took place at the Opera, in a sumptuous production by Serge Lifar, with Carina Ari in the main role. This performance, conducted by Philippe Gaubert, at last marked Honegger's official arrival at the Paris Opera, since Ida Rubinstein had, until now, rented the theater for her own productions, and *Icare* was, as we have seen, given under Szyfer's name. Despite the handicap of Lifar's preordained rhythms, the work is of a luxuriant sonority rare in Honegger's output and has always been underestimated. It was regularly revived all through the year. On the 13th, a brilliant company of actors rather than singers, including Saturnin Fabre and Marguerite Pierry, gave *Les Petites Cardinal* at the Bouffes-Parisiens. But the popular triumph of *Les Aventures du roi Pausole* was not repeated, and the production had to be written off as a partial failure.

On 14 February Paul Sacher, hopeful as ever, asked Honegger for the exact date of the *Jeanne d'Arc au bûcher* premiere at the Opera so that he could come to it. It should have been no surprise to find that Ida, in her capricious way, had postponed it once again.

On the 27th, Ibert wrote his operetta collaborator a long letter about the way some critics had panned *Les Petites Cardinal*:

> I've read the article by our friend Vuillermoz. . . . He's fixed us all right! I was expecting him to be cross, but his grumpiness in this case is too over-done to be entirely sincere. I'm sending you a second article, which appeared in *Candide*. I'm amused by its scandalized tone. For him to accuse us of not knowing how to harmonize, of being unable to write a scrap of melody, of being ignorant of orchestration, of having no sense of rhythm, and so on . . . that's strange. But for him to start giving us lessons in coun-terpoint . . . , I'm flabbergasted! Obviously he wanted to get it across to W. that he should have asked Reynaldo [Hahn], or Yvain, or Beydts to write the music for his play. And Vuillermoz's pretended indignation is prompted by his desire to serve the interests of his three friends. It's sad . . . and without importance.

He goes on to say that the box-office receipts are not too bad, and ends:

> Let's hope it lasts and, as you say, it'll be the best reply to the tendentious statements of those crabby individuals who will never accept that Corneille wrote *Le Menteur* as well as tragedies, and Racine also wrote *Les Plaideurs*. Reynaldo has written plenty of operas!

After a short visit to Basel, and then to Zug to see the family, on 28 Febru-ary the Honeggers stopped over at Beatenberg, on the terraced slopes over-looking Lake Thun, in central Switzerland.

Honegger was back in Paris on 10 March, where a letter from Paul Sacher, written on the 14th, reached him to ask about the difficult choice of soloists for *Jeanne d'Arc*, and especially about the tenor. He also asked about various problems over the pronunciation of the Latin, and wondered whether Claudel would agree to give an introductory talk. Four days later, on the 18th, Sacher wrote again, in desperation. He had had a letter from the publishers Sénart telling him that Ida Rubinstein was absolutely against having Claudel's libretto printed in the program, and that she would allow it only after the premiere on the stage of the Paris Opera. Sacher felt it was impossible to present the work without a libretto, especially in a concert version, and begged Honegger to act as a go-between. Honegger replied on the 26th that Rubinstein was, unfortu-nately, being obstinate. He suggested they should bypass the problem by putting into the program a detailed analysis of the work, scene by scene. As for Claudel, he had agreed to give the introductory talk.

On 28 March Honegger went for a short visit to Switzerland. *Amphion* was given in Bern, and the next day the Lausanne society, La clarinette, devoted an evening to his chamber music, with the participation of the Hungarian Quartet.

Back in Paris on the 31st, Honegger soon had another SOS from Sacher, dated 4 April. Was there really no way they could print Claudel's text in the program? Honegger sent a negative reply on the 14th, now suggesting to Sacher that he might ask permission at least to print a German translation, which Hans Reinhart would be very happy to supply. But in his letter of the 22nd, Sacher threw in the towel. He resigned himself to a scene-by-scene analysis and invited Honegger to the first rehearsal with the complete complement of soloists and orchestra, which was fixed for 9 May. It is strange that no one thought of the solution of getting Claudel to read his libretto in the course of his talk.

Before going off to Basel, Honegger was able to attend the first Paris performance of his *String Quartet No. 3* by the Pro Arte Quartet in a Triton concert on the 25th, and just as he was leaving he had an encouraging letter from Romain Rolland, dated 7 May: "Claudel is a marvelous symphonist, with breadth and variety. Your music becomes one with his words, with his humor, with his wings."

The date 12 May 1938 assumed a quadruple importance and marked the true establishment of Arthur and Vaura's friendship with Paul and Maja Sacher.

For that first performance of *Jeanne d'Arc au bûcher*, Paul Sacher conducted the Basel Chamber Choir and Orchestra, both reinforced for the occasion, together with Ida Rubinstein, Jean Périer as Brother Dominic, and a brilliant line-up of soloists, including Maurice Martenot on the ondes that he had invented. It was a huge success, and Claudel noted in his diary, "An audience of a thousand, endless ovations." Vaura, though, was burned by all the comings and goings, and the advance notice for that date in her diary reads: "Yes, until proved otherwise."

For Honegger, it was the most important event in his career since the first performance of *Le Roi David* seventeen years before. For the first time since 1921, he recovered that unanimity and contact with the general public that he had been missing so cruelly for years, at least in regard to a work he felt to be essential to his output, one that sprang from the depths of his being. It is true that he had again become a popular composer in the years since 1935, but only on the basis of his film music, his "social" music, and the works he had written as a young man. But now his journey through the desert was over, and the way of triumph opened up before him. It would never close again in his lifetime, but would lead from peak to peak, with *La Danse des morts* and the last four symphonies.

The day was no less important for Paul Sacher. His great patience had been rewarded, and he had at last been able to conduct the world premiere of one of his friend's works with his own choir and orchestra. And what a work! With many more to come.

The occasion also brought results in the matter of Sacher's future collaboration with Honegger. From it sprang Claudel's idea for *La Danse des morts*, and also the definite commissioning of the *Symphony for Strings*. Finally, that was the date of what Vaura, with an almost religious fervor, called their "first station at the Schönenberg." From now on, she and her husband and daughter would be regular guests at the Sachers' magnificent mansion, and the magic date of 12 May, together with Paul and Maja's birthdays, would be noted in all their future diaries.

With *Jeanne d'Arc au bûcher*, Honegger reached a high point that he would equal but never surpass. Today, it is, even more than *Le Roi David* and *Pacific*

2.3.1, his most universally popular work, and with justice. But Claudel played a large part in its success, and the composer was the first to recognize this.

Claudel had been greatly impressed by what he had seen in the museums and churches in Basel and had immediately had a vision of a new work that he wanted to write with Honegger, which would be to *Jeanne d'Arc* what a crypt is to a cathedral. After Honegger's return to Paris, he was therefore able to mention it to Sacher in a letter of 28 May (it was written from London, where Honegger had gone to discuss the music he had been asked to compose for Anthony Asquith's film based on George Bernard Shaw's *Pygmalion*):

> This is just a note to say that after our stay in Basel I've seen Claudel again and we've discussed the idea of a *Danse macabre*. He was so taken by the idea that a few days later he asked me to come and see him. He read me a scenario that would, I think, be remarkably suitable for an oratorio and which he is offering me. This dance of the dead is divided into three parts and is based on three ideas:
>
> > Man remember that thou art dust
> > Man remember that thou art spirit
> > Man remember that thou art rock and that upon this rock I build my church.
>
> The text contains long extracts from Ezekiel and Job, and the whole thing has an extraordinary grandeur about it.
>
> Of course, this adaptation goes considerably further than what I had originally envisaged. It would in fact be impossible to set this text with just a string orchestra. The length, too, would have to be increased, to forty-five minutes or an hour. There would be only two soloists and a narrator. I'd keep the orchestra as small as possible—double woodwinds, two trumpets, two trombones, two horns. The choir will have some highly novel and striking effects, but I'll keep the writing as simple as I can.

Honegger later described the meeting with Claudel to his publisher, Salabert:

> Opening his manuscript, Claudel said to me: "It begins with a huge clap of thunder, not a simple clap of theatrical thunder, but a musical thunder, prolonged, with the sound rolling around, coming and going, doubling back on itself, like the thunder you hear during the great spring storms." Then he read me the text. Long adaptations from the Bible, the vision of Ezekiel, fragments of Job, popular songs slightly altered, shouts, sobs, phrases in Latin, and everything organized, fitted together, and as it were surrounded by music.

Sacher replied enthusiastically on 8 June. He was delighted that *La Danse des morts* was taking shape and wanted to know whether the title referred to Basel or Holbein. He told Honegger that he could use a larger orchestra and suggested a line-up that the composer would follow almost exactly. He asked if the work would be finished by the end of the year, so that it could be programmed for the spring of 1939. He also told Honegger that Ida Rubinstein was proposing a tour of *Jeanne d'Arc au bûcher* through the whole of France, with Sacher's choir, if it was available. She was now talking about the premiere at the Paris Opera as definitely taking place in November, but Sacher no longer believed her. Who could blame him? Rubinstein would never play the part of Joan at the Opera, and the work was not given there until December 1950.

During June, Honegger was working on *Pygmalion*, his only English film venture, and he went to London to record it on the 23rd. But his sketchbook for this period also contains the first ideas for the grandiose *Selzach Passion*, which one might have been surprised to find dating from such an early period, were it not for the letter of 27 November 1937 from which I have already quoted.

From 13 July the Honeggers stayed with their friends the Iberts at Houl-gate and it was there that Arthur began serious work on *La Danse des morts*, first of all sketching out the overall plan and then filling in the detail. On 3 August, he was able to write Paul Sacher that of the seven sections he envisaged of the Totentanz (sic; this is the German title) the first two were already finished and the following three sketched out.

At the same period (in a letter simply dated August, Houlgate) he kept Claudel informed of his progress: he had got as far as the "Lamento" (No. 3), but the orchestration remained to be done. In setting the words of the "Danse" itself (No. 2), he had added to *La Carmagnole* and *Sur le Pont d'Avignon* a frag-ment of *Nous n'irons plus au bois* because of "the insinuating and persuasive qual-ity of 'Entrez dans la danse, voyez comme on danse,' etc." And he goes on:

> Right at the end, under a tumult of voices, part of the orchestra under-mines the 6/8 rhythm, which has been continuous so far, with a heavy waltz rhythm that finally wins out. . . . Everything after that is sketched but not yet worked out in full.

From Paris the Honeggers left once more for Montquin in the Morvan, to stay with their friend Jacques Thévenet, and there, on the 21st, Arthur finished the third part of *La Danse des morts*, the wonderful "Lamento." From Montquin he wrote Claudel again, describing the effect and the details of the opening roll of thunder, and going on: "In the 'Dialogue' (No. 1) the chorus goes from an almost spoken, simple unison to a more polyphonic texture before the orches-tra comes in."

Back in Paris, he finished the fourth section on 1 September, before leav-ing for Italy. He was in Rome on 9 September, conducting his *Nocturne* at the Venice Biennale, and then returned via Turin to Paris on the 14th. He spent several weeks with Vaura and Pascale at Mougins and finished the fifth section of *La Danse des morts* there on 22 September. On the 24th, Claudel wrote him:

> I've had an idea for the *Danse macabre* [sic]. We could use the rattle that replaces the bell at Mass on Good Friday. There are two sorts of rattle: one rather like the clapper that street vendors used to use, the other a funnel that turns round a wooden spindle with a grinding noise. It seems to me we could use both. At the Mikado's funeral, the coffin was carried in a char-

iot drawn by six black bulls and as the wheels turned they produced the nine noises stipulated by ritual.

This letter, among others, testifies to the extraordinary acuity of Claudel's ear. He was indeed a kind of great composer *manqué* and Honegger was able to bring his sound visions to life.

Honegger wrote only two film scores this year and the second of them, for which he was commissioned in October, was for the Swiss producer Max Haufler's *L'Or dans la montagne (Faux Monnayeurs)* (Gold in the Mountain, or Counterfeiters). This was based on C. F. Ramuz's novel *Farinet ou la fausse monnaie* (Farinet or the counterfeit money) and, as in his previous Ramuz project, *Rapt*, Honegger was helped by Arthur Hoérée.

After staying with Fernand Ochsé at Montfort-l'Amaury from 13 to 19 October, he completed *La Danse des morts*, apart from the orchestration, on the 25th. Almost immediately he was offered a new oratorio project, *Nicolas de Flue*, on the Swiss national saint who brought the divided Confederates together after their victories over Charles the Bold (the Duke of Burgundy from 1467 to 1477 who sought to free his duchy from dependence on France and restore it as a kingdom; the Swiss cantons allied with France and the Holy Roman Emperor against Charles the Bold). The oratorio was intended for performance by a group from Neuchâtel at the Zurich National Exhibition in the summer of 1939, and Denis de Rougemont was already at work on the libretto.

It is undoubtedly the most specifically Swiss of Honegger's major works, being German-Swiss in subject and French-Swiss in its text and in the performers for whom it was written. It is also the closest in spirit to the deliberately populist Festspiel—something that was bound to appeal to the composer. On 1 November, Denis de Rougemont wrote him that he had written part of the second act.

On 9 November Paul Sacher with his usual unquenchable optimism wrote Honegger to ask whether *Jeanne d'Arc au bûcher* was still scheduled to appear at the Opera on the 29th, as he would like to come. He also took the opportunity to remind him that he owed two years' subscriptions, for 1937 and 1938, to the Swiss Composers' Association, 22 francs in all. "Our president, Vogler," he wrote, "is very meticulous and quick to cross off any members who haven't paid."

On 10 November *L'Aiglon* was produced at the Théâtre de la Monnaie in Brussels, and was revived next day at the Paris Opera. On the 14th, Honegger replied to Sacher that *Jeanne d'Arc* had obviously been canceled and that "at the moment I'm on very bad terms with Madame Rubinstein." As well he might be!

On 24 November he finished the orchestral score of *La Danse des morts*. On the 28th, the pianist Nicole Henriot gave the first performance at the Salle Gaveau of a collection of pieces that had been published the year before, called *Parc d'attractions—Expo 1937: Hommage à Marguerite Long*. The composers were all French by adoption (Tcherepnin, Martinů, Mompou, Rieti, Ernesto Halffter, Tansman, Mihalovici, and Harsanyi), and Honegger was, typically enough, represented by a piece called *Scenic Railway*.

The same day, Sacher wrote him at length. He hoped that at least Ida

Rubinstein would keep her promise to come and perform *Jeanne d'Arc au bûcher* in Basel and Zurich on 11 and 12 May 1939. For the Zurich National Exhibition, he had had great difficulty in getting permission to engage a foreigner, and for that reason he had, for instance, had to replace the Italian soprano Ginevra Vivante. "How are you getting on with *La Danse des morts*? Have you completely given up on the work for strings? Shouldn't we warn Croiza in case Ida Rubinstein backs down at the last moment?" To which Honegger replied:

> *La Danse des morts* is absolutely complete. At the moment I'm working on some incidental music for someone from Neuchâtel, a *Nicolas de Flue*. If Selzach comes to anything, these two and *La Danse des morts* will probably be my last choral works. As to the string piece, various new projects have just come up, but the delay is getting to be longer than I would like. P.S. Today, Vaura and I will both be at the Opera, sitting on a jury.

Honegger was right. After *Nicolas de Flue*, his last large choral work would be *Une Cantate de Noël* (A Christmas Cantata), using material from the abandoned *Selzach Passion*.

On 2 December he had a second letter from Denis de Rougemont, who had worked out a detailed plan of his third act. Honegger also wrote down in his personal manuscript catalog, dated December 1938, a work called *L'Alarme* for soloists, choir, and orchestra. No trace of it survives—but then this catalog is full of gaps.

On 28 December Denis de Rougemont sent a third letter, containing the prologue to the first act, the "Pilgrims' Chorus" in the second, and the whole of the third "apart from a scene for which I don't have the historical information. I still have to do the 'Children's Song' in Act I." But by the end of December Honegger had completed the composition of the first act, apart from "The Climb up the Ranft," which he finished on 31 January 1939.

On the 30th, somewhat late in the day, as we can see, he confirmed to Claudel that "*La Danse des morts* is completely finished and orchestrated." And this highly productive year closed symbolically with the composition, on 31 December, of a short vocal piece on a poem by his publisher Maurice Sénart, called *Hommage au travail* (Homage to Work).

1939

On 12 January Denis de Rougemont sent a fourth and final letter, together with the final text of the second act, the scene of the Diet in Act III and the "Children's Song" from the first scene of Act I. Honegger now had everything he needed to complete his score. And he was hard at work on it when he wrote Sacher a little later, asking him to wait until 2 February for the private performance of *La Danse des morts* in the presence of Claudel, because he has not yet been able to get all his soloists together (his diary mentions rehearsals on 16 and 29 January).

It's great fun, and that goes for the orchestration too. A baritone, two women's voices (I'll choose them from among the chorus), and a narrator. The orchestra the same as for *Judith*, double woodwinds, two horns, two trumpets, two trombones, timpani, and percussion. Duration thirty-seven minutes. The whole thing is fairly easy to perform, apart from one short chorus. . . . I'm already deep into *Nicolas* and I've written a cheeky letter to the Exhibition. [He uses the word *frech*, which comes regularly in his German letters to Sacher.]

On the 17th Honegger was present at a film synchronization (probably of *L'Or dans la montagne*) and on the 21st, Sacher replied, saying he was sorry he could not come to Paris for the read-through of *La Danse des morts* on 1 February (in fact it took place on the 2nd), but that the first performance was planned to take place during the 1939–1940 season. And he was still concerned about the Basel and Zurich concerts, because he had not yet found a Brother Dominic.

Meanwhile, Honegger finished Act II of *Nicolas de Flue* on 28 January. Then, shortly after the read-through of *La Danse des morts* with Claudel on 2 February, he finished the third act on the 5th, apart from the delightful chorus of "The Companions of Follevie," which he added on 11 March. In his personal catalog, Honegger gives May 1939 as the date when *Nicolas* was finished, but this must refer to the orchestration in its original wind band form.

Like René Morax and Paul Claudel, Denis de Rougemont was astonished by Honegger's infallible instinct for translating accurately into music the nuances of a text or of an idea:

> Later I asked him to tell me the secret of this ability to divine the spirit of things, and he replied modestly: "I learn the words by heart and then I repeat them to myself continuously, in my studio, in the street, when I'm driving my Bugatti. Until the melody springs out of the words." Obviously, I believe him, but that's not the whole explanation. It's more than a psychological process of verbal transmission.[7]

On 2 February another anxious letter arrived from Paul Sacher. Ida Rubinstein was suggesting Jean Hervé as Brother Dominic, but he was afraid he would not get permission for this from Zurich because they were not accepting foreign soloists. This was followed by a telegram dated the 11th, urgently asking for the score of *La Danse des morts*. On the 14th, Honegger replied: "Since you ask my opinion, I have to say I'm not at all keen on Monsieur Hervé and suggest Jean Bard instead." Bard was Swiss, too. On the 21st, Paul Sacher wrote to say how enthusiastic he was after reading *La Danse des morts*: "The new work gives me enormous pleasure, even though I've only been able to look through it superficially."

Honegger spent most of March working on another film score, for *Le Déserteur (Je t'attendrai)* (The Deserter, or I'll Wait for You) by Léonide Moguy. There were a number of other composers involved, including Henri Verdun and Henri Christiné. On the 28th, Sacher announced the surprising news that Ida Rubinstein had actually authorized the broadcasting of the Zurich performance of *Jeanne d'Arc au bûcher*. Meanwhile, Honegger returned to song writing after a gap of fifteen years. On 31 March, he wrote "Sieste," the first of the *Three Poems of Claudel*, very different in atmosphere from his last collection, the *Six Poems of Jean Cocteau*.

Meanwhile, an important event was in preparation. Before the concert performances in Basel and Zurich, *Jeanne d'Arc au bûcher* would have its first performance in France. Symbolically, it was given, on the initiative of the mayor and the bishop, in the city of Orléans that played such a vital part in Joan's life. Rehearsals were well under way by 27 April. Next day, Honegger wrote Sacher telling him of the forthcoming performance, and adding that he would be coming to Basel directly afterward and that he would arrive on 8 May with Vaura, as well as "le Tartouillot [that is, Pascale] and her nurse." It was around this time that a revolting libel was published, which gives us some idea of the poisoned atmosphere in France in the weeks leading up to the Second World War:

> After the conquest of Orléans by the enemy, comes that of *Jeanne d'Arc* by the Jew Rubinstein. On 6 May next, M. Albert Lebrun and the Archbishop of Westminster will attend the capitulation of Orléans. The main event of these celebrations will be a performance of *Jeanne d'Arc*, with the participation of the Jew Rubinstein, the freemason Jean Hervé, and with music by the Jew Arthur Honegger.

Many years earlier a critic had written, with entirely laudatory intentions, that in view of the work's authentic tone "the composer of *Le Roi David* had to be a Jew."

Despite this smear, the performance of *Jeanne d'Arc au bûcher* in Orléans on 6 May was a triumphant success both with the public and with the critics. Louis Fourestier conducted the two fine soloists, the Félix Raugel Choir, and the Orchestre Philharmonique de Paris, and Alexandre Benois had designed backdrops, even though the performance was not staged.

Jeanne d'Arc had an equally enthusiastic reception in Basel on 12 May, exactly a year after the world premiere, and in Zurich on the 15th. And the Honeggers were back in Paris for the similarly warm welcome given the work there on 13 June (with a dress rehearsal the day before), when Charles Münch conducted it at the Palais de Chaillot. The overwhelming purity of Honegger and Claudel's work sets it on a plane far above all meanness. In the dark hours of the Nazi Occupation that were soon to engulf Paris, *Jeanne d'Arc au bûcher* would bring both life and comfort.

If Honegger had, for the moment, stopped crossing swords with Ida Rubinstein, this was not the case with some of his fellow composers, and he sprang firmly to their defense. On 1 June, he wrote to Jacques Ibert concerning *Jeanne d'Arc au bûcher*:

> The Opera has finally been abandoned, and that has led Darius to make a request of Ida. I think it would be a good idea if you joined him in canceling your commitments to her, because, like Darius, I consider her promise to put on your two works in November as just another of her wild ideas.

The works in question were Milhaud's *La Sagesse* and Ibert's *Diane de Poitiers*. Rubinstein would never perform in either of them, either at the Opera or elsewhere. Honegger's letter went on to mention a suggestion by Raoul Gunsbourg for a new collaboration between him and Ibert, this time based on Brantôme's *Dames galantes*, and Honegger wrote, "I assure you straightaway that I will only do it with you." But the war prevented the project from getting off the ground. Honegger ended by saying, "I bought the *Monde illustré* because the cover showed you resplendent in your diplomatic uniform, surrounded by important people."

This last prewar Paris season ended with the first revival for some years of *Le Dit des jeux du monde*, at a concert of La Sérénade on 21 June.

Honegger spent July working on his last film score before the war. This was for Raymond Bernard's *Cavalcade d'amour*. Honegger wrote it in collaboration with Milhaud, who used his music for it as a quarry for one of his most popular works, *La Cheminée du roi René* (King René's Progress). On 14 July Honegger wrote a kind of cantata for choir, *Possèdes-tu pauvre pécheur*, but this has remained in manuscript and we do not know for what occasion it was written.

The Honeggers seem to have stayed in Paris during that summer, while the storm clouds gathered. A letter from Paul Sacher, dated 19 August, announced that *La Danse des morts* had been definitely programmed for 2 March 1940 (when it would indeed be performed), gave a list of the soloists (who did indeed take part!), and said that the occasion would be broadcast not only by Beromünster (German Swiss Radio), but by the BBC. And he wondered whether French Radio would also be interested.

On 21 August Honegger wrote Hans Reinhart, who had just sent him his German translation of *La Danse des morts*. After thanking him, he went on:

> The translation is superb. I haven't had to change a single note, something that's never happened, I imagine, in a work like this. It's a masterly piece of work and I'll tell Claudel so when he gets back to Paris. I'm really keen to see the version of *Jeanne d'Arc* and send you my warmest thanks for that.

Because Ida Rubinstein for a long time refused to release Claudel's original text, that translation of *Jeanne d'Arc au bûcher* was not published until 1942, at the author's expense. That was shortly before the work's German-language premiere in Zurich.

Meanwhile, war was just about to break out. At the end of August, Switzerland too gave orders for general mobilization and on 2 September the army was ready for action. The box office was already open for the first performances of *Nicolas de Flue*, planned for the Zurich National Exhibition on 23 and 24 September, but these were now postponed till happier times.

On 6 October the Honeggers were at Montquin with the Thévenets, and we know from a letter Arthur wrote Claire Croiza in September that they had been there since the end of August. "For the moment," he wrote, "I'm not moving. I haven't been called up in Switzerland and I've got no work to do in Paris." They stayed at Montquin until 20 November.

That evening Honegger listened to a radio recording of a concert in Geneva in which Ernest Ansermet conducted the Suisse Romande Orchestra and included the *Prelude, Arioso, and Fughetta* and the *Cello Concerto*, with Richard Sturzenegger as soloist. The next day, Honegger wrote Ansermet:

> Dear Ansermet,
> My friends the Thévenets happened to call me to listen to the radio yesterday evening and I heard your voice saying some very nice, flattering things about me. Thank you, I was delighted. After that I heard, or rather deciphered through counterpoint from an English radio station, the works on the program.

After a brief stay in Paris at the end of November, the Honeggers went to Zurich (rehearsal and concert on 4 December), Biel (6th), Bern (7th), Radio Lugano (8th), then to Rome (dinner with Ibert on the 9th), Palermo (visit to Monreale on the 10th and concert on the 11th), Naples (rehearsals on the 12th and 13th, concert on the 14th), and back to Rome for a few hours on the 15th. Announcing his arrival to Ibert the day before, Honegger asked for his hospitality for a short time "to allow us to sort out our numerous parcels (eleven of them) and to give the ladies a chance to have a pee before the concert." Finally, they reached Venice and their tour ended there on the 16th.

From here Honegger wrote Sacher, giving him news of their success ("very generous press, except in Naples") and saying they would soon be back in Zurich. Vaura would spend a few weeks in Paris, no doubt to see her daughter, but Arthur would not leave Switzerland before the first performance of *La Danse des morts*. In reply to a letter from Sacher dated 21 December, in which Sacher inquired whether Claudel would again be willing to give an introductory talk on *La Danse des morts*, Honegger wrote that he was being asked for "a short piece of incidental music for Lausanne Radio," adding, "I've got work to get on with, which at this point is just as well."[8]

In fact, the cinema, which was his principal source of revenue, had been shut down by the war and he would not be able to work in this field until 1942, when the French studios opened once more. The "short piece of incidental music for Lausanne Radio" was *Christopher Columbus*, the first of his three large-scale collaborations with William Aguet. Like the other two, *Battements du monde* and *Saint François d'Assise*, this score is much more important than Honegger was prepared to admit for the time being. They would turn out to be three of the finest radio scores ever written.

1940

Before he began work on *Christopher Columbus*, Honegger checked with Claudel that neither he nor Milhaud would object to his working on this subject. This was being scrupulous indeed, and it shows how honest he always was in dealing with his friends. In Zurich he completed the *Three Poems of Claudel*, composing "Le rendez-vous" (No. 3) on 16 January and "Le delphinium" (No.

2) on the 18th. On 19 January he wrote Sacher, who was expecting him the following Tuesday, to say that Louis de Vocht would be putting on *Jeanne d'Arc au bûcher* in Brussels on 1, 2, and 3 March, that is to say, at exactly the same moment as the first performance of *La Danse des morts* in Basel. But, naturally, he was giving the latter priority. De Vocht would be an incomparable interpreter of *Jeanne d'Arc*, and made the first recording of the work on disc in 1943.

Another work written that month in Zurich was the *Partita for two pianos*, a very different work from the similarly titled one of 1929. The composer and Franz-Josef Hirt played it for the first time in Zurich on the 31st. After a concert in Geneva on 6 February, Honegger was in the audience for the first performance of Martinů's *Concerto for two string orchestras, piano, and timpani*, which Paul Sacher conducted in Basel on the 9th, and was moved to tears. The work is indeed one of the jewels among Sacher's rich haul of commissions. He then returned to Zurich and finished *Christopher Columbus* on the 21st. The next day in Paris, *Jeanne d'Arc au bûcher* was repeated at the Salle Pleyel with the same forces as the previous year in Orléans.

While preparations were being made in Basel for *La Danse des morts*, Honegger wrote Arthur Hoérée on 26 February, asking him to sort out the problems with *Musiciens du ciel*, a film for which Honegger had refused to write the music, but for which his name had nonetheless appeared on the credits, something he obviously could not allow.

After a series of introductory talks on the 24th and the dress rehearsal on 1 March, the first performance of *La Danse des morts* took place on the 2nd, with Jean Hervé as narrator. Honegger's first large-scale commission from Sacher made a deep impression on both the public and critics, who realized that they had witnessed the birth of a masterpiece. Meanwhile in Belgium, Ida Rubinstein played the part of Joan for the last time, first in Brussels on the evening of 1 March, with matinées on the 2nd and 3rd, and then in Antwerp, with an evening performance on the 2nd.

According to Honegger's manuscript catalog, March 1940 also saw the composition of a new and forceful homage to Switzerland under its most Alemannic aspect, a military march commissioned by Basel Radio for the fanfare of the Landwehr (the Swiss defense force) and entitled *Grad us* (Forward March). In Paris, on 9 April, Charles Münch conducted the first performance in France of the *Nocturne*, at the second concert of the Association de musique contemporaine. Then, on the 16th, Honegger was in Lausanne for the the first radio performance of *Christopher Columbus*, conducted by Ansermet.

During these months of the so-called phony war, Honegger continued to live a more or less normal life, except for spending more time than usual in Switzerland. As we now know, there was no forewarning of the catastrophe that was about to strike. On 7 May, three days before the mighty German offensive, Sacher wrote the composer that he had given Münch permission to conduct the first Paris performance of *La Danse des morts* in June (!), not, he added, with much lightness of heart, but because "this war may as easily last seven years as two" and he did not want Paris to have to wait so long to hear the work.

After the Germans broke through at Sedan, a new general mobilization was ordered in Switzerland on 11 May, and as a result the first performance of *Nicolas de Flue*, planned for that month in Neuchâtel, was postponed once again. On 12 May, Honegger finished a new ballet, *La Naissance des couleurs* (The Birth of Colors), commissioned by the Paris Opera. He had begun it in Morges, at the time of the first performance of *Christopher Columbus* in nearby Lausanne. But he would not orchestrate the work until eight years later, in quite different circumstances.

The German armies were approaching, and by the 13th at the latest the Honeggers were at Le Grand Mesnil with their friends the Winters. On the 16th, the two families left for Montquin to join the Thévenets, arriving there very much the worse for wear on the 17th at six o'clock in the morning. This second stage of their exodus lasted a month, but then they had to flee to the south. They hurriedly rented a large house on the banks of the Garonne, not far from Agen, at Saint-Hilaire-sur-Garonne. On 16 June, at one o'clock in the morning, the Honeggers, the Winters, the Thévenets, and the Mathelins left Montquin together. Francis Carco and his wife, who had stayed with them at Montquin, went their own way for the time being.

In the meantime, Switzerland had been spared by the cataclysm and, on 2 June, *La Danse des morts* was given at the Zurich Stadttheater in a staged version, using Hans Reinhart's German translation. Honegger had been able to write to William Aguet from Montquin on 10 June, saying how happy he was to hear that *Christopher Columbus* had been well received and agreeing enthusiastically to write a *Don Quixote* with him, although this never came to anything.

The same day, Sacher wrote to him at Montquin (the letter must still have reached him), asking if he would conduct a concert of his works at the New York World's Fair. Switzerland would take charge of the financial side and it would be regarded as an official occasion. Before receiving this letter, Honegger had already written Sacher on 12 June:

> I've been meaning to write you for some time, but I must confess I've been rather depressed by the grim events we're living through. My ballet for the Opera was finished. . . . I've had a letter from Lausanne Radio, asking me to collaborate on another small project with Aguet.

A few days later, he was making the dangerous journey south under the constant menace of German planes. He stayed for over four months at Saint-Hilaire-sur-Garonne, in a large house sheltering more than twenty people. A few days later, the group was joined by the painter Georges Wakhevitch.

On 15 August Honegger sent Sacher his news. He was not allowed to leave the area, but he hoped to get to Switzerland in September, as he was supposed to be conducting *Judith* in Perugia. He intended to go first to Paris "to pick up my best set of tails." And he went on:

> Here I'm leading a peaceful life and I have the feeling of being completely 'out of things.' I'm doing a lot of cycling again, which is useful for obtaining provisions. . . . It's a quiet, non-intellectual life, in which one's main preoccupation is finding things for lunch and dinner.

This letter reflects the absolutely unreal atmosphere of that summer of 1940 when anything seemed possible. Sacher replied on 29 August, saying that he had read in the papers that Erich Schild would give *Nicolas de Flue* on 27 October, which was another reason for Honegger to come to Switzerland. Sacher himself had not taken to cycling, but was going into town on foot or on the tram because there was no gasoline. He also asked about the work for strings and, as we know, his perseverance would soon be rewarded. But then the tone of his letter becomes more serious:

> Will Switzerland have an opportunity to play her part in the great tasks that lie ahead, or is she too destined to perish? As long as we can preserve the outward appearance of being intact, we must try to uphold a tradition that later will, perhaps, serve as a basis for reconstruction.

Honegger also had the pleasure of hearing from Jacques Ibert, who had managed to reach Antibes after traveling via Bordeaux, Morocco, and Algeria. Ibert wrote him on 16 September:

> I've just come back from spending several days in Vichy, where I was hoping to get enough information to enable us to make decisions. The Villa, as you've no doubt heard, has been sequestered for the time being and my students there are worried about what will happen to them. Unfortunately, it's very difficult to sort out their futures for them. . . . Maybe, if funds permit, I'll rent a villa here by the month where I can work, while I wait and see what happens. Even if the non-intellectual life we're leading has helped restore me to health, it's stupid and deadening in the long term. And my bad temper's not helped by seeing people who don't care and who can't see the fearful disruption that awaits our country. . . . Luckily, Provence is extraordinarily beautiful now that it's been purged of a large number of unwanted people!

Ibert, being firmly anti-German, would not see eye to eye with the Vichy government, and this led to him being harassed. As for Honegger, like hundreds of thousands of others, he finally resigned himself to returning to occupied Paris. He told Sacher of this decision on 18 October. If Paris "is too devoid of interest," he will try and return to Switzerland. "I'd also be grateful if you would tell the people of Selzach that I'm working and that they can always count on me totally." Finally, Honegger appoints Sacher "his moral and artistic representative in Switzerland for the duration of the war."

The Honegger family reached Paris on 26 October. That day and the next, Erich Schild, with William Aguet as narrator, gave the first performances of *Nicolas de Flue* in Solothurn.

At the bottom of page 30 of the third of the four books of sketches that are held by the Bibliothèque nationale in Paris, dated 1940, we find a first outline of the beginning of the *Symphony for Strings*. Even if France was beaten, Honegger was not. And his presence among the French, whose life he had shared for so many years, would afford them a powerful moral and spiritual comfort.

SEVEN

The War and After: Climax of a Career

In choosing to remain in occupied Paris, Arthur Honegger certainly made a brave decision and took a calculated risk. He could expect no favors from the Germans. The Nazi regime had banned his music as soon as they came to power, both in the Reich itself and in the annexed countries: Honegger's music would not be heard in Germany, Austria, Czechoslovakia, or Poland until 1945. And in any case, the composer of *Jeunesse*, the collaborator of Romain Rolland, Vaillant-Couturier, André Wurmser, and Jean-Richard Bloch was firmly classed as a "leftist," even if he always refused to support any party actively. If one had to choose one of those labels he hated, he could be defined nowadays as a kind of social democrat, while Vaura moved more and more to the right, even if she never became an extremist.

As for Claire Croiza, whose public career was more or less at an end by 1940, she was accused of being too friendly with Vichy, and this caused her serious problems at the Liberation. The truth is less cut and dried. A Vichy law had excluded her from taking her Conservatory class (the new regulation was that both one's parents had to be French, whereas, as we know, hers were Irish and Italian). The director, Henri Rabaud, had managed, however, to secure an exception in her case. But she never, as Marcel Delannoy has suggested, sang to the occupying forces. All she did was to have faith in Marshal Pétain (head of Vichy France during the Occupation) for a time, like most French people, although her attitude led to fairly lively discussions with Honegger.

Honegger had made his own position crystal clear as early as 1939 in the June issue of the magazine *Clarté*, the "organ of the World Committee against Fascism and War," which reproduced his message at the International Conference for Democracy, Peace, and the Human Individual on 13 and 14 May:

> Fascism denies the artist the playing out of his personal drama, his struggles, his search for new sources of inspiration, and his freedom to celebrate a creative spirit that is considered too threatening in its sincerity. It cannot deprive him of his place in the structure of society, but it leaves his inspiration no more than a narrow space, thereby limiting his freedom of expression so severely that his art becomes little more than an expression of those limitations. How can one remain indifferent to its threat?
> The creative man cannot reconcile his dignity as an artist with the slav-

ery that Fascism imposes. Art may be at the service of an idea, but the artist must preserve his right of criticism untrammeled.

It is from everyday life that art draws its strength. Life is vast, and manifold are the avenues it opens up. We refuse to submit ourselves to progress in one single direction or to be governed by *diktat*.

And he expressed his warmest wishes for the success of the conference, ending with the words: "May it result in Munich's never being repeated" (referring to the Munich Agreement of September 1938, signed by the European Powers, and its policy of "appeasement" toward Hitler and Nazi Germany). That is the attitude of a true, clear-thinking democrat, not of a bleating pacifist.

As I have said, he took a calculated risk. We must never forget that Honegger was Swiss, a citizen of a neutral country that was not at war with Germany, and that, because of this, his standing, and that of his family, was quite different from that of the French, whose hardships he had freely chosen to share. By remaining in France, he was subject to privations, cold, bombing and other acts of war, and all the unpleasantness of a life lived in occupied territory. On the other hand, as long as he was careful in what he did, said, and wrote, he did not risk either arrest or deportation. His purely diplomatic, passive presence at various meetings organized by the German cultural authorities in Paris certainly did not have the collaborationist significance it would have had for a Frenchman.

His activities as a critic on *Comoedia*—the periodical to which he had contributed regularly since the founding of Les Six—were given over entirely to the defense of French music against the overwhelming preponderance of German works. It was because of these too that he was asked to join the National Musicians' Front, a leftist, even communist, cultural organization that aimed to bring together all the "sane" elements of the intellectual world. As a Swiss citizen, he qualified from time to time for an *Ausweis* (permit) allowing him to leave France—he went once to Austria, twice to Switzerland, once to the Netherlands, twice to Belgium, and once to Spain and Portugal. Vaura and Pascale, on the other hand, were always kept as "hostages," although on the two occasions when Pascale took advantage of the Red Cross program for Swiss children in France to spend her holidays in Switzerland, it was her father who could not leave the country. Vaura would not leave France until the Liberation.

The much-discussed journey Honegger made to Vienna at the end of 1941, which earned him a certain amount of criticism at the Liberation, was taken for a very specific reason: to get the manuscript of his new *Second Symphony for strings and trumpet* (*Symphony for Strings*) to Switzerland. He did this under cover of writing a review of the festival to mark the 150th anniversary of the death of Mozart and the visit had nothing to do with his own music, which was, as we have seen, in any case banned in Austria. During these sad years, Honegger only conducted his music in neutral countries, such as Switzerland, Spain, and Portugal, or in occupied ones, such as France, Belgium, and the Netherlands. And if one or two meetings he had, which we shall discuss later, would have smacked of dangerous compromise for a Frenchman, they were entirely in order for someone who was Swiss. Despite one or two discordant voices when the great accounting took place in 1944–1945, Honegger's adopted country felt nothing but respect and gratitude toward him for not having chosen the easy way out when things got difficult. Those friends of his who were actively involved in the struggle against the Germans all remained loyal to him, and it was no accident that two of the film scores he wrote in those years of the Occupation, *Secrets* and *Un Seul amour*, were for films produced by Pierre Blanchar, then the leading light in the Resistance cinema.

The whole of Honegger's career had been split between France and Switzerland, but it was in Paris that he had lived since 1911 in a condition of cultural symbiosis, it was Paris whose stimulating atmosphere was still as necessary to him as oxygen. His attachment and gratitude toward France allowed him no hesitation, and it was once again his absolute loyalty, honesty, and courage that dictated such a difficult decision. Jean Maillard, who would later write an excellent study of his symphonies, remembers meeting Honegger during the winter of 1943–1944 and the composer saying: "The best moments of my life have been spent in Paris, I don't see why I should leave her at a time of misfortune. I'm not a rat who deserts the sinking ship!"[1] Moreover, he must obviously have been thinking of Claire Croiza and their son, whom he refused to abandon.

Using his status as a neutral and his friendship with a music-loving German officer[2] (who would finally pay for his leniency by being transferred to the Eastern front), Honegger also tried to help friends who were in danger. But, despite his desperate efforts, he did not manage to save one of the closest of them, Fernand Ochsé, who died an appalling death in Auschwitz.

Charles Münch, who was an untiring supporter of Honegger all through the Occupation, gave the first performance of the *Chant de Libération* (Song of Liberation), written in 1942, at one of his first concerts in a newly liberated Paris, in October 1944. Maurice Brillant, writing in *L'Aube* on 28 October, wrote of the work: "And to all its merits is added that of having been composed in 1942. For our joy and honor, Honegger was a composer of the Resistance." Honegger's popularity had never been so great as in those years when *Jeanne d'Arc au bûcher*, *La Danse des morts*, and the *Symphony for Strings* united packed audiences in enthusiasm and hope. Honegger did well to remain in Paris, risking, as he did, far more than just his material comfort. He made his decision simply, without pathos or fuss, obeying the voice of his conscience.

During that somber fall of 1940, while Paris came to terms with rationing, cold, dark, insecurity, and denunciation, Honegger began writing the *Selzach Passion* with the episode of Job. On the 21st, Jacques Ibert wrote him from Antibes on one of those sinister "inter-zonal" postcards, which were more like forms to be filled in. And on the 28th, Paul Sacher, his "moral and artistic representative in Switzerland," sent him an account of the first performance of *Nicolas de Flue*. It had been a great success, even if the original intentions of the authors had not been respected, chiefly in that there had been too many long pauses between narration and music. But "the whole musical community of Switzerland came together at Solothurn" to hear this message of peace amid such painful reality.

During December, Honegger continued his work on the *Selzach Passion*, finishing the long chorus "Lobet den Herrn" (Praise the Lord) and the "Procession of the Sick and Beggars." In a letter to his librettist Caesar von Arx (it is undated and was perhaps written a little later, but certainly by February 1941), he gave details of his progress. He had finished the beginning of the first part as far as Adam and Eve, then the Job episode as far as the end of the first part, the beginning of the second part, and various sketches for other movements.

That month Honegger also wrote his last considerable piece of chamber music, a *Sonata for solo violin* in four movements. This is an austere work, more like a suite than a sonata, and in it the influence of J. S. Bach is as clear as it is in the *Passion*. And on 28 December, he wrote the second of the *Three Psalms* for voice and piano, "O Dieu, donne-moi délivrance de cet homme pernicieux" (O God, Deliver Me From This Evil Man), based on Psalm 140 in Théodore de Bèze's Huguenot Psalter. One wonders who the evil man might have been who was oppressing Europe in those last days of 1940?

1941

The two other Psalms followed shortly after: No. 3, "Il faut que tous mes esprits" (I Shall Give Thanks with All My Heart), a paraphrase of Psalm 138 by Clément Marot, on 8 January, and No. 1, "Jamais ne cesserai de magnifier le Seigneur" (I Will Magnify the Lord Always), based on Théodore de Bèze's version of Psalm 34 and the nearest of them to Bach in tone, on the 20th. Before the year was out, Pierre Bernac and Francis Poulenc would give the first performance of this triptych.

The *Selzach Passion* was also making progress, with the Handelian "Laudate Dominum" and the "Christmas Episode," which was dated 24 January. The latter was the basis for the future *Une Cantate de Noël*, which would include the note "after the sketch of 24.1.41." Then, on the 31st, Honegger made a final version of the Job episode, and finally completed the very beginning of the work, "Am Anfang schuf Gott Himmel und Erde" (In the Beginning God made Heaven and Earth), which is dated 9 February.

While involved with this serious, religious work, Honegger found time to jot down a collection of easy variations for piano, *Petits Airs sur une basse célèbre*, dedicated "to Tartouillonnionet from her Papa," seven of them on January and the other five in February. They were published only recently.

On 26 January Charles Münch and the Paris Conservatory Orchestra, with Jean-Louis Barrault as narrator, gave the first performance in France of *La Danse des morts* in the Old Conservatory Concert Hall. This was postponed from June 1940 when, we may remember, Paul Sacher had given Münch his permission to perform it. It was such a success that the concert had to be repeated on 2 February and again on 23 March in the Palais de Chaillot. This was followed by a recording that has lost nothing of its extraordinary power and remains unequaled today, despite a brief cut that had to be made in order to accommodate the length of 78 rpm records. From now on, Münch and Barrault would be in the front line of Honegger interpreters, and Barrault would often turn to Honegger when he needed incidental music.

For the moment, Honegger's prolific work in this line during 1941 was for other producers. First there was *Mandragora*, for the play by Machiavelli, which he finished on 11 March, then almost immediately after that J. M. Synge's *L'Ombre de la ravine*, written on the 18th and 19th. Between these two, Honegger put the final touches to the central slow movement of the *Symphony for Strings*—the movement he composed first—and on 26 March he was present at the first Paris performance of his *Partita for two pianos* by Ina Marika and Monique Haas. *Mandragora* and *L'Ombre de la ravine* were performed by the Jeune Colombier troupe, directed by Jean-Jacques Aubier, at the Théâtre Monceau on 2 April,[3] with a talk by Honegger the day before. During April, the Honeggers stayed briefly with Charles Münch at his country house, Grosrouvres, at Louveciennes, not far from Versailles, to which they would often return.

On 10 April Honegger noted the name Heinrich Strobel in his diary. This brilliant German musicologist, who was then working on one of the most searching books ever written about Debussy, was an officer of the German forces occupying Paris and was in charge of the Department of Propaganda, whose job it was to promote Franco-German artistic collaboration. After the war, he would take over the Baden-Baden radio network (now Südwestfunk), set up by the French authorities in their occupied sector of the former Reich, as well as the famous Contemporary Music Days at Donaueschingen, which he revived with the help of the radio network after their disappearance during the Nazi regime. He would particularly favor French composers, including Messiaen and the young Pierre Boulez, who was indebted to Strobel for the first performance of *Le Marteau sans maître* in 1954. Strobel always claimed to be a passionate supporter of France and its culture, which was no doubt true, but his role in occupied Paris is not entirely clear, and according to some reports Honegger knew certain details in this area that he preferred to keep to himself. Strobel will reappear in our story in February 1942.

From 12 to 18 April Honegger wrote a short cycle of five songs, *Petit Cours de morale*. These five portraits of women, based on Jean Giraudoux's *Suzanne et le Pacifique*, are charming, light efforts that remind us slightly of the carefree early days of Les Six. Then, on the 20th, the Colonne Concerts revived the *Orchestral Suite* from *Phaedra*.

The first movement of the *Symphony for Strings* was finished on 8 May and all through the month Honegger was also working on a large incidental score, with choruses, wind band, percussion, and ondes Martenot, for Aeschylus's *Les Suppliantes* in the excellent translation by André Bonnard. They would collaborate on *Prométhée* five years later. The first chorus (No. 3) is dated 11 May and the entire score was finished on the 27th, even though the orchestration took him until 7 June.

Meanwhile in Switzerland, so near and yet so inaccessible, the first staged performance of *Nicolas de Flue* took place on 31 May. This was under the direction of the young Charles Faller, with the choirs of La Chaux-de-Fonds and Le Locle.

In June Honegger wrote some new incidental music for *Huit Cent Mètres* (800 Meters), a "sporting drama" by André Obey. Strange as it may seem, the first performances of both *Les Suppliantes* and *Huit Cent Mètres* took place together, on 5 July 1941 in the Roland-Garros Stadium, with the Yvonne Gouverné Choir and the Paris Conservatory Orchestra, conducted by Charles Münch.

In July began the great tour of *Jeanne d'Arc au bûcher* through the free southern zone of France. This represented the realization of a rather unusual project. The Committee for Struggle against Unemployment in the Vichy government got together an orchestra and a choir, under a young conductor, Hubert d'Auriol, and this "orchestral camp" took *Jeanne d'Arc* to more than forty towns in Vichy France as a traveling show. Jacqueline Morane was Joan, Jean Vernier played Brother Dominic, and the producer was Pierre Bertin. According to Pascal Lecroart, this tour "was beset by a number of difficulties, especially owing to provocation by militiamen. But it had a great success wherever it went."[4]

In the meantime, the Honeggers were able to spend a few days with Jacques Thévenet at Montquin from 23 July, then they returned to Grosrouvres to stay with Charles Münch on the 28th, before getting back to Paris on 3 August. Life under the Occupation was now becoming gloomier than ever, and culture and music provided the only respite, a life symbolized by a photo taken of Arthur on a bicycle pulling Vaura along in a wheelchair. Since her accident, she found it hard to walk for very long.

Everyone covertly supported the Resistance as best they could. Francis Winter designed and made a superb adjustable wrench decorated with a fake emerald for Dior and Piguet, and soon the whole of Paris was wearing it as a brooch, mocking the Nazis, who obviously did not understand the allusion. (The French term for an adjustable wrench is *clef anglaise*, or "English key.") For the moment, Les Six was incomplete, due to the absence of Darius Milhaud who, as a Jew, had found refuge in the United States. But Georges Auric abandoned his usual bantering attitude for the seriousness of his *Quatre chants de la France malheureuse*, including a setting of Aragon, and two years later Francis Poulenc would write his monumental unaccompanied cantata *Figure humaine* on poems by Paul Éluard, ending with his famous *Liberté*. But within a few weeks, Honegger would get in ahead of his friends with the victory chorale on the trumpet that crowns his *Symphony for Strings*.

From September dates a new incidental score for a play by Serge Roux, *La Ligne d'horizon*, first performed on 25 October at the Bouffes-Parisiens with Elvire Popesco in the principal role. That month Honegger also wrote a new song cycle, *Saluste du Bartas*—six villanelles on poems by Pierre Bédat de Monlaur, dealing with the life of a Protestant gentleman and poet in sixteenth-century Gascony.

On 16 September Paul Sacher wrote Honegger a long letter, saying how happy he was to learn that the *Symphony for Strings* was nearly finished—the Finale is in fact dated 13 October. He asked Honegger to send the score the moment it was completed, said that he intended to have the parts copied in

Basel, and set a date of 22 January 1942 for the first performance, at which he hoped the composer would be present. He was also planning a performance in German of *Jeanne d'Arc au bûcher* in Zurich, but was worried about the performing material, which had to be redone with Hans Reinhart's German translation, and about the impossibility of finding ondes Martenot in Switzerland or anybody to play them. As for Caesar von Arx, he had told Sacher that nothing could be done about the *Selzach Passion* until the end of the war, nor about constructing the special setting they had been planning for it. Nonetheless, Sacher asked Honegger to go on with his work.

The composer had managed to keep in contact with René Morax through his sister Toto (now Madame Stadler of Zurich), who herself had news of Honegger through Francis Winter's brother in Marseilles. Toto wrote to Morax on 20 October, sending a copy of Honegger's card, which had reached her by this roundabout route, and giving all the above information as well as two other points: that he was hoping to be able to go and conduct the Amsterdam Concertgebouw on 15 January with the pianist Franz-Josef Hirt, and that he had for some months been the music critic for *Comoedia*. We may note that an important anthology of his articles would be published in 1949 under the facetious title *Incantation aux fossiles* (Incantation to the Fossils).

On 15 November Pierre Bernac and Francis Poulenc gave the first performance of the *Three Poems of Claudel* at the Salle Gaveau and, on the 27th, Honegger left for Vienna to cover the Mozart Festival for *Comoedia*. He stayed there until 6 December and, on the 5th, the 150th anniversary of Mozart's death, he could not get out of attending an official dinner given by Baldur von Schirach. On 30 November, he wrote a long letter, in German, to Paul Sacher. He had handed over the photocopy of the *Symphony for Strings* to the conductor Franz von Hoesslin, who would take it over into Switzerland. Alfred Schlee, the director of Universal Edition, had kept another photocopy and was suggesting that his firm produce the performing parts. The composer did not think the work was very difficult to play, "but the tempo in the first movement needs to be relaxed slightly at the points where the polyphony becomes more dense."

Honegger would conduct at the Concertgebouw on 15 January and hoped to go directly from there to Basel. There were a number of Swiss present in Vienna for the event, and among the Frenchmen were Florent Schmitt, Jacques Rouché, René Dommange, and Gustave Samazeuilh. Honegger writes: "Otherwise, we're not doing too badly. Vaura and Tartouillot still have enough to eat, only the house isn't very warm." Finally, he mentions the splendid version of *La Danse des morts* that Charles Münch has recorded on disc. As for the German performing material for *Jeanne d'Arc*, it is now ready.

Honegger would be widely criticized for going to Vienna in 1941, but it seems as though he felt he had to make this tiny concession to mollify the German authorities, so that they would give him a permit to allow him to go and conduct his music. And it was the only way of getting a score of the *Symphony for Strings* to Paul Sacher.

On his return to Paris, Honegger wrote a little ballet, *Le Mangeur de rêves* (The Dream Eater), on a scenario by René Lenormand, the score of which has since disappeared. Sacher wrote him on 22 December: "I am absolutely delighted with the score of the *Symphony for Strings*, and I thank you most warmly for this splendid work." But the performing material did not arrive from Vienna and, much to his regret, he had to abandon the first performance he had planned for 22 January. He was now hoping to do it on 18 May in Zurich, with the Collegium Musicum. This performance did indeed take place, but unfortunately Honegger was not able to be present.

1942

In 1941 Honegger wrote a large amount of incidental music, which paid well and to some extent replaced the film scores that had momentarily dried up because of the war. When the Paris studios resumed their activities (and we know what masterpieces they would produce during the Occupation), Honegger went back to writing for the cinema from 1942 onward. Meanwhile, the year began with a brief stay in Amsterdam, where he conducted some of his works at the Concertgebouw on 15 January.

On 3 February Honegger made a note in his diary of the famous reception at the Ritz Hotel. An account of that occasion was given by Fred K. Prieberg:

> Heinrich Strobel was also present at the Ritz on 3 February 1942 for a reception of the Department of Propaganda for French composers. Honegger was suggesting a festival of his own works and had already submitted the program to the occupying forces some time ago in order to obtain their agreement. Piersig took advantage of this reception to try and dissuade Honegger from including the *Symphonic Movement No. 1, Pacific 2.3.1*, as being "degenerate" music. Honegger kept his right hand casually in his pocket while holding a cigar in his left. Piersig spoke to him with some animation and, behind him, one could see, smiling politely, the head of Éditions Durand and the director of H.M.V. Strobel used all his diplomacy as an intermediary. Also present were Piersig's collaborators, the music critic Hans-Georg Bonte and Dr. Waldemar Rosen, the cultural attaché with responsibility for foreign relations in the Ministry of Propaganda. Champagne was drunk, cake nibbled. Cameras flashed incessantly to ensure that the Nazi press had a permanent record of this extremely warm collaboration. After that, things moved quickly. *Pacific 2.3.1* was accepted and on 11 February Honegger's *Petit Cours de morale* on texts by Jean Giraudoux also obtained the necessary stamp from the German censors.[5]

The only censors' stamp I can find of this date is the usual one for the registration with SACEM (The Society of Authors, Composers, and Music Publishers). The Honegger Week was planned for the end of June and the beginning of July as a celebration of the composer's fiftieth birthday, but it was certainly not the composer himself who had submitted the program to the German authorities, since he had no part in putting this festival together. Quite apart from one or two details that prove this testimony comes to us second or third hand (Honegger smoked a pipe, not cigars, and Durand was certainly not his publisher), this account seems to me to be born of a desire to drag the composer's name in the mud. The writer deliberately fails to mention the most important fact, the composer's Swiss nationality, and the fact that his music was banned in Germany and the occupied countries. During this same period, Othmar Schoeck was having his operas performed in grand style at the Dresden State Opera, and operas by the young Heinrich Sutermeister were likewise being well received on the other side of the Rhine. There was no cause to blame someone who was trying bravely to survive and support his family in conditions that he had freely chosen to undergo. His presence at the Ritz and in the photographs was in no way proof of any collaboration—where are the concerts or the works to uphold any such claim? They were merely an act of necessary courtesy on behalf of a citizen of a country that was neutral and not at war with the Reich.

In any case, the indispensable permits did not always arrive, even when Honegger wanted to travel on his own. His diary contains proposed journeys to Lisbon by airplane on 11 February and a concert in Barcelona on the 23rd and, because no *Ausweis* was granted, both of them had to be postponed to the end of 1943. On the other hand, after the triumphant revival of *La Danse des morts* in Paris on the 8th, Honegger was able to go to Rennes for another performance on the 23rd. On 8 March, *Le Roi David* was repeated at the Pasdeloup Concerts, and on the 21st Noémie Pérugia gave the first performance of *Saluste du Bartas* at the Salle Gaveau, accompanied by Irène Aitoff.

In April Honegger wrote the *Chant de Libération*, which I have already mentioned. In his manuscript catalog it appears as "Song of B. Zimmer for the film." But which film? On 15 April, he wrote the second of the *Two Sketches for Piano* in Nicolas Obouhov's new, simplified notation, which he wholeheartedly supported. He was always in favor of any method of making the business of writing and reading music easier, as we can see from his long-established habit of writing his orchestral scores at pitch, eschewing the usual transpositions. The Sketch published as No. 1 would not be written until 9 October 1943.

On 17 April Éliette Schenneberg sang the *Three Psalms*, and shortly afterward recorded them with the composer at the piano. And before the month was out, Honegger resumed his work for the cinema, writing a score for Georges Lacombe's film on O. P. Gilbert's *Le Journal tombe à cinq heures*. He completed this in mid-May and the score was registered with SACEM on the 22nd.

On 3 May Honegger wrote Paul Sacher, as usual through the indispensable offices of the Winters in Marseilles, because it was no longer possible to communicate with Switzerland except through the unoccupied zone: he has his permit and will be able to travel to Zurich for the German-language premiere of *Jeanne d'Arc au bûcher* on 25 May (it would in fact take place on 13 June), but unfortunately not for the first performance of the *Symphony for Strings* on 18 May, because he has to conduct *La Danse des morts* in Poitiers on the 19th. But even if this important occasion had to take place without him, he had only to wait until 25 June to hear his work.

On 29 May he was in Zurich, his first visit to Switzerland for more than two years—since 18 April 1940, to be exact. A photograph taken on 5 June shows him in Zurich with Serge Lifar. On the 7th and 8th he was at the Schönenberg, and on the 13th, as planned, *Jeanne d'Arc* had its first staged performance in Hans Reinhart's German translation. The following day, Honegger described the occasion in a letter to Paul Claudel that was also signed by Paul Sacher:

> We've just had a very fine stage performance of *Jeanne d'Arc au bûcher* at the Theater of Zurich with choirs from Basel conducted by Sacher. Many of the stage effects came off splendidly and the whole work was a great success. I'm going back to Paris tomorrow to conduct another performance of *Jeanne d'Arc* at the Palais de Chaillot on the 25th.

René Morax was not able to attend, as he did not want to interrupt his work on *Charles le Téméraire*, which would be his last collaboration with Honegger at the Théâtre du Jorat.[6]

Honegger returned to Paris on 17 June and, on the 21st, was at the Salle Pleyel for the premiere of his ballet *Le Mangeur de rêves*. But this was just a little hors-d'oeuvre before the Honegger Week arranged in Paris to mark, albeit belatedly, his fiftieth birthday. The *Comoedia-Charpentier* series published a large special number, illustrated with dozens of photographs and containing articles and homages from Paul Claudel, Roland-Manuel, and Émile Vuillermoz.

On 25 June, at the Palais de Chaillot, Charles Münch introduced Paris audiences to the new *Symphony for Strings*. It was received ecstatically and would be, more than any other, the conductor's favorite piece—he recorded it no fewer than three times, not counting recordings made from radio performances. In the same program, *Jeanne d'Arc au bûcher* was given with a highly distinguished cast, including Marie-Hélène Dasté, Jean-Louis Barrault, Julien Bertheau, Jean Hervé, Éliette Schenneberg, Odile Turba-Rabier, and the Conservatory Chorus and Orchestra.

A concert given at the Salle Gaveau on 28 June included *Le Dit des jeux du monde*, *Pâques à New York*, the *String Quartet No. 2*, the *Three Psalms*, the *Six Poems of Jean Cocteau*, and *Prelude, Arioso, and Fughetta*. Pierre Bernac and Francis Poulenc also gave the first performance of *Petit Cours de morale*, and a facsimile of the score was published in the special issue of *Comoedia-Charpentier* that I have already mentioned. On 27 June, Jean Giraudoux wrote Honegger a letter, which Toné Winter religiously stuck on to the cover of the original manuscript, now, like so many others, in the collection of Paul Sacher:

> Dear Honegger,
> I'm delighted to see your attention drawn to Suzanne through her course in ethics. Perhaps one day you'll be won over by her course of physical exercises! I hope so. I'm happy too to have this opportunity to tell you the pleasure your music gave me, and to send you my best wishes.

The festivities continued on 29 June at the École normale, with Vaura playing the *Seven Short Pieces*, she and Honegger joining forces in the *Partita for*

two pianos, and André Navarra and Vaura performing the *Cello Sonata*. The celebrations ended on 2 July at the Palais de Chaillot with the composer conducting *Le Roi David* and *Pacific 2.3.1* (as we have seen, he finally passed *Jeanne d'Arc*
over to Münch), and at the same venue the next day, when Münch conducted *Le
Chant de Nigamon*, the *Concertino for piano and orchestra* (with Vaura, naturally),
and the first concert performance of the *Orchestral Suite* from *Regain*.

For Honegger, this was the final achievement, the apogee of his career.
Never had his popularity been so total. He was indeed an artistic and spiritual
beacon for the starving audiences of occupied Paris. Not that this affected his
equilibrium or went to his head in the slightest. In *Comoedia* on 11 July, he
merely remarked laconically: "In the old days, I was asked to spend the evening. Now I'm invited for dinner."

Meanwhile, on 5 July, René Morax came down from his mountain and gave
Werner Reinhart the news that *Charles le Téméraire* was finished. Honegger
was now at work, in collaboration once again with Arthur Hoérée, on his second film of the year, Richard Pottier's *Huit hommes dans un château* (Eight Men
in a Castle). He then had a peaceful stay at Migné-Auxence in the Poitou region
of western France, at "La Comberie," the house belonging to the Beignards
(M. Beignard was the director of the Poitiers Conservatory). Here, with the
Hoérées, Honegger wrote another film score for Henri Membrin's documentary *Les Antiquités de l'Asie occidentale*, produced by the French Office of Art and
History Films for the Louvre.

He returned to Paris in September and wrote some "orchestral pieces for
France Actualités," according to his private catalog, although these are hard to
identify among his unsorted manuscripts. He also wrote the songs for *Le Capitaine Fracasse*, a film by Abel Gance, for which the remaining music would not
be written until April 1943. He wrote two more film scores in October. For
the first, a documentary by Lucien Gasnier-Reymond called *La Boxe en France*
(Boxing in France), most of the music was composed by André Jolivet, with
Honegger merely contributing a *Hymne au sport* on words by his friend and
future biographer, the excellent Belgian musicologist José Bruyr. The second
was a much larger score for Pierre Blanchar's *Secrets*, based on Ivan Turgenev.

On 15 and 16 October Honegger attended the recording of the first two
movements of the *Symphony for Strings* by the Paris Conservatory Orchestra
under Charles Münch. The difficulties of the time meant that the Finale of this
powerful and expressive interpretation had to be recorded much later, on 1
March 1944.

On 26 October Honegger's diary mentions a meeting with Werner Egk, a
German composer whose *Peer Gynt* was being given by the Paris Opera and
who was a great admirer of Honegger's music. Egk would soon write an enthusiastic and intelligent article on *Antigone*, when it was taken into the Palais Gar-
nier's repertory on 26 January 1943. Rehearsals for this began on 17 November.
This same month had begun with another performance of *Le Roi David* at the
Pasdeloup Concerts on the 1st. On the 5th, the *Symphony for Strings* under
Ansermet was a success at the Victoria Hall in Geneva, following its domination
of the annual meeting of the AMS in Neuchâtel. The month continued with the

completion of another section of the *Selzach Passion* on the 16th, Honegger's paraphrase of the sublime chorale "O Haupt voll Blut und Wunden" from Bach's *St. Matthew Passion* (and work on this large enterprise went on into December). The month ended with a meeting between Honegger and a composer of whom he would soon have the opportunity to say kind words in *Comoedia*, Olivier Messiaen.

On 4 December Honegger went briefly to Brussels, where Louis de Vocht was again putting on *Jeanne d'Arc au bûcher* on the 5th and 6th, no doubt with a view to the recording he would make the following month. Back in Paris, Honegger took part in the making of the soundtrack for *Secrets* on the 14th and 15th, while rehearsals for *Antigone* continued. He went on working at the *Selzach Passion* and wrote a short orchestral piece that remains rather mysterious: *Le Grand Barrage*, which has the subtitle "Image musicale" and which was not published until 1966. This may have been music for a film—the mention of it in Honegger's diary as being recorded on 4 January suggests as much—but if so, it is not clear which film it was.

Honegger was not in Rome on the 20th for a concert performance of *Jeanne d'Arc* at the Teatro Adriano, but on the 30th he wrote Claudel a brief postcard: "I'm seeing Jean-Louis Barrault tomorrow morning to plan the music for *Le Soulier de satin*, which is due to be given in April." This would be the third and last of the great collaborations between the two artists. If it is not as well-known as the previous two, it is their equal in quality, at least in the poet's eyes. But the first performance would not take place until 27 November 1943 at the Comédie-Française.

1943

Nineteen forty-three began with the recording of *Jeanne d'Arc au bûcher* by Pathé Marconi in Brussels, in the composer's presence. It is quite an exceptional interpretation and a real landmark in recording history, even though obviously it does not include the Prologue, which was added by Claudel and Honegger in 1944. Louis de Vocht is an enthusiastic and inspired conductor and the excellent Belgian soloists include Marthe Dugard as Joan, Raymond Gérôme as Brother Dominic, and Frédéric Anspach as Porcus.

On 23 and 24 January, in Paris, Honegger wrote a radio score for Henry de Montherlant's *Pasiphaé*, a commission from the Studio d'essai, subtitled "a little musical decor." Hard on this followed the long-awaited premiere of *Antigone* at the Opera on 26 January—for some strange reason, Falla's *El amor brujo* (Love, the Magician) was chosen to complete the evening's entertainment. The conductor was Louis Fourestier and the fine cast included Éliette Schennenberg as Antigone and José Beckmans as Creon. The opera is a taxing and difficult work and did not carry everyone with it (nor has it ever done so since). But Werner Egk, after meeting Honegger on 3 and 5 February, wrote an extremely perceptive review in *Comoedia* on the 6th:

In the score of *Antigone*, the constructive element is especially powerful, even more powerful than in the composer's other works. The music is built deliberately on motifs that are extremely short. But it never gives the listener the impression of being cerebral. You remain completely under the spell of a violent temperament that lashes the audience. It would be tempting to describe the compositional technique in *Antigone* as anti-melodic. In refutation of this charge, it is enough to quote the moving cantilena of Antigone's farewell. This is proof of Honegger's great skill, in reserving this effect for a precise moment. . . . Throughout the opera, Honegger achieves a sound that is convincing and demonic in its impact. *Antigone* demonstrates that not all the possibilities of the modern orchestra have been exhausted.

The work would be revived regularly until the Liberation.

On 30 January the Touche Quartet gave another performance of the *String Quartet No. 2*, and on 8 February Honegger attended another session making the soundtrack for *Secrets*, which appeared at the Ermitage cinema on 17 March. On the 11th, he was involved in the soundtrack for *Pasiphaé*, but in the end it was not broadcast as Montherlant's subject was judged to be immoral!

In February Honegger made two short trips into the provinces, traveling to Toulouse on the 14th for a performance of *Le Roi David* on the 16th, and then staying in Nancy from the 20th to the 22nd for a concert on the 21st. But he also found the time to write a charming score for André Marty's animated film *Callisto, ou la petite nymphe de Diane*, which was recorded on 15 March. *Antigone* was repeated on 1, 21, and 29 March, while Honegger worked steadily on the incidental music for *Le Soulier de satin*. He saw Claudel to discuss this on the 31st.

In the preceding weeks, he also wrote one of his best film scores, for Louis Cluny's *Mermoz*. Recording sessions for this began in the Salle Gaveau on 1 April, and later Honegger extracted two fine concert suites from it. In April, he composed his large score for Abel Gance's *Le Capitaine Fracasse*, including the songs he had written the previous September. The heroic and picaresque tone of this music was new for Honegger's output, but perfectly suited to the subject. The first projection of the film on 20 April came at the end of a busy week for Honegger, which had included the synchronization of *Callisto* on the 15th and another performance of *Antigone* on the 17th.

In May Honegger wrote a work for voice, harp, flute, and string trio entitled *Céline*, on a poem by G. Jean Aubry. It has since disappeared, although it does figure in his manuscript catalog and although Aubry wrote Honegger in September 1945 asking him to set a poem called "Noémi," "for the same combination as *Céline*," which proves that it did exist. (A version for voice and piano turned up in 1993 and has since been published.) Also in May, Honegger went on working at *Mermoz*, as well as composing a *Panis angelicus* that would be first published in the October/November 1950 supplement of the *Revue de l'Opéra de Paris*. On 9 May he conducted *Jeanne d'Arc au bûcher* in the Salle Pleyel, with the National Radio Orchestra, Mary Marquet as Joan, and Jean Hervé as Brother Dominic. On the 18th Olivier Messiaen wrote him to thank him warmly for his review of *Visions de l'Amen* in *Comoedia*, saying: "The really great artists are simple and good: you have just proved this anew."

In June Honegger began writing his music for Pierre Blanchar's film *Un Seul amour*, based on the work of Honoré de Balzac. He wrote two sentimental romances for it, "Quand tu verras les hirondelles" (When You See the Swallows) and "Si le mal d'amour" (If the Pain of Love), as well as the "Ballet de la Sylphide." The rest would follow in September.

On 10 June Honegger left for Switzerland, and he did not return until the 27th. He was in Basel on the 11th for a concert given by the Schola Cantorum, Paul Sacher's ancient music ensemble, then on the 14th he went to Zurich for the performance the following day of Othmar Schoeck's new opera *Schloss Durande*. Honegger wrote a review of the work for *Comoedia* and this seems to have been the pretext for his journey. After spending several days with his family, he stayed in Bern from the 22nd to the 24th, with a quick trip to Lausanne and Morges, where he saw René Morax and collected the libretto of *Charles le Téméraire* from him.

On 25 and 26 June, before going back to Paris, he stayed at the Schönenberg, and it was there that he wrote his well-known commentary on the *Symphony for Strings*. The fragment reproduced below, on the other hand, is not so well-known because it was never published. It is nonetheless a very important document in any consideration of Honegger's general aesthetic stance:

> After writing a score, I find it absolutely impossible to explain or even remember the way it grew in my mind. I can only consider it objectively, and I have never been able to remember more than four measures by heart. When I have to accompany any of my songs, which is the only practical task I can accomplish, I have to work at remembering them as well as getting my fingers round the notes. When I state that I'm not very gifted musically, people are kind enough to object. But it is no more than the absolute truth.

Even if we need to take this declaration with a grain of salt, it is still true that Honegger belonged more to the Beethovenian camp than to that of the Mozarts and Schuberts of this world, with all their natural facility.

On 25 July Jacques Ibert wrote Honegger from Saint-Gervais, Switzerland, breaking a long silence. He had spent three "very busy" weeks in Switzerland with the Aguets:

> Aguet asked me to send you not only his best wishes, but the news that he was getting on with the work you're writing together for the Radio. He expects to finish it in mid-August and hopes to come to Paris to bring it to you himself. If that isn't possible, the Radio will send it to you through the official channels. I traveled with René Morax and he asked me to embrace you. Dear Morax, always so cheerful and smiling and lighthearted, like a butterfly. . . . I enjoyed his company.

This new collaboration between Honegger and William Aguet would be *Battements du monde* (Heartbeats of the World), written at the start of 1944.

Arthur and Vaura spent the summer at Grosrouvres with Charles Münch, from 9 August to 13 September. There the composer worked on a *Nativity* for another animated cartoon by André Marty, the creator of *Callisto*, but this project never came to anything. He then returned to Paris and finished the music for the film *Un Seul amour* between 13 and 22 September.

On 9 October he composed the first of the *Two Sketches for Piano*, written in Obouhov's simplified notation (the second one, we may remember, had already been completed on 15 April 1942). On the 11th the first performance took place, at the Théâtre Hébertot, of Giraudoux's *Sodome et Gomorrhe*, for which Honegger had written some rather strange incidental music for a group of trombones. On the 13th he recorded his *Cello Concerto* with Maurice Maréchal and the Paris Conservatory Orchestra at the Conservatory, and the day after it was the gala premiere of *Mermoz* at the Opera. Finally, on the 20th, he finished the substantial score of the ballet *L'Appel de la montagne* (The Call of the Mountain), commissioned by the Opera, which he had started at Grosrouvres in August. This is a colorful and entertaining piece, entirely Swiss in inspiration. Honegger takes the best-known tunes from Swiss folklore and works them in together in witty counterpoint. But it would not be performed until after the Liberation, on 9 July 1945.

After a concert of his works at the Salle des Agriculteurs on 22 October, on the 28th Honegger undertook a tour of Portugal and Spain. From Irun, the Swiss consul's car took him to Saint-Sebastian, from there to Madrid on the 30th, and then on to Lisbon, where he stayed for a month. Four concerts including music by him, on 4, 5, 11, and 12 November, formed part of a large Swiss exhibition. Two more concerts took place in Porto on the 16th and 17th, then he returned to Lisbon on the 19th, where the end of his stay was spoiled by a serious bout of influenza. On the 29th, he boarded a plane for Madrid, where there was a concert on 4 December, and from there he returned two days later to Paris.

During his absence, René Morax had arranged for the score of *Charles le Téméraire* to reach Switzerland via the diplomatic bag, as this was now the only way a parcel of this sort could leave Paris, and Honegger availed himself of this when he had completed his music at the end of February.

But he also missed the premiere of *Le Soulier de satin*, which took place at the Comédie-Française on 27 November. He was still laid low with influenza on the 7th, but he went to the performance on the 8th and wrote Claudel the next day. As to his own music, he was, as usual, self-deprecatory: "I'm very proud, rather like a flea in a lion's mane, to be associated with this occasion through a contribution whose limits and inadequacies I, unfortunately, recognize more clearly than anyone, but with which you are kind enough to declare yourself content." Claudel, as I have already said, was very far from sharing this opinion! The orchestra was conducted by André Jolivet.

Arthur and Julie Honegger with their children Arthur and
Marguerite, in Le Havre, 1895. Private collection.

Arthur and his locomotive,
with his father and his sister
Marguerite, circa 1895.
Private collection.

In Switzerland with his two sisters, circa 1913. Private collection.

On the rue Say, during the winter of 1913–1914. Private collection.

Vincent d'Indy's class in the Bois de Meudon, 10 June 1917. Honegger is seated, fourth from the left. "Everyone in this photograph won a prize at the Conservatory, except two: Vincent d'Indy and myself." Private collection.

Top: In 1921, writing *Le Roi David*. Private collection. *Middle:* In 1922 in Salzburg. From left to right: Aloys Mooser, Arthur Honegger, Egon Wellesz. On the right: Ernest Ansermet. Private collection. *Bottom:* In Annecy with Gabriel Fauré, 1923. Private collection.

The "sublime barn": the Théâtre du Jorat in Mézières. Private collection.

Claire Croiza as Judith. Private collection.

In Mézières at the time of *Judith*: René Morax, Honegger, Claire Croiza, and Pierre Alcover. Private collection.

Honegger and Claire Croiza.
Private collection.

In St. Petersburg, Russia, with Dmitri Shostakovich (bottom left), 1928. Private collection.

The singer Cobina Wright, Andrée Vaurabourg, and Honegger, during their U.S. tour in 1929. Courtesy of the Lipnitzki-Viollet Collection, Paris.

Aboard the *France*, with Henri and
Robert Casadesus, January 1929.
Private collection.

With Andrée Vaurabourg. Private
collection.

In Boston, in front of the locomotive *Knickerbocker*, January 1929. Private collection.

In Mézières with Fernand Ochsé, 1931. Private collection.

With Abel Gance. Courtesy of the Lipnitzki-Viollet Collection, Paris.

In 1932, at the wheel of the famous Bugatti. Private collection.

Andrée Vaurabourg. Courtesy of the
Lipnitzki-Viollet Collection, Paris.

The composer with his daughter
Pascale. Private collection.

The studio on the rue Duperré. Courtesy of the Lipnitzki-Viollet Collection,
Paris.

With Ernest
Ansermet and
Paul Hindemith.
Courtesy of the
Lipnitzki-Viollet
Collection, Paris.

Honegger with
Régine de
Lormoy, her
husband Arthur
Hoérée, and
the pianist
Pierre Maire.
Courtesy of the
Lipnitzki-Viollet
Collection, Paris.

The creators
of *Les Petites
Cardinal*, 1938:
Paul Brach,
Honegger,
Albert
Willemetz, and
Jacques Ibert.
Courtesy of the
Lipnitzki-Viollet
Collection, Paris.

In Paris during the war. From left to right: Ginette Mathelin, Andrée Winter, Lucien Mathelin, Andrée Vaurabourg, and Honegger. Private collection.

With the painter Jacques Thévenet and his wife, and (in the background) Henri Winter, 1940. Private collection.

With William
Aguet and
Ernest
Ansermet.
Private
collection.

Serge Koussevitzky. Private
collection.

Werner Reinhart. Private
collection.

In Gstaad in 1946, with Paul Sacher and Dinu Lipatti. Courtesy of the Paul Sacher Foundation, Basel.

With Ida Rubinstein and Paul Sacher in Basel, May 1938. Courtesy of the Paul Sacher Foundation, Basel.

The composer in 1949. Courtesy of the Lipnitzki-Viollet Collection, Paris.

The reunion of Les Six, in December 1951. Jean Cocteau at the piano and, from left to right, Darius Milhaud, Georges Auric, Honegger, Germaine Tailleferre, Francis Poulenc, and Louis Durey. Courtesy of the Lipnitzki-Viollet Collection, Paris.

Rehearsal for *Jeanne d'Arc au bûcher* at the Paris Opera, June 1954: Paul Claudel, Serge Lifar, Honegger, Ingrid Bergman, and Roberto Rossellini. Courtesy of the Lipnitzki-Viollet Collection, Paris.

In 1948 at the Théâtre Marigny, *L'État de siège*: Jean-Louis Barrault, Honegger, Balthus, Maria Casarès, and Albert Camus. Courtesy of the Lipnitzki-Viollet Collection, Paris.

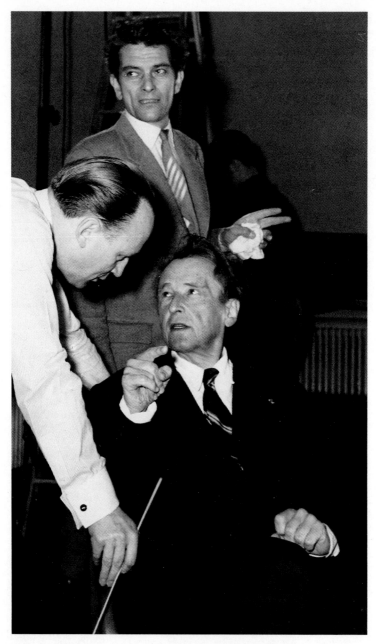

On 25 August 1954, with Paul Sacher and the film director Georges Rouquier. Private collection.

1944

For the people of Paris, the final winter of the Occupation was without doubt the hardest. On the material front, for all except collaborators and those with access to the black market, it was a time of cold and famine. In addition, there were more and more frequent air-raid warnings, as the Allied bombing, with the Liberation in mind, became more and more accurate and deadly. The culmination came with the attack on La Chapelle, only a few steps away from the Honeggers, on the night of 21 April. The only person pleased by this was Jean-Claude—when his father came to see him and Claire Croiza in the rue Spontini, he would pray that the warning would force Honegger to stay the night. No one, indeed, saw as much as they would have liked of Arthur, except perhaps Pascale, who was, as she says, given privileged treatment "because she made no demands" on the solitude so harshly and imperiously required by the act of creation.[7] Not all the great composers have had the bitter good sense to forego a family, voluntarily or not, as Beethoven did, and Schubert, Brahms, and Bruckner—who was asked one day by a friend why he didn't get married, and replied, "I can't, I haven't the time, I'm writing my *Fourth Symphony!*"

Loyal and brave as Vaura was, she was also hardened, embittered, and miserable. She had been like this for some time, and one might even question whether she was made to be happy. There are very few photographs that do not show her looking tragic or sour. She was a Puritan by temperament, and it was said that of the two of them, she was the Protestant, even the Jansenist. The terrible accident of 1934 had not made her life easier either: ever since, she had walked slowly and with difficulty.

She devoted herself entirely to her teaching. For some years she had had the reputation of being the most eminent professor of technique of her time and, even though she had never been a pupil of Gédalge, in counterpoint and fugue she was his worthy successor. Her diary was full of daily appointments with her numerous private pupils, since she would not teach at the École normale de musique until after the Liberation. Her 1944 diary has on its cover the words "Boulez Year One." This nineteen-year-old boy had arrived in Paris from Montbrison not long before, and the first weekly class he had with Vaura took place on 19 April at four o'clock. She very soon realized what an exceptional genius she had on her hands and was prouder of him than of any other of her students—she devotedly framed his wonderfully elegant counterpoint exercises.

The Honeggers were spared at least the round-ups, arrests, and tortures. But this was, alas, not the case for their numerous Jewish friends. And as Arthur's officer friend among the occupying forces had some time ago paid for his compliance by being sent to the Russian front, his efforts on their behalf were now as unavailing as they were desperate. Arthur was therefore unable to do anything for the wretched Max Jacob, hauled away from his retreat at Saint-Benoît (for the Nazis, conversion did not count, only race) and thrown into Drancy, where he died on 5 March 1944 at the age of seventy-eight.

But Honegger was absolutely desolated by the fate of Fernand Ochsé, his closest friend. For a long time Ochsé had thought he was safe in the modest family hotel in Cannes where he was hiding with his wife. Marcel Delannoy relates that only a few weeks before the Allied invasion there was a round-up, and Ochsé heard through the wall his neighbor, who had false papers, being arrested by the Gestapo.

> "Someone was led away. There was shouting. Fernand, in a more nervous, impressionable state than ever, lost his head, seized his own false papers, ran out of the room to dispose of them, and fell into the arms of a police-man who arrested him and his wife." A French policeman, needless to say.
> . . . Despite the intervention of Honegger and other friends, the two of them also found themselves in Drancy, where Arthur was able to get parcels to them through the baker's wife in Bobigny. But the worst hap-pened. The Ochsés were on the last convoy to Auschwitz, of accursed memory, in July 1944; they never returned. The composer never got over the loss. Always, when he finished a new work, he would ask himself: "What would Fernand have thought of it?"[8]

Throughout 1944, traveling was more or less impossible and everyone laid low, waiting for the invasion. The most Honegger could do was go for three days to Reims to conduct a concert on 26 January. The cinema studios had to close once again, but luckily Honegger managed to survive thanks to commis-sions from Switzerland. In January and February he tackled two of them. The first was *Battements du monde*, the new work for radio by William Aguet, who had brought Honegger the text in person the previous autumn. Radio Lau-sanne had been given the commission by the International Children's Union and Honegger finished the orchestration in March. It is a simple, but deeply moving work, ending with the prayer: "My God! Hear us little children, grant our prayer, for these wretched little ones who claim to be big."

On 24 February Honegger sent the score of *Charles le Téméraire* to René Morax, by diplomatic bag, as they had agreed:

> Altogether there are eight choruses, three fanfares, and a number of rhyth-mic pedals as a background. The scoring is for two trumpets, two trom-bones (with the second being a bass trombone), timpani, bass drum, and tam-tam. There are also the fifes, and that's why I thought it was better for the Swiss march to take a real Swiss tune that the players would already know and that would have some meaning for them. I'd very much like to come for the performances and if you can make an official request, that would help me in getting visas.

And he was even hoping to get visas for Vaura and Pascale, so that they could all spend the summer in Switzerland. But in vain.

On 24 February he also composed a song on Verlaine's poem "Un grand sommeil noir," which would be the third of his *Four Songs for Low Voice*. And on 1 March, Charles Münch was at last able to record the Finale of the *Symphony for Strings* and thus complete the recording that had been suspended since October 1942.

While a fruitless correspondence took place with Saint-Georges de Bouhélier about a new ballet that never came to anything and, on 17 March, a new song was written, "Odelette bachique," which would become the fourth of the group for low voice, the Honeggers did not forget their friends and sent Werner Reinhart warm greetings for his sixtieth birthday.

Arthur was able to hear a performance of *La Danse des morts* at the Conservatory on 30 April, as well as two of *Antigone* on 8 and 21 May, but the Germans refused him the visas for Switzerland and so he missed both the first performance of *Battements du monde* at Lausanne Radio under Ansermet on 18 May, and the one of *Charles le Téméraire* at Mézières on the 27th, conducted by Carlo Hemmerling. Hans Reinhart was very shocked that a Swiss citizen should be prevented from traveling to his own country, while any number of French artists continued to go there without any problems. Writing René Morax on 14 May, Reinhart said in surprise: "What's the reason he has to stay in Paris, when Charles Münch is free to leave it at any time and come and conduct concerts in Switzerland?" So much for the rumors that were shortly to go around about Honegger being favored by the Nazis.

In Paris, on 21 May, in the Salle du Conservatoire, Ginette Guillamat and Pierre Sancan gave the first performance of three of the *Four Songs for Low Voice*. Honegger had now added the second of the set, "Derrière Murcie en fleurs," taken from the music he had written in 1940 for William Aguet's *Christopher Columbus*, while the first song, "La douceur de tes yeux," would not be composed until December 1945.

Honegger stayed on in Paris and on 29 June served as a member of the jury for the final examinations at the École normale, just as he had been in the habit of doing for those at the Conservatory.[9]

Nothing happened during the summer, as Paris waited for the arrival of the Allies. On 16 August, shortly before they reached the city and the day after they had landed in Provence, Paul Claudel wrote Honegger from Brangues, his house in the Dauphiné:

> My dear Honegger, where are you? And where will this letter reach you, in the terrifying and exciting times we're living through? In August 1940, in the depths of our misery, I put on paper the sketch of an introduction to *Jeanne d'Arc*, then I forgot it. Just recently I came across it again, and its character seemed to me so appropriate to this moment that I had the idea of reworking and developing it. I enclose it herewith. Do with it what you will. The suggestions I've added are merely my own ideas. But of course you have absolute authority to change whatever you like. Heartfelt greetings. P. Cl.

A few days later, Paris was liberated. Honegger noted in his diary on 24 August: "Entry of the French and Americans at 9:30 PM," and on the 26th "de Gaulle's procession. Fighting in the Montmartre cemetery. German bombing." Honegger could see the Montmartre cemetery from his windows.

From the end of September life began to return to normal and appointments began to build up in the diary that had so long been empty. Honegger was able to see friends he had lost sight of years before: Claudel on the 26th, Ibert on the 28th. Meanwhile, Vaura's diary includes the entry for 9 October: "Meeting at the École normale." This marked the start of her regular teaching at the institution, where Arthur would join her two years later. On 22 October, Charles Münch gave the first performance at the Conservatory Concerts of the *Chant de Libération*, with Jacques Rousseau as soloist. The work was enthusiastically encored.

Shortly after this, the first postwar letter from Paul Sacher arrived, dated 30 October. Pascale had spent the summer and autumn on holiday in Switzerland and Sacher commented "she is a particularly adorable and charming person." He was keen to put on *Antigone*, but there were problems over the performing material and he was insisting on using the German version. He was thinking of including Roussel's *Bacchus and Ariadne* to complete the program, but here again there were the same problems as for Roussel's *Psalm*, which he wanted to give in English. On 28 November, Honegger could tell Claudel: "I've finished the score for the prologue" (of *Jeanne d'Arc au bûcher*). He certainly was not expecting to have to wait until February 1946 to be able to hear it.

In December Honegger wrote the "Scène du paradis terrestre" (dated the 25th), which would be his last contribution to the *Selzach Passion*. But he would not definitely abandon the project until 1949, when Caesar von Arx committed suicide the day after his wife's death, as he had said he would. Honegger then did nothing with the work until 1952, when he used his large stock of sketches for his last composition, *Une Cantate de Noël*. In the same way, Jean Giraudoux's death earlier in the year had put an end to the idea of a "grand, ceremonial opera" on the story of Alceste.

Now that the initial euphoria had faded, the Liberation began to show its unpleasant aspect. It was the time of settling scores, of mean acts of personal revenge, of the self-promotion of the mediocre, and of the spirit of "move over, that's my place," all in the name of purification. On 22 December Claudel wrote to Honegger, suggesting that as an answer to the accusations aimed at him, he should arrange a performance of *Jeanne d'Arc au bûcher* with Prologue, first of all in Belgium (as he in fact did) or in Switzerland. As he saw it, the accusations against Honegger were based mainly on his journey to Vienna in 1941, his continued links with the magazine *Comoedia*, and his articles on German composers (even if they were far fewer than the ones he wrote supporting French ones). On 29 December, Honegger replied:

My situation is somewhat comical. They don't want to bring me before a commission of purification because apparently they've got no charges against me. But one or two totally well-meaning colleagues think that "in my own interest it's not a good idea for my music to be played at the moment" (sic!). . . . I can assure you that in the depths of my conscience I can find nothing to reproach myself with. It was as a result of my articles in *Comoedia* that people came asking me to join the National Front in 1941, so it's hardly logical to reproach me with them now.

It is true that for some months, until the summer of 1945, Honegger's name would practically disappear from the billboards of Paris—a real boon for his less talented and more opportunistic colleagues. Honegger was ready with a creative reply. In January 1945 he began the De profundis of his *Third Symphony, Symphonie liturgique* (Liturgical Symphony).

1945

In January 1945 Honegger also wrote a short song on a poem by Henri Martin, *O Temps suspends ton vol*, which remained unpublished until very recently. There was little activity to report during that terrible winter, during which Paris was colder and hungrier than ever. In an undated letter, Honegger told Claudel that the gala performance of *Jeanne d'Arc au bûcher*, which was to have taken place on 27 April, had been postponed until May. "The Prologue will be ready. The chorus parts have been printed and the orchestral ones will be copied by the end of this month." Claudel replied on 27 April that this delay would enable him to hear the new Prologue. He also said that he had just come across an old poem he had written in Tokyo in 1926, "in which I found all the ideas I later put into *Jeanne d'Arc*."

In the end, the gala never took place. Hard luck for the Parisians, who would not hear *Jeanne d'Arc* with its Prologue until June 1947, after Brussels, Strasbourg, Vienna, Milan, London, and even Rouen.

Honegger was not slow to resume his work for the French cinema, which was now beginning to arise from the ashes. As for Pierre Blanchar, who was head of the Resistance in this field, he had evidence in plenty of Honegger's moral and political integrity! On 27 May, Honegger wrote the *Chant de la Délivrance* (Song of Deliverance), which would find a place in Raymond Bernard's *Un Ami viendra ce soir* (A Friend Will Arrive This Evening). He wrote the rest of the score in July.

On 13 June, Honegger wrote Maja Sacher to say that he would probably be coming to spend August in Switzerland for a composition course he was being asked to give in Lucerne. Vaura had not yet made up her mind whether or not to go, because she was scared by the cost of living in Switzerland: "You know," said Arthur, "how hard she is to persuade." Between then and July he had to write his ballet for the Opera (this would have been *Chota Roustaveli*, unless he still had to finish the orchestration of *L'Appel de la montagne*, the work he had begun in 1943). And he added: "Life is not pleasant here. Everything's fluid, nobody's in charge at the Opera, it's all chaotic, and as a result you can't be certain what's going to happen or count definitely on anything."

On 22 June he wrote a *Morceau de concours pour violon et piano* (Competition Piece for violin and piano)—published finally in 1984—for the Conservatory competition, which took place at the rue Bergère on 6 July. Between two visits with Vaura to Charles Münch at Grosrouvres, on 9 July he attended the premiere of *L'Appel de la montagne* at the Opera, conducted by Louis Fourestier.

The work had very bad press, however—obviously the Parisians did not appreciate its specifically Swiss sense of humor.

During July Honegger wrote the first and fourth tableaux of a large ballet, *Chota Roustaveli*, for a performance by Serge Lifar at the Nouveau Ballet de Monte-Carlo. The two central tableaux were composed by Alexander Tcherepnin and Tibor Harsanyi. Even so, Honegger's contribution came to fifty minutes of music for large orchestra. He also wrote a very beautiful *Paduana for solo cello*, which remained unpublished until 1992. This is the only extant movement of a projected suite.

After an abortive departure on 2 August at three o'clock in the morning, the Honeggers finally left for Switzerland on the 7th, at the same ungodly hour. Even so, because the network was still in tatters, the trains were slow. Arthur and Vaura did not reach Zurich until the following day after spending the night at Neuchâtel (the direct Paris-Basel line had not yet been reopened). They went to a Münch concert in Zurich on 10 August and then went on to Sils-Maria, in Upper Engadine, where they stayed a full week. There Arthur went on with the De profundis of the *Third Symphony*, which he had started in Paris in January. Then, from 20 August to 5 September, he gave the six composition lectures in Lucerne, as planned (20, 21, 25, 29, 31 August, and 5 September). The family spent the whole of September in Switzerland, and it was in the train going from Basel to Bern one day that Honegger had the vision of the Dies irae that would be the first movement of his *Third Symphony*. In the same way, the opening theme of his next symphony, the *Deliciae basilienses*, came to him one day in June 1946 on a number 92 bus between the Place de l'Étoile and the Alma. As Marcel Delannoy says, the spirit bloweth where it listeth.

On 24 September the Honeggers went to stay with Werner Reinhart at the Rychenberg for the first time since before the war, although their pleasure at seeing him again was diminished by his poor state of health.

Before leaving the Rychenberg for Paris with his wife and daughter on 3 October, Honegger finished the De profundis that would be the heart of his new symphony and had caused him so much trouble. It is one of the high points of his output. Later he would recall:

> What tribulation this movement cost me! I wanted to develop a melodic line without using formulae or systems. No side-tracking, no harmonic progressions, none of the dodges that are so handy for those who've got nothing to say! I took over the question at the point where the classic masters left it. To go forward, to walk without looking back, to extend the initial curve without repetitions or interruptions: ah, how difficult that is![10]

It is worth quoting what Honegger wrote in the Sachers' visitors' book at the end of his stay:

> Maja and Paul are two lunatics who have the crazy idea of giving their friends everything they could want. Beside those terrible lunatics who have given us five years of war, they re-establish an equilibrium and restore our confidence in life. How could one ever thank them enough?

Back in Paris, Honegger wrote a little piece in a quite different style, light and charming, in the old manner of Les Six: on 15 October, he finished his *Sérénade à Angélique*, a commission from the German Swiss radio station in Beromünster and a witty and tender tribute to his great friend Jacques Ibert, quoting a passage from his comic opera *Angélique*. Vaura's diary shows that on the 21st there was an evening meeting of the Union des Républicains et de la Résistance, and on the 28th the composer wrote Paul Sacher to say that he had finished the *Sérénade à Angélique* and mentioned "another piece that is rather important for me and that I worked on at Pratteln"—obviously the De profundis, but Honegger was not going to count his chickens just yet! He finished by saying: "Two film scores are waiting for me and a shower of newspaper and periodical articles." He was back in the swing.

Paul Sacher, though, knew that something was in the air, writing on 5 November: "Your large new symphony also seems to have made progress." Honegger went to a lecture by Claudel on the 12th, but he was not able to attend two first performances of his works in Switzerland. On 14 November the suite he had extracted from *L'Appel de la montagne*, called *Schwyzer Fäschttag* (Swiss Holiday), was conducted by Ansermet at Winterthur, and on the 19th Scherchen conducted *Sérénade à Angélique* on Radio Zurich. During the latter part of the month Honegger's energies were absorbed by the cinema. He was helping with the soundtrack of *Un Ami viendra ce soir* on the 28th, 29th, and 30th, and, on the 29th, looking at a film by Yves Allégret called *Les Démons de l'aube* (Demons of Dawn), on which he was again helped by Arthur Hoérée.

In December he finally wrote the one missing song from the *Four Songs for Low Voice*, "La douceur de tes yeux" (The Sweetness of Your Eyes), which would be No. 1 in the printed volume. The poem was by the Armenian Tchobanian, whose "La mort passe" he had set in March 1916. But, most important of all, on 5 December Honegger finished the Dies irae of the *Symphonie liturgique* and completed the orchestration on the 18th. This *Third Symphony* was still not out of his hands before a fourth one appeared on the horizon. In a letter of 10 December, Paul Sacher asked him to write a new work for the twentieth anniversary of his Basel Chamber Orchestra, which would be celebrated on 21 January 1947. Martinů had already accepted and Sacher was hesitating between Stravinsky and Hindemith. At the same time, Pro Helvetia wanted to commission a work from Honegger, and Sacher had suggested a symphony, as he was just writing one! The fee would be between 7000 and 10,000 Swiss francs.

The composer replied immediately, in a letter of 12 December, saying he was delighted to accept the two commissions. He had Münch in mind for his new symphony (the *liturgique*) and hoped that Pro Helvetia would agree to let him conduct the first performance, which would obviously take place in Switzerland. He went on: "My stay in Switzerland and especially with you has given me back the courage to attack a score of this kind. I've written the first two movements." He was planning to go to Italy, where he would conduct in Milan, Florence, and Rome. Otherwise, in Paris, there's often no electric light, no heating, food is hard to find and outrageously expensive, there are threats of having lodgers billeted in our apartments, taxes rising all the time, no domestic help, in short everything you could lump together under the heading "a damned nuisance."

Sacher was delighted that Honegger had accepted the commission, writing (in German) on the 26th:

You must know that your music is the closest to my heart, and that I love and venerate "the old composer"! . . . [*Sérénade à Angélique*] is full of charm, and so serene and cheerful, one would never guess the unpleasant conditions in which you wrote it.

Even if Switzerland was lucky enough to escape such unpleasant conditions, elsewhere they were far from over.

1946

In his determination to avoid the aforementioned conditions he was met with in Paris, Honegger made 1946 a year of travel; he spent only four short periods of time in that city, adding up to less than six months in all. But in the midst of tours and incessant traveling, this year would also be a red-letter one, with the completion of the *Third Symphony* and the composition of the whole of the *Fourth*. At the age of fifty-four, Honegger was at the height of his career. Shortly before his death, in an unpublished article on his *Symphonie liturgique*, he would write: "Together with the *Fourth*, and for quite different reasons, this is the symphony of mine that I like the best. I think it was at that moment that I was most completely in possession of my powers."

On 8 January the family left for Geneva at the start of a tour of Switzerland, Belgium, and Italy, which lasted until 10 March. They reached Geneva on the 9th and the next day Arthur had lunch with Claudel, who had come from Brangues. Then, on the 12th, he had lunch with René Morax at Morges, before they all went the following day to the Schönenberg. He wrote in the Sachers' visitors' book: "Short and undistinguished visit by a purulent sufferer of sinusitis." He would complain more than once of sinusitis attacks from this point on, which may well have had something to do with his "very muffled voice." The family left for Zurich on the 17th, then on the 21st went on to Unterwasser, a small winter-sports center in the Toggenburg, in the mountains near St. Gallen, where Honegger had a fall while skiing on the 26th. But despite that he was still working and on the 30th he finished the chorus of the Oceanides, "Terrible est la haine des dieux" (Terrible is the Hate of the Gods), intended for Aeschylus's *Prometheus*. Paul Sacher confirmed in a letter of the 31st that Pro Helvetia was offering 7000 francs for the symphony but was insisting on the first performance being conducted by a Swiss citizen. Why not Honegger himself?

Honegger's fall cannot have been a serious one, because on 3 February he attended the first German-language performance of *Nicolas de Flue* in the Zurich Tonhalle. But he left immediately for Brussels and arrived just in time to hear the last of four concerts (on 2, 3, 4, and 5 February) at which Louis de Vocht conducted the first performances of *Jeanne d'Arc au bûcher* with the new Prologue, using the same solo singers as in the memorable 1943 recording. Claudel was there, giving a talk on the work on the 5th, and in his diary he noted: "Admirable performances by the Antwerp Coecilia Choir and by Louis de Vocht. . . . Enthusiastic ovations. Queen Elisabeth was there for the last two evenings."

The tour of Italy followed on straightaway, with Honegger conducting in Milan on the 12th and again on the 16th. Meanwhile, French Radio put on *Judith* and *La Danse des morts* and Jean-Louis Barrault asked Honegger to write incidental music for Shakespeare's *Hamlet*, in André Gide's French adaptation.[11] Honegger would do so in August and September. From Florence, where he had a concert on 24 February, he wrote Sacher that he was very pleased with the tour, that the orchestras were excellent and cooperative, and the audiences enthusiastic. He urged Sacher to agree to conduct in Italy, which Sacher had always refused to do until then.[12] Certainly, a fourteen-hour journey from Milan to Florence in packed, dirty carriages, with planks instead of windows, did not measure up to Swiss railways! We may note too that, because the Italian postal service was so unreliable, Honegger was weighed down with suitcases containing all the orchestral parts for his concerts: in retrospect, the disaster of the following year was not that surprising. In Florence he had met Luigi Dallapiccola twice, on the 20th and 21st, and on the last postcard to Sacher he told the nice story of the famous German conductor in Italy: "Ich, guter Kapellmeister, Sie, gutes Orchester, Beethoven, guter Komponist, also warum probieren?" (I'm a good conductor, you're a good orchestra, Beethoven's a good composer, so why rehearse?)[13] After a concert in Rome on 3 March, Honegger started on the return journey, stopping off in Zurich and at the Schönenberg, and reaching Paris on 10 March, his fifty-fourth birthday.

Apart from a concert at Le Puy on 7 April and a stay at Grosrouvres from the 18th to the 29th, Honegger now stayed in Paris until 4 May, composing a large score of incidental music for chorus, wind instruments, and percussion for performances of André Bonnard's translation of Aeschylus's *Prometheus* in the Roman theater at Avenches, in the Swiss canton of Vaud. The chorus sections seem to have been written some time earlier and, as we have seen, one of them was completed on 30 January. But his most important work was on the Dona nobis pacem that concludes his *Symphonie liturgique*: he finished the short score on Easter Sunday, 21 April, and the orchestration eight days later. He had spent more than fifteen months on this, the largest and most monumental of his five symphonies, and could now turn to its successor.

The dedicatee of that next symphony, Paul Sacher, had given the first performances in Italy of *Jeanne d'Arc au bûcher* at the Teatro Civico in Milan on 19, 21, and 23 April, in the concert version. Stage performances would follow at La Scala a year later. Honegger himself now went on another tour south of the Alps, which took him and Vaura to Lugano (concert on the 7th), Basel, and then Bern (concert on the 9th). After returning to Basel on the 10th to hear

Frank Martin's *In terra pax*, they left for Zurich on the 14th for a Collegium Musicum concert on the 17th. On the 19th he completed the Finale of *Prométhée* and traveled from Lausanne to Milan on the 20th. Meanwhile, on the 12th the *Symphony for Strings* was played at the Théâtre des Champs-Élysées and *Le Roi David* at the Palais de Chaillot, while Charles Münch conducted triumphant performances of the *Symphony for Strings* at the first Prague Spring Festival on 27 and 28 May.

Honegger, having reached Turin, found time on the 21st to get to Monte Carlo and see *Chota Roustaveli* danced by the Nouveau Ballet.[14] The director was Serge Lifar, who had been dismissed from the Paris Opera but brought all its best dancers with him. The composer then returned to Turin to conduct there on the 24th and in Trieste on the 31st. Finally, after one more concert, he returned to Paris, without having seen the premiere of *Prométhée* at Avenches on 5 June. On that day he wrote Sacher from Paris: "Jean-Claude has just lost his mother Claire Croiza."

Claire Croiza's death had occurred on 25 May while Honegger was away on tour. It was not unexpected. Croiza had been deeply affected by the war and the Occupation, and still more so by the "purification" that had removed her from her Conservatory class. By the time the news reached her that she had been rehabilitated and restored to her former position, she was fatally ill with a brain tumor. In 1955 Honegger would die at almost exactly the same age, with only six days' difference.

Croiza's death must have upset Honegger profoundly, stirring up memories of the love he once had for her. Even so, life, and composing, had to go on. In response to Sacher's commissions, both Stravinsky and Martinů were writing concertos (a *Concerto for string orchestra* and a *Concerto da camera* respectively, although the latter was finally called *Toccata e due canzoni*). As a result, Sacher asked Honegger not to call his work a concerto—so Honegger decided to write another symphony. In his diary, on Pentecost Sunday, 9 June, he noted: "Began Paul's symphony," and the same day he wrote him a long letter. After emphasizing how distressed Jean-Claude was at his mother's death, Honegger went on:

> I'm beginning to think seriously about your piece, which I'm finding quite hard, because I'm convinced I shall only come up with rubbish or platitudes. I don't want to be shown up too obviously by Igor and Martinů, and above all I want to write something you'll like. After the *Symphonie liturgique* I'd like to compose something clear and simple, like life at the Schönenberg, but I'm afraid of the banal or the facile. Anyway, we'll see!

What would be seen, a few months later, was the most delicately modeled, the most affectionately shaped of all his works, the "Symphony of the Delights of Basel," which in an incomparably more mature fashion, recaptured the open-air freshness of Honegger's youthful *Pastorale d'été*. This charming work was a kind of oasis in the middle of those desperate postwar years. Its Mozartian ease of movement gives the lie to the most profound craft that underpins it, reminding us of Rameau's ideal of "the art that conceals art."

In parallel with this, Honegger continued the work he had begun in March on Christian-Jaque's film *Un Revenant*, a sharp satire on the monied bourgeoisie of Lyons and in which Honegger has a brief appearance in his real role of composer. The preliminary showing was on 12 June and work on the soundtrack lasted from 26 June to 2 July. Also on 12 June, there was news from Jacques Ibert, who had returned to his position as director of the Villa Medici: "We continue to relish the charms of the Villa in Rome, despite all the things that are happening, for the moment without serious consequences." Ibert had in mind Italy's turbulent transition from a monarchy to a republic.

After a short, trouble-free period of gestation, Honegger finished the first movement of his new symphony on 7 July. Although it was written entirely in Paris, starting, we may recall, with the birth of the opening theme on the 92 bus, this long, incomparably graceful movement is wholly impregnated with the ambience of the Schönenberg, as is confirmed by the commentary the composer wrote for the first performance:

> The first movement, written in 1946, is a very precise expression of a state of mind. In the midst of the hateful and stupid living conditions imposed on us, it describes the hope engendered by the prospect of escaping from this atmosphere for a time, and spending the summer in Switzerland surrounded by the affection of close friends, for whom music still has a role to play. These expectations revive the composer's creative faculties.

In fact, this prospect was very soon realized: the Honeggers would spend several weeks in Switzerland from 16 July to the beginning of October.

At Sils-Maria and throughout Upper Engadine, where the Honeggers had stayed briefly the previous year, there was a flourishing musical life, and its pleasures alternated pleasantly with those of tourism, as we can see from Honegger's diary. On 20 July there was a concert at Silvaplana, on the 21st at the Kurhaus in St. Moritz, on the 22nd an excursion to Vicosoprano, on the 23rd to the Bernina, with a recital by Pierre Fournier and Dinu Lipatti in the evening, on the 24th a trip to Zuoz (an old Engadine village with its facades decorated with graffiti), on the 25th to Muottas Muragl (with fine views over the landscape below), on the 26th to Lake Staz and the Swiss National Park, and on the 27th to the Waldhaus in St. Moritz (a concert with Sacher and Lipatti). In the middle of all this activity, Honegger managed to orchestrate the first movement of his symphony.

On 30 July the Honeggers embarked on a grand Alpine tour, starting with the Julier pass and Andermatt and going on the next day via the passes of Furka and Grimsel toward Interlaken and Gstaad, where the Loewenguth Quartet was giving an evening concert. On 1 August they went through the Pillon and Les Mosses passes and went up in the cable car to Wassergrat, above Gstaad, where Paul Sacher was giving a concert on the 3rd. Honegger had finished his orchestration the day before and sent his friend an amusing card from Gsteig, quite near there. It was in fact written by Vaura, but Honegger added a postscript: "The bath house with its various kinds of water (mineral and *eau de vie*) was especially remarkable." Then the tour continued via Zurich, where they spent a few days with Honegger's relatives, then Unterwasser on 7 August (where he had fallen skiing in January), and returning to St. Moritz through the Fluela pass on the 8th. On the 12th there was an excursion to Lenzerheide and Chur, coming back through the Albula pass to Sils-Maria, and they then spent the evening with the Münchs and had lunch with them the following day at the Waldhaus. They finally got back to Zurich on the 14th.

Münch gave the world premiere of the *Symphonie liturgique*, which is dedicated to him, at the Zurich Tonhalle on 17 August. So, obviously, Pro Helvetia had agreed after all to allow a non-Swiss conductor, given that he had long been a favorite along the banks of the Limmat. After that the Honeggers seem to have stayed in Zurich until the early part of September. Arthur set about obtaining new Swiss passports for himself and his family, and it was on this occasion that Pascale, accompanying her father to the relevant office, noticed him putting down the name Jean-Claude. Never having heard the name before, she was highly intrigued, and so it was at the age of fourteen that she suddenly discovered the existence of a half-brother. She would soon meet him in Paris and from then on Jean-Claude would play a full and open part in their family life.

Arthur, Vaura, and Pascale spent September at the Schönenberg and Honegger worked simultaneously on the incidental music for Jean-Louis Barrault's *Hamlet* and on the Finale of his symphony. Contrary to his usual habit, Honegger left the short slow movement until last. He finished the Finale on 16 September, and this conclusion resounds with the merry noise of the fifes and drums of the *Basler Morgenstreich* (the traditional tune of the Basel carnival). But it was now time to return to Paris, and there, very quickly, Honegger completed the symphony. A letter to Paul Sacher dated 9 October, some five days after his return, announced that he had come to the end of the brief, mysterious central Larghetto, with its nostalgic reference to the old song *Z'Basel an mi'im Rhy* (In Basel on the Bank of My Rhine), which was the signature tune of the local radio station: "The second movement of the symphony is finished and I hope you'll like it. We're getting acclimated to this city where one only survives by grab." He finished orchestrating the symphony on 20 October. Three days earlier *Hamlet* had its premiere at the Théâtre Marigny.[15]

On 24 October Arthur and Vaura were again in Switzerland, first in Basel and then in Zurich, but he went on alone to Milan, where he conducted the *Symphonie liturgique* at La Scala on 3 November. His diary entry for 8 November makes the first mention of a course at the École normale. It had been intended, in principle, that these classes would take place twice a month. But in fact they would be rather irregular because of all the traveling he did.

In Milan, news reached Honegger that the city of Basel had awarded him its music prize (Basler Musikpreis), and in a letter of 6 November he thanked Paul Sacher for it. He ought not to accept, but what could he do? And he offered to write whatever Sacher wanted, for orchestra or choir or both together. "But you'll soon be crushed under the weight of my outpourings!"

Vaura returned to Paris on her own. Clearly, all was not well between them. She seems to have been less a part of Arthur's life during these years and to have turned in on herself, devoting her energies entirely to her teaching. It was only the serious crisis in Honegger's health in August 1947 that brought them together again.

On 11 November Sacher wrote to ask: "Have you, with Professor Staiger's help, found a good Latin title for the symphony?" It was in fact Emil Staiger, a professor at Zurich University, who came up with the title *Deliciae basilienses*, which fits the character of the work so well. Meanwhile, on 14 November, the *Symphonie liturgique* had its first Paris performance under the passionate direction of Charles Münch.

On the 22nd another letter came from Paul Sacher. He would conduct the stage version of *Jeanne d'Arc au bûcher* in four performances at La Scala, in Milan, from 4 to 10 April 1947. And the following day Honegger could tell his friend that the performing material of the new symphony would soon be ready, but that breakdowns in the electricity supply were hampering the printers. And he added: "I'm still quite shaken by the Basler Musikpreis."

In December Honegger composed one of his most striking vocal works, *Mimaamaquim*, a transliteration of the original Hebrew of Psalm 130, the De profundis, written for the exceptionally deep voice of the contralto Madeleine Martinetti. He would make an orchestral version of it the following June. On 4 December Tibor Harsanyi conducted the French Radio Orchestra in the first performance in France of the *Sérénade à Angélique*; on the 7th Charles Münch and the BBC Symphony Orchestra gave the first British performance of the *Symphonie liturgique* (two days earlier, Ernest Ansermet and the Suisse Romande Orchestra had done the same for Geneva); on the 14th and 15th *La Danse des morts* was revived at the Théâtre des Champs-Élysées; and on the 19th Jane Évrard gave another performance of the *Symphony for Strings* at the Palais de Chaillot with her women's orchestra.

This busy year came to an end with another letter from the composer to Paul Sacher, dated 22 December: "It's really quite cold here and my studio's rather like a refrigerator. The main aim is to stay in bed as long as possible." He did not go to Brussels, which also hosted a performance of the *Symphonie liturgique*, the reason being that there was no mention of it in the press. "There too my name is subject to official silence."

1947

Nineteen forty-seven was the critical year, the turning point, when suddenly everything was thrown into turmoil.

The pattern of early January was curiously similar to that of the previous year. After a lecture at the École normale on the 3rd, Honegger left again for Basel on the 12th for rehearsals and the first performance of his new symphony. Vaura was unable to join him until the 18th and would leave again on the 23rd—from now on her teaching duties at the École normale would normally prevent her traveling except during the vacations. Her timetable was clearly fuller and more demanding than Arthur's.

Following two other first performances, of Stravinsky's *Concerto in D* and Martinů's *Toccata e due canzoni*, that of *Deliciae basilienses* on 21 January was the high point of the Basel Chamber Orchestra's anniversary concert. Paul Sacher was as delighted as one would expect, the reception was enthusiastic, and the symphony would soon become popular. Honegger wrote in the Sachers' visitors' book: "*Deliciae basilienses* isn't the name of a Läckerli biscuit, an old Basel specialty, but the symbol of the Schönenberg." The composer spent another week in Switzerland, first in Zurich, where he attended a Bernanos conference on the 23rd and a performance on the 24th of Othmar Schoeck's *Penthesilea*, a work he very much admired, and then a visit to Lausanne Radio on the 30th. After that he returned to Paris and must have reached it on the 31st.

There was another concert of his music at the École normale on 10 February, and the day after that Strasbourg audiences had their first opportunity to hear the *Symphonie liturgique*, directed by Fritz Münch. Honegger did not attend as he had already left for Monte Carlo, where he conducted the same symphony followed by *Le Roi David* on 13 February; he gave Sacher news of this concert in a letter dated 15 February. From the 23rd to the 27th, Honegger was in Strasbourg for three performances of *Jeanne d'Arc au bûcher* on the 24th, 25th, and 26th. Apparently these were the first occasions in France where the work was given with the Prologue. Sacher meanwhile announced his intention of conducting *Jeanne d'Arc* at the Vienna Music Weeks on 16 and 17 June and the concerts should start with the *Symphonie liturgique* conducted by the composer. But this last plan never came to anything. Honegger replied by return. He was just back from Strasbourg and would be at Lugano Radio on the 20th and in Milan on the 21st. On 4 March he had lunch with Paul Claudel, then his journey went ahead as planned.

In Lugano he was greeted by a veritable festival. He conducted three concerts there on 23, 27, and 30 March, and on the 28th a film was made about him. The next day Paul Sacher came to see him on his way through to Milan, and on the 31st there was a general reunion in the Lombardy capital, with Vaura and Pascale arriving from Paris as well as Claudel. On 4 April Sacher conducted the first performance of *Jeanne d'Arc au bûcher* at La Scala, with three further ones on 6, 7, and 10 April. Even if Claudel was happy with the singing and playing, he had reservations about the production and noted in his diary: "Eight hundred people on the stage! It's better as an oratorio. The end didn't come off. Two scenes were a success: the card game and the *kermesse*" (scene 8).

After these performances, Arthur and Vaura had to return to Paris to fulfill their teaching commitments and they came back together on 13 April. So the composer was not present at the first performance of *Jeanne d'Arc au bûcher* in England, which took the form of a radio broadcast, in English, on 16 April, conducted by Basil Cameron. Nor did he manage to get to Prague for Sacher's highly successful performance of the *Third Symphony* on the 24th. In a letter of 20 April Sacher informed Honegger that he would be conducting it again in Vienna in June, and in Budapest and Baden-Baden in September. So the work was finding a place in the repertory with unusual speed for a new score, and by the end of the year Honegger could count no less than seventeen performances. Also in April, Honegger wrote an *Intrada for trumpet and piano*, commissioned for the Geneva International Performance Competition.

On 31 May, the date on which Joan of Arc died more than five centuries earlier, Honegger's oratorio was given under the composer's direction at the Théâtre-Cirque in Rouen, with Jacqueline Morane in the title role. A few days earlier, on the 23rd, the Honeggers had caught up with an old friend, Georges Enesco, at the house of Hilda Gélis-Didot, Pascale's godmother and one of the Honeggers' closest friends. They would see more of Enesco in the years that followed, and Hilda Gélis-Didot's name would appear regularly in their diaries, especially Vaura's.

June was extremely busy. On the 4th, in the Salle Gaveau, Philippe Strubin put on *Le Roi David* for the first time in Paris in its original instrumentation, which Honegger always preferred, and on the 8th he completed his orchestration of *Mimaamaquim*. Meanwhile, on the 7th, Louis de Vocht and his usual forces chose The Hague as the starting point of a grand tour with *Jeanne d'Arc au bûcher*. After Amsterdam on the 8th and Utrecht on the 9th, the complete work in this definitive interpretation finally reached Paris and the Théâtre des Champs-Élysées on 14 June. It was about time!

From 15 to 20 June Honegger was in Brussels, and on his return he found a letter from Paul Sacher, written in Vienna on the 19th. His friend was sorry that the composer had not been present at the great triumph of *Jeanne d'Arc* at the Vienna Konzerthaus on the 16th (the *Symphonie liturgique* had also been on the program). He was still looking for a Creon for *Antigone* and someone had suggested Morane (in fact, Camille Maurane); what did Honegger think?

But Honegger's thoughts were already elsewhere. On 25 June he attended the recording of the incidental music he had written for André Obey's translation of Sophocles's *Oedipus*, and the next day he was at another recording session, this time for a disc of *Mimaamaquim* and Nos. 2 and 4 of the *Four Songs for Low Voice* (on words by William Aguet and Paul Verlaine), which would be sung by Madeleine Martinetti with orchestral accompaniment. And in a letter written on 22 June, Honegger told Serge Koussevitzky he would be arriving in New York on 5 July.

His old friend and early champion had invited him to spend the summer on the other side of the Atlantic and to take part in the well-known summer courses at Tanglewood, the summer residence of the Boston Symphony Orchestra, which comes every year to this beautiful spot in the Berkshires, amidst the finest hills and woodland scenery in New England. After these weeks of courses and conferences, Honegger intended to make a huge tour of the United States, Mexico, and South America. He hoped indeed to get down as far as Tierra del Fuego and play *Le Chant de Nigamon* to the Patagonians. As he said with a smile to Marcel Delannoy just before he left Paris: "After all, it's just a story about American Indians."[16]

Man proposes, but God disposes. The man who climbed aboard the airliner *Star of Madrid* at seven o'clock in the morning on 5 July bound for New York, and who reached New York that same day at four o'clock in the afternoon local time, after regulation stops at Shannon in Ireland and Gander in Newfoundland, was a man in the prime of his life, at the height of his physical and creative powers. But on the other side of the ocean, Death in person stood waiting to greet him.

EIGHT

Catastrophe and Reprieve: The Final Harvest

To begin with, everything went well in the States. On 6 July, the day after his arrival, Honegger moved in at Lenox, Massachusetts, near Tanglewood, where the courses he had agreed to teach would be given. The first one, on the *Symphonie liturgique*, took place on the 8th, and two more followed on the 11th and 12th. But preparations had to be made for the South American tour, and for that he had to obtain the visas that he detested so violently. On the 20th Honegger drove in an automobile to New York, in the stifling heat which that huge city suffers every summer, with a humidity count that overwhelms anyone who is not used to it. On the 21st, at the Mexican consulate, he suddenly felt so ill that he had to go immediately and see a doctor—something that ordinarily never happened to him. Dr. Taylor of Park Avenue immediately realized how serious the situation was and sent him back to Lenox with orders that he should have absolute rest and not move. It is true that, as he would admit to Arthur Hoérée in a letter written on 24 September, he had been exhausted when he left Paris. But now it was his heart that was failing, and in a month's time it would be worse.

Fifty-five is a critical age for all men, but particularly for someone who has never looked after himself, who lives a frenetic life, and who, in addition, does not intend to renounce any of the joys of existence. After the privations of the war, Arthur launched himself at anything that could banish the memory of doubtful pâtés and stews of unknown parentage, with the result that he put on weight with dangerous rapidity.[1] Corpulence, cholesterol, hypertension, and intolerable heat: a combination of all the conditions necessary for a serious warning shot.

In reply to a letter from Darius Milhaud, announcing that on 12 or 13 August he would be returning to France for the first time since the war, Honegger told him what had happened:

> My dear Darius,
> The stupidest thing of all is not just being here, but being stuck in bed waiting for permission to ring your number in three or four days' time. What happened was that a few days after my arrival I went to New York for my Mexican visa, and found myself so out of breath, I had to be taken to a doctor, who ordered me to bed. I've overtaxed a muscle in my heart.

So no Mexico, and no stairs! There we are. . . . I embrace you meanwhile, and I'll call you as soon as I'm allowed to go down the stairs. Yours ever, Arthur.

A much more detailed report to Paul Sacher likewise testified that Honegger's good humor was intact. As long as he had absolute rest, the situation did not seem worrying, and on 7 August Vaura felt she could leave Paris for a holiday at Grasse and Mougins. On the 15th Honegger wrote Sacher:

> So, after traveling on the superb Constellation airliner *Star of Madrid*, I arrived in New York around four in the afternoon New York time, a bit disoriented and green about the gills but proud of having crossed the Atlantic without throwing up. I got down to work the next day and explained in American to the young composers of this hemisphere that a trombone should not be confused with a piccolo and that the interest of a piece was not necessarily a function of the number of notes poured out onto the lovely transparent manuscript paper we've both seen examples of.
> I then went to the Mexican consulate in New York for my visa and I had the feeling all was not well. Then, accompanied by a helpful young person who spoke French, I went to see a doctor who looked as though he'd stepped out of an American film. An hour later I came out again not feeling very cheerful and thinking perhaps the first thing I should do was send you a farewell card. I've been put to bed for three weeks solid. Adieu Mexico City and your 7000 feet. Koussevitzky sent for a specialist from Boston and, as every cloud has a silver lining, I was staying in a house where the aunt and her niece are both qualified nurses. So I've been looked after, and still am being, as though I was a particularly important newborn baby. I'm washed, shaved, combed, perfumed, the whole Boston Symphony Orchestra takes turns coming to play me solos, I have presents of wine, fruit, books, candies. To begin with I slept an incredible amount, day and night for hours at a time, as happy as a well-fed pig in his sty. Things are going better now. I get up every day and people speed east and west to do my bidding.

He was still hoping to be able to leave for Miami at the beginning of September and from there to fly to Buenos Aires in stages, if the doctors permitted. He saw a lot of Martinů, who had also had an accident while teaching at Tanglewood the previous summer, when he fell from a high terrace and fractured his skull. The *Symphony for Strings* was played at Tanglewood to an audience of twelve thousand people.

On 20 August he wrote Pascale a very affectionate letter, belatedly wishing her a happy fifteenth birthday, but without mentioning his health.

But suddenly, what had been no more than a serious warning turned to tragedy. During the night of 21 August, and then again in the morning of the 22nd, Honegger suffered a grave triple infarctus, and his diary for that day is marked with a simple but terribly impressive funerary cross. The diagnosis was not encouraging and it seemed that his days were numbered: coronary thrombosis, pulmonary embolism, and a number of complications including circulatory and cardiovascular problems, embolisms, and phlebitis. Telegrams were sent at once to Vaura and the Winters, and Vaura managed to obtain her visa for the United States on the 26th. But airplanes were infrequent and fully booked, and written confirmation from Pierre Bourdan, the Minister for Youth, Arts, and Letters, that the composer was dying was influential in obtaining for her the necessary priority. When she arrived on the 30th, she was appalled by what she saw. Two days later she wrote the Winters at length, at the same time asking them not to alarm Pascale:

> I found our poor A. much changed. He recognized me and smiled at me, then suddenly he started to talk without stopping. It was difficult for him (problems with his facial muscles more than with his breathing) and he complained about any number of boring little things, regularly interrupted by the remark: "you can see the state I'm in, you can see what they've managed to do!" Those few moments terrified me, because A. was talking as though none of the muscles in his mouth were working properly and he was talking sense interspersed with nonsense.
>
> As far as I could understand him, it seems as though he feels persecuted. The problem is partly that in America no one ever tells the patient what's wrong. It's such an ingrained habit that here patients never ask any questions, but let themselves be treated without saying anything. Unfortunately, A.'s brain is working and rebelling against this. He's said to me several times: "They're playing a devil of a game with me, they're making me play a devil of a game."
>
> After this visit, I had a long talk with Dr. Forsley. . . . His first attack was due to his heart muscles that contracted out of fatigue, affecting the veins and arteries in the heart. This was improved by his long rest. The second attack was of the sort called "coronary thrombosis." This serious crisis happened in three stages during the night of 21 August and on the morning of the 22nd. Following his first attack he has been looked after by two nurses working in relays, so that from the start everything necessary and possible has been done. Then A. spat blood, which showed that there was a clot in the lung. There's also a little clot in his right leg, which has caused phlebitis. . . . The fact that his brain is working away, making him tell me the most extraordinary stories, and that his face muscles, especially those round his mouth, are restlessly and distressingly distorted, that comes from the morphine. This morning Dr. Forsley was delighted to find him so much better. Everything is relative, and personally I'm distraught at seeing our poor A. like this. . . . Perhaps it would be better if Toto didn't tell Jean-Claude the whole truth; the poor boy has already lost his mother. . . . Before the Boston doctor left, he said to me: "the heart is much, much better. Mr. H. is still very ill, but he has a fifty percent chance."

Two days later, Honegger's condition had visibly improved, as Vaura wrote the Winters on 3 September:

> Arthur had a good day yesterday. He slept till five o'clock in the afternoon, although they had to wake him from time to time to get him to drink—he has to drink a lot. I made him a little café au lait and, as he

wanted a piece of toast, I made him some as quickly as I could. Unfortunately, by the time he raised it to his lips he no longer wanted it. But never mind, it's the first time he's wanted anything to eat, and that's something.

Last night the doctor was so pleased with him, he said to me specifically: "Your husband now has a sixty percent chance. If there are no setbacks by the end of the week, that'll go up to seventy-five percent, and if the same applies by the end of next week, it'll be one hundred percent." I find these "percentages" irritating, but I pass them on, since those were his very words. . . . I'm very happy to see him sleeping peacefully. Until Monday, he seemed to be suffering in his sleep, he was very restless and talking unintelligibly. He was also singing a lot, but that's stopped now and his brain seems at last to be calm. Yesterday he told me he thought he'd been delirious and that in this state he had "gone through all the classical symphonies." Basically I'm sure this heart attack is the result of physical and mental exhaustion. . . . But what a difference between now and Saturday evening and Sunday! If things had gone on for long like that, I think I'd have gone mad.

Three days after that letter, on 6 September, Vaura noted in her diary: "Dr. Forsley today said: another six or eight weeks in bed, can't travel for two or three months." The worst was now behind them. All that was required was patience, and two whole months would pass before he could return to France. Obviously the South American tour was now out of the question, and in any case the medical expenses in America were terribly high. Luckily, in Paris his friend Albert Willemetz had meanwhile put on a revival of *Les Aventures du roi Pausole*, which brought the composer in substantial royalties, and Koussevitzky had been a very generous helper.

On 18 September a get-well card arrived from Honegger's old friend Werner Reinhart, and on the 20th Vaura wrote Jean-Claude:

> Your papa is doing well, very well in fact. It's miraculous to see him so well after he's been so ill, and if it wasn't for his bad leg he'd be running around like a two-year-old. But perhaps the phlebitis is a blessing in disguise, because he has to stay lying down instead of going on with his tour, as he would have done otherwise.

On 22 September Arthur was able to write for the first time. The letter was to Toné Winter:

> Today I'm picking up a pencil for the first time. . . . And for the first time since 21 August I've got out of bed, because I'm now much better. As they sing in *Manon*, I am "still quite dizzy" by what happened to me so suddenly. The doctors claim that I'll come out of it all renewed, revived, restored, and in better shape than ever.

And Vaura added as a postscript:

> What A. doesn't say is that he got up this morning for a few minutes. He didn't go far, obviously, just from his bed to an armchair a few feet away,

and then using only his good leg. But all that without feeling ill in the slightest and without any disturbance of his pulse.

Replies were called for to any number of messages of friendship and sympathy. On 24 September, it was Arthur Hoérée's turn: "I'm only now beginning to get up for the first time since 21 August, and I've become as slim as you are, even if not as elegant." He then expressed his regret over the grand tour, which had now been canceled, and went on:

> Anyway, I might have died. Which would have been another way out of the situation. According to the doctors, this event has been postponed and I've been restored and mended like an old tire. Let's hope so. . . . A cable from the Winters tells us that some of the newspapers were printing bad news about me. It's too late, or perhaps too early, and for the moment I'm busy convalescing.

On 26 September he wrote Paul Sacher in the same vein, talking about his return to France. Sacher had conducted *Deliciae basilienses* for the first time in Venice in the course of the Biennale at Teatro La Fenice on 15 September, and on the 28th he would conduct the *Symphonie liturgique* on Baden-Baden Radio, before reviving *Jeanne d'Arc au bûcher* at the Vienna Konzerthaus on 9 October.

Also on 26 September, a letter went off from Lenox to Pascale from both her parents. It was, naturally, reassuring and full of details about the American food that was impossible to get in the France of 1947: white flour, sugar, rice, fruit, and so on. The temptation to fill their suitcases with it all must have been almost irresistible.

As the weeks passed, Honegger's health continued to improve, slowly but surely. On 25 October Vaura could write to Werner Reinhart:

> Arthur is now doing well, very well . . . it's a miracle! He's already been out two or three times—in an automobile. He enjoys these trips amid this splendid scenery. The weather's magnificent and the forests, with the maples in their fall colors, are splendid.

The previous evening, Koussevitzky had given another triumphant performance of the *Symphony for Strings* in Symphony Hall in Boston.

Vaura's diary entry for 31 October gives us the first glimpse of what would become the *Concerto da camera*. In fact, it was three months earlier that Honegger had received a commission from Elizabeth Sprague Coolidge for a piece—either a sonata or a chamber work—that would treat the English horn as a soloist. In early August the composer accepted, subject to progress in the state of his health. For the moment, according to Vaura, he felt he would rather write a concerto. And indeed his exquisite masterpiece in this form was completed a year later.

The date of his return was now approaching. Of course, air travel was out of the question and would remain so—likewise, the summer of 1946 had been the last Honegger would ever spend up in the mountains. On 4 November he wrote Arthur Hoérée to tell him that he would be sailing soon:

> Our departure is very near now—we leave on the 8th on the *Mauretania*, bound for Cherbourg. I've had a good day here with Hindemith, who came specially from New Haven with his wife, and another one with Charles Münch, who brought me news from Paris. My *Symphony for Strings* is making my American tour for me. In this month alone there have been three performances in Boston and five in New York. A dozen or so other cities have put it on their programs. The *Jeanne d'Arc au bûcher* in Buenos Aires also went very well, with five performances, but without me, alas.

Honegger, in fact, was supposed to have been conducting those performances.

On 14 November, Arthur and Vaura disembarked at Cherbourg and the following day they were back in Paris, which Honegger had left four and a half months earlier. A welcome telegram from Sacher was waiting for them, and they had already received in Lenox a very touching letter from Milhaud, who had reached France some weeks before them:

> I thought of you all through the forty days this Norwegian cargo ship took to bring me back to France. The Germans had totally cleared out my flat and I spent a day putting in order some of the odds and ends you'd found. Thanks to you, Sauguet, Déso, and Jacques Denoël, I've discovered some books, a little music, some pictures. You'd brought over to my flat the small collection of things you'd been looking after in yours, and it was as though you—my friend for thirty-five years—had come to greet me here in person. The news reached me at the same time that you were better. Speaking as someone who has got used to illness, I can imagine how depressing it must be when it suddenly descends on those who have hitherto been spared. Dear Arthur, look after yourself and come back soon. And I, who was away for seven years, will be the one to greet and embrace you!

And so this man of an iron constitution, of Herculean energy, returned home permanently dispossessed of his health and strength. Despite that, Honegger would for years fly in the face of reason, determined to ignore the evidence. His traveling schedule would often go back to its earlier frenzied pace, notably in 1949, and only very gradually did his activity as composer and conductor show signs of abating. He was reluctant too to renounce the pleasures of life, especially of the table. His poor heart did the best it could under this onslaught, and during the early part of these last years, Honegger's decline was still interrupted by periods of recovery, albeit temporary. Only during the sad epilogue of his final three years were his activities and traveling severely limited, so that inevitably he lost the appetite for life. We can see this very gradual deterioration in photographs of him. There is a vast difference between the face and silhouette of 1948, both practically normal, and the terrifying images— almost like a premature death mask—of the last months of 1955.

But this is to anticipate—a rich harvest was still to be reaped. For the moment he could even comfort himself with illusions, as we can see from his letter of 15 December to Serge Koussevitzky: "I'm feeling better every day. The head of the faculty's cardiology clinic has done a new electrocardiogram on me that is very reassuring. My heart is absolutely back to normal."

On 18 December Jacques Ibert wrote him from Rome an affectionate message full of confidence and optimism. On the 19th the first performance took place, at the Théâtre des Champs-Élysées, of the Sophocles/Obey *Oedipus,* for which Honegger had pre-recorded the music just before flying to the United States. And his diary for this year's end contains two complementary, symbolic entries.

First, a victory tally, of the number of performances of the *Symphonie liturgique* since the first one—seventeen in all: in Zurich, Milan, and Paris during 1946, and in 1947 in London, Amsterdam, Brussels, New York, Geneva, Strasbourg, Monte Carlo, Prague, Vienna, Budapest, Baden-Baden, Jerusalem, Tel Aviv, and Haifa. And second, under the heading "distractions," a compendium, possibly made in Lenox, of sensible advice in which one may detect some irony: "No climbing, no running, no efforts. Swim next summer as long as you don't get tired. No fat or oil, no sweet wine or cocktails. Rice is fine, but only unsalted. Hot lemon good. Above all, don't worry." On 21 December Arthur, Vaura, and Pascale went to join Paul and Maja Sacher at the Schönenberg, and we can well imagine what an emotional meeting it was at the end of a year so full of drama. Honegger stayed at the Schönenberg until 16 March.

1948

On 3 January 1948 the Prague audience gave an enthusiastic welcome to the first Czech performance of *Jeanne d'Arc au bûcher,* conducted by Walter Ducloux, and in Paris Honegger's music was no less popular. *Pacific 2.3.1* was given at the Pasdeloup and Lamoureux Concerts on the same day, 18 January (in his articles for *Comoedia* Honegger was forever condemning this kind of doubling-up!), then on the 25th Eugène Bigot conducted the *Symphonie liturgique.* On 6 February Honegger was back at the Schönenberg and went to an English concert, preceded by a lunch with the performers, Benjamin Britten and Peter Pears. On the 11th he wrote Jacques Ibert a calmly euphoric letter:

> My dear Jacques,
> I'm spending a peaceful, happy time here and I think it'll put me back on my feet for good. Already I'm feeling absolutely fine and it's only out of obedience to the doctor that I avoid certain things like climbing stairs, drinking, and smoking, all of which are now forbidden me. I'm not working at all and I'm afraid I may have got into the habit of total idleness. But then, when it comes to it, nobody asks one to write so much music, and it gets round the unpleasant business of playing it.

But, as we may imagine, these good resolutions did not last for long.

On 7 March Vaura returned to Basel for an important concert—rehearsals would begin the day after, with the concert itself on the 12th. For this, Paul Sacher programmed together two of Honegger's favorite works, his two most radical and difficult masterpieces: *Horace victorieux* and *Antigone*. Then, on 16 March, Arthur and Vaura returned to Paris. From there, Honegger wrote Paul Sacher on the 21st about a book he had just been shown, in which his own youth had been described with such whim that he could hardly believe he was the subject of it! (This must have been the book by José Bruyr in which, for all its warmth, enthusiasm, and keen musical judgments, one has to sort out the wheat from the chaff among an almost excessive abundance of detail.) Honegger was not able to attend the first performance in Winterthur, on 31 March, of *Deliciae basilienses*, conducted by Hermann Scherchen.

From 16 May to 8 June, Honegger underwent a thermal cure at Bagnoles de l'Orne in Normandy, and while he was there he orchestrated his ballet *La Naissance des couleurs*. He had finished this on 12 June 1940, but now it was due to be performed at the Paris Opera.

"It's getting me back into the way of writing notes. I'd more or less forgotten where to put a B or a D. I'm also having to use glasses," he wrote Paul Sacher on 30 May. In fact, it was the first time since his heart attack that he had written anything on manuscript paper. Shortly before, he had had an inquiry from Sacher about progress on the *Concerto da camera* intended for Mrs. Coolidge. "Alas," he replied, "no sufficiently brilliant ideas have yet sprung from my poor head. I don't dare begin." But he noted the orchestral forces, which would remain the same: flute, English horn, and strings.

Because *Amphion* had been totally forgotten, Honegger decided to transcribe the last and best part of it for orchestra alone. He called the triptych *Prelude, Fugue, Postlude*, and it is one of the most powerful, if alas one of the most widely neglected, of his orchestral works. Ernest Ansermet took a great interest in it, and Honegger wrote him on 22 June:

> I'm delighted by your wish to introduce the Americans to the *Prelude, Fugue, Postlude* that I've just taken from *Amphion*. I think it will stand up fairly well as an entity. It lasts thirteen minutes and could be used as a program opener.
>
> I'm also very pleased to know that you're still interested in that old *Horace victorieux*, of which you gave the first performance in Lausanne, twenty-seven years ago, alas! But we don't give a damn about that—we're as young as ever, whatever fools may say. I've been following your great success in America and I'm absolutely delighted. I was intending to send you postcards from Mexico, but I'm afraid my doctor was dogmatic: "Mexico 6000 feet . . . you dead."

From now on Honegger began to receive honors—which he would always accept with his usual detachment and modesty. He wrote to Paul Sacher on 4 July, after being given a doctorate *honoris causa* from the University of Zurich:

> At the same time, I had a letter from Jaujard telling me that my buttonhole had lost its virginity and that I had been elevated to the rank of Officer of

the Legion of Honor (not bad for an ordinary third-class Fusilier). So, thanks to my great age, I'm entering the era of honors and distinctions.

Honegger then spent a month in Ireland, from 15 July to 15 August, with Vaura, Pascale, and the Sachers, twenty-one years after his previous visit with Werner Reinhart and René Morax. This holiday in peaceful countryside and in the company of those dear to him seems to have had a real therapeutic effect. Almost as soon as he got back to Paris, he began the *Concerto da camera* for Elizabeth Sprague Coolidge and completed the first movement at great speed, before the month was even over. The beautiful Andante was written in September, interrupted only by a brief trip to the festival of Besançon, where *La Danse des morts* was given on the 13th.

Meanwhile, *Jeanne d'Arc au bûcher* was repeated in Buenos Aires during September and October and the *Symphonie liturgique* was played on French Radio on 30 September. Paul Sacher wrote again to ask about progress on the *Concerto da camera* and passed on a request from Heinrich Strobel for Honegger to conduct a concert of his own works in Baden-Baden. Sacher urged him to accept because he knew the orchestra to be excellent, having been formed and trained by Hans Rosbaud. Honegger replied on 17 October, saying he was happy to accept the offer from the Südwestfunk radio network, and the concert duly took place on 29 May 1949.

Honegger went on to say: "I've started the concerto. I've finished two movements and am working on the third," and that he had been burgled, losing all his suits and coats—a significant loss at a time of shortage. "Here," he continued, "burglary is becoming a national institution. Whatever the government doesn't steal from you is entrusted to the care of these fly-by-nights." He was also working on incidental music for Albert Camus's *L'État de siège* (State of Siege), which Jean-Louis Barrault was putting on at the Théâtre Marigny.[2] Honegger was invited to Naples, Genoa, and Milan to conduct his music, while Charles Münch was playing the *Symphonie liturgique* with the French National Orchestra in the United States. Honegger had just been elected president of CISAC (International Confederation of Authors' and Composers' Societies), and on 28 October he finished the last movement of his *Concerto da camera*. He wrote Elizabeth Sprague Coolidge on the 29th: "I've just finished the little work I've been writing for you. . . . Will you give me permission to entrust the first European performance to my friend Sacher with the Musikkollegium of Zurich in May?"

This concerto was his first real creative effort since his heart attack. Proof that he had fully recovered his compositional gifts is offered in abundance by the sparkling naturalness of the outer movements, and by the touching seriousness of the central meditation, a gentler sister of the De profundis from the *Symphonie liturgique* and well worthy to be compared with the "Lamento" of *La Danse des morts*.

Honegger did not attend Ansermet's performance of the *Prelude, Fugue, Postlude* in Geneva on 3 November, but left on the 10th for Milan and then on to Genoa where, on the 16th and after seven rehearsals, he conducted "energetically and without fatigue"[3] a long program that included *Horace victorieux*, the *Symphonie liturgique*, *Pacific 2.3.1*, and *Chant de joie*. He then spent two days with his friend Ibert at the Villa Medici. It was from here that he wrote Sacher confirming that the *Concerto da camera* was finished and that Mrs. Coolidge was happy to have Sacher conduct the first European performance (in fact, the first anywhere) in May 1949.

Meanwhile, Honegger's tour continued, with concerts at the San Carlo Theater in Naples on the 22nd, at La Scala in Milan on the 26th, and at La Fenice in Venice on 5 December.

He was back in Paris by the 7th. On 20 November a collection of his articles and reviews for *Comoedia* was published by Éditions d'Ouchy in Lausanne under the provocative title *Incantation aux fossiles* (Incantation to the Fossils). We can find on every page evidence of Honegger's attractive personality, his absolute intellectual honesty, and his loyalty. One can also see how completely disinterested he was in praising his fellow-composers, whether they were insufficiently recognized talents of an earlier generation, like Enesco or Ropartz, or younger men, among whom Messiaen was a particular favorite.

The Honeggers spent Christmas Eve at May-en-Multien, at the country house of their faithful friends the Winters.

1949

Hardly had Honegger returned to his series of classes at the École normale de musique when he left for Prague on 12 January 1949. Even if his music had long been popular on the banks of the Vltava, it was the first time he himself had been to Czechoslovakia, which, after its long and glorious musical history, had fallen under the sway of Stalin's communists in February 1948. It was not as an interpreter of his music that he went, but as a guest at the famous cultural congress that would lay down Zhdanov's social-realist doctrines as official policy for all adherents of "progress."

How could Honegger have made such a mistake? No doubt through naiveté and idealism. At first sight, he too believed in the idea of music for the masses, free of high-flown jargon, stifling coteries, and ivory towers; he too maintained that, to survive, music would have to change and become "simple and straightforward." Obviously, it was the Honegger of *Jeunesse*, of the "social" compositions written at the time of the Popular Front, that the Marxist ideologues were trying to capture for their cause.

Honegger had failed to see the trap. But he was swiftly brought to his senses by the party line and the suffocating absence of creative freedom within the Stalinist regime. It is true that his music would remain widely played and recorded in the Eastern bloc, and that he would soon return to Prague for one last time as composer and conductor. But it was made very clear to him that they had no patience for his scruples or his displays of emotion, and that he was merely a bourgeois. He left in a rage, never to return. Happily, though, party politicians, ideologues, and functionaries were only a minority, and the audiences remained faithful to him. To this day Prague has remained one of the strongest bastions of Honegger's music in the world, just as in the Russian states themselves he has always had his enthusiastic champions.

His brief stay in Prague included a meeting with Czech composers on 18 January as well as several concerts, including one by the Czech Philharmonic Orchestra on the 20th. He did not, of course, see his friend Martinů, who had chosen exile rather than live under Stalinism, as he had when faced with Hitler in 1938; he would die without seeing his homeland again. On 22 January Honegger was back in Paris, just in time for the concert broadcast on the 24th from the Salle Gaveau, in which Paul Sacher conducted the *Symphonie liturgique* and then Willy Burkhard's magnificent oratorio *Das Gesicht Jesajas* (The Vision of Isaiah)—the latter to a Paris audience that remained totally impassive.

On 4 February a letter from Paul Sacher sounded a warning shot: a Swiss newspaper attacked Honegger violently for having visited Prague and, as all totalitarian regimes used the names of visiting artists as publicity, Sacher himself had decided not to go there, and indeed never did cross the "Iron Curtain."

After two further seminars at the École normale on 31 January and 7 February, the composer received invitations from the two ends of Europe. He conducted in Copenhagen on 17 February and Göteborg on the 22nd, and then traveled to Barcelona for a concert on 9 March at the Teatro de la Comedia with the Orfeu Català. These exhausting sessions, duly reported in a letter to Paul Sacher of 7 March, were hardly suitable for someone nursing his health. It is hard to believe that Honegger did not realize he would have to pay the cost, sooner and more dearly than he imagined.

On 14 March he gave another seminar, and the same evening in Paris a Dutch orchestra played the *Symphony for Strings*. On the 17th Sacher wrote to tell him that the *Symphonie liturgique* had been a triumphant success in Frankfurt, and went on to ask anxiously whether the *Concerto da camera* had been performed yet.

After conducting three staged performances of *Jeanne d'Arc au bûcher* in Rome (on 16, 20, and 23 April at the Opera), Honegger was present at the first performance of the *Concerto da camera* on 6 May in Zurich with André Jaunet (flute) and Marcel Saillet (English horn) as soloists, and the Collegium Musicum conducted by Paul Sacher.

The concert Honegger conducted during the famous Prague Spring Festival on 22 May included *Le Chant de Nigamon*, the *Concertino for piano and orchestra* (with Vaura), the *Fourth Symphony*, and *Judith*. We can see from this vast program that he was still not taking life easy. This concert was followed by a meeting with Czech composers the next day.

On 24 May Arthur and Vaura left Prague for Stuttgart, from where a special train took them to Ravensburg for an official reception at the headquarters of the French occupying forces, and then on to Baden-Baden where, on the 24th, Honegger conducted the orchestra of the Südwestfunk, of which Hans Rosbaud was the chief conductor. The concert included *Prelude, Fugue, Postlude, Schwyzer Fäschttag*, the concertino (with Vaura), *Horace victorieux, Sérénade à Angélique*, and *Pacific 2.3.1*. The next day they were in Frankfurt, where the performance of *Jeanne d'Arc* was followed by a supper given by the Swiss consul. Finally, they both returned to Paris on the 31st and Honegger resumed his seminars the next day.

It was Heinrich Strobel, who was the director of Baden-Baden Radio under the aegis of the French Occupying Forces in Germany, who set up this ambitious project, giving it a large-scale, official profile and proving his credentials as a Francophile—even if the object of his attentions was Swiss! For all Strobel's personal interest in the tour's success, the Honeggers were delighted to be welcomed so warmly. On 25 May, a telegram from Paul Sacher announced that their next musical reunion would be in Vienna where, on 23 June, he would conduct *Prelude, Fugue, Postlude, Horace victorieux*, the *Concertino for piano and orchestra*, the *Fourth Symphony*, and *Pacific 2.3.1*.

Meanwhile, Honegger continued to lead a full life. He met with Georges Enesco at Hilda Gélis-Didot's house on 8 June and then went immediately to Lausanne for the rehearsals under Ernest Ansermet of an important new work, *Saint François d'Assise* (Saint Francis of Assisi). This must have been written the previous autumn, since there seems no way the composer's hectic schedule in the early months of 1949 could have left him time to write such a long work. It was the third and last of his radio collaborations with William Aguet; it is also the largest and musically the finest. The recording, with the Carlo Boller Choir and the Suisse Romande Orchestra, took place at Lausanne Radio on 11 June, and the work earned its creators the Grand Prix of Swiss Radio.

Vaura and Arthur were in Vienna as arranged for the concert conducted by Paul Sacher on the 23rd and were back in Paris by the 25th. Arthur missed the delayed premiere of *La Naissance des couleurs* at the Opera on the 22nd, but attended the second and last performance on the 29th. Unfortunately, like many of Honegger's ballets, it suffered from a production and choreography that were very far from ideal.

Honegger's teaching commitments for the session ended with a final seminar on 29 June, followed by two days on a jury. On the 30th, the Sachers arrived in Paris.

On 3 July Honegger wrote to thank Ansermet for his interpretation of *Saint François*, adding with his usual modesty: "Thanks to you I got a favorable impression of my work. This may be an illusion, but I'm grateful to you for having created it." He also mentions another radio work, this time for French Radio:

> I am in fact intending to write incidental music for a radio production of *Guillaumet*. But I haven't started it yet and it won't be a symphonic work, just an illustration of various parts of the text. So it won't be suitable for concert performance.

This was a commission from the Studio d'Essai, the experimental section of French Radio, called *Marche contre la Mort* (March Against Death), on a text by Saint-Exupéry written in memory of the pilot Henri Guillaumet, "the eagle of the Andes." No trace survives of the score or of any performance of it, but it is listed in the composer's manuscript catalog.

Arthur and Vaura spent 7 to 10 July with Georges Enesco, then Honegger served as a member of the final Conservatory panel on the 11th. He saw Paul and Maja Sacher the same day. On the 24th he left for the Aix-en-Provence Festival, where *Prelude, Fugue, Postlude* was on the following day's program. He stayed in the area until some time in the middle of August, and on 15 August took part in a public discussion about "Mediterranean Music,"[4] organized as part of the Festival. From the 22nd to the 26th he was in Switzerland for a concert on Zurich Radio. After a brief stay in Paris, he traveled to the Besançon Festival on 5 September. Here he took on the difficult task of trying to gain a sympathetic hearing for *Cris du monde*, the most controversial of his large-scale works and for that reason the closest to his heart. But the concert on 7 September showed that this implacable work was still too much for the public to accept.

On 10 September Arthur rejoined Vaura at Le Tréport (on the French shore of the English Channel) and seems finally to have allowed himself some respite. At any rate the next indication that he had returned to Paris was not until 23 October, when he and Vaura had dinner with the critic Jacques Feschotte. Also present was the doyen of French music, Guy Ropartz, whose liking and admiration for Honegger was reciprocated. The next day Honegger resumed his teaching at the École normale de musique. On 4 November he recorded for French Radio an interview about Gabriel Fauré, another great composer whom he had adored since his youth; it marked the twenty-fifth anniversary of Fauré's death.

On 27 November Honegger conducted *Cris du monde* at the Colonne Concerts, and again the audience was divided. He could not know—and nor could anyone else—that, six years to the day before his death, he had conducted a public concert for the last time. He would make a recording of *Le Roi David* on disc in October 1951, but that was in a studio. He had abused his strength, and his heart now began to take its revenge.

On 3 December the first public performance of *Saint François d'Assise* took place at Lausanne Radio, with William Aguet himself, Hugues Cuénod, the Tour-de-Peilz Choir, and the Suisse Romande Orchestra conducted by Ernest Ansermet. But Honegger was in Paris that day, teaching at the École normale; he would give another session on 19 December. He was in Strasbourg on the 7th, when Fritz Münch celebrated the twenty-fifth anniversary of his Saint-Guillaume Choir by conducting *La Danse des morts* (its first performance in Strasbourg) and *Le Roi David*. During the final weeks of 1949, Honegger worked again on a play by Paul Claudel, a radio adaptation of *Tête d'Or* (Head of Gold), intended for French Radio. This quite considerable score would be finished in Zurich in early January. The Honegger family once again followed their pattern of spending the end of the year at the Schönenberg. The composer spent three whole months in Switzerland.

1950

The year 1950 can be divided into two unequal parts. The first and longer spell was fairly uneventful, while the second, from August onward, saw the final kindling of Honegger's creative flame. The first and most important result of this latter stage was his *Fifth Symphony*, entitled *Di Tre Re*. The last of his products in the genre, it was completed by the end of the year.

Two works that we cannot precisely date were composed in the early months of the year. *De la musique* is described in Honegger's manuscript catalog as a "little ballet for the Thomson Houston company"; the score has disappeared and there is no record of any performance. The other work was the music for René Lucot's documentary film *Bourdelle*.

Vaura returned to Paris on 6 January for her teaching and so was alone in attending the recording of the music for *Tête d'Or* at French Radio on the 16th. On the 26th she and Pascale went back to Basel for the first performance there of the *Concerto da camera* under Paul Sacher on the 27th. Sacher also conducted *Jeanne d'Arc au bûcher* for Bavarian Radio on 7 February, while Paris had its first chance to hear *Deliciae basilienses* on the 25th.

Honegger was not present at either of these two occasions because his health had again deteriorated, as might have been foreseen after his crazy workload of the preceding year. He did not return to Paris until 22 March. At the same time as Ernest Ansermet and the Philharmonic Orchestra were preparing for the first English performance of the *Concerto da camera* on 10 April, two letters bear witness to the precarious state of Honegger's health. On 6 April he wrote to Wolfgang Steinecke, the director of the famous summer courses at Darmstadt, declining his invitation to teach there in July; he would again refuse the following year. And he sent Paul Sacher the result of a new electrocardiogram: "hypertrophy of the right ventricle, but no trace now of the thrombosis. . . . Apologies for these long, boring reports on the condition of this old, worn-out composer."[5]

Even so, he intended to go and conduct in Algiers and Tunis before staying in Zurich at the beginning of June. But this tour would not take place, and Vaura crossed out in her diary the program already agreed for the "Honegger Festival" in Tunis on 20 May, which consisted of *Le Chant de Nigamon*, *Schwyzer Fäschttag*, *Pacific 2.3.1*, *Prelude, Fugue, Postlude*, and the *Symphonie liturgique*. On 12 April, Paul Sacher wrote to say he was going to conduct this last work in Berlin.

On 19 May Honegger wrote the speech he was going to make for the fiftieth anniversary of the Association of Swiss Composers. In a letter of 22 May to Maja Sacher, announcing his arrival at the Schönenberg for Pentecost (the 27th), he described a number of his medical examinations and ended by saying: "Your old retired composer is waiting with a touch of skepticism for his breath to return." Allusions of this sort would become ever more frequent in his letters.

Vaura and Arthur were both at an important ballet evening in Zurich on 2 June, consisting of *Le Cantique des cantiques*, *La Danse des morts*, and "The Dance

Before the Ark" from *Le Roi David*. On the 4th they were both at the Fluh, where they were probably seeing their old friend Werner Reinhart for the last time.

According to Vaura's diary, it was in July, after a short trip to Italy, that Honegger finished recording the series of interviews with Bernard Gavoty on French Radio, which would be the basis the following year for the well-known book *Je suis compositeur* (I Am a Composer). The French Radio archives give September–October as the date, but this must have been the date when the interviews were edited, or possibly broadcast. The book consists of bitter, disillusioned musings on the lot of the creative artist, and their pessimism has been attributed to the author's failing health. In fact, one can find traces of it already in *Cris du monde*, in the notorious article "Pour prendre congé" of February 1932, and, disguised by irony and humor, in many of his articles for *Comoedia*.

In July Honegger went to the Aix-en-Provence Festival, as he had the year before. Among the works he heard were Poulenc's new *Piano Concerto* (the famous "cheeky" concerto [*concerto en casquette*]) on 24 July, with the composer as soloist and Charles Münch conducting, and, the day after, the first performance in France of Messiaen's enormous *Turangalîla Symphony*, to which he gave an immediate response in a brief interview now in the French Radio archives.

Honegger returned to Paris on 29 July and, although at first glance August might appear to have been empty, by 5 September he had completed the first movement of his new *Fifth Symphony*, subtitled *Di Tre Re*. He had said nothing about it to Sacher when they had dinner together at Véfour's on 31 August. But one day, probably in October, his friend and biographer Marcel Delannoy went to see him and found the work in progress.

> Just as I came through the door, I saw a sketch, a musical one, on the desk. "Ah!" I said. "Mmm," said he, "you know the story, I've no idea if it's true, of Berlioz being inspired by Sylphs during the night? Well, that's rather what's just happened to me. An idea, then another one to match the first." "And?" "Well, maybe a *Fifth Symphony*. But as you know, with me, working it out's a slow, difficult business. Anyway, I'd rather you didn't say anything about it in your book."[6]

Bernard Gavoty gives us plenty of details about this new work, and it does seem to have been the product of sleepless nights caused by increasingly severe problems with his breathing. He completed the second movement of the symphony on 1 October, but his duties as president of CISAC forced him to interrupt his work in order to attend its biennial congress. That year the congress took place in Madrid. The Honeggers left Paris on 3 October, with a bullfight among the welcoming festivities on the 5th. Honegger presided bravely over all the working sessions, but on the 15th he and Vaura returned to Paris, where his symphony was waiting for him. Vaura was left behind to represent the family for the sightseeing part of the trip in Seville.

The return of Honegger's creative appetite did not remain a secret for long. On 27 October Paul Sacher passed on a commission from the Zurich Tonhalle to mark the six-hundredth anniversary of that city's entry into the

Swiss confederation. Sacher had managed to extract 5000 Swiss francs from the Zurich authorities instead of the 2000 originally envisaged. And, as Honegger was accepting commissions once more, Sacher suggested he write something either for his sixtieth birthday concert in March 1952, or for the 1951–1952 season, which would be the twenty-fifth anniversary of the Basel Chamber Orchestra. It could be either a fifteen- to twenty-minute work for orchestra alone, or a half-hour one with chorus as well. The fee would be 5000 francs for the first, 10,000 for the second.

Work on the new symphony proceeded apace. On 28 October Honegger finished orchestrating the first movement, on 10 November he finished composing the Finale, on the 23rd orchestrating the second movement, and on 3 December orchestrating the Finale. The whole work had thus been composed in four months. As soon as it was done, Honegger started on a more modest piece, the second movement of his final so-called insomnia trilogy, the *Suite archaïque* (Archaic Suite), which had been commissioned by the Louisville Orchestra. He began with the third of the four planned movements, then going on to the first. He completed this on 17 December.

The next day came the great occasion that had been eagerly anticipated for fifteen years: the entry of *Jeanne d'Arc au bûcher* into the Paris Opera's repertory. This masterpiece received a production worthy of it: Claude Nollier was a wonderful Joan, Jean Vilar, and later Henri Doublier, were her equals as Brother Dominic, the producer was Jean Doat, the designer Yves Bonnat, the choreographer Serge Lifar, and the conductor Louis Fourestier. The production was revived on 22 December and would have more than fifty performances until Easter 1953. It then went on tour to Rouen, Vichy, and Metz, and after that to Rio de Janeiro and Buenos Aires. It was a belated but splendid justification of the work's value, and brought to a triumphant end this year in which Honegger's creative powers were miraculously restored. Alas, the miracle would not last.

1951

The new year of 1951 continued the mood of energy and optimism that closed out the previous one, with Honegger working on the second and fourth movements of the *Suite archaïque* and completing it on 15 January. But, despite his still poor health, he was already thinking of the next work, for the Zurich Tonhalle. In a letter to Paul Sacher of 13 January, Honegger mentioned the work he had nearly finished and the one he was planning, and asked his friend for technical advice—over Jass, the Swiss version of pinochle, which he was playing furiously with Vaura and Pascale.

Four days later, on the 17th, came another letter, this time deeply pessimistic and evidence of further deterioration in his health:

I was very sad not to be able to be at your dinner on 20 December, but I really felt so rotten, bed was the only place for me. Vaura must have told you how I nearly threw up my innards and what's left of my lungs all over President [Vincent] Auriol. He's a very nice man and talks far more intelligently about music than some people who aren't presidents of the Republic.

He had to stay in bed, and then in his bedroom, but he took advantage of this enforced imprisonment to finish the *Suite archaïque*, which he described in some detail,

> Rather overconfidently, I'm already thinking about the piece for the Tonhalle and I think perhaps I'll be able to manage it. I've also got a little book to write and I'm looking for a text for a "choral work dedicated to the Basel Chamber Choir." After that, I shall consider my activity at an end and will wait patiently until the idiocy of those who have taken upon themselves the task of leading nations puts a full stop to our civilization, and probably to our existence at the same time.

All through the last years of his life Honegger was haunted by the vision of a nuclear apocalypse, although he used to say he was less afraid of the bomb than of "the terrifying stupidity of mankind." It is this anxiety that lies beneath the surface of the *Symphonie liturgique* as well as of the *Fifth Symphony* and of the forthcoming *Monopartita*.

On 22 February Honegger for a second time refused an invitation to teach the summer course in Darmstadt. He wrote the director Wolfgang Steinecke as follows: "Confined to my bedroom for more than two months now after a congestion of the lungs, following on a pulmonary embolism." Even so, Honegger would give several more sessions at the École normale (his diary notes the dates of 26 February, 12 and 19 March, and 2 April).

On 28 February Robert Whitney gave the first performance of the *Suite archaïque* with his Louisville Orchestra. On 2 March the irrepressible *Le Roi David* was given again at the Pasdeloup Concerts in Paris, and on the 9th Charles Münch gave the first American performance of the *Fifth Symphony* in Boston. The work was written for the Koussevitzky Music Foundation in memory of Nathalie Koussevitzky. The next day, Münch wrote the composer a heartfelt letter:

> My dear Arthur,
> And so your most recent, lovely child has seen the light of day. I can't get over the fact that I was the one who was able to bring it to life for the first time. How can I thank you, or express to you my emotion and gratitude? Once again, thanks to you, all the miseries, anxieties, efforts, and sacrifices of a troubled existence find a recompense that provides consolation for everything and gives it all meaning. I'm not good at putting these things into words and it's almost impertinent of me to write to you, but your music moves me, and the mystery that surrounds it. I have a lump in my throat and tears in my eyes.
> Another seven weeks and I'll be able to come back to Paris. And if you like, I'll come and see you again and sit with you, even if I don't say anything important—certainly nothing very intelligent. On Monday, *Di Tre*

Re will be heard in Hartford, on Tuesday in New Haven, on Wednesday in New York, on Friday in Brooklyn, and on Saturday for a second time in New York. The reviews in general have been excellent. I take the liberty of sending you a sample. . . . For ever, Ch.

But this composer, who, from a body in ruins, could draw sonorous and spiritual substance enough to provoke tears, was already well on the way to finishing his next work. On 15 March he wrote a long letter to Maja Sacher. He had just finished the piece, with the orchestration still to do, but he was still looking for a title. "I started out on a quite different version that was beyond my capabilities. A touch of megalomania, when I was aiming to play my little Johann Sebastian Bach. So the title *Ricercare* no longer fits."

He went on to talk about the first and subsequent performances of the *Fifth Symphony* in America, telling her that Koussevitzky would be playing it in Paris in May[7] and Münch again at the Strasbourg Festival. He also mentioned the "successful" first performance of the *Suite archaïque* in Louisville, and went on:

No doubt you'll think I'm getting a bit uppity, but I want to write for the Chamber Choir as though I were still composing something just for my own convenience. But I'd still like to do it. I thought perhaps a secular oratorio like *Cris du monde*, but on a more lighthearted subject and with a certain logic in the way it develops. It's quite hard to find.

But this idea of a secular oratorio never came to anything. After a very long delay due to illness, Honegger could manage only a reworking of various fragments from his unfinished *Selzach Passion*, in the form of his *Une Cantate de Noël*. It would prove to be his musical and spiritual testament.

On 26 March he finished orchestrating the work for the Zurich Tonhalle. He decided to call it *Monopartita*, because its various contrasted episodes follow on one another so as to form a single entity. In the course of eight months he had completed his last great orchestral trilogy. There are profound affinities between the three works, and their spare, bitter grandeur and concise, monumental form present all the characteristics of a late style—one that would not be taken further. It is sad that the wide popularity of the *Fifth Symphony* should have left its two more modest companions in the shade, since they are its equal in quality. The *Monopartita*, especially, must be classed as one of his unacknowledged masterpieces.

In a letter dated 8 May, Ernest Ansermet asked about the new symphony, which he wanted to put into his Geneva program the following winter, inquiring about how long it was and wanting to see the score. This was still being engraved, but Honegger promised to send it soon, replying in a letter of 12 May: "I've been in poor shape from February through November, but now things are going much better and I've gone back to work with a certain effrontery."

While *Jeanne d'Arc au bûcher* was being revived at the Paris Opera on 14 April and the Capelle Quartet was playing the *String Quartet No. 3* at the École normale on the 27th, Paul Sacher was getting to know the new works. He was enthusiastic:

Many thanks for the scores of both the *Suite archaïque* and the *Fifth Symphony*. You've never written anything more beautiful than these two works and I hope to be able to perform them soon and as often as possible! The symphony is really magnificent, and I like the suite just as much. If the oratorio you want to write for us turns out to be a major masterpiece like these two (and I have no doubt it will), then its first performance will provide the worthiest possible means of celebrating your sixtieth birthday and our twenty-fifth anniversary.[8]

On 7 May Charles Münch conducted the first European performance of the *Fifth Symphony* in a concert broadcast by the French National Orchestra in Paris. The same day, José Bruyr sent his congratulations to Honegger for a work that was, as he so rightly said, so "simple, straightforward, moving, and strong." On the 9th the Honeggers had lunch with Paul Claudel, and the same evening Pierre Fournier played the *Cello Sonata*.

On 3 June, there was another performance of *Jeanne d'Arc au bûcher* at the Opera, and now Honegger set to work on his last two film scores. First, in June, he collaborated with Tibor Harsanyi and Arthur Hoérée on George Rony's documentary *La Tour de Babel* (The Tower of Babel). This would have only a brief public career because it made use of classified military information. Then, on 18 July, Honegger finished a score to go with a film by André Gillet about Paul Claudel.

Arthur, Vaura, and Pascale went to Zurich for the first performance of the *Monopartita* on 12 June, with Hans Rosbaud conducting the orchestra of the Tonhalle. The work's fierce, untrammeled energy was too much for some of the more conservative local critics, and it has to be said that it was not the sort of festive offering the commission might have been expected to yield. On the 25th Honegger came to the Strasbourg Festival from the Schönenberg and was present at the triumph of the *Fifth Symphony* under Charles Münch's inspired conducting. This was really the first performance in France, since the Paris concert on 7 May was only a broadcast, and the symphony went on to worldwide success. Honegger then returned to Paris and attended a meeting of the École normale jury on the 27th.

In July 1951 *Je suis compositeur* reached the bookstores. Honegger spent the whole month in Paris, where a letter from Paul Sacher dated 5 July reached him asking about the oratorio the composer had in mind:

Will you now be using Strobel's text, or will you be satisfied with the Easter Cantata? I'm sure you know Saint-Exupéry's *La Citadelle*. A friend recently mentioned to me that he thought parts of it would lend themselves particularly well to a musical setting.

This was the first mention of a projected Easter Cantata, for which it was hoped that Claudel would write the words, and which was discussed at length until illness forced Honegger to abandon the idea. But we have found no other allusion to a libretto by Heinrich Strobel. As for Saint-Exupéry's *La Citadelle*, we may note that in 1957–1958 Martinů would use it as the source of the text for the first two movements of his last great orchestral work, the triptych *Paraboles*, written for Charles Münch.

On 12 July Ernest Ansermet wrote to Honegger at length about the *Fifth Symphony*, subjecting it to his usual sharp, analytical insight:

> I must congratulate you, and that's why I felt I had to write. At Münch's rehearsal I was sure your second movement was full of contrapuntal secrets, but now that I've seen and made certain of everything, I must tell you how astounded I am. This movement is a contrapuntal masterpiece worthy of the Renaissance masters. But at heart it could be taken as a joke at the expense of twelve-tone composers—a way of saying to them (and all the more pointedly since it doesn't give the impression of being anything much): "You're always doing it to us, and we too, we know how to write imitations in crab motion. But we write music at the same time."
>
> I must confess to you, your first movement gives me food for thought. I can quite see the point of a heterophony of lines, but I'm not yet convinced that this sort of heterophony of chords is viable, even though there's no denying it makes an effect. But I'm always suspicious of effect—that scoundrel Meyerbeer was always good at it. As for the third movement, the most impressive thing for me is the "form"; and the whole symphony, from the point of view of form, is extraordinary. I've done no more than glance at the *Monopartita*. But it's from the same vintage! I hope all that will speed your recovery. I think about you all the time.
>
> Yours most affectionately, E. Ansermet.

On 10 July *Le Roi David* was given in Lyon-Fourvière with three hundred performers, while in Paris Honegger was present for the projection of the film about Claudel. He finished the music for it the following week, on the 18th, on the day Ansermet conducted the *Fifth Symphony* in Geneva as part of a Wednesday concert on Sottens Radio.

On 20 July Jean-Louis Barrault approached Honegger for some new incidental music for Alfred de Musset's *On ne badine pas avec l'amour* (Do Not Trifle With Love), which he was going to put on at the Théâtre Marigny. The extremely detailed outline that he enclosed suggests that this stage score would have been on a large scale. Unfortunately, it has not so far been found. The music for the film *Paul Claudel* was recorded on 24 July, and on the 27th and 28th Ansermet conducted a successful performance of the *Fifth Symphony* at the Aix-en-Provence Festival. At the end of the month Honegger left his wife and daughter to spend the whole of August taking in the waters at Bagnoles-de-l'Orne. On 13 August a telegram arrived from Paul Sacher asking what title he wanted for the new cantata. But Honegger had not yet thought of one and suggested that he simply put "Cantata."

On 29 August 1951 Werner Reinhart died suddenly at age sixty-seven. With the passing of the "man with the hands of gold" came the end of an era. René Morax paid him a suitably poetic homage:

> Like the Medicis, the great Merchant Princes,
> You lavished on Art the treasures of a Sage of Old.

In a letter of 29 September to Sacher, who was about to visit Paris, Honegger said he had arranged a meeting with Olivier Messiaen, and emphasized how shaken he was by Reinhart's death.

During the first three days of October, Honegger mounted the conductor's rostrum for the last time to record *Le Roi David*. On 3 October Ansermet conducted the *Fifth Symphony* at a subscription concert in the Victoria Hall in Geneva. He confirmed to the composer that the work had made a big impact on the audience and on the critics, but at the same time he suggested that the central movement might go at a faster speed than the one marked on the score (eighth note 132 to 138, instead of 126), which he thought would give it "a certain bite—like scorpions."[9] His instinct seems to have been right, since most later conductors have agreed with him. On 7 October the same symphony had a triumph under Hans Rosbaud at the Contemporary Music Festival at Donaueschingen. All the musicians present sent Honegger a joint letter, with a particularly affectionate note from Messiaen: "As always, you're the strongest of us all." We should note that on 10 September of the previous year, Donaueschingen had included in its first postwar season the first performance in Germany of the *Concerto da camera*.

Honegger gave the first two seminars of the season at the École normale on 13 and 20 October, and on the 18th the film *Paul Claudel* had its press showing at the Studio des Champs-Élysées. Honegger then left Paris for Italy to sit on the jury for an opera composers' competition with Giorgio Federico Ghedini at La Scala in Milan. There he had a letter from Sacher saying the *Fifth Symphony* had been a great success under his baton in Frankfurt and telling him of the concerts planned for his sixtieth birthday. They would be given on 7 March in Basel and on the 14th in Zurich. Sacher also expressed the hope that the birthday itself, 10 March, might be celebrated at the Schönenberg, even though he knew that Honegger would also have a concert in his honor that day in Paris.[10]

Honegger's reply, sent from Milan on 28 October, shows him in happy, even deliriously high spirits. Sacher had sent him a questionnaire about the soloists in *Cris du monde*, which would be the climax of the birthday concert in Basel—and one needs to read the exchange in its original German to get the full flavor. Sacher: "Ich denke an Rehfuss oder Ochsenbein" (I'm thinking of Rehfuss or Ochsenbein) [two singers whose names mean "deer's foot" and "ox's leg"]. Honegger's reply reads: "Oder Kalbshaxe, Osso Buco, oder Stierenschenkel, Rinderknie, du hast ja eine ganze Metzgerei aufgemacht!" (Or Knuckle of Veal, Osso Buco, Bull's Thigh, Cow's Knee, that gives you a whole butcher's stall!). Ghedini added a postscript: "Honegger è sempre fresco come una rosellina di maggio, io un po meno (perchè lui è piu virtuoso di me!)" (Honegger is always fresh as a rose in May, I rather less so—because he's more virtuous than I am!).[11]

Honegger returned to Paris on 7 November, and so was not able to attend the first night of the film on Bourdelle for which he had written the music.

Three works of varying importance occupied Honegger during November and December. The first was a short toccata for orchestra intended as an overture for a joint work called *La Guirlande de Campra* (The Garland of Campra), which would be played as a homage to the great composer from Aix-en-Provence at the next festival there. The other contributors were Daniel-Lesur, Roland-Manuel, Germaine Tailleferre, Francis Poulenc, Henri Sauguet, and Georges Auric. Then came the incidental music for Jean-Louis Barrault's production of *On ne badine pas avec l'amour*, which would have its opening night at the Théâtre Marigny on 12 December. And the final work was Honegger's last radio score, *La Rédemption de François Villon*, on words by José Bruyr, which was put out by French Radio for the first time on 30 December.

On 21 November Honegger wrote at length to Paul Sacher about the Easter Cantata. Claudel had warned him:

> You must treat me warily. Francis Jammes used to say: "If you ask Claudel for a bunch of flowers, he brings you a virgin forest." . . . The text will be in three parts: Morning, Midday, and Evening. Almost entirely in Latin, which certainly doesn't bother me. This morning I received an outline of Part I. I told him I was "hoping" still to be able to write this work with which to finish my career, but I warned him that I should need time, because I can't work fast any more and I should also have to focus my energies in order to produce something worthwhile.

On 24 November he wrote to Claudel along the same lines:

> I'm now going to focus on this text and do my best to realize your intentions. It may take some time, so don't blame me, but I want you to be satisfied with this score and for me to give up composing afterward without regret. As always, your conception of the piece is novel and grand.

On 26 November Paul Sacher wrote Honegger that he had just conducted the *Suite archaïque* at Winterthur and that in Munich he had had a huge success with the *Fifth Symphony*. On the 30th Honegger wrote about the cantata: "Claudel has sent me his completed text. I must think about how to tackle it, if it's still within my powers."

On 1 December Igor Markevitch wrote him after conducting a highly successful performance of the *Fifth Symphony* in Stockholm. It was the first Honegger work Markevitch had ever conducted, but now he was intending to perform it ten times in Israel, then give the first performance in Rome on 27 February 1952, then in Germany, and so on.

Arthur and Vaura spent a few days in Zurich, where *Jeanne d'Arc au bûcher* was revived on 8 December.

The year ended with a slightly gruesome letter to Sacher:

> I'm busy at the moment casting *Antigone*, which is going to be revived with *Jeanne d'Arc* at the Opera at the beginning of February, and also with *Oedipus* at the Comédie-Française. After that I shall come and take refuge at the Schönenberg, which will be nearer and more convenient for the crematorium.[12]

1952

The *Oedipus* mentioned by Honegger was his last piece of incidental music, for Thierry Maulnier's translation of Sophocles's *Oedipus Rex*. He finished it in April of 1952. It should not be confused with his incidental music for André Obey's adaptation of the same play, which dates from 1947.

On 5 January 1952 Honegger resumed his seminars at the École normale, which he would continue as best he could, with some interruptions, until the summer of 1953. In a letter to Maja Sacher, dated simply "Saturday," he thanked her for the present of yet another fine bookshelf, and he ended the letter with one of those rather sour, ironical observations that his state of health so often provoked: "I'm still moldering in bed, but as soon as I'm up I'll start sorting out the books and I hope everything will be in order for the day of my funeral."

From the 21st to the 28th, Arthur and Vaura were again in Basel, this time for the twenty-fifth anniversary of the Chamber Choir, with concerts on the 24th and 25th and a banquet on the 26th. But the cantata would not be finished for some time yet, and then not in the form planned with Claudel. On 1 February the Honeggers returned to Paris and went to hear *La Danse des morts* in a concert given by the students of the Conservatory. Paul Sacher arrived to conduct the commercial recording of the *Suite archaïque* and the *Monopartita* at the Théâtre des Champs-Élysées, and on the 8th the revival of *Antigone* took place at the Opera, inevitably eclipsed, to Honegger's great chagrin, by *Jeanne d'Arc au bûcher*, which brought the evening to an end.

The musical events to mark Honegger's sixtieth birthday were now close at hand. On 27 and 28 February, Vaura's diary mentions a reunion of "Arthur's friends," but the birthday itself would be celebrated in Switzerland. After another performance of *Antigone* and *Jeanne d'Arc* at the Opera on the 29th, the Honeggers left for Zurich on 5 March. On the 7th Paul Sacher conducted the Collegium Musicum there in a program that included the *Suite archaïque*, the *Concerto da camera*, the *Concertino for piano and orchestra* (with Vaura), and the *Symphony for Strings*. On the 9th everyone returned to Basel, and Honegger's birthday on the 10th was indeed celebrated at the Schönenberg, as Sacher had hoped. Here preparations were in hand for a second concert on 14 March, and certainly a more important one for Honegger, containing as it did the *Fifth Symphony* and *Cris du monde*. Meanwhile in Paris, the birthday itself was marked by a concert given by the French National Orchestra, conducted by Ernest Bour. Once again *Cris du monde* was on the program, this time preceded by *Pacific 2.3.1* and *Prelude, Fugue, Postlude*. On the 17th Honegger was in Zurich with his family, while Vaura made a quick journey back to Paris. But she was back with her husband just above Montreux on the 20th. A deterioration in Arthur's health meant he had to go into a clinic above Territet and only a step away from Glion, at Val-Mont where Milhaud had stayed in 1924.

For four and a half years, Honegger had enjoyed the benefit of a precarious and often questionable improvement in his health. But he had refused to face the facts and had led an exhausting and, for him, more or less "normal" life. Now that his final harvest of works was almost entirely gathered in, the result was total exhaustion. In view of the all-too-frequent little warning symptoms and the outbreaks of black humor in his letters, this came as no great surprise.

We now come to the last, saddest, and most depressing chapter in Honegger's story. In the years of his health and strength, he had tasted the fruits of existence to the fullest; now he would have the leisure to experience Turenne's ideal of having some years between his life and his death. But not in the way the writer had in mind. Bernard Gavoty remembered Honegger often saying "I'm already living the life of the dead," and life from here on would play a cruel game of cat-and-mouse with him—in which Honegger, with no chance of escape, was subject to life's whims and its offerings of false hope. Not that the tally of his works was quite complete. *Une Cantate de Noël* was still to come and there were three and a half years of decline left to him. But from the time of his first visit to the clinic, Honegger would lead the life of a serious invalid, increasingly in pain. Although he would continue to provide accounts of his happier moments, their tone became more and more pathetic. From now on, news of his health would take the place of new scores.

NINE

Epilogue: Life's Setting Sun

The title of this final chapter—"La décroissance crépusculaire" (crepuscular decrease) in the original French—is taken from Victor Hugo's *Les Misérables*, where the author uses it to describe Jean Valjean's last agony and death, and it perfectly describes the gradual descent into darkness and the equally gradual slowing down of activity in a man whose daily task from then on was to find enough breath.

While Arthur was in the experienced hands of Dr. Jacquot, Vaura, and sometimes Pascale as well, stayed in the Hôtel Victoria in Glion, from where a short walk through the woods would take her every day to her husband's side. He also had other visitors, such as William Aguet and his wife on 27 March. A cryptic remark in Vaura's diary for the 31st suggests the gravity of the situation: "Does one tell her, or is she to be left in the dark?"

But Honegger continued working. On 3 April he finished the incidental music for *Oedipe-Roi* (Oedipus Rex), by no means a small score, at the Comédie-Française. Meanwhile, without any proposal on his part, he had been made a foreign member of the Institute of France, filling the chair once occupied by Haydn. Letters of congratulation immediately began arriving at Val-Mont with every mail delivery. On the 18th, just before his stay at the clinic ended, Arthur had a visit from the Sachers. On the 20th he returned to Paris, for the moment out of danger. For the moment. He wrote Sacher on the 26th:

> For your birthday on Monday, I send you all the best wishes you can imagine. When you get to my age of fatal respectability, I'm afraid I shan't be there to congratulate you and celebrate as you have done for me. But I hope you won't have forgotten and that you'll remember your old composer and friend.

On 6 May Charles Münch was at the Paris Opera with his Boston Symphony Orchestra. His concert included the *Symphony for Strings*, which he then took on to Brussels on the 12th and Metz on the 19th. Since the 6th, Honegger had been present at the rehearsals of *Oedipe-Roi* at the Comedie-Française and the first performance took place on the 14th. On the 17th Ansermet and the Suisse Romande Orchestra gave the *Fifth Symphony* at the Théâtre des Champs-Élysées as part of the "Twentieth-Century Music Festival" organized by Nicolas Nabokov under the aegis of the Congress for Freedom and Culture. Two days later, on the 19th, *Antigone* and *Jeanne d'Arc au bûcher* were again given at the Opera, and on the 24th Honegger managed to hold another seminar at the École normale (and again on the 28th). Meanwhile, on the 26th, Charles Münch, continuing his tour with the Boston Symphony Orchestra, gave an acclaimed performance of the *Fifth Symphony* at the Royal Festival Hall in London. And on the 27th there was an evening of Honegger's chamber music at the Salle Érard. This cascade of concerts ended with a performance of *Judith* on French Radio on 5 June.

From 10 to 23 June, Arthur and Vaura were in the Netherlands for the biennial congress of CISAC. It was a succession of festivities, banquets, receptions, visits, and concerts, including *La Danse des morts* at the Amsterdam Concertgebouw on the 19th and *Jeanne d'Arc* at the Scheveningen Kurhaus on the 22nd. There were also work sessions, and at the end of it all, as Vaura noted in her diary, "the return from Amsterdam and the burial of delegates dead with fatigue." There was much anxiety about Arthur's heart, but it would hold out more or less until October.

From 11 to 21 July, the Honeggers were on vacation with Mica Salabert at Grez-sur-Loing, on the edge of the forest of Fontainebleau. On the 22nd they left for Switzerland and went straight to the Sonnenberg, Dr. Bircher's famous clinic just on the outskirts of Zurich, and a stone's throw from the house belonging to Tati, Arthur's younger sister. There they underwent a regime of *Birchermüesli*[1] and fruit juice, of which details are found in their diaries. Even though Arthur was already very thin, he had to lose still more weight to take the strain off his heart, and on this diet he went down from 163 lbs on 23 July to 144 lbs on 14 August.

All through the summer, the Honeggers, including Pascale, traveled back and forth between Zurich and the Bürgenstock, near Lucerne, for the music festival there. Vaura also went on her own to Winterthur on 29 July—a kind of pilgrimage to a place she loved. Werner Reinhart was no longer there, but his brother Hans had survived him.

Obviously Honegger was not able to attend the first performance of *La Guirlande de Campra*, which took place at the Aix-en-Provence Festival on 31 July, with Hans Rosbaud conducting the Conservatory Concert Society. On 11 August, still in Zurich, he wrote the speech he would make the following month in Venice for the World Congress of Artists organized under the auspices of UNESCO. On 29 August he wrote Maja Sacher to tell her of this Venice trip with Vaura and Pascale, in the car belonging to his publisher, Mica Salabert. And he added: "As soon as I get back to Paris, I'll take an objective look at those passages of the *Passionspiel* (Passion play) that Paul spoke to me about, and if it's not too stuffy and pitiful I'll try and arrange it for you."

He was in fact becoming less and less sure of whether he had the strength to write the Easter Cantata according to Claudel's plan, and Sacher now suggested to him for the first time that he might make a cantata out of his unfinished *Selzach Passion*.

Honegger stayed in Dr. Bircher's clinic until 10 September, with excursions round the lake on 26 August, to Regensberg, Kaiserstuhl, and Eglisau on the 28th, and to Stein-am-Rhein, Ermatingen, and Frauenfeld on 5 September. He had to avoid high altitudes. At the same time, his humor remained black. Vaura noted in her diary on 30 August: "A. talks to me about our 'future' underground."

Mica Salabert arrived on the 14th, and on the 16th they all left for Venice, via Como, Milan, and Verona. The Congress was held from 19 to 28 September at the Teatro La Fenice, although the official opening did not take place until the 22nd, in the Doges' Palace, where Honegger gave his talk. Then the traveling resumed, now purely for the sake of tourism: Ravenna on 29 September, Florence on the 30th, where they stayed until 6 October (with Pascale leaving for Paris on the 2nd), and then Naples. Honegger had been there about ten days, when his health suddenly worsened. On 18 October Dr. Burkhard, of the international hospital, ordered an immediate transfer back to Paris, where, from the 20th onward, a succession of different doctors looked after him. After a few months of relative respite, his illness had taken a further serious turn for the worse. From the purely clinical point of view, it is perhaps here that our last chapter ought to have begun.

By 12 November, Arthur had recovered sufficiently to be able to accompany Vaura to the premiere of *Jeanne d'Arc au bûcher* at the Théâtre de la Monnaie in Brussels, with Marthe Dugard and Claude Étienne, under the direction of Corneil de Thoran. It ran for eleven performances. The next day, after lunch at the French Embassy with Claudel, they returned to Paris in time to go to a concert at the Salle Gaveau in which Fernand Oubradous conducted the *Concerto da camera*.

On 25 November Paul Sacher, now back from South America, inquired about *Une Cantate de Noël*. Honegger's immediate reply, written on the 27th, is one of the most pessimistic letters he ever penned, and shows how much worse his health had become since the Naples crisis in October:

> In my vegetable state I don't even know what day it is, and I'm often so tired I can't decide on the smallest gesture. . . . I haven't yet been able to make a decision about the *Cantate de Noël*. I find everything I've done so bad that I'm discouraged and it seems the best thing to do is not to compound the error. But I'll spend a little longer thinking about it.

In the same dispirited letter, Honegger calls the *Suite archaïque* a "little piece of trash." The composer Albéric Magnard used to say the same about all his pieces, small or large. Those self-critical composers who are for ever dissatisfied, he would say, always appear to themselves to be living "in the suburbs of their ideal." But on this occasion Honegger's resentment is also directed at something else. He confessed himself appalled at the stupidity and frequent errors in what he had so far read of the manuscript Willy Tappolet sent him of the biography he was writing, and Honegger begged Paul Sacher to prevent publication until he had read the whole thing himself. He was *niedergeschmettert* (crushed). Everything was wrong, about him and about the whole period from

1918 to 1925. "Why write on something you know nothing about? Help! . . . Hell and damnation, as that old fraud Berlioz would have said. I embrace you and hope to see you again before leaving for the crematorium, which is beckoning me."

This virulent criticism was directed at a work that has been taken as authoritative for over forty years and in which, to judge by the number of mistakes it still contains, the author does not seem to have paid much attention to the composer's corrections.

The day after Honegger wrote this savage letter, 28 November, Bernard Gavoty introduced *Le Roi David* at the Salle Gaveau under the auspices of the Université des Annales.

On 2 December the composer began a new homeopathic treatment, which had an immediate effect on his mood, to judge by the more confident tone of the letter he wrote Paul Sacher on 7 December, still on the subject of *Une Cantate de Noël*:

> For some days I've been feeling a bit better, I'm sleeping, I no longer get leg cramps in the night, and I'm recovering a little from my comatose state. I've had the courage to look at the whole passage of the *Passionsmusik* that would go into *Une Cantate de Noël*. After mature reflection, I think (which means "still") that I'll be able to do it. Obviously, almost all of it will have to be reworked, but the outline is coming, as I'm now able to think about it in a concentrated manner. It won't be twelve-tone writing in the least, as that wouldn't go with the use of popular tunes, but I'll do my best to see that it isn't too senile or infantile, or too disappointing for you. As I see it at the moment, it will last a good half hour and will certainly need an organ. I can already see that there's still a host of difficulties to get around, but they don't terrify me as they did some time ago.

Returning to the subject of the previous letter, Paul Sacher informed Honegger on 10 December that he had given Willy Tappolet a copy of his manuscript with all the composer's corrections in Honegger's own writing. I have not managed to see this corrected version of Tappolet's book.

That December also saw the belated Parisian premiere of *Nicolas de Flue* conducted by Philippe Strubin and, on the 16th, a revival of *L'Aiglon* at the Opera. On 27 December Honegger wrote Sacher again, with more details on *Une Cantate de Noël*, which he was now working on:

> As I told you, everything has to be redone and I've started work along these lines. One thing that's concerning me is the difficulty of including an organ, because the very concept of the piece demands an obbligato organ part, which it's almost impossible to replace by anything else.
>
> As I now envisage it, this score is going to be quite sizeable. I shall need a children's choir, as much of it is written in five parts. It will be very tonal since its central focus is on a succession of popular Christmas carols, which it would be ridiculous to treat in the twelve-tone manner, as well as being too superficial from the technical point of view. This is the form of the work as I see it: [the next passage was written in German]

1. Large chorus of lamentation, with an orchestra gradually making itself heard more insistently (perhaps a brief organ introduction), leading to:
2. Chorus and chorus of angels "O come Emmanuel!"
3. Transition (bass solo) "Fear not . . . "
4. Christmas carols, one after the other, then one combined with the other as far as the mid-point, when they are all mixed together and spread out round the entire world like a veil.
5. Transition (bass solo) "Glory to the Lord"
6. Laudate Dominum
7. Postlude, in which the orchestra gradually fades out, leaving the organ on its own.

[Here Honegger returns to French.]

That's it. I'd like your advice on just one point. Do you think the opening choral lament that rises to such a pitch of violence is comprehensible for the listener and that the following chorus "Come Emmanuel" is enough to explain it? Or would you think it better just to start at that point? There are other details I'd like to go over with you score in hand, so as to reach the clearest layout for the passage where all the popular songs are superimposed on each other.

On the last day of the year, Ernest Ansermet, in reply to a letter from Honegger, expatiated on his book *Les Fondements de la musique dans la conscience humaine* (The Foundations of Music in Human Consciousness), which had been occupying his thoughts for many years and would continue to do so until 1961. He tried to explain to the composer the quadruple significance he attached to a melodic line, and concluded:

I never imagined one could explain everything to oneself about this extraordinary thing called music, but this is about explaining it to other people. Those who are born musicians, like you, have no need to have it explained to them and my explanations won't give them anything new, except the satisfaction of having been right and of knowing that in fact other people have been wrong.

From an extract like that we can see what a deep gulf separated the speculative theorist, brilliant though he may have been, from the practicing, creative artist.

1953

During the three years of life left to him, Honegger's health inexorably pursued its downward path. Its most notable impact on this narrative is that his travels, which in the past followed one another at a hectic pace, now more or less came to an end. During 1953, he stayed in Paris until 12 July and from then remained in Switzerland until 26 May of the following year. He became increasingly short of breath, especially in very cold weather, and climbing stairs became such a problem for him that finally he would refuse to leave his large third-floor studio on the boulevard de Clichy. Jacques Feschotte remembers one of the doctors saying that Honegger was "living with a third of a heart."[2] His survival was a miracle! "Recipes" like the following, from one of Honegger's notebooks of the time, make poignant reading:

> *To climb stairs.* Press the elbows against the body at the level of the breastbone, the palms open and facing upward. Fill the lungs before moving. Breathe out in short puffs on each step. Stop as soon as one is out of breath.

Clearly, nothing was wrong with his spirit. He marked the first day of the new year by writing a moving letter to Charles Münch, who had just been conducting Schumann's wonderful *Second Symphony.* This had prompted Honegger to reread the score:

> You are too generous in comparing my works, even faintly, with ones like this. I confess most sincerely that when I reread them, I feel myself to be totally inept and pretentious. But when a man like yourself, for whom music is his entire life, gives me words of encouragement, that is for me the only real, great, inward pleasure and I feel less ashamed of being so far from what I should like to write. My excuse is that I have, at least, done my best with what Providence gave me.

The same day he wrote to his old friend Jacques Ibert, who had been so deeply affected by the tragic death of his daughter:

> My dear Jacques,
> To you and to Rosette I send my affectionate thoughts and wishes for the New Year. May it bring you peace, a little happiness and health, and the possibility of good work to bring you consolation.

And he added:

> Here the weather is horrible, cold, snow, and frost. I don't go out because I can't take a dozen steps without getting out of breath. . . . I'm following my homeopathic treatment, but I still can't sleep. Oh well!

On 7 January Honegger's official reception into the Institut took place, followed by dinner in his apartment with Paul and Maja Sacher. Shortly afterward (the letter is undated, but it must have been written in January) he told Milhaud that he was now feeling a little better: "I'm less of a vegetable, the edema is now returning more slowly and I'm eating and sleeping better. What I lack is breath, especially outdoors and in the cold."

On the 19th Sacher wrote to say that he was thinking of performing *Une Cantate de Noël,* with Schütz's *Christmas History* in the first part of the concert. Six days later, on 25 January, Honegger finished the cantata, but it would be many months before he could summon up the strength to orchestrate it.

Some question remains as to whether it was in fact Honegger's last work. Geoffrey K. Spratt, in his book *The Music of Arthur Honegger,* maintains that the cantata was followed by the minor work *Romance for flute and piano*, published this same year. But we do not know when this was written. In any case, the *Romance* is no more than a charming miniature.

On 24 January, contrary to all expectations, Honegger resumed his teaching, which he now did in his apartment in the boulevard de Clichy. Because he could no longer travel, these classes would be more numerous and regular than before. There would be ten in all (24 January, 7 and 21 February, 7 and 21 March, 11 and 25 April, 9 May, 6 and 20 June) and they were the last he gave.

I had the privilege of attending them—the only time I ever got close to the composer. He was very kind, certainly, but also severe when it was necessary, though he would always explain how to correct one's errors. But he had no time for pretention, for false intellectualization, or for "paper music." I remember one day, when he was faced with one of those sterile twelve-tone works that were beginning to be the fashion, he asked two of us to sit at the piano and sight-read the thing (it was a string quartet), and whispered to the one playing the bass to transpose the viola part down a tone. The poor "composer" didn't notice—which showed he couldn't hear his own music.

Vaura's diary entry for 7 February mentions "Reception at the Institut," but perhaps this was merely one of their regular meetings. On the 12th Paul Sacher sent a telegram: "Many thanks for short score *Cantate de Noël*. Am happy to have received this fine work. Warmest best wishes."

Paul Claudel, in a letter of 19 February, had asked Honegger to send him back the text of the Easter Cantata, and with a heavy heart, we would imagine, the composer did so. But he had not entirely given up hope of the project, as we can see from his letter of the 22nd:

> I don't despair of being able to take it on. I'm looking at some passages of my abandoned *Selzach Passion* to try and get my brain working again. Might I, if there's a "renaissance," ask to have the material back again?

It was not to be. The *Passion* might contain all that was needed to write something on a Christmas theme, but nothing in the remaining fragments was relevant to Easter.

It looks as though Vaura went to Toulouse for a revival of *Jeanne d'Arc au bûcher* on 7 and 8 March, but Arthur did not accompany her. He did, however, attend the recording of *Nicolas de Flue*, conducted by Georges Tzipine, from 11 to 16 March.

It was during this period that the Lausanne writer and musicologist Jean Matter began writing a book on the composer, *Honegger, ou la quête de joie* (Honegger, or The Quest for Happiness), which would be published in 1956. A letter Honegger wrote him, probably in April, shows the depth of his exhaustion: "I've got no composing plans. I think I've said all I had to say. I'm tired. I can't play rugby football any more. There comes a time when you must make way for the young. You must let them have their chance."

On 23 April René Morax wrote from Rome to say that the score of *La Belle de Moudon* had at last been found in the Bern National Library and that the work would be played in Lausanne on 12 May, the day after his eightieth birthday. In fact, Morax lived on another ten years.

On 29 May Paul Sacher confirmed that *Une Cantate de Noël* was programmed for 18 December, but expressed concern at not yet having received the orchestral score—for which there was one very good reason! On 13 June, two days after a visit from his old friend Paul Hindemith, the composer replied: "Rather slowly, I've made a start on orchestrating the little cantata. . . . I'm intending to spend a little time in Switzerland in July." On 16 June Sacher asked what the orchestral forces would be for the cantata, which he reckoned would last about twenty-five minutes. He added that he had had a great success in Vienna with the *Monopartita* and that he was going to conduct the *Concerto da camera* in Aix-en-Provence.

On 12 July the Honegger family, together with the composer's brother Zigo, left for Zurich. While Vaura and Pascale stayed with Toto, Arthur preferred to stay with his younger sister, Tati, who understood and respected his fierce desire for independence. Meanwhile, as a fringe event at the summer course in Darmstadt, the local theater put on *Antigone* with Christa Ludwig in the title role. The director was Harro Dicks and the conductor Richard Kotz.

But suddenly, Honegger's health gave new cause for alarm. On 22 August, the sixth anniversary of his original heart attack, he was rushed into the Kantonsspital (District Hospital) in Zurich and had to stay there three whole months. While he was there he received a touching letter from Paul Claudel, written from Brangues on 20 August, most probably in reply to a letter that has been lost and whose content is therefore unknown:

Dear Honegger,
How kind you are! Your sincerity goes straight to my heart! You too, you are for me a brother I admire, and the collaboration you have three times granted me has been the great opportunity of my life! May God bless you! With all my heart, P. Cl.

Meanwhile, Paul Sacher, knowing that Honegger was incapable of putting pen to paper for the time being, wrote Vaura on 8 September to ask about the forces used in the cantata. She wrote back on the 11th, adding:

After being drowsy for so long, Arthur had a marvelous "awakening" yesterday afternoon. I found him armed with a piece of paper and a pencil, working out various menus that might provide the most agreeable means of assuaging his hunger. I was so pleased to see him like that, being actively grumpy.

That letter is the last in the thick folder containing the Sacher-Honegger correspondence, testimony to an unparalleled friendship and a mutual artistic understanding. After that, Honegger remained almost continuously at the Schönenberg until October 1954, which explains the absence of letters. But none have been found covering the last year of the composer's life, which he spent entirely in Paris.

Vaura returned to Paris on 4 October, no doubt feeling somewhat reassured. But from the 10th to the 12th, Honegger was again in serious condition in the hospital and she came back to his bedside. By dint of superhuman efforts, he managed to finish the orchestration of *Une Cantate de Noël* on 16 October. The autograph score bears a dedication to Paul Sacher, which Honegger added the day after the first performance. It is less a dedication than a letter:

> Here, my dear Paul, is the score completed with difficulty in room F33 of the Kantonsspital in Zurich. It owes its existence to your affectionate insistence, because without that it would have remained at the bottom of a drawer. It is therefore to you that I am grateful for a last performance of my music that has given me much joy, through your affection and talent. Thank you with all my heart.

Vaura's diary over the following weeks records the sad tale of the ups and downs in Arthur's health: "26 October: A. very depressed. 2 November: A. doing very well. A very nice afternoon. 8 November: Ansermet visited the Kantonsspital. 10 November: the Hindemiths, and again on the 15th. 17 November: A. gloomy and tired. 18 November: A. better."

And he remained better, so that on 23 November he could at last leave the hospital and go to the Schönenberg. But the letter he wrote Milhaud on 2 December nevertheless makes painful reading: "I've at last left the Kantonsspital after three months. . . . Suddenly I've turned into a little old man like Gandhi, a sack of old skin hanging on a scaffolding of dry bones. I've lost 22 lbs and I still feel fairly tired." Then, changing the subject to the question of operas and the problems of staging them, he wrote: "It's the manpower that absorbs all the time and money, and there's nothing left for the works themselves."

One may wonder what this fragile, emaciated man, now down to between 130 and 145 lbs, must have felt on rereading the powerful text Claudel wrote in Basel on 11 June 1938, under the impact of the *Danses macabres* that were the starting point for *La Danse des morts*:

> What joy! So this earthly body in which we find ourselves entangled, and from which we draw less pride, pleasure, or profit than irritations of all kinds, bravo! it is only temporary! We need not take it too seriously! . . . So be at ease, you sluggard! What joy to be disencumbered not only of clothes, but of your skin and of this clumsy, ridiculous personality! "I am nothing but bones," lamented the prophet Job. Well, that is at least something!
>
> This spry, unclothed gnome makes me think of a ballet master who, in order to train his troupe, strips down to his shirtsleeves. . . . Under the influence of this agile master of ceremonies, inviting and drawing them in, the ball has begun! How thick, heavy, and clumsy all these living people seem! . . . And not only what they're wearing, but these cheeks, these stomachs, these breasts, these buttocks, these folds of fat and intestines, all these prejudices, all this tallow.

But life had one last consoling triumph in store. On 18 December Paul Sacher conducted the first performance of *Une Cantate de Noël*, with Derrik

Olsen as soloist. Basel Radio put out a recording of it on the 21st. Then Honegger enjoyed a peaceful Christmas Eve at the Schönenberg, and on Christmas Day itself he wrote a second dedication, this time on the original short score:

My dear Paul,
　　I am happy to dedicate this score to you and your Chamber Choir, in memory of all the fine performances you have given me, from *Le Roi David* to this cantata, with your talent, your devotion, and your brotherly affection. I embrace you and thank you. Your grateful A. H. Christmas 1953.

The year ended on a happy note at the Zurich Stadttheater, which, after so many years, finally put on *Les Aventures du roi Pausole*, for the first time in the German translation. The premiere took place on 30 December and the performances continued on into the New Year.

1954

　　On 7 January 1954 Vaura and Pascale left Arthur at the Schönenberg and went back to Paris for the first performance in France of *Une Cantate de Noël*, at the Théâtre des Champs-Élysées on 10 January with the Elisabeth Brasseur Chorale, the Orchestra of the Conservatory Concert Society, and Pierre Mollet as soloist, under the direction of Georges Tzipine. Over the following two days the same performers recorded the work in the church of Saint-Eustache. The work made a profound emotional impact. As Jacques Feschotte says: "We knew Honegger was listening on the radio. And an enormous, interminable ovation carried the gratitude of his faithful Paris audience to him over the airwaves."
　　The same day, Jacques Ibert wrote him:

Dear old Arthur,
　　When they said just now that you were listening, I wanted to jump up on the stage and shout: "Bravo, Arthur! We all embrace you." But I'm sure you felt the surge of enthusiasm that swept through the entire hall after the end of your cantata, and that explosion of joy that eradicates all doubt—if there ever was any!—and strengthens hope.
　　I won't say any more, but I wanted to waste no time in assuring you of the profound emotion and admiration felt by all the musicians who were there, before the pure, serene beauty of your piece. From the low organ pedal and insistent sounds of the sub-basses at the start, to the final choral paragraph and the silvery counterpoint on the trumpets, your sure and masterly hand was everywhere in evidence.

During the day of 24 January, Honegger twice spat blood. From midnight to two o'clock in the morning he felt so ill that a quarter of an hour later he was rushed to the hospital in Basel. Vaura quickly came back from Paris to find him "much better" on the 26th, to the point where on the 28th he could dictate to her a succinct report to be read out at the congress in Rome on the legislation over authors' rights. On 1 February she wrote "very good day, the best"; on the 2nd, "A's health today less continually good"; but on the 7th, "A's health better," and on the 8th, "much better." On 3 February Honegger wrote Francis Poulenc to tell him of "a new little annoyance in the form of a pulmonary embolism." In fact, he was not allowed back to the Schönenberg until 9 March, the day before his birthday. He celebrated this with the Sachers, Vaura, his two sisters from Zurich, and Pascale, who stopped off for a couple of days.

On 7 March he wrote Aloys Mooser, the widely feared Geneva critic who had been one of his earliest supporters and who was now suggesting a new work from him: "This Nyon project strikes me as interesting and I would have seized on it with enthusiasm . . . several years ago. Now I'm a useless, clapped-out old devil, who's quite happy to give way to others." And he ends by wishing Mooser "happy festivals of dung-shaped twelve-toneries."

On 23 March Theophil Kaufmann, the Federal German consul in Basel, came to the Schönenberg to give Honegger the Richard Strauss Medal, and on 5 May Arthur was the recipient of a little "serenade from the Pratteln Music Society in honor of the composer Monsieur Arthur Honegger"—Pratteln being the little town that lies directly below the Schönenberg. Meanwhile, on 22 April, at La Scala in Milan, Ingrid Bergman gave her first performance in the title role of *Jeanne d'Arc*, which she would soon repeat at the Paris Opera.

On 10 May Honegger wrote Poulenc, who had just sent him a copy of his *Conversations with Claude Rostand*:

> In the middle of the fashions, systems, and slogans that the impotent have tried to impose, you have remained true to yourself with a rare courage that commands respect. Our temperaments are, I think, very different, but I feel I share with you a love of music rather than a love of success. From opposite points of view, we express ourselves in similar terms. . . . I hope you won't think me too presumptuous if I bracket us together and say: we are two "honest men." I embrace you with brotherly affection. Yours, A. Honegger.

Meanwhile, he felt well enough to go with Vaura on one last long journey to Bergen in Norway for the biennial congress of CISAC, of which he was still president. On leaving the Schönenberg, he wrote in his hosts' visitors' book: "My heart is attached to yours, weak and tired though it be. As long as it beats even slightly, please know that it will be for you."

Honegger returned to Paris on 10 June, for the first time in eleven months. He was getting ready for a great event, the revival of *Jeanne d'Arc* at the Paris Opera in a quite new production, directed by Roberto Rossellini and with his wife, Ingrid Bergman, in the title role. The premiere took place on the 21st in the presence of the composer and Paul Claudel, who both attended three of the four performances. In 1956 Rossellini put this outstanding production on film.

On 1 July Honegger met the filmmaker Georges Rouquier to fix with him the details of a film Rouquier wanted to make about him. With Vaura, he then left for Bad Nauheim, a German spa well-known for the treatment of heart conditions. He stayed there undergoing a cure for six weeks, until the middle of August. While he was there, he started on the last of the notebooks he had been keeping for some time. In them, one finds a disorganized collection of reflections, anecdotes, press cuttings, literary and philosophical quotations from various epochs, complaints about the pressure put on artists by the tax authorities, some analytical notes on his own works, and "naughty" rhymes. And also the following, which begins the new notebook in striking fashion:

> In *La Danse des morts*, Claudel paraphrases Job and writes: "What is Man that You should magnify him and that You should take him to Your heart?" Reply: "a water-skin full of pus, urine, and detritus. A bag of dung. And yet it is from this that temples, works of art and science, from the pyramids to the calculator, have sprung. A miracle!"

Words to set beside Sophocles's hymn to the greatness of Man, which Jean Cocteau kept in his libretto for *Antigone*.

At the end of Honegger's treatment, he and Vaura returned to Zurich. Here, on 25 August, in the little hall of the Tonhalle, the rushes of Georges Rouquier's film took place, with Paul Sacher and the orchestra of the Collegium Musicum. On the 28th they both returned to the Schönenberg.

As he was too tired to write himself, on 31 August Honegger dictated to Pascale a letter to Arthur Hoérée, who was thinking of writing a book about him. In the end this never materialized, any more than the one planned by Bernard Gavoty, but the one by Willy Tappolet did finally appear ("luckily, in German," remarked Honegger). And overall the composer was slightly alarmed by this profusion, which he did not feel he had in the least deserved. His letter finishes with the now ritual complaint: "I'm absolutely exhausted and have no urge to undertake anything."

Vaura's diary records the sad daily round at the Schönenberg:

1 September: A. tired. Letter from Mihalovici to say that Enesco is paralyzed.
2 September: Heavy storm during which Dr. Lang (in place of Dr. Scholer) gives A. an intravenous injection that has no effect.
3 September: Very bad day (Dr. Scholer doesn't get back until the middle of the night).
4 September: A. very ill. Transfer to the hospital in Basel mercifully avoided. Professor Staub arrived at 5:30 AM with Scholer, who spent the afternoon at the Schönenberg.
5 September: Maja arrived from London at 2 AM. A. is better.
6 September: Well.
7 September: Paul arrived from London.
19 September: Visit from Jean-Claude.
20 September: Pascale returns to Paris on her own.
23 September: 137 lbs in black socks and beige sweater.

On 28 September Arthur and Vaura returned to Paris for the last time. He would not leave the city again. He was now too ill to live on his own and, as he did not want to leave his studio on the boulevard de Clichy, his wife moved in with him. He would from this point on be receiving goodwill messages almost every day, and on 13 October his weight rose to touch the 143-lb mark. But on the 26th he was ill again from an overdose of mercury after injections of thiomerine.

René Morax came to see him on 5 November, and on the 26th *Jeanne d'Arc au bûcher* was revived at the Opera. On 2 December Honegger was promoted to the rank of Grand Officer in the Legion of Honor and letters of congratulation arrived from the Institut, from the Association of Swiss Composers, and from Ernest Ansermet. The ceremony took place at the Centre Marcelin-Berthelot under the presidency of Edgar Faure, the French Finance Minister—Honegger, as an enemy of all taxes, no doubt appreciated the irony.

1955

During this last year of Honegger's life, Paul and Maja Sacher often came to see him in Paris, as he could no longer travel. The year began with a recording on disc of a talk, *Arthur Honegger vous parle* (Arthur Honegger Speaks to You), that he made in two sessions in his studio on 18 and 25 January.

On 23 February 1955 Paul Claudel died at the age of eighty-six. No loss could have affected Honegger more deeply, and the same day he went with Vaura to see Claudel's widow. But because Arthur could no longer tolerate the cold, Pascale took his place at the funeral in Notre-Dame on the 28th. Later in the year, when Albert Einstein too passed away, Honegger would note in his diary: "Claudel is dead. Einstein is dead. I've got Albert Schweitzer left." The great Catholic, the great Jew, the great Protestant—these were perhaps the three men he most admired.

On 23 March, with Bernard Gavoty, he took part in a session on *La Danse des morts* for the youth group Jeunesses Musicales, and on the 28th he gave a radio interview with Jean Cocteau. On 25 April he noted "In bed all day asleep."

On 7 May another great friend, Georges Enesco, died. The month of June was given over to recordings: *Le Roi David* for the Club National du Disque, and the first recording of all three string quartets by the Lespine Quartet, with *Pâques à New York* as a filler. From 11 to 23 July, Georges Rouquier's film on the composer was completed in the boulevard de Clichy studio. It contains terrifying pictures of Honegger, veritable death masks recalling the words of the soldier in Stravinsky's *The Soldier's Tale*: "I am a dead man among the living." Ordinary human decency should prevent them from being reproduced.

Otherwise, these last, empty months passed without any major crises. It was the classic "peace before the end." Many visitors came to see him, including the Iberts, Marcel Delannoy, the Winters, Arthur Hoérée, Mica Salabert, his brother Zigo, Albert Willemetz, and, of course, Paul and Maja Sacher, who came on 30 and 31 July.

On 31 August, at the casino in Vichy, Louis de Froment revived the unjustly neglected score of *Les Mille et Une Nuits*. In other times, Arthur would no doubt have been there.

Honegger now entered a period of great calm, a mixture of serenity and resignation. On 26 September he wrote Aloys Mooser one of his last letters—perhaps the very last. He thanked him for an article in which he recognized "Mooser's iron hand in a horsehair glove." Honegger went on: "I keep going as best I may, I read and listen to the works I like on disc and on the radio. All in all, it's a good life."

On 28 September he was visited by the Milanese musicologist Luigi Rognoni. On 20 October he went to the Institut for Jean Cocteau's reception there. On the evening of the 24th Bernard Gavoty came to see him, followed by Marcel Mihalovici on the 26th. On 6 November it was Paul Hindemith's turn, who, knowing Honegger was seriously ill, gave up the opportunity of attending a festival of his own works in Baden-Baden to be able to see his friend one more time. On the 10th Honegger had lunch at the Closerie des Lilas to mark the publication of the discs of *Le Roi David* recorded in June.

On 13 November he was present for the last time at a performance of one of his works, *La Danse des morts* at the Lamoureux Concerts. On the 14th, 15th, and 16th he chaired meetings of the Académie du disque français, of which he was president, but he would not live to take part in the lunch on 8 December, duly noted in his diary. His last visitor seems to have been Bernard Gavoty. A few days before his death, he supervised the recording on disc of his *Symphonie liturgique* under Georges Tzipine.

During these last months, Honegger often went to see his old friend Darius Milhaud. For that, he only had more or less to cross the boulevard, even though there still remained the terrible problem of stairs, which were the only obstacle to his visits.

After so much suffering, the pangs of a death agony were spared him, and he died quickly and peacefully. On 27 November, at 4:20 in the afternoon, he felt a little better and wanted to get out of bed. He asked Vaura to help him raise himself, but he immediately fell back and died in her arms. The "third of a heart" had, after so many trials, ceased to beat.

I was at that time a student at the Paris Conservatory. The next day, in our music history class, Norbert Dufourcq said gravely and simply: "Honegger died last night." Spontaneously, we collected ourselves in silence. The young of today cannot imagine what Honegger meant to their elders forty years ago.

The funeral took place at the Temple de l'Oratoire on Friday, 2 December. Fritz Münch, who was a priest as well as a musician, conducted the service and chose for music the "Lamento" from *La Danse des morts*, followed by the Alleluia from *Le Roi David*—a perfect choice. At the cremation in the Père Lachaise cemetery, it was Jean Cocteau who found the right words. After his heartfelt cry, "Arthur, you have been a wonderful friend. Today is the first time you have caused us pain!" he concluded:

Arthur, you have succeeded in gaining the respect of a disrespectful age. You combined the knowledge of an architect of the Middle Ages with the simplicity of a humble cathedral workman. Your ashes burn and will never grow cold, even if this earth ceases to be. For music is not of this world and its reign will never end.

Arthur Honegger was the first of Les Six to enter the valley of the shadow of death. A little over seven years later, Francis Poulenc followed him, almost at the same age, and then Jean Cocteau a few months after that. They were joined by Darius Milhaud in 1974, Louis Durey in 1979, and Georges Auric and Germaine Tailleferre in 1983. Vaura survived almost a quarter of a century after her husband, acting as his executor until her death on 18 July 1980.

Part Two
INVENTORY OF WORKS

The catalog of Arthur Honegger's works includes well over two hundred items and embraces every genre. The present volume does not attempt any detailed analysis, which can be found in a separate, specialized volume, together with a true *catalogue raisonné*.[1] For the present volume, two approaches suggested themselves: either a superficial glance at every work, or else a more profound analysis of the more important works within a more general perspective. I have chosen the latter, although all Honegger's compositions receive at least a mention, sometimes with just a few words of commentary.

The choice of works to be examined in more detail was dictated not only by their intrinsic importance, but also by the likelihood of the reader hearing them, either in the concert hall or on disc. Together with these two considerations is my continuing intention of rehabilitating those important works that are still underestimated or unknown, in the hope that this book will encourage those responsible for putting on concerts and for choosing music to go on disc to give the works the hearing they deserve. Reference to scores will always be a valuable adjunct for those readers with access to them. Music examples have been chosen according to two, often overlapping criteria: the first, to present thematic outlines that are either typical or memorable, and the second, to establish the presence of cyclical links. Such links may exist either within a single piece—which is especially the case for larger structures such as symphonies, oratorios, and so on—or between one work and another, where the presence of links underlines the profound unity of Honegger's output, despite what seems at first sight to be its bewildering diversity.

"I have, in fact, written a lot." This calm statement, which Honegger made to his biographer José Bruyr at the end of their joint labors, gives some idea of Honegger's typical blend of modesty and humor. He knew perfectly well the respective value of each of his compositions, including those unpopular ones that were, understandably, dearer to him than the others—I am thinking of *Cris du monde* and *Antigone*.

But from the most spectacular stage work to the most modest bagatelle, from the most profound symphony to the lightest popular song, from the slow movement of a string quartet to a tango or a blues, the same professional conscientiousness is to be found, the same respect for technical expertise on which Honegger is so insistent in his writings. In every case we find the stamp of the

231

good workman, and this care over construction is no doubt a mark of Honegger's Swiss ancestry. Ravel's biographers often attribute his "Swiss watchmaker's" perfectionism to the fact that his father's family came from Versoix, near Geneva. As soon as the young Honegger decided he wanted to be a composer, he concentrated on acquiring an utterly solid technique, with all the slow, grinding labor that requires.

He was far more anxious to acquire the knowledge necessary for his craft than he was to collect official marks of approval. His correspondence with his parents confirms that he chose his teachers with this in mind, knowing full well that those fellow students who coveted a first prize could achieve their heart's desire in another class. When he left the Paris Conservatory, he did so having won only one second prize, but in the knowledge that he had learned there what he needed to learn, even if that was still far from sufficient.

As for the rest, Arthur Honegger successfully became his own teacher through unremitting hard work. He would always emphasize that he was not naturally gifted, and envied his friend Milhaud on this account—not that it was necessarily true, if we look at the speed with which he was able to write occasional music for stage and screen. For that, his apprenticeship gave him a dexterity that ensured he never wasted his time banging his head against brick walls. It was indeed in his most cerebral, ambitious works that we find him struggling, as Beethoven had done before him (and Poulenc in our own day, for all the apparent spontaneity of his music).

He was, too, an extremely clear-headed judge of his own work. He spoke proudly of the "technical progress" accomplished in his *String Quartet No. 3* as compared to its predecessors, and that of the *Deliciae basilienses* compared to the *Symphonie liturgique*. The truth is, he was absolutely right in both cases! At the end of his career, he could celebrate the most glorious victories of a technique that was no longer submitted to any strain, and I think of the tours de force of the Finale of *Deliciae basilienses*, the Scherzo of *Di Tre Re*, or the final chorus of *Saint François d'Assise*. Here, as in all truly classical works, technique is neither self-satisfied nor pedantic, but elegant and discreet: "the art that conceals art," as Rameau used to say.

Elegance is not a word that has been much used to describe this "sturdy, strapping Swiss," the rugby enthusiast in his leather jacket, the lover of locomotives. And yet, one cannot help but admire the unparalleled calligraphic beauty of his scores, which are masterpieces of presentation, clarity, taste, and economy, with never a single page or staff too many, and which are far more rewarding to look at than the comparatively banal printed editions. The same elegance could be found in his choice of everyday and ornamental objects for his studio, where they were set off by the room's almost Spartan austerity, and in his carefully relaxed dress as well as in his easy use of invertible counterpoint. For sure, it was Gédalge who inculcated this feeling for the elegant solution to a technical problem, a state of mind that was much stressed in the Conservatory's teachings. But certainly Honegger acquired this skill only later, and after considerable effort. That particular brand of elegance is not in evidence in either the *String Quartet No. 1* or *Le Chant de Nigamon*, but only, at this early stage in his Conservatory studies, in works of a less ambitious nature, such as some of his songs. This may be why he failed to win a first prize—a failure that now strikes us as so undeserved.

After his simple childhood efforts, Honegger's official output began with the *Three Pieces for piano* published in Le Havre in 1910. He would later disown these and would never take any steps to have them republished. From here he went through several years of experimentation, from which little has survived. Certainly, the few pieces from before 1914 that have come down to us represent no more than a tiny proportion of what he committed to paper during those years. His *String Quartet No. 1*, begun in June 1913, was the first important work of his that he would later recognize, although we should also remember the ambitious, if immature, violin sonata of 1912. But his continuous output began really in the fall of 1914, when he was twenty-two, so he could hardly be called exceptionally precocious. From that point to the completion of the orchestration of *Une Cantate de Noël* in the Kantonsspital in Zurich on 16 October 1953, there stretched a creative life of just under forty years, during which the composer wrote the 222 works considered in this volume, some of which have disappeared. To this total we could add several other pieces that we do not know of from his time at the Conservatory.

His production was spread over the years with remarkable regularity and with very few breaks. Those breaks that occurred between the completion of *Antigone* in September 1927 and the composition of *Rugby* in August 1928, and then during the early months of 1929, can be explained by his extensive tours of Russia and the United States respectively (though the spring of 1929 may also have seen the start of his work on *Amphion*). The period between the completion of *Cris du monde* and *La Belle de Moudon* at the end of March 1931 and the beginning of the *Sonatina for violin and cello* in September 1932, however, was a real gap of nearly eighteen months, coinciding with Honegger's serious crisis of self-questioning (discussed in Chapter 5 of the biographical section of this book). His output was still on the slow side for most of 1933, but from the fall of that year onward, Honegger threw himself with manic energy into his new career as a cinema composer. Until the Second World War, there would be no more than a couple of brief pauses to catch his breath, from January to June 1938 and from August to November 1939.

The two interruptions that followed were the result of circumstances that the Germans (who were, as it happened, responsible for them!) would call *höhere Gewalt* (force majeure): his absence from Paris between mid-May and the end of October 1940, and the events leading up to and following the Liberation, between April and the end of October 1944. After that Honegger worked continuously until the catastrophe of the summer of 1947, which paralyzed him for more than a year. He gradually returned to work in mid-May 1948, orchestrating *La Naissance des couleurs* and the *Prelude, Fugue, Postlude* from *Amphion*, and then moved on to composition proper with his powers undiminished, as we can see from the *Concerto da camera* begun in August 1948. But as his health declined during this last period, which ended with his final incidental music for *Oedipe-Roi*, his production slowed. Slowly and painfully, the sick man put the finishing touches to *Une Cantate de Noël* between the end of 1952 and 16 October 1953. After that came two years of silence.

Neither these rare interruptions in his creativity, nor the natural breaks that have allowed us to split up his life into the nine chapters of biography in Part One, correspond with distinct stylistic phases. With Honegger, there are no "manners" or successive styles, but a single, straight, ascending line in pursuit of the same aesthetic and spiritual ideal.

He found his own voice very early, in the summer of 1915 at the latest, and it is impossible to confuse the songs of this period or the *String Quartet No. 1* with the works of any other composer. There were some early influences, both Germanic (Strauss, Reger, first-period Schoenberg) and French (Debussy), but these soon fell away, at the latest by the time Honegger left the Conservatory. The influence of Stravinsky, too, has often been mentioned, but to me it seems practically nonexistent. On the other hand, Honegger, having taken a long time to appreciate Gabriel Fauré's hermetic music, bore the clandestine, subterranean imprint of that music until the very end of his life. Even so, his work forms an astonishingly homogeneous whole and, in its impermeability to outside influences, it remains almost as isolated a phenomenon as the music of Messiaen.

This is also the reason why criteria of modernity or avant-gardism do not really apply to Honegger's music. As a result, there has been much misunderstanding and irritation on the part of those who see history in the light of determinism and artistic progress. It is true that *Le Dit des jeux du monde* and *Horace victorieux* were in no sense backward works by the most advanced standards of their time, and the same could be said a few years later of *Antigone* and the *First Symphony*. But Honegger was never interested in being avant-garde or in employing any musical language for its own sake, only in what it needed to be in order to be expressive and functional. The fact that *Horace victorieux* could date from the same period as *Le Roi David*, and his film music from the same period as the last two string quartets, proves how profoundly indifferent he was to modernity for modernity's sake—the interest of which anyhow extends only as far as its first four letters ("mode" in the sense of "fashion"). Honegger's modernity was deeper and truer, rooted in the human community of his time and devoted to trying to express its problems and anxieties. In that sense, the composer of *Cris du monde* is an out-and-out modernist. But the listener who does not know the date of a composition can never use modernity as a clue. The *Pastorale d'été* of 1920 is as harmonious, consonant, and tonal as the *Deliciae basilienses* of 1946; and the violent atonality and grinding dissonances of the Dies irae of the *Symphonie liturgique* echoed those of *Horace victorieux* a quarter of a century earlier. In the interviews he gave late in life, Honegger recorded his conviction that with the twelve-tone chord, music had reached its apogee of complexity—he never envisaged the thirteen-tone-plus music of so many of today's composers. But long before then he had realized the inanity of the intellectual position that tried to equate avant-gardism with the degree of dissonance or atonality. And yet we have had to wait until the last years of our century to see that he was right.

In the course of his career, Honegger tried his hand at nearly every musical genre, even if with one or two of them, such as organ music, he did so only once. It is certainly a cause for regret that Honegger the violinist did not leave us a concerto for his own instrument. But apart from unaccompanied choral music, so richly provided for by his friends Poulenc and Milhaud, there is no grouping that he ignored.

My complete catalog, published separately, contains no less than seventeen categories, some subdivided. They are listed in that volume as follows:

1.   Piano, two pianos, organ
1A. Piano music derived from stage works
2.   String quartets
3.   Sonatas and sonatinas
4.   Chamber music, various works
4A. Chamber music derived from stage works
5.   Symphonies
6.   Concertos
7.   Other orchestral works
7A. Orchestral music derived from stage works
8.   Songs
8A. Songs from stage works
9.   Popular songs
9A. Popular songs from stage works
10. Cantatas and oratorios
11. Operas
12. Operettas
13. Ballets
14. Incidental music
15. Radio scores
16. Film scores
17. Various, unclassifiable

For the present volume, practical considerations have led me to regroup Honegger's works in a slightly different order. In Part Two of this book, the categories of works will be discussed under the following five main headings:

Chapter 10, Chamber Music: categories 1, 1A, 2, 3, 4, 4A, 8, 8A
Chapter 11, Orchestral Music: categories 5, 6, 7, 7A
Chapter 12, Theater and Musical Frescoes: categories 10, 11, 13
Chapter 13, Incidental Music: categories 14, 15, 16
Chapter 14, Light Music: categories 9, 9A, 12, 17

I believe this reordering is certainly clearer and more attractive for the nonprofessional reader; for a complete catalog, however, the traditional order of instrumental music, vocal music, stage music must be retained.

Each category's chapter begins with a summary introduction, after which the works are presented in chronological order of composition. Each of them carries a brief factual heading, a shortened version of that which appears in the complete catalog, and this consists of the following items:

Opus number and precise title
Date of composition
Dedication or commission (where relevant)
Names of collaborators, librettists, and others (where relevant)
Place and date of first performance, with names of principal artists
Vocal or instrumental forces
Overall length (broken down into movements where possible)
Publication details

A brief descriptive commentary follows, or, where justified by the work's importance, a more detailed analysis. Conclusions as to the music's aesthetic character, its historical position, or the composer's musical language are left until the third and last section of the book.

TEN

Chamber Music

Arthur Honegger began his creative life in the most traditional way possible: by writing piano pieces, songs, and chamber music. His first modest attempt at an orchestral work, the *Prelude* for *Aglavaine et Sélysette*, dates from the end of 1916 and bears the number 10 in my chronological catalog. But Honegger's most prolific chamber music period, both instrumental and vocal, came to an abrupt end during the summer of 1923, when he finished two works that he had been working on for some time: *Le Cahier romand* and the *Six Poems of Jean Cocteau*. Certainly, he would later compose two important string quartets, two sonatas, and one or two shorter pieces, as well as several more songs at the start of the Second World War. But chamber music would now assume no more than a marginal place in his output and there would be none written during the final years. There are no last sonatas or last quartets—a lack much to be regretted. His pessimism over the small audiences attracted to the genre no doubt contributed to this, and unfortunately, he died too soon to see the resurgence of interest that took place, largely due to recordings, during the 1960s.

In fact, this avenue of inspiration was diverted and reached its goal in another direction. Just as the frustration he felt over the future of opera after the lukewarm reception of *Antigone* led him to write oratorios with a strong visual input (*Jeanne d'Arc au bûcher* being the prime example), similarly one could say that the *Second Symphony* (*Symphony for Strings*) marks the ultimate expression of his quartet writing. There is, therefore, no call for undue regret. The harvest is still a fine one, as we shall see.

Category 1: Music for Piano, Two Pianos, and Organ

1. *Three Pieces for piano* (*Scherzo, Humoresque, Adagio*)
8. *Toccata and Variations*
14. *Fugue and Chorale for organ*
23. *Three Pieces for piano* (*Prélude, Hommage à Ravel, Danse*)
25. *Seven Short Pieces*
26. *Sarabande*, from the *Album des Six*

237

43A. *Suite* from *Three Counterpoints*
52. *Le Cahier romand*
69. *Hommage à Albert Roussel*
81. *Prelude, Arioso, and Fughetta on the name BACH*
95. *Berceuse* for *Le Bal des Petits Lits blancs*
115. *Scenic Railway*
145. *Petits Airs sur une basse célèbre*
173. *Two Sketches for Piano*
213. *Très modéré*

Honegger's piano output is fairly small, comprising less than an hour and a half of music, including transcriptions. Being a violinist by training, he had no natural affinity with the piano, even though he played it less badly than he claimed—well enough, in any event, to accompany his songs and play his part in the *Partita for two pianos* (see Category 1A). But he never risked solo performances on what he would often refer to as the "wooden beast." Nevertheless, some of his piano compositions are fine works, even though he never pursued the quest for a large piano work after the experiment of the *Toccata and Variations.*

1. *Three Pieces for piano*

1909–1910
"To Monsieur R. Ch. Martin"
Duration: 8 minutes
Desforges

The only interest in this youthful essay lies in the fact that it was Honegger's first published work. The brief *Scherzo* (molto vivace) is the least ambitious and certainly the most successful of the three pieces. It is reminiscent of Felix Mendelssohn, while the *Humoresque* (allegretto) recalls Grieg with its insistent fifths. As for the *Adagio* (molto ed espressivo), a desperately Beethovenian funeral march, it sounds too much like a reduction of an orchestral piece.

8. *Toccata and Variations* for piano

May–September 1916
"To the memory of my uncle O. H." (Oskar Honegger)
First performance: 15 December 1916, Andrée Vaurabourg, Salle Oedenkhoven, Paris
Duration: 12 minutes 20 seconds
Salabert

This powerful diptych is evidence of the young Honegger's inclination toward formal rigor and polyphonic complexity. It is his only attempt at a large-scale piano work, and in it he brings a stringency and a new lucidity to a chromatic language derived from post-romanticism. Latin influences (Debussy and Fauré) are already more noticeable than Germanic ones.

The Toccata (vif–lent–tempo primo) in B-flat major is in the classical mold of ABA′ and coda. Beneath the agitated sixteenth-notes of the right hand, the left announces a vigorous theme that, typically, dies away on a descending whole-tone phrase (Example 1).

Example 1

This is followed by a brief but almost exact quotation from the Toccata by Debussy. Throughout, the basic tritonal opposition (B-flat/E) replaces the traditional dominant; this is a logical consequence of the theme's whole-tone profile. After a short, slower central section in more reflective, chromatic style, the six periods of the first part are repeated in a different order and in different keys. The Toccata concludes forcefully with a brief coda, which returns to the initial phrase of the theme.

The Variations (in fact, a theme and five variations) are based on a kind of somber chorale nineteen measures long, the beginning of which especially betrays its model, Fauré's *Theme and Variations*, Op. 73. The two main sections of the theme pass through numerous fleeting modulations in a mixture of chromaticism and modal diatonicism, and the beginning of the second phrase even recalls the opening of Ravel's *String Quartet*. The key of the theme wavers between B-flat minor and E-flat minor, and Honegger seems to have been happy with this sense of indecision. The first variation is somber, stormy, and chaotic, with iambic rhythms typical of the composer, and harks back to Debussy's *What the West Wind Saw*. The second variation, animé in 9/8, is more classical in effect and recalls the ninth of Paul Dukas's *Variations on a Theme of Rameau*.

The calm third variation, in E-flat major, is like a clearing in the undergrowth and is entirely modal and diatonic. At fifty-six measures long, the fourth variation, in B minor, is larger than its neighbors: an "amplification" in the Beethovenian sense. It is dominated by an ostinato, the dotted rhythms of which finally invade the theme itself. The cycle ends with the long, lyrical, expressive epilogue of the fifth variation. Here the tonality is initially veiled by the exuberant richness of the chromatic passing notes, but gradually a steady, luminous diatonicism wins the day.

Despite the influences I have mentioned, *Toccata and Variations*, written when Honegger was twenty-four, is his first successful instrumental work. Although he had begun the ambitious *String Quartet No. 1* in 1913, he would not finish it until October 1917.

14. *Fugue and Chorale for organ*

September 1917
Fugue: "To Charles-Robert Martin"; Chorale: "To Andrée Vaurabourg"
Duration: 5 minutes 20 seconds
Chester Music

This diptych is Honegger's only organ work, and it makes us wish he had written for organ again. Its chromatic polyphony is extraordinarily dense and complex. Of all Honegger's works, the *Fugue and Chorale for organ* is the one that is closest to Max Reger, who seems to have been the model here, rather than César Franck or any of his pupils. The Fugue (moderato), in C-sharp minor, is built on a three-measure subject that lies within the narrow range of a minor seventh, moving entirely by step except for one leap of a tritone. There is a regular exposition with four entries, followed by a modulating episode that develops the various motifs of the subject. Then comes a further exposition on the tonic, profoundly modified (there are only two entries), and finally a short coda.

The Chorale (lento sostenuto) only affirms D minor after the hesitant Prelude, interspersed with pedal points. Then comes the Chorale proper. The tune is basically diatonic, with a modal seventh, but it includes a number of chromatic passing notes. The four sections of four-part writing show a clear and precocious technique. A varied and abbreviated repetition of the Prelude leads to a coda on a tonic pedal in D major, once more stating the opening measures of the Chorale.

23. *Three Pieces for piano* (*Prélude, Hommage à Ravel, Danse*)

November 1915 (*Hommage à Ravel*); May 1919 (*Prélude* and *Danse*)
Prélude: "To Walter Morse Rummel"; *Danse*: "To Ricardo Viñes"
Duration: 7 minutes
Salabert

The *Prélude* (lourd et grave) is a titanic piece in 9/8—dark, rough, atonal, and highly dissonant. It is somewhat reminiscent of the Prelude from Roussel's *Suite*, Op. 14, for its unresolved tritonic tensions and looks forward to the opening of Honegger's own *Judith*. The piece, ternary in form with an abbreviated reprise and coda, develops mostly in the darkest low register. In the central section, occasional right-hand sorties into the treble seem to be aimed at helping the music to escape from the murk. In the recapitulation, the climax is reached with an orchestral texture on three staffs, covering the whole range of the instrument. A strident chord with trills precedes the final abrupt chord. Throughout, the complex harmonic aggregates are built over Honegger's typically vigorous fifths in the bass, providing rich resonances and a solid tonal foundation.

This exercise in German expressionism is followed by the limpid clarity of the *Hommage à Ravel* (modéré), a graceful and dreamily tender little piece. It is curiously effective in integrating typically Ravelian harmonic fingerprints and sonorities (as well as occasional distant echoes of Debussy) with Honegger's own easily recognizable personality. Once again the form is ternary followed by a coda. The first section exposes three contrasting ideas (the capricious third, in a rapid staccato, is the one reminiscent of Debussy). They are developed in a central part in which tension grows toward a brief, passionate climax, very much like the one in Ravel's *La Belle et la Bête*. It is indeed *Mother Goose* that seems to have attracted Honegger the most of all Ravel's works, and not just here. In the coda, we should note the delightful cadence (B-flat major–B minor) preceding the final resolution into E major—a surprise of truly Ravelian elegance.

In the final *Danse* we return to an atonal idiom, based on the whole-tone scale. The robust perpetuum mobile (rapide) in 6/8, with its harshly percussive whirling motion, gives way briefly to a staccato middle section in 2/4, before launching once more into its mad gyrations in shortened note-values and firing up in strident tremolos. In comparison with the *Toccata and Variations*, the *Prélude* and the *Danse*, at least, adopt a language that is far more daring and modern.

25. Seven Short Pieces

October 1919–January 1920 (No. 1: October 1919; No. 2: November 1919; Nos. 3, 5, 6, and 7: January 1920; No. 4: December 1919)
No. 1: "To Rose Martin-Lafon"; No. 2: "To Mina Vaurabourg"; No. 3: "To Andrée Vaurabourg"; No. 4: "To Marcelle Meyer"; No. 5: "To Mytyl Fraggi"; No. 6: "To Mme. E. Alleaume"; No. 7: "To Robert Casadesus"
First performance: 4 March 1920, Andrée Vaurabourg, Salle Gaveau, Paris (SMI concert)
Duration: 6 minutes
Salabert

These seven lovely miniatures are perhaps Honegger's best piano pieces. They are concise, well contrasted, unfailingly interesting, and radical in their sound and their harmonies, and together they make up a remarkably unified cycle.

The first piece (Souplement) presents a graceful tune supported by bittersweet harmonies that are vaguely bitonal, leading to an unexpected cadence in G-sharp minor.

The chromatic second piece (Vif), like a little passing squall, lasts a mere twenty seconds. The third piece (Très lent), on the other hand, takes up almost a third of the duration of the entire group. It is a sort of funeral procession, with somber and highly complex chromatic and atonal harmonies, full of six- and seven-note aggregates leading to an unexpected resolution into C major.

The fourth piece (Légèrement) is as short as the second. Sixteen measures of caustic polytonality set one's teeth on edge. This marks the nearest Honegger ever came to the style of his friend Milhaud.

The fifth piece (Lent) is a languid, nostalgic piece in the form of a tango or habanera. Its obsessive pedal fifth to some extent recalls Debussy's *Soirée dans Grenade*. It is informed by three rhythmic elements: the slow habanera rhythm, leaning on its opening fifth; a brief motif of staccato, repeated 32nd-notes; and finally a triplet motif bearing the melodic material of the piece.

The launch of the sixth piece (Rythmique) on a "classical" motif in the style of Bach suggests that it will be an "invention" of some kind, but it turns into a sort of clumsy, primitive jazz, rather like Debussy's *Minstrels* or *General Lavine*. The cycle concludes with a spicy A major contaminated by harmonic clusters. This final piece is the nearest of the seven to the aesthetic of Les Six. It is a percussive and ultradissonant homage to jazz as seen by Stravinsky, and to the cult of the fair and the music hall that was dear to Cocteau but in general very far from Honegger's own concerns—even if the locomotive of *Pacific 2.3.1* also shows its snout here. The flow of the deliberately trivial, strident tune is interrupted by a number of breaks in hammered-out sixteenth-notes in the manner of 1920s jazz.

26. Sarabande, from the *Album des Six*

January 1920 (but see commentary below)
No. 2 of the *Album des Six* (No. 1: *Prélude* by Georges Auric; No. 3: *Romance sans paroles* by René Durey; No. 4: *Mazurka* by Darius Milhaud; No. 5: *Valse* by Francis Poulenc; No. 6: *Pastorale* by Germaine Tailleferre)
Duration: 1 minute 20 seconds
Salabert

Frédéric Robert's research suggests that Honegger's *Sarabande* for the *Album des Six* may have been written some four years earlier as part of a suite that has remained unpublished, a collective work written at the instigation of Maurice Emmanuel and consisting of a prelude by Milhaud, a minuet by Pierre Menu, and a gigue by Jean Déré.[1] Honegger's *Sarabande* is a delightful miniature. Its texture is densely polyphonic and its harmonies rich and complex, although the overall key of B-flat major is felt throughout.

43A. *Suite* from *Three Counterpoints* for piano duet

Date unknown
Hansen

The *Suite* from *Three Counterpoints* is a transcription by the composer for piano duet. The *Three Counterpoints* (described under Category 4 later in this chapter) date from October–November 1922, though the date of this transcription is unknown. There exists a later arrangement for two pianos, made for Honegger's American tour in 1929. The first performance of this two-piano version was given in Seattle on 2 February 1929 by Honegger and Andrée Vaurabourg.

52. *Le Cahier romand*

July 1921–July 1923 (No. 1: September 1921; No. 2: July 1923; No. 3: July 1921; No. 4: June 1923; No. 5: April 1922)
No. 1: "To Alice Ecoffey"; No. 2: "To Jacqueline Ansermet"; No. 3: "To Miquette Wagner-Rieder"; No. 4: "To Paul Boepple"; No. 5: "To René Morax"
First performance: 30 January 1924, Andrée Vaurabourg, Salle Érard, Paris (SMI concert)
Duration: 6 minutes 20 seconds
Salabert

Le Cahier romand is a second collection of miniatures that comes close in quality to the *Seven Short Pieces*. But, apart from the burlesque antics of the fourth piece, the writing here is simpler and more transparent, and there is a feeling of a relaxed, pastoral idyll, reflecting the happy times Honegger had spent in western Switzerland with the friends to whom the pieces are dedicated.

The superb opening piece (Calme), compound form with coda, is implicitly in B-flat, disguised by a multiplicity of chromatic passing notes. This is essentially a contrapuntal piece, and its expressive intensity looks forward at times to the wonderful duet "Espérance dans la Croix," the sixth movement of *La Danse des morts*. By contrast, the second piece (Un peu animé) is a graceful, disarming little dance in D major. It combines considerable chromaticism in contrary motion with melodic invention, superb counterpoint, and tender lyricism.

The masterly polyphony of the third piece (Calme et doux) leads to an atmosphere of concentrated but gentle gravity. The key of B major is hidden almost until the final measure by the chromatic language, but this is not really dissonant, apart from a number of fine suspensions that obey the traditional rules. The fourth piece (Rythmé) contrasts with its neighbors not only in its rhythmic vigor, but also in the freedom of its form and language. It is a powerful and boldly syncopated caprice, and its opening gesture, as Alfred Cortot has pointed out, derives from the second tableau of Stravinsky's *Petrushka*. From this grows a first theme that is gradually ousted by a second, which comes to dominate the middle of the piece. We find here an exact premonition of the opening syncopations of the *Concertino for piano and orchestra*. The last piece (Égal) is a tranquil, almost popular monody, like a soothing lullaby, over evasive modal harmonies. The form alternates two periods, both in simple conjunct motion, and the mood of inexorable, hypnotic placidity—very rare in Honegger's music—makes one think of Stravinsky's *Easy Pieces* for piano duet.

69. Hommage à Albert Roussel

13 (or 18?) December 1928
For Roussel's sixtieth birthday
First performance: 13 April 1929, Pierre Maire, Festival Roussel, Salle de l'ancien
Conservatoire, Paris
Duration: 1 minute 30 seconds
Salabert

The *Hommage à Albert Roussel* is built on a theme made out of the thirteen letters of the name Albert Roussel (A–F-sharp–B-flat–E–F-flat–A-flat / F-flat–C-flat–B-flat–G-flat–G-flat–E–F-sharp). This jagged melodic outline is powerfully harmonized with chords of a decidedly Rousselian cast, as is the remainder of the piece. This robust, highly rhythmic homage, firmly anchored in D major, quotes in its middle section the Valse from Roussel's *Le Festin de l'araignée* (The Spider's Banquet), compressed into binary rhythm. The coda quotes the soloist's theme from the slow movement of Roussel's *Piano Concerto*, Op. 36, completed only the previous year.

81. *Prelude, Arioso, and Fughetta on the name BACH*

October 1932
First performance: 26 November 1932, Andrée Vaurabourg, Salle de Géographie, Paris (children's concert)
Duration: 6 minutes 10 seconds
Salabert

This fine, short triptych is today best known in the transcription by Arthur Hoérée for string orchestra (H81A, Category 7). The brief Prelude (allegro) develops the four notes B, A, C, H in swift, toccata-like arpeggios, with octave jumps in both directions. During the first sixteen measures it rises through all twelve semitones before returning in the opposite direction.

The expressive Arioso (grave), in three periods, is built on long, drawn-out lines, like the "Lamento" from *La Danse des morts* or, even more closely, the Larghetto from the *Fourth Symphony*. Here the motif B–A–C–H, in half-notes, becomes a sort of harmonized cantus firmus and acts as accompaniment to a beautiful decorated cantilena. Overall, the principle is more or less that of a passacaglia.

A brief cadenza accelerates to a whirlwind of 32nd-notes, alluding to the Prelude, and leads to the sprightly Fughetta (allegro), a two-part invention (which does not preclude the subject and countersubject being treated both in straight and inverted form, not to mention a counterexposition and even a stretta!) (Example 2). After various partial octave transpositions of the B–A–C–H motif, it is finally presented in a chorale-like version, culminating in a ringing B major chord.

Example 2

95. *Berceuse* for *Le Bal des Petits Lits blancs*

Early June 1935
First performance: 4 June 1935, Cercle Interallié, Paris
Duration: 1 minute
Unpublished

An unpretentious sixteen-measure trifle in F-sharp major. Its cheerful popular melody is heard over a bell-like basso ostinato.

115. *Scenic Railway*

1937 (most likely in the summer)
"To Marguerite Long"
First performance: 28 November 1938, Nicole Henriot, Salle Gaveau, Paris
Duration: 1 minute 30 seconds
Salabert

A piece of musical realism "describing" a roller coaster. Six introductory measures lead to the main Allegro, in which the two hands move in dizzy parallel chromatic lines, rising and falling over a wide range of the keyboard, with breathtaking rallentandos, especially before the final tumble.

145. Petits Airs sur une basse célèbre

January–February 1941 (Nos. 1–7: January; Nos. 8–12: February)
"To Tartouillonnionet from her papa"
Duration: 11 minutes
Salabert

The work *Petits Airs sur une basse célèbre* is dedicated to Honegger's daughter, Pascale, who was eight years old at the time it was written. It is his only contribution to piano teaching literature for the young, and it consists of twelve short pieces on an extremely simple bass, written initially in the form of a little waltz. Practically all the pieces are in a two-part texture. The sixth is a march, the eighth a sicilienne, the tenth a highly expressive arietta full of sighs, and the last a very modest exercise in virtuosity using chromatic sixteenth-notes. This little collection, which was published a long time after its composition, is worth the attention of music teachers.

173. Two Sketches for Piano (in Nicolas Obouhov's new, simplified notation)

15 April 1942 (No. 2); 9 October 1943 (No. 1)
No. 1: "To Madame Aussenac de Broglie"; No. 2: "To Yvette Grimaud"
Duration: 5 minutes 20 seconds
Salabert

Until these two pieces are rewritten in standard notation, they will remain imprisoned in a notational system for which Honegger showed enthusiasm at the time, but which never caught on. The first piece, written entirely in dense, dissonant clusters that were no doubt suggested by the notation, is a somber, austere piece of limited interest. The second piece, which was written first and in standard notation, is more tonal and, frankly, more attractive. Continuous sextuplets in the treble register unroll over the left hand's gentle, diatonic cantus firmus of quarter-notes in the middle register.

213. Très modéré for piano

Date unknown. Possibly contemporary with the *Seven Short Pieces* or *Le Cahier romand*
Duration: 50 seconds
Salabert

Très modéré is a brief bagatelle that could have been included among the *Seven Short Pieces*. This unobtrusive, slightly caustic piece seems to dance with the lightest of feet before disappearing with an ironic pirouette.

Category 1A: Music for One or Two Pianos from Stage and Film

60B. *La Neige sur Rome*, from *L'Impératrice aux rochers*
60C. *Suite (Partita) for two pianos*, adapted from *L'Impératrice aux rochers*
76A. *Suite for piano*, adapted from *Les Aventures du roi Pausole*
110A. *Orgue dans l'église*, from the film *Marthe Richard au service de la France*
139. *Partita for two pianos*
166B. *Three Pieces* from the film *Le Capitaine Fracasse*
183A. *Three Pieces* from the film *Un Ami viendra ce soir*

This category contains one of Honegger's most important piano works, the *Partita for two pianos* (H139).

60B. *La Neige sur Rome* (Snow in Rome), from *L'Impératrice aux rochers*

Transcription of the Prelude to Act II, No. 7 of the complete score (H60, Category 14)
Duration: 2 minutes 50 seconds
Salabert

60C. *Suite (Partita) for two pianos*, adapted from *L'Impératrice aux rochers*

Arranged, possibly with the help of Andrée Vaurabourg, for Honegger's tour of the United States in 1929; Nos. 4, 12, 25, and 14 of the complete score (H60, Category 14)
First performance: 26 January 1929, Arthur Honegger and Andrée Vaurabourg, Detroit
Duration: 12 minutes 35 seconds
Unpublished

Not to be confused with the *Partita for two pianos* (see H139); only the Finale of that work is the same as that of this one.

76A. *Suite for piano*, adapted from *Les Aventures du roi Pausole*

Late 1930 or early 1931
Duration: 11 minutes 45 seconds
1. "Ouverture" (No. 1); 2. "Ritournelle de la mule" (No. 12); 3. "Les adieux de Pausole" (No. 25); 4. "Air d'Aline" (No. 17); 5. "Le chocolat espagnol" (No. 23)
Salabert

110A. *Orgue dans l'église* (The Organ in the Church), from the film *Marthe Richard au service de la France*

c. 1910–1911 (the handwriting and musical style are close to that of the *Sonata for violin and piano in D minor*, H3). Included in the film score *Marthe Richard au service de la France* (H110, Category 16); the rest of the music from that score dates from February 1937. This piece is No. 14.
Duration: 3 minutes 35 seconds
Choudens

Orgue dans l'église is a very early piece for organ, very naive in its academic four-part writing, with correct modulations to keys close to the tonic E-flat major. Interesting only as evidence of Honegger's earliest composing years.

139. *Partita for two pianos*
January 1940 (finished before 31 January)
"To Franz-Josef Hirt"
First performance: 31 January 1940, Arthur Honegger and Franz-Josef Hirt, Zurich
Duration: 10 minutes 40 seconds
Salabert

After fourteen newly composed measures, the initial Largo of the *Partita for two pianos* is taken from scene 4 of the first tableau of *Sémiramis* ("Entry of the Idols of the Vanquished"). The Vivace–Allegretto links episodes 2 and 3 of scene 3 of this first tableau ("The Queen Descends from the Chariot and Leaps on to the Throne" and "Toilette of the Queen"). The second Largo uses the beginning of the first Interlude (Nocturne) between the first and second tableaux of *Sémiramis*, while the final Allegro moderato consists of No. 14 ("The Return of the Emperor") from *L'Impératrice aux rochers*, which Honegger had already used as the Finale of the unpublished *Suite (Partita) for two pianos* (H60C).

For reasons that had nothing to do with the music, this powerful four-movement work was not published until 1987. It consistently opposes large, harshly percussive, dissonant block chords with passages of delicately pastoral cantilena interspersed with airy bell sounds, and deserves a place of honor in the rather limited two-piano repertory.

The cyclopean character of the opening Largo recalls the *Prélude* of *Three Pieces for piano* (H23) of 1919. After the mysterious crawling phrases at the beginning, the movement develops in a fiercely atonal style with extremely harsh, percussive sounds, but enclosing a long central melody. A brief Vivace introduction in very fast, fleeting eighth-notes in 6/8 time leads to a ternary Allegretto. This begins with a delicate, diatonic, almost Ravelian theme, harmonized with light touches of bitonality, from which it proceeds to other melodies of a similarly peaceful limpidity. The middle section is much tougher and more symphonic, like the opening Largo, alternating blocks of syncopated, dissonant chords with percussive triplet eighth-notes. After this, the opening passage returns, enriched with brilliant glissandos and rushing countermelodies in sixteenth-notes. The second Largo is a kind of paraphrasal development of the middle section of the first.

The *Partita for two pianos* ends with the Allegro moderato, a grand finale in A major (presented almost always in its first inversion). This ternary movement is of symphonic dimensions that bring it close to being a sonata form, and it is much more tonal than what has gone before. It takes the form of a march with rather gawky dotted rhythms over a steady quarter-note accompaniment. The theme (Example 3) is present throughout, even under the long lyrical melody of the middle section. The reprise is decorated with vertiginous glissandos covering the whole extent of the keyboard and culminates in a grand ceremonial coda.

Example 3

166B. *Three Pieces* for piano from the film *Le Capitaine Fracasse*

April 1943
Duration: 8 minutes
1. Matamore (largamente–moderato); 2. Isabelle (andantino); 3. Danse de Scapin
Éditions Josette France

Unlike the rest of the published score of the extended music Honegger wrote for Abel Gance's film, these three pieces were brought out in a separate edition prepared with particular care. Although they were intended as concert pieces, they have been wholly ignored. Nonetheless, "Matamore," the longest of the three, is a very fine, serious piece. It provides a good contrast with the graceful arietta of "Isabelle" (andantino), a piece that is classically inspired despite its many modulations, and with the final "Danse de Scapin," which is a lively passepied.

183A. *Three Pieces* for piano from the film *Un Ami viendra ce soir*

July 1945
No. 1 (Souvenir de Chopin): "To Jacqueline Potier-Landowski"
Duration: 8 minutes 30 seconds
1. Souvenir de Chopin; 2. Jacques au piano; 3. Prélude à la Mort
Salabert (No. 1)

One of the heroes of Raymond Bernard's film *Un Ami viendra ce soir* is a mad pianist, which explains the presence of these three pieces. In "Souvenir de Chopin," Honegger wrote a successful pastiche of impeccable style and taste. It is a kind of melancholy impromptu, exuding a bittersweet nostalgia highly reminiscent of Chopin, even if the brief middle section makes a bow in the direction of Liszt or even Wagner. The two other pieces are not so successful ("Jacques au piano" recalls part of the first piece in its final measures). They are too closely tied to their film context to have a life of their own, and they remain unpublished.

Category 2: String Quartets

15. *String Quartet No. 1* in C minor
103. *String Quartet No. 2* in D
114. *String Quartet No. 3* in E

I have written a certain number of "challenging" works, as people call those compositions that constitute a particular tax on one's creative powers. . . . I regard them rather as by-products of Beethoven, so to speak. "Poor man's Beethoven," you may say. I agree, but even so, that is the area in which my true nature expresses itself. Within this category I have a secret preference for certain pieces that have not always been much appreciated: these include the quartets, and especially the first because it exactly reflects the character of the young man who wrote it in 1917. It has its faults and its *longueurs*, but in it I recognize myself as though I were looking in a mirror. From the technical point of view, I would mention the *String Quartet No. 3*, which marks some progress in economy of means and in compositional skill.

This sober objectivity is typical of the way Honegger used to talk about his own music. It is a matter for considerable regret that he wrote no more than three string quartets, and in particular that he did not return to this genre at the height of his maturity, after writing his five symphonies. In his quartets he wrote without compromise in a terse, sharp, forceful style, and was able to blend his specifically Alemannic traits with a concision and clarity that belonged more to the Latin side of his make-up. In short, they demonstrate a synthesis of two cultures that is particularly fitting in a Swiss composer. Although these quartets are rarely played today, they are his most important pieces of chamber music and are some of the finest works in this medium written in the twentieth century.

15. *String Quartet No. 1* in C minor

First version: June–September 1913 (first movement); November 1915 (third movement)
Second version (first movement only): nearly finished by 17 March 1915
Final version: July 1917, Paris (first movement); March–April 1916, Paris/Le Havre (second movement); October 1917, Paris (third movement)
"To Florent Schmitt"
First performance: 20 June 1919, Capelle Quartet, Paris (SMI concert)
Duration: 25 minutes (6:30 + 11:00 + 7:30)
La Sirène/Max Eschig

The 1915 version of Honegger's first string quartet must have included a first draft of the second movement, but this is now lost.

We should also mention that the original (1913) version of the first movement is followed by the beginnings of a Scherzo in 3/8. Honegger later used this, completely transformed, as the basis for the "Pantomime" that forms the second movement of the *Suite archaïque* (H203) of 1951.

The *String Quartet No. 1* merits particularly close attention because the different completed versions of two of the three movements give us an insight into Honegger's working methods at the time he was a student and was fashioning his own style.

Early Attempts

FIRST MOVEMENT (FIRST AND SECOND VERSIONS)

The first two versions of the first movement have the same number of measures (263), that is to say, forty-two more than the final version. It is essentially the same piece, but in almost every measure there is at least one change of detail, and many measures are entirely rewritten. Honegger's aim was to turn the texture into a true four-part polyphony, with interesting countermelodies replacing the numerous tremolos, which smacked too much of orchestral writing. In their stead, Honegger put rhythmic figures (eighth-note triplets) or real tunes, eliminated obsessive and tiresome rhythms, and gave more character to melodic outlines by means of accents, rhythm (often dotted), and articulation. In short, he made the whole movement more intense and alive. At certain points he also filled out the sonority with chords and double stopping.

FIRST MOVEMENT (SECOND AND THIRD VERSIONS)

The final version of the first movement shows further progress in the direction of true polyphony, with the elimination of the last vestiges of orchestral writing. Of particular note is the change from the traditional sonata form, with the suppression of forty-two measures, to the specifically Honeggerian type of sonata form with reversed recapitulation that he would henceforth use in almost every case. Certain passages are entirely new. He suppressed some fifty measures of the recapitulation *after* the first theme, so that the appearance of the second theme, which was originally part of the central development section, now becomes the start of the reversed recapitulation. This second theme has finally reached its definitive form, complete with its descending element.

THIRD MOVEMENT (FIRST AND SECOND VERSIONS)

In the case of third movement, Honegger's recomposition was more radical. The movement is also shortened by no less than seventy-one measures (269 instead of 340). Once again, the traditional sonata form is replaced by that with reversed recapitulation. Only frequent guiding-marks allow us to stake out the two courses. The two expositions are the passages that remain the closest to one another. In the first version, the final return of the first theme functioned as a coda, being preceded by a long passage of calm. This passage is totally removed in the definitive version, no doubt because it made the movement too long and preempted the effect of the marvelous slow epilogue.

Final Version

The language of the quartet is one of widely extended tonality, with considerable chromaticism and numerous sharp dissonances. Indeed, the basic tonalities (C minor, with E major in the Adagio) are often hard to perceive. It must be the only work written in France at that time (and by an adopted Frenchman) that recalls Max Reger in its hectic, dense polyphony. The dedication to Florent Schmitt may be taken as symbolic, since Schmitt was the nearest to German romanticism of the French composers of the time. Like all Honegger's large instrumental works, the quartet is in three movements, all in sonata form with a reversed recapitulation. The last movement has three themes.

Whatever Honegger himself may have thought about the work, it stands as his first real masterpiece, on an equal footing with the symphonies of his maturity. As such, it demands analysis in some detail.

FIRST MOVEMENT: APPASSIONATO (VIOLENT ET TOURMENTÉ)

The first movement is of an extreme intensity, as suggested by its complete title. The counterpoint is masterly, and the breadth and flow of the argument allow for no weak points or relaxation. A chromaticism derived from *Tristan* via Reger alternates with a modal style in the manner of Fauré and Ravel.

The rich thematic material remains consistent thanks to the presence of motifs *a* and *b*, fragments of ascending and descending scales respectively, which grant the piece's cohesion and unity. The upward thrust and dotted rhythms of the passionate first theme (Example 4), rising to the heavens ("himmelsstürmend," as the Germans would say), recall the opening of Schoenberg's *First String Quartet*, which Honegger must certainly have known.

Example 4

The choice of the melodic minor (or Dorian mode on D) underlines the diatonic aspect of the melodic style, which is in permanent conflict with the chromatic polyphony. Honegger's typically solid fifths underpin the structure, matched against the agitated eighth-note triplets in the second violin. The consequent of the theme (measure 3) embraces the Neapolitan sixth, the attraction of which toward the tonic C minor underlines the latter's dominant role. An energetic fanfare motif (an addition of the final version only) will later be used in the development section. For the moment this leads to a break, followed by the first passage of calm in the movement, a bridging theme of a peculiarly

French cast. This is developed through dense polyphony, and, as in César Franck's *String Quartet*, all musicians are playing the entire time, without respite. After further incidents, the real second subject appears at measure 66 (Example 5). Its gentle scales are a curious premonition of the second theme of the first movement of Fauré's *String Quartet*, not written until 1924. Schoenberg and Fauré—these are the two opposite poles between which the young composer's inspiration seems to move.

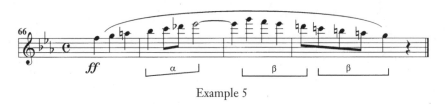

Example 5

The music now reaches the relative E-flat major, and the opening theme is heard first on the viola and then on the first violin. But the feeling of security is short-lived. The development follows at once at measure 85, consisting of a stormy contrapuntal scuffle that develops the opening theme both straight and inverted, and then in stretto, driven ever onward by the fanfare motif. A false recapitulation of the first theme in B minor precedes the reappearance of the second (which has not been developed), and this (measure 155) marks the beginning of the reversed recapitulation. Emerging from a low menacing rumble of triplets, the first theme springs in quadruple imitation and in three successive bursts. It is only with the third of these, at measure 185, that it appears in the main key and in a powerful *fortissimo*.

An abrupt break ushers in the coda at measure 197. This unfolds entirely over a tonic pedal and in a spectral, disembodied *pianissimo* that looks forward to the "dumbfounded and terrified" conclusion of the *Fifth Symphony*. Sometimes the triplets in eighth-notes become quarter-notes—a sign that the movement's physical energy is getting exhausted. Finally, the opening theme fragments itself, disintegrates, and is reduced to its initial anacrusis. The music dies a natural death.

SECOND MOVEMENT: ADAGIO (TRÈS LENT)

The extended Adagio of the second movement is the longest Honegger would write until the De profundis of the *Symphonie liturgique*. Overall, this second movement is more tonal than the first, and the passages of chromaticism (the introduction and the second theme) are more strongly contrasted against the diatonic ones (the first theme). The succession of dominants occupy for the first time the predominant place they would continue to hold in Honegger's musical rhetoric. Fourteen introductory measures of utterly *Tristan*-like chromatic hesitations, interspersed with fermatas, grope in search of the first theme, which is finally heard at measure 15 (Example 6). This long and wonderfully sinuous E major tune can be heard as the fruit of Gédalge's teaching in the way it develops without repetition or padding. For the first time Honegger had succeeded in realizing an ideal that he would always hold dear, as in the De profundis mentioned above. But more memorable still is its brief consequent (Example 7), with its successive dominants of A and B-flat. It is curiously reminiscent of Ernest Bloch, and probably the only point of contact between two composers who never met.

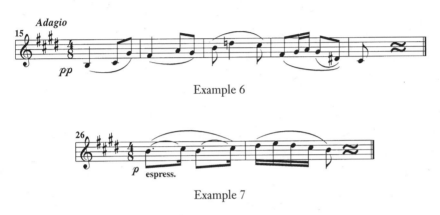

Example 6

Example 7

A rhythmic ostinato leads to the second theme at measure 42, heard high on the cello but almost obscured by the figurations derived from the ostinato. It is more clearly heard at its second appearance on the first violin, in a strident climax followed by a break. The calm passage that ensues, closing the exposition, quotes, no doubt unconsciously, a motif from the second movement of Debussy's *Sonata for flute, viola, and harp* (written shortly before this piece). At the beginning of the development at measure 60, this is transformed into an ostinato, almost in the manner of a funeral procession. This development is split into two absolutely equal halves, on the first and second themes successively, and this last section expands into figuration of an almost orchestral exuberance, in which Florent Schmitt, to whom the piece is dedicated, might well have seen a homage to himself! The implacable buildup of the huge crescendo reaches a tension that is almost unbearable. This, from measures 78 to 95, is the climax of the movement, indeed of the whole quartet. A sudden lull inaugurates the recapitulation at measure 96. For once, this is not reversed, although Honegger does reverse the order of the two elements within the first theme itself, beginning with its consequent (Example 7). This recapitulation is a faithful repeat of the exposition, changes of tonality aside, and it leads to a coda on the first theme in the tonic E major at measure 129. This is followed by an epilogue that corresponds exactly with the *Tristan*-like introduction, only this time it resolves peacefully into E major.

THIRD MOVEMENT: ALLEGRO (RUDE ET RYTHMIQUE)–ADAGIO

This Finale is close in character to the first movement, sharing its key of C minor. But it is in 3/4, and its structure, based on three ideas, is more complex. We can analyze it either as a sonata form, with a brief development starting at measure 93 and a reversed recapitulation at measure 140, or else as a binary form with a long developing recapitulation through measures 93 to 222, followed by a brief final development and the slow coda. In any event the form is irregular, and the polyphonic flux is even more intense than in the first movement. After an opening twofold gesture, like a motorcyclist impatiently revving the engine, the first theme makes its entrance (Example 8). The pattern of four nervous, energetic sixteenth-notes will be the basic motor element of the piece, in company with the ascending motif *c*. The first theme proper at measure 6 includes the dotted rhythm that we observed in the first movement in Example 4, but now adapted to triple time. The eighth-note triplets also create an organic link between the two movements. The rough bridging theme (Example 9), with its wide fifth and octave leaps, is percussive and orchestral in character, like Roussel's later 3/4 allegros.

Example 8

Example 9

As in the first movement, the tension abruptly relaxes for the entry of the second group of themes at measure 55, a more flowing, limpid, and melodic passage in the relative E-flat major. The first of this group, a cheerful ascending idea, incorporates *c*, then at measure 74 we hear a twinging canon between viola and cello in their high registers, a pattern that would haunt Honegger right up to the duet "Espérance dans la Croix" of *La Danse des morts*. The peaceful cadential group foreshadows the end of the work.

The extremely compact development section excludes the second group of themes, relying on canons and inversions. At measure 140, the forceful bridging theme (Example 9) dominates the scene and, although we may possibly regard this as marking the start of the recapitulation (for it shall never come back), the play of counterpoint continues ever more vigorously until a *fortissimo* paroxysm high in the treble. Then comes the recapitulation of the second group, but again the contrapuntal development includes elements of the first group. Only the arrival of the cadential group brings a brief respite. But the motorcyclist is already stepping on his accelerator and at measure 223 the first theme returns, now in C-sharp minor, ready for the final polyphonic conflict.

The tension builds through long, ultra-dissonant chords in the high register, and then deconstructs itself in measures 246 to 251, six measures of an extraordinary decrescendo in register, intensity, and speed that strikingly looks forward to the end of *Pacific 2.3.1.* We then reach the sublime adagio coda, at measures 252 to 269, in which ever-diminishing chromatic interruptions gradually leave a serene C major in possession. Here we come across an echo of that most Fauréan of Ravel's inspirations, "The Fairy Garden" from *Mother Goose*— Reger and Schoenberg are exorcised, nowhere to be seen! If we look closely at the two sections of this epilogue, we can see that they are relaxed, diatonic transfigurations of the first theme and the bridging theme respectively. In the final morendo, Honegger adds the second and the sixth to the closing C major chord. He would have this epilogue very much in mind when writing the conclusion to his *First Symphony*.

103. *String Quartet No. 2* in D

1934/1935 (first and second movements); June 1936 (third movement)
"To the Pro Arte Quartet"
First performance: September 1936, Pro Arte Quartet, Venice Biennale
Duration: 18 minutes 45 seconds (6:30 + 6:15 + 6:00)
Salabert

Honegger's *Second* and *Third String Quartets* are very similar to one another, *String Quartet No. 3* having been begun very shortly after the completion of *String Quartet No. 2*. Both are in three movements and are shorter than the *String Quartet No. 1*; both make compelling listening through the sheer force and energy of their allegros and the deeply expressive tension of their adagios; both may be considered as decisive steps along the road to the *Symphony for Strings* of 1941, which built an epic, monumental edifice on the ground they had conquered. Both quartets, and especially the *Third* (which the composer rightly preferred), deserve a place in the modern chamber music repertory.

In the *String Quartet No. 2*, and especially in its first two movements, one is struck by the importance of pedal notes, whether adorned or plain, and by the ostinatos that invade the accompaniments and even play a part in the formation of themes. Some secondary elements in the opening Allegro (eighth-note triplets, widely leaping dissonant chords) form the basis of main themes in the Finale.

First Movement: Allegro

This sonata movement is concise and economical in its form. The three sections are of almost equal length (59, 50, and 65 measures). The solo cello begins with repeated quarter-notes that sound like an accompaniment figure, but in fact constitute the beginning of the principal theme (Example 10), while the eighth-note pattern in the second measure will, despite appearances, be no more than accompanimental. The melodic, rather sullen second theme does not appear until measure 36, polarized like the first around the note D. The development, with a long E pedal at its center, does not deal at all with the second group of themes, but the first half of the reversed recapitulation fills this gap. The return of the first theme is punctuated by strange glissandos, and the movement ends as it began on the cello's low Ds. Eight measures of a più lento coda act as a link to the second movement, which begins without a break. This transition establishes a thematic link between the two movements, the repeated quarter-notes anticipating, in augmentation, the ostinato in the middle of the Adagio. It also effects the tritonal modulation from D to the Adagio's basic key of G-sharp minor.

Example 10

SECOND MOVEMENT: ADAGIO

The outer sections of this ternary form (37, 39, and 34 measures) are entirely in G-sharp minor. Above discreet ostinatos on the two violins, the viola unfolds its long modal lament, expressing an irremediable despair. The central section momentarily reasserts D minor in rich triple-stopping from the cello. There is a passionate, if dissonant, duet for the two violins high up, and this is soon joined by an obsessive ostinato on the viola, the acute tension of which looks forward to the trumpet ostinato in the first movement of the *Fifth Symphony*. After a return of the opening lament, now expressed more forcefully, the music rises to a huge, almost orchestral climax, followed by a long decrescendo toward the varied recapitulation of the first section. This now incorporates the ostinato of the central section, before fading away on a unison G-sharp.

THIRD MOVEMENT: ALLEGRO MARCATO

The *String Quartet No. 2* ends with a strident, impetuous toccata, pursuing the conflict between the poles of D and G-sharp. This prefiguring of the Finale of the *Symphony for Strings* is particularly striking in the coda. Unlike Willy Tappolet[2] and Geoffrey Spratt,[3] I see the form of the movement as that of a well-balanced sonata structure, with a much-condensed recapitulation (56, 46, and 35 measures).

The opening gesture is purely rhythmic. Dissonant groups of two tied eighth-notes, on and off the beat, are set against eighth-note triplets, then with Honegger's favorite iambic rhythms, recalling his particular way of accenting the French language. At measure 24, a new idea (now in G-sharp) makes enormous, giant-like leaps, interspersed with rasping syncopations. Finally, at measure 32, a new melody enters in the guise of a second theme, returning us to D minor. This melody, symphonic in character, with its chaotic rhythms, is destined to become the basis of the work's final triumphal measures.

The cadential group makes further allusions to the "giant leaps," and the return of these, transposed into E minor, will mark the beginning of the recapitulation at measure 103. This occurs after a varied and complex development section, which cannot be described in detail here, but which brings in a new, simple theme in F-sharp major (Example 11). If we examine this theme closely, we can see that it is merely the diminution of the main theme of the first movement. The second theme returns at measure 114, sailing on the first violin high above the forest of triplets, and establishes D major, which will now be the key until the end of the work. The triumphant atmosphere is close to that of the end of the *Symphony for Strings*, and this work is anticipated even more closely in the final intervention of the "giant leaps." The movement ends exactly as it began, providing the work with a worthy conclusion.

Example 11

114. *String Quartet No. 3* in E

September 1936–June 1937 (first movement: 5 June 1937; second movement: May
     1937; third movement: September 1936)
"To Madame Elizabeth Sprague Coolidge" (who commissioned the work)
First performance: 22 October 1937, Pro Arte Quartet, Salle de la Réformation,
     Geneva
Duration: 16 minutes 40 seconds (5:30 + 6:10 + 5:00)
Salabert

Although Honegger's *Third String Quartet* is similar to its predecessor in size and shape, it is undoubtedly a better work. It is far more polyphonic, and contains real melodic counterpoint, in place of superimposed ostinatos, and considerable thematic work. The composer himself knew it was a better work, due to its truly lapidary conciseness.

FIRST MOVEMENT: ALLEGRO

The first movement is in 6/4 time and, like the other two, is based on E. It is also entirely dominated by three elements: the two from the opening theme, *a* and *b/c* (Example 12), with particular emphasis on the initial descending third, and the rhythmically insistent five quarter-notes of the bridging theme at measure 24 (Example 13). This bridging theme assumes the "masculine" role here, and looks forward to the faster sections of *Monopartita* (H204). The musical language of the movement is dissonant and barely tonal, despite one or two passages, especially toward the end, where a key is discernible. As in the Finale of the *String Quartet No. 1*, the development and recapitulation are combined.

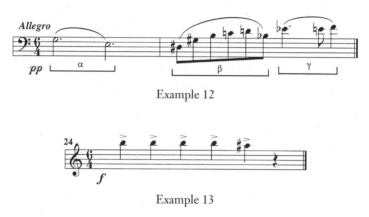

Example 12

Example 13

The brief central development section, from measure 49 to measure 74, uses only the first group of themes, followed by a "developing recapitulation" of the second group, including two distinct themes (heard at measures 32 and 41). Deeper analysis reveals a capacity for continuous development worthy of Schoenberg or Mozart. Particularly noteworthy is the triple affirmation of the complete first theme, beginning at measure 84, in imitations and in B-flat minor (a tritone away from E), constituting a powerful and decisive "false recapitulation." We should also note the final appearance in measure 140 of this same theme in a four-part stretto-canon in C minor. The coda at measure 156 blends this theme with the rhythms of the bridging theme (Example 13). Finally, the dying oscillation of the minor third (*a*) brings the movement to an end in an atmosphere of gray, melancholy resignation that foreshadows the end of the first movement of the *Symphony for Strings*.

SECOND MOVEMENT: ADAGIO

It is, however, the beginning of the *Symphony for Strings* that is called to mind by the somber, fourth-based chords that open the Adagio. They are encircled with grazing funeral wreaths or garlands (sul tasto, estinto), which play a role rather similar to that of the delicate supporting atmosphere at the beginning of the Adagio of *String Quartet No. 2*. But the form of the present movement is quite different. Eight chords establish the foundation of a four-measure structure that will be used as a chaconne or passacaglia bass. There are seven variations leading up to the center of the movement (occupying measures 30 to

46), then four more after the center. A brief recall of the central section in measures 63 to 68 precedes a twelfth variation, followed by a two-measure cadence as coda.

The succession of the chords does not set up any clear tonality and their pitch is changed in each variation by transposition. This defines two other cycles (variations 7 to 11 correspond to variations 2 to 6). The harmonic structure of the variations that come after the center (from No. 8 onward) is slightly more developed than that of the preceding ones, and the rhythms are more distinctive, in shorter and more complex note values. There are also more precise rhythmic correspondences between certain variations (2 and 7; 3 and 5; 4 and 6; 8 and 10). The third variation marks the beginning of a broad melody covering the three variations that follow. This magnificent seventeen-measure tune (Example 14), a processional both grand and sad, is constructed of phrases that deliberately fail to coincide with the variations themselves. This melody is carried on into the seventh variation by a more checkered idea on the viola. Rhythmic ostinatos once again contribute to the great ascent of the middle section, the language of which is more tonal. But here, too, we find more dense thematic working, incorporating even the weaving garlands of the start.

Example 14

After the long melody is repeated in its entirety in variations 8 to 11, together with some of the motifs from the central section, it is the "garlands" that bring the movement to an end, the final variation being identical with the first. But no analysis can do justice to the immense emotional power of this Adagio, which is one of the high points of Honegger's music.

THIRD MOVEMENT: ALLEGRO

We can find still more premonitions of the *Symphony for Strings* in the impetuous, hammering eighth-notes of the Finale. It begins with furtive pizzicatos on the cello outlining what looks like a twelve-tone row. But Honegger is only pretending to be serial. Then the rhythm gradually gets itself organized, although the real first theme does not appear with full assurance until measure 21, in a highly chromatic E major. Further on, at the bridge passage in measure 29, a dissonant and syncopated idea is heard that will reappear in the first movement of the *Symphony for Strings*, and also a triumphant harmonic progression that will underpin its Finale. Under a twofold shifted texture of eighth-notes in canon, the second theme of this sonata-form movement enters (Example 15).

This great C-sharp major paean of victory, of masculine joy, is then repeated in canon in B-flat. For a moment, helped by the presence of the

ff marcato

Example 15

eighth-notes, it looks back to the gigantic Fugue from *Amphion*. The central development section is dense and complex, full of contrapuntal prowess. The recapitulation, reversed as always, begins with the bridging passage, followed by the triumphant second theme repeated a semitone higher. The cadential group is omitted and replaced by a long, final development of the opening theme, complete with stretto. Finally, a triple, victorious appearance of the main theme (Example 15) leads to the coda. This consists of a canon on the first theme at three different speeds. The slowest version, in half-notes, takes on the identity of a majestic chorale—yet another analogy with the *Symphony for Strings*. But here the triple-stopping on the first violin cannot palliate the absence of the large orchestra the music demands. Perhaps, after all, Honegger realized that here he had reached the limits of what the string quartet medium could provide? As in the *Symphony for Strings*, a few measures of toccata follow up the impetus, tumbling down to the brief, final common chord.

Category 3: Sonatas and Sonatinas

VI. *Six Sonatas for violin and piano*
3. *Sonata for violin and piano in D minor* ("No. 0")
4. *Sonata for cello and piano*
17. *First Sonata for violin and piano in C-sharp minor* (*First Violin Sonata*)
24. *Second Sonata for violin and piano in B* (*Second Violin Sonata*)
28. *Sonata for viola and piano* (*Viola Sonata*)
29. *Sonatina for two violins in G*
32. *Sonata for cello and piano in D minor* (*Cello Sonata*)
42. *Sonatina for clarinet and piano* (*Clarinet Sonatina*)
80. *Sonatina for violin and cello in E minor*
143. *Sonata for solo violin in D minor*

Honegger was a violinist by training, and according to him, he wrote as many as twenty sonatas for the instrument even before entering the Zurich Conservatory. A collection of six of these youthful attempts has survived. After a very interesting D minor sonata, which has remained unpublished, he returned to the chamber music medium on the threshold of his first maturity, in the period from 1916 to 1920, with a cycle of four sonatas—two for violin and piano, one for viola and piano, and one for cello and piano. These, together with the *String Quartet No. 1* and the two sonatinas of the same period, established Honegger's reputation as an accomplished writer of chamber music. Thereafter he returned only twice to the sonata form. This was many years later, and he chose not to use the piano on either occasion. In turning away from the sonata, he was at one with most of his composing colleagues—only Milhaud, Martinů, and Hindemith remained loyal to the sonata after the 1930s.

VI. *Six Sonatas for pianoforte [sic] and violin*

March–July 1908 (No. 1: 8 March; No. 2: 25 April; No. 3: undated; No. 4: 16 June;
    No. 5: 25 June; No. 6: 3 July)
No. 1 in C minor (4 movements): 14 minutes 25 seconds
No. 2 in F major (3 movements): 12 minutes 20 seconds
No. 3 in C minor (4 movements): 22 minutes 35 seconds
No. 4 in B minor (4 movements): 17 minutes 15 seconds
No. 5 in A minor (3 movements): 12 minutes 30 seconds
No. 6 in G major (4 movements): 12 minutes 25 seconds
Unpublished

This touchingly clumsy collection of early attempts at sonatas comes to us in the form of a handsome bound volume. At the end, an index in both German and French shows the sixteen-year-old composer's serious approach to the matter at hand. He had just discovered Beethoven, and these sonatas aim to copy this prestigious model, to the exclusion of any later influence—Honegger would not discover the "modern" music of his time until he got to Zurich. From all this, it should be clear that these sonatas are of no more than documentary interest.

3. *Sonata for violin and piano in D minor*

1912 (first movement: 12 February; second movement: 22 June; third movement: 23
    October)
Duration: 25 minutes (11:30 + 6:30 + 7:00)
Unpublished

Honegger had been a student at the Paris Conservatory since the previous autumn, and the *Sonata for violin and piano in D minor* is a very interesting product of his formative years. The language is not yet highly personal, but this is the only example we have of a large work before the *String Quartet No. 1*, and it already shows Honegger in command of a respectable technique and with a remarkable sense of form and proportion. It is easy to see why Honegger never published this piece, but it deserves an occasional airing, and certainly in the context of any complete survey of his chamber music on disc. Debussy's early *Piano Trio* is far less worthy of revival.

The first movement (Largo–Agitato) is almost as long as the other two combined and takes on an air of deep pathos (on the model of Franck) that is not without a certain forcefulness in places. The Agitato, whose *Sturm und Drang* atmosphere is a far less accomplished forerunner of that in the first movement of the *String Quartet No. 1*, already presents a telescoped recapitulation, minus the opening theme. The Molto adagio in A major is in ABABA "lied" form, one that Honegger would not use often. It alternates a gently singing theme, including chromatic harmonies that are again reminiscent of César Franck, with a kind of funeral march in E minor.

The Finale (Sostenuto–Allegro) is the most accomplished and characteristic of the three movements. After a slow introduction, it launches into a fast, rhythmical three-in-a-measure, very like the Roussel of the next decade. It is in sonata form with two themes very similar to each other and is distinguished by delicate, effective counterpoint—less than a year after the start of Honegger's studies with Gédalge. The movement concludes with a cyclic coda (maestoso), recalling the principal theme of the first movement, in the best tradition of Schola Cantorum. It is worth noting that this sonata provides no indication whatsoever of Germanic influence.

4. *Sonata for cello and piano*

c. 1912 or 1913
Lost

This piece probably dates from 1912 or 1913. We know from Honegger's correspondence with his parents that this work, now lost, was performed first in Le Havre on 31 March 1913, and then again in Paris in December 1915.

17. *First Sonata for violin and piano in C-sharp minor (First Violin Sonata)*

July 1916 (first movement); 28 February 1917 (second movement); February 1918
 (third movement)
"To Andrée Vaurabourg"
First performance (first two movements only): 19 January 1918, Arthur Honegger
 and Andrée Vaurabourg, L'Université Interalliée du Parthénon, Paris
First complete performance: 19 March 1918, Hélène Jourdan-Morhange and Andrée
 Vaurabourg, Théâtre du Vieux-Colombier, Paris
Duration: 19 minutes (7:00 + 4:00 + 8:00)
Salabert

Honegger's *First Violin Sonata* is more or less contemporary with his *First String Quartet*. Although it was finished four months after the quartet, the sonata had been a long time in the making. As well as being longer than the sonatas that were to follow, it is also simpler and more traditional in its melodic and harmonic language. Honegger aims for a new and original formal balance by inserting a lively Scherzo between two movements in moderate tempo. The last movement adopts this very ternary form.

FIRST MOVEMENT: ANDANTE SOSTENUTO

The first movement is a broad, lyrical, dreamy movement in sonata form. The recapitulation is, of course, reversed. In the first theme, piano chords fill in the rests in the solo part, and the key hovers between C-sharp minor and A major. The second theme, in B major, is more firmly tonal and also of a more sustained melodic character. The opening theme is treated at length in the development, and thus figures only briefly in the recapitulation.

SECOND MOVEMENT: PRESTO

After this fresh, limpid vision of spring comes a marvelous scherzo—also contrasting by its tonality (F major), and remarkable for its rhythmic and contrapuntal verve. A brief introduction takes the music from C-sharp minor to F major, leading to the bucolic vigor of the tune (Example 16). This is the closest Honegger came to a certain side of the music of Roussel and, especially, of Albéric Magnard.

Example 16

After a contrasting, more chromatic idea, in which the canonic games continue, the theme tries to reassert itself. But after two unsuccessful attempts we move on to B major for a tuneful Trio. The return of the scherzo begins with the chromatic idea presented in the form of a fugue. At the end of the movement, the Trio theme is briefly heard high on the violin, leading to a boisterous coda (più presto). A wonderful movement!

THIRD MOVEMENT

The two outer Adagios are ostinatos of the passacaglia type on a short phrase that, as Georges Auric was the first to point out, is similar to the "Carillon de Laon" in *Jeanne d'Arc au bûcher* (Example 17). There are twelve variations in the first Adagio section and seven in the second, both of them sharing the same somber, funereal atmosphere, with a melancholy, expressive countermelody on the violin. A transitional passage in 6/8 for piano alone (quasi allegro) gradually adumbrates the main theme of the Allegro assai. This is heard on the violin at measure 37, in C-sharp minor without a leading tone. A second, cantabile theme very quickly intervenes and is followed by a group of vigorous, cadential chords reminiscent of the Finale of Debussy's *String Quartet*. The development consists of dense, modulating counterpoint in which Example 17 is also heard.

For once, the recapitulation follows the standard pattern, beginning with the first theme. This accelerates toward a gigue in the manner of Vincent d'Indy, before returning to the serious passacaglia theme, now harmonized in C-sharp major. It is repeated (for the only time) by the violin in E minor, and

Example 17

then goes back to the original key. But the added minor sixth in the final chord prolongs to the end the opening ambivalence between C-sharp minor and A major.

24. *Second Sonata for violin and piano in B* (*Second Violin Sonata*)

April–November 1919 (first movement: April–May; second movement: August; third
     movement: November)
"To Fernande Capelle"
First private performance: 8 January 1920, Arthur Honegger and Andrée
     Vaurabourg, Darius Milhaud's apartment, Paris
First public performance: 28 February 1920, the same artists, Société nationale, Salle
     du Conservatoire, Paris
Duration: 13 minutes (5:00 + 5:00 + 3:00)
Salabert

The *Second Violin Sonata* is more concise than its predecessor, but its simple form and structure is in contrast to its harmonic complexity—it is one of Honegger's most polytonal works.

FIRST MOVEMENT: ALLEGRO CANTABILE

The first movement is a broad, lyrical movement in 9/4. The violin soars high above piano arpeggios and evokes a kind of bitonal Fauré, with B major and F major sounding simultaneously. The form is Honegger's usual sonata form, with reversed and condensed recapitulation, and with the second theme absent from the central development section.

SECOND MOVEMENT: LARGHETTO

In this intense, concentrated, and highly chromatic second movement, the key of D minor remains vague. A "searching" introduction leads into the two themes, the second of which is rather like an old-fashioned sarabande. The dreamlike coda resolves surprisingly into D major.

THIRD MOVEMENT: VIVACE ASSAI

The short, witty Finale pursues the B/F ambiguity outlined in the first movement. It is in sonata form with a normal recapitulation. The jaunty, memorable first theme (Example 18) is followed by a sunnier second one in G major.

Example 18

After four measures of dreamy lento, which are an augmentation of the first theme, a hectic coda-stretto (presto) on the same theme leads to an abrupt ending.

28. Sonata for viola and piano (*Viola Sonata*)

January–March 1920 (first movement: March; second movement: January; third
  movement: February)
"To Henri Casadesus"
First performance: 2 December 1920, Henri and Robert Casadesus, SMI, Paris
Duration: 14 minutes 30 seconds (6:30 + 4:00 + 4:00)
Max Eschig

This is one of the best sonatas ever written for the restricted viola repertory, and a finer work than any of Honegger's previous sonatas.

FIRST MOVEMENT: ANDANTE–VIVACE

The first movement is the longest of the three. Two tempos alternate three times—an andante in 3/4 and a vivace in 3/8—as in the Dumkas of Antonin Dvořák and his compatriots. Each of these pairs corresponds to one of the sections in a kind of sonata form. Despite beginning and ending on A, the movement is barely tonal and the virtual A minor is obscured by numerous appoggiaturas and passing notes. The work's Finale is not in A, but in C major.

The first idea (Andante) is curiously reminiscent of Scriabin in its harmonies (measure 4 makes one think of *Prometheus*). Here two passages for solo piano alternate with two passages for solo viola that foreshadow the first of the two themes in the Vivace. The second one is rhythmic and percussive and is taken over into the second Andante in the form of a smooth, gentle variant. Unlike the first, this second Andante brings the two instruments together. Like the second Vivace, it serves as a development section, while the third Andante is a kind of recapitulation and the third Vivace a brief coda ending on tiptoes.

SECOND MOVEMENT: ALLEGRETTO MODERATO

This gentle and leisurely intermezzo makes a solid impact, thanks to Honegger's absolute technical mastery and to his use of original, clear-cut ideas. The form is simple ternary. The outer sections, in a modal A minor, with narrow intervals gravitating round three notes like some mournful popular litany, contrast with the sunny middle section (poco più allegretto), which looks forward to the Finale in its limpid diatonic structure and straightforward character. Its main theme, also pentatonic, will be based on chords of the same kind. But that is not all. When the first section is repeated, the piano recalls the rhythmic ideas of the first movement's Andante. This Allegretto therefore has cyclic links with both the movements that surround it.

THIRD MOVEMENT: ALLEGRO NON TROPPO

This Finale is in sonata form with two related themes and a reversed recapitulation. Its vigorous affirmation of C major shows us Honegger's popular, festive side, with peals of "Easter" bells, reminding us of the shortly forthcoming Alleluias of *Le Roi David* and of *Chant de joie*. All share the same deliberate gait, and a certain frank, square solidity. The robust diatonic structure of the loud piano chords at the start recall Milhaud. The first theme (Example 19) is like some cheerful, ceremonial procession. It holds its own against both the sweeter, more legato second theme and the capricious rhythms of the viola (marcato poco scherzando), and its triumphal progress finally leads to a broad peroration of truly symphonic breadth.

Example 19

29. *Sonatina for two violins in G major*

March–June 1920 (first movement: March–April; second movement: June; third
    movement: May)
"To Darius Milhaud"
First performance: 29 November 1920, Darius Milhaud and Arthur Honegger, a
    concert of works by Les Six, Théâtre des Champs-Élysées, Paris
Duration: 7 minutes 50 seconds
Max Eschig

For Honegger, 1920 was indeed his "sonata year." It was also the year in which, during his well-known interview with Paul Landormy,[4] he affirmed his predilection for chamber music.

The composition of the *Sonatina for two violins* followed directly on that of the *Viola Sonata* and led without delay into that of the *Cello Sonata*. It is a charming piece, shorter and lighter than the others round it, and it marks the closest Honegger came to the aesthetic of Les Six, especially in the miniature sonata form of the opening Allegro non tanto. This movement (in G major, like the last movement) seasons its diatonicism with a discreet but piquant bitonality, rather like the *Pastorale d'été*, which Honegger was to compose a few months later. It is written in the spirit of a real *bicinium*, with the two violins frequently exchanging material. The Andantino in D minor, in simple ternary form, is played using mutes. It is a gentle, plaintive reverie, and its opening theme is related to that of the first movement in its brief anapestic motif. The final Allegro moderato provides a strong contrast with the two preceding movements, in both its chromaticism and its contrapuntal texture. It is a fugue, starting with a real three-voice exposition of a long, sinuously descending subject, beginning as illustrated in Example 20. Episodes, augmentations, strettos, and canons follow one another without the slightest hint of pedantry or ponderousness and, after a final progression in which the arpeggios offer due homage to J. S. Bach, the subject brings the work to an end in the form of a broad, solemn chorale. Here Honegger obeys the credo of Les Six, uniting lightness with the cult of Bach.

Example 20

32. *Sonata for cello and piano in D minor* (*Cello Sonata*)

June–September 1920 (first and third movements: September; second movement: June–July)
"To René Gosselin"
First performance: 23 April 1921, Diran Alexanian and Andrée Vaurabourg, concert of the Société nationale, Salle du Conservatoire, Paris
Duration: 14 minutes 40 seconds (5:35 + 5:00 + 4:05)
Max Eschig

This final, full-length sonata crowns the Honegger cycle. It is a real masterwork, concise and powerful, and it deserves to be in the repertory of every cellist. Even though its language is increasingly dissonant and chromatic, all three movements are based on the key of D. These return to the fast–slow–fast pattern of the *Second Violin Sonata*.

First movement: Allegro non troppo

The first movement, a masterly but modified sonata form, is especially rich in melody. As we shall see, its unified flow is based on two complementary, related themes that share a short four-note descending motif (minor second, then two minor thirds), which begins the first theme and concludes the second. Despite short outbreaks of violence, we can trace the influence of Fauré in the rocking 9/8 meter, recalling the first movement of his *Second Violin Sonata*. The piano begins the movement on its own, low and mysterious in the bass, and then decorates the cello's continuous legato lines, sometimes with arpeggios and figuration, sometimes with counterpoint. Two brusque, violent measures introduce the second theme, heard high on the cello with the piano playing syncopated repeated chords that sound more than ever like Fauré. The passionate development of the first theme, starting at measure 37, is unexpectedly followed by the recapitulation of the second at measure 67. Then the development resumes at measure 78 and continues at length, bringing the two similar themes together. After an impressive triple *fortissimo* and a long, very gradual decrescendo, the first theme is finally repeated at measure 113, before fading to a gloomy close at measure 128.

SECOND MOVEMENT: ANDANTE SOSTENUTO

The second movement is a profound and powerfully expressive meditation that features canonic writing, and it illustrates in the clearest possible manner Honegger's self-proclaimed leaning toward the sober and the austere. Its ternary form offers a contrast between the restrained and introspective chromaticism of the outer sections and the clear, consoling diatonic light of the middle section that, after a number of more agitated measures, breaks out into a great *fortissimo* cry of anguish. The movement ends, nevertheless, in D major, together with Honegger's favorite added second and sixth.

THIRD MOVEMENT: PRESTO

The wildly whirling Finale is at the same time impetuous and harsh. It is launched by the initial impetus of the piano tumbling down the length of the keyboard with ninths and sevenths, like the lash of a whip, and setting in motion an ostinato of dotted rhythms and eighth-note triplets. Only later does a tune emerge, of a popular cast (Example 21), belonging to the same family as that in the Finale of the *Second Violin Sonata* (Example 18). It is the first real melodic idea in the movement, which will contain two further principal themes of a similarly straightforward kind.

Example 21

With these three ideas, and by means of some of his most ingenious counterpoint, Honegger constructs a concise argument, even if its form is fairly complex. It is not a rondo-sonata, as Willy Tappolet suggests,[5] but there are a number of other possibilities. If we call the themes A, B, and C, then it could be either a succession of three cycles of A + B + C, followed by a coda, or a ternary form in which two A + B sections enclose an inner cycle C + A + B + C, or, finally, it could be a Honeggerian kind of sonata form with exposition (A + B + C), development (A + B), recapitulation (C + A + B), and coda (C). It is not a matter of great import, as the music's wonderful vitality defies pedantry, and the opening "whiplash," ending the movement exactly as it began it, seems fitting punishment for any pedant who gives too much credence to such academic minutiae.

42. Sonatina for clarinet and piano (Clarinet Sonatina)

October 1921–July 1922 (first movement: July 1922; second movement: October 1921; third movement: November 1921)
"To Werner Reinhart"
First performance: 5 June 1923, Louis Cahuzac and Jean Wiéner, Wiéner Concert, Salle Pleyel, Paris
Duration: 6 minutes 30 seconds
Salabert

These three miniatures are dedicated to the "Maecenas of Winterthur," Werner Reinhart, who was an excellent clarinetist and for whom Stravinsky wrote his *Three Pieces*. They show Honegger at the closest he ever came to the spirit of Les Six. The miniatures did not become a sonatina until Honegger eventually added the first movement.

The first movement, Modéré, is a charming piece in simple ternary form. It flows nonchalantly, even lazily, and its atmosphere is bittersweet and discreetly polytonal. In the middle there is the contrast of a brief, sparkling contrapuntal development, using a good staccato tune, of which the composer regrettably does not make more.

Example 22

The second movement (Lent et soutenu) is a delightfully beguiling reverie, for all its uncertainty of key. It is a delicate cantilena in four sections, free in form.

For the last movement (Vif et rythmique), Honegger comes up with a playful, impertinent little joke of a piece, even nearer to the spirit of Les Six than the other movements. In its syncopated verve it comes close to the jazz or, to be more accurate, the ragtime of the period, complete with clarinet glissandos. From time to time a tiny stereotypical motif cuts across the bar lines, interrupting the argument, which finally stops abruptly on a pirouette, in less time than it takes to describe it.

80. *Sonatina for violin and cello in E minor*

September 1932
"For Albert and Anne Neuburger"
First performance: 16 December 1932, Roth and van Dooren, Triton concert, École
    normale de musique, Paris
Duration: 15 minutes 10 seconds (5:30 + 6:10 + 3:30)
Salabert

The happy, relaxed, and entertaining character of this work for violin and cello explains the title "Sonatina," although in length it qualifies as a sonata. Its polyphony is luminous and transparent, and it is far more in the classical mold than the string quartets that were to follow. It marks not only the composer's return to chamber music after a gap of nearly ten years, but also his return to creative work after the seventeen-month depressive crisis that followed the completion of *Cris du monde*.

FIRST MOVEMENT: ALLEGRO

The first movement, in a flowing 6/8 meter, contains no fewer than three themes. The first, in unison, prolongs the ambivalence between E minor and its relative major, while the third, in C major, looks back to the energetic, "Eastertide" character of the Finale of the *Viola Sonata*. But there is only a brief allusion to this in the usual reversed recapitulation. The short development section unleashes lively contrapuntal games involving the first theme, which brings the movement to a peaceful conclusion.

SECOND MOVEMENT: ANDANTE

The second movement, in D major, is a successful synthesis of andante and scherzo. Honegger would return to this idea (with the materials interchanged) in the second movement of his *Fifth Symphony*. The Scherzo (doppio movimento) occupies the even-numbered sections in the five-part plan. Its second appearance, varying in detail the jolly fugato of the first, is cleverly grafted onto the continuation of the Andante. The rich sonority that results is, with just two instruments, a tour de force.

THIRD MOVEMENT: ALLEGRO

This E major rondo, in a concentric form A-B-A-C-A-B-A, is disarmingly simple in the rigorous symmetry of its proportions. With its contrapuntal alacrity and cheerful energy, it brings the work to a sparkling, witty conclusion. Its rondo theme (Example 23), in humorous dialogue between the two players, seems like a double homage to the Beethoven of the Rondo Finale of the *String Quartet*, Op. 130, and to the Ravel of the Finale of his incomparable sonata for the same pair of instruments.

In the B section, the violin (in the recapitulation, the cello) declaims a kind of grand recitative-cadenza in a deliberately pompous, overblown manner,

Example 23

while the central C section pays homage to Haydn. The final return of the rondo refrain (prestissimo) is a hectic coda-stretto leading to the pizzicato ending. This is the unbuttoned Honegger, so to speak, and how delightful it is to find, in this wonderful sonatina, that Honegger's creative appetite had returned, and with it his appetite for life.

143. *Sonata for solo violin in D minor*

November–December 1940
First performance: Christian Ferras, Paris. Date unknown
Duration: 12 minutes (5:00 + 2:00 + 1:30 + 3:30)
Salabert

In this severely classical work, a few scattered reminiscences of romantic music combine with the obsessive, overpowering presence of Bach. Honegger found this exercise in discipline necessary when he returned to Paris from exodus at the end of 1940. He was working at the same time on his *Selzach Passion*, another homage to Bach—what better refuge could he have turned to from the understandable disarray in which he found himself?

It is a relatively impersonal work, one of craft rather than of inspiration, and makes one think of the late suites of Ernest Bloch. It could be that Honegger felt the need to escape from himself at this time, although the earliest sketches for the *Symphony for Strings* are exactly contemporary. The inclusion of four movements is unusual for Honegger and places the work in the domain of the suite or partita, rather than that of the true sonata. The opening Allegro, which is by some way the longest movement, is a veritable catalog of violin techniques and, from this point of view, makes an excellent study piece. Honegger clearly knew his instrument. The unusual form (A-B-B'-A'), the same as that of the Finale, corresponds to a Honeggerian sonata form without a development section.

The Largo in G minor is a purely classical sarabande, differing from those of Bach only in its constant modulations. The A major Allegretto grazioso recalls a Bach gavotte in its seductive grace, with a central musette in A minor and its repeat in diminution, in the manner of the traditional "double." After the quasi-allemande of the first movement, then the sarabande and the gavotte, the final Presto takes the role of a gigue. It is a brilliant, incisive movement, with virtuoso violin writing recalling Paganini's *Caprices*, especially in the way it develops through large ascending and descending arpeggios.

Category 4: Other Chamber Music

2.   *Adagio for violin and piano*
6.   *Trio for violin, cello, and piano in F minor*
13.   *Rhapsody for two flutes, clarinet, and piano (or two violins, viola, and piano) in F*
22.   *Furniture Music*
33.   Hymn for Ten String Instruments in B minor
36.   *Cadenza* (for violin solo) for the *Cinéma-Fantaisie* based on Milhaud's *Le Boeuf sur le toit*
43.   *Three Counterpoints*
59.   *Hommage du trombone exprimant la tristesse de l'auteur absent*
79.   *Prelude for sub-bass and piano in C major*
89.   *Petite Suite for two instruments and piano*
179. *Morceau de concours pour violon et piano*
181. *Paduana for solo cello in G major*
193. *Intrada for trumpet and piano in B-flat major*
211. *Romance for flute and piano*
214. *Arioso for violin and piano*

Apart from his string quartets and sonatas, Honegger's chamber music consists only of some short pieces, of varying importance. For these, brief introductions will suffice.

2. *Adagio for violin and piano*
c. 1910
Lost

Written around 1910, this *Adagio* is now lost. One of the few works Honegger wrote during his time at the Zurich Conservatory.

6. *Trio for violin, cello, and piano in F minor*—first movement only
August–October 1914
Duration: 6 minutes
Salabert

The movements following this initial Allegro vivace are either lost or were perhaps never written. It is in a taut sonata form and the first theme—a rhythmic idea in 9/8 meter—is already almost banished from the recapitulation. The second theme, a more melodic one in E-flat, is fairly conventional. The young student showed this movement to his teacher Widor, who understandably found it more to his taste than various more recent and daring compositions.

13. *Rhapsody for two flutes, clarinet, and piano (or two violins, viola, and piano) in F*

April 1917
"To Monsieur Ch. Widor"
First performance: 17 November 1917, Manouvrier and René Le Roy (flutes), Tournier (clarinet), and Andrée Vaurabourg (piano), L'Université Interalliée du Parthénon, Paris
Duration: 9 minutes
Larghetto–Allegro–Tempo primo
Salabert

This delightful and seductive triptych is nowadays unaccountably forgotten, but when it first appeared it was one of the most frequently played of the young composer's works. The two slow sections, based on a pattern of 3 + 2 + 3 eighth-notes, are evidence of Honegger's deep admiration for Debussy, both in the whole-tone scales of the first and in the more tonal writing of the second. In the middle comes a robust but graceful Allegro in a modal C-sharp minor. This adds a discreetly Ravelian touch to the ensemble, and a faint reminiscence of it is heard in the reflective coda.

22. *Furniture Music* (Musiques [Pièces] d'ameublement)

End of March 1919
First performance: 5 April 1919, Salle Huyghens, Paris
Performing forces: flute, clarinet, trumpet, string quartet, piano
Duration: flexible
1. *Vif* (without strings); 2. *Lent* (without trumpet); 3. *Modéré* (without second violin or viola)
Unpublished

These three tiny miniatures (of 6, 4, and 9 measures) were intended to be repeated ad infinitum during an interval, in line with Satie's well-known idea. They would seem to correspond to a work mentioned in a manuscript catalog by Honegger under the title *Entrée, Nocturne et Berceuse*, wrongly identified by Geoffrey K. Spratt, in his 1987 study of Honegger, as a lost piano concerto. The third piece is a little collage, combining the lullaby *Fais dodo Colas mon p'tit frère* with tunes by Benjamin Godard, Chopin, and Fauré.

33. Hymn for Ten String Instruments in B minor (*Hymne pour Dixtuor à cordes*)

9 October 1920
Commission from Léo Sir
First performance: 17 October 1921, Léo Sir's Dixtuor, Concert Art et Action, Paris
Performing forces: ensemble of instruments invented and constructed by Léo Sir:
   super-soprano in F *in alt*, violin, mezzo-soprano, alto, contralto, tenor, baritone,
   cello, sub-bass in G, double bass. Transcription for standard instruments: four
   violins, two violas, two cellos, two double basses
Duration: 7 minutes 35 seconds
Salabert

This Hymn for Ten String Instruments owed its inception to Léo Sir, a
violin maker from Marmande, but his newly invented instruments never made
any permanent headway. At the same time, Milhaud wrote the fifth of his *Little Symphonies* for the ensemble. This Hymn is a serious and beautiful work that
may once more find a place in the repertory, now that it has finally been transcribed for standard instruments.

The form is that of a varied "lied" (A-B-A-B-A-coda). The real Hymn is
heard in the B sections, a richly harmonized lament, and the first in a line that
would include the De profundis from the *Symphonie liturgique* and the Andante
of the *Concerto da camera*. On its repeat it is played in canon, as it is when it
recurs one last time in the coda.

36. *Cadenza* (for violin solo) for the *Cinéma-Fantaisie* based on Milhaud's *Le Boeuf sur le toit*

Possibly the summer of 1920, or a little later
First performance: 26 May 1921, M. Benedetti, Paris
Solo violin
Duration: 2 minutes
Max Eschig

This brilliant demonstration of Honegger's mastery of the violin (which
makes us regret that he never wrote a concerto for this instrument) was
intended to form part of the violin and piano transcription of Milhaud's celebrated piece. Around the two themes from *Le Boeuf sur le toit*, the violin lets off
a fireworks display of triple and quadruple stopping, harmonics, trills, glissandos, and agile figuration of all kinds.

43. *Three Counterpoints*

October–November 1922 (Nos. 1 and 2: October; No. 3: November 1922)
No. 1: "To Maurice Jaubert"; No. 2: "To Jacques Brillouin"; No. 3: "To Marcel
   Delannoy"
First performance: 16 February 1925, Fleury (piccolo), Gaudard (oboe and English
   horn), Krettly (violin), Pierre Fournier (cello), SMI concert, Salle Érard, Paris
Performing forces: flute, oboe (English horn), violin, and cello
Duration: 5 minutes 50 seconds
Wilhelm Hansen, Copenhagen, 1926

These three attractive miniatures, ingeniously written and full of original color, are by no means negligible. The *Prélude* is a vigorous invention, with sharp dissonance and considerable rhythmic interest. The *Choral*, in which fleet counterpoint on the strings encompasses a cantus firmus on the English horn, is a precise realization of the ideal propounded by Honegger in his 1920 interview: Bach's textures applied to modern harmony and tonality.[6] The best of the three pieces is undoubtedly the final *Canon*. This unfolds in three voices over a cello ostinato, and the third section in its A-B-A form is the exact mirror of the first. There is no hint of scholastic aridity in this little group of pieces, and they illustrate well Honegger's natural gift for polyphony.

59. Hommage du trombone exprimant la tristesse de l'auteur absent (Homage of the trombone to say how sorry the composer is not to be present)

June 1925
"For Serge Koussevitzky"
First performance: June 1925, in the offices of the journal *Comoedia*, Paris
Performing forces: trombone and piano
Duration: 1 minute 10 seconds
Unpublished

A lighthearted trifle.

79. Prelude for sub-bass and piano in C major

February 1932
"To André Laurent"
Duration: 5 minutes
Leduc (version for double bass and piano)

Honegger's *Prelude for sub-bass and piano in C major* was intended for the sub-bass, the Léo Sir instrument that was pitched between the cello and the double bass. In fact, it is perfectly well playable on the latter and could be used to fill out the double bass's rather thin repertory. Unfortunately, it is not a very interesting or inspired piece, and its banality only illustrates the composer's depressive state in the early months of 1932.

89. Petite Suite for two instruments and piano

August 1934
"For Yvonne and Pierre Stadler"
For two melody instruments *ad libitum* and piano
Duration: 4 minutes 15 seconds
Le Chant du Monde

This tiny triptych is shorter and simpler than the *Three Counterpoints*. It is a jewel of a work and an ideal teaching piece. After an expressive cantilena in G minor comes a *bicinium* in F major in which a popular-sounding tune is heard over an unchanging ostinato C-D-F-D. Finally comes a short, cheerful carillon in G major and 7/8 meter.

179. *Morceau de concours pour violon et piano* (Competition Piece for violin and piano)

22 June 1945
For the final competition at the Paris Conservatory
First performance: 6 July 1945, by the various competition candidates
Duration: 2 minutes
Salabert

A violin solo in the style of a virtuoso romantic recitative. The title says it all.

181. *Paduana for solo cello in G major*

July 1945
Duration: 3 minutes
Salabert

The *Paduana for solo cello* was intended for a solo cello suite that was never finished. To judge from this splendid movement, the intended suite would have been distinctly superior to the *Sonata for solo violin*. With its majestic dotted rhythms, its widespread chords encompassing the whole instrument, its pizzicatos, and ethereal harmonics, it is one of the best of Honegger's posthumously published works.

193. *Intrada for trumpet and piano in B-flat major*

April 1947
For the Geneva International Competition in Musical Performance
Duration: 5 minutes
Salabert

The *Intrada for trumpet and piano in B-flat major* is another competition piece, but very much more successful than its predecessor. Trumpeters have been quick to take advantage of this windfall. It is a joyful piece, and very characteristic of its composer in the diatonic language with frequent pentatonic inflections, and with the fourths and fifths that suit the trumpet so well. Two slow sections (Maestoso), the second much shortened, enclose a lively toccata in 3/4 meter (Allegro), culminating in the indispensable virtuoso passage in rapid repeated notes.

211. *Romance for flute and piano*

1952 or 1953
Duration: 2 minutes 30 seconds
Billaudot

This piece in a rather elusive G minor is marked by an exquisite melancholy and harmonic refinement. In atmosphere it recalls once more the Andante of the *Concerto da camera*. The piano here is an active partner and not just an accompanist, as in the competition pieces, so that the *Romance* may be called a true chamber work. This jewel of a piece is perhaps Honegger's last composition.

214. *Arioso for violin and piano*

Date unknown (late 1920s)
"To Lipnitzky, with warmest memories and my thanks for the fine photos"
Duration: 2 minutes 15 seconds
Salabert

A piece of some interest, in which somewhat tortuous chromaticism is interrupted by two diatonic oases. It might have served as the slow movement of a sonatina.

Category 4A: Chamber Works Derived from Stage and Film Music

IA.   *Overture* to *Philippa*
IIIA.   *Overture* to *La Esmeralda*
39.   *Danse de la chèvre*
45.   *Antigone* (incidental music)
56.   *Prelude and Blues for four chromatic harps*
62.   *Pour le cantique de Salomon*
73.   *Berceuses for Bobcisco*
74.   *J'avais un fidèle amant*
163.   Music for *Pasiphaé*
215.   *Andante for four ondes Martenot*
216.   *Colloque* for four instruments
217.   *Introduction and Dance for flute, harp, and string trio*

Apart from the popular *Danse de la chèvre*, these pieces have remained unpublished until recently and merit no more than a brief mention.

IA. *Overture* to *Philippa*

23 August 1907, Le Havre
Unpublished

IIIA. *Overture* to *La Esmeralda*

1907, Le Havre
Unpublished

Arrangements for two violins and piano of the overtures to these two child-hood operas.

39. *Danse de la chèvre* (The Goat Dance)

Probably November 1921 (and not May 1919, as was believed previously)
"To René Le Roy"
Written for the dancer Lysana, for Sacha Derek's play *La Mauvaise Pensée* (The Evil
    Thought)
First performance: 2 December 1921, Nouveau Théâtre, Paris
Solo flute
Duration: 3 minutes 20 seconds
Salabert

As we can see from its entry in the disc catalog, this little piece, together with Debussy's *Syrinx*, Varèse's *Density 21.5*, and Jolivet's *Incantations*, is one of the pre-1940 classics for solo flute. A slow, dreamy introduction outlines the memorable theme of the dance proper (vif in 9/8 meter)—a skipping, truly goat-like theme in a chromatically altered F major (Example 24). A more melodic subsidiary idea is heard no more than twice, and in the final repeat of the initial lent, now only five measures long, we hear again the outline of the principal theme.

Example 24

45. *Antigone*—incidental music

December 1922
Incidental music for the Cocteau play that would inspire Honegger to write his opera
    of the same name (H65, Category 11)
First performance: 20 December 1922, Théâtre de l'Atelier, Paris
Performing forces: oboe (or English horn), harp
Duration: 2 minutes
Salabert
Published in the music supplement to *Feuilles libres*, January 1923

56. *Prelude and Blues for four chromatic harps*

1925 (?)
Arrangement for four chromatic harps by Jeanne Daliès from an original that can no
    longer be identified (perhaps the lost blues from the ballet *Vérité? Mensonge?*,
    H34).

First performance: 24 March 1925, Casadesus Harp Quartet, Salle des Agriculteurs, Paris
Unpublished
Lost

62. *Pour le cantique de Salomon* (For the Song of Solomon)

May 1926
Commission from the narrator Chochana (Suzanne) Avivitt, to accompany a recitation of fragments from *Le Cantique des cantiques*
First performance: 16 June 1926, Chochana Avivitt and members of the Golschmann Orchestra, conducted by Vladimir Golschmann, Salle Gaveau, Paris
Performing forces: two flutes, two clarinets, trombone, gong, string quintet. The strings may be doubled (in which case the work would appear in Category 7A, Music for Chamber Orchestra).
Duration of music: 5 minutes 10 seconds; with recitation: 12 minutes
Unpublished

Pour le cantique de Salomon is in the same biblical and "oriental" vein as *Le Roi David* and *Judith*, with the same fluctuations between the pastoral and nostalgic on the one hand and the raucous and twinging on the other. There are four movements, and at times they are surprisingly close to Vaughan Williams's *Flos Campi*, which dates from the same year and is also inspired by *Le Cantique des cantiques*. Both successfully recapture the appropriate "Shulamitic" atmosphere.

73. *Berceuses for Bobcisco*

December 1929
Music for the cinema club founded by Honegger's friends under the name "Bobcisco" (see Chapter 4)
Performing forces: violin, flute (or second violin), trumpet (or viola), cello, and piano
Duration: 30 seconds
Unpublished

74. *J'avais un fidèle amant* (I Had a Faithful Lover)

December 1929
Music for the cinema club founded by Honegger's friends under the name "Bobcisco" (see Chapter 4)
Performing forces: string quartet (or string orchestra)
Duration: 2 minutes 40 seconds
Unpublished

The *Berceuses* are only a few measures long and are of little importance, but *J'avais un fidèle amant* is a little group of variations on a popular song of this name from France's Morvan region, passed on to Honegger by his friends the Thévenets, with whom he often stayed in the village of Montquin in the Morvan. The composer was sufficiently fond of this piece to have performed it, in the string orchestra version, at a concert he conducted in Paris on 15 December 1932.

163. Music for *Pasiphaé*

23–24 January 1943
"A little piece of musical decoration" for a radio transmission of Henry de
    Montherlant's *Pasiphaé*. It was a commission from the experimental studio of
    French Radio, but the broadcast never took place, as the censors found the text
    to be "immoral" (this was, after all, during the Occupation)
Performing forces: two oboes, two clarinets, alto saxophone, two bassoons
Duration: 4 minutes 15 seconds
Salabert, Paris 1983

Three miniatures in very simple modal and diatonic style.

215. *Andante for four ondes Martenot*

Probably January 1943
Short musical illustration for a documentary film on the ondes Martenot
Duration: 1 minute
Unpublished

216. *Colloque* (Conversation) for four instruments

Date unknown
Undoubtedly title music for an unidentified film
Performing forces: flute, celesta, violin, viola
Duration: 2 minutes 15 seconds (Poco largo–Andantino–Allegro)
Editions Papillon, Geneva

A very pretty little work, enticingly colored. A melancholy tune on muted
viola leads to a sprightly little dance.

217. *Introduction and Dance for flute, harp, and string trio*

Date unknown
Probably a piece of incidental music (rather than film music)
Performing forces: flute, harp (or piano), violin, viola, cello
Duration: 4 minutes 40 seconds
Salabert

A very attractive piece that would go well in concert. A brief Introduction
in dialogue outlines the theme of the graceful, nonchalant Dance. The form of
this is absolutely concentric, and at the end of the central development section
there is a modest climax with virtuoso writing for the harp.

Category 8: Art Songs (Mélodies)

V. Three Early Songs
5. *Two Songs* (including *Barcarolle*)
7. *Four Poems for Voice and Piano*
9. *Three Poems of Paul Fort*
11. *Nature morte*
12. *Six Poems of Apollinaire*
30. *Pâques à New York*
51. *Six Poems of Jean Cocteau*
54. *Chanson de Ronsard*
70. *Vocalise-Étude*
137. *Possèdes-tu, pauvre pécheur*
138. *Three Poems of Claudel*
. 144. *Three Psalms*
148. *Petit Cours de morale*
152. *Saluste du Bartas*
168. *Céline*
169. *Panis angelicus*
178. *O Temps suspends ton vol*
184. *Four Songs for Low Voice*
192. *Mimaamaquim*
222. *La Nuit est si profonde*

If we include the few items written for the stage (see Category 8A), Honegger wrote some sixty art songs (*mélodies*), plus some forty lighter *chansons*, or popular songs (Categories 9 and 9A; see Chapter 14), mostly intended for films. While this does not compare with the output of Milhaud, or of Poulenc (whose songs occupy a central place in his work), Honegger's best settings nonetheless assure him an eminent place among the song composers of the first half of the twentieth century—the last song composers, it would seem, since this genre of composition seems to have died out. There were two periods especially during which Honegger concentrated on songwriting. The first lasted until 1924, that is to say, during his piano and chamber music period. The second lasted from 1939 until 1947, a period during which he was inspired by various excellent singers.

Honegger's gifts particularly predisposed him to songwriting. He had a natural feeling for the voice, for the curve of a vocal line, and he possessed the ability both to come up with striking images and to make an immediate and often startling transformation of a visual stimulus into a musical effect. He could also match the form of a poem with an equally elegant musical structure. Regarding his early *Four Poems* (H7), he said he had sought in André Fontainas and Francis Jammes "the subject of a musical construction that could parallel the literary one," and, when he set some of Apollinaire's *Alcools* he admitted, in a 1925 interview in the journal *Dissonances*, "'Automne' satisfies my need for geometry as much as my need for emotion," indicating a wholly Latin, indeed classical, approach to the problem of setting poetry.

Honegger's choice of poets reveals his remarkable literary taste: first of all, Jules Laforgue and Francis Jammes, then very soon after that, Paul Fort, Guillaume Apollinaire, Blaise Cendrars, Jean Cocteau, and, later still, Paul Claudel and Jean Giraudoux—the list speaks for itself. Some of them, like Cocteau and Claudel, were close friends of Honegger's. On the other hand, apart from Ronsard, whose poetry he set twice, and Shakespeare, in the French translation by Guy de Pourtalès, he never set poets of the past.

Honegger's earliest songs, dating from his adolescence and early manhood, have disappeared, and the earliest surviving song, "Sur le basalte" (the first of the *Four Poems for Voice and Piano*), dates from November 1914. Apart from the early piano pieces printed privately in Le Havre, it is also Honegger's earliest published piece still on sale today. During the summer of 1915, between two periods of military service, Honegger's genius suddenly broke through, and one after the other he wrote "Prière" (on Jammes) and "Automne" (on Apollinaire). These were his first two masterpieces, written a year before his first considerable instrumental work, the *Toccata and Variations*, and two years before the final completion of the *String Quartet No. 1*. We may therefore say that, like Debussy and Schubert, the young Honegger found himself in the field of song.

The support of a literary text is certainly useful for an inexperienced composer, but the composer also needs to be gifted with a specifically poetic imagination, which was certainly the case with Honegger. The fact that he turned to song in his early years also throws a revealing light on the melodic, lyrical roots of his inspiration, which was closely bound up with words. The dialectic between geometry and emotion, as expressed in the composer's own words just quoted, also explains the apparent contradiction between his "taste for chamber and symphonic music in its most serious and austere manifestations" and in the cynical question he asked in his last years: "Pure music—what purity is that? The purity of emptiness?"

V. Three Early Songs, on poems of Moréas, Hérold, and Guillard

c. 1906–1908
Lost

5. *Two Songs* (*Barcarolle* and "one other")

pre-1914 (mentioned in a letter of 15 December 1915)
Lost

7. *Four Poems for Voice and Piano*

November 1914 (No. 1); July 1915 (No. 3); March 1916 (No. 4); May 1916 (No. 2)
"To Madame Jane Bathori"
No. 4 orchestrated by Arthur Hoérée in 1930

Duration: 9 minutes 30 seconds
Chester Music

Jane Bathori was the first of Honegger's important interpreters, followed shortly by Rose Armandie, Rose Féart, Gabrielle Gills, and especially Claire Croiza, then Régine de Lormoy. Notable singers among the second wave, from 1939 to 1947, would include Pierre Bernac, Éliette Schenneberg, Noémie Pérugia, and Madeleine Martinetti. It is important to mention these names, because Honegger always wrote his songs with a particular voice in mind.

For this, his first collection, the young Honegger chose a group of symbolist or post-symbolist poems (as defined by their publication by the *Mercure de France*) in which the atmosphere is often somewhat decadent and *fin de siècle*. The influence of Debussy is more dominant here than in the instrumental works of the same period, and we can find no traces of German models, as though the French language had extirpated them. We can trace to Debussy the constant successions of dominant major ninths, which become almost a mannerism, as well as the sense of melodic recitative. But, with the exception of "Sur le basalte" (No. 1), the harmonic language is more chromatic and tortuous and less tonal. There is a noticeable contrast between the simplicity of the vocal line and the occasionally excessive luxuriance of the piano part.

1. "SUR LE BASALTE"

The poem is taken from the collection *Vergers illusoires* (Imagined Orchards) by the Belgian symbolist poet André Fontainas. It is a typically decadent product, overflowing with precious, artificial verbosity, and this inevitably weighs on the music, which is on the long side and rather too far-fetched. Although it follows Debussy in its static treatment of tonality, its ternary form already shows Honegger's concern for architectural rigor.

2. "PETITE CHAPELLE"

This song, on a poem by Jules Laforgue, was the last of the four to be written. It is more personal in expression and, like the following one, strikes us by the depth of its religious feeling—one of the most basic essentials in the art of a man who nonetheless considered himself an agnostic. The form is once again ternary, with an overall doleful and weary atmosphere and complex and tortured chromatic harmonies. These are lightened in the diatonic central section, beginning with the words "Ardente apothéose."

3. "PRIÈRE"

For this song Honegger set the Preface to Francis Jammes's collection *De l'angélus de l'aube à l'angélus du soir* (From the Dawn to the Evening Angelus). It is his only Jammes setting and is the finest and best-known of the set. It seems as though the amateur soldier who was then spending his time safely and ingloriously in the Swiss federal army identified with some parts of the poem ("I walk down the road like an ass"), just as he did with Apollinaire's "knock-kneed peasant" in "Automne," written immediately afterward. Later, according to José Bruyr, Honegger would consider "Prière" his "best song, the most melodious I've written," even though it is in fact a long, syllabic recitative in the Debussy manner (Example 25). The harmonies are so changeable and complex that one can hardly speak of keys but only of dominants, since the chromatic instability rests on resonances of chords of the ninth. The final sound—the crystalline evocation of the angelus bells in the treble of the piano—is suspended on a ninth. The language is in fact very close to that of the Adagio of the *String Quartet No. 1*, and its notation is not without its problems. By retaining four flats in the key signature while he moves into distinctly sharp-side tonalities, Honegger lays himself open to the same charges he would later level at Dukas's opera *Ariane et Barbe-bleue* in a famous article republished in his book *Incantation aux fossiles*.[7] The unity of the song is achieved both by the declamation and by an important accompaniment figure, blending eighth-notes, sixteenth-notes, and syncopation.

Example 25

4. "LA MORT PASSE"

Apparently Anatole France had a high opinion of the "proud, tender soul" of the Armenian poet Archag Tchobanian. Honegger would return to Tchobanian's poetry once more in 1945 in "La douceur de tes yeux." Here the poet gives rise to the shortest and lightest of the four songs, based entirely on a pedal fifth on C-sharp. The free and supple declamation is heard over a lightweight, mobile accompaniment with gently clashing false relations.

9. *Three Poems of Paul Fort*

August–November 1916 (No. 1: August; No. 2: October; No. 3: November)
No. 1: "To Mademoiselle Madeleine Bonnard"; No. 2: "To Rose Armandie"; No. 3: "To Élisabeth Vuillermoz"
Poems taken from Paul Fort's *Complaintes et Dits* (Laments and Verses)
No. 1 orchestrated by the composer (performing forces: 2.2.2.2.–2.0.0.0.–harp; suspended cymbal; strings)

First performance of this version: 25 January 1930, Lina Falk, Pasdeloup Orchestra, conducted by A. van Raalte, Théâtre des Champs-Élysées, Paris
Duration: 7 minutes
Salabert

Paul Fort, the "Prince of Poets," inspired Honegger to write much simpler, more straightforward music than in the earlier *Four Poems for Voice and Piano*. G. K. Spratt finds that the piano parts of this collection smack too much of orchestral reductions, but this criticism really applies only to "Le chasseur perdu en forêt," which the composer indeed orchestrated, and in a delicate fashion moreover. It is the only one of his songs that he orchestrated before 1944. Later he would orchestrate two of the *Four Songs for Low Voice* (H184) and *Mimaamaquim* (H192).

1. "LE CHASSEUR PERDU EN FORÊT" (THE HUNTER LOST IN THE FOREST)

As the subject would suggest, "Le chasseur perdu en forêt" is the most romantic and "Germanic" of the three songs. In the first of its two sections (animé), the voice is surrounded by two complementary motifs: a typical horn call and a dotted ostinato in the bass outlining fifth and octave in an arpeggio. But the words "Adieu chasse, adieu galops" lead to a long, dreamy, mysterious nocturnal epilogue. Here the preceding motifs vanish, but the tonality establishes itself as the Lydian mode, with the sharpened fourth so typical of the hunting horn.

2. "CLOCHE DU SOIR" (EVENING BELL)

In "Cloche du soir" one detects the influence of Ravel in the bell resonances. This is particularly the case at the end, when the Honeggerian chorale, already heard in the central section of this ternary form at the words "l'angélus va mourir," takes on pentatonic form for the epilogue. We should note that at this period the young Honegger was attracted to graveyards in the dusk, the angelus, and bells in general. These would appear for the last time in the last of the *Six Poems of Apollinaire*, in a quite different poetic context.

3. "CHANSON DE FOL" (SONG OF THE FOOLISH FELLOW)

"Chanson de fol" has the fresh and lively character of a popular song. It unfolds against an accompaniment of ostinato sixteenth-notes, the bitonality of which recalls *Ronde*, the third of Ravel's *Three Unaccompanied Part Songs for Mixed Chorus* (as discussed in Chapter 2, we may remember that Poulenc and Honegger had sung these shortly after the score came out). Another strong influence is Debussy's last song, *Noël des enfants qui n'ont plus de maison*. In the middle section of "Chanson de fol," the solo piano plays some stubborn figuration, and the piece ends with the pirouette of two arpeggios going in different directions and remaining ironically suspended in the air.

11. *Nature morte* (Still Life)

February 1917
Poem by Vanderpyl
Duration: 1 minute
Published in issue No. 2 (July 1919) of the review *L'Arbitraire*, with the caption
"music by Honniger" (sic!)
Republished by Salabert

A charming description of a table decorated with fruit and a single flower.
Why did this delightful bagatelle remain unpublished for so long?

12. *Six Poems of Apollinaire*

August 1915–March 1917 (No. 1: May 1916; No. 2: March 1916; No. 3: August
    1915; Nos. 4 and 6: March 1917; No. 5: January 1917)
"To Fernand Ochsé"
First performance (Nos. 1–3 only): 11 July 1916, Rose Armandie, CMDI concert,
    Salle Oedenkoven, Paris
First performance of the complete cycle: 15 January 1918, Jane Bathori and Andrée
    Vaurabourg, Théâtre du Vieux-Colombier, Paris
The cycle (with the exception of No. 2) was orchestrated by Arthur Hoérée. First
    performance: 25 January 1930 (see H9)
Duration: 8 minutes
Salabert

On these six poems, taken from Apollinaire's collection *Alcools*, Honegger
composed a veritable masterpiece. It shows marked progress in concision, economy, accuracy of depiction, and an independence between voice and piano
achieved without any loss of unity.

1. "À LA SANTÉ" (AT THE PRISON OF LA SANTÉ)

The song gravitates round the immutable note A, the dominant of D
minor, to which the permanent accompaniment figure A -C-sharp-F -G lends
a whole-tone atmosphere (augmented fifth), suspending the feeling of tonality.
The high eighth-note figure in parallel fourths is heard in strict alternation
with the voice.

2. "CLOTILDE"

The unsettled, undulating tonality and the fleet arpeggios in high quintu-
plets make this Honegger's most Fauréan composition.

3. "AUTOMNE"

Honegger himself would later declare (in *Dissonances*, 1925): "I saw what I
wrote, I was Apollinaire's knock-kneed peasant during that tedious, inglorious
period when I was doing my national service in Switzerland." And José Bruyr
comments: "In this first true meeting of sound and soul . . . the scene is admirably caught in its dull, thick, ochre and gray coloring."[8] Even if the influence of

Debussy is still present, this modal, syncopated atmospheric song is nonetheless a masterpiece (Example 26).

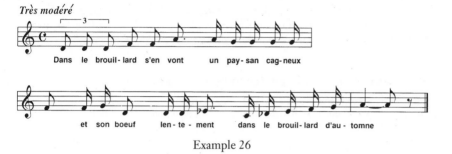

Example 26

The middle of the song is rather clearer and more lively, because suddenly, at the words "En s'en allant là-bas le paysan chantonne" (As he makes his way there the peasant sings to himself), the silhouette takes on substance and character. Note the lovely modulation to B minor at the words "une chanson d'amour" and the moving nostalgia of the cry "Ah l'automne!"

4. "SALTIMBANQUES" (THE TRAVELING CIRCUS)

This placid, if slightly grotesque procession, with its nonchalant, slightly limping gait, is another little gem. The tonality is deliberately blurred and we can sense the discreet presence of black minstrels, no doubt through the mediation of Debussy's *Minstrels* and *General Lavine*.

Example 27

5. "L'ADIEU"

"L'adieu" is not really Fauréan, as claimed by Spratt, nor atonal, as claimed by Delannoy, but subtly polytonal. It gives off an atmosphere of muted pain, of mourning, and autumnal melancholy. Is the voice singing in the Dorian mode, or in the Lydian? Honegger is happy to leave us unenlightened.

6. "LES CLOCHES" (THE BELLS)

"Les cloches" is perhaps the most Debussyan of the six songs, with the piano's joyful carillon in rapid waltz rhythm preserving the ambivalence between 3/4 and 6/8 meters that is so much a part of Debussy's Spanish style. The capricious rhythms of the central section are even a direct reference to *Ibéria*, and Debussy would again seem to be the source of the whole-tone scales, the very free vocal line, and the brief, half-tearful, half-mocking eruption of sentiment at the words "Tu seras loin, je pleurerai" (You will be far away, I shall weep), with the piano's ironical echo of the word "peut-être."

30. *Pâques à New York* (Easter in New York)

March–July 1920 (Nos. 1 and 2: March; No. 3: July)
Three excerpts taken from Blaise Cendrars's *Du monde entier*
First performance: 24 February 1922, performers unknown, New York
First European performance: 24 January 1924, Rose Féart and the Pro Arte Quartet,
     Nouvelles Auditions, Geneva
Performing forces: mezzo-soprano and string quartet
Duration: 5 minutes 30 seconds
Carl Fischer, New York, 1923

Marcel Delannoy wrote:

> In Arthur Honegger's subconscious there exists, and always has existed, a kind of dream of Easter: luminous, gentle, a Maurice Denis fresco but with more vigor in its volumes. The sharp conflicts in his nature are drawn toward it as to a peaceful resolution.[9]

Delannoy goes on to refer to Honegger's daughter's first name, the *Cantique de Pâques*, the end of *Le Roi David*, the Finale of the *Viola Sonata*, and so on. José Bruyr, speaking of *Pâques à New York*, mentions "tender emotion" but also "dense lyricism"; Willy Tappolet mentions "wild, despairing chromaticism" but also "seraphic ecstasy"; and Jacques Feschotte praises Honegger's genius "in its brightest light, which is that of spirituality and faith." If these judgments seem to contradict each other, they are in fact complementary, because, at least in the first two songs, the "Easter" serenity is achieved through intense struggle. *Pâques à New York*, based on Cendrars's fine poems, is one of the high points of Honegger's output. It is a work of exemplary concision and, regrettably, the only one in which he combined the voice with a chamber ensemble.

1. "C'EST À CETTE HEURE-CI"

A long rising phrase on the cello underpins the dissonant, bittersweet counterpoint on the other instruments, and the voice is integrated into this texture. But this harsh climate changes abruptly at the word *coeur* ("tombe sur votre coeur"), with the otherworldly light of harmonics that preserve the key of D major until the end of the song.

2. "FAITES, SEIGNEUR"

The tormented violence and dense, chromatic polyphony of "Faites, Seigneur," full of dotted rhythms, recall the *String Quartet No. 1*. The tension mounts implacably as far as the dramatic downward leap in the voice on the words "désespoir farouche" (fierce despair). This is followed by an instrumental interlude that forms a gentle introduction to the most beautiful and moving section of the song: "Je suis triste et malade, peut-être à cause de vous" (I am sad and ill, perhaps because of you). The mood is one of controlled suffering, which reaches a sublime resolution into C major.

3. "DIC NOBIS MARIA"

Paradoxically, it is in this song written in Zurich, and not in the previous song written in Aix-en-Provence, that we hear the sound of crickets in the very high tremolos on the first violin. Within the atmosphere of dazzling light, the calm psalmody of the voice part becomes more halting, illustrating in a highly realistic manner the "blancheurs, éperdues *palpitantes* comme des mains" (bewildered whitenesses *beating* like hands). In the epilogue, note the wonderful appearance of E major on the last word of "tressaillir dans mon sein" (shiver in my bosom).

It is worth quoting a short unpublished commentary by Honegger himself:

> The first song is a serious meditation in which the poet remembers an old Protestant chorale describing "the beauty of your face under torture," which must be the well-known "O Haupt voll Blut und Wunden" (O sacred head sore wounded). The second song is an explosion of violent despair, which becomes calmer toward the end. The last is an evocation of the Annunciation in the spirit of an Italian Primitive; it forms a little triptych on its own, with the same question asked three times, each time eliciting a different response.

51. *Six Poems of Jean Cocteau* (Six Poésies de Jean Cocteau)

May 1920 (Nos. 1 and 2); June 1920 (No. 3); January 1923 (No. 6); June 1923 (Nos. 4 and 5)
"To Rose Féart"
First performance: 17 November 1924, Claire Croiza and the composer, Salle Pleyel, Paris
Arranged by Arthur Hoérée with string quartet (first performance, 12 December 1930, Régine de Lormoy and the Brussels Quartet, Brussels Conservatory), and with string orchestra (first performance, 5 December 1936, Hugues Cuénod, Jane Evrard's Ladies' Orchestra, Salle Gaveau, Paris)
Duration: 5 minutes 15 seconds
Salabert

These tiny, entertaining parodies (the longest lasts a minute) were called "trifles" by Honegger himself and, of all his groups of songs, these are the nearest to the style of Les Six. "Le nègre" combines a "classical" concerto grosso theme with a ragtime, full of cross-accents—what Bruyr describes rather well as "Bach's humor seasoned with a clove of jazz."[10] "Locutions" begins almost like Poulenc, but this is then denied by the song's increasing harmonic complexity. The delightful "Souvenirs d'enfance" partakes of a popular song à la Debussy.

After the brief declamation of "Ex voto" comes "Une danseuse," a grotesque poem comparing a female ballet dancer to a crab! The latter is described first of all in a chromatic, atonal style, before the dancer arrives in E-flat major, with a waltz motif in the left hand. As Honegger himself said: "For the crab, dry, rhythmic music, in opposition to that for the dancer, which is gentle and singing." Finally, in "Madame," Honegger recalls Chabrier in poking fun discreetly at grand opera. A little pirouette concludes this charming cycle, which is often sung in place of some of Honegger's more important works.

54. *Chanson de Ronsard*

February 1924
"To Charles Panzéra"
Pierre de Ronsard's poem *Plus tu connais que je brûle pour toi* (The More You Know
    That I Burn With Love for You)
For the supplement to the May 1924 issue of the *La Revue musicale* ("Tombeau de
    Ronsard"), in which the song was published for the first time
First performance, version for voice and piano: 15 May 1924, Claire Croiza, *La
    Revue musicale* concert, Théâtre du Vieux-Colombier, Paris
First performance, version for voice, flute, and string quartet: 24 January 1925,
    Régine de Lormoy, A. Blanquart, Poulet Quartet, conducted by Arthur Hoérée,
    Paris
Duration: 1 minute 30 seconds
Salabert

The homage on the occasion of the four-hundredth anniversary of the birth of Pierre de Ronsard featured contributions from Honegger, Dukas, Roussel, Louis Aubert, Caplet, Roland-Manuel, Maurice Delage, and Ravel. Ravel and Honegger were undoubtedly the composers who came closest to recapturing the Renaissance spirit.

The modal language of this delightful little masterpiece seems to make a bow in Ravel's direction, especially in the harmonies on the words "Plus tu connais que je vis en émoi" (The more you know that I live in turmoil). But under the double arabesque of voice and flute, the string quartet outlines a four-part chorale. The quintet version of the song is greatly superior.

70. *Vocalise-Étude*

1929 (before June)
Written for the final examination at the Paris Conservatory in 1929
"To Berthe Seroen"
Duration: 1 minute 40 seconds
Leduc

As an examination piece, the *Vocalise-Étude* understandably brims with technical difficulties, in intonation and rhythm, and demands a supple voice. But it is a very attractive piece of real musical quality. We may imagine it sounding effective on flute, oboe, or clarinet, like the two *Vocalises* by Roussel.

137. *Possèdes-tu, pauvre pécheur* (Do You Possess, Poor Sinner)

14 July 1939
Duration: 40 seconds
Unpublished

Possèdes-tu, pauvre pécheur is a canticle for unison choir and harmonium (or piano) on words of unknown origin. We may wonder what prompted Honegger to write these seventeen measures, on Bastille Day, 14 July!

138. *Three Poems of Claudel*

31 March 1939 (No. 1); 16 January 1940 (No. 3); 18 January 1940 (No. 2)
"To Pierre Bernac"
First performance: 15 November 1941, Pierre Bernac and Francis Poulenc, Salle Gaveau, Paris
Duration: 7 minutes 30 seconds
Salabert

The *Three Poems of Claudel* is without doubt the most undervalued of Honegger's song cycles, and yet it is certainly of more value than the *Six Poems of Jean Cocteau*, for example. If the Apollinaire settings are perfect miniatures, what we have here are three songs of broad and imposing dimensions, in keeping with the character of the poet. But commentators on Honegger's works have found little good to say about them. G. K. Spratt concedes that "Le delphinium" is the most beautiful and perfect of all Honegger's songs, but he has distinct misgivings about the other two.

1. "Sieste"

Claudel's description of the torrid heat of a provincial Sunday afternoon is deliberately prosaic and objective, like a still life. The declamation is very sober and syllabic, with an accompaniment that varies between high chords in an ostinato of seven quarter-notes within the 6/4 meter and more complex counterpoint, but the low register is not reached until the end of the piece. Its tonality of E (first minor, then major) establishes its cohesion.

2. "Le delphinium"

Bright, luminous sonorities and an accompaniment evoking the sounds of a harp describe the dazzling, majestic flower of Claudel's poem, "an enormous, blue torch that revels in life to the point of persuading us that, if called upon, it could cure the boredom of God." An animé in 7/4 and a modéré in 4/4 alternate in the order A-B-A-B-A. The use of the Lydian sharpened fourth further heightens the color. Would Messiaen, with his ability to see sounds as colors, have agreed on blue here?

3. "LE RENDEZ-VOUS"

"Le rendez-vous" comes as a total contrast, with its evocation of a menacing, nocturnal forest scene, of old age and death, and of an almost over-the-top romanticism. Against this is set the resolution of the hero, who, at the end, braves thunder and lightning to reach a rendezvous with, one supposes, his loved one. This image of Claudel's inspired Honegger to write a song even less well understood than the previous two—Bruyr himself speaks of "violence with a touch of over-emphasis."[11] Even so, we only have to compare it with the juvenile "Le chasseur perdu en forêt" (H9) to see how far Honegger had progressed.

Before looking at this undeniably complex piece, one would do well to reread Claudel's poem, preferably out loud, in order to get the measure of its amazing musicality, which must have fascinated the composer. Following the dramatic, declamatory nature of the text, Honegger several times has recourse to his particular style of word setting with accents on the first syllables of words—a style he normally reserved for oratorios and music for the stage. With this in mind, he chose iambic and anapestic rhythms for the piano accompaniment, within a disrupted, even chaotic 9/8 meter. And we may note that this, for once, truly orchestral accompaniment leads Honegger exceptionally to write on three staffs for the final storm. The tonality here is vague due to the somber, growling chromaticism, and the vocal line at times takes on the outline of a gasping, hectic recitative. At the height of the climax, at measure 39, the "thunder" breaks: the voice rises for the one and only time to a high G and delivers the word *tonnerre* (with the accent on the first syllable, naturally) in rhythmic unison with the iambus in the piano part. From here the tension relaxes swiftly through the epilogue's decrescendo. In my opinion, these three Claudel songs mark the apogee of Honegger's song output.

144. *Three Psalms*

December 1940–January 1941 (No. 1: 20 January 1941; No. 2: 28 December 1940; No. 3: 8 January 1941)
"To Éliette Schenneberg"
Texts from the Huguenot Psalter
First performance: 17 April 1942, Éliette Schenneberg, Paris
Duration: 5 minutes
Salabert

Willy Tappolet records that in the Bible Honegger received at his confirmation, the priest in Le Havre wrote: "Continue thou in the things which thou hast learned and hast been assured of" (2 Timothy, 3, 14).[12]

The triptych of *Three Psalms* belongs to the period of reflection and self-examination that followed Honegger's return to Paris after his exodus, during which he also wrote the austere *Sonata for solo violin* and extensive sketches for the *Selzach Passion*. There is a marked contrast between the confident jubilation of Nos. 1 and 3, which are of an even purer Bach-style classicism than the passages in *Le Roi David*, and the intensity of the central lament (written first) over the miseries of war. In Part One of this book, I have already suggested that, in

Honegger's eyes, the "evil man" (*homme pernicieux*) of the Psalmist could be none other than Adolf Hitler. The piano, especially in Nos. 1 and 3, is treated like an organ, and the work is perfectly performable in that form.

1. PSALM 34: "JAMAIS NE CESSERAI DE MAGNIFIER LE SEIGNEUR"

Most of the psalm is based on the principle of a response, with each of the eight phrases of the sung chorale preceded by a few measures of strict, Bachian, three-part counterpoint, which has no thematic links with the chorale. Only the last four phrases of the chorale are accompanied.

2. PSALM 140: "O DIEU, DONNE-MOI DÉLIVRANCE DE CET HOMME PERNICIEUX"

The entire first page of this poignant and expressive psalm in F minor is an admirably molded declamation over harmonies. The central section for piano alone replies with the chorale "I know that my Redeemer liveth," already used in *La Danse des morts*. A barely perceptible echo of this is heard in the bass in the final three measures.

3. PSALM 138: "IL FAUT QUE TOUS MES ESPRITS"

This psalm is the closest to the Calvinist psalms of the Reformed Church. The traditional melody is treated in canon between voice and piano (Example 28). The notes marked with a cross suggest that this might have been one of the sources for the chorale that crowns the *Symphony for Strings* (see Example 42).

Example 28

148. *Petit Cours de morale*

April 1941
"To Elsa Scherz-Meister"
Texts taken from Jean Giraudoux's *Suzanne et le Pacifique*
First performance: 28 June 1942, Pierre Bernac and Francis Poulenc, Honegger Festival, Salle Gaveau, Paris
Duration: 3 minutes 50 seconds
Salabert

After the two previous serious and grave sets of songs—*Three Poems of Claudel* and *Three Psalms*—come two sets of a lighter, more amusing character. In these, and especially in the *Petit Cours de morale*, Honegger seems to have intended a friendly homage to his old comrade Francis Poulenc. As José Bruyr remarks, none too seriously, the first names of the five young girls described by Giraudoux "make up an alexandrine."[13] Each has elicited a little poem of six lines. "Jeanne" unfolds in a modal E minor through an almost unbroken series of sixteenth-notes. In "Adèle," irony is joined with realism in a brief narrative—the composer's light-winged fantasy makes any description seem cumbersome! "Cécile," with its added sixths and waddling rhythms, brings us close to the delightful "naughty" world of the cabaret. The singer celebrates the slightly perverse charms of "Irène" over an unchanging fox-trot rhythm, but the lines "Irène, petite Irène, l'amour c'est la grande peine" (Irène, little Irène, love is great suffering) twice provoke a broad, impassioned phrase roguishly recalling grand opera. Finally, "Rosemonde" is another sideways glance at Poulenc. The vocal line is languorous and slovenly against the steady, placid chords of the accompaniment and its deliberately kitsch romantic modulations. The implicit key of D major is disclosed only in the last two measures, and the song ends with the words "Veux-tu découvrir le monde? Ferme les yeux, Rosemonde!" (Do you want to discover the world? Close your eyes, Rosemonde!) on a delightful melodic wink.

152. *Saluste du Bartas*—Six Villanelles

September 1941
"To Noémie Pérugia"
Poems by Pierre Bédat de Montlaur
First performance: 21 March 1942, Noémie Pérugia and Irène Aitoff, Salle Gaveau, Paris
Duration: 7 minutes
Henri Lemoine

Saluste du Bartas is another set of wonderful miniatures, but this time with an archaic accent, as befits the subject. Saluste du Bartas (1544–1590) was a Protestant Gascon gentleman, a poet, an ambassador, and a fighting compan-ion of Henri IV. He was mortally wounded at the battle of Ivry (though he was able to write about the incident before he died) and had tender feelings toward his protectress, Queen Marguerite of Navarre. The poet Pierre Bédat de Mont-laur described du Bartas in a series of villanelles, a verse form that he claimed to have revived, proclaiming himself its standard-bearer. He published a collection of twenty-six of these and all were set to music by various composers, although Honegger was the only famous one to do so. A villanelle has six lines, with the last identical to the first. In this present cycle, Honegger employs bold but nat-ural-sounding modulations to get back to the opening tonality for the last line.

1. "LE CHÂTEAU DU BARTAS"

Dotted rhythms have been a symbol of ceremonial since Lully's day, and this little processional march suggests the pride of the Gascon knight with a nice irony.

2. "TOUT LE LONG DE LA BAÏSE"

A sinuous, chromatic line of eighth-notes in 6/8 meter evokes the flow of the Baïse River and the bank where the gentleman poet takes his promenade. Here, announced by bright chords on the piano, the queen poet comes to join him.

3. "LE DÉPART"

"Le départ" is a light canter, with sprightly rhythms and supple, natural, almost Debussyan modulations.

4. "LA PROMENADE"

A rather formal procession of the beautiful queen through her gardens.

5. "NÉRAC EN FÊTE"

The piece "Nérac en fête" is simply an excuse for a joyful celebration.

6. "DUO"

"Duo" describes the last meeting between the poet, symbolized by a rhythmic motif on the piano, and the queen, whose name, Marguerite, is sung three times as a ravishing vocalizing. This slow, languorous, and sensuous procession suggests the fulfillment of the lovers' happiness.

168. Céline

May 1942 (version A); 15 May 1943 (version B)
Poem by G. J. Aubry
Performing forces: version A: voice, flute, harp, and string trio; version B: voice, piano
First performance (version A): 9 May 1942, Leila Ben Sedira, Paris
Duration: 1 minute 40 seconds
Salabert (version B)

Version A remains lost. Version B turned up unexpectedly in 1993 and was subsequently published. It is a little gem of a piece, of exquisite elegance, in a very classical E minor.

169. Panis angelicus

May 1943
Latin liturgical text
Duration: 2 minutes 20 seconds
Facsimile of the autograph published in the music supplement of the *Revue de l'Opéra de Paris* (No. 2, October/November 1950)
Salabert

Panis angelicus is a very attractive piece in B major in the Fauré tradition that was never far from Honegger's mind. It modulates with the ease and originality that were the two traits the composers had in common.

178. *O Temps suspends ton vol* (O Time, halt your flight)

January 1945
Poem by Henri Martin
Duration: 2 minutes 20 seconds
Salabert

The vocal range of *O Temps suspends ton vol*, from C-sharp up to F, is too high for this song to have formed one of the *Four Songs for Low Voice*, but it is still strange that Honegger should not have published this very beautiful song. It is one long recitative, in a single outpouring without joins or repetitions, and it is certainly a *mélodie* (art song), not a *chanson* (popular song). The poem itself is also extremely fine.

184. *Four Songs for Low Voice*

February 1940 (No. 2; No. 12 in *Christopher Columbus*, H140); 24 February 1944
    (No. 3); 17 March 1944 (No. 4); December 1945 (No. 1)
No. 1: "To Elsa Cavelti"; No. 2: "To Madeleine Martinetti"; No. 3: "To Éliette
    Schenneberg"; No. 4: "To André Gensac"
First performance (Nos. 2, 3, and 4 only): 21 May 1944, Ginette Guillamat and
    Pierre Sancan, Salle du Conservatoire, Paris
No. 2 was originally written for voice, clarinet, and harp; No. 3 was orchestrated by
    the composer
Duration: 4 minutes 50 seconds
Salabert

The first two songs are actually *chansons* and really belong in Category 9, while the last two are true *mélodies*. This makes for a certain lack of unity in the cycle and can lead to misunderstandings.

1. "LA DOUCEUR DE TES YEUX" (THE SWEETNESS OF YOUR EYES)

"La douceur de tes yeux" is an irresistibly charming love song over a syncopated accompaniment. Here Honegger returned to the work of the Armenian poet Archag Tchobanian, whom he had already set in "La mort passe" (see H7). Even in such a light piece as this, Honegger does not hesitate to accentuate the first syllable of words when he feels the text demands it (*"mor*telle des *bles*sures"; *"ter*rible *bles*sure," and so on).

2. "DERRIÈRE MURCIE EN FLEURS" (BEHIND MURCIA IN BLOOM)

"Derrière Murcie en fleurs" is a Spanish song in a typically Phrygian B minor, with the feeling of an improvised serenade. It comes from the score to

William Aguet's radio play *Christopher Columbus* (H140, Category 15), where it appears as No. 12.

3. "Un grand sommeil noir" (A Long Dark Sleep)

"Un grand sommeil noir" is Honegger's only setting of the poet Verlaine. The poem is a particularly gloomy one that Ravel had also set to music as a young man in 1895. As we might expect, it is an oppressively sad song that never leaves C-sharp minor.

4. "La terre les eaux va buvant" (The Earth Drinks Up the Waters)

This is Honegger's second and last setting of Ronsard, twenty years after the lovely *Chanson de Ronsard* of 1924. A lively, captivating little song on a dance rhythm that owes nothing to the Renaissance and everything to 1944. A sure-fire encore hit.

192. *Mimaamaquim*

December 1946; orchestration completed 8 June 1947, in Paris
"To Madeleine Martinetti"
Transliteration of the Hebrew text of the first verse of Psalm 130 (De profundis)
For low contralto going down to F-sharp
Orchestral performing forces: flute, oboe, clarinet, bassoon, horn, harp, and strings
Duration: 3 minutes 30 seconds
Salabert

Mimaamaquim, Honegger's last song, is one of the high points of his output. With his extraordinary ability to assimilate influences, he recalls in this overwhelmingly passionate litany the profoundly Jewish atmosphere of *Le Roi David*—which, as mentioned previously in Chapter 6, had caused one critic of the time to say "the composer of *Le Roi David* must be a Jew." Certainly, Honegger must have studied Jewish music to be able to capture the characteristic intonations of synagogue chanting, such as we hear in the opening Recitative (Example 29). The simplicity of its A-B-A-B-A form only compounds the emotion. The piece is even more beautiful in its orchestral form.

Among the sketches for the unfinished *Selzach Passion* is a quite different, equally fine setting of *Mimaamaquim*, dated 31 January 1941. Whether in French, in Latin, or in purely instrumental music such as the second move-

Example 29

ment of the *Symphonie liturgique*, the idea of the De profundis haunted Honegger continually.

222. La Nuit est si profonde (The Night Is So Profound)

Date unknown, but probably before 1920
Author of the text unknown
Voice and orchestra (two flutes, two oboes, two clarinets, two bassoons, strings)
Duration: 3 minutes
Unpublished

The subject of *La Nuit est si profonde* is once again a nocturnal rendezvous in the forest, as in the *Three Poems of Paul Fort* and the *Three Poems of Claudel*. Exactly when Honegger wrote it, and for whom, remains an enigma, although it might appear to be the scene from an opera. Details of the handwriting and notation confirm the stylistic evidence, indicating that the work must date from before 1920, and one can even detect the influence of Ernest Chausson, which is rare elsewhere in Honegger's output.

Category 8A: Art Songs from Stage and Film

48B.   *Two Songs for Ariel*, from *The Tempest*
63.   *Three Songs of the Little Siren*
136A. *O Salutaris*, from the film *Cavalcade d'amour*

The numerous popular songs written for film are described under Category 9A in Chapter 14.

48B. Two Songs for Ariel, from the incidental music for The Tempest

April 1923
No. 1: "To Gabrielle Gills"; No. 2: "To Joy MacArden"
Shakespeare's texts in the French translation by Guy de Pourtalès
First performance: 18 November 1925, Joy Demarquette-MacArden, Strasbourg
    Municipal Orchestra, conducted by Arthur Honegger, Palais des Fêtes,
    Strasbourg
Performing forces: 2.1.2.2.–2.2.0.0.–celesta, harp, strings
Reduction by the composer for voice and piano
Duration: 3 minutes 10 seconds
Salabert

These famous words have often been set to music, but rarely so well as here. The orchestral versions are indispensable. The first song follows every detail of the text with that heightened feeling for imagery that Honegger always displays, ending with the magic, bitonal tinkling of submarine bells on the celesta. The second song is shorter and more unified, and here rapid harp arpeggios combine with syncopation on high, divided violins and a rapid, supple vocal line.

63. *Three Songs of the Little Siren*

End of 1926
"To Régine de Lormoy"
Words by René Morax, for a show based on Hans Christian Andersen's *The Little Mermaid*
First performance: 26 March 1927, Régine de Lormoy, the flautist Réon, and the Roth Quartet, conducted by Arthur Honegger, Durand Concert, Salle Pleyel, Paris
Two versions: with flute and string quartet; with piano
Duration: 2 minutes 30 seconds
Salabert

These three delicate miniatures are more effective in the original quintet version. In the "Chanson des sirènes," the bitonality at a minor-ninth distance of the pizzicatos and string harmonics is indispensable in depicting the rustling of the waters, while the voice declaims a free recitative. Likewise, in the very brief and fresh "Berceuse de la sirène," the complex multiple rhythms of the muted strings recall the 6/8 section of the first movement of Debussy's *La Mer*. The tiny "Chanson de la poire" (Song of the Pear) is over in a flash. José Bruyr found the right words when he called it a *"beurrée d'automne* grafted off Stravinsky"[14]—*Pribaoutki* and *Tilimbom* come to mind.

136A. *O Salutaris*, from the film *Cavalcade d'amour*

July 1939
"To Ginette Guillamat"
First performance: 9 October 1943, Noémie Pérugia, Church of Saint-Séverin, Paris
Two versions: for voice and piano (or harp); for voice, organ, and piano (or harp) *ad libitum*
Duration: 1 minute 40 seconds
Heugel

A clever and attractive pastiche of Fauré, in that master's favorite key of D-flat major, with harp arpeggios and modulations one would expect. This is church music in the style of Honegger's *Panis angelicus* (H169), and none the worse for that. Honegger the professional did what he was asked to do, and the result is faultless.

ELEVEN

Orchestral Music

With the five symphonies forming a compact and imposing chain on the horizon, the central massif of Honegger's orchestral works consists of more than
forty peaks of varying sizes. Together with the "grand frescoes"—that is to say,
the oratorios—it is essentially on these orchestral works that Honegger's reputation rests, and rightly so. He made a prudent and sensible entry into this
field with works of modest dimensions, such as *Aglavaine et Sélysette* and *Le
Chant de Nigamon*, and gradually turned the orchestra into his favorite medium
at the expense of chamber music, which had been predominant at the start of his
career, but which retreated into the background after 1923.

Clearheaded realist that he was, Honegger made no early forays that were
beyond his powers: there was no grandiose project for a symphony subsequently
stillborn or abandoned. *Horace victorieux*, which was by far the largest of his
early orchestral works, was originally conceived as a ballet and therefore is based
on a detailed scenario. He waited, then, until he was thirty-eight years old
before tackling the supreme challenge of a symphony, with a fully accomplished
work that bears the opus number 75 in his chronological catalog. Before that,
a number of his works, notably the Symphonic Movements *Pacific 2.3.1* and
Rugby, are at least as elaborately structured as this *First Symphony*, the first
movement of which is the most complex he ever wrote.

But as the years pass, it is increasingly the orchestral music to which we
should turn in order to grasp Honegger's true, essential message. What the
String Quartet No. 1 expresses at twenty-five, the De profundis of the *Symphonie
liturgique* expresses at fifty. The *Concerto da camera* and *Deliciae basilienses* are
amplifications and sublimations of chamber music, while the *Symphony for
Strings* is the culmination of the quartets. Certainly, we may regret that Honegger abandoned chamber music at the height of his artistic maturity, but this
has been the case with other great symphonic writers of this century, such
as Jean Sibelius, Carl Nielsen, and Vaughan Williams. Perhaps one has to be a
Beethoven to manage the two simultaneously.

Among the essential symphonic gifts that Honegger possessed, first and
foremost was that of inventing thematic outlines that were striking and also
capable of being elaborated and developed. His main themes are memorable
not only just as tunes, beautiful though they may be, but also as living organisms
containing possibilities of growth and regeneration. Of all the composers of

his time, Honegger was one of those most deeply concerned—preoccupied, even—with problems of perception and hearing. He was well aware that, for a nontonal theme to engrave itself on the memory, it must compensate for its lack of tonality by other parameters: by rhythm, accentuation, the specific quality of its intervallic structure, or by its harmonic coloring.

Honegger had an exceptional feeling for the length and proportions of a work. His pieces are almost always admirably concise, to the point that occasionally (I think of *Monopartita*, which could have become a sixth symphony) we may regret that he did not expand them further. But that is so much better, and so much rarer, than the other way round!

This paring-down—a process that does not exclude a certain degree of complexity—can also be seen in a style of orchestration that often strikes us as severe when compared with the extravagance practiced by many of his contemporaries, but which is entirely at the service of the music it clothes. This born symphonist never thinks of the orchestra, as Richard Strauss did, as having a value of its own, and he even observed the traditional practice, now more or less obsolete, of leaving the orchestration until after he had written the notes. In certain specific works where the musical substance required it (I think in particular of ballets such as *Sémiramis* and *Le Cantique des cantiques*), Honegger proved that he was a complete master of the seductive "impressionist" style, but it is typical of him that beyond the context of the stage, in his large orchestral works and especially in his symphonies, he did not resort to "special" instruments like the saxophone or the ondes Martenot, although he was fully familiar with their capabilities and, in the case of the ondes, had introduced them into the orchestra.

This stand against pretty, picturesque sound detail that might obscure the actual music is echoed in his sober use of percussion. As with his great model, Beethoven, feeling was more important than sensation. We can only admire the elegance of the gesture by which he excluded all percussion from the violent hurly-burly of *Rugby*, where the subject would seem to have demanded it most. Similarly, he never had recourse to the extravagantly large orchestras of the post-romantics. On the other hand, the chamber orchestra in the *Deliciae basilienses* has the sonority of a large body of players, while at the same time preserving the advantages in transparency of reduced numbers. And the *Symphony for Strings* draws its extraordinary power from its very austerity.

Even if the *First Symphony* has still not made a permanent position for itself, the other four, together with the three Symphonic Movements, have gone round the world and could now fairly be called popular. But too many of Honegger's other orchestral works, of considerable musical value, remain largely unknown. I hope, in this chapter, to draw attention to these and to show that in this field, as in others, Honegger's failure rate is extremely low, despite his prolific output.

I shall look firstly at the symphonies, then the concertos, the miscellaneous orchestral works, and finally at those derived from stage works and films.

Category 5: Symphonies

75. *First Symphony in C*
153. *Second Symphony for strings and trumpet in D* (*Symphony for Strings*)
186. *Third Symphony* (*Symphonie liturgique*)
191. *Fourth Symphony in A* (*Deliciae basilienses*)
202. *Fifth Symphony in D* (*Di Tre Re*)

For more than a century now, well-meaning commentators have periodically been announcing the death of the symphony. Nevertheless, it has remained alive and well, and today composers of all ages continue to cultivate it. When Debussy declared rather rashly that "since Beethoven's Ninth the uselessness of the symphony has been established," the many examples by Schubert, Schumann, Mendelssohn, Brahms, Bruckner, and Dvořák, not to mention those of the Russian and French schools, had already proved him wrong. And if we take the word "symphony" in a broader context, then surely Debussy's *La Mer* must count as one of the most perfect symphonies ever written. Even so, it is true that when Honegger's generation began writing, after the First World War, music was turning away from symphonic perspectives. Gustav Mahler, who died in 1911, seemed to have reached the outer limits of the genre, from the point of view both of the symphony's formal and temporal dimensions (works lasting an hour and a half or more) and of its performing forces (including voices). As musical language pushed at the borders of tonality, so the thematic working had reached the ultimate in length and complexity.

The future would indeed show that an extreme position had been reached. Like Beethoven's immediate heirs a century earlier, those of Mahler, with Shostakovich at their head, would remain on this side of their model's broken boughs.

Meanwhile, Mahler's great rival and antipode Jean Sibelius, who survived him by nearly half a century, struck out at a tangent that could not seem other than marginal and anachronistic in the eyes of the musical world of the time. Only in our own time has the transcendent value of his approach become fully apparent. Sibelius's language seems traditional and consonant, and the orchestral forces he asks for go no further than Beethoven's, but the models he proposed of formal integration, and of a thematic growth that is equivalent to a real biological process in sound, illustrate the possibilities of emancipating the technique of development from its inherited forms, with a concision unequaled since the classics.

But neither Honegger nor any of his contemporaries then knew of these crucial compositions, the impact of which is only now being felt on young composers. If nearly all the composers of his generation turned their backs on large forms like the sonata and the symphony, it was because the most influential among their immediate elders had turned their attention to other problems and other forms. No possible solutions for a budding symphonist were forthcoming either from the Debussy of *Images* and *Jeux*, from the brilliantly revolutionary Stravinsky of *The Rite of Spring*, or from the Schoenberg of *Pierrot lunaire*, who seemed to have broken music down into its smallest components. The breakup of tonality seemed to have sounded the death knell of the forms to which it had given rise, based on the idea of theme and development. From Beethoven to Brahms, then to Bruckner and Mahler, the increasing invasion of tonal language by chromaticism brought with it a progressive obfuscation of the clarity of thematic shapes, so that it was harder and harder for the listener to remember themes. This incompatibility reached breaking point in the sonata movements of Max Reger.

Honegger wrote his five symphonies between the years 1930 and 1950, at the same time as a number of other important symphonic composers. In France, after the early death of the truly great symphonist Albéric Magnard, so much admired by Milhaud, the name that comes to mind is that of Albert Roussel. His last three symphonies (dating from 1921 to 1934), and especially the last two, were way ahead of all rivals. In these, Roussel treated the great classical forms with unusual conciseness and allied this with a tonal language expanded through polytonality. He also gave counterpoint the priority over harmony, as against the approach of the whole generation of French composers that succeeded Debussy and Ravel. Roussel was, it is true, six years older than Ravel, but he was a slow developer and at the age of sixty found himself the leader of those who were a generation younger than himself. Honegger as a symphonist was to some extent a member of this movement. As for Milhaud, Honegger's friend and comrade-in-arms, he did not try his hand at a symphony until later, writing twelve of them between 1939 and 1961. The spirit of these, and their determinedly Mediterranean, melody-based language, are very far from Honegger's rough, Beethovenian power, whose varied successors in this respect would prove to be (to mention only French composers) André Jolivet, Henri Dutilleux, and Marcel Landowski.

The same period also saw the composition of Sergei Prokofiev's symphonies. The three "Paris" symphonies (Nos. 2, 3, and 4 of 1924–1930) are much closer to Honegger's than the three "Soviet" symphonies (Nos. 5, 6, and 7 of 1944–1952). Dmitri Shostakovich, who was a great admirer of Honegger, partakes of the same dramatic power and epic tone, even though his musical language is more traditional and, especially, his forms are longer and, it has to be said, looser. One should also mention Paul Hindemith, even if he was certainly less of a symphonic composer than Honegger because of the absence in his music of dynamic forms, thematic transformations, and dramatic tension. Some among the English school of symphonists—Vaughan Williams, in particular—also have undeniable affinities with Honegger. But the man who must be considered, with Honegger, as the most eminent symphonist of his generation, Bohuslav Martinů, showed a totally different spirit and style in the six symphonies he wrote between 1942 and 1953.

But back to Honegger—and to what seems, at least, to be the paradox of a symphonist in the Beethovenian mold existing within the ranks of Les Six, and hence under Cocteau's patronage. We can be in no doubt that he was the least characteristic member of the group, if we look at his taste for long, well-structured movements and at the serious tone of his music in the chamber works of the early 1920s. His German-Swiss ancestry can only partly explain his firm attachment to the romantic tradition, which meant that he never shared his friends' enthusiasm for Satie, let alone their hatred of Wagner. In the crucial interview he gave to Paul Landormy on 20 September 1920, Honegger was obviously determined to set the record straight without delay. And we could say that the famous statement that ended his article of 1 February 1922 in *Le Cour-rier musical*—"It is pointless to break down doors that one can open"—sums up in one pithy phrase his attitude, which was open-minded and evolutionary rather than revolutionary. It shows too that he was one of the few of his gener-ation who was born to be a symphonist.

Nonetheless, as we have seen, Arthur Honegger waited until he was nearly forty, and until he was absolutely in command of his technique, to write his first essay in the symphonic form. What's more, another eleven years would pass before he tried his hand at another. His symphonies belong, therefore, to the period of his maturity (for the most part the war years and those immedi-ately after it), and he devoted much of the last part of his life to this genre, which, at the time, had become the most difficult and problematic of all. These problems are also felt in the *First Symphony*, which, though by no means the least fascinating, is the most "experimental" of this family of five.

A family it is indeed, and one of unusual unity with many links running from one to the other like so many lines of force. And yet Honegger did not intend the five to form a cycle—it was originally his intention to make the *Fourth Symphony* his last. The *Fifth* may today sound to us too much like a tes-tament not to stand as an epilogue, but it seems as though only death then pre-vented Honegger from continuing the cycle.

The language of the symphonies is recognizably constant, even if we can clearly hear the evolution between the dense, complex, churning textures of the *First* and the concise, yet grandiose simplicity of the *Fifth*. The idyllic *Fourth* is the only point of repose in a cycle that deals above all with the dramatic ten-sions of a terrible epoch. Honegger stood as a lucid, compassionate witness to it all.

The musical language in these works is basically tonal, but the tonality is decidedly complex and much expanded, with any number of harmonic aggre-gates and polyphonic superimpositions that are hard to explain by means of traditional harmonic functions. The themes themselves often escape beyond the bounds of tonality, with their enormous leaps and wide, expressionist inter-vals, recalling at times those of the Second Viennese School. It is possible to dis-tinguish a tonal center in all the symphonies, except perhaps in the *Third*: C for the *First*, D for the *Second* and *Fifth*, A for the *Fourth*. But this center is no more restrictive than those in, for example, Bartók's middle period quartets. The harmonic tension is usually extreme, and the dissonances frequently under-lined by the roughness and violence of the orchestration. With the exception once again of the *Fourth Symphony*, this music certainly sounds more harshly dissonant than much music that leaves tonality far behind.

The symphonies last for between twenty and thirty minutes, the *First Sym-*

phony being the shortest and the *Third* the longest. That is to say, they go back, as do those of Roussel and Sibelius, to pre-Beethovenian dimensions, in reaction against the gigantic size favored by Bruckner and Mahler. All five of Honegger's symphonies are in three movements, but the balance of size and speed is different from one symphony to another. The *Second* and the *Fourth* have a slow introduction before the first Allegro, and the first movement of the *Fifth* is slow throughout. As a result, this last symphony has a Scherzo as its second movement, interrupted by two slow Trios, whereas the middle movements of the remaining symphonies are all slow. The Finales are all fast. In the *First* and *Third Symphonies*, they culminate in a slow epilogue, while in the *Fourth* the swift flow is interrupted by two slow intermezzos. But Honegger's usual feeling for proportion sees to it that the presence here of slow episodes in the outer movements is compensated for by the fact that the central slow movement is the shortest of the five.

Honegger remains faithful to the sonata form with two themes or two groups of themes, but with his own variant in the form of the reversed recapitulation that we have already seen in his chamber music. This gives the movements a symmetrical, or rather concentric form, especially as the second group is not usually taken up in the central development section. Certain movements diverge from these norms. The Adagio of the *First Symphony* is a vast diptych, the second half of which is a free retrograde of the first, in eight sections, like the briefer Larghetto of the *Fourth*, on the model of a passacaglia; the Adagio mesto of the *Second* and the opening Grave of the *Fifth* are simple varied da capos; and in the Finales of the last three symphonies, development and recapitulation are telescoped into a single unit, even if in a different way each time.

Three of the five works demand a full symphony orchestra, but the *Second Symphony* uses strings alone, preferably a largish body, with a trumpet in the Finale. The *Fourth* is written for chamber orchestra (nine wind instruments, a small percussion section, piano, and small complement of strings). As I have already said, Honegger's use of percussion is unusually discreet for a twentieth-century composer. It is totally absent from the *Second*, confined to a few touches on the bass drum and tam-tam in the *First Symphony* and to the three fateful Ds on timpani in the *Fifth*, and has a slightly larger role in both the *Third* and the *Fourth*. In the latter two, the presence of a piano lends a distinctive coloring. There are no parts for other keyboard instruments or for harp.

Honegger's orchestration has been the target of criticism, and not always without reason. As with the orchestration of Schumann and of Brahms, it is hard to make Honegger's orchestration "sound." The bass lines are sometimes clogged and heavy, and the violins at the other extreme are exposed in high positions, often with difficult, dangerous figurations to manage. As for the brass, in Honegger's hands their energy sometimes becomes overpowering. In this respect, as in others, the charming *Fourth Symphony* is an exception, showing that the thickness and earnestness elsewhere is not the result of faulty technique, but a deliberate choice made for expressive reasons.

That said, it needs a first-class orchestra under a supreme conductor to do justice to these scores, bursting with music as they so often are, and vibrating with the electricity generated by the message they have to convey. It is the overwhelming intensity of that message that places these works in the authentic line from Beethoven. Honegger, modest as always, used to speak of his quartets as "*ersatz* Beethoveniana" or "poor man's Beethoven." His five symphonies are no less worthy of their ancestor, even without their composer's restrictive qualifying statements.

Before I go on to examine the symphonies in detail, here are some of the points they have in common:

First and *Third*: a violent opening Allegro, a long, intense, dramatic slow movement, then a slow epilogue. These two opening movements and the Finale of the *Fifth Symphony* belong to the same family, as does the Finale of the *Third* if it is taken, not at quarter-note = 88, as in the printed score, but at quarter-note = 112, following Honegger's later manuscript notes. This faster tempo accords better with the nature of the music. The slow movements of the *First* and *Fourth Symphonies* are linked by their structure in eight sections and their passacaglia-like character.

The Finales of the *First* and *Fourth Symphonies* are both in ternary meter (6/8 and 9/8) and are scherzo-like in mood. Both begin furtively in the bass, with the themes taking shape gradually.

There are also thematic links that we shall note as we go through, such as those between ideas in the opening movements of the first two symphonies. In general, the *Second* and the *Fifth* are more independent of the others.

As for tonality, the most classical is the *Fourth*, with its slow movement in the subdominant, while the tonality of the *First Symphony*'s Adagio is related tritonally to its neighbors. The *Second* and *Fifth* are monotonal. Only the *Third* lacks tonal unity. Finally, the longest movements are the first movements of the *Second* and *Fourth Symphonies* and the slow movement of the *Third*, all of which last between eleven and twelve minutes. The opening movement of the *First*, the Finale of the *Second*, and the central Larghetto of the *Fourth* each last around five or six minutes.

75. First Symphony in C

December 1929–May 1930 (first movement: completed 10 March 1930; second
    movement: completed 3 April 1930; third movement: December 1929–February
    1930); orchestrated April–early May 1930
"To the Boston Symphony Orchestra and its conductor Serge Koussevitzky"
Commission from Koussevitzky for the orchestra's fiftieth anniversary
First performance: 13 February 1931, Boston Symphony Orchestra, conducted by
    Serge Koussevitzky, Boston
First European performance: 2 June 1931, Straram Orchestra, conducted by Arthur
    Honegger, Salle Pleyel, Paris
Performing forces: 3.3.3.3.–4.3.3.1.–bass drum, tam-tam–strings
Duration: 21 minutes 25 seconds (6:00 + 8:15 + 7:10)
Salabert

Honegger's *First Symphony* was one of the group of important works commissioned to celebrate the Boston Symphony Orchestra's jubilee, together with Stravinsky's *Symphony of Psalms*, Roussel's *Third Symphony*, Prokofiev's *Fourth*, and Hindemith's *Concert Music*, Op. 50, among others. In broaching finally this long-postponed problem, Honegger adopted the bold, uncompromising style of *Horace victorieux* and *Antigone*. It is written in a rougher, less clearly delineated language than its successors and is undoubtedly the hardest of them to play and to understand—despite its masterly form, which testifies to its place at the point of transition between youth and maturity.

The *First Symphony* may be heard as an introductory synthesis to the cycle, just as the *Di Tre Re* is a concluding synthesis. Its general atmosphere, the abrupt and concentrated impetuosity of the first movement, the slow, heartfelt procession of the Adagio, the peaceful, ethereal conclusion of the Finale: all these look forward to the *Third Symphony*. At the same time, more localized thematic references seem to anticipate the *Second*, and the open joyfulness of the last movement will find its partner in the Finale of the *Fourth Symphony*.

But here everything is more youthful, perhaps less "committed," with a "sporty," physical bluntness overshadowing the spiritual humanism of the later symphonies. This bluntness, harshness even, is a specifically German-Swiss quality obviously not found in the other members of Les Six, or indeed in any other French composer except Roussel. It does, however, link Honegger with compatriots like Willy Burkhard, Conrad Beck, and, nowadays, Klaus Huber. These particular Swiss sonorities, however, conjure up rocks, snow, and scree. It is not until the *Fourth Symphony* that we find gentle meadows and Alpine slopes dotted with flowers.

1. ALLEGRO MARCATO

Honegger throws us into the thick of things with a violence and an impetuosity that has no counterpart in the symphonies that follow. We are reminded of the wild unleashing of the scrum in *Rugby*, like young dogs fighting over their prey. Despite the latent presence of a tonal center of C, this is the most atonal symphonic movement Honegger ever wrote and also the most polyphonically complex. There are at least half a dozen themes and most of them contain several elements—a show of exceptional prodigality for a movement lasting barely six minutes, but one that is in no way detrimental to its iron sense of unity (largely determined by its rhythmic pulse).

The first idea, with its abrupt outline and rough repeated notes, is the richest of the themes (Example 30). This consists of four elements (*a, b, c, d*)—only the second of which insists on the tonic C. The first element contains in embryo the elements of the third (*c*), the most important and memorable of the four. With its wide, atonal leaps, this forms part of a family with later motifs that I shall quote from the *Symphony for Strings* (see Example 39), from the Dies irae of the *Third Symphony* (see Example 45), and from the Finale of the *Fifth Symphony* (see Example 66). These four elements will be developed separately and will also serve as countermelodies to other ideas.

The bridge passage at measure 15, with its rasping, dissonant syncopation, consists of a premonition of the fast version of the opening idea of the *Symphony for Strings* (see Example 37). Although the second phrase of the bridge passage,

Allegro marcato

Example 30

at measure 42, is close to the first theme in its wide intervals, it establishes a much more tonal, diatonic atmosphere, confirmed by the cheerful trumpet fanfare that makes up the second real theme (Example 31). This rises by semitones in the Honeggerian manner, up to the forceful cadential group that prefigures one of the two new elements that will dominate the development. Both of these are derived from elements already encountered. The development (measures 90–172) combines Beethovenian procedures of thematic deformation, notably by expanding intervals, with the most extreme resources of Bachian polyphony.

Example 31

The recapitulation at measures 173–239 begins, of course, with the second theme, in pastoral manner on the flute in a limpid, consonant C major. But this is only a momentary respite. The contrapuntal scuffle soon returns, leading to its climax at measure 226 with the aid of a crescendo on the bass drum, the only use of percussion in the movement. This climax superimposes the repeat of the first theme in its entirety upon the two themes from the development section in a masterly stretto that definitively re-establishes the tonic C. From here on, it is never again challenged. A final development-cum-coda in measures 240–284 tries to revive the conflict by quoting the bridge passage, but the combined forces of the four elements of the opening theme reduce it to silence, and motif *c* (Example 30) remains master of the field. Its intervals contract, its energy finally begins to dissipate, and the music deconstructs itself, gradually disintegrates, and finally comes to rest in the extreme depths of the orchestra.

2. ADAGIO

The Adagio is the expressive heart of the work. It has the character of a highly moving slow procession, but one thinks less here of a march of penitents (such as that of the De profundis of the *Third Symphony*) than of the measured, heroic tread of Alpine climbers crossing a glacier. The steady ostinato basses that underpin the music recall Bach, as often with Honegger. The movement is as firmly in F-sharp as its predecessor was in C, and if its language remains chromatic, it is no longer atonal as was the first movement. Formally, it consists of eight groups of slightly different lengths (between eleven and fourteen measures) in two cycles of four, the second repeating the first in a free retrograde.

The first two sections are heard over an ascending chromatic bass covering an octave from F-sharp. At first this is combined with a long melodic line with wide, jagged intervals, recalling Anton Webern, that form a link with the first movement (Example 32). Around it float wispy arabesques on the woodwinds, looking forward to the Larghetto of the *Fourth Symphony*, where the Alps will be reduced to harmless wooded hillsides. The second section is a tuneful contrapuntal episode for strings alone, moving by magnificent modulations from one dominant to another, as often with Honegger. The third abandons the chromatic bass and introduces a new, more restful tune in eighth-note triplets on the muted trumpet, followed by a lovely melodic clearing on the violins ("There is hope"). The dotted rhythms of a procession take over in the fourth section, from which a virile horn theme slowly emerges (Example 33).

Example 32

Example 33

A crescendo leads to the long and powerful *fortissimo* of the fifth section at measure 47, built on two ascending diatonic scales of B major and then B-flat minor. These heroic octave leaps, like giants mounting an assault on the heavens, combine the horn theme (Example 33) and the tune of Example 32, which is here repeated. The sixth and seventh sections are free retrograde versions of the second and third ones. The eighth and final section is a coda that at once balances the first one and works into it material from the fourth. At the end, everything disintegrates and fades out on a mysterious, barely audible touch on the tam-tam—the only time the instrument is heard in the whole symphony.

In an unpublished comment to Bernard Gavoty, Honegger said of this Adagio:

Here I abandoned myself to what people smilingly refer to as "my *roman-ticism*"; it's a crime I don't repent at all. The song takes wing, the tunes embrace, then separate, the song comes to earth again, and it's all over.

3. PRESTO–ANDANTE TRANQUILLO

Close to the ground, furtive double-bass pizzicatos and bassoons outline a dancing 6/8 rhythm. Honegger wanted to give this movement the character of a divertimento, or Scherzo, in which the straightforward diatonic language contrasts with both the aggressive atonality of the first movement and the straining chromaticism of the second. But a certain Swiss roughness remains, making the pebbles roll under the walker's foot. After the hard climb, we now come to the relaxed, if sometimes bumpy waddling of the descent. The movement is in sonata form with a brief central development section and a longer one at the end, leading to a slow epilogue. The movement begins in E minor and remains there for the thirty-two measures of the introduction before turning to C major. The first theme is a grotesque canon between clarinet and bassoon. Was Honegger perhaps thinking here of *The Sorcerer's Apprentice*?

The exposition, from measures 33 to 126, presents the first theme in com-plete form (Example 34). This, likewise on horns but transposed from E-flat to C, is exactly the melodic outline of the opening theme of Sibelius's *Fifth Sym-phony*. A simple descending figure on bassoon (Example 35) will later play an important role. After a capering bridge passage comes the second theme at measure 62—a blazing carillon on horns, which is the most memorable theme of this Finale and will be its dominant element (Example 36). There is also a complementary theme, again on horns, with iambic rhythms typical of Honeg-ger and a cadential passage in regular dotted quarter-notes, before the exposi-tion closes on the dominant of E with an allusion to the introduction.

The short development section, from measures 127 to 172, is a polyphonic working of continuous eighth-notes derived from the first theme (Example 34), and this is then combined with an imitative version of the cadential theme. Then comes the repeat of the introduction, but now transposed from E into C minor. The recapitulation, from measures 173 to 242, combines the two prin-cipal themes (Example 34 in augmentation on the trombone, and Example 36) in a bright C major, after which the other elements are themselves repeated. The capering little tune leads to the long final development in measures 243 to 317, and a grand tutti at measure 264, again combining Examples 34 and 36 in C major, is the climax of the whole movement. Then at measure 272 the descending motif of Example 35 appears, in a double attempt to take us toward E minor, the key of the opening. But a smart dig in the ribs, typical of the pipe-smoking Honegger, pushes us back into C major with assistance from trom-bone glissandos.

The tutti of measure 264 is firmly repeated, the brashness of the writing in the brass recalling Milhaud. But the movement's energy gradually ebbs and a diminuendo-rallentando leads unexpectedly to seventeen measures of coda in andante tranquillo (measures 318–334). This relaxed, poetic epilogue, with not

Example 34

Example 35

Example 36

a cloud in the sky, is in the noble, pastoral tradition of the epilogue to the *String Quartet No. 1*. Ever shorter and more evanescent fragments of Examples 34 and 36 come together, dissolving into the evening hush of Example 35, which has the last word. As in all Honegger's symphonies (with the sole and tragic exception of the last) an overwhelming vitality is finally subsumed into a spiritual peace.

153. Second Symphony for strings and trumpet in D (*Symphony for Strings*)

1940–1941 (first sketch: November 1940; first movement: completed 8 May 1941; second movement: completed 15 March 1941; third movement: completed 13 October 1941)
"To Paul Sacher"
Commission from Paul Sacher for the Basel Chamber Orchestra
First performance: 18 May 1942, Collegium Musicum, conducted by Paul Sacher, Zurich
Duration: 25 minutes 15 seconds (11:30 + 8:00 + 5:45)
Salabert

Eleven years separate the *Second Symphony* from its predecessor. These years were devoted mainly to the great oratorios that established the composer's popular reputation (*Jeanne d'Arc au bûcher*, *La Danse des morts*, and *Nicolas de Flue*), but also to his two final quartets. As I have already said, the *Second Symphony* is the continuation and expansion of these chamber works on an orchestral scale. There are reasons for regarding this symphony as Honegger's masterpiece and it is gratifying to see that none of his works, not even *Pacific 2.3.1*, has been recorded so many times. Charles Münch alone has left us five versions of the work.

Paul Sacher had for many years been asking Honegger to write a string orchestra piece for the Basel Chamber Orchestra, and the *Largo for string orchestra* (H105) of September 1936 was an abortive attempt at such a work. Honegger began the symphony in the extremely difficult conditions of the first winter of the Occupation: cold, hunger, and fear all left their mark on the work. I have described in Chapters 6 and 7 the circumstances of its composition, the way the manuscript was smuggled through to Paul Sacher, and the first performance in Zurich, followed some weeks later by its Paris triumph on 25 June 1942 under Münch and his superb first recording of it even before the Liberation.

It is a somber, tragic work of a depth and solidity reminiscent of Beethoven, and its powerful material is cast into a structure of rare perfection. There is hardly one other score that draws such expressive tension from strings alone. The players, who should be fairly numerous, are stretched to the limit and, because of this, the work can be performed only by the best orchestras. The highly chromatic language is complex and dissonant, with a predilection for tritones and minor seconds, in opposition to fourths and fifths. Consonant intervals such as thirds and sixths remain relatively rare.

1. MOLTO MODERATO–ALLEGRO

The first movement, in the symphony's overall key of D, is by far the longest of the three. It is broad and complex in its structure, which most commentators have described as a rondo. Even so, despite the periodic returns of the slow introduction, it is indisputably in sonata form, and one of his most masterly examples of it. Confusion has probably been caused by his characteristic use of the reversed recapitulation.

The slow introduction is based on an ostinato theme (Example 37), repeated no less than twelve times, first on solo viola, then on all the violas, with the aching intensity of a litany, surrounded by dark, plaintive chords and immediately breaking with the key of D. The exposition of the Allegro, from measures 30 to 104, begins with a harshly percussive eight-measure theme, a closed structure (Example 38). Of the four segments *a*, *b*, *a'*, and *c*, *a'* expands the intervals of *a*, *b* is a consequent, and *c* the conclusion. These elements will for the most part be developed separately, and constitute a rich but economical stock of ideas. Its presentation in unison accentuates its latent violence.

As it is one of Honegger's very finest, this theme merits more detailed analysis. The element *a* shares with the introductory theme (Example 37) both the pattern of repeated notes and the oscillation between notes a second apart. It also contains the tense, rising diminished octave, from D to D-flat, which

Molto moderato

Example 37

Example 38

will be a determining factor in the work's harmonic style. Segment *b* contains two distinct cells: an energetic start followed by a longer, sinuous inflection, while *a'* expands the intervals of *a*, with the semitone of the four repeated quarter-notes becoming a tritone. It also reverses the direction of its final notes, which are now ascending instead of descending. Finally, *c* breaks the regularity of the beat with its groups of three eighth-notes (the third of each being a rest). As it descends, the intervals contract from a tritone to a minor second. We may note that *a* and *a'* are ascending, while *b* and *c* are descending.

A brief polyphonic development leads to a bridge passage at measure 54 in which we hear a preliminary outline of the theme that will form the basis of the cadential group (Example 39). The second theme, on the other hand (un poco meno mosso at measure 70), is a short, melancholy episode, a pale and delusive lighting that is no more than passing and is never developed. The cadential group beginning at measure 78 consists of two elements. The first is the one adumbrated in Example 39, with its initial triplet and its descent in large, atonal, extensible leaps—these leaps, which belong to the family mentioned in connection with the *First Symphony* (Example 30*c*), will be developed separately. The second element, in eighth-notes, is a synthesis of Examples 37 and 38*a* and of the second theme.

Example 39

Imitative treatment of Example 39 leads to a powerful buildup, culminating in a double canon. The accumulated tension is released for the final part of the exposition at measure 97, where an accelerated version of the theme of Example 37, now set to savagely dissonant harmonies, is combined with the quarter-notes of Example 38*a* hammered out in the bass. A decrescendo leads to the development section at measure 105. This employs every contrapuntal resource in combining elements of Examples 37, 38, and 39, up until the return of the Molto moderato in measure 154. Here Example 37 returns eight times, surrounded by warm harmonies and splendid countermelodies, with ever greater division of the strings. This ends with four measures of dominant-tonic harmony clearly underlining the main key of D.

This is immediately followed by the bridge section at measure 176 and, as it never returns in this form, it is arguable that the recapitulation begins here rather than at the reappearance of the second theme in measure 190. This recapitulation is in fact a developing one. The themes, played in reverse order as usual, are put through all manner of contrapuntal techniques in which canon reigns supreme, culminating in the eightfold repetition of the accelerated Example 37. This acts as a transition to the final return of the Molto moderato at measure 253, where this theme is again repeated six times and finally combined with the second theme.

The movement ends with a short, now reticent and almost furtive coda (Allegro, measures 268–284) based on Example 38. Element *b*, finally reduced to its sinuous inflection, sinks down onto its unison *pianissimo* Ds in a mood of gray resignation.

2. ADAGIO MESTO

The atmosphere of the symphony, far from clearing at this point, now becomes darker still with the heartbroken lament of the second movement. The form is a simple A-B-A′, with A′ including a memory of B as a coda. The first section, from measures 1 to 24, consists of three periods. First, eight long and heavy 3/2 measures of dissonant ostinato, sounding like sobs, establish a kind of passacaglia ground. Over this is heard a beautiful long lament on the cellos, and then a consoling, "celestial" melody on the violins, descending in equal notes. The central episode (B, measures 25–52) is a very harsh, dissonant, rhythmic crescendo that is remarkably reminiscent of the climactic passage linking the last two movements of Roussel's *Sinfonietta*. This episode reaches its apogee and breaks off at measure 44. Above ghostly tremolos a strange double-bass solo unfolds, high and husky—the cup has been drained to the dregs.

But then, at measure 49, the "celestial" consolation returns, this time in peaceful, diatonic context ("There is hope," now and always!). This relief is, however, short-lived, and soon absorbed by the oppressive mist of the opening. In measures 53 to 74 we hear a varied repeat of this (A′) including, at measures 61 to 67, an echo of B. The music dies away on a desolate, solitary fifth (D/A) over which the solo viola superimposes a last leap from A-flat to F, an "ultra-minor" nuance with the diminished fifth A-flat.

3. VIVACE NON TROPPO–PRESTO

Suddenly, it's daylight—or rather a raw, shivering dawn. A lively 6/8 tempo and a high texture on the strings are elements we have so far been firmly denied, and now they create a totally new atmosphere. This Finale is in sonata form with reversed recapitulation and coda, and it is all the more powerful for its brevity. The exposition (measures 1–94) immediately establishes a horizon in the form of a polyrhythmic, polytonal ostinato high on the violins, with pizzicatos in a pentatonic C-sharp major and 2/4 set against repeated chords in D major and 6/8. Beneath this we hear the first theme of prodigious energy in the double basses (Example 40). Its athletic vigor, with its huge leaps, links it to the theme of the first movement exposition (Example 38), and like that theme it is a fine example of Honegger's melodic craft, consisting of four phrases. But, despite the expanded intervals, we are now clearly in D major because they can all be interpreted as appoggiaturas, either unresolved or resolved irregularly.

Example 40

The bridge passage introduces two subsidiary elements. The first, with its repeated eighth-notes, stands out against a polytonal ostinato (Example 41), which prefigures the one that will support the second theme. The second element, at measure 53, follows a counterexposition of the first theme (Example 40) and is heavy and massive in its harmonies, duplets, and dotted rhythms. The second theme, at measure 65, is heard against two ostinatos, one of ten eighth-notes (Example 41) and the other of five. The meter is still 6/8. This theme, in the classical dominant key of A major, has the broad character of a hymn of resurrection, announcing a new future of freedom that will finally be embodied in the chorale.

The development, from measures 95 to 174, is full of incident and modulates constantly. Among its elements is the first theme (Example 40) complete

Example 41

and inverted, and it elaborates all the exposition material with every possible contrapuntal device, while the ostinato accompaniment unfolds at length in canon. At measure 135 we hear the radiant buildup that will later usher in the chorale. But it is not time for this yet and the climax subsides, with the music tumbling from the heights to the very depths. This marks the beginning of another long ascent, at the end of which the ostinato (Example 41) becomes jostling and exasperated, compressing its nine eighth-notes into eight, and then into seven. This accelerating effect leads on naturally into the recapitulation.

The recapitulation, which lasts from measures 175 to 240, begins as usual with the second theme, in the tonic D major. After this, at measure 200, comes a five-voice stretto on the ostinato. The resultant chaos is, in fact, organized by the numerous accentual displacements caused by the interaction of the cycles of ten eighth-notes with the 6/8 meter. This tumultuous gradation rises to the new presto tempo at measure 214 and the slightly modified recapitulation of the first theme (Example 40). A repeat of the bridge passage takes the music immediately to the victorious crescendo of measure 135, and this time it does lead on to the chorale, which acts as a coda.

One of the sources of this straightforwardly D major chorale (Example 42) is undoubtedly the third of the *Three Psalms* (H144; see also Example 28). It consists of six periods, grouped in pairs. The tonal scheme is as follows: tonic, relative minor of the dominant (F-sharp minor), and return to the tonic via the subdominant G. This tune is heard over dense, vigorous counterpoint on elements *a* and *b* of Example 40—these are heard in straight and inverted form, and in combination with other motifs.

Example 42

Honegger directed this chorale to be played with a trumpet *ad libitum*, doubling the violins like an extra stop on the organ. But from the point of view of color and expression, it is a most indispensable obbligato that crowns the symphony—the only one of the five that ends *forte*—with peremptory evidence. After the end of the chorale, the strings are carried forward by their own momentum and continue for another twelve measures (measures 288–299). They are finally halted by the modulation of the 6/8 meter to 3/4 and then hurtle down a series of fourths on to a final D major chord with added second and sixth.

186. *Third Symphony* (*Symphonie liturgique*, or "Liturgical" Symphony)

1945–1946 (first movement: completed 5 December 1945, orchestration completed
   18 December; second movement: January–October 1945; third movement:
   completed 21 April 1946 (Easter Sunday), orchestration completed 29 April)
"For Charles Münch"
Commissioned by the Communauté de Travail "Pro Helvetia"
First performance: 17 August 1946, Tonhalle Orchestra, conducted by Charles
   Münch, Zurich
Performing forces: 3.3.3.3.–4.3.3.1.–piano–timpani, percussion–strings
Duration: 28 minutes 55 seconds (6:30 + 11:30 + 10:55)
Salabert

The triumphant cry at the end of the *Second Symphony* would never be
heard again. The symphony that followed would escape despair only by taking
refuge in prayer, and in the utopian vision of a better world. Like Prokofiev's
Sixth Symphony (its contemporary), the *Symphonie liturgique* (Liturgical Symphony) tells of a future that is painful rather than pleasant. The price of victory
has been too high, with all its bereavements and sufferings, leaving behind a
world ravaged and desolate in which mankind has become no better than it was
before. After its first performance in Zurich and then its triumph in Paris on 14
November 1946 (both performances under Charles Münch) this symphony
quickly toured the world. For a decade or so, it was one of the most frequently
played of contemporary works, catching as it did the feelings of the time. Nowadays it has regained that status, and rightly so, since its subject matter is, alas,
still relevant to our world.

The *Third* is the longest and most imposing of Honegger's five symphonies, and the only one that has an acknowledged "program" for each of the
three movements. This program, though, exists only in a general sense—this is
pure music, constructed with the same rigor as in its four companions. The
epithet "Liturgical" refers simply to the work's religious character as expressed
in the titles of the three movements (all borrowed from the Roman Catholic
liturgy). But they are interpreted in a far from conventional manner and there
is no allusion whatsoever to Gregorian plainchant.

In the course of the well-known series of interviews with Bernard Gavoty,
Honegger explained the work's motivations very precisely, but I should like
first of all to quote an unpublished description, dating from 1954 and found
among the composer's papers.

This *Third Symphony* is, like most of my symphonic works, in the form of
a triptych. It is in direct reaction against the fashion for so-called objective
music. Each of the three parts tries to express an idea, a thought which I
would not want to call philosophical—that would be pretentious—but
which represents the personal feeling of the composer. I have therefore
had recourse to liturgical subtitles and called the symphony "Liturgical,"
hoping in that way to make myself better understood.

   I. Dies irae: this poses no problem, since we have all lived through the
years of war and revolution with which those who preside over the des-
tinies of peoples have rewarded them.

II. De profundis clamavi ad te: everything that remains in mankind of purity, clarity, and confidence tends toward that force which we feel to be above us. God, perhaps, or that which each of us bears with passion in the secret depths of his soul.

III. Dona nobis pacem: the inescapable rise of the stupid things of the world: nationalism, militarism, red tape, administration, customs duties, taxes, wars, everything that man has invented to persecute man, to cheapen him, and turn him into a robot. The terrifying crassness that finally provokes this cry of despair: "Dona nobis pacem." And it ends with a brief meditation on what life could be: calm, love, joy—the song of a bird, Nature, peace.

I had been thinking for a long time about this symphony. Slowly the melodies of the Adagio formed within me and grew together. I already had the central kernel, the "De profundis clamavi ad te Domine" [Honegger here quotes Example 47] that would well up from the depths of the abyss until it turned into shrill cries of despair before falling back, growing quieter, and finally dying out. The first movement tornado came to me suddenly, in its entirety, on the short train journey from Basel to Bern. I wrote out a complete rough draft before going to bed that evening.

The Finale came to me just as quickly, although I forget when. Naturally, the basic idea of this ascent toward a cry of despair was already firmly fixed in my mind. So was the slow coda, but I then worked at it for a long time, except for the phrase in F-sharp for violin and cello, which I jotted down one day just as I was about to go out to lunch, with my overcoat on and one knee on a chair. It is my favorite symphony, together with the *Fourth*, which I like for quite different reasons. I think this was the moment when my faculties were operating at their optimum.

With Bernard Gavoty, Honegger expressed himself in very similar terms:

My intention in this work was to symbolize the reaction of modern man against the morass of barbarism, stupidity, suffering, machine-mindedness, and bureaucracy that has been besieging us for some years now. I have reproduced in musical terms the combat that is joined in man's heart between yielding to the blind forces that enclose him and his instinct for happiness, his love of peace, his apprehension of a divine refuge. My symphony is, if you like, a drama played out between three characters, whether real or symbolic: misery, happiness, and man. These are everlasting themes. I have tried to give them new life.

1. DIES IRAE: ALLEGRO MARCATO

This first movement returns to the abrupt violence and the irresistible dynamism of the opening movement of the *First Symphony*, but here the sparser texture lends more emphasis to the lines of force and produces an atmosphere of intense tragedy. Although practically atonal, it is vaguely organized around the pivotal note A, the key in which the movement ends. Its structure is that of a clearly defined sonata form with a varied and developing recapitulation. Honegger described the movement to Bernard Gavoty as follows:

In the Dies irae, I was concerned with depicting human terror in the face of divine anger, with expressing the brutal, unchanging feelings of oppressed peoples, delivered to the whims of fate and seeking in vain to escape the cruel snares of destiny. Day of anger! The violent themes crowd in upon each other without leaving the listener a moment's respite. No room for breathing or thinking. The storm sweeps all before it, blindly, angrily. . . . Then finally, at the end of the movement, the bird makes its appearance.

The exposition (measures 1–113) takes up almost half the movement. The somber stirrings, with subterranean noises from the double basses, are uncannily reminiscent of the opening of the final "Dialogue of the Wind and Sea" from Debussy's *La Mer*—a similar evocation of the elementary violence of a natural phenomenon. A strident, abrupt rhythm stands up high in the woodwinds, under which the strings proclaim a fiercely energetic opening theme. Its intervals are wide and atonal, and the final measures on horns sound out, according to Honegger himself, the terrible words "Dies irae, dies illa" (Example 43).

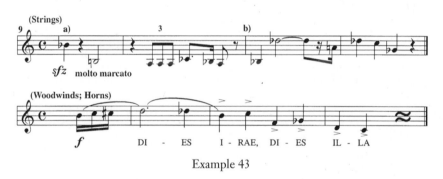

Example 43

A threefold presentation of this theme leads to the bridge passage at measure 33. This passage is made up of two elements. The first consists of a counterpoint of chords (a procedure that would reach its most imposing form in the opening of the *Fifth Symphony*) leading to the heavy tread of quarter-notes in the low brass. The second, a descending chromatic phrase at measure 41, is very important as it will be one of the two cyclic elements in the symphony as a whole (Example 44). In particular, this phrase will become the dying fall of the "Ad te Domine" of the De profundis (see also Example 47). We may note that it consists of seven beats, thereby negating the bar line.

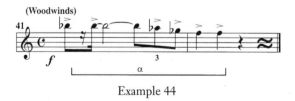

Example 44

The second theme itself, with its enormous atonal leaps, is like a huge terrifying grimace (Example 45). It will be used in both its straight and inverted form, this latter including it as a member of the family already described in the earlier symphonies (see Examples 30c, 38c, and 39). But before the development, the cadential theme is heard at measure 71. This is the only melodic element in the movement: a long, tortured, chromatic lament, punctuated by sharp accents that are often syncopated. The relatively short development section, from measures 114 to 168, is essentially based on the first theme. From the very beginning it creates tension through the abruptness and scarcity of musical events, which are reduced to the status of brief interjections. It sounds like a single entity and is a marvelous example of how the composer's iron control and discipline can be employed in describing an antithetical chaos.

Example 45

The recapitulation from measures 169 to 224 is altered, condensed, and of course reversed. Since the first theme has been the basis of the development, it is not fully restated here. The form marks a return to the preclassical conception of a sonata movement as a binary structure, with development and recapitulation together being the same length as the exposition. This approach would be confirmed in the two symphonies that followed. The coda (measures 225–246) introduces a broad, dark-hued, diatonic cantus firmus, sounding like a kind of macabre chorale (Example 46). This plunges the music back into the abyss from which it had risen. It is the second cyclic element in the symphony and the initial form of the bird theme of which Honegger speaks. Here, though, the bird is a large, raucous crow or some other harbinger of death.

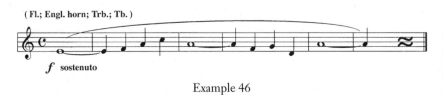

Example 46

2. DE PROFUNDIS CLAMAVI: ADAGIO

The storm has passed and is followed by the immense, sublime Lamento, one of the high points of Honegger's oeuvre, and a movement in which he succeeded totally in the aims he expressed:

It is the sorrowful meditation of mankind abandoned by the divinity—a meditation that is already a prayer. What tribulation this movement cost me! I wanted to develop a melodic line without using formulae or systems. No side-tracking, no harmonic progressions, none of the dodges that are so handy for those who've got nothing to say! I took over the question at the point where the classic masters left it. To go forward, to walk without looking back, to extend the initial curve without repetitions or interruptions: ah, that's difficult! It is hard, too, to put into the mouths of men a prayer without hope. At one point the double basses, the contrabassoon, and the piano—all the deepest, most mysterious instruments in the orchestra—proclaim the funeral text "De profundis clamavi ad te, Domine." Toward the end of the movement I have repeated the bird theme more obviously. Man can do no more, he is at the lowest point of his distress. God, who once thundered and threatened, is now deaf to the prayers that rise to Him. Heaven is closed off, but. . . . But, as Claudel wrote in our *Jeanne d'Arc au bûcher*: "There is Hope that is stronger than all things! There is Joy that is stronger than all things! There is Love that is stronger than all things!" That is the message of the dove, the olive branch it holds in its beak, the promise of peace that it symbolizes amid disaster.[1]

After that commentary, the direct and overwhelming expressive power of this movement does not call for much in the way of technical analysis. Its language is entirely tonal, once more demonstrating the fact that Honegger's melodic/harmonic ideal derives from late Fauré, and ultimately from "The Fairy Garden" of Ravel's *Mother Goose* suite. It is in a spacious but very simple ternary form, with an introduction and coda. The aggressive atonality of the Dies irae gives way to a language that is much more consonant and harmonious, based on the tonic E.

The twelve-measure introduction sees the gradual emergence of themes— a procedure begun in the Finale of the *First Symphony* and taken much further in the outer movements of the *Fourth*. Here we find tentative fragments of periods 1 and 5, the De profundis in fragmentary and then in complete form, and finally the bird motif. In the first long section, from measures 13 to 88, the amazing melodic curve unfolds in six extended periods, with the fourth and fifth briefly repeated before we hear the sixth. Discounting the ensuing conclusion, these amount to sixty-eight measures of faultless invention, the easily flowing line giving no indication of the trouble they caused to write. A brief allusion to "clamavi" completes the final period, after which the conclusion confirms the tonic E and allows us a moment of repose. The central section (B, measures 89–120) is a development modulating by ascending chromatic progressions based on the De profundis proper, which we have already heard in the introduction (Example 47). This is punctuated twice by the theme of the bird, in a metamorphosis of Example 46 (Example 48).

This is an extraordinarily dramatic development, broken up by sighing and sobbing similar to that in *La Danse des morts*, together with an increase in tension using the motif quoted in Example 47 in the form of a bitonal canon. The climax is reached in a paroxysm of grief. The bass drum hammers out the rhythm of Example 47 and this, coinciding with the emphatic return of the first

Example 47

Example 48

period, marks the beginning of the third section (A′, measures 121–197). After just two measures of a dissonant tutti, the first period is heard again, complete this time, and purified, as though the tears on a face have suddenly been wiped away by grace. This third section is a varied, developing recapitulation of the first. There is no partial return of periods 4 and 5, as there was the first time. Instead, inserted before period 4, comes a development in measures 155 to 172 of the De profundis (which has in any case been present to some extent throughout in a fragmentary form), of period 5, and of period 1. This development once again stirs up anguish for a moment, but this is soon dispelled by the radiant reappearance of period 4, emerging from this passing cloud.

The whole of this recapitulation is enriched with admirably inventive counterthemes. The final period now leads to a brief coda in measures 198 to 205. The long procession of human suffering is at an end and the melody quoted in Example 48, which had been flying over it from time to time, now glides freely on its way—an aerial arabesque on the flute that the composer described as the "fluttering of the innocent bird piping above the ruins."

3. Dona nobis pacem: Andante–Adagio

The last movement rests perhaps more firmly than its predecessors on an extra-musical explanation. Otherwise, the level of its inspiration—the epilogue excepted—runs the risk of seeming slightly inferior to that in the rest of the work. I turn one last time to Honegger's own words:

> Have you noticed that misery is a poor counselor, and that suffering mankind is often unpleasant and uncouth? There is nothing so stupid as barbarism unleashed in a civilization. What I wanted to express at the beginning of the third movement was precisely this increase in collective stupidity. I had the idea of a heavy march, and for this I deliberately wrote a tune that is idiotic, played first by the bass clarinet: boueh-boueh . . . boueh . . . boueh . . . boueh . . . boueh-boueh-boueh! It's the march of the

robots against the bodies and souls of men. It's people standing in line outside stores in the rain and snow, for hours at a time. It's interminable, useless formularies. It's pestering, unnecessary regulations. It's the revolt of the beast against the spirit. The imbecilic march continues, and the straggling flock of mechanical geese waddles along in time to it.

But now a feeling of rebellion surfaces among the victims. The revolt takes shape and grows. Suddenly an immense clamor, three times repeated, escapes from the lungs of the oppressed: "Dona nobis pacem!" And then, as though the cup of suffering were full and the desire for peace had finally gotten the better of the horror of disorder, I wanted to find a long, cantabile phrase that would express suffering humanity's wish "to be delivered from all this," and that would suggest the vision of a peace so long wished for. As to what that peace might be, I accept no responsibility. For some, it is eternal repose, celestial bliss. For others, it is paradise on earth, the humble paradise of beauty, the modest happiness to which all of us aspire, saying "After all, life could be like that!" The clouds part and, amid the glory of the rising sun, for the last time the bird sings. In this way the song of the bird hovers over the symphony, just as once the dove hovered over the immensity of the waters.[2]

The movement is in binary form, without a recapitulation. Its place is taken by the development, after which a brief, climactic transition leads to the peaceful coda. The effect of the movement is altered, one has to say, depending on whether it is played at quarter-note = 88, as on the printed score, or at quarter-note = 112, as Honegger suggested later in some notes on its interpretation, which have remained in manuscript. The second option, which most conductors tend to adopt instinctively, brings the speed close to that of the Finale of the *Fifth Symphony*. But Honegger never altered the indication andante—andante, and not allegro.

In this dull, exhausted atmosphere, the double basses sound out the footsteps of an immense procession, of a crowd on the march. Against this is heard the "idiotic" theme (Example 49), the goosestep of His Most Brainless Majesty, which Honegger described elsewhere rather more forcefully as the "theme of human b . . . dy-mindedness" (*thème de la c . . . rie humaine*). Ten quarter-notes long, it conflicts rhythmically with the bar line.

Example 49

In measure 31, we at last hear the first sonata subject, a bitter but determined call to rebellion on the horns (Example 50). This is followed by a heartrending chromatic lament on strings, evoking all the world's irremediable ills. Both themes incorporate the cyclic cell of Example 44. We may be reminded of the "Hunger March" that ends Vaughan Williams's *"London" Symphony* of 1914, or Shostakovich's overwhelming *Thirteenth Symphony* of 1962—both testimonies to the disasters of this terrible century.

Example 50

We are surrounded by descending chromatic glissandos on the woodwinds, which have already been heard in the Dies irae. At measure 67 the goose step returns, over an inexpressive melodic idea: a sort of sardonic, unfeeling military tune for robots. The strings respond with further lamentation, expressing their bitter impotence through harsh, bitonal clashes. The second section begins at measure 87 with the idiotic theme of Example 49, now more insolent than ever in its incurable stupidity. It develops in its own fashion—that is to say, idiotically. The listener has already been warned that the beauty of pure music is not the criterion here.

The whole of this varied recapitulation leads the exasperated rebellion on ever further, and we are beaten down and drenched under a flood of glissandos. Suddenly, at the Pesante of measure 165, the triple call Honegger spoke of breaks out. This colossal "enough-of-it" outcry, sounding out the Dona nobis pacem, is played by the whole orchestra in rough clusters, and the effect is of a giant voice, both single and multiple. Twice the idiotic theme of Example 49 replies, but the third call, albeit reduced to exhaustion, succeeds in reducing the theme to a dull pulsing. And now the unhoped-for happens. From the tonic E, which has held sway so far, the music eases gently into F-sharp major and the beginning of the sublime Adagio epilogue. This is an Elysian vision of peace, with its simple, diatonic ascending melody on cello solo, doubled by the violins. Its passing similarity to the Adagio of Saint-Saëns's *Third Symphony* was surely involuntary.

A further modulation soon takes us into C-sharp major, where the music will remain. The idiotic theme, now exorcised and harmless, stammers on flutes and oboes, and at measure 196, with a change of meter to 3/4, we pass into "the sunlit peace of divine love," to quote Messiaen, where the slender, redemptive outline of the song of the bird rises to the heavens. At measure 204 we hear on solo violin the complete De profundis of Example 47: the prayer has been answered and mankind, exhausted but alive and safe, has reached its goal. The final chord is one of C-sharp major, to which Honegger adds not the second nor the sixth, but the leading-tone. The symphony's program is an explanation of why this is the only one of Honegger's symphonies not to end in its original tonic.

191. *Fourth Symphony in A* (*Deliciae basilienses*, or "The Delights of Basel")

9 June–10 October 1946 (first movement: 9 June–7 July; second movement: completed 9 October; third movement: completed 16 September); orchestration completed 20 October 1946 (first movement: July–2 August)
"To Paul Sacher and to the Basel Chamber Orchestra for its twentieth anniversary."
Commissioned by Paul Sacher
First performance: 21 January 1947, Basel Chamber Orchestra, conducted by Paul Sacher, Basel
Performing forces: 2.1.2.1.–2.1.0.0.–piano–cymbal, glockenspiel, Basel drum, tam-tam, triangle–strings (small group)
Duration: 25 minutes 30 seconds (11:00 + 5:30 + 9:00)
Salabert

No greater contrast could be imagined than that between this symphony, written apparently without any trouble in only a little over four months, and its predecessor, which had taken sixteen months of hard labor. This contrast was deliberate on Honegger's part, as he explained:

In the miserable year of 1946, we were living in unhappy times. In every country, governments were asking their peoples to pay for the effects of the war. In the middle of the hateful, stupid conditions that were imposed upon us, this symphony mirrors the hope generated by the thought of escaping this atmosphere for a moment and spending the summer in Switzerland, surrounded by the affection of close friends for whom music still has a role to play. The first movement was sketched out in this frame of mind.[3]

And, Honegger continues, "After the *Symphonie liturgique*, I wanted to write something as clear and simple as life at the Schönenberg."

Not that the symphony was begun there—the whole of the first movement was conceived in Paris and the opening theme came to him on a number 92 bus traveling between the Étoile and the Pont de l'Alma (as Marcel Delannoy pertinently remarked, the spirit bloweth where it listeth)! But the spirit of the Schönenberg infuses the whole work, together with that of the city of Basel, which is alluded to by specific musical quotations in the last two movements. The suggestion of Emil Staiger, a professor at Zurich University, that it should be called *Deliciae basilienses* was therefore a highly appropriate one.

It is easy to underestimate the beauties of this light, discreet, and apparently modest score. The work was not heard in Paris until 25 February 1950—three years after its first performance in Basel—and the list of recordings is relatively short. But these "Delights of Basel" make up what is undoubtedly the most perfect of the five symphonies, the most lovingly shaped and crafted in detail, and the most refined in the field of timbre and harmony (even if it is also the most consonant and tonal). It is a marvel of technique, and exhibits a sovereign mastery of the most recondite resources of counterpoint. Formally, too, it is perfect, even though asymmetrical, with free employment of cyclic principles binding the themes together and making for overall unity.

Here Honegger is working on a scale not normally associated with him, given his tendency to produce grand, epic frescoes. But he himself admits the difference: "If the *Symphonie liturgique* is more in the tradition of Beethoven, being essentially dramatic and full of passion, the *Fourth Symphony*, on the other hand, follows in the footsteps of Haydn and Mozart in its spirit and in its form." It does indeed favor clear, luminous textures, delicate watercolor tints, and elegance in its melodic outlines, to the extent that its transparency of sound and relaxed atmosphere tend to make us forget the ingenuity of its polyphonic writing. In the Finale, this reaches an apogee of complexity, even if Honegger does not advertise the fact.

Deliciae basilienses is pure music, and it is significant that the composer's fairly long commentary on the work is exclusively technical in character. It is Honegger's "Pastoral Symphony" and, a quarter of a century later, it returns in a more extended, personal, and profound way to the happy vein of the *Pastorale d'été* of 1920. A final work from the same source would be the wonderful *Concerto da camera* of 1948. None of the symphonies lends itself more readily to a detailed analysis. There are no less than five cyclic motifs contributing to the work's "biological" unity.

1. LENTO ET MISTERIOSO–ALLEGRO

"Biology in sound" might well be the best phrase to describe the thirty measures of slow introduction to the first movement. With its 407 measures, it is the longest movement of the work, and indeed the longest movement in any of the five symphonies. The supremely gentle and delicate introduction is based on the key of A minor. In the course of it, the various themes gradually take shape, almost always in the bucolic woodwinds, following a process of "thematic growth" that recalls Sibelius.

There are six ideas in all. The first of these, heard in the second measure, is built of four chords that harmonize the famous C-D-F-E motif from Mozart's *"Jupiter" Symphony*—this is the only one of the themes that is restricted to the slow introduction. The other five ideas are the first subject of the sonata allegro, its brief afterthought, the two bridging themes, and the second sonata subject. This last theme, for instance, is heard complete on the flute, but in reduced values, at measure 16 in what will be its own key of E-flat—a tritone away from the tonic A.

This, of course, is the key in which the Allegro begins. The exposition, measures 31 to 177, keeps the triple pulse and the basically lyrical, cantabile character of the preceding passage. The broad opening theme (Example 51) is presented in the form of a canon, simultaneously with its little pentatonic complement on the clarinet (Example 52). The bridge passage, starting at measure 87, offers a contrast with its more capriciously rhythmic character, and the piano is treated like a glockenspiel, adding its bright tinkling to the ensemble. This passage consists of two ideas (Examples 53 and 54) separated by an episode of jerky, dissonant, almost Stravinskyan chords that cut across the bar line. Calm returns with the lyrical, cheerful second theme (Example 55), followed almost at once by the cadential passage (measure 145), which is based initially on the jerky chords of the bridge passage—linked by spidery figures on the violins—and then on Examples 54 and 52.

The relatively succinct development, measures 178 to 262, is composed of two sections. In the first of these, the first theme is heard at length on bassoon, then horn, over clarinet undulations that suggest the torpid heat of summer. The second section, beginning at measure 199, is the still center of the move-

Example 51

Example 52

Example 53

Example 54

Example 55

ment. Over a long pedal E (supporting a first inversion of C major), violins and violas weave a perpetual three-voice canon on the first theme (Example 51). Over this, flutes, trumpets, glockenspiel, and piano pick out a bright, pentaphonic carillon in irregular rhythms, reproducing the sound of a gamelan. Close study reveals this to be an augmentation of the complete bridge theme of Example 53. A slightly shorter sequence of the same material follows, modulating imperceptibly into E major. Suddenly, at measure 263, the midday siesta is shattered by the cheerful return of Example 54 in B-flat major, marking the beginning of the reversed recapitulation, which is varied and subjected to new contrapuntal acrobatics. The first theme, however, is repeated complete in its original form, only transposed from A into D major (measure 305). This is a unique instance in Honegger's output, but the music is so good that we are delighted to hear it again. In any case, the twentieth-century phobia about repetition has now led to the opposite extreme in so-called minimalist or process music.

At measure 375 the slow introduction returns, greatly modified (since its function as a pre-exposition is now over) and at half its original length. The movement ends with the superimposition of the two main themes (Examples 51 and 55) at measures 375 to 407. This acts both as a final development and as a coda, remaining throughout in A major. We may note the miraculous ease with which Honegger incorporates first a triple, and then even a quadruple stretto into this peaceful, serene conclusion, ending *pianissimo* low in the orchestra.

2. LARGHETTO

The Larghetto movement, in the classical subdominant key of D minor, is a short procession over a dotted passacaglia theme (even if the meter is quadruple). The atmosphere is one of mysterious twilight, with arabesques in the woodwinds. The movement consists of eight sections.

From the very beginning, the low strings establish a theme that, despite its large intervals, does not disturb the D minor tonality (Example 56). At measure 9 begin the circling figures on the woodwinds that conceal the intervals of the Basel theme to be heard later. The figures conceal the intervals so well that one would never have known, had the composer not mentioned them in his commentary on the work. With the beginning of the third section, the first theme (Example 56) becomes intermittent. Meanwhile, the violins unfold a long melody that is then taken up by the flute—this contains the descending motif from Example 51. In the fourth section the theme of Example 56 is even more discreet and a new woodwind arabesque appears, like the song of a bird, together with a mysterious diminished fifth pedal. This begins to undulate strangely during the fifth section, and now the theme of Example 56 has entirely disappeared.

But the theme reappears in the sixth section, while the march past strange silhouettes is continued, reaching a modest climax in the seventh section. Here, over the simultaneous sounding of the preceding motifs, the horn intones in F major the old Basel tune *Z'Basel an mi'im Rhy* (In Basel on the Bank of My Rhine), which has for many years been the signature tune of the local radio sta-

Example 56

tion (Example 57). The eighth and final section is similar to the second, and the conclusion is left hanging over a low A on the clarinet.

Example 57

3. ALLEGRO

The Finale, in 9/8 meter, has some affinities with the first movement. It is likewise in triple rhythm and in the tonic and, even though this is the tonic minor, the mood is one of unclouded gaiety. Mendelssohn, among others, had already shown that the minor mode is not synonymous with drama by ending his *Fourth Symphony* (also in A major) with a whirling saltarello in A minor. For all its liveliness and carelessness, this movement conceals beneath its diverting exterior a form which is both original and complex, and which has inspired any number of comments. Indeed, the composer himself has contributed to the debate by referring to a compromise between a rondo, a passacaglia, and a fugue. In fact, the structure of the movement is perfectly clear once one has understood that, like the Finales of the two surrounding symphonies, it is in a sonata form without a recapitulation, or rather with its place taken by a development section.

As in the first movement, an introduction (measures 1–58) allows us to hear the gradual emergence of four of the six themes, although this time the tempo is fast from the start. (Of these six themes—a further link with the first movement—I shall quote only those more important ones that contribute to the cyclic links with the preceding movements.) The introduction is in the form of a mysterious instrumental dialogue and its weft becomes gradually more continuous. It offers prefigurations of theme 1 (Example 58) and theme 4, but already includes complete versions of themes 2 (Example 59) and 3 (Example 60).

At the very beginning there are echoes of *The Sorcerer's Apprentice* in the bassoon, and especially in Example 59 played on muted trumpet. The exposition proper (measures 59–158) suddenly presents theme 1 (Example 58) complete from top to bottom on the violins. This lighthearted, capricious farandole covers sixteen measures in a single phrase, passing through seven keys and

Example 58

Example 59

Example 60

including two crucial cyclic cells, *a* and *d*. Then come theme 5 (lyrical on the clarinet) and theme 4 (energetic in D major), the jerky rhythms of which recall the Stravinsky-like episode from the first movement. These then go completely against the bar lines, producing a curious limping, disorganized effect. In fact, though, they are grouped as a four-measure ostinato, the whole central section of which is even symmetrically "non-retrogradable" in the manner of Messiaen.

Meanwhile, the cellos introduce the broad, highly melodic sixth idea, above which we hear the first theme on the oboe and the non-retrogradable ostinato—a little foretaste of the contrapuntal ingenuities to come. But soon a rallentando leads to an adagio episode at measures 159 to 179. This oasis of tender, caressing lyricism is written in chromatic melodic counterpoint, even though C major is clearly its tonal basis. It also contains a fleeting allusion to the beginning of the theme of Example 58.

After this gentle episode, the witty round resumes (measures 180–285), and we come to the most astonishing part of the symphony. The return of the first theme (Example 58), in A minor on the bassoon, suggests a recapitulation. To this, five of the six themes are added in an amazing stretto, with only the fourth theme being absent (we shall see why). Both the second and third themes

(Examples 59 and 60), which have not been heard since the introduction, are included. This extraordinary example of polyphony, made up of five themes, is worthy of comparison with the famous stretto that crowns Mozart's *"Jupiter"* *Symphony*. It lasts, without any apparent sign of strain, for seventy-five measures and ends in the apotheosis of measure 255, and the triumphant entry of the *Basler Morgenstreich*—the traditional early morning tune of the Basel carnival, and one which is said to date back to the Middle Ages, although the nature of the tune must cast doubt on this assertion (Example 61).

Example 61

The tune sounds three times in a straightforward A major, on piccolo and Basel drum, and is then repeated as an echo by trumpet, glockenspiel, and piano, over a triple canonic stretto of the motif from Example 58, without any of the other themes. Gédalge's lessons at the Paris Conservatory bore fruit!

From measure 279 onward the cheerful tumult subsides, and piccolo and flute take turns to muse a little over the carnival theme. Meanwhile, fragments of Example 58 are scattered around in the light of dawn, and one thinks again of *The Sorcerer's Apprentice*. Nine measures of sublime reverie (measures 286–294) lead to the very brief six-measure coda (measures 295–300). This is the ultimate synthesis of Example 58, which Honegger called "a little cloud of dust that flies away"—an enigmatic pirouette very close to the ending of Debussy's *Jeux*, which shares the same key and color. And so the work fades quietly into silence.

I am tempted to place this masterpiece at the head of my list of favorite Honegger works. And we may, lastly, note how finely balanced the Finale is. Whereas it is dominated by its first theme, the second and third themes appear in their complete form in the introduction and are then not heard in the exposition. The fourth theme (Example 61) is the only one that appears complete both in the introduction and the exposition, and that is why it is the only theme not heard in the recapitulation.

202. Fifth Symphony in D (Di Tre Re)

August–December 1950 (first movement: August–5 September, orchestration
    completed 28 October; second movement: September–1 October, orchestration
    completed 23 November; third movement: October–10 November,
    orchestration completed 3 December)
"For the Koussevitzky Music Foundation. Dedicated to the memory of Nathalie
    Koussevitzky."
First performance: 9 March 1951, Boston Symphony Orchestra, conducted by
    Charles Münch, Boston

First European performance: 7 May 1951, Orchestre national, conducted by Charles
  Münch (on radio); then in the concert hall, 25 June 1951 by the same forces,
  Strasbourg Festival
Performing forces: 3.3.3.3.–4.3.3.1.–timpani (*ad libitum*)–strings
Duration: 23 minutes 40 seconds (8:00 + 9:20 + 6:20)
Salabert

Honegger's final symphony was written in response to a commission three
years earlier from the Koussevitzky Foundation, which the composer did not
then think he would be able to fulfill because of illness. And so, thirty years
after the cycle of symphonies began, it came to an end. This *Fifth Symphony* is
dedicated, like the *First*, to the Boston Symphony Orchestra. Honegger explained to Bernard Gavoty the difficult conditions in which it was composed: "I
was suffering from dreadful insomnia. To get rid of my gloomy thoughts, I
wrote them down. . . . These turned into sketches! After I'd joined them
together, I realized they made a symphony; so I orchestrated it."[4] As for the
rather puzzling subtitle he gave to it:

> When a composer reaches the stage of writing his fifth symphony, it would
> be overweening to call it simply that. For many years, the only *Fifth Sym-
> phony* has been Beethoven's. That's why I added the subtitle *Di Tre Re* to
> the score that bears this number, as a handy reference. It is not an allusion
> to the Three Kings of the Nativity, or any other kings, but simply to the
> final three low Ds in each movement on pizzicato double basses, and on
> the timpani *ad libitum*, which has only these three notes to play.[5]

Although Honegger would write an epilogue to his symphonies in his
orchestral testament, the *Monopartita* of 1951, this work marks the true conclusion of the series in that it returns to the tragic and oppressive atmosphere of
the *Second* and *Third Symphonies*, but more harrowingly in that it leads to a pessimistic conclusion. The *Symphony for Strings* ended with a song of victory, and
the *Symphonie liturgique* with a confident prayer, but *Di Tre Re* leads to nothingness and seems to illustrate the gloomy remarks Honegger made at the time
to Bernard Gavoty:

> I have the very clear impression that we are at the end of a civilization—the
> end of our musical civilization, which anticipates by only a little the end of
> our civilization in every respect. We must have the courage to envisage it
> lucidly, as one does when one awaits one's death.[6]

Forty-five years later, the world is still in existence and so is music. But only
thanks to humankind's ability to adapt to the worst circumstances, an ability
that Honegger, being ill and exhausted, had not given it credit for.

The symphony *Di Tre Re* is distinguished from the previous symphonies by
a sparse, lapidary grandeur, a direct simplicity of utterance that nonetheless
conceals a technical mastery (of polyphony especially) that shows Honegger's
genius at its height. The layout of the three movements is an original one. A
long slow movement is followed by a Scherzo containing two slow Trios, and
then the fast Finale.

1. GRAVE

Like some giant organ, the orchestra hurls at us the vehement cry of its immense chorale, with bitonal chords moving in contrary motion (Example 62). This gradually sinks in pitch and intensity through the first section of the movement (measures 1–32), which is in simple ternary form plus coda. (Unlike G. K. Spratt and Jean Maillard, I do not see this as a sonata form.)

Example 62

Only the horns are absent from this tutti, in correspondence with the "gap" between the two ranks of chords. The chorale is firmly homophonic in its grandiose, granite-like nakedness, and it will be echoed in both the Scherzo (measures 83 and 289) and the Finale (measure 38). The middle section, from measures 33 to 77, introduces rapid dotted motifs that bind together the scattered texture, against which a melody rises, from the depths, on bass clarinet (Example 63). This is in three periods, the second of which, passing to the English horn, is more halting, interrupted by sighs and lamentations. We may note that measures 37 and 38 of this movement are repeated exactly as measures 125 and 126 of the Finale—not a cyclic repetition, merely a little secret link that is not intended to be heard by the listener or picked up by the analyst, like those initials and monograms that an architect or a sculptor tucks away in a corner of his work.

Example 63

Unlike the opening section, this central section consists of a crescendo moving toward the treble. In the course of it, from measure 53 onward, the tune gathers an accompaniment of dissonant, nightmarish trumpet fanfares (Example 64). These turn into an ostinato that, as the Dutch composer Alphonse Stallaert has rightly said, is reminiscent of the "La Malinconia" movement from Beethoven's *String Quartet*, Op. 18, No. 6. Jean Matter likens it to the expression of the damned man in the famous Autun tympanum, whose hands cover his ears to stop him from hearing. At the climax in measure 71 the chorale returns in force, still with obsessively strident trumpets insisting on their high F-sharps. At measure 77 the tutti is interrupted and the trumpets continue to climb up to a high G-sharp. This is held as a high pedal and then, as it reaches the A, everything stops.

Example 64

Here begins the third section of the movement (measures 78–105), which is a complete repetition of the chorale in a ghostly *pianissimo* in the strings. Meanwhile, the woodwinds interlace dotted rhythms in both 9/8 and 3/4, giving the effect of two different tempos. In the coda, from measures 106 to 121, Examples 62 and 63 briefly alternate. The latter disintegrates and the movement ends on pizzicatos that outline the skeleton of the chorale. The hollow low D on timpani sets the seal on the argument.

2. ALLEGRETTO–ADAGIO–TEMPO PRIMO

The second movement is a macabre Scherzo, interrupted by two funereal Trios. Here Honegger's prodigious technical skill is employed to summon up the evil world of robots, which the composer had campaigned against from *Cris du monde* up to the Dona nobis pacem of the *Third Symphony*. Marcel Delannoy described it well as "a learned, very ambiguous game of knuckle-bones played by laboratory robots." And this laboratory is devoted to an expressive and spiritual void. The mixture of irony and pedantry in this 3/8 movement recalls some of Max Reger's fugues. All Honegger's technical virtuosity is let loose on a twelve-tone theme (Example 65). The composer makes use of all the processes beloved by serial composers, but his skill in doing so is never deployed in defiance of the needs of musical reality. There are, in addition, a number of non-contrapuntal interludes that are not based on the theme (Honegger knowing to not exhaust the listener). The three Allegrettos correspond to the three sections of a Honeggerian sonata form with reversed recapitulation.

The first of these sections (measures 1–126) is divided into no less than seven parts, forming a triptych. The first panel presents the theme (Example 65) successively in its four forms: straight (clarinet), inverted retrograde (bassoon), inverted (flute), and retrograde (English horn and oboe), surrounded by delicate, organic counterpoint. In the central panel (measures 37–95), a roughly accented interlude is followed by a new, simple, and even tonal idea (echoes of this will be found in *Monopartita*), and finally by a homophonic tutti, a transformation of the first movement chorale and the first *forte* in the movement. A

Example 65

shortened and varied repetition of the opening, incorporating this tutti, leads via a rapid imitative decrescendo to the first Trio, an adagio in 4/4 (measures 127–145).

A window opens, but on nocturnal shadows. A desperate, chromatic, athematic lament forms a pathetic interlude, full of harsh, cavernous sounds, among which a muted trombone stands out, rasping at the bottom of its register. The Allegretto suddenly resumes its course, heading for the main central development section (measures 146–254); the six sections of this make up another triptych. In the first panel there is an alternation, heard twice, between a canon in contrary motion, setting out the four versions of the theme in pairs, and a homophonic toccata deriving from the central portion of the first Allegretto.

Now comes the climax of the entire movement (measures 193–218): three strettos on the four versions of the beginning of the theme. The first is in triple augmentation, on brass and then woodwinds; the second is in simple augmentation (giving the effect of 3/4 inside the 3/8 meter); the third is in normal values—and all three develop over a swell of string tremolos. There follows a calm, relaxed plateau (measures 219–254), playing with measures 5 and 6 of the theme in a graceful dialogue. A diminuendo takes the texture toward the bass and leads to the second Adagio (measures 255–264), which is shorter than the first, but the Allegretto continues simultaneously in the form of an arabesque that conducts a fantastic dialogue with the woodwinds, based on the twelve-tone theme (Example 65).

Finally, in measures 265 to 359, the last Allegretto repeats the first one in retrograde, section by section (even the quadruple presentation of the theme of Example 65 is reversed). It ends with a coda, starting at measure 349, in which we hear two more quadruple strettos on the beginning of the theme, one in prime form, the other in inverted retrograde. The decrescendo leads to the discreet timpani D.

3. ALLEGRO MARCATO

The third movement is a sort of synthesis of the Dies irae and Dona nobis pacem of the *Third Symphony*, even if the language is more tonal and its delivery less jerky and chaotic than in the Dies irae. Mustering all his strength for the last time, Honegger here gives one last cry of revolt. The full power of the orchestra is unleashed, with the brass much in evidence, and the virtuoso writing demands players of the highest caliber. The form is the most dramatic in all Honegger's output. The sonata structure is deprived of a recapitulation, being literally cut short by the catastrophe at measure 172, which is a terrifyingly realistic portrayal of his own heart attack. Nonetheless, Honegger's architectural genius assimilates this dramatic collapse into an amazingly satisfying structure, and we shall see the exceptional role played in this movement by the Golden Section.

Measures 1 to 79 correspond to an exposition, beginning with a 21-measure introduction in A minor, which has a cadential function leading into the principal key of D. The toccata-like eighth-notes of the trumpets, studded with brutal accents on the horns, the iambic cries of the woodwinds, and the rising tide of hammered sixteenth-notes on the strings, all set the scene for the eruption of the first theme at measure 22 (Example 66). This theme, one of Honegger's most powerful, consists of three elements, the last two of which in their distended intervals make this theme the last in a line going back to the *First Symphony* (Example 30). The forward drive is halted by a polytonal chordal theme acting as a bridge passage, and stemming from the first movement's chorale. The two appearances of this both end in collapse, each time rescued by the tumultuous revival of the sixteenth-notes.

Example 66

Then comes the second theme (Example 67) in F-sharp minor (measure 52), in two phrases, the second of them expressing a desperate determination close in tone to the theme of revolt in the Finale of the *Symphonie liturgique* (Example 50). After the cadential group, the development at measure 80 begins by hurling the themes at each other in a furious scuffle, the ultimate tragic transformation of the athletic vigor that had once propelled *Pacific 2.3.1* along its nightly track. And here, suddenly, amid the lowering clouds, the horns flash out a kind of grand diatonic chorale, its almost Gregorian outlines bringing hope (Example 68). This entry occurs exactly at the Golden Section point of the movement (measure 117). It stresses the dominant of F major, then A minor in an already subdued consequent on strings (this is the "secret link" with the first movement).

The repetitions of the phrase *c* of Example 66, however, become more and more noticeable and lead to the return in force of the toccata-like sixteenth-notes (measure 139). Then they swell to an immense augmentation, trying at all costs to halt the theme of hope. This theme will appear twice more, but its victory is no more than temporary—like an airplane momentarily glimpsed

Example 67

Example 68

between clouds. It is the final echo of the great hope raised by Joan of Arc, but this time it will not prove to be "the strongest of all." Like the blade of a guillotine, the hammered eighth-notes of the brass fall at measure 164, assisted by the string sixteenth-notes rising from the double basses. The iambic cries mount a decisive assault, ending in the catastrophe of measure 172.

The recapitulation would normally arrive at this point, but this "truncated" sonata form is far more striking in its dramatic concision. What follows, in measures 172 to 190, is a coda marked *pianissimo subito*. After the continuous *forte* of the preceding music, it comes as what the composer himself called a "conclusion muffled as though in terror." There is no real tune, only fragmentary quotations from the introduction, to which it forms a symmetrical counterpart. The motor energy begins to dissipate, the eighth-notes become intermittent and then cease. These last nineteen measures are a shattering, merciless, clinical description of an agony that Honegger had suffered in heart and mind. The final D on the timpani is Death.

So ends in darkness the work that Marcel Delannoy called "the least Christian of his works, the one in which the light of Easter never manages to pierce the clouds."[7] Some conductors slacken the tempo at this coda. It is quite clear, however, that there must be no such slackening here, any more than there should be at the end of Sibelius's *Fourth Symphony*, with which Honegger's final work has a strange similarity—Sibelius wrongly believing, when he wrote it, that he was dying of throat cancer.

Category 6: Concertos

Compared with the powerful body of his symphonies, Honegger's three concertos form a fairly modest group. He never considered writing a grand romantic concerto and his three works in the genre last only between eleven and seventeen minutes. They also use a small orchestra—strings only, in the case of the *Concerto da camera*—and all three could, like the first, almost be called "concertino." From the point of view of quality, though, the situation is quite different. Even if they were written at different periods, none of them is a minor work and the *Concerto da camera* in particular is one of his most delightful pieces. The *Concertino for piano and orchestra*, too, is an irresistibly fresh and charming piece, dating from the "roaring '20s" when Les Six were in the full bloom of youth.

55. *Concertino for piano and orchestra*

September–17 November 1924
"To Andrée Vaurabourg" (this dedication does not appear on the published score)
First performance: 23 May 1925, Andrée Vaurabourg, orchestra conducted by Serge Koussevitzky, Paris Opera
Performing forces: piano solo; 2.2.2.2.–2.2.1.0.–strings
Duration: 11 minutes 25 seconds (4:15 + 2:00 + 5:10)
Salabert

Of all Honegger's works, the *Concertino for piano and orchestra* is perhaps the one most clearly influenced by Les Six, with its neoclassicism flavored with jazz idioms (especially in the Finale). The short Larghetto seems to be a straightforward homage to Poulenc, but the whole work is also very close to what Martinů would write between 1925 and 1930. The three movements are played without a break.

1. ALLEGRO MOLTO MODERATO

Everything is symmetrical in this simple ternary form in E major. The first section is a strict dialogue. Each measure of syncopation in the orchestra is followed by a naive, diatonic theme on the piano in the manner of a popular song (Example 69). It is only in the central section (measures 21–62) that the two partners play together. A repeat of the opening, followed by a decrescendo codetta, leads to the next movement.

Example 69

2. LARGHETTO SOSTENUTO

In this brief G minor arietta, with its charming turn toward G-flat major (in the manner of Poulenc), the piano calmly unfolds its cantilena over placid *Alberti* bass figures. Meanwhile, little pastoral motifs in the woodwinds look forward to the bird arabesques in the Larghetto of the *Fourth Symphony*.

3. ALLEGRO

Suddenly, low, dry, col legno chords start in the strings, followed by descending chromatic triplets on the clarinet—such an exact premonition of the Allegro of Ravel's *Concerto for the Left Hand* that the possibility of coincidence must be discounted. This G major introduction ushers in the longest of the three movements in A-B-A'-B' form. It is a thoroughgoing imitation of 1924 jazz (now delightfully old-fashioned) with its muted trumpet, its modal, sleepily syncopated piano tune complete with "blue note" (*Rhapsody in Blue* had just reached Europe), its poco vibrato trombone figure, and its second theme with a sort of boogie-woogie bass. The coda is based on a real "walking bass," above which the themes disintegrate and gradually disappear in a manner that obviously has nothing in common with the tragic end of the *Fifth Symphony*. An off-beat *fortissimo* chord adds a final exclamation mark to this little work, which, for all its modest ambition, remains one of the few in this style that do not show their age.

72. *Concerto for cello and orchestra in C major* (*Cello Concerto*)

August 1929; orchestration completed November 1929, in Paris
"To Maurice Maréchal"
First performance: 17 February 1930, Maurice Maréchal, Boston Symphony
    Orchestra, conducted by Serge Koussevitzky, Boston
First European performance: 16 May 1930, Maurice Maréchal, Orchestre
    Symphonique de Paris, Pierre Monteux, Salle Pleyel, Paris
Performing forces: cello solo; 2.2.2.2.–2.2.0.1.–timpani, cymbals, triangle–strings
Duration: 16 minutes 45 seconds (6:00 + 5:25 + 5:20)
Salabert

The *Concerto for cello and orchestra* is only a little longer than the concertino and uses a fairly similar orchestra, with tuba replacing trombone, and with the addition of both a little percussion and Honegger's favorite bass clarinet. It is above all a lyrical, charming composition that continues in the divertimento vein already mined in the concertino.

1. ANDANTE

An eighteen-measure introduction presents a sort of leitmotif or motto, peaceful and pastoral in character, opposing the soloist's iambic rhythms to the rising chords in the orchestra. The following section may be termed an Allegro because of the doubling of the tempo, even though the word does not appear on the score. It is in sonata form with a much abbreviated recapitulation. The first tune is nonchalant in tone, syncopated and lightly swung, and close to being light music with its oscillation between two notes in the style of 1929 jazz (Honegger had just started writing *Les Aventures du roi Pausole*). A second tune is slightly sharper and more decisive. After the return of the introduction's leit-motif and a final dreamy allusion by the soloist to the swung theme, we move on at once to the next movement.

2. LENTO

The distance of a tritone between the F-sharp minor of the second move-ment and the principal key of C is the same as that in the *First Symphony*, on which Honegger started work immediately afterward. This Lento is darker in mood than the movements that surround it. The cello theme is pentatonic and its rhythms and intervals confirm Honegger's fascination for the music of American Indians, first evidenced more than a decade earlier in *Le Chant de Nigamon*. It is taken as the subject of two variations separated by an accompa-nied cadenza, and the second variation is scherzo-like in character. The cadenza proper, written by Maurice Maréchal, leads directly into the Finale.

3. ALLEGRO MARCATO

In this sonata form, the recapitulation is reversed and the development deals briefly with the opening theme and its obsessive quarter-notes on the note C. The music is seasoned with cheeky dissonances in 1929 jazz style. As a contrast, the second theme in F-sharp major (note the impeccable tonal logic!) is a broad cantabile, repeated in canon. It will open the recapitulation, in E major, with the flutter-tonguing tuba giving an irresistible growl, and clarinet in canon adding truculent appoggiaturas to its line. A diminuendo leads to the coda, which is a poetic reminiscence first of the opening leitmotif, then of the swung theme from the first movement. A brilliant stretto on the repeated quarter-note theme of the Finale provides a forceful, triumphant ending.

196. *Concerto da camera* for flute, English horn, and strings

August–October 1948 (first movement: August; second movement: September; third
    movement: completed 28 October)
"To Mrs. Elizabeth Sprague Coolidge" (who commissioned the work)
First performance: 6 May 1949, André Jaunet (flute), Marcel Saillet (English horn),
    Collegium Musicum of Zurich, conducted by Paul Sacher, Zurich
Duration: 16 minutes 30 seconds (5:30 + 7:00 + 4:00)
Salabert

This delicious little masterpiece is a kind of condensed, decanted version of the *Fourth Symphony*. It marks the all-too-brief revival of Honegger's creative powers after his heart attack, which had prevented him from writing anything since June 1947. There is no tonal unity between the three movements, which are in E major, F minor, and B minor respectively. It is an orthodox concerto in the sense of being a dialogue both among the soloists and between the soloists and the strings.

1. ALLEGRETTO AMABILE

The overall atmosphere is rural and pastoral, and the themes also have a popular, unsophisticated air. The form is a mixture of sonata and irregular rondo based on three groups of themes (A, B, C), which can also be arranged in two sections. The following table should make things clear:

A	B	C	A	B	C	A	B	A	B
19	20–36	37–48	49–66	67–80	81–90	91–105	106–117	118–127	128–133
position			Development				Recapitulation (108)		
st section					Second section				

The two Golden Section points are at measure 51 (very near the start of the development) and at measure 82 (very near the start of the second section).

From the point of view of tonality and modulation, this piece marks Honegger's most accomplished management of dominants and of the links between them.

The movement begins with syncopated string chords divided into ten parts, and these chords recur frequently throughout. They introduce the two melodic ideas of group A (Example 70), on English horn, with its wide seventh and octave leaps (Example 71) and on flute—a livelier idea and a witty homage to the "Gavotte" from Fauré's *Masques et bergamasques*. Each one successfully stakes out its instrumental identity.

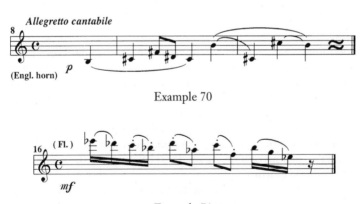

Example 70

Example 71

Once the syncopated chords have been abandoned, group B begins with a naive popular tune over offbeat pizzicatos (Example 72), interrupted by a vigorous tutti interjection on a variant of Example 71 (this will be the only musical idea given to the strings). The dialogue continues in delicate textures (English horn above flute) until the appearance of group C, a concluding theme on the flute, its large intervals, deriving from Example 70, gradually closing up and getting faster (Example 73). This theme is linked with the second theme of the Finale (see Example 76), but it will not be repeated in the recapitulation of the first movement, and this leads me to prefer seeing the structure as binary. Once these ideas have been presented, there is no real point in pursuing a detailed analysis; all is grace and spontaneity, and the movement ends discreetly, without a coda or even a final chord.

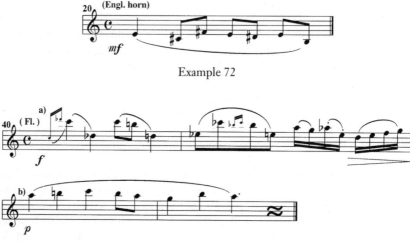

Example 72

Example 73

2. ANDANTE

Undoubtedly, the second movement of the *Concerto da camera* is one of the high points of Honegger's oeuvre in its sustained melodic inventiveness, polyphonic mastery, and, above all, in an intensity and expressive warmth comparable with what we find in the De profundis of the *Symphonie liturgique* or the "Lamento" of *La Danse des morts*. Two themes suffice (Examples 74 and 75), and the melancholy atmosphere manages to achieve gravity without falling into heavy-handedness. The themes are freely varied in the course of eight sections divided into two groups of four. Again, their relative lengths are determined by Golden Section proportions.

The first of the two themes opens the movement on low unison strings (Example 74). Although it gives the impression of being a chaconne or passacaglia bass, it will not in fact be either. The second theme (Example 75) is a delicate lament on flute, with the descending chromatic tail of which Honegger was so fond, following Debussy's *Sonata for flute, viola, and harp*. At the end of the fourth section, at measure 48, we may note a short panting passage on strings that is very close to the famous *beklemmt* (oppressed) figure in the

Example 74

Example 75

Cavatina of Beethoven's *String Quartet*, Op. 130—identified by one doctor as the rhythm of a weak heart. Then, at the beginning of the second section (measure 51), the two soloists play together for the first time since the beginning of the movement.

3. VIVACE

The third movement is a lighthearted Scherzo with a fairly short middle section (Trio; measures 89–123) and a shortened recapitulation (measures 124–181). The first theme is sketched out by the flute but is not heard in complete form until played by all the strings at measure 23, followed by its consequent. In the same way, the "heehaws" of the second theme, which bring it close to theme C in the first movement, are sketched out several times before the theme is heard complete on the flute at measure 51 (Example 76).

Example 76

After an interlude for the tutti, the "heehaws" introduce the short Trio. Rhythmic figures in the lower part of the orchestra are derived from earlier material, while in the treble the flute performs acrobatic arabesques in sixteenth-notes. Between these, the English horn intones a melody that is too much like a popular tune to be called a cantus firmus. After the shortened recapitulation comes the coda. There is one last "heehaw," a cadential, dominant-tonic gesture, and, as lightly as a feather, the work takes its leave.

Category 7: Other Orchestral Works

10. *Prelude* for *Aglavaine et Sélysette*
16. *Le Chant de Nigamon*
31. *Pastorale d'été*
47. *Chant de joie*
53. *Pacific 2.3.1* (*Symphonic Movement No. 1*)
67. *Rugby* (*Symphonic Movement No. 2*)
81A. *Prelude, Arioso, and Fughetta* (transcription for string orchestra)
83. *Symphonic Movement No. 3*
92. *Radio-Panoramique*
102. *Nocturne for orchestra*
105. *Largo for string orchestra*
107. *Les Mille et Une Nuits*
162. *Le Grand Barrage*
182. *Sérénade à Angélique*
203. *Suite archaïque*
204. *Monopartita*
207. *Toccata on a Theme of Campra*
218. *Chevauchée*
219. *Pathétique*
220. *Vivace (Dance)*
221. *Allegretto*

The pieces on this list of "Other Orchestral Works" vary considerably in importance and in the frequency with which they are played. I shall concentrate on those of the highest quality. Priority will be given, therefore, to *Le Chant de Nigamon*, *Pastorale d'été*, *Chant de joie*, and the three Symphonic Movements, all pieces that are often played and recorded. But I shall also consider in some detail the *Nocturne*, the *Suite archaïque*, and *Monopartita*, which deserve to be just as well known.

10. *Prelude* for *Aglavaine et Sélysette*

November–23 December 1916; orchestration completed 1 January 1917
Inspired by Maurice Maeterlinck's play
First performance: 3 April 1917, conducted by Honegger, Paris Conservatory
    orchestral class
First public performance: 1 June 1920, Golschmann Orchestra, conducted by
    Vladimir Golschmann, Salle Gaveau, Paris
Performing forces: 1.1.2.2.–2.1.0.0.–strings
Duration: 6 minutes 45 seconds
Salabert

This utterly Debussyan piece was the composer's first orchestral work, for
which Honegger specified forty-three players (nine woodwinds and thirty-four
strings). He never conducted it again, and it was not published until after
his death. The same was true of the *Interlude* for *La Mort de Sainte Alméenne*
(which follows the same stylistic path) and for their later successor, the ballet
Sous-marine.
    The form is ternary, but the repeat is no more than a coda fifteen mea-
sures long, in which the tonality is deliberately vague ("Drown the tonality,"
said Debussy). The central section contains no more than a hint of contrast,
although it has the only *fortissimo* in the movement, at measure 104. There
would be much more of a contrast between sections in the *Rhapsody* (H13), written a few months later. But the control of color is already remarkable here,
even if Honegger has not yet quite found his own personality.

16. *Le Chant de Nigamon* (The Song of Nigamon)

September–December 1917 (completed before 19 December)
"To Rhené-Baton"
Based on an episode from Gustave Aimard's novel *Le Souriquet*
First performance: 18 April 1918, conducted by Honegger, Paris Conservatory
    orchestral class
First public performance: 3 January 1920, Pasdeloup Orchestra, conducted by
    Rhené-Baton, Cirque d'Hiver, Paris
Performing forces: 3.3.2.3.–4.2.3.1.–timpani, cymbals, bass drum, triangle–strings
Duration: 9 minutes 50 seconds
Salabert

As in the *String Quartet No. 1* (also in C minor), Honegger has here found
his own voice, despite the relatively traditional harmonic and tonal language.
He also continued to recognize the work and often conducted it. We can hear
a slight debt to Richard Strauss's *Elektra*, and the strident piccolos recall d'Indy.
The composer quotes three authentic American Indian themes, which he found
in Julien Tiersot's *Notes d'ethnographie musicale.*
    The form of the piece is fairly complex. It looks like a sonata structure with
slow introduction and coda, but the three American Indian themes either interrupt this scheme or else are sounded in conjunction with it (from the development section only). Before examining the music in detail, we must read the
scenario, as printed at the head of the score:

Tareah the Huron had spared Nigamon and the other Iroquois chiefs in order to burn them alive. The fire was put to the stakes. When the flames began to rise, Tareah leapt through them, mercilessly scalped Nigamon and his companions, and began to thrash them with their own hair. Then the Iroquois began their death chant, but when Nigamon began his, the others fell silent in order to hear it.

The score follows this scenario faithfully. In this respect, *Le Chant de Nigamon* is thus a real symphonic poem, and the only such work from Honegger's pen, even though it works perfectly well as a piece of pure music. It consists of seven sections.

1. A slow introduction (measures 1–15) creates an atmosphere of mystery and suspense, thanks to Honegger's typical use of C minor as the dominant of F. We hear the fanfare motif, which will appear throughout (Example 77), and the outline of the first theme of the exposition.

Example 77

2. The exposition of the Allegro (measures 16–77) is launched by a crash on timpani and cymbals, and violence is unleashed, with lightning flashes from the piccolo amid the fanfares. After this beginning, no less than three themes are heard (measures 34, 43, and 65), the most striking of which is the last, which has a cadential function (Example 78). This is played at length by the violins in F-sharp minor, and the choice of a tritonal instead of a dominant relationship with the tonic will remain typical of the composer.

Example 78

3. The development (measures 78–140), with fanfares continuing, is based initially on the first theme, and then on the third (from measure 114). But it is interrupted midway (measures 100–108) by the first Indian theme ("a Huron war dance, collected in Lorette, Canada, by J. Tiersot"). This is in a jerky 12/8 meter, in pentatonic minor on low strings. The background is provided by a brilliant toccata on trumpets, of which the raucous, fifth-based harmonies recall

Ernest Bloch's *First String Quartet* and *First Quintet*—Bloch, too, often turned to American Indian sources.

4. Between the development and the recapitulation we hear the second Indian theme (measures 141–158). This theme (an "Iroquois warriors' song, collected by H. E. Krehbiel") is given an imposing rendition by horns on the three notes A, C, E, which are then treated in canon and punctuated by the fanfare motif.

5. The recapitulation (measures 159–204) is reversed as usual and superimposes the continuation of the second Indian theme, in bitonal canon, with the second and third themes of the exposition. But a pre-echo of the third Indian theme at measure 174 reduces the rest to silence ("the others fell silent in order to hear it"). Beginning in measure 177, this theme ("The Warrior's Last Word," an Iroquois melody taken from "Wa-Wan"), receives a grandiose treatment (Example 79). It is a magnificent tune of epic grandeur and, after a brief intervention from the first sonata theme, it is repeated *fortissimo* in D minor by trombones (measure 195). This is the climax of the work, after which the theme fades slowly and dies.

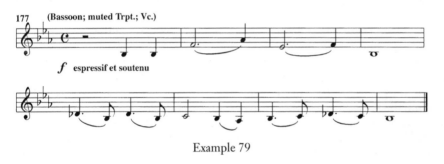

Example 79

6. In a final development (measures 205–217), the long decrescendo continues and leads imperceptibly into the epilogue.

7. The slow epilogue (measures 218–227) is a symmetrical counterpart to the slow introduction, except that there are no more fanfares. The extraordinary final chord is worth noting: C minor with added major sixth and seventh.

The Golden Section point, both of the work as a whole and of the sonata allegro, comes at measure 140, exactly at the appearance of the second Indian theme, the chant of collective death.

31. *Pastorale d'été* (Summer Pastorale)

August 1920
"To Roland-Manuel" (this dedication does not appear on the published score)
First performance: 17 February 1921, Golschmann Orchestra, conducted by
    Vladimir Golschmann, Salle Gaveau, Paris; the work was awarded the Prix
    Verley on that occasion

Performing forces: flute, oboe, clarinet, bassoon, horn, strings
Duration: 7 minutes 45 seconds
Salabert

A simple, unpretentious piece, *Pastorale d'été* was the fruit of a happy summer holiday spent at Wengen in the Bernese *Oberland*, at the foot of the Jungfrau mountain. The piece was, understandably, an immediate success and at its first performance it won the Prix Verley, awarded by the audience (with a huge majority). This success has never waned and the work continues to delight chamber orchestras, even those of modest standards, thanks to its being relatively easy to play. At the head of the score stands a brief quotation from Rimbaud: "J'ai embrassé l'aube d'été" (I embraced the summer dawn). This idyll is in a simple A-B-A' form, with the third section superimposing the material of the first two—a procedure that Honegger was fond of, and which he would use often, thanks to his technical mastery.

The work is a perfect example of Honegger's feeling for the dominant. The three sharps in the key signature seem to suggest A major. But as the music is mostly in the dominant of A, Honegger allows an ambiguity to persist between this key and Mixolydian E major (that is, the mode on G without a leading tone).

Over a gently undulating accompaniment made up of three different figures, the horn plays a long, calm melody that begins as shown in Example 80. It is repeated in canon and leads to a crescendo that recalls Debussy's *Prélude à l'après-midi d'un faune*. This in turn leads to the lively central section (Vif et gai, measures 48–107) in the main key of B-flat major. A lively pastoral call from the bassoon gives rise to two new tunes, both clearly written in homage to Beethoven's *"Pastoral" Symphony*, whom Honegger, alone among Les Six, would continue to admire. The first tune, on the clarinet, is an echo from the first movement of the "Pastoral" (Example 81), while the second, on the violins, recalls the 2/4 Trio of its Scherzo. The slightly bitonal staccato accompaniment here is the only "modern" touch in the score. Between the two tunes, a passing modulation into F-sharp minor provides a sudden breath of fresh air, as though a little cloud had passed across the sun. These two tunes are heard together at the only *fortissimo* in the piece—a very modest one at measure 96—after which the music fades toward the third and final section.

In the final section, at measures 108 to 141, the lively arabesques based on the motif in Example 81 are superimposed on the dreamy opening tune. Then, in a wonderfully poetic passage, the calls grow more and more distant and a beautiful modulation (surely inspired by the end of Debussy's *Prélude*) takes us through D-flat/C-sharp and D major to E major. This is the first emphatic statement of the tonic, with the theme of Example 81 played on the flute. Even so, the final chord remains ambiguous: E-B-D-F-sharp-A, that is, E major without the third, but with the D-natural still showing that it is the unresolved dominant of A.

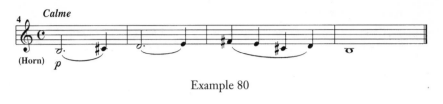

Example 80

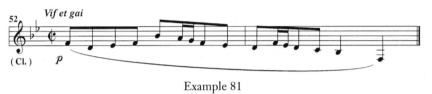

Example 81

47. *Chant de joie* (Song of Joy)

November 1922; orchestration completed January 1923
"To Maurice Ravel"
First performance: 7 April 1923, Suisse Romande Orchestra, conducted by Ernest
    Ansermet, Victoria Hall, Geneva (twenty-fourth meeting of the AMS
    [Association of Swiss Composers])
Performing forces: 3.3.3.3.–4.3.3.1.–cymbals, bass drum, celesta, harp–strings
Duration: 6 minutes 15 seconds
Salabert

Willy Tappolet, in describing this short, straightforward work, rightly
compared the work's sense of the festive with that of the procession in the *Mas-*
tersingers Prelude, and he called *Chant de joie* "a hymn or overture for a sporting
festival." It appears to be one of Honegger's simplest scores. In fact, it is one
that most easily allows us to study the principles behind his rich and complex
harmonies. These might be called "pantonal" or "metatonal," in the sense that
they are enriched (like uranium) by the use of total chromaticism, even if the
result remains diatonic. At the same time, these harmonies are generated by
Honegger's intense and masterly employment of contrapuntal lines. The
orchestra includes harp and celesta, both rare with Honegger. Again, the form
is an obvious A-B-A′.

The rhythmic, vigorous opening section launches at once into a heroic
theme, played by the horns in full swing in the plainest of D majors (Example
82). This is dominated by Bach's favorite dactylic rhythms and backed up by
crunchy harmonies, enriched by widespread string chords. The central section
(measures 48–93) is calmer and more consonant. Its pastoral arabesque on the
clarinet (Example 83) is in E major, one of the composer's favorite keys, and
sounds like a memory of the Alleluia from *Le Roi David*.

With much use of double and even triple canon, the woodwinds stand out
against rapid scales passing between strings and harp. The third section (measures 94–143) to a large extent reverses the order of material in the first, following Honegger's usual principle, and reaches the recapitulation of the heroic
theme (Example 82) only in measure 107. This comes at the end of a crescendo

Vigoureux et rythmé

(Horns) *f*

Example 82

Calme

52

(Cl.) *p*

Example 83

that looks forward in its dissonance to the middle of the slow movement of the *Symphony for Strings*. But the two themes are now superimposed, with the second being slightly modified and reduced to its first period. In the final apotheosis (Large) the two ideas are reunited, with the second in triple canon-stretto. The work ends in a radiant burst of sound, crowned by a final chord of D major.

53. *Pacific 2.3.1* (*Symphonic Movement No. 1*)

March–December 1923
"To Ernest Ansermet"
First performance: 8 May 1924, conducted by Serge Koussevitzky, Paris Opera
Performing forces: 3.3.3.3.–4.3.3.1.–side drum, cymbals, bass drum, tam-tam–strings
Duration: 6 minutes 30 seconds
Salabert
Pacific 2.3.1 has inspired two films: one by Tsekhanuski (Soviet Union, 1931), the
    other by Jean Mitry (France, 1950)

It is a pity that the excessive popularity of *Pacific 2.3.1*, together with the descriptive aspect of its title, have brought it into disfavor and even contempt with the so-called specialists and cognoscenti. It is one of Honegger's most original, radical, and carefully constructed works. Some of the misunderstandings have been furthered by the composer's manifold comments, some of which have been contradictory, suggesting that he was embarrassed by the work's huge success (which threatened to overshadow the rest of his output). Honegger never intended to rival the naively imitative, "noise-ist" compositions of Italian futurists such as Russolo and Balilla Pratella, or to exalt the machine at the expense of human beings—we have already seen that any such idea was totally contrary to his beliefs. We can see, first of all, that there are affinities with the paintings Fernand Léger was producing in those same years, but beyond that we must begin by examining those notorious statements:

> I have always been passionately fond of locomotives. For me they are living beings and I love them as others love women or horses.[8]

What I was after in *Pacific* was not the imitation of locomotive noises, but the translation of a visual impression and a physical delight through a musical construction. It is based on objective contemplation: the tranquil breathing of the machine in repose, the effort of getting up steam, then the gradual picking up of speed, culminating in the lyrical, engrossing vision of a train weighing 300 tons hurtling through the night at 75 miles an hour. I chose as my subject the locomotive of the "Pacific" type, with the symbol 231, used for heavy, high-speed trains.[9]

At first I called this piece "Symphonic Movement." But on reflection I found this rather dull, and suddenly a romantic idea came to me. When I'd finished the work I wrote the title *Pacific 2.3.1* over the top. This indicated locomotives for heavy, high-speed trains, but now this type has been superseded by and sacrificed, alas, to electric trains.[10]

This last comment was made some years after the work's composition and has to be taken with a grain of salt. The piece was not entirely the fruit of an abstract project. The Prelude that survives from the music for Abel Gance's film *La Roue* (H44), which dates from November or December 1922, contains unmistakable sketches for certain ideas in *Pacific 2.3.1*, most notably for measures 109 and 118, which are marked with words like "locomotive" and "rail." *La Roue* was, then, the breeding ground for the ideas of *Pacific*. Honegger left the following account of his protracted struggles to give the work its rigorous, carefully planned construction:

> In *Pacific* I was after an extremely abstract and wholly ideal notion: that of giving the impression of a mathematical acceleration of rhythm while the speed itself decreased. From the musical point of view, I composed a kind of large chorale variation, shot through in the first part with alla breve counterpoint and conjuring up the style of Johann Sebastian Bach.[11]

The subtitle "Symphonic Movement" is doubly justified here. It is a "movement" in the sense of sounding like part of a symphony or a sonata, but also in the sense of being a kinetic study in motion, based on the dialectic between agogics and tempo, with both being variable. *Rugby* would also illustrate the two senses of the word movement, in a very different manner.

It is possible to analyze the work according to four different but simultaneous criteria.

1) Rhythmic structure and tempo. Throughout the eight main sections of the piece, we can distinguish passages that are unstable (sections 2, 4, and 8) and stable (sections 3, 5, 6, and 7), with the slow introduction (section 1) being outside the system. The unstable passages, where the durations undergo change, are an early, successful example of the principle of metric modulation found in the work of Elliott Carter and foreseen by Charles Ives.

2) Development and metamorphoses of what Honegger calls a chorale. This is in fact a long cantus firmus, firmly anchored to C-sharp (one of Honegger's favorite keys) and extending in its complete version to no less than forty-one whole-notes. It appears six times in all, but the only complete versions are

the first (measure 27, section 3) and the triumphant fifth, heard a semitone down in C minor (measure 169, section 7).

3) The "normal" parameters of themes, keys, and form. There are five principal themes, almost all growing like suckers from the parent cantus firmus. The similarity is found in two basic elements: A (the principle of intervallic expansion) and the melodic outline B. The successive exposition of themes lasts from measure 39 (the middle of section 3) to measure 131 (the middle of section 6), and their development from measure 132 to measure 217 (the end of the piece). As in the sonata movements of the later symphonies, there is no real recapitulation.

4) The figurative, illustrative aspect. This certainly exists, whatever Honegger may have said later when he had grown tired of having provoked so many anecdotal commentaries that obscured all the work's essential qualities.

In fact, *Pacific 2.3.1* stands out from all the so-called mechanical works so popular at the time. While they have vanished into oblivion, *Pacific* lives on because of its value as a piece of expressive pure music. It is true that its pretext, as it were, resides in an object of the real world. But surely, for the children of the twenty-first century, the steam locomotive has joined the fairy-tale dragon as a common archetype of the collective unconscious?

SECTION 1 (MEASURES 1–11)

This brief slow introduction, outside the main tempo, describes the "tranquil breathing" of the machine at rest. But the tuba is already beginning to accelerate its note values.

SECTION 2 (MEASURES 12–26)

The mighty engine ponderously begins to move. The whole-notes become half-note triplets, while the intervals begin to expand.

SECTION 3 (MEASURES 27–53)

The first "plateau" of stable note values (quarter-notes breaking down into eighth-notes), and the first exposition of the cantus firmus (Example 84), followed by the first of the contingent themes.

SECTION 4 (MEASURES 54–72)

Another unstable passage of accelerating values, illustrating the acceleration of the train, with the second contingent theme.

SECTION 5 (MEASURES 73–117)

The train races on through the night to the rhythm of its regularly pulsing eighth-notes, and these spill over into the third contingent theme (Example

Example 84

85). This looks forward to the first theme in the Finale of the *Fifth Symphony* (see Example 66). It is followed by the fourth theme at measure 91, and the extended intervals here link it with the family already described in my examination of the symphonies (Examples 30, 39, 45, etc.). Then comes a stretto on the third theme, a development of the first, and a partial repeat of the cantus firmus.

Example 85

SECTION 6 (MEASURES 118–168)

Another long passage of metric stability, based now on swirling eighth-note triplets, which mark the fifth and final contingent theme (Example 86). This, incarnating the joy of speed, is an arabesque belonging to the "alleluia" family of which we have seen another prototype in *Chant de joie* (Example 83). From measure 132, the five themes and the beginning of the cantus firmus are developed, either together or separately, in a passage of wonderful polyphony.

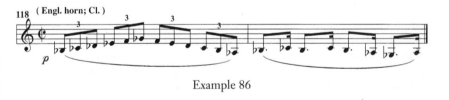

Example 86

SECTION 7 (MEASURES 169–203)

The climax of the work is reached with the cantus firmus blazed out on full brass in C minor. It has now become a broad, lyrical melody sung at the top of the orchestra's voice and surrounded by the other themes, which are now reduced to the status of countersubjects or satellites to its triumphant progress. All this counterpoint resolves gradually into the superimposition of different rhythms, and the visual aspect of the score at this point (especially at measures

195 to 200) is a perfect reproduction of the gears and pistons of the machine. Finally, the cantus firmus reaches its conclusion in a huge *fortissimo* uproar.

SECTION 8 (MEASURES 204–217)

The coda, taking us back to C-sharp minor, is astonishingly brief and an exact retrograde of the events of section 2. The final deceleration is obviously shorter than its counterpart and is a tangible embodiment of the enormous braking force necessary to halt this mass of steel, which finally comes to rest on the final, unique unison C-sharp.

67. Rugby (Symphonic Movement No. 2)

August 1928; orchestration completed September 1928
"To René Delange" (this dedication does not appear on the published score)
First performance: 19 October 1928, Orchestre Symphonique de Paris (inaugural
        concert), conducted by Ernest Ansermet, Théâtre des Champs-Élysées, Paris
Performing forces: 3.3.3.3.–4.3.3.1.–strings
Duration: 7 minutes 45 seconds
Salabert

The composer wrote:

> I'm very fond of football, but rugby is closer to my heart. It seems to me more spontaneous, more direct, closer to Nature than football, which is more scientific. Certainly I'm not insensible to football's carefully prepared moves, but I'm more keenly attracted by rugby's rhythm, which is savage, abrupt, chaotic, and desperate. It would be wrong to consider my piece as program music. It simply tries to describe in musical language the game's attacks and counterattacks, and the rhythm and color of a match at the stade de Colombes. I thought I ought to be honest and indicate my sources. That's why this short composition has the title *Rugby*.[12]

Structurally, and above all rhythmically, *Rugby* is one of Honegger's most complex works, but also one of the most approachable for the listener. He rarely showed such rhythmic imagination, which here is totally free, not mathematically organized as in *Pacific 2.3.1.* In using all his compositional rigor and discipline to describe the apparent anarchy of a rugby match, Honegger reveals the logic and order that lie below its anarchic surface. The main key is D major, but this is not reached until the second "half," and the first theme is initially presented in G major. Apart from its jerky, broken rhythms, the work's other characteristic is the use of huge melodic intervals to express athletic vigor. The fact that these intervals are often simple (thirds, fourths, fifths, octaves, and their multiples) means that the infrastructure is diatonic, even though the score is one of Honegger's most dissonant.

This paradox is not uncommon with him and is joined here by another, the luxury that I have already commented on: the total absence of percussion in a work dedicated to muscular strength. It has been called a free rondo, but the

structure is complicated by the fact that there are two important, intercon-
nected refrains (Examples 87 and 88). The periodic return of the introduction
suggests that it is possible to divide it into two halves and a period of overtime.
In sporting terms, this overtime is unjustified (at the end of the second half the
first theme is leading by four "tries" to three [a rugby "try" is roughly equivalent to American football's "touchdown"]), but Honegger prefers to let his referee commit a serious error and gives priority to purely musical considerations!
As in *Pacific 2.3.1*, the two main themes are of the cantus firmus type and some,
but not all, of the secondary themes are connected to them.

Example 87

Example 88

In the introduction (measures 1–11), a unison on the leading-tone C-sharp
describes the tension of anticipation. A quick ascending run of the strings is followed by a rapid triplet descent. The referee has blown his whistle, unleashing
a disorganized rush of sound, like that of a pack of young dogs after their prey.
    The first half (measures 12–121) begins with a double exposition of the first
theme (Example 87) on trombones, then on horns (the whole work relies heavily on the brass section). This is followed by a long central section in two parts,
each of them on a new secondary theme (the second of them uses the metric
modulations practiced in *Pacific 2.3.1*). The final section is an extended and more
emphatic repeat of the opening theme, surrounded by new motifs, figurations,
exuberant outbreaks, runs, and accelerations in dotted rhythm, all of which
evoke the energy of the game and put the orchestral players to the test.
    A return of the introduction, reduced now to five measures (122–126) gives
the signal for the second half (measures 127–259). The second main theme is
now heard for the first time, played with extreme gusto by strings and confirming D major as the tonic for the first time. Like the first theme, it is repeated
in canon. Then comes a second episode, orchestrated in a strangely pointillist
manner, in which the meter changes for the first time from 3/4 to 4/4. The

return of the second theme is superimposed over this, and then we reach the third and final episode. This is the longest of the three and is based on a metamorphosis in rapid note values of the first theme, preceding the return of the theme itself.

But this episode, like the first, is in two parts. In the second part we find the motif treated as an accelerando by means of metric modulations—this brings back the second theme, and the score is now three tries each! But, at measure 241, the first theme reappears in full force, and even in augmentation, on trombones and in D major, as at the start. Four tries to three!

Despite that, then comes the surprise of the brief return of the introduction (measures 260–262), signaling overtime. This passage (measures 263–284) is quite rightly short. After a final chasing stretto on fragments of motifs derived from the episode themes, and a last appearance of the beginning of the first theme, the referee blows his whistle for the end of the game.

The coda lasts for a mere seven measures (285–291). We hear again the unison C-sharp of the opening, but this time it resolves in a blaze of D major, and the loud sixteenth-notes on trumpets and the progression of the last three chords both vividly recall the end of Debussy's *Ibéria*.

81A. *Prelude, Arioso, and Fughetta on the name BACH*—transcription for string orchestra

Arrangement of H81 for string orchestra, by Arthur Hoérée. H81 was composed in October 1932. The arrangement must date from 1936.
First performance: 5 December 1936, Orchestre féminin de Paris, conducted by Jane Évrard, Salle Gaveau, Paris
Duration: 6 minutes 30 seconds
Salabert

For an analysis of the original solo piano version of the *Prelude, Arioso, and Fughetta*, see the discussion of H81 (Category 1, in Chapter 10). The work has become more popular in the form of this excellent arrangement, which enriches the all-too-meager repertory of Honegger's works for strings.

83. *Symphonic Movement No. 3*

30 October 1932; orchestrated December 1932–January 1933
"For Wilhelm Furtwängler and the Berlin Philharmonic Orchestra" (commission)
First performance: 26 March 1933, Berlin Philharmonic Orchestra, conducted by Wilhelm Furtwängler, Berlin
Performing forces: 3.3.2.3.–alto saxophone–4.3.3.1.–cymbals, tam-tam, bass drum–strings. N.B. The composer prefers if possible a double bass clarinet to a contrabassoon.
Duration: 9 minutes 40 seconds
Salabert

Honegger's *Symphonic Movement No. 3* is structurally and formally much simpler than *Pacific 2.3.1* or *Rugby*, but it remains relatively unknown due to the composer's self-professed "lack of imagination" over its title. In its broad sweep, it looks forward to the symphonies, and if the Allegro seems to mark the end of the preceding period, the long lament of the Adagio begins a series that will end in the central movement of the *Fifth Symphony* and especially of *Monopartita*. It had already been prefigured in the Postlude to *Amphion*, both in this respect and in the use of the saxophone (which Honegger rarely employed in his purely orchestral works but frequently in his stage works and oratorios). It occupies a rather lonely place in the depths of the great depression at the beginning of the 1930s, but nothing of this comes through in the technique or the inspiration. G. K. Spratt even goes so far as to regard it as the best orchestral work Honegger had written up to this point. It is also the only work written to a commission from Germany, with the exception of the music he wrote a little later for the movie *The Demon of the Himalayas* (H93).

The Allegro marcato is in very simple ternary form, and at the beginning of its first section (measures 1–67) two measures of violent scales introduce its principal subject, establishing the key of C-sharp minor (Example 89). It is one of Honegger's finest and most powerfully etched themes, virile and energetic, with its modulations typically passing through minor keys and describing a perfectly symmetrical cycle. The main tune is repeated in the double basses under an equally impassioned countersubject on violins. A jerky, dissonant chordal theme with iambic accents establishes a 3/4 meter inside the 4/4 and this looks forward to the central section B, the theme of which is also anticipated. But before this, a sudden *piano* (the first) ushers in a fluid, atonal, almost twelve-tone figure in a livid woodwind unison. This precedes the second theme proper, which is a long lyrical theme on violins.

Example 89

The middle section (poco più pesante in 3/4, measures 68–114) is built around a horn theme that, in its insolent defiance, recalls the "Entry of the Horatii" in *Horace victorieux*, over heavy accents on strings. It is then repeated in triple stretto, and this polyphonic working is taken over by the whole orchestra. Following a familiar Honeggerian pattern, it turns into an ostinato, and a dissolve leads into the varied, extended recapitulation of the first part (measures 115–195). During this, an irresistible crescendo builds up until the tutti at measure 182, which is the high point of the work, superimposing the principal theme (Example 89) in stretto, the theme of the central part, and other motifs. The tension accumulated by this prodigious machinery is resolved by a series of explosions marked by trombone glissandos and separated by ever more widely spaced silences.

At this point the Adagio supervenes (measures 196–244). This vast epilogue, a long lament once more in C-sharp minor, is almost a movement in itself. The saxophone theme, taken up at length by the other instruments, is one of the composer's finest melodic inventions; Example 90 shows the beginning. In his favorite manner, Honegger surrounds it with various fragments of themes from the Allegro marcato, and Example 89 is even heard complete in quicker note values. The brief, cold, skeletal coda at measure 237 is a veritable death agony of sound, prefiguring the "conclusion muffled as though in terror" of the *Fifth Symphony*.

Example 90

92. *Radio-Panoramique*—symphonic movement

January 1935
For Geneva Radio on the tenth anniversary of its foundation
First performance: 4 March 1935, various soloists, Suisse Romande Orchestra, conducted by Hermann Scherchen, Salle du Conservatoire, Geneva
Performing forces: 1.1.1.1.–alto saxophone–1.1.1.0.–timpani, bass drum, cymbals, side drum, tenor drum, piano, organ, soprano and tenor soloists, mixed choir–strings (the choir and organ are optional)
Duration: 9 minutes
Unpublished

Radio-Panoramique is another "symphonic movement," but very different from its predecessors. The subtitle hardly seems appropriate, and indeed Honegger did not give it the number 4! A lighthearted little piece, it treats with humor the subject that had been taken seriously in *Cris du monde* and would be again in the *Nocturne for orchestra* discussed below. That subject is noise pollution, and the invasion by noise of solitude and man's inner world. The butt of the satire here is a radio station of the kind that commissioned the piece, with listeners endlessly trying to find a different station, or merely distressed by the vagaries of fading signals.

The piece consists of a true collage, which nowadays could be achieved by juxtaposing strips of tape. The combination of brevity and large forces has ensured that the work has been excluded from the normal repertory. Here, in crazy succession, are a popular ditty, a jazz tune, a serious Protestant chorale for choir and organ (this was for Geneva Radio, let us remember), on the same intentionally idiotic words that will serve for the other sung passages, some Oriental bazaar music, a slow, sleepy waltz, a classical organ solo, an equally classical passage for string quartet, an imposing tenor aria, a romantic piano cadenza, a cabaret song that the organ deigns to join, and heaven knows what else. This riotous potpourri ends with sensational violin glissandos.

102. Nocturne for orchestra

March 1936
"To Hermann Scherchen"
First performance: 30 April 1936, Brussels, conducted by Hermann Scherchen
Performing forces: 3.3.3.3.–saxophone–4.3.0.1.–triangle, cymbals, woodblock, side
    drum, rattle, tambourine–harp–strings (one of the trumpets is a high trumpet in
    D)
Duration: 8 minutes
N.B. The entire central section (measures 32–208) is the First Interlude from
    Sémiramis (H85, Category 13)
Boosey and Hawkes

The *Nocturne for orchestra* is one of the most unjustly neglected of Honegger's works. It is contemporary with *String Quartet No. 2* and *String Quartet No. 3* and is the only purely orchestral work written between the *Symphonic Movement No. 3* and the *Symphony for Strings*. It is a perfect little piece in the familiar A-B-A' form, with A' being abbreviated and including echoes of B, which is itself a scherzo-type intermezzo in concentric form.

Of the title, Honegger said to his friend Arthur Hoérée:

It is a night of repose, such as one would like to spend in the countryside. But this ideal is quickly shattered by the reality of nighttime in the city— hence the fast middle part. After all the excitement, a desire for calm brings back the opening theme as a conclusion.

The first section is in A major, but over a pedal sixth (measures 1–31). It is close to being a pastoral reverie, and in this the tonality is a help just as it would prove to be in the first movement of the *Fourth Symphony*. Divided violins weave a pattern of three chromatic ostinatos, alternating in dialogue with a tranquil saxophone line and a long tune on flute and oboe. Suddenly, a brisk interruption on woodwinds disturbs the serenity. What follows (measures 32–208) is the middle section mentioned by Honegger (taken directly from the First Interlude from the ballet *Sémiramis*, written three years earlier). The saxophone line is transformed into an irritating motif on muted trumpet, whose ostinato aggressiveness destroys the peaceful atmosphere. It is the incarnation of the city, passing from one instrument to another like an annoying mosquito and refusing to go away.

Then comes a kind of caricature of jazz, with a tuba doing a waddling elephantine dance (replacing the ondes Martenot of *Sémiramis*). The "mosquito" returns in force with support from the woodblock, and the tension mounts. Suddenly, we are back with the calm music of the opening (measures 209–230), interrupted ever more feebly by the irritating trumpet motif. This is finally transformed back into the gentle saxophone motif from which it grew, and which seems almost to anticipate Example 54 from the *Fourth Symphony*. The violins' chromatic ostinato has the final word.

105. *Largo for string orchestra*

September 1936
Duration: 2 minutes 30 seconds
Salabert

A letter to Paul Sacher of 19 September 1936 allows us to identify this short piece of fifty-six measures as the first, abortive attempt at the future *Symphony for Strings*. It was never used again. Even though it is so short, its rich, complex, and dissonant harmonies would make it well worth playing on its own. It may be heard as a modest anticipation of the impressive chordal counterpoint at the start of the *Fifth Symphony*.

107. *Les Mille et Une Nuits* (The Thousand and One Nights)

December 1936–3 January 1937
For the Festival of Light and Water on the Seine, as part of the Paris Universal
    Exhibition of 1937
Text by Dr. Jean-Claude Mardrus, after *The Arabian Nights*
First performance: 9 July 1937, Germaine Cernay, Édouard Kriff, orchestra
    conducted by Gustave Cloëz, on the banks of the Seine (relayed by
    loudspeakers)
First concert performance: 4 December 1937, conducted by Robert Siohan,
    Concerts Poulet, Paris
Performing forces: soprano, tenor; 2.0.2.2.–3 saxophones–0.3.3.0.–piano, celesta,
    harp–anvil, cymbals, rattle, side drum, tenor drum, tam-tam, triangle,
    woodblock–4 ondes Martenot–10 violins, 6 violas, 6 cellos—43 players in all
Duration: 22 minutes
Unpublished (on rental from Salabert)

Since it was conceived for open-air performance, *Les Mille et Une Nuits* is perhaps the least easily classifiable of Honegger's works. Even though the two voices are often active, they generally confine themselves to commenting briefly on the images suggested by the music, so that it certainly cannot be classed as one of the cantatas. The orchestration is light and original in texture, and shows Honegger's short-lived interest in color, as in the ballets of these years (*Sémiramis*, *Le Cantique des cantiques*, *La Naissance des couleurs*). Even if it is not a major work, it makes very agreeable listening. It consists in effect of a succession of sound images in the style of high-class atmosphere music, with the occasional touch of witty Orientalism. It is the product of a seasoned professional who, at the time, was turning out film and stage scores in considerable quantity.

162. *Le Grand Barrage*—musical image

6 December 1942
First performance: 4 January 1943 (recording)
Performing forces: 3.3.3.3.–4.3.3.0.–harp, celesta–bass drum, tam-tam, cymbals,
    triangle–strings
Duration: 4 minutes
Salabert

We do not know the occasion for which Honegger wrote this short piece, but in spite of the fact that *Le Grand Barrage* is scored for very large orchestra, it may well have been written for the cinema, especially as his diary mentions a "recording." It may possibly have been one of the "pieces for France-Actualités" mentioned in his manuscript catalog. It is a brief, evocative, coloristic, and glowingly orchestrated diptych. After a somber, majestic first section comes a luminous, glistening second section. Each section contains a broad melody. It is a fine piece, close in style to a fresco like *Mermoz*.

182. Sérénade à Angélique

15 October 1945, Paris
"For Beromünster" (commissioned by German Swiss Radio)
First performance: 19 November 1945, Zurich Radio Orchestra, conducted by
    Hermann Scherchen
Performing forces: 1.1.1.1.–saxophone–2.1.1.0.–harp–side drum, suspended cymbal–
    strings
Duration: 6 minutes 30 seconds
Salabert

A delightful piece, *Sérénade à Angélique* is a genuine example of light music and totally unpretentious, even if fashioned with a master's skill. It is a homage to his friend Jacques Ibert and to his opera *Angélique*, in which the heroine defies her name by tyrannizing her husband Boniface in the most appalling fashion. He tries in vain to rid himself of her by putting her up for sale! The tripping accompaniment introduces the main theme, which is popular in character, and its imperturbable placidity alternates with music that is polytonal and spicy in no very serious way. The underlying tonality of E-flat major is never in doubt.

The orchestration throughout is marvelous and the bassoon plays a particularly important role. The parodistic element is evident in a number of passages: in a dolorous trombone recitative in grand opera style, in a Larghetto in which short phrases on the saxophone (un poco troppo espressivo) are heard over a jazz accompaniment, in a short but riotously polytonal passage in 6/8, and in a mini-recapitulation of the opening. This latter is punctuated by *lagrimando* sighs from the violins before coming to an ironic, understated conclusion. But, just before the Molto vivace in 6/8, Honegger gives us seven measures of pure poetry, which seem to have been taken from the future *Fourth Symphony*. They are in A major, too!

203. Suite archaïque (Archaic Suite) in E minor

December 1950–January 1951 (first movement: 17 December 1951; second
    movement: January 1951; third movement: December 1950; fourth movement:
    15 January 1951)
"Dedicated to the Louisville Philharmonic Society" (commissioned by the Louisville
    Orchestra)
First performance: 28 February 1951, Louisville Symphony Orchestra, conducted by
    Robert Whitney, Louisville (Kentucky)
First European performance: 7 March 1952, Collegium Musicum of Zurich,
    conducted by Paul Sacher, Zurich

Performing forces: 2.2.2.2.–0.2.2.0.–strings
Duration: 14 minutes (4:30 + 2:00 + 3:30 + 4:00)
Salabert

The *Suite archaïque* is certainly the feeblest and least inspired of the three works in Honegger's final orchestral trilogy. At times he seems to be using up discards that had not found a place in the *Fifth Symphony*. The composer even described it as "merde" (shit) in one of his letters. (We may recall that the ever unsatisfied Albéric Magnard would call all his works "ordures" [garbage] and even gave them numbers as such!) But that would obviously be going rather too far in this case, since certain passages are well up to Honegger's standard. The two outer movements are both ritual and hieratic in tone, and sparse and emaciated in texture. Their material is very alike, too, and in earlier days Honegger would never have allowed two such similar movements to appear in the same work. And yet, for all its spare bitterness, the *Suite archaïque* is not without a certain grandeur, and its third movement breathes a very individual atmosphere.

The musical language is predominantly modal and diatonic, but includes a number of rough dissonances. The orchestra is not very large and does not include horns—a decision made, as at the beginning of the *Fifth Symphony*, with a view to eliminating anything that might smooth over the abrupt asceticism of the texture. The title is explained in strictly musical terms by the presence of characteristically modal cadences. The composer commented further: "I rather imagine this suite as a festival taking place in an unknown country long ago."

1. The Overture (largamente; modal on E)

Entirely homophonic, the Overture becomes rather wearisome at this slow tempo. The form is simple ternary, and the "archaic" effect is due also to antiphonal groups of woodwinds, brass, and strings answering each other in the manner of the sixteenth-century Venetian *cori spezzati*. The central section quotes two phrases from Psalm 143, which are taken (like the *Three Psalms* of 1940–1941) from the Huguenot Psalter, and harmonized in four parts on muted brass in a pure counterpoint worthy of Bach.

2. The Pantomime (presto; 3/8 in B minor)

A light-footed Scherzo that is over in a flash. Surprisingly, its origins can be traced to the sketch for a Scherzo in the first, 1913 version of the *String Quartet No. 1*, the manuscript of which was covered with orchestral indications. Other ideas seem to have come from the second movement of the *Fifth Symphony*. The 3/8 meter is often blurred by disjointed rhythms. Brief as it is, the movement exploits no less than five different kinds of material, arranged in a more or less concentric pattern: pizzicatos, flutter-tonguing on flutes and trombones, nimble sixteenth-notes, violent chords, and finally, as a mini-Trio, a charming modal tune alternating between flute and oboe.

3. Ritornello and Serenade (Andantino, più lento, rubato; G major)

Without a doubt the most attractive of the four movements, with its delightful and memorable modal ritornello (Example 91). This alternates three times with a recitative for cello, viola, and violin solo successively (for some reason, Honegger calls these recitatives "Serenades"). These recitatives are slightly reminiscent of late Bartók, both in their rhythmic shaping (although the iambic rhythm was also one of Honegger's favorite fingerprints) and in the way the other strings provide a tremolo background. The final return of the ritornello unexpectedly cadences in A minor, with a final falling pizzicato fifth from B to E. One is perhaps reminded of the conclusion to Satie's *Socrate*.

Example 91

4. Processional (Largo)

In the Processional, we return to the musical ideas of the Overture, now in a different orchestration. Honegger adds unison scales in sixteenth-note sextuplets but, instead of the Huguenot chorale, we now have a dozen measures of modal but modulating polyphony for strings alone (measures 17–28). Here, suddenly, is Honegger at his greatest. The final chord, like that of the Overture, confirms E major.

204. *Monopartita* in F-sharp minor

Mid-February–end of March 1951 (composition completed 15 March; orchestration
    completed 26 March)
"Dedicated to the Zurich Tonhalle Society." Commissioned by the Tonhalle for the
    600th anniversary of Zurich's entry into the Swiss Confederation
First performance: 12 June 1951, Orchestra of the Tonhalle, conducted by Hans
    Rosbaud, Zurich
Performing forces: 2.3.3.2.–4.3.3.0.–timpani–strings
Duration: 12 minutes
Salabert

Honegger's native city of Zurich certainly took its time in honoring him with this, its first and only commission from him. *Monopartita* is one of the most undervalued of contemporary masterpieces and provides a fine conclusion to Honegger's career as an orchestral composer—as a composer, indeed, since all the music in *Une Cantate de Noël* dates from 1941 or earlier. It is clearly from the same stable ("from the same barrel," as Ernest Ansermet used to say) as the *Fifth Symphony*. In fact, there was enough material here to make a sixth symphony, but it literally "imploded," as *Antigone* had imploded a quarter of a century earlier, and turned into one of Honegger's most powerfully concentrated compositions.

The musical invention, whether of granitelike grandeur or overwhelming emotion, is of the highest caliber throughout. As for the slightly curious title, Honegger explained: "It may seem contradictory, since the prefix *mono-* means single, while *partita* refers to a collection of movements. In fact, it does consist of a collection of pieces, but they are linked and form a whole."

The structure is very simple: Introduction–Allegro–Recitative–Adagio–Continuation of the Allegro–Continuation of the Adagio–Recitative–Repeat of the Introduction as a conclusion. The tonal plan is, for Honegger, exceptionally classical, with the subdominant B minor being used for the Allegros and the dominant C-sharp minor for the Adagios. Note also the restricted but crucial role of the two timpani, playing the notes F-sharp and A. There is no other percussion.

In the opening Largo (measures 1–21), one is struck immediately by the importance of Honegger's favorite dotted rhythms, sometimes double dotted, whether iambic or trochaic. These give this initial majestic statement the air of a French overture (Example 92). The long unison lines of the strings establish a gray horizon of F-sharp, broken by dotted caesuras upon which the brass build their dissonant, chordal counterpoint. This arrangement of instruments is reversed for a shorter repeat in C minor, and in a darker hue. Hard on this follows the Allegro marcato (measures 22–92), a toccata in triple rhythm, beginning with a clear statement of Example 93 on timpani. The entire beginning of this violent, hot-headed piece is a reworking of the "Panic Dance" from the incidental music for Aeschylus's *The Suppliants*, written in 1941 (H149).

Secondary motifs are now developed, leading to an impassioned, anguished chromatic call on strings. The music comes to rest on a strident dissonant chord held by the woodwinds, acting as a *fortissimo* pedal point, and this leads to a dramatic Recitative (measures 93–111), gradually giving rise to a jolting descending dotted motif. The final form of this serves as an accompaniment for the sublime lament of the Adagio (measures 112–143, Example 94). This is one of Honegger's most touching cries from the heart. With its finely crafted modulations, the music here creates an atmosphere very close to that of the Andante of the *Concerto da camera*.

The second Allegro (measures 144–227) is a kind of extended development of the first. One of its passages (measures 171–187) is extraordinarily close, both in its line and in its harmonies with added leading-tone, to a fragment from the Scherzo of Bruckner's *Ninth Symphony*. This link is practically unique in Honegger's output.

It is impossible here to describe every detail of the polyphonic texture. Like the second Allegro, the second Adagio (measures 229–259) is a development of the first, with much use of canon. The second Recitative is very short (mea-

Example 92

Example 93

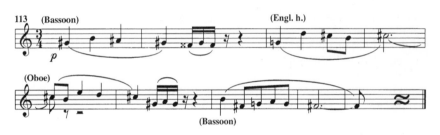

Example 94

sures 260–265) and focuses on three measures of "ghostly" arpeggios on *pianissimo* strings, preparing the final return of the Largo in measures 266–279. This repeat is a condensed, shadowy version of the initial music, like the recapitulation in the first movement of the *Fifth Symphony*. The woodwinds are silent, the brass muted, and the whole work ends, again like the *Fifth Symphony*, on low, unison pizzicatos, with timpani tapping out the minor third (A–F-sharp) shown in Example 93.

207. *Toccata on a Theme of Campra*

November 1951
The first number in a composite work, *La Guirlande de Campra*, based on a theme from André Campra's opera *Camille*. The other contributors were Daniel-Lesur, Roland-Manuel, Tailleferre, Poulenc, Sauguet, and Auric

First performance (of the whole work): 21 July 1952, Conservatory Concert Society Orchestra, conducted by Hans Rosbaud, Aix-en-Provence Festival
Performing forces: 2.2.2.2.–2.2.0.0.–strings
Duration: 1 minute 30 seconds
Salabert

This little Allegro moderato in G major lasts a mere forty-one measures. It is a charming bagatelle and contents itself with decorating the sarabande rondo theme with quick running sixteenth-notes.

218. Chevauchée

Date and destination unknown. Possibly a piece of incidental music or, more likely, film music
Performing forces: 1.1.1.1.–saxophone–0.2.2.0.–piano–tenor drum, bass drum–strings
Duration: without repeat, 1 minute 50 seconds; with repeat, 3 minutes 20 seconds
Unpublished

219. Pathétique

Date and destination unknown. Possibly a piece of incidental music or, more likely, film music
Performing forces: 1.1.1.1.–0.2.1.0.–piano–cymbals, bass drum–strings
Duration: 2 minutes 10 seconds
Unpublished

These two pieces are perhaps extracts from film music now lost. The second piece sounds rather like a signature tune.

220. Vivace (Dance)

Date and destination unknown. The composition of the orchestra, the character of the music, and the presence in the blank spaces of the autograph of counterpoint exercises seem to point to a date before the summer of 1918. It could be a fragment of a ballet or of incidental music.
Performing forces: 1.1.2.2.–2.0.0.0.–timpani–strings
Duration: 3 minutes 30 seconds
Salabert

Vivace (Dance) is a good piece, far more interesting than the preceding two, and deserves to be played more often. With its almost popular, direct expression, it would fit well as the Scherzo of some sinfonietta or chamber symphony. Its meter is 6/8, its key G minor. The form is that of a sonata with two themes, containing a short central development section, a normal recapitulation (beginning with the first theme), and a tiny coda.

221. *Allegretto*

Date and destination unknown
Performing forces: flute, oboe, English horn, clarinet, bassoon, 2 trumpets, strings
Duration: 1 minute 55 seconds
Salabert

The handwriting and layout of the autograph of *Allegretto* suggest a date not earlier than 1937–1938. The character and orchestration of the music do not suggest that it was written for a film. Perhaps it forms part of one of the lost ballets, such as *Le Mangeur de rêves* or *De la musique*. It is complete and has recently been published.

It is a very attractive little character piece in E-flat major, almost counting as light music. It is in ternary form with a coda.

Category 7A: Orchestral Works from Stage and Film

Into this category come works of a wide diversity of origin and importance, although all of them, originally written for stage or screen, are suitable for concert performance. For the most part, they are suites or extracts chosen or arranged by the composer himself with this in mind. The two exceptions are undoubtedly the two most important works in this category: *Le Dit des jeux du monde* and *Horace victorieux*. They are included here because their real career has taken place away from the stage. As for the film music, to the suites from *Les Misérables*, *Regain*, and *Mermoz* (all created by Honegger himself), I have added all that remains from his work for silent films, *La Roue* and *Napoléon*—two works that have also made a name for themselves through concerts and recordings.

It would certainly be possible to make concert pieces out of a number of other fragments from his ballets, and from his stage and film music. We shall discuss these possibilities when dealing with the works in question. For the moment only a few works on this long list justify a detailed analysis. The most obvious of these, apart from *Le Dit des jeux du monde* and *Horace victorieux*, already mentioned, are the triptych *Prelude, Fugue, Postlude* from *Amphion* (one of the composer's most powerful orchestral works) and the extracts from *Phaedra*, an impressively dramatic but unjustly neglected score. We should be absolutely clear on one point: all these works have value as pure music, on par with those discussed in the preceding sections. The only distinction between them lies in their origins.

19. *Le Dit des jeux du monde*

May–6 November 1918 (No. 1: undated; Nos. 2, 7, 9: August; No. 3: September; Nos. 4, 5: May; No. 6: June; Nos. 5, 6: completed in August; No. 8: July–August; Nos. 10, 13: October; No. 11: August–September; No. 12: end of October–6 November)
Ten Dances, two Interludes, and an Epilogue for chamber orchestra, for the poem by Paul Méral
"To Fernand Ochsé"
First stage performance: 2 December 1918, sets and costumes by Guy-Pierre Fauconnet, conducted by Walther Straram, Théâtre du Vieux-Colombier, Paris
First concert performance: 4 January 1921, Golschmann Orchestra, conducted by Vladimir Golschmann, Salle Gaveau, Paris
Performing forces: flute (and piccolo), trumpet, 4 percussionists (timpani, bass drum, cymbals, side drum, bouteillophone or triangle), 4 violins, 2 violas, 2 cellos, 2 double basses—16 players in all
Duration (music only): 45 minutes 10 seconds
Salabert

The evening's entertainment contains three quarters of an hour of music and it was, for all that it employs a small orchestra, by far the largest and most ambitious project completed by Honegger up to that time. After the *String Quartet No. 1*, which summed up his early years, and *Le Chant de Nigamon*, his first accomplished orchestral work, *Le Dit des jeux du monde* opens up a new period of experiment that would be taken further in *Horace victorieux*. The text by the young Belgian poet Paul Méral is somewhat cloudy and overblown in its post-symbolist pretensions, so the work is probably no longer viable in its original form (excerpts from the composer's letters, quoted in the biographical chapters of this book, give some idea of this). But when we listen again to the music by itself, we may recall that the scandal of December 1918 was due above all to the staging. As had happened with *The Rite of Spring*, there were no problems at all on the occasion of the first concert performance in January 1921. Even the movements for percussion alone seem quite acceptable beside Milhaud's *Choéphores* or *L'homme et son désir* (both of which had been written earlier, even if they had not yet been performed at the time). It seems unlikely that Honegger knew these pieces, given that Milhaud was with Claudel in Brazil and also that Honegger's work still contains elements drawn from the romantic tradition, especially in the slow, lyrical movements.

Most Honegger commentators find in *Le Dit des jeux du monde* traces of Stravinsky's influence. Despite the role of the percussion, nothing could be further from the truth. On the contrary, no work of Honegger's is nearer to Schoenberg in his free atonal period, and perhaps to Berg as well (although little of his music was known at the time). These influences show up also in *Horace victorieux*, while the atonality in *Antigone* would be of an altogether different character.

Le Dit des jeux du monde remains one of Honegger's most fascinating scores, even if it is impossible to classify it either as a ballet, a piece of music theater, or an audio-visual poem. It is in fact a work that contains elements of them all. The table below sets out the instrumental dispositions for each of the movements. In this respect, it is vital not to expand the double string quintet to the dimensions of a string orchestra, as is done sometimes:

umbers	1	2	3	4	5	6	7	8	9	10	11	12	13
ute	x		x	x	x			x	x	x	x (piccolo)	x	x
rumpet	x		x	x	x			x	x	x		x	x
rings	x		x	x	x			x	x	x		x	x
rcussion		x		x	x	x	x		x		x	x	

1. "LE SOLEIL ET LA FLEUR" (THE SUN AND THE FLOWER)

A lyrical, largely atonal movement, with two ideas: the first on the flute, the second on the trumpet.

2. "LA MONTAGNE ET LES PIERRES" (THE MOUNTAIN AND THE STONES)

A brief triptych for percussion instruments alone.

3. "L'ENFANT ET LA MER" (THE CHILD AND THE SEA)

A very beautiful movement, beginning with a flute recitative. Even if the cantabile polyphony of the strings is highly chromatic, it remains fixed around the dominant of A major.

4. "L'HOMME TOURNANT SUR LE SOL" (MAN REVOLVING ON THE GROUND)

This is the first movement involving the full complement of instruments, and its power and sweep are truly symphonic. The introduction heavily stresses the tonic C, the earthly attraction of which the music tries to escape. Soon we hear a passionate theme on viola (repeated on muted trumpet), which will be the most important in the movement. But the whole central section is a brilliantly scored dance in 9/8 meter, in the sudden light of E major, with decorative runs on piccolo. The coda is broad but violent, with the trumpet proclaiming the opening of the theme three times.

5. "L'HOMME FOU" (THE MADMAN)–FIRST INTERMEZZO

Here Honegger introduces the bouteillophone, an instrument of his own invention and one he subsequently used often. Made of tuned bottles, it is a modern adaptation of the *Glasharmonica* (glass harmonica) employed by Gluck and Mozart. The gay and lively toccata theme in D major (Example 95) is very typical of the composer and passes from one instrument and from one key to another.

Example 95

6. "LES HOMMES ET LE VILLAGE" (MEN AND THE VILLAGE)

The held superimposed string chords of the introduction create an atmosphere of mystery. Then follows a broad cantus firmus on trumpet, preceding a wonderful passage of post-romantic polyphony on strings that looks back to Schoenberg's *Transfigured Night* (a similar passage occurs earlier, in "L'enfant et la mer"). A tumultuous central episode full of ostinatos leads to the return in reverse order of the ideas already heard.

7. "LES HOMMES ET LA TERRE" (MEN AND THE EARTH)

This second movement for percussion alone begins with a slow introduction, after which we hear a "tala" of the timpani and bass drum and, on the bouteillophone, a rhythm consisting of eighth-notes, eighth-note triplets, and sixteenth-notes. The two elements alternate and are then superimposed, producing a gradual crescendo that continues uninterrupted until the end of the movement.

8. "L'HOMME ET LA FEMME" (MAN AND WOMAN)

The percussion is silent in this extraordinary Adagio—a movement that is a single entity and one of the young Honegger's greatest achievements. The wild, exacerbated chromaticism derives ultimately from *Tristan*, via early Schoenberg and even Scriabin. It is a piece of pure German expressionism such as nobody in France has written, either then or since. The movement is atonal, but F-sharp major is vaguely hinted at from the start and the piece ends in this key. Of the two chromatic themes, the first (Example 96), representing Man, is heard immediately on cellos alone, while the second (Example 97), representing Woman, is heard only after a gradation on violins. The second section brings with it a brusque outburst of passion, the most carnal, "sexual" music Honegger ever wrote: a cry of desire from the Woman is heard on cellos and an aggressively erotic cry from the Man on trumpet, in the manner of Scriabin. This is an abbreviated form of Example 96 (Example 97 is a kind of mirror of this), and panting syncopated string figures form a background to the whole.

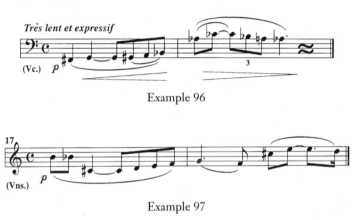

Example 96

Example 97

Suddenly, in the *pianissimo subito* of the coda, we reach a luminous, blissful fulfillment, with violins playing a theme that is a sort of fusion of the two heard earlier. A series of continually prolonged and postponed resolvent cadences leads to the final chord of F-sharp major (plus second and fourth), upon which the sated lovers finally break free of each other. In a mere sixty-three measures, the young Honegger has produced one of the great erotic passages in all music. But who knows it?

9. "L'HOMME QUI LUTTE ET CONDUIT" (MAN STRUGGLING AND DRIVING)–SECOND INTERMEZZO

Only the interdependent first and last sections are in C-sharp minor, while the rest of the movement is atonal. After the introduction, the slow, sad procession sounds like a description of Golaud in Debussy's *Pelléas et Mélisande* or, even more, like part of *The Martyrdom of Saint Sebastian*, with its similarly bitter dissonances. From this springs a somber, savage dance, to jerky stampings broken by abrupt halts like pedal points. The procession is repeated before the conclusion.

10. "L'HOMME ET L'OMBRE" (MAN AND THE SHADOW)

The shadow takes the form of a canon and this movement, which is another long, slow, expressionist movement in the tradition of Schoenberg, is a triumph of canonic writing in which there is no hint of academic dryness. The winner of the second mention in counterpoint at the Paris Conservatory reveals himself as a precocious master of technique. The opening of the main theme is easily remembered thanks to its initial ascending leap of a seventh. The sound of the ending looks forward to the last chord of the Andante of the *Concerto da camera* (a trumpet playing low and quietly sounds very like an English horn).

11. "LE RAT ET LA MORT" (THE RAT AND DEATH)

Rolls on the bass drum serve as a background for the extraordinary piccolo solo, the opening of which might be mistaken for a passage from Edgard Varèse's *Octandre* of 1923. This is then developed with its intervals expanded. A new protagonist, the side drum (death) pursues the rat/piccolo, catches it, and joins with it in perfect synchronization. When the side drum stops, it is because it no longer needs to persecute its victim, whose death agony is depicted at the end of the movement. Throughout, dull rolls on the bass drum continue unconcernedly.

12. "L'HOMME ET LA MER" (MAN AND THE SEA)

This piece is one of the most symphonic and yet simplest movements; it is all of a piece. Above a chromatic swell on strings is heard a long trumpet tune based on C minor. The contours are highlit by shrieks from the piccolo and, in striking anticipation of the *Prelude* for *The Tempest* (H48A), the music evokes the unleashing of the elements. The end conjures the power of a full orchestra.

13. EPILOGUE

Only ten measures long, the epilogue does not reach a conclusion but remains suspended on a complex, unresolved dissonance, followed by a long, unbroken silence.

20A. *Interlude* from *La Mort de Sainte Alméenne*

Honegger worked on *La Mort de Sainte Alméenne* until December 1918, leaving the orchestration unfinished; he took from it this *Interlude*, which he then orchestrated, probably shortly before its first performance in October 1920
First performance: 30 October 1920, Colonne Orchestra, conducted by Gabriel Pierné, Théâtre du Châtelet, Paris
Performing forces: 1.1.2.2.–2.1.0.0.–strings
Duration: 5 minutes
Salabert. A manuscript note ("No. 25. Prisons") suggests that it may have been used later as music for a stage production or film

Honegger took the original Interlude between the two scenes of the little opera *La Mort de Sainte Alméenne* and added to it the first five measures of the second scene and the last six measures of the whole work. This is the Honegger of *Aglavaine et Sélysette*—Honegger, the doting, even slavish admirer of Debussy. The form of the piece is ternary with a coda. It seems never to have been replayed after its first hearing in 1920, at least until 1992.

35. *La Noce massacrée* (The Ruined Wedding) from *Les Mariés de la tour Eiffel* (The Couple Married on the Eiffel Tower)

February 1921
No. 7 of the ten movements in this collective work by five of Les Six (Louis Durey did not contribute), text by Jean Cocteau
First performance: 18 June 1921, Rolf de Maré's Ballets Suédois, conducted by D. E. Inghelbrecht, Théâtre des Champs-Élysées, Paris
Performing forces: 2.2.2.2.–2.2.3.1.–timpani, muffled side drums, cymbals, bass drum–strings
Duration: 3 minutes 40 seconds
Salabert

La Noce massacrée is no more than a bagatelle, but even so Honegger's concern for craft ensures that it is nonetheless both beautifully written and superbly orchestrated. It is a funeral march for the old general, proud of his exploits, who is swallowed by a lion. This was the only stage work on which members of Les Six collaborated, on a text by their friend and spokesman Jean Cocteau. The introduction gathers up all the traditional clichés of a funeral march, to be followed by a deliberately old-fashioned tune, then by a whimpering violin solo. In the final solemn apotheosis for full orchestra, this is superimposed on a version of the waltz from *Faust*, stripped of its rhythm, on the double basses.

38. *Horace victorieux* (Horace Triumphant)—Symphonie mimée

November 1920–18 February 1921; orchestration completed August 1921
"To Serge Koussevitzky"
Ballet-pantomime by Guy-Pierre Fauconnet, based on Livy
First performance (in concert): 31 October 1921, Suisse Romande Orchestra, conducted by Ernest Ansermet, Lausanne
First staged performance: 11 January 1928 (or 28 December 1927), production and choreography by Jans Keith, conducted by R. Schulz-Dornburg, Stadttheater, Essen (Germany)
Performing forces: 3.3.3.3.–4.3.3.1.–timpani, cymbals, bass drum, side drum, tam-tam, rattle–harp–strings
Duration: 18 minutes
Salabert

Horace victorieux was written just before *Le Roi David* but orchestrated after it. Even though it figures in the recording catalog or in concerts only scantily, it is certainly Honegger's most important orchestral work next to the five symphonies. It is his most radical and daring masterpiece, and the furthest he would go in his approach to atonality, even if tonal substrata remain perceptible, together with tonic and, especially, dominant functions.

There are two families of themes, and therefore two sorts of music. On the one hand, there are lyrical, expressionist slow passages, in which the chromaticism and wide melodic leaps recall the Second Viennese School—they derive too from the slow movements of *Le Dit des jeux du monde*, but have become much tougher and more experimental. Example 98 shows a characteristic example. On the other hand, there are passages of athletic, violent, fast music that is brutally rhythmic rather in the manner of *The Rite of Spring*. These can be found earlier in *Le Chant de Nigamon*, which also contains very wide intervals. Here, though, they have a different, physical, sporty significance that looks forward to *Rugby*. *Horace victorieux* is also a veritable mine of information in terms of the study of Honegger's harmony, with its reliance on added notes and *acciaccaturas*. The introduction, a mere five measures long, leads to a solid construction in eight episodes. Although these episodes are tied to the stage action, there are a number of links and reminiscences between them.

Example 98

INTRODUCTION

The Introduction is a brief, violent gesture affirming the dominant of C minor, which will (at least by implication) be the tonic key. Then comes a piling-up of brass in the manner of Varèse, forming an eight-note chord of tritons and perfect fourths. The four missing notes of the chromatic spectrum are to be found in the harmonics of the following movement.

1. "CAMILLE ET CURIACE" (TRÈS LENT; MEASURES 6–83)

This great love scene between Camilla and Curiatius is a grippingly intense and expressionist Adagio. It consists of an introduction, followed by a sonata structure typical of Honegger, with reversed and abbreviated recapitulation. The introduction sets the scene of a cool, airy dawn, on the horizon of which appears a viola solo (the theme of Camilla in love). This spreads to the whole string section in a wonderful wide-leaping, atonal melody (Example 98) worthy of Alban Berg—who was still working on *Wozzeck* at this time. After a crescendo, we hear the theme of Curiatius at measure 35, again on violas. The basic cell of this theme will recur in the Curiatii fanfare in the fourth section of the work, when it will be integrated into their collective identity. The powerful central development section culminates in dramatic syncopations.

2. "ENTRÉE DES HORACES" (RYTHMIQUE; MEASURES 84–124)

The Entry of the Horatii introduces music of the second type defined above. The Horatii are all biceps and bulging muscles and stride past to an exaggeratedly dotted motif (Example 99). This is presented in a series of four fugal entries (their old father is leading the procession!).

Example 99

3. "ENTRÉE DE LA FOULE PRÉCÉDANT LES HÉRAUTS" (ASSEZ ANIMÉ; MEASURES 125–155)

The Entry of the Crowd Preceding the Heralds is a confused jostling, shot through with fanfares, leading via a crescendo to the following episode.

4. "ANNONCE ET PRÉPARATIFS DU COMBAT" (UN PEU PLUS LENT; MEASURES 156–219)

The two rival fanfares of the Horatii (underpinned by the rumbling dotted motif of Example 99) and the Curiatii confront one another in the Announcement and Preparations for the Combat. Both fanfares are for three voices (corresponding to the number of protagonists). Then the adversaries defy each other, stamping their feet to an astonishing rhythmic motif (recalling the warriors depicted in the works of the Swiss painter Ferdinand Hodler) amid bellicose sounds with brutal accents on the brass. The combat is preceded by a passage of calm (measure 204) that brings back Camilla's theme in canon between bassoon and viola.

5. "LE COMBAT" (TRÈS ANIMÉ; MEASURES 220–321)

The Combat is the heart of the work, and the first of its three sections presents an athletic theme, derived from the Hodlerian idea and punctuated by offbeat accents that call to mind blows from clubs and swords. A rapid crescendo ends in a *fortissimo* marking the fall and death of the first of the Horatii (measure 240). The second phase of the combat (measures 244–262) is faster and more breathless, and leads in similar fashion to the death of the second Horatius. The surviving brother reflects and gathers himself together to a fugue on a toccata-like subject with repeated notes (Example 100). The three entries of this symbolize the three wounded Curiatii fleeing at different speeds.

The two expositions are followed by a double stretto (on the subject and on the Hodlerian motif). The wild fury of this passage marks the absolute summit

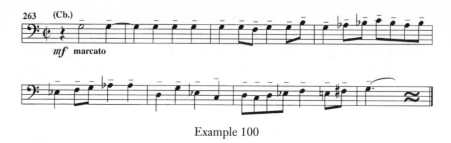

Example 100

of the work, leading to a measure of dramatic silence. Horatius, at the end of his breath, contemplates his victory in a state of stupefaction. Willy Tappolet makes an excellent comparison here with Hodler's *William Tell*.[13]

6. "Triomphe d'Horace" (un peu plus large; measures 322–356)

In Horatius's Triumph, a shrill, strident hymn of unbridled joy builds up on a seven-note chord: a dominant thirteenth based on the note A. Over this is heard a cheerful motif in 6/4 meter on horns and trumpets in A-flat major, one of the rare "diatonic islands" scattered over this atonal sea. The enthusiastic crescendo grows right up to Camilla's lamentations.

7. "Lamentations et imprécations de Camille" (très lent, expressif et douloureux; measures 357–373)

Camilla's Lamentations and Curses, a gloomy reminder of the first movement, acts as a kind of pendant in the form of a very free and condensed recapitulation of it. But the brass section outlines the obsessive memory of the Curiatii fanfare, in the form of an ostinato. The curses gather momentum and the tension becomes unbearable.

8. "Meurtre de Camille" (très vif et en pressant beaucoup; measures 374–378)

Suddenly, Horatius strikes his sister four times and kills her: a moment of brutal realism, followed by a horrified silence.

Epilogue (très large; measures 379–388)

A shrill eight-note chord in the Epilogue is succeeded by high, tense trills on woodwinds and the sound of the rattle and the icy flame of the suspended cymbal. Then a series of abrupt chords, like a body being dismembered, ushers in the long final chord of C minor. This is enriched with added second, sixth, and leading note, together with *acciaccaturas* to the fifth and sixth, and is prepared by a long "dominant" pedal on G. Willy Tappolet is right to speak of a "very crude sonority, ending in a sort of glacial numbness."[14]

44. *Overture* from the film *La Roue* (The Wheel)

November or early December 1922, Paris
The only piece of music that survives from the music for Abel Gance's film, on
    which Blaise Cendrars worked as an assistant
Performing forces: flute, clarinet, bassoon (all doubled *ad libitum*)–strings
Duration: 3 minutes 50 seconds
Salabert

The *Overture* for Abel Gance's film *La Roue* is a rather strange piece, made
up of heterogeneous material and, from the formal point of view, badly put
together. The eight brief episodes are different in character and language and
there is no repetition of material. The instrumental forces are the same as for
the ballet *Vérité? Mensonge?* (H34), the music for which is largely lost. It is possible that this music was used again in that work.

It is difficult to find a common denominator between some of the material.
The noble gravity of the modal counterpoint in measures 1 to 8 or 23 to 33
bespeaks the real Honegger ("modern" and richly dissonant) as does the sudden
pastoral idyll of measures 34 to 51, in which one dominant follows another in
a limpid atmosphere that looks forward to the *Deliciae basilienses*. (Honegger
used this passage again as measures 25 to 43 of the opening Calme of his music
for the film *Napoléon*.) On the other hand, there is the remainder of the music,
which is, to say the least, more disparate. The most interesting moments are the
premonitions of *Pacific 2.3.1* in measures 52 and following, corroborated by
verbal indications like "locomotive" and "rail." In fact, they were even clearer
in a passage of twelve measures that appeared between measures 58 and 59 in
the edition produced by Adriano, and in which one finds not only the cantus firmus (Example 84), but also the last theme (Example 86) complete. The editor
claims these were only incomplete sketches. In fact, the writing in two or three
parts is almost self-sufficient. The penciled additions simply show Honegger
bringing these measures to the state they reached in measures 118 and following in *Pacific 2.3.1* All this evidence confirms the "railroad" origins of this
famous work, despite the composer's denials.

48A. *Prelude* from *The Tempest*

February 1923
"To Madame L. Maillot"
The earliest contribution to the important incidental music for Guy de Pourtalès's
    French adaptation of Shakespeare's *The Tempest* (H48, Category 14). Honegger
    continued to work at this music sporadically until the end of 1929 or even the
    beginning of 1930
First performance (of the *Prelude*): 1 May 1923, Straram Orchestra, conducted by
    Walther Straram, Théâtre des Champs-Élysées, Paris
Performing forces: 2.2.2.2.–4.2.3.1.–cymbals, bass drum, triangle, tam-tam–strings
Duration: 6 minutes
Salabert

This piece, marked "lourd et agité" in 6/4 meter, is the only part of the
incidental music for *The Tempest* to use the full orchestra. It is naturalist writing, evoking most successfully a stormy sea, showing the skill that made Honeg-

ger such a good film composer. It is interesting to compare this to Sibelius's work of the same name, written a little later in 1925. The texture and techniques are very similar: chordal counterpoint in contrary motion, ostinatos, and so on. In Honegger's version, we may note the chromatic whistling of violin harmonics, representing the wind. There is no motivic working or even melodic invention, both of which would be out of place in this movement, which is all of a piece. The form is irregularly concentric (A-B-C-D-E-C-B-D-A) and only the C sections contain anything one could call a melody.

60A. *Orchestral Suite* from *L'Impératrice aux rochers*

Incidental music written 5 August–13 November 1925
"For Ida Rubinstein" (who commissioned the work)
Incidental music for the drama in five acts and a prologue by Saint-George de Bouhélier
First performance: 18 February 1927, Ida Rubinstein, soloists, Paris Opera Chorus and Orchestra, conducted by Philippe Gaubert, Paris Opera
First concert performance of *Suite*: 18 May 1928, Straram Orchestra, conducted by Arthur Honegger, Paris (this performance also contained Nos. 6 and 26 of the complete incidental music)
Performing forces: 3.3.3.3.–4.3.3.1.–celesta, harp–cymbals, tam-tam, bass drum–strings
Duration of *Suite*: 17 minutes
Salabert

The music for *L'Impératrice aux rochers* is Honegger's longest piece of incidental music, lasting nearly sixty-five minutes. It contains twenty-six movements, seven of which are condensed to form the five movements of the present *Suite* (see further details under H60, Category 14, in Chapter 13). "La Neige sur Rome" has also been published in a piano transcription (H60B, Category 1A), and No. 14 of this huge score ("Return of the Emperor") was also transcribed to become the Finale of the *Partita for two pianos* (H139). It would easily be possible to make a second orchestral suite out of these and other remaining movements. The five movements of this suite are atmospheric pieces, showing Honegger's masterly skill at creating an ambiance instantly and economically—an ability he so often turned to good effect on stage, on radio, and in the cinema.

"La Chasse de l'Empereur" (The Emperor's Hunt) combines Nos. 2 and 3 of the incidental music. Galloping rhythms and archaic, modal fanfares approach, pass across the stage, and disappear over the horizon. "La Neige sur Rome" (Snow in Rome; No. 7) is a delicately atmospheric piece over a pedal B, as the dominant of E, decorated with Ravelian harmonies and diaphanous orchestration. "L'Orage" (The Storm; No. 16) is an onomatopoetic piece in the style of the *Prelude* for *The Tempest*, full of realistic effects. Only in the middle section (slightly calmer) does a broad melody blossom. The tender, poetic evocation of "Le Jardin" (The Garden; No. 11), on the other hand, employs two long melodic curves over a "fairy" accompaniment of flutter-tongued flute figuration, slow arpeggios on celesta, rapid arpeggios on harp, and tremolos *sul ponticello* in the second violins. The strange coda departs from the key, bringing with it an air of cold and gloom.

"L'Orgie" (Nos. 17 and 18) is boisterous and cheerful. A syncopated three-note ostinato (E-flat-D-C), with cross accents, sets up a 4/4 pattern inside the 3/4 meter, which is sustained only by the lively woodwind ritornello. The central section is a kind of Trio for reduced forces (originally played on stage by flute, English horn, clarinet, bassoon, trumpet, tambourine, and strings). It draws entertaining asides from the obsessive opening theme. The repeat of the opening brings this simple, direct piece to a forceful conclusion.

61A. *Orchestral Suite* from *Phaedra*

March–10 April 1926
"To André George"
Incidental music for Gabriele d'Annunzio's *Phaedra*. Commissioned by Ida
    Rubinstein. The *Suite* contains most of the score, except for three very short
    pieces.
First performance: 19 April 1926, Ida Rubinstein, conducted by Arthur Honegger,
    decor by Léo Bakst, Teatro Costanzi, Rome
First concert performance of *Suite*: 19 December 1928, conducted by Arthur
    Honegger, Utrecht, The Netherlands
Performing forces: 2.2.2.2.–2.2.3.1.–timpani, cymbals–strings (and eight contraltos in
    No. 3)
Duration of *Suite*: 22 minutes
Salabert

The music for d'Annunzio's *Phaedra* is a more profound and dramatic work than its predecessor, and Jacques Feschotte describes it as "harsh and passionate." The *Orchestral Suite* includes the essence of the whole and deserves an honored place among Honegger's orchestral output.

1. Prelude to Act I

The powerfully tragic tone of this movement recalls the opening of *Judith*. The insistence of the ostinatos and the roughness of the counterpoint contribute to its dissonant ferocity. And here, for once, Honegger does not employ ongoing development, but a static montage technique in the manner of Stravinsky. Four different types of music alternate and overlap within a framework that is nonetheless clearly ternary with a coda.

2. "Cortège des suppliantes" (Procession of the Suppliants)

The orchestra is reduced here to six woodwinds, two horns, and strings. A twinging chromatic theme on the oboe is treated in three-part canon, and this kind of texture will predominate until the end of the piece. The form is ternary, as in the previous movement.

3. Prelude to Act II

The first section of this masterly movement in ternary form presents a basso ostinato made up of four chords (D-A-D; sixth chords in E-flat major, then in G-flat major; then D-A-D again) spread out over the whole tessitura above a roll on cymbals—a magical, sidereal effect, amazingly close to the beginning of Albéric Magnard's *Third Symphony*. Then come four variations, the first and last of which include a flute arabesque that looks forward to the birds in the Larghetto of the *Fourth Symphony*.

The middle of the piece marks an abrupt change. The ostinato is in fact abandoned in favor of music that is melancholy, tormented, and chromatic. The violas play an impassioned recitative (expressing Phaedra consumed by illness) in a style close to that of Camilla in *Horace victorieux*. But this soon gives way to the eight contraltos in unison singing an expressive melody in a Phrygian B minor surrounded by obsessive accents in anapestic rhythm (Example 101). The recitative is repeated and extended on violins before the return of the four-chord ostinato. These now sound even more insubstantial, being played with tremolos, and they are followed by four new variations, the second of which is rather reminiscent of Example 101. In the coda, an echo of this is combined with that of the flute arabesque, and the music fades on a chord of D major.

Example 101

4. "Imprécation de Thésée" (Theseus's Curse)

A short, violent movement, building up to an energetically dotted martial theme. It forms a stark contrast with the movements around it.

5. Prelude to Act III

This Prelude returns to the harsh, dissonant mood of the first one. After a somber introduction, which we hear again at the end, there is a threefold alternation of stark, polytonal polyphony on woodwinds with a chromatic motif on muted trombone. The next movement follows without a break.

6. "Mort de Phèdre" (Death of Phaedra)

A short but exceptionally intense movement. The first seventeen measures establish an eerie, fanciful atmosphere, built entirely of long-held harmonics on muted violins and violas—very hard to play well. Above the ensuing funereal accompaniment we hear the solo violin playing Phaedra's theme, played in the second Prelude by the viola, complete with its initial ascending minor ninth. At the end, the procession is halted, and divided strings intone a mysterious, *pianissimo* ten-note chord. Finally comes the gentle conclusion in D minor, with flute and oboe indulging one last time in a dialogue on the opening phrase of Phaedra's theme.

64. *Suite* from the film *Napoléon*

Late 1926–early 1927. Number 3 ("Danse des enfants") dates from November 1920, probably being intended for the ballet *Vérité? Mensonge?* (H34). Also, measures 25–43 of No. 1 ("Calme") are taken from the *Overture* to *La Roue* (H44), and as happens more than once in Honegger's film music, it cannot be ruled out that other movements were taken from pieces he had composed earlier.
Music for the film by Abel Gance, to whom Nos. 7 and 8 are dedicated on the manuscript
Film premiere: 7 April 1927, gala evening at the Paris Opera
Performing forces: 2.2.2.2.–2.3.3.1.–timpani, tenor drum, cymbals, bass drum, tamtam, triangle–strings. N.B. In his published edition, Adriano specifies four horns instead of two. In the original version intended for stage rather than concert performance, No. 8 ("Les Mendiants de la gloire") required a military band and male chorus
Duration: 21 minutes 15 seconds
Salabert

The reconstituted version of Abel Gance's monumental film lasts considerably over five hours and, as it was a silent film, music was played practically throughout. As with Gance's *La Roue*, Honegger proceeded largely by adapting and reorchestrating music already in existence, either classical, popular, or of his own composition. These eight pieces are all that have come down to us. The order is that intended for concert use and was certainly not the order in which they appeared in the film. This is hard to reconstruct, since the running order has been lost. But Nos. 1, 2, 4, 5, and 6 are numbered in Honegger's own hand.

1. "CALME"

An idyll in the style of *Pastorale d'été*, with a happy modulation from the initial B major to the middle section, taken from *La Roue*.

2. "LA ROMANCE DE VIOLINE"

A piece of romantic pastiche. For the only time in his work, the beginning could easily be taken for something unknown by Mahler! But it reverts to a French style thereafter.

3. "DANSE DES ENFANTS"

Here Honegger conjures up a light, rustling style in the manner of Messager. These first three movements may surprise the uninstructed listener in that they are anything but Napoleonic.

4. Interlude et Final

Here the tone changes. In the Interlude (in A-B-A form), the mysterious atmosphere of whole-tone scales and syncopated undulations almost suggests Debussy's *La Mer*. But in the distance we hear the *Ça ira*, and suddenly the *Carmagnole* bursts out in the brass, soon combined with the *Ça ira*. A crescendo on the rhythm of the latter leads to the Finale in 6/8 meter, first on the couplet of the *Carmagnole* ("Madam'Veto avait promis"), then, after a noisy crescendo, superimposing the two songs once again in a brilliant tutti.

5. "Chaconne de l'impératrice"

This is more of a slow, sultry waltz than a chaconne. It sounds like an homage to Fauré or Messager, and makes one think perhaps of the lovely Trio from *Les Aventures du roi Pausole* (No. 16).

6. "Napoléon"

I feel this may well have been the title music for the film. The hero is symbolized by a proud trumpet theme, rising in perfect fourths, and recalling the famous opening of Schoenberg's *First Chamber Symphony*, which Honegger had known well ever since his days as a student.

Example 102

7. "Les ombres" (The Shadows)

This is a genuine chaconne, on an eight-measure ostinato of mysterious common chords on strings. It generates four variations.

8. "Les mendiants de la gloire" (The Beggars of Glory)

The first of this movement's two sections seems to want to begin like a fugal exposition, but the fourth entry of the subject is replaced, on trumpets playing *piano*, by the *Chant du départ* in its entirety. The second section brings in the *Marseillaise* over the top of it, on full brass. In the film, the military band and male chorus join in for the *Chant du départ*, which ends up being submerged, and its refrain—"La République nous appelle" (The Republic Calls Us)—is suppressed. Honegger borrowed the whole of this final passage (measures 54–92), unchanged, for the end of Act IV of *L'Aiglon* ("La plaine de Wagram").

66A. *Blues* from *Roses de métal*

Probably 1928
For a ballet by Élisabeth de Gramont
First performance: 3 June 1928, Xavier de Courville's "La petite scène," Salle
    Oedenkoven, Paris
Performing forces: 1.1.1.1.–1.1.0.0.–strings
Duration: 2 minutes 10 seconds
Salabert

The ballet score of *Roses de métal* was much longer and was written for dynaphones (early electronic instruments) and percussion (see Chapter 4). This Blues piece must be a transcription by the composer of a fragment of the score, which has disappeared, together with the rest of the music. It is an entertaining little item in the style of 1928 jazz, with the clarinet in the role of soloist (probably replacing the dynaphone of the original score).

68A. *Suite After J. S. Bach*, from *Les Noces d'Amour et de Psyché*

Summer–Fall 1928 (perhaps even the end of 1927)
Commissioned by Ida Rubinstein for a ballet based on the music of Bach,
    orchestrated by Honegger
First performance of ballet: 22 November 1928, Ida Rubinstein Ballet Company,
    Paris Opera
First performance of *Suite*: 5 February 1933, Orchestre Symphonique de Paris,
    conducted by Gustave Cloëz, Poulet Concerts, Paris
Performing forces: 2.2.2.2. (first clarinet doubling on soprano
    saxophone)–4.3.0.0.–celesta, harp–strings
Duration: 11 minutes 30 seconds
1. Anglaise (based on the fifth movement of *Third English Suite*; in the ballet, No. 2,
    "Entrée de Mercure"); 2. Sarabande (based on the third movement of *Sixth
    French Suite*; in the ballet, No. 3, "Entrée d'Apollon"); 3. Gavotte (based on the
    fourth movement of *Fifth French Suite*; in the ballet, No. 7, "Entrée de Vénus");
    4. Minuet (based on the fourth movement of *First French Suite*; in the ballet, No.
    5, "Entrée de Minerve"); 5. Gigue (based on the seventh movement of *Fifth
    French Suite*; in the ballet, No. 4, "Entrée de Diane")
Universal Edition

In the *Suite After J. S. Bach* written for *Les Noces d'Amour et de Psyché*, Honegger respects Bach's notes and confines himself to the role of orchestrator, but he scores them for a modern ensemble, including saxophones—which are, after all, no more anachronistic for Bach than clarinets. The scoring is different for each piece. In the Anglaise, the soprano saxophone takes the limelight, whereas in the Sarabande it is the bass clarinet, accompanied by trumpets and harp. The harp, and especially the celesta, take on the cheerful dialogue of the well-known Gavotte, and the low reed instruments are the melodic protagonists in the Minuet. The Gigue is the most brilliant movement, with the four horns and two trumpets used for the one and only time.

68B. *Prelude and Fugue in C Major by J. S. Bach*, from *Les Noces d'Amour et de Psyché*

For details, see 68A above. This is an orchestration of the *Prelude and Fugue* BWV
545 for organ
Performing forces: 3.3.3.3.–2 saxophones (S, A)–4.3.3.1.–bass drum–strings
Duration: 5 minutes 45 seconds
1. Prelude (in the ballet, No. 1, "Prelude"); 2. Fugue (in the ballet, No. 15b,
"Apotheosis")
Universal Edition

In the *Prelude and Fugue* for *Les Noces d'Amour et de Psyché*, Honegger
employs a full modern symphony orchestra, including two saxophones. It would
be interesting to compare this orchestration with the exactly contemporary
orchestration made by Schoenberg of the *Prelude and Fugue in E-flat major*,
BWV 552.

71A. *Prelude, Fugue, Postlude* from *Amphion*

Spring 1948 (before 15 May); *Amphion* originally composed in August 1929
Amphion is dedicated to Ida Rubinstein, who commissioned the work
First performance of *Amphion*: 23 June 1931, Paris Opera (see H71, Category 13)
First performance of *Prelude, Fugue, Postlude*: 3 November 1948, Suisse Romande
Orchestra, conducted by Ernest Ansermet, Victoria Hall, Geneva
Performing forces: 3.3.3.3.–alto saxophone–4.3.3.1.–cymbals, bass drum, tam-tam–
harp, celesta–strings
Duration: 13 minutes
The work is played without a break. The passages shared with *Amphion* are as
follows:
measures 1–19: *Amphion* measures 365–383
measures 20–223: *Amphion* measures 403–608
measures 224–256: *Amphion* measures 615–647
Salabert

Amphion is one of Honegger's great unknown masterpieces—like *Horace
victorieux* and *Monopartita*—and from it he took for concert use the last and
finest section. He put together this powerful triptych during his convalescence
after his 1947 heart attack, introducing a bare minimum of changes into the
original score. It includes his longest fugue, a cyclopean example of the form,
and illustrates his harmonic language at its peak, with chains of dominants, of
minor chords a third apart, chords with added notes, and so forth. Matching
Valéry's "Apollonian" subject, however, this language is far less dissonant and
more tonal than that of *Horace victorieux* or *Antigone*—not that we can in any
sense speak of "regression," in the sense understood by Theodor Adorno's
pupils in their enslavement to the doctrine of historical determinism in music.

1. PRELUDE

The Prelude begins with the majestic theme of three sidereal chords, the
third of which, representing Apollo, is variable. Then, among fragments of
future ideas, we hear a lovely pastoral dialogue on woodwinds that evokes the

freshness of morning. From this, at measure 22 over a chain of dominant chords, emerges the broad theme on alto saxophone representing Amphion—one of the most beautiful melodies Honegger ever wrote (Example 103).

(Alto sax.)

Example 103

After a double *fortissimo* over a pedal point comes the second, fast section of the Prelude (allegro marcato, measure 43). This is an imaginative feast of scales, moving in every possible direction and at every possible speed. This part is a double diptych (A-B-A'-B'), with the B sections consisting of a consonant stretto on four-part strings in continuous eighth-notes, as in Bach's Toccatas. Soon these are joined by Amphion's theme sailing above them (Example 103).

The play of scales resumes (A', measure 76) with blocks of syncopated bitonal chords, in possibly the most Stravinskyan passage in Honegger's output, but belonging to the later Stravinsky of the *Symphony of Psalms* or the *Symphony in Three Movements*. Amphion's theme for a second time dominates the swell from the strings, and then an irresistible crescendo ushers in the Fugue.

2. FUGUE

The subject of the Fugue, heavily introduced by the double basses in the main key of C minor, is of prodigious length and of Herculean power (Example 104). In its octave leaps and rhythmic articulation, it is strongly reminiscent of the first theme in the Finale of Bruckner's *Fifth Symphony*, also treated in fugue form. It soon collects two countersubjects, and the first of these is equally incisive and important. With the end of the exposition, strict fugal writing gives way to fugal writing of a more symphonic kind (with the subject played, for instance, in chordal blocks), but the technique is no less dense or rigorous for that. Episodes and stretto passages based on this rich material duly follow, with a calmer, cantabile reworking of the second countersubject on the trumpet.

Example 104

After two triple strettos, the fugal texture turns into superimposed osti-natos, as is often the case with Honegger (compare the end of *Pacific 2.3.1*). The accumulated tension is resolved at measure 187 in a 3/2 largamente *fortis-simo* passage, with a powerfully harmonized stretto on the augmented subject (reminiscent of the coda of Sibelius's *Fifth Symphony*). At the height of the cli-max, two statements of Apollo's chordal theme on the brass combine with a double stretto on subject and countersubject. This grandiose moment leads finally to a *pianissimo* in C major. There is one final stretto, but now transfigured into a fairy-tale texture of flute, celesta, harp, and high violins. An expressive tune on saxophone leads without a break into the brief Postlude.

3. Postlude

Suddenly a cloud seems to pass across the sun. A lovely flute melody (Example 148), which has already been heard in the complete ballet, unfolds over modulations through descending minor chords. The epilogue proper con-sists of a long saxophone cantilena, taken over by English horn, around which the shadows, and the pitch, continue to fall. The bass clarinet has the last word, and the music dies on a double bass pizzicato.

I have deliberately treated this work as a piece of pure music, leaving dis-cussion of the story to the entry for the whole ballet (see Category 13, Chapter 12). But it would be flouting Honegger's wishes not to reproduce the short quotation from Paul Valéry that he wanted at the head of *Prelude, Fugue, Postlude*:

> Amphion, a man, receives the lyre from Apollo. Music grows from under his fingers. At the blossoming sounds, the stones move and join together: architecture is created. As the hero climbs toward the temple, a veiled fe-male figure appears and bars his way. Amphion hides his face in the bosom of this figure, who is Love or Death, and allows himself to be led off by her.

88A. *Orchestral Suite* from the film *Les Misérables*

1934 (the music for the film: November 1933–summer 1934)
First performance of *Suite*: 19 January 1935, conducted by Robert Siohan, Siohan Concerts, Salle Rameau in the Paris Conservatory, rue de Madrid
Performing forces: 1.1.2.1.–1.1.1.0.–suspended cymbal, bass drum, tenor drum–harp, piano–strings (without double basses). Second clarinet also doubles bass clarinet and alto saxophone.
Duration of *Suite*: 19 minutes 35 seconds
Salabert

The complete music for Raymond Bernard's trilogy based on Victor Hugo's *Les Misérables* lasts an hour and is Honegger's longest film score. He called this the "First Symphonic Suite" but, although there is no shortage of material, he never put together a second suite.

The title music is a steady procession, almost a funeral march, on two of the three main cyclic themes, both in E minor: a rising theme for Jean Valjean and, for the convicts, a theme with an obsessively falling minor third G-E. Whereas the first, for all its gloom, expresses noble aspirations, the second depicts absolute, irredeemable misery, and even looks forward in tone to the De profundis of the *Symphonie liturgique*. The two short passages that follow the title music here come from the second number of the complete film, "Jean Valjean sur la route" (Jean Valjean on the Road). They are in a classically French, popular, and rustic style.

"Dans les égouts" (In the Sewers), one of the longest and most impressive movements in the *Suite*, is again in E minor and is based on a continuous rhythm of pairs of slurred eighth-notes, expressing superhuman effort. It is in the form A-B-A-B-A and the A sections are punctuated by the watchful but unseen presence of Javert (a motif of detached quarter-notes in the bass of the piano). The B sections consist of slow, chromatic crescendos.

As a total contrast, the brief "Musique chez Gillenormand" takes us back to an idyll of the rococo period, in one of those pastiches that Honegger was so good at, and that send the standard-bearers of the avant-garde into such a rage. It is an agile, sprightly 6/8 section in G major. The only slight departure from the eighteenth century comes in the Trio, where clarinet and trumpet play a picturesque duet, with the trumpet confining itself to comic scales and fanfares.

"La mort de Jean Valjean" (The Death of Jean Valjean) is an adagio in C minor on a lovely tune imbued with feeling. For some unknown reason, however, Honegger has not used the last nine measures in the *Suite*. In these, a moving allusion to the third main cyclic theme of the score, depicting the love of Cosette and Marius, is combined with the theme of Jean Valjean.

The *Orchestral Suite* concludes with "L'émeute" (The Riot), a violent allegro in A minor. This is epic battle music, at the climax of which the convicts' theme is heard at full strength (because the revolution intends to set them free). This passage leads straight into the brief coda of "La fuite de Jean Valjean" (The Escape of Jean Valjean), after the death of Fantine, where his theme is superimposed on that of the convicts.

Among the most striking of the movements that might have made up a second suite, one may mention particularly the ghostly "Tempête sous un crâne" (Brainstorm; No. 4), the love music for Cosette and Marius (Nos. 8, 11, and 12), and, by way of contrast, the "Fête à Montfermeil" (No. 9).

104. *La Marche sur la Bastille* (March on the Bastille), from the show *14 Juillet*

June 1936
No. 6 of the seven numbers of Romain Rolland's collective show *14 Juillet*; this is the
　　Prelude to Act III
First performance: 14 July 1936, conducted by Roger Désormière, Théâtre de
　　l'Alhambra, Paris
Performing forces: wind band (4.2.3.3.–3 saxophones–5.3.4.3.–side drum, cymbals,
　　bass drum)–chorus *ad libitum*
Duration: 5 minutes
Chant du Monde

Together with *Grad us* (H141, Category 17) and the original version of *Nicolas de Flue*, the *La Marche sur la Bastille*, from the show *14 Juillet*, constitutes Honegger's contribution to the repertory of the wind band. It is an extremely dramatic and descriptive piece, building up tension through a series of linked dominants in the context of a highly chromatic B-flat minor. It is deliberately cinematographic in spirit and culminates in a *pianissimo* "open" ending, leading directly into the *tableau vivant* that follows.

111. *Prelude à la Mort de Jaurès*, from the show *Liberté*

April 1937
Prelude to the thirteenth and penultimate scene of the collective show *Liberté*
First performance: 2 May 1937, as part of the show put on by *May 36*, the Popular
      Movement of Art and Culture, produced by Léon Ruth, conducted by Maurice
      Jaubert, Théâtre des Champs-Élysées, Paris
The music is lost

117A. *Orchestral Suite* from the film *Regain*

4–28 September 1937 (film music)
First performance of *Suite*: 21 December 1937, conducted by Jacques Chailley, Salle
      Gaveau, Paris
Performing forces: 1.1.1.1.–saxophone–0.2.2.0.–bass drum, cymbals, rattle, tam-tam,
      tenor drum, triangle–piano–strings
Duration of *Suite*: 14 minutes
Salabert (only the *Suite*, and that only on rental)

Marcel Pagnol's film *Regain* is a cinema classic and still very much with us. It is one of the best, and best-known, of the films in which Honegger was involved. The score, lasting around thirty-five minutes, is a little shorter than the one for *Les Misérables*, but it is perhaps of higher quality. It is a masterpiece of the genre and the whole score, not merely the *Orchestral Suite*, is worthy of revival on disc, even though it has not survived quite complete. None of Honegger's other film music possesses this earthy flavor, this sense of pastoral well-being, and it is also one of the most "French" scores he ever wrote. It is a great pity that the *Suite* does not contain either the unforgettable "Chanson d'Aubignane" or pages like "Été" ("Panturle au soleil" or Panturle in the Sun; No. 8) or "Nocturne" ("Panturle et Arsule près du ruisseau" or Panturle and Arsule Near the Brook; No. 11), not to mention the splendid title music (No. 1), all of which are as good as, if not better than, those that are in fact included.

"Le Panturle" combines two different but complementary pieces. The first is No. 6, "Panturle—Le village sur la colline" (Panturle—The Village on the Hill), lively, rhythmic music presenting the theme in characteristically iambic guise to depict Pagnol's uncouth peasant. The second occurs in the middle section: the vigorously athletic No. 5, "Panturle coupe les arbres" (Panturle Cuts Down the Trees). By contrast, "Hiver" (Winter) is a slow, sad, emaciated movement, lightened by the beautiful dialogue for clarinet and saxophone in "Printemps" (Spring). Then appears the unforgettable silhouette of Fernandel in a bowler hat ("Gédémus le Rémouleur" or Gédémus the Knife-grinder), with his comical, limping bassoon. It lies somewhere between King Pausolus on his mule and Louis XI (in *Christopher Columbus*) on his! We finish on the healthy, vigorous C major of *Regain*, introducing Panturle's theme in its most complete form, culminating in ten grandiose measures (still enhanced in the *Suite*), which will serve as music for the final credits.

167A. *Two Suites* from the film *Mermoz*

May 1943
First performance: gala film premiere 14 October 1943, Paris Opera; general release 3 November 1943. On the soundtrack, Honegger himself is conducting the Paris Conservatory Orchestra
Performing forces: 1.1.1.1.–saxophone–0.2.2.0.–bass drum, cymbals; (*Second Suite* only) tam-tam, triangle–piano–strings
Duration: 18 minutes 30 seconds (*First Suite*: 9 minutes 30 seconds; *Second Suite*: 9 minutes)

Louis Cuny's film is no longer viable these days because of its grandiloquence, the extreme chauvinism of its spoken commentaries, and the old-fashioned manner in which these alternate with dialogues that are themselves extremely stereotyped. But the score is one of the best Honegger wrote for the cinema, and happily one of the best-known, thanks to the *Two Suites* he made from it. In all there were a good fifty minutes of music, but only these *Two Suites* survive in full score.

The music is entirely dominated by one of the composer's broadest and grandest themes (Example 105). The music for the film *L'Équipage* included an early sketch of this in 1935, but it found its definitive form in May 1937 in the forgotten ballet *Un Oiseau blanc s'est envolé*, all of the music for which was reused in *Mermoz*. For the most part, the music is entrusted to the trumpet. It divides into three main periods, not counting a codetta, and each of these contains distinct motifs that are developed separately. As a result, it is the seed bed for most of the score. It is in a radiant, "white" C major and returns to this after many a modulatory excursion. In Honegger's usual manner, its directness and grandeur conceal a rare complexity and subtlety.

The *First Suite*, "La Traversée des Andes" (Crossing the Andes), consists of six musical sequences that follow one another without a break. The first one, corresponding in essence with the title music, lets us hear Example 105 in full and in canon, over an accompaniment of swaying chords depicting the swirling of the air beneath the airplane. Fragments of its first period are then developed over an ostinato of chromatic trills. In the second sequence (measures 51–98; "Sur les Andes"), three long, modulating progressions of Wagnerian proportions (we may be reminded here of the beginning of the last scene of *The Twilight of the Gods*), built on a dotted rhythm and intervals of a second, are combined with elements of Example 105—*a* for the second progression, *b* and *c* for the third. Suddenly, a chromatic, nonthematic, atonal passage signals that "Le vent se lève" (The Wind is Rising; third sequence, measures 99–167), in ever more violent and rapid figurations (sixteenth-note sextuplets).

In the fourth sequence (measures 168–189), element *a* from Example 105,

Example 105

now low on trombone, forces its way through the mist, while the tempo grows ever slower and heavier. Suddenly, in the fifth sequence (measures 190–206), we reach a magnificent "Lever du jour" (Dawn), with majestic major chords on brass linked by rising thirds—no longer Wagner, but something between Bruckner and the Sibelius of *Nightride and Sunrise*. Having reached the dominant of C, we enter on the Finale (measures 207–224), a real Brucknerian coda and an apotheosis of the period of Example 105 in C major, surrounded by rich figuration. It is reminiscent of the coda of Bruckner's *Fourth Symphony*, with only a few added seconds betraying that it belongs to the twentieth century.

The *Second Suite*, "Le Vol sur l'Atlantique" (The Flight Over the Atlantic) also consists of six sequences, the first of which is simply a curtain raiser establishing the key. The second (measures 7–55) again opens on wide-open spaces, this time of the endlessly undulating waves in sextuplets in parallel thirds. Here we are nearer to Sibelius than to Bruckner. Over a broad ascending scalic theme on double basses unfold the three periods of Example 105 in a true thematic development. The harmonic movement is intentionally slow (Honegger has learned a lesson from Wagner) and the music reaches a state of passing euphoria. With the third sequence (measures 56–83), darkness descends abruptly. It is the doldrums feared by all pilots, a chromatic, atonal flux in the midst of which rises a long, moving theme on strings. It is also a brief moment of human subjectivity in the middle of the music of Nature, as Mermoz receives a radio message from his mother.

Suddenly, in the fourth sequence (measures 84–96), the lightning flashes and the music becomes discordant and jagged. With the fifth sequence (measures 97–119) we return to the chromatics of the howling wind, as in the third sequence of the *First Suite*. Through these, Example 105 (even though it is almost obliterated by the fury of the elements) is heard complete, still in canon on the brass, but now with a modulatory course as though it were affected by the storm. At the climax we come to the abrupt rhythms of the previous sequence, followed by a *fortissimo* pause on a string tremolo, held as a high pedal point. Suddenly, in the sixth and final sequence (measures 120–155), sunlight breaks in the coda-apotheosis. Example 105 is heard for the last time complete and extended by the opening title music, but now the orchestration is much grander, proclaiming C major at some length. The care and masterly inspiration with which Honegger handles this "popular" music makes it, to my mind, his best film score.

174A. *Schwyzer Fäschttag* (Swiss Holiday), Orchestral Suite from the ballet *L'Appel de la montagne*

Ballet composed summer–20 October 1943; orchestrated June–July 1945
Scenario by R. Favre le Bret
First performance of ballet: 9 July 1945, conducted by Louis Fourestier, Paris Opera
First performance of *Schwyzer Fäschttag*: 14 November 1945, conducted by Ernest Ansermet, Winterthur
Performing forces: 3.3.2.3.–4.3.3.1.–timpani, cymbals, side drum, tenor drum, triangle, woodblock–celesta, piano–strings
Duration of Suite: 20 minutes 35 seconds
Salabert

In 1943, Honegger was separated from Switzerland by the war and was unable to visit it. In *L'Appel de la montagne* he regards his homeland with an irony not devoid of tenderness, but it would be a great mistake to look down on the work snobbishly, as the French did at the time. With trifles like the cabaret song *Tuet's weh?* or the military march *Grad us*, this is the cheerful, lighter side of Honegger's German-Swiss inheritance, which we also find, in a more powerful and harsher guise, in *Horace victorieux*, *Monopartita*, and the *First Symphony*. The complete ballet also includes a Scottish element, connected with the character of MacGuire and represented, like the Swiss element, by popular tunes. Apart from a very short passage just before the "Alpeglüe," however, that Scottish element is missing from this Suite, which (as the Swiss-German titles indicate) remains entirely Swiss.

"Am Fäschtplatz" (Festival Square) is the first number of the ballet, and it is also repeated almost exactly as No. 5. It is a vigorous clog dance in 3/4, with diatonic dissonances rather in the style of Stravinsky. In the middle is a jolly waltz theme on piccolo and celesta, answered by unison strings sounding, for the only time in Honegger's work, like Chabrier. The composer reused the heavy, robust "Buretanz" (Peasant Dance, No. 2 in the ballet) from his 1934 music for the film *Rapt*, which was set in the Swiss mountains. Its memorable, slightly Mahler-like tune is one of the best he wrote in popular vein (Example 106).

"D'Sänne chömmed" (Entry of the Shepherds, No. 4 in the ballet) is built on a deliberately unpolished march theme in the double basses, later combined with the well-known tune "Ich bin ein Schweizer Knabe" (I Am a Swiss Boy) on the trombone.

By contrast, the "Ländler" (Swiss Waltz, No. 7 in the ballet) is a lilting, sensuous waltz, punctuated by glissandos that call to mind the swirl of raised petticoats. It belongs to the family of well-bred light music, which Honegger composed in quantities for his films. A short tucket on the brass, heard again in echo, leads to the highly realistic description of the throwing of the stones,

Example 106

"Schteischtosse" (Nos. 8 and 9 in the ballet). The rising glissandos on low strings describe the effort of lifting them up, and these alternate with music that is deliberately square-cut and clumsy (one might, not entirely seriously, compare it with the "Combat of the Horatii").

The episode of the "Hoselupf" (Battle in Underpants, No. 10 in the ballet), depicts the other traditional sport of the hefty Bernese cattle drovers and is, perhaps, a little long-drawn-out for the concert hall. It finally accelerates to become a kind of toccata in which we may recognize a vague pre-echo of one of the themes of the Dies irae in the *Symphonie liturgique*.

Lastly, we come to the "Fäschtabschluss" (End of the Festival, No. 11 in the ballet). This describes the crowd happily dispersing, after the distribution of the prizes, to a popular martial tune. There follows a very short moment of calm during which the Scottish theme is heard. In the complete ballet, this accompanies MacGuire while he is climbing the Jungfrau mountain (see H174, Category 13, in Chapter 12, for a brief account of the story).

The music moves on without a break to the "Alpeglüe" (No. 12 in the ballet), the magic of the sunset over glaciers and fields of snow. This cheeky fricassee of five well-known Swiss popular songs, in D major, is the exact equivalent of Honegger's more familiar tour de force with Christmas carols in *Une Cantate de Noël*. (The sketch for the *Selzach Passion*, which already existed at the time of this ballet, juxtaposed them but did not yet superimpose them.) Here, Honegger's mastery turns them into charming color (one might even say Technicolor) postcards.

Among the recognizable tunes are "Han an einem Ort es Blüemli gseh" (I Saw the Little Flower in a Particular Spot) as a cello solo, the very popular "Lueget wo Bärgen und Tal" (See Where Mountains and Valley) on trombone, then, simultaneously, a rapid echo on bassoon of "Ich bin ein Schweizer Knabe" (I Am a Swiss Boy) and, on the flute, the "Liauba" from the *Ranz des Vaches* (Cow Call) of the Gruyère region. Finally, sparkling and witty in fast notes on the piccolo, the cheerful and equally well-known "Vo Luzern uf Weggis zue" (On the Way from Lucerne to Weggis). These tunes alternate and blend over gentle string harmonies and then, just as in *Une Cantate de Noël*, there is a gradual diminuendo as night falls, with fragments of tunes scattering toward the horizon. We may well wonder why the critics dealt so harshly with this work, and why a Swiss popular song should be inferior to a Christmas carol.

TWELVE

Theater and Musical Frescoes

From this point on, the divisions between musical genres become less and less watertight, and the classification of works becomes more and more a matter of personal choice. The title of the present chapter alludes to the fact that the oratorios that have established Honegger's greatest claim to fame were generally defined as "grand frescoes." But they often consist of a succession of short scenes that are as concise as they are suggestive, showing Honegger's genius as an "illustrator" in just as marked a manner as does his incidental music or his music for radio and films (to be examined in the following chapter).

In any case, *Le Roi David* and *Judith* were originally written as incidental music, while the largest of the radio scores, in particular *Christopher Columbus* and *Saint François d'Assise*, are true oratorios, intended for radio and not for the concert hall. Most of the works in Category 10 (Cantatas and Oratorios) have been staged, in general proving more effective in that guise and, in the case of *Judith*, reaching in it their ultimate form—the exceptions (the *Cantique de Pâques*, *Cris du monde*, and *Une Cantate de Noël*) are also those works without spoken text. In this way, *Le Roi David* and *Nicolas de Flue* have passed from the stage to the concert hall, while *Jeanne d'Arc au bûcher* (although intended originally for the theater) and *La Danse des morts* have gone in the opposite direction. Only *Judith* has made the round trip, as it were, through its three successive versions.

But that is not all. In the case of the ballets, four of them demand vocal soloists and chorus, while *Amphion*, wrongly labeled a "melodrama," remains a fascinating hybrid of ballet and oratorio-cantata; and the same might almost be said of *Le Cantique des cantiques*. The key to this confused situation, to these fluid identities, is found in a brief sentence from the composer: "My dream would have been to compose nothing but operas."[1] That is why I have refused to separate these works from his oratorios and ballets, many of which are "opéras manqués."

Honegger was not alone in this. We know that Mozart too would have liked to write nothing but operas, and that Hector Berlioz lived his whole life in a similar state of frustration, as *The Damnation of Faust* and *Romeo and Juliet* testify. It is significant that these works too, after his death, found their way on to the operatic or balletic stage, with greater or lesser success. We know that the monopoly exercised by Rossini, and then by Meyerbeer and Halévy, ruined

393

Berlioz's chances of a career as an opera composer. During the first half of the twentieth century, even for a composer as well-known and well-established as Honegger, the situation in France was no better. The only real difference was that the monopoly had long passed into the hands of the dead. If we consider that the Paris Opera took seventeen years to stage *Antigone* and thirteen to find room for *Jeanne d'Arc au bûcher* (which was destined for it), then we can understand why the marginal careers, to say the least, of *Judith* and *Antigone* did not encourage a composer to persevere—especially one who was keen above all else to communicate with the widest possible audience.

And then, even if *Antigone*, that unique "white dwarf" of the operatic repertory, is profoundly innovative and does far more than stand as a "small monument" (as Honegger himself modestly put it[2]) to the composer's name, he was of course far from being the only one to write operas. So, as soon as *Le Roi David* was somewhat unexpectedly transformed into an oratorio for the concert hall, the composer found himself, equally unexpectedly, propelled into the position of being the renovator of a genre that had fallen into disuse. Honegger became the leading composer in the field of the oratorio, and others duly followed in his footsteps. For the general public, even today, Honegger is above all the master of the oratorio, even if, in the strictest sense of the word, only *Cris du monde* and perhaps *La Danse des morts*, brief though it is, conform to the exact definition of the genre.

Category 10: Cantatas and Oratorios

IV.   *Oratorio du Calvaire*
18.   *Cantique de Pâques*
37.   *Le Roi David*
57.   *Judith*
77.   *Cris du monde*
99.   *Jeanne d'Arc au bûcher*
131. *La Danse des morts*
135. *Nicolas de Flue*
177. *Selzach Passion*
212. *Une Cantate de Noël*

If we leave aside the youthful *Oratorio du Calvaire*, the brief curtain raiser of the *Cantique de Pâques*, and the huge unfinished project of the *Selzach Passion*, Honegger's so-called grand frescoes are seven in number. Only three of these last longer than an hour, while two others last less than half an hour. Once again, we are faced with his innate love of concision, so that while we may sometimes be sorry that a Honegger work is so short, we never feel it to be too long. It says something about his attitude that his longest piece is the operetta, *Les Aventures du roi Pausole*.

Being a Swiss composer, Honegger belonged to a culture in which choral singing holds an important place—far more important than in France. Furthermore, his Protestant ancestry contributed to forming his role as a renovator of the oratorio. He began writing his *Oratorio du Calvaire* at the age of sixteen, and (as mentioned in Chapter 3) he said of the commission to write *Le Roi David*: "I accepted with pleasure because the subject suited my 'Bible-loving' tendencies." Since Honegger always claimed to be an agnostic, we are talking here of a cultural tradition that meant that Johann Sebastian Bach was much closer and more familiar to him than to his French Catholic colleagues.

One has to have lived in the Reformed cantons of Switzerland to appreciate the extraordinary impact Bach's Passions and Cantatas have on the musical life of the general public. That Protestant heritage, expressed through the frequent presence of chorales, did not prevent Honegger from collaborating with the greatest French Catholic poet of the century, Paul Claudel, in what are perhaps his two most spiritual masterpieces: *Jeanne d'Arc au bûcher* and *La Danse des morts*. Nor did it prevent him from honoring the Swiss national saint, Nicolas de Flue, in company with the Protestant Denis de Rougemont, or, ten years later, from writing his *Saint François d'Assise*. This broadly ecumenical attitude was shared by Milhaud, who was Jewish and who also collaborated with Claudel.

Honegger had an extraordinary genius for mimicry, and this enabled him to conjure up with equal ease the Biblical atmosphere of the stories of David and Judith and the heartrending cry of *Mimaamaquim* (the critic Mainsieux stated, in the journal *Le Crapouillot*, that only a Jew could have written *Le Roi David!*), or the profoundly Catholic France of *Jeanne d'Arc au bûcher*, or the archetypal Switzerland of *Nicolas de Flue*. We shall have occasion to mention again that Honegger partook, not merely of two, but of three cultures, since the world of French-speaking Switzerland, to which his collaborations with René Morax and, much later, with William Aguet belonged, is as distinct from that of France as it is from German-speaking Switzerland.

Honegger's adaptation of the *Le Roi David* theater score revived or at least injected new blood into the oratorio. As a musical genre, it had been languishing for some time. After the masterpieces of the eighteenth century, including the Bach Passions and the oratorios of Handel and Haydn, the romantic era had done nothing to renew the genre, which was that of an opera in concert form on a sacred subject. Felix Mendelssohn's *St. Paul* and *Elijah* achieved a certain inspired nobility in developing their classical inheritance, but his successors— whether German, French, or English—rarely rose above an undistinguished academicism. Neither Elgar's *The Dream of Gerontius* nor Franck's *Les Béatitudes*, for all their undeniable beauties, could form the basis for any renewal. It is also interesting to note that the most direct and formative precedent for *Le Roi David* was Debussy's *The Martyrdom of Saint Sebastian*—another work that had migrated from the stage, in which form it had been overwhelmed by an extravagantly long spoken text and had had only a limited impact.

There were also, at the beginning of the century, some large psalm settings with orchestra, such as Max Reger's *Psalm 100* and Florent Schmitt's monumental *Psalm 47*, both of which certainly inspired Honegger. His example in turn inspired Albert Roussel's *Psalm 80* and William Walton's *Belshazzar's Feast*, to cite only two works from the same decade. Zoltán Kodály's large-scale *Psalmus Hungaricus* was written at the same time as *Le Roi David*, and therefore independently of it.

The reason why the oratorio flourishes in Switzerland lies beyond the presence of a Protestant tradition, in the profoundly communal and civic character of the Swiss social life based, as it is, on an extremely decentralized political structure that encourages local initiative. In the twentieth century, Switzerland has given the world, apart from the oratorios by Honegger, masterpieces such as Hermann Suter's *Laudi*, Willy Burkhard's *Das Gesicht Jesajas* and *Das Jahr*, Frank Martin's *In Terra Pax*, *Golgotha*, *Mystère de la Nativité*, *Pilate*, and so on, and more recently, the astonishing *Erniedrigt, geknechtet, verachtet, verlassen* by Klaus Huber. The oratorio is certainly the field in which Swiss music has flourished most vigorously.

IV. *Oratorio du Calvaire* (Calvary Oratorio)

1907
The text was undoubtedly by Honegger himself and consisted of seven sections: 1. Prelude; 2. Chorus "Jerusalem"; 3. Aria "Une épée te transpercera le flanc" (A sword shall pierce thy side); 4. Arioso "Jesus-Christ tout puissant" (Jesus Christ all-powerful); 5. Aria "Eli lama sabacthani"; 6. Chorus "O terreur" (O terror); 7. Epilogue
Lost

The straightforward titles of the *Oratorio du Calvaire* show Honegger, at the precocious age of fifteen, already drawn to the austerity of Biblical subjects, having come under the overwhelming influence of discovering the Bach Passions. We also know that the performance, given in the family circle, was entrusted to amateurs, fellow students, and others, and that those playing the tutti did not have to venture beyond open strings. This is an early example of the practicality that Honegger was to show all through his career. We may note that Vaughan Williams adopted the same procedure in his *Concerto grosso* (1950), which also mixes professionals and amateurs.

18. *Cantique de Pâques* (Easter Canticle)

July 1918; orchestrated in November 1922
"To Robert Godet"
Text (very short) by the composer
First performance: 27 March 1923, conducted by Arthur Honegger, Toulouse (other details missing)
Performing forces: soprano, mezzo, and contralto soloists; three-part female chorus; orchestra: 2.2.2.2.–2.2.0.0.–celesta, harp–strings
Duration: 7 minutes
Salabert

Although this is Honegger's first choral work, and a significant step on the road to *Le Roi David*, the *Cantique de Pâques* has remained one of his lesser-known pieces. It is all that is left of an *Easter Mystery*, projected for the Théâtre du Vieux-Colombier in collaboration with Fernand Ochsé. It is similar to *La Mort de Sainte Alméenne*, both because it was never completed and also because Honegger would later rescue a usable fragment from it to be orchestrated for the concert hall. As in *Sainte Alméenne*, Debussy's influence is still predominant. But the formal construction already reveals the sureness and perfection of the mature Honegger, enabling us to discern six distinct sections within its barely one hundred measures.

The introduction (measures 1–10) is a fugal exposition for the three unaccompanied vocal soloists, on a modal subject in A minor. It shows the influence of the clear textures of *The Martyrdom of Saint Sebastian*. Section A (measures 11–28) begins in C major and already demonstrates the beauty of modulations progressing through chains of dominants. Here Honegger combines peaceful orchestral arabesques in triplet eighth-notes with sung Alleluias (but it is the orchestral triplets that look forward to the Alleluias in *Le Roi David*). The chorus appears for the first time in section B (measures 29–52), with a new theme in 3/4 time in A-flat major. A modulating progression leads to the central, climactic section of the work (measures 53–68). This is a development, combining the themes of sections A and B in a masterly and complex polyphony, at full volume.

The varied reprise of section B (measures 69–88) takes place in D (a tritone away from the previous A-flat major), with an expressive countersubject passing from the cello to the solo violin. The work then fades out in a mysterious coda over a long pedal on the tonic C (measures 89–98). After the final choral Alleluia, over a reminiscence of theme B in augmentation, the orchestra concludes the work on its own. In the final perfect triad, the second and sixth are added, exactly as in the epilogue of the *String Quartet No. 1*, finished the previous year.

37. *Le Roi David* (King David)

A. First version: Biblical drama by René Morax
25 February–28 April 1921; orchestration completed 20 May 1921. The first piece written was No. 11, the last Nos. 13, 17, and 27
First performance: 11 June 1921, conducted by Arthur Honegger, Théâtre du Jorat, Mézières (Vaud). Some of the movements had been performed before the first performance, with piano accompaniment: 2 June 1921 (Nos. 2, 8, and 18 by M. Scheridan, SMI concert, Salle Gaveau, Paris) and 7 June 1921 (Nos. 6, 9, and 21 by the tenor Hubbard, Paris)
Performing forces: soprano, contralto, tenor, mixed chorus; 2.1.2.1.–1.2.1.0.–celesta, piano, harmonium–timpani, percussion (cymbals, side drum, bass drum, gong, tambourine)–double bass (cello *ad libitum*)—17 instrumentalists in all; numerous spoken parts
The performance, with a single intermission after Act III, lasted more than four hours and was divided into five acts, or "degrees": 1. The Shepherd; 2. The Captain; 3. The Chieftain; 4. The King; 5. The Prophet. As for the music, the present No. 3 came at the end, just before "The Coronation of Solomon" (present No. 26), while Nos. 15 and 17 were interchanged on either side of No. 16, "The Dance Before the Ark."

B. Second version: symphonic psalm in three parts, based on the drama by René Morax

German text by Hans Reinhart, English text by Edward Agate

"To my parents"

First performance: 21 January 1923, conducted by G. M. Witkowski, Lyons

Performing forces: see first version, though all the roles spoken by actors were replaced by a narrator. The order of the movements was that of the definitive score (see analysis below). The music is identical to that of the first version.

Duration: 67 minutes (including 57 minutes of music), in 27 numbers grouped into three parts (29:00 + 12:30 + 25:30)

Foetisch Frères

C. Third version: for large orchestra

Reorchestrated: July–August 1923

First performance: 2 December 1923 (in German), conducted by Ernst Wolters, with Clara Winz-Wyss, Lisa Appenzeller, Carl Seidel, Municipal Chorus and Orchestra of Winterthur, Winterthur Stadthaus

First French performance: 14 March 1924, conducted by Robert Siohan, with Jacques Copeau (narrator), Gabrielle Gills, Cellier, Charles Panzéra, La Chorale française and L'Art choral, Salle Gaveau, Paris

Performing forces: 2.2.2.2.–4.2.3.1.–timpani, percussion (bass drum, cymbals, side drum, tambourine, tam-tam, triangle)–celesta, harp, organ–strings; narrator and voices (see versions A and B). The music is the same.

Foetisch Frères

The biographical section in Part I of this book relates in detail the birth, development, and performance of the work that propelled Honegger into the limelight, thereby turning him, almost overnight, into "King Arthur." As has been said many times, Le Roi David is both the fruit of a happy concatenation of circumstances and the prime example of a work born under a lucky star. It also needed fertile soil on which to cast its light, and it came at just the right time, thanks to the efforts of the right man (or rather "men," because we must not forget the vital contribution of René Morax, who was also the project's instigator).

Le Roi David is remarkably close to the oratorios of the eighteenth century in its musical constituents: sections for orchestra, large choruses, arias, and chorales, but all treated with unusual conciseness. One essential difference lies in the recitative, which in classical oratorio was sung, but which in Honegger's music is spoken. This speeds up the action considerably. It is this role of speech, found in most later oratorios, that enabled the genre to find new life as a musical form, and to keep pace with the psychological tempo of our century.

For his text, René Morax took his inspiration largely from the Old Testament (I and II Samuel, I Kings), but also from the Huguenot Psalter, which contains the Psalms of Clément Marot and Théodore de Bèze. The Biblical drama of the first version lasts more than four hours and contains no less than twenty-five episodes, or tableaux (some without music), grouped in five acts or "degrees." But in the concert version the story moves at a rapid pace, tracing the life of David from his adolescence in the countryside to his final glory. The work captures wonderfully the rustic yet warlike atmosphere of the Israel of three thousand years ago. The extreme concentration of the storytelling provides a kaleidoscopic and slightly dizzying succession of contrasting episodes, passing in flashes from jubilation to despair, from glory to defeat, and from peace to war. The role of the music is to fix these moments by means of brief but striking formulae. This was, perhaps, the most difficult problem facing the composer, and he resolved it triumphantly. Cocteau once described his version of *Antigone* as "a photograph of Greece taken from an airplane," and Morax, too, in revising his text of *Le Roi David* for the concert hall, seems to have viewed his subject from a more compact, aerial perspective.

The score consists of twenty-eight numbers, with a brief fanfare standing as No. 3a. Eight of these numbers are purely orchestral, while the other twenty contain a sung part, with nine for chorus alone, six for soloists, and five for both together. No less than ten of these are psalms and four others are canticles. Numbers 18 and 22 are also near to being canticles in spirit, so that only four numbers in all possess any dramatic sense and move the story onward. Three of those four (Nos. 14, 16, and 26/27) are the longest numbers in the score and require the participation of the narrator (who otherwise alternates with the music).

In the original version for small forces, the instrumentation is different for each number, just as in Bach. The performing forces required for each number will be noted at the head of each, as it is discussed. These numbers are mostly extremely short: Nos. 4 and 19 are only thirteen measures long, and only three of the numbers (Nos. 14, 16, and 27) are longer than fifty measures. Only "The Dance Before the Ark," with 305 measures, can be called a real cantata, and it includes development that allows Honegger to demonstrate his epic qualities. Elsewhere, Honegger achieves grandeur through the concentrated intensity and extraordinary vigor of each individual passage.

This "symphonic psalm" consists of three parts, the second being much shorter than the other two. As Willy Tappolet rightly observes, "the contrast between the pagan character of the first part and the Christian inspiration of the last is sufficiently marked so that the symmetrical disposition as a triptych is not some pre-established plan but the result of an internal necessity."[3]

There remains the question of whether to choose the original version or the one for full symphony orchestra. The latter has long eclipsed the former, and the first Paris performance of the original version was not given until 4 June 1947, on the initiative of Philippe Strubin. But Honegger always preferred this early version, and now it has moved up in popularity alongside its more brilliant junior rival. It avoids some of the more powerful effects, which sometimes border perilously on grandiloquence, and restores to the work some of the rural atmosphere, the youthful freshness, and the inimitable blend of roughness and tenderness that contributes so much to the authenticity of Honegger's vision of Biblical antiquity. But even in the larger orchestral version the composer was careful to preserve the music's primitive color, underlining what he himself referred to as its "unpolished and slightly barbarous character" by retaining the predominance of wind instruments.

An extremely detailed analysis of *Le Roi David*, far exceeding the frame of reference of this book, is to be found in a book written (in German) by Hans Dieter Voss, *Arthur Honegger: Le Roi David* (Munich, 1983). This volume also deals with a few variants in details made necessary by the 1923 reorchestration. The following commentary is based on the original version. In conclusion, I shall briefly look at the advantages (or, indeed, disadvantages) of the reorchestrated version.

First Part: David as Shepherd, Chief, and Military Leader

1. INTRODUCTION (ALL WINDS, PIANO, TIMPANI, BASS DRUM, DOUBLE BASS)

In the space of a few measures, Honegger sets the scene. In the overheated atmosphere, the twinging, vaguely Oriental oboe cantilena is heard over dark, plodding bass notes. We are in the land of Israel three thousand years ago. The second section of this introduction is slower and of a strange, archaic gentleness, with the oboe in measure 18 recalling Debussy. This section introduces the entry of the narrator: the prophet Samuel goes up to Bethlehem to find the young shepherd David, who has been chosen as King of Israel.

2. "CANTICLE OF THE SHEPHERD DAVID" (CONTRALTO, TWO FLUTES, BASSOON, HARMONIUM)

The diatonic simplicity of a fresh, tender pastoral melody stands in contrast to the slightly dissonant chromaticism of the transparent harmonies that surround it. A high bassoon introduces a special color. Honegger here expresses the confident abandon of the boy to his God.

3. PSALM (UNISON CHORUS, BASSOON, HORN, TWO TRUMPETS, DOUBLE BASS)

There are clear references to Bach and Handel in the forceful rhythmic drive, the plain diatonicism (the sole modulation is a classical one to the relative minor), and the strong, straightforward two-part counterpoint. The words ("Praised be the Lord, full of glory") are by Clément Marot.

3A. FANFARE (HORN, TWO TRUMPETS, TIMPANI)

This short bitonal fanfare, in the keys of B-flat major and D-flat major, is modeled on one in Florent Schmitt's *Psalm 47*. Here it announces Saul assembling the Israelite warriors going off to confront the Philistines. Goliath (represented by a brief trombone solo) falls beneath David's sling.

4. "SONG OF VICTORY" (FOUR-PART CHORUS, TIMPANI)

Thirteen measures of fierce, exultant joy, with splendidly violent accents (*Sa*ül; *dix* mille). These measures will be repeated after No. 5. Note the near-quotation from Debussy's *Fêtes* at measures 6–9 ("The Eternal has chosen him, the Eternal supports him").

5. "Procession" (brass, piano, double bass)

Quadritonal fanfares (trumpets in E in parallel fourths, horn in D minor, trombone in F-sharp major, double bass ostinato in F minor). These combine 4/4 and 12/8 meters. The victorious Jewish army approaches.

6. Psalm (tenor, all woodwinds, horn, piano, double bass)

The spirit of evil has entered into Saul, and he tries to kill David with his bow as he sings and plays the harp. But David's belief remains unshaken ("Fear nothing and put thy trust in the Eternal"). After a brief central section of agitated modulations, culminating in the realistic whistling of the arrow, turned aside by the hand of God, the serene melody reappears intact. But David has to escape into the desert.

7. Psalm (soprano, all winds, piano, cymbals)

This delightful movement, one of the high points in the score, describes most movingly David's nostalgia at being separated from his family and friends ("Oh, if I had the wings of a dove!"). Honegger's choice of harmonies, the finely balanced *sicilienne* rhythm, and his use of flute and oboe reveal his admiration for Fauré, whose influence is especially noticeable in the seductive languor of the instrumental interludes (measures 6–9 and 14–17). In the stage version, this Psalm comes after No. 8.

8. "Canticle of the Prophets" (two-part male chorus, clarinet, bass clarinet, bassoon, gong, double bass)

Saul's envoys find David amid the prophets, who meditate gloomily on the ephemeral fragility of existence ("Man that is born of woman hath but a little time to live"). The exclusive use of low registers and of "organum-type" intervals (fourths, fifths, and seconds) for the male chorus underlines the weighty, austere character of the musical ideas.

9. Psalm (tenor, all winds, double bass)

David has been driven into the mountains by Saul's men and cries out in distress ("Have pity on me, my God!"). The bitterness of this appeal is emphasized by the Phrygian minor and by the sonority of the English horn. But his prayer is answered, and suddenly the character of the music changes to a robust Allegro marcato in the manner of Bach. The music is buoyed up by ascending modulations, expressing unshakable confidence ("My heart is firm"). God delivers up to David Saul's army, which is plunged in a deep sleep.

10. "Saul's Camp" (clarinet, bass clarinet, bassoon, horn, two trumpets, double bass)

A brief but evocative description of a calm night, disturbed by the sentries' distant polytonal fanfares. The atmosphere is one of mystery and suspense. Then comes a renewal of the fighting between Hebrews and Philistines—the latter now supported by David. Saul's army nevertheless affirms its belief in the Eternal.

11. Psalm (mixed chorus and complete instrumental ensemble)

Honegger began the composition of the work with this chorus. Its dynamic oppositions suggest some passionate dialogue of the soul with itself, as affirmation alternates with replies in a pale *pianissimo* and in Debussyan harmonies. All is resolved once more in a decisive Allegro in Bachian style ("When the wicked advance in great numbers"), and this hymn of faith is combined with both the text and the music of the initial affirmation ("The Eternal is my infinite light"). This leads to a brilliant conclusion in D major.

Abandoned by everyone, Saul goes by night to the witch of Endor and asks her to raise up the ghost of Samuel from Sheol.

12. "Incantation" (female narrator and complete instrumental ensemble)

The measured declamation is set off against a prodigiously powerful and dramatic orchestral interlude—a slow but irresistible crescendo and accelerando with broken rhythms and incantatory percussion. The atonal language here stands in deliberate contrast to the clear, diatonic idiom of most of the oratorio. These forty-seven measures reveal the young Honegger's symphonic talents to the full.

As Samuel's oracular pronouncement had foretold, the Israelite army is defeated on Mount Gilboa and Saul and his sons are killed.

13. "March of the Philistines" (piccolo, bassoon, brass, percussion, double bass)

The Philistines triumph, to music that is strident, heavy, vulgar, and puffed up with pride—Nazi music before its time! It is through this disaster that David inherits Saul's crown, brought to him by a messenger. His reign begins in sorrow. He tears at his clothes and weeps before his people, and they join in his affliction.

14. "Lamentations of Gilboa" (narrator, soprano, contralto, two-part female chorus, complete instrumental ensemble, except trombone)

This fine long movement brings the first part of *Le Roi David* to an impressive close. The melismas of the vocal soloists are then repeated by the chorus, and owe their Oriental atmosphere to their deliberate monotony, which underlines their desolation. Hans Dieter Voss has, in the aforementioned work, established links with both the cantillations of Yemenite Jews and the liturgy of the Comtat Venaissin. Could it be that Honegger became acquainted with the latter through Milhaud?

The arabesques of the wind instruments increase the passage's expressiveness. This magnificent threnody, one of the great funeral laments in all music, takes us far from Paris or Mézières, to the bare, ravine-pitted mountainsides of Judea. The aching woodwind dissonances of the introduction are like sobs, continually refusing to resolve. Then the first of the three forms of the lamentation theme (Example 107) reveals itself as a kind of disturbing negative of the future Alleluia (see Example 109).

Example 107

The mournful procession sets off at measure 17 with the second form of the theme. The chorus sopranos and contraltos alternate, in contrary motion, in an inexorable harmonic litany, with discreet modulations from the accompanying instruments. Under the garlands of triplets in the voice parts, the third form of the theme finally appears (Example 108). This is the most memorable of the three, both in its Oriental instrumental color (piccolo, flute, oboe) and in the searing dissonances of its contrary motion, set against the voices singing "Pleurez *Saül*." At measure 49, the second form reappears, in close imitations over descending piano arpeggios: a passage very similar to Debussy's *Sirènes*. The motif of Example 108 returns for the brief coda, which finally combines the three variants.

Example 108

Second Part: David as King

At the center of *Le Roi David* stands the impressive edifice of the temple of Joy. Preceded by its narthex, the "Festive Canticle," this provides all the material for the second part, and is a veritable summer solstice in the work: a long, ecstatic point of repose between the two lengthy, epic narratives that surround it. The composer's intuition testifies to his architectural genius. David the King enters the festive streets of Jerusalem, accompanying the Ark that will find a permanent home there, and dancing before it.

15. "FESTIVE CANTICLE" (SOPRANO, FEMALE CHORUS, PICCOLO, OBOE, PIANO)

Introduced by the bright, acid call of the oboe, the solo soprano's fresh, exultant vocalise invites the daughters of Israel to rejoice. It is superimposed on their song, before soaring away on its own in a sunlit conclusion. Under the fast, high piano arpeggios, the anapestic rhythms of the girls suggest unheard castanets and tambourines, and their Hebrew tone is close to that of popular dances found in Israel today—Honegger's intuition told him that the Shulamite belongs to every age. Numbers 15 and 17 are reversed in the stage version.

16. "THE DANCE BEFORE THE ARK" (NARRATOR, SOPRANO, SIX-PART MIXED CHOIR, COMPLETE INSTRUMENTAL ENSEMBLE)

This huge fresco brings the whole population of Israel into the action: shepherds, harvesters, winegrowers, then priests and warriors follow one another in an uninterrupted procession. The harsh sunlight intensifies the excitement of both bodies and minds, an excitement that slowly intensifies to become a furious ecstasy, a sacred *raptus*. Through this, the celebration of the Eternal God of Hosts joins the great initiatory mysteries of the ancient Orient, in which bodily frenzy acts as a conduit for experience parallel with that of the spirit. Honegger brings a wonderfully sure touch to this rendering of the festivities of a civilization that is both warlike and pastoral.

The length of the movement (eleven minutes of continuous music) allows Honegger to proceed by large symphonic steps, based on well-defined thematic elements. We can distinguish six main sections:

a) (measures 1–39) The narrator declaims his text over a calm, solemn orchestral introduction, modulating twice by intervals of a semitone. This typically Wagnerian procedure (see, for example, Brünnhilde's awakening in the last act of *Siegfried*), leads each time to a pastoral arabesque on the flute. Then the music gradually becomes livelier through the intervention of dance rhythms and fanfares, until it becomes a joyful polytonal tumult.

b) (measures 40–105) The male chorus makes its entrance with the passionate, almost threatening appeal "Jehovah, come to us!" in B-flat, with energetic dotted rhythms. The women immediately reply to the sound of tambourines, in F-sharp ("Come to us, Eternal One, light of the morning!"), taking up the anapestic rhythm of the "Festive Canticle." This is developed at length, in sporadic counterpoint with a broad, ascending, triumphant theme from the basses, in the middle of the polytonality of the orchestra. Syncopations of a frenzy that almost recall Stravinsky's *Rite of Spring* introduce the warriors' harsh interlude ("All peoples have waged war against me"). This is surrounded by ecstatic cries of "It is Jehovah!" from the women and leads through a modulation rising by whole tones to four measures of Largo in 3/2 meter. These launch us unexpectedly into the dance proper.

c) (measures 106–229) This section is in a rigorously emphasized 3/4, continually modulating by rising tones. It begins brightly in the women's voices ("Sing to God, the strong and merciful"), before becoming ever wilder and faster. The frantic repetition of the same words on the same notes drives the whole throng to a sacred hysteria.

d) (measures 230–252) At the return of the 4/4 meter, the tone becomes insistent, even brutal. Within the ascending chromatic movement, the voices are arranged in layers: basses in repeated quarter-notes, tenors in eighth-notes, and women in sixteenth-notes. Then a repeat of the dance marks the high point of the liberation from all restraint. At the climax, a vast allargando suddenly halts the music on a *fortissimo* chord of F major.

e) (measures 253–270) In the startling silence we hear, for the first time in the work, the tinkling sounds of the celesta and, rising from it, the soprano voice of the Angel, who announces that it will not be David who builds the temple, but his son Solomon.

f) (measures 271–305) Now, radiant and collected, soprano voices softly strike up the airy vocalise of the Alleluia. This theme is, in its classical simplicity, the most inspired and memorable in the entire score (Example 109). It proceeds on its leisurely, unhurried way, passing from one voice to the other, over basses in conjunct descending quarter-notes. From D major there is a marvelous modulation to E major, then to a stretto in A-flat. The soprano's ecstatic vocalise is added above the polyphonic texture and settles into a dazzling F-sharp major. After a premonition on piano and woodwinds of the "Easter" carillons in fourths that will end the work, the soprano line slowly fades into the distance, into a dream world. Never before had Honegger achieved such a masterstroke.

Example 109

Third Part: David as King and Prophet

This third section is an account of David's entire reign, up until his death. In its evocation of the many events of this reign, both happy and sad, it returns to the rapid narrative rhythm and short movements of the first section.

17. "CANTICLE" (UNISON CHORUS, BASSOON, BRASS, TIMPANI, BASS DRUM, HARMONIUM, DOUBLE BASS)

The three verses of this hymn of praise have a straightforward energy that is underlined by trumpet figures and by a sudden, passing change of harmony from the dominant of B-flat to E major. The last verse expands to end in a brilliant peroration in G major, delivered with an utterly Brucknerian vigor.

But at the height of David's power, sin enters his heart: he desires Bathsheba, the wife of his general Uriah, whom he has seen from the height of his terrace.

18. "SONG OF THE SERVANT GIRL" (CONTRALTO, FLUTE, TWO CLARINETS, HORN, PIANO)

Both the words and the music of this touching, voluptuous melody were inspired by *The Song of Songs*, with the voice intertwining itself amorously with the broad horn theme.

David arranges Uriah's death and takes Bathsheba as his wife. But their son dies, the victim of divine anger. There follow two psalms of penitence and contrition, of very similar inspiration.

19. "PSALM OF PENITENCE" (TWO-VOICE MIXED CHORUS, ENGLISH HORN, BASSOON, BRASS, DOUBLE BASS)

The quarter-note chords in the orchestra oppose the gray bitterness of their heavy 6/4 meter against the floating, desolate, 12/8 lament of the chorus. The effect is one of scraping and dragging. Unresolved dissonances on brass drive the music on to the final *fortissimo*.

20. PSALM (FOUR-VOICE MIXED CHORUS, ALL WINDS, PIANO, HARMONIUM, DOUBLE BASS)

In the introduction to this second lament, the English horn quotes Claude Goudimel's melody "I am disinherited," from Psalm 51 in the Huguenot Psalter. It is a penitential procession that looks forward to Frank Martin's *Golgotha* and accentuates the dejection and contrition of the previous movement. Note the descent in measures 19 to 21 to the words "greatly sinned," which sounds like a huge sigh. In measure 30 there begins the long progression in close imitation on the theme of the preceding psalm. Acrid pillars of minor ninths on the orchestra seek in vain for resolution, and prolong the vocal supplications. This is music of ashes, reeking of death, and foreshadowing the last great symphonies, *Symphonie liturgique* and *Di Tre Re*.

David's trials are not yet at an end. The revolt of his son Absalom forces him once more to seek refuge in the desert.

21. PSALM (TENOR, WIND INSTRUMENTS EXCEPT TROMBONE, DOUBLE BASS)

This paraphrase of Psalm 121 ("I will lift up mine eyes unto the hills") expresses trust in God and hope. It is divided into two sections. The first is undecided in tone, but the second is anchored to a stable rhythm and tonality (6/4 and C major). However, it resolves in modal fashion, on to a surprise final chord of A major.

Absalom's army is defeated in the forest of Ephraim. But, while David mourns the death of his son, the women of Israel sing.

22. "THE SONG OF EPHRAIM" (SOPRANO, CHORUS CONTRALTOS, FLUTE, TWO CLARINETS, HORN, TIMPANI, TAMBOURINE, PIANO)

This charming song is heard over a flickering, lightly bitonal accompaniment. The vocal interest alternates between the soprano and the contraltos, who echo her phrases in vocalise. The tambourine beats a steady rhythm throughout.

23. "MARCH OF THE HEBREWS" (ALL WINDS EXCEPT BASSOON, TIMPANI, PERCUSSION, DOUBLE BASS)

Once more we hear polytonal fanfares built on fourths. The victorious Jewish army marches (in the key of E minor) past the old king, racked with grief. He nonetheless interrupts the procession to express his gratitude to his warriors—a brief moment of serenity, taken up by the following psalm.

24. PSALM (FOUR-VOICE MIXED CHORUS, WOODWINDS, HORN, PIANO, HARMONIUM, DOUBLE BASS)

The text ("I shall love you, Lord, with a tender love") is by Clément Marot. Honegger gives a gentle, Fauréan cantilena to voices in alternation, the contraltos prolonging each soprano phrase with a sensuous arabesque. The lilting, transparent harmonies are briefly interrupted by a dash of dramatic, chromatic polyphony at the words "Like a torrent, they hoped to surprise me." But this outburst leaves no trace on the serene opening music when it returns.

The old king's pride, which leads him to number his people as a measure of his power, brings divine anger upon Israel for one last time, in the shape of the Angel of death, who brings pestilence.

25. PSALM (UNISON CHOIR, COMPLETE INSTRUMENTAL ENSEMBLE)

This is a vision of terror on Marot's words "In this fear, the great God whom I adore." They are declaimed, almost spoken, in a brusque, violent recitative, accompanied by a chaotic orchestral storm, almost Stravinskyan in tone, and looking forward to the Dies irae of the *Symphonie liturgique*. At the end, the chaos comes together into a frantic hammering of repeated chords. The whole movement is atonal.

The time has come for pardon, and also for the end of this long, active life. David abdicates in favor of his son Solomon.

26. "CORONATION OF SOLOMON" (NARRATOR, ALL WINDS, TIMPANI, DOUBLE BASS)

This short interlude has an august grandeur, with its noble trumpet call repeated by trombone, and for a moment one thinks of *Parsifal*. It leads without a break into the final scene.

27. "THE DEATH OF DAVID" (SOPRANO NARRATOR, MIXED CHORUS, COMPLETE INSTRUMENTAL ENSEMBLE)

This is the second climax of the score. Honegger's great problem here was to supersede the first climax, "The Dance Before the Ark." Although this final movement now seems to us supremely evident, it took him ten days to find the solution—and we may remember what a single day meant for him in his tight schedule.

The narrator concludes the whole story supported by twelve measures of light woodwind chords. Then we hear the pure voice of the solo soprano singing the Angel's prophecy, which is none other than the Messianic prophecy of the Virga Jesse. Since Morax here introduces a New Testament element into the story, it was logical that the composer should try to do the same with the music. This he achieved by giving the Angel's melody, when it is taken over by the female chorus, the feel of a chorale, thanks to a simple change in its rhythm (Example 110).

The origin of this chorale may lie in two well-known tunes, both used by J. S. Bach: *Wie schön leucht'uns der Morgenstern* (How Brightly Shines the Morning Star) and *Wachet auf, ruft uns die Stimme* (Sleepers Awake, a Voice is Calling), itself stemming from the Gregorian *Magnificat*. The chorale has six periods. The male voices punctuate it with Alleluias in detached sixteenth-notes, *pianissimo*. Then suddenly comes the surprise of the return of the Alleluia from "The Dance Before the Ark" (Example 109) and the fulfillment of our intimate hope. The abrupt arrival of A-flat major is an effect that will never pall.

With the return to D major, the chorale theme is heard in the basses in long values, like a cantus firmus. Although this procedure is standard in the works of Bach, we should not underestimate the contrapuntal skill it requires, especially when the harmonies flow as naturally as they do here. The super-

Example 110

imposition of the two themes fits perfectly inside the music's modulatory structure, with the highly chromatic course of the Alleluia preserved intact. The only change is the transposition of the fourth phrase of the chorale down a tone—an adjustment that passes totally unnoticed. Honegger had reason to be proud of such an achievement.

The tone of radiant joy grows more emphatic as the music modulates upward one tone at a time. As the chorus reaches the peak of an irresistible crescendo, it comes to rest on a D major chord. But the orchestra (as it will later after the trumpet chorale in the *Symphony for Strings*) has five more measures to play, and the Easter carillon rings out in major scales harmonized in brilliant parallel fourths.

Finally, I should say a few words about Honegger's rescoring of the work for large orchestra in 1923. The addition of strings did not affect every movement by any means: there are no violins or violas in Nos. 3, 4, 5–8, 10, 13, 15, and 19, and no violins in Nos. 6 and 18. In No. 7, the harp is obviously more suitable to the movement's Fauréan character than the piano. Likewise, harp and celesta are preferable to piano in measures 49 and following in the "Lamentations of Gilboa" (No. 14), as well as in No. 15, which otherwise Honegger left as it was.

The movements that benefit from a large orchestra are the more extended, "symphonic" ones (Nos. 12, 14, 16, 25, and 27). The full string band is irreplaceable in the slow introduction and in the whole of the enormous central section of "The Dance Before the Ark," as well as in the middle of No. 26 and in the slow beginning of No. 27. The organ, happily, intervenes only at the climax of "The Dance Before the Ark" (sections *d* and *e*; but not in the Alleluia), in the powerful Canticle No. 17 (where it takes the place of violins and violas), at the climax of No. 20 (measure 30 and following), and in the last fourteen measures of No. 27.

Otherwise, it is to be regretted that in No. 18 Honegger replaced the solo horn with solo viola and English horn in alternation—it is duller, and there was no need for it. On the other hand, the high violin pizzicatos are excellent for doubling the woodwinds in the E minor "March of the Hebrews" (No. 23), and the strings are a welcome addition in No. 24. In short, as I have already said, both versions deserve to survive and are to a certain extent complementary.

57. Judith

A. First version: Biblical drama by René Morax
December 1924 (or January 1925)–5 April 1925; orchestration completed late April 1925.
"To Claire Croiza." Commissioned by the Théâtre du Jorat.
First performance: 13 June 1925, Claire Croiza (Judith), Mme Andréossi (Serving Girl), Pierre Alcover (Holofernes), chorus and orchestra, conducted by Arthur Honegger, Théâtre du Jorat, Mézières (Vaud)
Performing forces: soprano (Serving Girl), mezzo-soprano (Judith), three chorus soloists (soprano, tenor, baritone); mixed chorus; orchestra: 2.2.2.2.–2.2.2.0.– percussion (bass drum, cymbals, side drum, tam-tam, triangle)–harmonium, two pianos–strings; numerous speaking roles
The whole work lasts an evening, with about 32 minutes of music
Act I: 1. Lamentation; 2. The Horn of Alarm; 3. Prayer; 4. Funeral Dirge; 5. Invocation
Act II: 6. Incantation; 7. Fanfare; 8. Scene by the Well; 9. Festive Music
Act III: 10. Nocturne; 11. Canticle of Battle; 12. Canticle of the Virgins; 13. Canticle of Victory

B. Second version: serious opera
See H57B (Category 11, Opera)

C. Third version: "action musicale" (oratorio)
Probably arranged shortly before the first performance in 1927
"To Claire Croiza"
Premiere: 16 June 1927, Berthe Seroen, Evert Cornelis, chorus and orchestra, conducted by Arthur Honegger, Rotterdam
Same performing forces as for the first version, with the addition of a narrator
Duration: 47 minutes (including about 40 minutes of music)
This version extends No. 2, also No. 4 slightly, inverts the order of Nos. 6 and 7, adds voices to No. 8, and contains three new movements: 9a. The Death of Holofernes; 10a. Return of Judith; 11a. Interlude. It contains 711 measures of music in all, as against 576 in the dramatic version. All these additions are taken from the second, operatic version.

None of Honegger's other works had such a complicated compositional history. To make matters worse, the autograph orchestral scores are not available, being owned by a collector who refuses to let them be seen. But the autograph vocal scores in the possession of the composer's son, Jean-Claude, have allowed me to shed some light on the composition of the three versions, with the operatic version preceding that of the oratorio.

I have already related in the biographical section of this book the story of how Judith was composed (even though we have very little evidence because of the absence of letters) and of the premieres of the different versions.

Judith is the transitional work par excellence. It is no longer Le Roi David and it is not yet Antigone, and it is searching for an identity between oratorio and opera. This is not to discount its musical qualities—such problematic turning points are often works of great value and fascination, as we know from Mozart's Idomeneo and Bruckner's Third Symphony. But in order to illustrate this hybrid quality I have deliberately separated discussion of the operatic version from that of the two others, as its thrust is utterly different. If Judith as an oratorio finds a place beside Le Roi David, as an opera it comes directly before Antigone. The reader will find a brief summary after my treatment of the operatic version.

The third (oratorio) version being the most often played (and so far the only one on disc), I shall discuss this first, following the pattern of *Le Roi David*. The story of Judith and Holofernes may be a more concentrated, unified one than that of King David, but it lacks its variety of incident and its broad human significance. René Morax's response to it was a libretto with a number of weak and tedious patches, some way from the spontaneity and freshness of that which he wrote for *Le Roi David*.

And finally (as discussed in Chapter 4), for all the fine musical qualities of Honegger's score, *Judith* did not suit the rustic surroundings of the Théâtre du Jorat. The original version (that which was performed at Mézières) contained only thirteen numbers, making up barely more than half-an-hour's music (half the length of *Le Roi David*). Even if these numbers are generally longer, none of them reaches the dimensions of the two great pillars of the preceding work, "The Dance Before the Ark" and "The Death of David." There were also none of the many brief but sharply etched choruses that had done so much to give *Le Roi David* its immediate popularity. In short, those who looked for a repetition of the characteristics of the previous work were disappointed, and the innovations *Judith* had to offer were met with a lack of understanding and rejection. For all that, the work is more mature and profound, more unified stylistically, more personal in its expression, and more modern in its musical language—all of which attributes Mézières did not find to its taste.

Both the original dramatic version and the oratorio version I shall be discussing here use only two main vocal soloists: Judith and the Serving Girl. Male voices are used only in the operatic version. There is no male chorus before the second act, and no full chorus before the third. Before looking at the score in more detail, we should remind ourselves once again how much Honegger was attracted to female characters of a heroic disposition: apart from Judith, to Antigone, Joan of Arc, and even Semiramis.

Act I

1. "Lamentations" (Judith, female chorus)

Right from the start we are gripped by strident, dissonant trills. In measure 5, a motif appears on two muted trumpets, repeated immediately by voices. This will be one of the main leitmotifs of the whole work (Example 111).

This entire, extremely harsh opening gravitates around D-sharp/E-flat minor. The female chorus alternates with Judith, whose strong accents

Example 111

("*colère*," "*désir*," and even "*faiblesse*") contribute to the air of tension and bitter determination, together with the use of the Neapolitan sixth on the tonic. The music modulates by descending minor triads, but after a return of the opening now reduced to five measures, it concludes abruptly and unexpectedly in C minor. Within a short space of time, Honegger manages to convey an oppressive atmosphere of despair, and to evoke the unmistakable character of the Middle East of Biblical times.

2. "THE HORN OF ALARM" (JUDITH, THE SERVING GIRL, A SOPRANO)

The voices figure in the second half of the number only (the last 29 of 56 measures). These were added for the second and third versions. The sepulchral dialogue of trombones and horns in long, irrational values stands out from the dark web of chromatic ostinatos in a tonality centered around F minor. The discreetly lyrical, yet intense dialogue of the two women takes place in a captivating nocturnal atmosphere. This is a conversation that is sung in the manner of opera, marking a fundamental difference with *Le Roi David*. This added section brings in the two other most important leitmotifs on the orchestra: the victorious, pentaphonic, ascending motif associated with Jehovah (Example 112)—Messiaen would revive a memory of this in the "Regard de l'esprit de joie" in his *Vingt Regards sur l'enfant Jésus*—and the twinging dissonant motif (Example 113) characterized by its contrary motion. In the final measures, Jehovah's motif (Example 112) rises gently in crystalline notes on the piano, and leads without a break into the next number.

3. "JUDITH'S PRAYER" (JUDITH)

"Judith's Prayer," the best-known passage in the work, is in E minor (perhaps the main tonality of the work), with a bright, confident conclusion in E major. It is a contemplative, searching movement, with a brief outburst of violence ("Lift Thine arm, crush their strength!") in the middle. A simple figure on the oboe introduces the song. The figure then moves to the flute and other woodwinds, marking out the different periods and acting as a conclusion. It also appears in the epilogue of the operatic version. The energetic Example 112 emphasizes, in Honeggerian manner, such words as "*Jéhovah*" and "*Éternel*," and acts as a constant support to the prayer. Even the word "*faiblesse*" (weakness) is accentuated in this way—Judith explains, "But it is my weapon." The blocks of parallel chords and pentatonic structures are strongly reminiscent of the diatonic modal but dissonant style of contemporary works by Vaughan Williams, such as *Flos Campi* and *Sancta Civitas*. This prayer is a masterpiece.

4. "FUNERAL DIRGE" ("FUNERAL SONG" IN THE ORIGINAL VERSION) (SOLO SOPRANO AND FEMALE CHORUS)

The three opening measures, added later, serve to link this number in B minor with the preceding number by a sung repeat of the work's opening theme

Example 112

Example 113

(Example 111). This dominates most of the movement, its ending suddenly calling to mind the "Lamentations of Gilboa" in *Le Roi David*. Example 111 is now heard on flutes. The modal color characteristic of Vaughan Williams persists, but it is rather Stravinsky one thinks of in passing when the instrumental bass line plays in 12/8 under the words "From the house our fathers built."

5. "INVOCATION" (FEMALE CHORUS)

This female chorus is surrounded by strident, painful dissonances on high violins, repeating Example 113 (which is itself a variant of Example 111). As the tempo increases and note values become shorter, the harmony progresses upward from E minor to A major. The rapid repeated notes in parallel thirds suggest the Stravinsky of *Oedipus Rex* or *Persephone*, although the harmony here is more attractive. The second act follows without a break.

Act II

6. "FANFARE" (NO. 7 IN THE ORIGINAL VERSION)

This short fanfare establishes the scene of Holofernes's camp. It is both polytonal (trumpets in E-flat and G-flat, horn in D-flat, trombone in A-flat, all over a pedal F-sharp) and polyrhythmic (the theme imitated in simple and double augmentation).

7. "Incantation" (No. 6 in the original version) (male chorus)

This violent, percussive number is marked by the first appearance of the male chorus. It is a kind of toccata that modulates from the initial E minor, and its brutal, vulgar tone (like that of the Philistines in *Le Roi David*) contrasts sharply with everything that has gone before. This underlines the striking contrast between the pagan way of hectoring their gods (who, it is clear, do not respond) and the Hebrews' passionate pleading with Jehovah. The climax is followed by a quieter, yet still menacing, coda.

8. "Scene by the Spring" ("Scene by the Well" in the original version) (Judith, the Serving Girl: their voices were added to the second version during the first 28 of the 44 measures of the movement. In both versions, a tenor voice is also heard at the beginning and at the end, vocalizing in the distance)

By adding the two women's voices, Honegger turned this simple instrumental interlude into one of the most moving pages in the score. Once again, his astonishing power of evocation creates an atmosphere of nocturnal anxiety. The somber introduction on strings is overlaid by Judith's long monologue in E minor—the key that represents her submission to God. Suddenly, she is afraid and her courage fails ("My only hope is death") and she suffers the momentary weakness that will one day afflict Joan of Arc as well. Meanwhile, Example 111 is heard in a chromatic, obsessively dissonant dialogue between woodwinds and strings. The final section repeats the Fanfare (No. 6). Over a held chord of F-sharp major, it now sounds both distant and menacing. It is followed by a brief reminder of the tenor vocalise.

9. "Festive Music"

This purely instrumental movement, in a moderate 6/8 meter and in B minor, is scored for a chamber ensemble of oboe, clarinet, two trumpets, two trombones, piano, and divided violas playing *col legno* and pizzicato respectively. This orgy in Holofernes's camp is a frankly sinister affair, with a sketchy accompaniment of ostinatos on violas and piano and acidulous, Oriental melismas alternating between oboe and clarinet.

9A. "Death of Holofernes" (the Serving Girl, Judith, a Sentinel-tenor)

From here to the end of the work all the numbers follow one another without a break, sometimes over the continuation of the spoken narrative. Here, for the only time, one may be reminded of Satie and *The Death of Socrates*, with its low, monotonous eighth-note octaves on the piano. The music very gradually accelerates in an ascending chromatic progression, while the Serving Girl comments in terror on that which she hears but cannot see: namely the murder of Holofernes. Her growing fear is underlined by the modified reminder of Example 111 on divided violins, the ghostly harmonics, first on violas and then on violins, and the unearthly glissandos on cellos ("Who hath groaned?"). The tension is made all the more unbearable by the deliberate scarcity and lack of eventuation in the musical material. It explodes abruptly at the appearance of Judith, who bursts upon the scene out of breath and holding in her hand the bloody head of Holofernes. After the two women's brief passage past the Sentinel, who luckily lets them through, the music ends as it began, because the Jews are still unaware of Judith's success.

Act III

10. "NOCTURNE"

Here again the sparse texture, slow pace, and high degree of dissonance create an atmosphere of aching expectation that sets the nerves on edge. Anxiously, the women of Bethulia wait for a sign in the night. After the twinging motif of Example 113, we hear the edgy voice of the English horn dominating the nocturnal woodwind dialogue.

10A. "RETURN OF JUDITH" (JUDITH, A SOLDIER-TENOR, A VOICE-BARITONE, MIXED CHORUS)

A rapid crescendo leads at last to the liberating *fortissimo* that we have been expecting for so long, an explosion of joy on the dominant of G, based on Jehovah's victory theme (Example 112). It is here, as Judith appears before her people, that the full mixed choir, carefully held in reserve until this crucial moment, makes itself heard for the first time. Its almost chaotic tumult is an expression of fierce joy. After the blaze of light on the dominant of G, Judith returns fittingly to the E-flat minor of the opening of the work, at the words "All of you look at this man, he is the enemy!" The hectic chords accompanying her words "I know one thing further" (on the victorious theme of Example 112 played at three different speeds), prepare us for the battle into which we are now led by a rapid, powerful crescendo.

11. "CANTICLE OF BATTLE" (MIXED CHORUS)

This movement is in a hectic 3/2 meter, with brusque rhythms derived from *The Rite of Spring*—powerful, martial music reminiscent of Ferdinand Hodler. The triumphant canticle in long values in 9/4 meter poses a textual problem that will only be solved when the autographs become accessible. It appears that in the first version the canticle was given to the sopranos (this is supported by the 1927 recording with Claire Croiza, conducted by Louis de Vocht). But in the second it was given to the tenors, which works less well, as they strike less of a contrast with the warriors' fierce cries of "Ho! Ho!" Michel Corboz, in his recording, opts for the compromise of doubling sopranos and tenors at the octave, which blurs the tutti even more. Whatever the solution adopted, this canticle succeeds through its typically Honeggerian use of meter and accent. This is especially true at the varied repeat, when Jehovah's theme (Example 112) blazes forth in all its glory and, after an electrifying crescendo, the violins in rapid, ascending scales in eighth-note tremolo triplets clash like swords and lances. The movement ends on a radiant chord of B-flat major.

11A. INTERLUDE

These nineteen measures in a pentatonic A-flat major are serene and dreamy. Discreet allusions to the theme of the following number are inserted in slightly clashing keys.

12. "CANTICLE OF THE VIRGINS" (SOLO SOPRANO, FEMALE CHORUS)

This delightful movement is the only one that recaptures the simple freshness of the canticles that are scattered throughout *Le Roi David*. The name that comes most readily to mind is that of Milhaud, both in the popular tone of the melodic ostinato in the voice parts (Example 114) and in the harmonic pedals of the accompaniment, which maintain to the end the ambivalence between D-flat major and its dominant A-flat. After a middle section that modulates to sharp keys, the varied recapitulation is adorned with new, lively countermelodies in the woodwinds. The final cadence comes unexpectedly in the real tonic D-flat, and is a moment of true grace.

Example 114

13. "CANTICLE OF VICTORY" (JUDITH, MIXED CHORUS)

This long, powerful finale is the climax of the work. A wild orchestral introduction sweeps Example 112 along like a river in spate, and accompanies the final appearance of the narrator calling upon the people to celebrate the victory. The chorus bursts in with vigorous "Hosannas," again supported by Jehovah's theme (Example 112, with a stretto on trumpets). At Judith's words "His name is Jehovah" this theme expands in D major. Its first three notes, augmented to quarter-notes, form a large anacrusis, followed by a much shorter accent and falling-away—a convulsive phrase shape expressing a joy that is exultant, wild, and almost spasmodic. It is one of the rare passages in *Judith* in which Honegger employs his well-known manner of word-setting.

The chorus briefly imitates the soloist (with the anacrusis now reduced once more to eighth-notes), then the tempo accelerates in sunny eighth-note triplet arabesques on women's voices, and in rough polytonal chords from the whole ensemble at the words "Holy, holy, holy is the Lord." This gives rise to a healthy bout of frenzy. In the midst of an orchestral tumult, the triplets join a fugal exposition on a new, rhythmic theme, based on three conjunct descending notes at the words "Glory to God the all-powerful!" The entries in this exposition are arranged successively in thirds (E, G, B-flat, C-sharp), rather than in fifths and fourths. Two strettos lead to a powerful unison on Example 112, and the orchestra on its own brings the work to a close with six measures of heavy chords that twice hammer out the Neapolitan sixth E-flat, before finally reaching an unambiguous D major. This ending is very close to that of *Le Roi David* (and in the same key), although its orchestral color is again reminiscent of Milhaud. We shall see that in the operatic version there is an extra epilogue, a quiet, melancholy passage in which, despite everything, Judith repents her action. In the concert hall the original ending is undoubtedly far more impressive.

77. *Cris du monde* (Cries of the World)

November or December 1930–1 March 1931; orchestration completed 24 March
    1931
"Dedicated to the Cecilian Society of Solothurn and to its conductor Erich Schild as
    a token of friendly gratitude"
Text by René Bizet (English version by Edward Agate; German version by Gian
    Bundi), inspired by John Keats's "O Solitude."
First performance: 3 May 1931, Berthe de Vigier, Pauline Hoch, Carl Rehfuss,
    Cecilian Society Chorus and an orchestra, conducted by Erich Schild, Solothurn
Performing forces: soprano, contralto, baritone soloists, mixed chorus; orchestra:
    3.3.3.3.–4.3.3.1.–bass drum, cymbals, side drum, tam-tam, triangle, woodblock–
    piano–strings
Duration: 54 minutes 25 seconds

Cris du monde was very well received at its first performance, but in Paris a month later it was greeted with incomprehension combined with hostility. To this day it remains perhaps Honegger's most difficult and problematic work. It is a bitter testimony to a profound personal crisis and to a general crisis provoked by the deep economic depression that followed the Wall Street crash of 1929, with the resulting unemployment and misery for millions of desperate people—easy victims for Hitler and other totalitarian ideologues. Beyond that, *Cris du monde* is a prophetic warning about matters that then had no name, but now have their own government departments: quality of life, the environment, pollution, enlistment, mass culture, pressure of noise, of the media, of collectivism—in short, everything that contributes to the destruction of the soul and the death of the individual. In 1931 the warning from this all-too-prophetic Cassandra came too early not to upset a civilization that was unwittingly dancing on the edge of the volcano due to destroy it a few years hence.

But the work retains a burning and sinister relevance. In *Cris du monde* Honegger expressed for the first time the terrible pessimism that would dominate his last symphonies. It is not an easy message to take direct and this, together with the tough, tense musical language that it called for, explains why

Cris du monde will never be a popular work. The subject, as Honegger himself described it in the review *Plans* in December 1931, is "the rebellion of the individual against the crowd that is crushing him." This implies a retreat into an inner life that we would be wrong to interpret as egoism or indifference. On the contrary, it is the reaction of someone who is too sensitive to the suffering around him, and who is obeying the need to distance himself so that he can preserve the spiritual space indispensable to his activities as a creative artist.

Unlike *Le Roi David* or *Judith*, the score of *Cris du monde* does not consist of separate numbers, but is a continuous work of a symphonic nature, lasting some fifty-five minutes. It is also, with the late *Cantate de Noël*, the only choral/orchestral work of Honegger's that does not include the spoken voice. Of the three solo singers, the soprano and baritone are treated as a couple, with the female voice representing the soul of the baritone-as-individual. The contralto's role, for all its beauty, is episodic, representing Woman, the final temptation of the individual.

The structure of the work can be summed up as follows: (1) dream prologue; (2) reality of the morning; (3, 4) ways of escape, cosmic; (5, 6) ways of escape, human; (7) reality of the night, a free recapitulation of that of the morning.

1. INTRODUCTION

The introduction is in two sections, the first of which is purely orchestral. A sinuous, atonal, almost serial line is crawling in the double basses, only vaguely defining C minor, which shall be the basic and final tonality of the work. Sepulchral, muted trumpets play an important dotted motif in fourths and fifths. It is like a spectral, deformed version of the triumphant tonal motif that would appear in *Mermoz* (see Example 102). These two elements alternate several times with the addition of countermelodies.

Suddenly, at the beginning of the second section, with the baritone's entry, the atmosphere changes completely, with a clear E major expressing hope. We may note right away Honegger's very personal treatment of words, which had only been touched on in the previous oratorios but had meanwhile been developed in the opera *Antigone*: the accents on the first syllable of words, falling on the first beat of the measures, instead of the usual anacruses that the French language produces naturally. These iambic rhythms violate the traditional rules of prosody, but give the text an extra vigor and impact. During this second half of the introduction, the baritone and soprano alternate before joining forces in a passage of spiritual aspiration already shot through with anxiety: "Every day I hear the disputing voices of doubt and faith. Have I raised up my soul, or destroyed it?"

2. "VOICE OF THE MORNING–VOICES OF THE OTHERS"

The Morning's reply is terrifying. Instead of producing the expected vision of peace and harmony, the orchestra, through abrupt and disjointed rhythms, progressively builds up a polyphonic, polyrhythmic fabric of no less than seven layers. In case we have not understood the message, the choral entry explains it: "Breathing of factories, panting of machines!" (Example 115). After this come the wretched "Voices of the Others," of men in general, miserably calling out for help: "There is no cure for poverty, and we collapse beneath its burden" (Example 116).

Souf - fle des u - sines—— ha - lè - te - ment des ma - chi - nes

Example 115

La mi - sè - re est sans re - mè - de

Example 116

Then come the Soldiers. In this biting, sardonic satire on a military march past ("the voice of the crowd acclaims your fatherland regiment by regiment"), the Honegger of 1931 expresses his unceasing hatred of war, nationalism, and goose stepping. After the Soldiers come the Workers, whose slogans combine with the military marching past to the strains of a searing canon between violins and voices. The baritone briefly intervenes to say that he has understood, but that he dreams of peace and solitude. The chorus of machines is repeated, now combined with mankind's laments and the Soldiers' cries in a passage of extraordinary polyphony, then the baritone delivers his final lament: "I can no longer hear the beating of my heart."

3. "Voices of the Sea and the Mountain"

Each of the four "ways of escape" that the world suggests to man will meet with the same refusal. First of all, it is the Sea—a gray, Nordic sea ("I am the route you must travel"), then the hieratic music of the Mountain ("My summits are the thrones of your wise men"), amazingly close to the later Honegger of the *Suite archaïque* and *Monopartita*. It is a mighty mountain, certainly, but austere and bereft of sun. The two then alternate, with ever-more-pressing arguments, but heard as though through a haze that gives these images a ghostly grandeur. A piercing dissonance from the strings breaks the atmosphere, and first the baritone then, after the return of the Mountain's solemn chorale, the soprano refuse to hear these calls, and once again unite in prayer: "But thou, silence at the gate of Heaven, listen to the burden of my song"—and the atmosphere suddenly clears.

4. "Voices of Space"

A wild, "cosmic" tumult of dense chromaticism on strings leads to a mighty wind and piano *fortissimo* in a pentatonic E. This is combined with the threefold ascending vocalise of the chorus. A very slow crescendo on unison voices ushers in a second "cosmic" wave, this time in G and more subdued in texture. The second section of this movement establishes a rapid 12/8 meter and chromatic harmony, alternating with a more sostenuto vocal line over a more finely detailed orchestral texture. Finally, the chorus turns itself into a kind of orchestra with glissando trills and rapid tremolos that suggest flutter-tonguing. The third section is a short synthesis of the two preceding ones and then, as in each of these "ways of escape," comes the response of the Individual. This time it is longer and it alternates, no less than four times, two passages of opposing character: first, one of consonant polyphony on strings in long note values, looking forward to the best moments in the De profundis of the *Third Symphony*, and then the vocal recitatives of the two soloists, offering up a passionate prayer that ends with the disillusioned statement: "Caught between two storms, at my feet and on my head, I walk at the pace of a wild beast, without knowing whether God hears me."

5. "Voices of Unknown Cities"

The next section follows without a break. A long unison line on all the strings combines with the choral recitative. Then, suddenly, the woodwinds break out into music of an impressionist stamp in pentatonic arabesques. The chorus enters, evoking the fabulous Orient in an A major studded with "Arab" chromaticisms, although the C-naturals give the curious effect of being "blue" notes (the color of Turkestan carpets, perhaps?). The middle portion of this concentrically constructed movement is a lively, forceful episode describing the frantic activity of ports ("Everywhere is full of shouts and chains"); then comes a reversed and shortened recapitulation. This blends into another "response of the Individual," with the soprano gently rejecting the lure of distant cities, and the baritone doing so more emphatically, as he demands silence and "a sky without faces."

6. "Voice of Woman"

This is the last and strongest temptation. The music underlines the perfidious sweetness of the trap by becoming suddenly sentimental and languorous. It is not only the words ("The springs and summers have gone without love") that recall the Ernest Chausson of the *Poème de l'Amour et de la Mer* and the *Chanson perpétuelle*. Here the contralto has her one great solo, splitting the eight lines of the text into four long paragraphs, separated by the vocalises of the female chorus (there are no male voices in this movement).

Honegger's treatment of words is here used to suggest a vocal line broken by sobs. The female voices weave a network of vocalises with a grace that betrays Honegger's profound debt to Fauré. After much meandering that modulates again with a Fauréan grace, the music settles in A minor. For the last time we have the "response of the Individual." Faced with the Woman, the baritone remains a long time on his own. The soprano, his "soul," does not join him until the very end. His long lament ("black dove with starry wings") invokes the night. Then, for the first time, we hear the work's final prayer ("Surround me, isolate me, deliver me"), provoking a reply from the chorus, gently humming. The soprano takes up the same prayer more eagerly, and a further reply from the chorus suddenly vanishes into the shadows, from which, confusedly, emerge the "Voices of the Night."

7. "Voices of the Night"

The gloomy orchestral introduction fixes the rhythmic pulse before the entry of the spoken chorus, enunciating the text in a way that directly anticipates its treatment in *Jeanne d'Arc au bûcher*. A double vocal polyphony develops, incorporating spoken rhythms and long sung notes ("Come, come with us"). This urban polyphony gradually crystallizes around E minor and is joined by a repeat of the "Breathing of factories" (Example 115) from the second section. There is a sudden interruption by "vulgarly" commercial music in D major, completely against the beat. The four phrases of a music-hall song call to mind the cinema ("Images that speak, images that move"). They are accompanied by jazz syncopations and dry dotted rhythms on the woodblock, while the whole ensemble is held together by obsessive shouts from the chorus of "Listen to us, look at us!" (Example 117).

Poco più animato

E - cou - te nous,   E - cou - te   nous

Example 117

Soon the pitiable cry from the second section, "There is no cure for poverty" (Example 116), more urgent than ever, adds itself to the uproar. To the supplications of the soprano and baritone, the chorus adds its plea of "Pity on us!" The pandemonium begins again even more loudly, mixed with interjections and spoken shouts. In the midst of the orchestral turmoil we hear the signals of different radio stations—a direct forerunner of Bernd-Aloys Zimmermann's *Linguals*. The two soloists are caught up in an ever-more-breathless whirl, until in the final climax all the main themes return, with the music-hall tune turned into a cantus firmus—a very Honeggerian touch! The baritone sinks beneath it all, but the solo soprano sails above it with her desperate prayer.

The phrase "Come with us" crystallizes three times into huge, dissonant chords. We may think of the climax of the Dona nobis pacem in the *Symphonie liturgique*, but here there will be no final catharsis, only three measures of *strepi-*

toso on "Come! Come! Come!" (drawing the music down, whereas the invocations "Come!" in *Jeanne d'Arc* draw it up to heaven). The work ends with a *fortissimo* orchestral sledgehammer blow in C minor.

99. *Jeanne d'Arc au bûcher* (Joan of Arc at the Stake)—dramatic oratorio

3 January–30 August 1935; orchestration completed 24 December 1935, Paris;
    Prologue completed 28 November 1944, Paris
"To Ida Rubinstein" (who commissioned it)
Text by Paul Claudel (German translation by Hans Reinhart; English translation by
    Denis Arundell)
First performance: 12 May 1938, Ida Rubinstein (Joan), Jean Périer (Brother
    Dominic), Serge Sandos, Charles Vaucher, Ginevra Vivante, Berthe de Vigier,
    Marianne Hinsig-Löwe, Lina Falk, Ernst Bauer, Paul Sandoz, Maurice
    Martenot (ondes Martenot), the Boys Choir of the Reformed Evangelical
    Church, the Basel Chamber Choir and Orchestra, conducted by Paul Sacher,
    Basel
First stage performance, in German: 13 June 1942, conducted by Paul Sacher,
    Zurich State Theater; in French: 18 December 1950, Claude Nollier (Joan),
    Jean Vilar (Brother Dominic), produced by Jean Déat, decor by Yves Bonnat,
    choreography by Serge Lifar, conducted by Louis Fourestier, Paris Opera
First performance with Prologue: 2 February 1946, conducted by Louis de Vocht,
    Brussels, Palais des Beaux-Arts
Performing forces, *spoken roles*: Joan of Arc, Brother Dominic, numerous other roles
    that can be taken in the concert hall by two narrators; *sung roles*: the Virgin
    (soprano), Margaret (soprano), Catherine (contralto), Porcus (tenor)—in the
    concert hall, the tenor also takes other minor roles, and a bass, a soprano
    (prologue), and a child's voice are also required; *chorus*: mixed chorus, children's
    chorus; *orchestra*: 2.2.3.4.–3 saxophones–0.4.4.0.–timpani, 2 percussion players
    (tam-tam, side drum, tenor drum, bass drum, cymbals)–celesta, 2 pianos, ondes
    Martenot–strings
Duration: 69 minutes 30 seconds
Salabert
There is a film version, produced in 1956 by Roberto Rossellini, with Ingrid
    Bergman playing the role of Joan

The story of the composition of the dramatic oratorio *Jeanne d'Arc au bûcher* can be found in Chapter 6 in the biographical section of this book. Thanks in particular to the research of Pascal Lecroart,[4] it has been possible to correct the chronology and certain dates wrongly given by both composer and librettist. For example, on the Decca disc of an interview about *Jeanne d'Arc* brought out by Bernard Gavoty, Claudel says he began the libretto in April 1934, when he met Honegger and Ida Rubinstein in Brussels at the Belgian premiere of *Sémiramis*. But *Sémiramis* was premiered in Paris on 11 May 1934, and in Brussels not until 26 January 1935, by which time the libretto of *Jeanne d'Arc* had been finished for more than a month, being datable from the second half of December. Likewise, Honegger cannot have started writing the music in October 1934, as he says, because the libretto was not yet in existence.

Jeanne d'Arc au bûcher is today Honegger's best-known and most often played work, together with *Le Roi David*, and is incontestably his most inspired masterpiece. It was his sixth and last collaboration with Ida Rubinstein, and the first work on which he collaborated with Paul Claudel. This meeting of the two men was a vital one for Honegger, both for his public career as a composer and for his psychological health: it was *Jeanne d'Arc* that finally rescued him from the depths of depression so dramatically signaled in *Cris du monde*.

Claudel's brilliant, intuitive stroke—which had already been applied in his *Christopher Columbus* set to music by Darius Milhaud—was to use a chronology in reverse, like a cinema flashback. Time goes backward until the crucial moment when the earthly present and the spiritual come together in the devouring flames—that final moment when those who are about to die relive in an instant the whole course of their brief existence. The stake in Rouen is at the same time a point of departure and of arrival, at the meeting point of the utter solitude of martyrdom and the redemption extended to all those for whom Joan sacrifices herself.

Claudel's text is by turns grandiose and boisterous, mystical, and popular. You find the most terrible puns rubbing shoulders with the sublime. It is a veritable cathedral in its power, bringing together the capital and the gargoyle, going from Rabelais to *The Imitation of Christ*, from *The Romance of the Rose* to *The Canticle of the Creatures* and Saint Bonaventure, and from François Villon to the minutes of the trial in Rouen. It is a real scenario in the cinematographic sense, and unique of its type. We can therefore easily understand why Honegger set about his task with such enthusiasm, even if he was being too modest when he later said,

> Claudel's input was so important, I don't regard myself really as the composer, but simply as a collaborator. If performances of the work produce any emotional effect, then it is only right to give Claudel a large part of the credit. All I did was follow his indications and put my technical know-how at his disposal, so as to try my best to realize the music he himself had imagined.[5]

It needed a composer as malleable and receptive as Honegger, and one as closely in tune with Claudel's thinking, for this extraordinary osmosis to work. And it is true that, in the libretto of *Jeanne d'Arc au bûcher*, Claudel reveals himself as a kind of great composer in embryo.

The two main roles, Joan and Brother Dominic, are spoken ones. There are a number of others, but the musical continuum is interrupted only three times (in the middle of scenes 2 and 8 and before scene 6) and never for more than two or three minutes. While all the spoken roles contribute to the narrative flow of Claudel's text, the lyrical, visionary sections are expressed in singing. This applies especially to the Virgin Mary and to Joan's "voices" (Saint Catherine and Saint Margaret). There are a few other sung roles, all fairly short, such as Porcus (Cauchon, the Bishop of Beauvais), who is somewhat of a parody of a high tenor.

As for the orchestra, Honegger replaces horns with three saxophones. There is no harp, but there are two pianos, and in the gambling scene these turn into harpsichords by means of rods placed on the strings. Finally, Honegger's favorite ondes Martenot play an important part. We hear it most clearly in the passage of the dog howling in the night (scenes 1 and 5), containing one of the cyclic themes that run through the work. Some of these are interlinked: for example, the sequence of four chords simulating bells (Example 118), which we hear in the Prologue and then in scenes 7, 9, and 11. The bass line here is a transposition a tone lower of B-A-C-H, while the harmonic movement is perhaps an unconscious memory of the chimes in the coronation scene of *Boris Godunov*. It goes on to serve as the underpinning for other themes, such as the "Daughter of God, onward, onward!" (in the Prologue, but without the triple call of "Joan," then in scenes 7, 9, and 11) (Example 119), and for the "Spira, spera" in scenes 7, 8, 9, and 11 (Example 120), in which the typically Honeggerian intervals and iambic rhythm again evoke the sounds of bells, particularly in the harmonized variant quoted above. More bell sounds appear in the "Carillon of Laon" in scene 8, with its authentic popular song "Do You Want to Eat Dumplings?" (Example 121).

The other popular song is "Trimazo," in scenes 1, 9, and 10 (Example 122),

Example 118

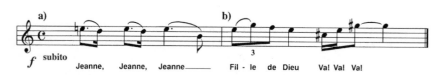

Example 119

Example 120

Example 121

which normally has a codetta "It is May, lovely May" (Example 123). This is closely related to Example 121. There are also examples of folk tunes that Honegger has invented or imagined, the most memorable being Heurtebise's robust tune in scene 8 (Example 124). The composer also borrowed two themes from plainsong, one of which, the "Donkey's Prose," is a sarcastic parody of a medieval *conductus* by the Beauvais students (scene 4), and the other, calm and meditative, is the antiphon "Adspiciens a longe" (scene 8).

Example 122

Example 123

Example 124

There is one purely rhythmic theme for the spoken chorus, when they become Joan's accusers and executioners ("Heretic, witch, relapser"). This appears in scenes 3, 5, 7, 8, 9, and 11 and is in striking contrast to the final group of themes, which are lyrical, mystic, and uplifting.

Three of these are particularly beautiful. First, there is the theme of Hope, with its rising fourths (Example 125)—traces of this theme are already discernible in the Prologue and then it appears in full shape in scenes 9 and 10. Then there is the theme of Love in scene 9, associated with Spring (Example 126), and finally the wonderful theme that is heard three times in succession at the end of the work (Example 127). And at the opposite extreme from the howling dog where we began, let us not forget the cyclical call of the "nightingale," which comes in the Prologue and again in the final measure—an early version of the "bird" of the *Third Symphony* (Example 128).

Il y a l'es - pé - ran - ce, qui est la plus for - te

Example 125

(Vns.)

f sost.

Example 126

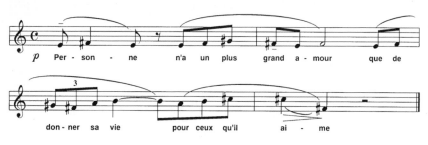

p Per - son - ne n'a un plus grand a - mour que de

don - ner sa vie pour ceux qu'il ai - me

Example 127

(The Nightingale) (Fl.)

pp dolce

Example 128

PROLOGUE

The text of the Prologue quotes from Genesis and compares the darkness that preceded the Creation with that covering occupied and divided France, both in 1940 and during the Hundred Years' War. God answers men's prayers by sending them "a girl called Joan." The dog howling in the night symbolizes the horror of physical torture, while the bells are Joan's "sisters and friends."

The whole of the opening is deliberately murky and low in pitch. The woodwinds establish the rhythm eighth-note/quarter-note/dotted quarter-note of the word "*té*nèbres" (the first word of the text, accentuated in Honegger's own manner). It is sung first by the choral basses, then imitated by the other voices. The remainder of the text is accentuated similarly, but with some subtlety. At the words "Et l'*E*sprit de Dieu planait sur le chaos" (And the spirit of

God floated above the chaos), "Esprit de Dieu" fixes a key, E minor, for the first time, but "chaos" remains unaccented. On the other hand, in "le *cha*os des âmes et des volontés" (the chaos of souls and wills), chaos does have an accent because it is the chaos of wills! Note also that the expression "[Et la France était] inane et vide" will be found again in the initial Dialogue of *La Danse des morts*.

Suddenly there resounds the solo soprano's passionate prayer "From the depths of the gulf"—Claudel's paraphrase of the De profundis—on a preliminary version of the theme of Hope (see Example 125). It lasts no more than six measures, but it is a cry from the heart. The chorus launches out on a brief faster passage, interrupted by the first entry of the narrator: "There was a girl called Joan." The soprano, electrified, repeats these words and the energy of their sixteenth-notes communicates itself first to the chorus, then to the orchestra, like fire taking hold on brushwood, bringing the violins to a state of incandescence. Attempts are made at "Daughter of God" (Example 119*b*) and the "bells" (Example 118), but they remain sketchy. They reach their definitive form only at the end of this Prologue, after a long, tortured procession accompanied by dotted rhythms that will later accompany the joyful coronation procession in scene 8. Left on his own, the narrator for the last time makes the clear statement: "There was a *virgin* called Joan." The drama can begin.

SCENE 1: "VOICES OF HEAVEN"

Honegger liked to quote as an example the veritable "scenario" that Claudel gave him for this first scene, and which he had only to translate, as it were, into musical sounds, helped by his extraordinary feeling for visual stimuli, which had been further refined by his experience of writing film music:

> We hear a dog barking in the night. Once, twice. The second time, the orchestra joins the howling with a kind of sob or sinister laugh. The third time, the chorus join in. Then silence. Then "the voices of the night in the forest," combined perhaps with the faint sounds of the song of Trimazo and the limpid call of a nightingale. Then silence and a few measures of melancholy meditation. Then, again, the chorus humming. Crescendo. Diminuendo. Then voices calling distinctly "Joan! Joan! Joan!"

The composer followed these indications to the letter. The twofold howling of the dog (the second time with chorus and the striking first appearance of the ondes Martenot) is a Wagnerian iterative gesture that Honegger had favored ever since *Le Roi David*. Then, beneath the flute/nightingale's arabesque (Example 128), soprano and tenor sing a dialogue based on Examples 123 and 122 (Trimazo). All this culminates in a very gentle threefold call of "Joan!"

SCENE 2: "THE BOOK"

The Maid appears, in chains, and soon the music ceases. Enter Brother Dominic, a large book in his hand: it contains the whole of Joan's life, which she will now live in reverse. Since she is unable to read, it is he who will read it out to her.

SCENE 3: "VOICES OF EARTH"

Brother Dominic intones in a parlando the rhythmic idea "heretic, witch, relapser," which is repeated by a horrified Joan and then by the chorus of her accusers. They reiterate these imprecations, by turns in French and in Latin, in a kind of rhythmic fugato on a single note, unleashing a bestiality that is all too human. Note the pun "assez, assez, assassez" (enough, enough, murder her), which is typical of Claudel. The bass and then the tenor declaim "Latin of Fouarre" (a pun on the Norman town of that name and on "foire" [a fair], "latin de foire" meaning "kitchen Latin") in a heavy, pedantic counterpoint parodying Bach. Joan remembers with horror "the fire that hurts" (lacerating glissandos on ondes Martenot), but Dominic explains to her who these so-called prelates really are. It is not men who are vilifying her in this way; like her sisters in pagan Rome, she will be delivered to the wild beasts, and they will judge her. A grotesque parody using spiky jazz rhythms on the woodblock conjures up the sarcastic horrors of the following scene.

SCENE 4: "JOAN DELIVERED TO THE WILD BEASTS"

To the sound of fanfares in Honegger's usual fourths, the herald (a spoken role) tries to set up the court. The tiger (trombone), the fox (saxophones), and the snake (piccolo and E-flat clarinet) refuse in turn. Finally, a candidate presents himself to preside over the trial, to the accompaniment of a massive rising arpeggio of G major, followed by an ornate cadence. This high tenor is Porcus, otherwise known as Cauchon, the Bishop of Beauvais. At the top of his voice he sings a grotesque aria in the style of 1935 jazz ("I, I am the pig"), supported by a chorus teeming with verbal and musical puns. There is no shortage here of added sixths, syncopations, and percussion, and the tune is deliberately vulgar, sarcastic, and complacent. But being a good-for-nothing takes practice! Like Mozart, Honegger manages to describe vulgarity without himself being vulgar, and his contrapuntal expertise cannot be ignored, especially in the central episode.

At the moment when the assistant judges are being chosen, the fanfare literally "deflates" with the entry of the sheep and their realistic bleating. The donkey presents himself as clerk of the court with enormous vocal leaps imitating "heehaws," and these are greeted with uproarious laughter from the chorus, to the sound of the rattle and a glissando on the ondes Martenot. The basses intone the medieval "Donkey's Prose," which is treated as a cantus firmus amid a merry, swarming polyphony, while the ondes Martenot bray to their heart's content. A second appearance of the "Donkey's Prose" in the sopranos confirms this unexpected abduction of Bach's organ chorales, which Honegger knew so well. Accusation and verdict are then delivered in a flash—as in Stalin's show trials—in a hasty declamation decorated with an untimely repeat of the "Donkey's Tale." The "wooden language" is here replaced by "Latin of Fouarre," in which Cauchon and his henchmen wallow as in a trough. All this is accompanied by the wild energy of an ironic pseudo-baroque ritornello combined with fragments of Porcus's aria, fanfares, and jazz. The reason is clear: Joan has been aided by the Devil, and she must burn.

SCENE 5: "JOAN AT THE STAKE"

Scene 5 presents a brief reminder of the fearful reality at this moment of the imminent flames. We hear again the twofold howling of the dog in the night. This is the second purely spoken episode, and here Brother Dominic explains to Joan that she has gotten here as the result of a game of cards. This is the topic of the scene that follows.

SCENE 6: "THE KINGS, OR THE INVENTION OF THE GAME OF CARDS"

The two pianos take the lead. They are transformed into harpsichords by the simple but effective device of a metal rod laid on the strings. (A very similar technique was used by Hanns Eisler and the musical collaborators of Bertolt Brecht. By sticking thumbtacks—*punaises*, in French, which also means "bedbugs"—into the hammers, they transformed the piano into what they called a *piano à punaises*, or *Wanzenklavier*, "bedbug piano," in German.) The two heralds announce the protagonists. The kings (of France, representing Stupidity; of England, Pride; and the Duke of Burgundy, Avarice) are depicted by a ceremonial, chromatic motif, full of arrogance. This is varied slightly for the fourth king, Death, accompanied by his lady, Luxury, suggested by a melting passage on high violins.

But the game is played by the jacks, that is to say, by the French nobility. After three games, the prize—Joan herself—is won by the English king. Honegger turned this scene into disquietingly mechanical ballet, reminiscent of the dancing clock jacks of medieval belfries. A pseudo-baroque ritornello in C major is played three times, in invertible counterpoint on three simultaneous themes. It comes first in three parts, then in four (the tune moving the second time to the relative minor). The technique here is superlative and the instrumental scoring is also different on each occasion. In a brief, mocking epilogue, the jacks take their leave as the piccolo plays a sped-up version of the end of the ritornello. By this time the double basses are already just audible, playing the opening of the next scene.

SCENE 7: "CATHERINE AND MARGARET"

In total contrast, the music in scene 7 is lyrical and serene. Joan again hears her beloved Voices and, to the sound of bells, they beg for divine assistance on her behalf. The bell theme (Example 118), on the two pianos and divided double basses, does duty as a pedal point, or rather group, to which is added the accent of the ondes Martenot on the upper pedal C, reinforcing the bell effect. Over these deeper bells, we hear smaller ones on two pianos and celesta playing iambic rhythms (Example 120, in fact a diminution of Example 118). Margaret is the first to give them words ("Spera, spira, Jesus, Mary!"), while the austere figure of Catherine, a contralto, sings the De profundis and the basses dimly intone their "comburatur igne." Then, a third higher, the two saints join in singing "Daughter of God, onward, onward, onward!" (Example 119) for the first time in its complete form. Now Joan relives the coronation of the dauphin Charles, and Honegger's effortless counterpoint stealthily introduces in shortened note values the future dotted motif accompanying the royal procession, into which we are ushered through an exciting orchestral crescendo.

SCENE 8: "THE KING WHO GOES FORTH TO RHEIMS"

This long scene marks the climax of the score's more extrovert tendencies. It is a lively, colorful popular fresco in five sections. To begin with, altos and tenors in the distance sing the "Bells of Laon" (Example 121) in augmentation in a modal C minor, with the bell theme (Example 118) as a regular background. Then the bells, which have acted as a link with the preceding scene, fall silent. Children's voices take up the melody in shortened note values in A minor. They are followed by a jaunty entry from the basses on "la la la," sounding like a minor variant of the *Carmagnole*.

Suddenly, in the midst of the crowd's rejoicing, the two halves of France, divided for so long, are at last reunited in what Claudel, in a superb phrase, has called a "national communion in both kinds." The two halves are symbolized by Heurtebise (the character is a windmill representing the corn-rich North) and the Mother of the Barrels (from the wine-growing regions of the South of France). Heurtebise's solid, plebeian 6/8 (Example 124), a striking example of invented folklore, gets under way in G major, harmonized with "popular" added sixths. This is followed by a more melodious theme in E-flat, depicting the Mother of the Barrels, and finally the two are combined. After spoken dialogue from the two protagonists over an orchestral accompaniment, a fast, lively popular dance is heard in D major, with florid decorative figures on brass and percussion, and over these, Example 128 is heard in long notes.

Suddenly, a loud sixth chord on strings would seem to be announcing a recitative. It is the third and last of the long spoken sequences: a cleric admonishing the crowd and inviting it to meditate and sing the antiphon "Adspiciens a longe," in order to greet the arrival of the royal procession. A solo flute first plays the Gregorian melody, in the Aeolian mode transposed on to B, and then it is taken up by the cleric on his own. Finally, it is heard on the chorus in unison, doubled by the woodwinds, in a medieval coloring, and then surrounded by held modal harmonies.

The royal procession is acclaimed by the crowd, as it approaches with joyous piping, sprightly trumpets, and invigorating drums. It passes before us, joined by the cleric's and the people's ecstatic Gregorian vocalises. At its climax it is combined with the bell theme (Example 118), then by Example 120, and, to crown the astonishing contrapuntal edifice, the "Bells of Laon" (Example 121) in long notes. The whole ensemble is carried off with beguiling assurance.

While the priest finishes his antiphon and the procession disappears into the distance, Joan rejoices: "It is I who did all that!" But Brother Dominic puts her right: "It is God who did all that!" To which she replies: "God with Joan!" But she must now face her enemies' opposition, muted at first, then increasingly violent. Their accusing voices are heard once more, to music that has suddenly turned gray and atonal. But this fury is calmed, and Example 120 announces the next scene.

SCENE 9: "JOAN'S SWORD"

Scene 9, "Joan's Sword," is even longer than the previous one, comprising six lengthy sections. After Margaret has repeated the motif of Example 120 very quietly, and it has been echoed at length, a long G major pedal is installed. During this, Joan, accompanied by the nightingale from scene 1 (Example 128), sees Normandy once more in its springtime splendor, while she thinks all the time of her native Lorraine. The chorus sings a long vocalise of ideal peacefulness. Margaret's gentle call (Example 120) ushers in a dream sequence: in the midst of glissandos on ondes Martenot and rapid, fleeting figuration on muted strings, Catherine's low voice addresses Joan with "Daughter of God, onward, onward, onward" (Example 119) in very long notes. Margaret and the chorus take up this melody at its initial length, in a game of echoes around Joan's enthusiastic exclamations, "I go, I shall go, I have gone!" in which past and future come together with the present.

When Brother Dominic asks Joan where her sword came from, she finds herself again at Domrémy in May, when the sword was given to her. But, she says, for Brother Dominic to understand this sword, he would have to be transformed into the little girl from Lorraine that she then was, singing "Trimazo" with the other children. A delicate dissolve touches on fragments of the tune, heard on the oboe and then on children's voices, before piccolo, flute, and E-flat clarinet play the beautiful tune in its entirety (Example 122), in a delightful modal harmonization that recalls the sound of a country organ. We may note the tune's unusual structure, of two measures of five beats, two of four, and one of three. A child's voice repeats it all in another harmonization that is just as well-finished, then it is taken up by all the children with Example 123 as a concluding ritornello, combined with a dotted countermelody on the flute.

In a calm but highly emotional atmosphere of bucolic repose, the men in the background hum the tune, remembering the time when they were boys. The vision slowly fades, and now Joan remembers winter to the sound of cold, dank, undulating thirds. At this point a solo baritone suddenly introduces for the first time the admirable theme of Hope (Example 125), harmonized in fourths—that is to say, with its own melodic intervals. Immediately there is a reply from the nightingale (Example 128), followed by Example 119 and by a powerful crescendo based on Example 125, now harmonized in the dominant, its "natural" resonance.

Suddenly we find ourselves in a straightforward E-flat major with the flute playing the theme of Spring (Example 126, but still without its inflection).

Joan's description of it is surrounded by a woodwind dialogue in dotted notes over a string tremolo—a passage that looks forward to the *Fourth Symphony*. A section of more martial music in A major with fanfares and drums, but still light and transparent in texture, illustrates the breaking of the chains, and leads, after an irresistible crescendo, to the full-throated lyrical apotheosis of Example 126 in its entirety, played by all the strings.

The effect of the modulation from A to E-flat is electrifying, underlining the words "This sword is not called hate, it is called love." It brings tears to the eyes and proves that in the hands of a composer of genius the resources of classical, tonal harmony have lost none of their power. The dazzling warmth gently becomes subdued. The children repeat "Trimazo," but this time the cadence does not resolve and the chorus goes on to call out the name "Rouen," the very sound of which is like a deep knell. Again the scene darkens and the hateful voices begin to build up. But now we have a weapon: Hope. Its theme (Example 125) is sung by Catherine as a vocalise, while Joan speaks its words.

Taken up by the basses and combined with Example 119, this theme informs a wonderful polyphonic buildup. At this point, Margaret greets us (Example 120) and takes us up to Heaven. In this she is assisted by a vertiginous swoop on the ondes Martenot and, beneath the high G of this, Joan, practically fainting with joy, declaims her act of faith in a decrescendo: "There is God, there is God who is the strongest." As a solo child's voice repeats Example 123 in the distance, the light begins to fail.

SCENE 10: "TRIMAZO"

This very short scene, during which Joan's voice tries to sing the song and bursts into sobs, is the decisive turning point in the whole work. Joan seems to wake from a long dream, and the book from which Brother Dominic has been reading to her is closed again, and the wheel of time has come full circle. She is faced with the terrible reality of the present, and of the stake. The hour of the final sacrifice has come.

SCENE 11: "JOAN OF ARC IN THE FLAMES"

The massive final scene consists of five long sections. The trumpet plays a firm, decisive tune, taken over by the trombone, while the Virgin sings "I accept this pure flame" on a variant of the theme of Hope (Example 125). Then begins a long tumultuous allegro in 3/4 in which Joan's enemies and supporters face one another in an inextricable scuffle of brutal imprecations and clear diatonic songs of praise. The basses sing the "Eulogy of fire" that Claudel took from Saint Francis of Assisi's *Canticle of the Creatures*. Then, as the chorus comments "She is waking as though from a dream," Joan gives vent to her sudden anguish. Brother Dominic has left her and, in the face of her fearful solitude, she knows the same brief faintness in her faith that Christ suffered on the Cross.

A long climb through minor keys, a tone apart, resembles an ascent to Calvary. Joan cries out "I am alone!" Despite the Virgin's reply of "Joan, Joan, you are not alone" over a broadened version of "Daughter of God" (Example 119) and followed by echoes from the chorus, the Maid refuses to die and confesses that she is afraid. The chorus comments immediately "She was only a poor child." Several measures of atonal nonmusic accompany the priest, who tries to make Joan abjure her faith, but already the theme of Hope (Example 125) is supporting her, as she replies that love and truth bind her hands and prevent her from signing. The Virgin encourages Joan to entrust herself to the fire that will deliver her from her chains and from the sufferings of her body. We hear again the "Eulogy of fire," with high eighth-notes on woodwinds and piano illustrating the flames.

Timpani strokes mark the fifths in the huge ascending march, combining the canticle of the fire in close imitation, the music of the flames, and the dialogue between the Virgin and Joan. It leads finally to the slower, triumphant affirmation of D major at the words "Praise be to our sister Joan, who is holy and upright." Above this float the song of the Virgin and the unreal sounds of the ondes Martenot. Their spectacular glissando supported by the whole orchestra leads us on to a new level.

The chorus in unison in the dominant of G (from this point Honegger employs strings of dominants in his usual manner) sings "Louée soit notre soeur Jeanne qui est debout pour toujours comme une flamme au milieu de la France" (Praise be to our sister Joan who stands for ever as a flame in the midst of France), in which we may note the typical accentuation of the words "*de*bout" and "*tou*jours." Here Claudel deliberately brings together praise of Joan and of the fire. Every resource is now summoned to assist Joan in making her great leap into salvation. Catherine, Margaret, and the Virgin return to Example 119, and the Virgin, for the first and last time, sings not "Onward, onward, onward!" but "Come, come, come!" A crescendo through a series of dominants on the theme of Hope, sung in imitation by the chorus, leads to three huge, long-held triple *fortissimo*s over a pedal point. These involve the dominants of G, D, and E, supported by modulating strettos on Example 125. Joan makes the transition to eternal life ("I come, I have broken through"), while the chorus holds the word "Dieu" (God).

The enormous tension now gradually relaxes. The imitations based on Example 125 become progressively less dense, before vanishing altogether in a purified atmosphere. Example 120 now re-emerges as a vocalise, in gradually decelerating rhythms. A gentle decrescendo on Joan's last words, "There is God who is the strongest," swooning in bliss, leads to the final, sublime catharsis of the ecstatic epilogue and a triple affirmation of the theme (Example 127) on the words "Greater love hath no man than to give his life for those he cherishes." This defines Joan as a saint, as an imitator of Christ. The phrase is sung first by Margaret and children's voices in E major, then played in D major by the ondes Martenot, while the chorus sings the words and harmonizes the melody "as though spelling out an inscription." Finally, we hear the phrase in C major sung by low voices, and this leads to a magnificent final cadence in D major, decorated by the nightingale's song on the flute and its bittersweet "blue" minor third. Few twentieth-century works have moved such vast audiences and few, probably, carry such a religious impact. Claudel had good reason to say that *Jeanne d'Arc au bûcher* was born under the sign of grace.

131. *La Danse des morts* (The Dance of the Dead)—sacred cantata

July–November 1938 (first sketches and No. 1: July 1938; No. 2: 8 August 1938; No. 3: 21 August 1938; No. 4: 1 September 1938; No. 5: 22 September 1938; No. 6: not indicated; No. 7: 25 October 1938); orchestration completed 24 November 1938
"To Paul Sacher" (who commissioned it)
Text by Paul Claudel (German version by Hans Reinhart; English version by Edward Agate)
First performance: 2 March 1940, Jean Hervé, Ginevra Vivante, Lina Falk, Martial Singher, Basel Chamber Choir and Orchestra, conducted by Paul Sacher, Basel
First stage performance (in German): 2 June 1940, conducted by Paul Sacher, Zurich State Theater
Performing forces: narrator, baritone, soprano, contralto, mixed chorus; orchestra: 2.2.2.2.–2.2.2.0.–four timpani (two performers), two percussionists (bass drum, cymbals, rattle, side drum, tam-tam, triangle, woodblock)–piano, organ (in the absence of an organ: double horns, trombones, and bassoons)–strings
Duration: 29 minutes 35 seconds
Salabert

La Danse des morts is the second major work to come out of the collaboration between Honegger and Paul Claudel. It is one of the composer's most perfect, concise, and finely balanced works, and it has the advantage too of a fine text, taken largely from the Bible. The genesis and early history of the work, especially as regards Claudel, have been outlined in Chapter 6 in the biographical section of this book. Chapter 9 also includes excerpts from a truculent text from Claudel inspired by his discovery of the *Danses macabres* (Dances of Death) in Basel. Another fragment from this text runs as follows:

> What struck me was not nearly so much the sinister or, as it is usually described, the macabre aspect of these interferences of the Bony Fellow into the lives of his successive customers, as their cheerful, attractive, and musical side. . . . What a contrast between this nimble, relaxed Harlequin and the gross creature whose chevalier servant he has become!

Claudel's text concludes with the statement of the threefold idea that is the basis for *La Danse des morts*: "Remember, man, that thou art dust, a dust that my breath hath scattered to the four corners of Heaven, but which it is equally capable of bringing together again." "Remember, man, that thou art Spirit!" "Remember, man, that thou art stone, and upon this stone I shall build, I shall rebuild my church, this good fellow who is a church all on his own! And the sob of despair becomes an exclamation of wonder!"[6]

Claudel's "good fellow" is obviously Peter, the subject here of a familiar pun. As he had already done in *Jeanne d'Arc au bûcher*, Claudel accompanied his libretto with very precise instructions (see Chapter 6) which had a decisive effect on Honegger's approach. He realized straightaway that he would be unable to stay within the narrow limits suggested by Sacher—basically, a string orchestra with chamber choir. This much became clear as early as the opening clap of thunder! Even so, the dimensions of the orchestra are not excessive.

After this initial thunder and its prolonged resonance, the work is in seven linked sections. Below are the extracts from the Bible that Claudel incorporated. The largest portions come from the famous vision in Ezekiel 37 of the plain filled with bones, as well as long extracts from Job 7, 10, 14, and 19. Shorter extracts belong to Genesis, Isaiah, and to the Gospels according to Matthew and John:

1. Dialogue. Narrator: Ezekiel 37, 1–10; Chorus: Job 10, 9; Genesis 1, 9; Job 19, 25–26; Genesis 1, 2.

3. Lamento. Job 10, 9; 19, 21; 19, 20; 7, 17–19; 7, 7; 14, 1–6; 19, 25–26.

4. Sobs. Job 10, 21–22 (in Latin).

5. God's Reply. Ezekiel 37, 11–14.

6. Hope in the Cross. John 20, 20, 25, and 27 (free paraphrase); Isaiah 49, 15; Matthew 11, 29; John 17, 21; Ezekiel 37, 16, (17 modified), 22–23, and 26–28 (28 in Latin).

7. Affirmation. Matthew 16, 18.

1. Introduction (orchestra) and Dialogue (narrator, chorus, orchestra)

The initial lightning flash is followed first by a short silence, then by the atonal chaos of the roll of thunder in a long crescendo and diminuendo, made of superimposed ostinatos in anapestic rhythms typical of Honegger. The Dialogue is divided into three sections, with narrator and chorus alternating. The chorus is interpolated into the narrative of Ezekiel's vision of the plain full of bones, and its first commentary (Job 10, 9) affirms the first of the work's three fundamental propositions: "Remember, man, that thou art dust."

The chorus then turns to speech ("Let the waters that are beneath the heavens") and returns to sung declamation ("And thus it came to pass") before finally delivering the work's choral leitmotif (Example 129) on the old tune from the cantata by Erdmann Neumeister ("I know that my Redeemer liveth"), used in the cantata numbered BWV 160 attributed to Bach, but in fact by Telemann. Honegger's treatment of it is, anyway, a long way from being traditional, since the second and third of its four phrases are in measured recitative. An energetic choral stretto ("Lord God, do You think that these bones are alive?") introduces the second sequence ("A kind of noise and movement"), a purely rhythmic passage in which bassoons dryly outline the motif (in Honegger's "locomotive" style) that will set the dance in motion. Notice the sudden C-sharp minor at the words "And the earth was without form and void," a verse from Genesis that will occur again in the 1944 Prologue to *Jeanne d'Arc au bûcher*. Suddenly we are in the third sequence with the anapestic rhythms of the initial thunder. The breath of the Holy Spirit begins to blow (high string harmonics imitated by woodwinds, over a suspended cymbal) and unleashes a mighty choral crescendo combined with the narrator shouting "It was an immense army." These six measures of massive tutti, in which the "locomotive" idea goes further than anything in *Pacific 2.3.1*, lead into the dance.

Je   crois   que   mon   Ré - demp - teur   vit

Example 129

2. "DANCE OF THE DEAD" (NARRATOR, CHORUS, ORCHESTRA)

The scenario envisaged by Claudel placed this, the most spectacular section of the work, very near the beginning. It needed all of Honegger's lyrical genius in the "Lamento" and then in "Hope in the Cross" both to prevent the structure's becoming unbalanced and to ensure that its spiritual impact built continuously to the end. In *Jeanne d'Arc*, by contrast, the equivalent grand fresco of "The King Who Goes Forth to Rheims" came at the beginning of the second half of the work, and the addition of the Prologue improved the balance still further.

Here we have a scene bursting with life, a *quodlibet* in which Honegger fits together a number of popular tunes with his usual astonishing contrapuntal skill, as he does in Joan's coronation procession, in *Une Cantate de Noël*, and in the "Alpeglüe" of *L'Appel de la montagne*. To begin with, a light, transparent texture in a brisk 6/8 surrounds the chorus's monotonal psalmody, while in the motto phrase whispered by the sprightly skeletons, "Souviens-toi, homme, que tu es esprit, et la chair est plus que le vêtement, et l'esprit est plus que la chair, et l'oeil est plus que le visage, et l'amour est plus fort que la mort" (Remember, man, that thou art spirit, and the flesh is more than clothing, and the spirit more than the flesh, and the eye more than the face, and love is stronger than death), the words are accented in the Honeggerian manner—"*sou*viens-toi," "*esp*rit," "*vê*tement," "*vi*sage," "*a*mour"—as they pass from one voice to another in a kind of rhythmic fugato.

While the orchestral texture becomes gradually more dense, the narrator summons the Pope, the Bishop, the King, and the Knight, all of them equal in the face of death, and all of them caught up by the lighthearted, friendly, chaffing skeletons in the irresistible hubbub of the dance. The popular tunes now enter successively in different keys: *Sur le pont d'Avignon*, now changed to *Sur le pont de la tombe* (On the Bridge of the Tomb), the *Carmagnole*, and the refrain only of *Nous n'irons plus au bois* (included by Honegger because of its persuasive invitation to "Enter into the dance"). The tunes then combine in a frantic stretto that drives on to the triumphant return of the *Carmagnole* in canon ("Long live the sound of the cannon"—how could the composer have resisted it?). Meanwhile in the orchestra we hear a heavy, grossly obscene waltz rhythm (a 3/4 "oom-pah-

pah" against the prevailing 6/8), while *fortissimo* trumpets and organ intone the Dies irae in long notes. After a brief interruption, a roll on the side drum launches the brief coda-stretto, incorporating the last appearance of the chorus's motto, this time cut short on the shouted word "death."

3. "LAMENTO" (BARITONE SOLO, ORCHESTRA)

We can find the model for this wonderful movement in the aria "Of love shall my Savior die" from Bach's *St. Matthew Passion*. At the end of his life, Honegger said of the movement, "I am presumptuous enough to hope that this piece will lead me to be forgiven for a number of others." And indeed he was never more inspired than in this overwhelming lament. Its form is that of a varied da capo with coda, for baritone with solo violin obbligato (following Claudel's indications) in the main key of G-sharp minor. The violin solo is based mainly on a simple motif of three quarter-notes (Example 130). The appoggiatura will undergo various intervallic expansions and these, together with rests, come to sound like the suppliant's sighs.

Example 130

The opening of the baritone's finely flexible line (Example 131) underlines every nuance of the text, which is an extraordinary montage of verses from the book of Job. The whole piece is built in the Bachian manner over the quarter-note ostinato in the violins, which descends chromatically through an octave every two measures.

Example 131

The orchestral texture is a little fuller in the central section ("How long wilt Thou forget to spare me?") at the subdominant C-sharp minor, where the English horn plays a faster countermelody in sixteenth-notes, the accompanying quarter-notes turning into double-bass pizzicatos. In the varied recapitulation (on different words, naturally) the texture is thickened by the addition of all the violins in unison and the chromatic bass is multiplied through octave leaps. After the coda, in which the baritone, returning to the chorale (Example 129) makes a fervent profession of faith, Honegger builds an instrumental epilogue on the chromatic bass, with the motif of Example 130 passing from solo violin to low flute and finally to bassoon.

4. "Sobs" (chorus, orchestra)

This movement is a brief chorus, but charged with tension. The dynamics are a constant *fortissimo* and the orchestration is harsh and heavy. As Example 132 shows, Honegger stays close to his librettist's wishes: "The cry, heavy with despair, then the broken sobs, the final gasp of the strangled throat." Two periods succeed each other over a chromatic, two-measure bass with wide leaps. In the depths, the gloomy text from Job (in Latin) evokes the darkness of Scheol, combined with the sobbing motif of Example 132. In the second period the counterpoint is reversed, with the women singing the Latin and the men being given the sobs.

Example 132

5. "God's Reply" (narrator, orchestra)

The repeat of the opening thunderclap, without the lightning, introduces the spoken narrative in which the Lord, through the mouth of his prophet, responds to humanity's cry: "I exist!" Over chromatic eddy from the orchestra, he tells the children of Israel of their coming revival and their return to the Promised Land. The trumpet plays the theme of the return from exile, to be heard in the next movement.

6. "Hope in the Cross" (soprano, contralto, baritone, chorus, orchestra)

This long movement is divided into two highly contrasting halves. The first of these, separated from the first by a long silence, goes on from the "Lamento" to become the work's second great lyrical climax. Claudel has in fact written a Stabat mater, showing the holy women at the foot of the cross, and Honegger has treated this as a powerfully expressive duet for soprano and contralto over a chromatic ostinato on muted strings, consisting of two alternating bitonal chords. It accompanies the dialogue of the two women: the soprano's piteous lament, itself chromatic, and the contralto's diatonic, modal reply ("My son, I have given you my heart"). A brief, violent interjection from chorus and orchestra ("Open, eternal gates") interrupts this dialogue, which then resumes over a humming Chorus.

Suddenly the baritone enters in the role of Christ ("Learn from me that I am gentle") in a bright C major, followed by the invocation of the two women in rhythmic unison ("So that I may be one in You"—a development, by Claudel, of John 17, 21). This great desire for the indispensable unity with God is underlined by a particular chord at each of the four proclamations of the word "One." Played by divided strings over a range of five-and-a-half octaves, it consists of the notes A-sharp–E-sharp–C-sharp–D-sharp–A-sharp–G-sharp–C-sharp. Dissonant though it is, this neutral, fourth-based chord does not demand resolution. The first half ends with an instrumental coda.

The second half offers a total contrast. Over rough, medieval-sounding music for brass, the baritone makes a vigorous entry on the words "Take a piece of wood," a phrase taken from Ezekiel 37, 16. But it was Claudel's idea to turn the wood into a cross, thereby once again linking the Old Testament and the New. This solo is brutally punctuated by the chorus at the words "Judah" and "Ephraim." The episode ends with the fourth phrase of the chorale followed by the confident, almost popular chorus of the children of Israel singing of their promised return from exile. Their simple, robust tune in B major also sounds like a chorale and has already been heard at the end of the previous movement. Punctuated by short, violent, enthusiastic Amens, it modulates by ascending tones with ever greater orchestral panache until a massive crescendo unleashes the final thunderclap. In the midst of the rumbling clouds, the chorus declaim in unison, and in Latin: "And they shall know that I am the Lord." The short final movement follows without a break.

7. "AFFIRMATION" (SOLO SOPRANO, CHORUS, ORCHESTRA)

The chorus hammers out with elemental power the work's third basic proposition, "Remember, man, that thou art Stone" (Matthew 16, 18). These words are emphasized by brutal chords on the orchestra. The word "Stone" is shouted, but at the words "I shall build my church" we return to the chorale style with one last repetition of the work's basic phrase (Example 129). This culminates peacefully in the solo soprano's ecstatic vocalise, melting wonderfully into the final resolution on a chord of C major—a worthy ending, and one close to those of *Jeanne d'Arc au bûcher* and the *Symphonie liturgique*. If *Jeanne d'Arc* is a cathedral in sound, then *La Danse des morts* is its crypt.

135. *Nicolas de Flue*—dramatic legend in three acts

December 1938–May 1939 (Act I: December 1938; Act II: completed 31 January 1939; Act III: completed 5 February 1939, apart from No. 21, which was composed 11 March 1939); orchestration for wind band completed 4 May 1939; reorchestrated for symphony orchestra December 1939
"To the five hundred inhabitants of Neuchâtel who, under the aegis of the Neuchâtel Institute and its president, M. Claude du Pasquier, took part in the performance of *Nicolas de Flue* during the 1939 Swiss National Exhibition in Zurich" (Dedication was not changed when the Zurich Exhibition had to be canceled)
Libretto by Denis de Rougemont (German version by Hans Reinhart)

First concert performance: 26 October 1940, William Aguet (narrator), Solothurn St. Cecilia Choral Society, Bern Municipal Orchestra, conducted by Erich Schild, Solothurn

First stage performance: 31 May 1941, du Locle and La Chaux-de-Fonds Choral Societies, conducted by Charles Faller, Neuchâtel

Performing forces: narrator, children's chorus, mixed chorus; also, in the stage version, a number of spoken roles; wind band: 2 flutes, 2 clarinets, 4 saxophones (doubling), saxhorns (bugles, alto, baritone, bass, contrabass saxhorns, all doubling), 2 bassoons, 4 horns, 4 trumpets (including 2 cornets), 3 trombones, tuba, timpani, 2 percussionists (bass drum, bells in E-flat and A-flat, side drum, tenor drum, cymbals, suspended cymbals, rattle, tam-tam, tambourine, triangle, woodblock), 8 double basses; symphony orchestra: 2.2.2.2.–2.3.3.1.–timpani, 2 percussionists (as earlier)–strings

Duration, stage version: a full evening; oratorio version: 65 minutes (25:00 + 19:00 + 21:00)

Act I: 1. Prologue; 2. Children's Song; 3. Fanfare; 4. Chorus "Remember"; 5. Chorale "He is on his way"; 6. Celestial Chorus "Alone"; 7. Nicolas's Prayer; 8. Recitative "Heavy is the pain"; 9. Chorale "He is on his way"; 10. The Climb to the Ranft

Act II: 11. Pilgrims' Song; 12. Double Chorus "Morning star"; 13. Watchman's Narration; 14. Celestial Chorus "It is God's will"; 15. Processions; 16. Recitative and Chorale; 17. Recitative and Chorale; 18. Chorus of Powers; 19. Chorus "Victory and Misery"

Act III: 20. Ambassadors' March; 21. The Companions of Follevie; 22. Fanfare of the Diet; 23. Recitative "Tomorrow comes war"; 24. Chorale "Nicolas, remember"; 25. Recitative "Among us, the people"; 26. Celestial Chorus "Alone"; 27. Chorale "He is descending"; 28. Celestial Chorus "Earth and Heaven, give ear"; 29. Recitative "Hear me, my people"; 30. Recitative of the Bells and Final Chorus

Foetisch Frères

Nicolas de Flue is the most specifically Swiss of all Honegger's works, being German-Swiss in its subject but French-Swiss in its libretto, its first performers, and in its commissioning. Its unmistakably national character means that it has never traveled much beyond the confines of Switzerland, nor does it seem likely that it will ever do so. It is only within the special context of Swiss democracy, with its largely decentralized civic and community life, that this kind of nationalistic *Festspiel* is still tolerable—elsewhere it is more likely to be greeted with irritation and sarcasm.

The subject is the life of Switzerland's national saint, who re-established peace among the nation's confederate states after the serious quarrels between town and country elements over the booty collected after the sweeping victories over Charles the Bold. The idea came to Denis de Rougemont as a result of the false euphoria following the Munich peace agreement in September 1938— and we know only too well what the outcome was of that. In fact, an arguably more important reason for the conflict between the confederates in 1481 had been the admission of two new cantons, Fribourg and Solothurn, to the confederation. This seemed likely to give too much power to the town elements, and the country cantons, which had until then been in the majority, accepted the new deal only thanks to Nicolas de Flue's mediation. He was too weak to journey in person to the diet of Stans, but he sent, as a powerful and explicit symbol, his lightly knotted girdle—easy to undo, provided the two parties did not pull on their respective ends.

Denis de Rougemont had heard Honegger conduct his *Nocturne* at the Venice Biennale on 9 September 1938 and he accepted the commission from the Neuchâtel authorities (the work was intended to represent the canton of Neuchâtel at the National Exhibition in Zurich in September 1939) only on condition that Honegger would write the music. Honegger for his part was attracted by a subject that chimed in with his profound pacifism and, immediately after *La Danse des morts*, he was keen to write a work for groups of amateurs representing an entire community. It is interesting to note that he would return to the same historical setting in 1944 with *Charles le Téméraire*, his final collaboration with René Morax and the Théâtre du Jorat; the musical resources would be more modest, with *Nicolas de Flue*'s rich orchestra of wind instruments replaced by a rustic brass ensemble. The dramatic circumstances connected with the outbreak of the Second World War, which forced the premiere to be postponed twice and which finally prevented the composer from attending it, have been described in the biographical section of this book (see Chapter 7). Given the work's subject matter, they assume a certain symbolic significance.

The work's musical style is simple, popular, and completely tonal, and Honegger returns to the large number of short movements he had favored in *Le Roi David*. The only movement of any great length is "The Climb to the Ranft," which ends the first of the work's three parts. Several of the movements return like leitmotifs, such as the two chorales "He is on his way" (No. 5, strophes 1 and 2, No. 9, and No. 27), "Nicolas" (Nos. 16b, 17, 24, 30b) (Example 133), the Pilgrims' Song (Nos. 11 and 15), and the Celestial Chorus "Alone" (Nos. 6 and 26) (Example 134).

As their language is so direct and straightforward, the thirty movements do not call for detailed analysis. Although there are no vocal solos of any kind, the choruses are in constant use, with or without the narrator. Apart from *Cris du monde*, which has such a different atmosphere, no other Honegger oratorio affords the chorus such an important role.

The first act traces Nicolas's life up until his retirement: how he left the

Example 133

Example 134

army after being unable to prevent soldiers under his command from ransack-
ing a convent and setting fire to it; how he resigned from being a judge after
being unable to prevent sentence being passed on a poor man who was innocent, but whose accuser was rich; and how finally, after the age of fifty, he left
his farm, his wife, Dorothy, and their ten children in response to God's call,
summoning him to the solitude of the mountain hermitage of the Ranft.

   This first act includes some of the leitmotifs, such as the chorale "He is on
his way" and the unaccompanied Celestial Chorus "Alone," with its memorable modulations (Example 134). It also contains one movement in a delightfully popular style, the chorus sung by Nicolas's children (No. 2, "From morning till night, what is my song?"), in which Honegger seems to cast a look in the
direction of such popular Swiss composers as Jaques-Dalcroze or Canon Bovet.
We may notice also Nicolas's beautiful prayer (No. 7) and especially the powerful "The Climb to the Ranft" (No. 10), the four sections of which deserve a
closer look.

   Pizzicatos pick out a simple ascending motif in the rhythm of a slow march,
the natural pace for a mountain-dweller going uphill (Example 135). This is
the motif of the final chorus of the piece, and a younger brother, as it were, of
the theme of Hope in *Jeanne d'Arc au bûcher*. Then the chorus enters with a
rhythmic variant of "Alone." As Nicolas climbs, he comes through the brief
visitation of demons (a choral declamation over ugly, atonal sounds from the
orchestra), but he soon leaves them below him. He is summoned by the celestial chorus, while Example 135 is heard in imitation on winds. Suddenly, the
children's chorus intones "Let us praise the Eternal One of the celestial Hosts"
in a Lydian D major, and the celestial chorus replies, again in the tone of a Dal-
crozian popular song. The spoken recitative is supported by a fine progression,
a succession of dominants based on Example 135. The final strophe of "Let us
praise the Eternal One" serves as a majestic, brilliant peroration, with brief
Amens delivered *fortissimo*.

Example 135

   In the second act, Nicolas, in his mountain retreat, receives numerous pilgrims who come to ask his advice. He sees terrible danger lying ahead for the
Swiss people. They are being asked by their powerful neighbors, France and
Austria, to take up arms against Charles the Bold. What Nicolas fears is that the
confederates will win, and that intoxication and wealth too easily acquired will
sow discord among them. But his warnings are in vain. They prefer to believe
the false prophecies of the great astrologer of Bern, who is in the pay of France
and Austria. As the narrator bitterly exclaims: "Woe to the people who believe
a soothsayer rather than a saint!"

The act ends in the midst of furious fighting. It brings in other leitmotifs, such as the austerely modal chorale of the Pilgrims' Chorus and the second chorale "Nicolas! Take care!" (Example 133). This is an especially beautiful and memorable movement, with its classical suspensions and appoggiaturas and its expressive modulations. We may also mention the double chorus "Morning star" (No. 12), the ethereal, alpine atmosphere of which brings it close to certain moments in *Le Roi David*. Then there is the bellicose Chorus of Powers (No. 18), with its pounding eighth-notes in the trombones—"armored" music in its rough, dense textures, broken by cries of "Ho there, the Swiss!" Finally, there is the broad concluding chorus "Victory and Misery" (No. 19), in three sections. Over a ground of somber, tragic chromaticism and beneath a lowering sky in which the glare of fires is already visible, the narrator sees the messenger of war. Over this hectic, barbarous music we hear the lamenting vocalises of the women. The recitative ends over what sounds like a knell, adorned with cries of "Nicolas!" from the chorus. After a rapid crescendo the act comes to an abrupt conclusion.

The third act begins with the Ambassadors' March (No. 20), one of the best military marches ever written by a "classical" composer. It is unusually rich in melody and in contrapuntal interest, including even a fugal exposition, as well as a short, more legato trio section. This is followed by the attractive "Companions of Follevie" (No. 21), recalling the composer's best popular songs and sung by a band of merry brigands. At the meeting of the diet of the cantons, discord reigns and there is the threat of civil war (recitative "Tomorrow comes war," No. 23, with female lamentations over sinister sounds from the side drum). How to defuse the situation? A delegation goes off to find Nicolas in his retreat. He is exhausted by fasting and age and collapses on the way down the mountain. But by means of his girdle, as discussed previously, he sends a message of peace. The lesson strikes home and peace is saved (No. 30). After a solemn procession punctuated by bells and the final verse of the chorale "Nicolas!" (Example 133), the work ends with a loud chorus glorifying the saint. A Handelian fugue subject in E-flat major is abandoned after the second entry in the tonic, and gives way to a joyful, festive texture in the traditional style of nineteenth-century *Festspiele*. Its directness of impact is sufficient to counter any grumbles on grounds of academicism.

177. *Selzach Passion* (Das Selzacher Passionspiel)

Passion in two parts (lasting a day) on a German libretto by Caesar von Arx
Uncompleted project
First sketches in a notebook from June 1938; further work from November 1940 to 9 February 1941, from 16 November to December 1942, and in December 1944 (up to 25 December)
Order as found in vocal score:
A. *First part*, The Creation of the World: 1. Prelude for organ and narrator; 2. Narrator and orchestra; 3. Chorus "Gloria in excelsis Deo." Dated at the end: Paris, 9 February 1941
B. *First part*, Adam and Eve: The Garden of Eden: 1. Narrator with orchestra; 2. Larghetto for orchestra alone; 3. Satan and the Demons (orchestra); 4. The

Archangel Michael; 5. Chorus and orchestra (without words, then De profundis). Dated at the end: Paris, 25 December 1944
C. *Beginning of the second part*, Annunciation of the Birth of Christ: 1. Narrator and organ (Prologue from the Gospel according to John); 2. Unaccompanied chorus (Benedictus, Jesus Christus, Agnus Dei, Hosanna); 3. Chorale "Nieder Herr die Himmel neige"; 4. Recitative with orchestra; 5. Funeral music for Jairus's daughter; 6. Chorale "O sacred head sore wounded"; 7. Adagio in dialogue (Agnus Dei). Dated at the end: 16 November 1942
D. *End of the first part*, Job: 1. Chorus and orchestra "Praise the Lord"; 2. Tenor solo (Job) and orchestra; 3. Chorus on Psalm 150 (dated at the end: December 1940); 4. Chorus and orchestra (Mimaamaquim); 5. Procession of the sick and beggars (orchestra alone; dated at the end: 17 December 1940); 6. Orchestra with Job's spoken recitative. Dated at the end: 31 January 1941
E. *Second part*, The Nativity: 1. Chorus and orchestra ("O come, O come, Emmanuel"); 2. Christmas Carols (orchestra alone); 3. Crescendo (orchestra alone); 4. Chorus and orchestra (Laudate Dominum); 5. Epilogue for orchestra alone (Largo). Dated at the end: Paris, 24 January 1941
B5 and E would be used in *Une Cantate de Noël* (H212), 412 measures out of the original 986. Order of composition: D, E, D, A, C, B. Order in the final work: A, B, D, C, E. The duration of the music not reused (A, B1–4, C, D) can be estimated at around 35 minutes.
Unpublished

The *Selzach Passion* would have been the crowning glory of Honegger's output, but fate decreed otherwise. The project was delayed by the Second World War and, when circumstances allowed it to be reconsidered, it was finally put to rest by the composer's illness and by the librettist's suicide in 1949. Honegger found himself with a good hour's worth of music that was worked out to the last detail, but not orchestrated. Slightly less than half of it was reused in *Une Cantate de Noël*, but the rest has remained unpublished and unknown to this day. Even G. K. Spratt does not seem to have examined this material, which is full of excellent things. It would certainly be worth orchestrating those parts that the composer did not. In the meantime, though, any detailed discussion of this music obviously lies outside the scope of this volume, and I shall limit myself to a few succinct remarks, split under two headings.

1. Music Reused in Une Cantate de Noël

The passages in *Une Cantate de Noël* taken from the *Selzach Passion*, sometimes with considerable changes, are sections A (not the introduction), B (not the first seven measures), D, F, and G. The newly composed passages are A (introduction, Largo, 13 measures), B (beginning, first crescendo, 7 measures), C (first Interlude with the baritone, Poco meno largo, 16 measures), and E (second Interlude with the baritone, Largo, 36 measures)—about five minutes of music out of the total twenty-five.

2. Music Not Reused in Une Cantate de Noël

A. "The Creation of the World"

The modulating introduction to "The Creation of the World" on solo organ is similar in kind to that of *Une Cantate de Noël*, but the notes are totally different. The spoken narration of the Creation, soon supported by a powerful orchestral crescendo, leads to the appearance of Light and then to a serene choral Gloria in C major.

B. "Adam and Eve: The Garden of Eden"

The appearance of Adam and Eve is accompanied by a somewhat agitated 9/8 section. Then they kneel down to the sounds of an Andantino while the narrator continues. The Larghetto in D minor provides contrast in its dissonant harmonies and sharply dotted rhythms. There are a few realistically unsettled measures for the appearance of Satan, and solemn brass chords for that of the Archangel Michael. The wordless chorus and the De profundis would supply section A of *Une Cantate de Noël*, minus the first thirteen introductory measures.

C. "Annunciation of the Birth of Christ"

In the "Annunciation of the Birth of Christ," the second section for unaccompanied chorus is a striking illustration of Honegger's ecumenism. The Benedictus in D major adopts a neo-Gregorian style, while the Jesus Christus in B-flat is treated as a Protestant chorale and the Agnus Dei in A minor is in chordal recitative. The Hosanna returns to the key and style of the Benedictus. The chorale "Nieder Herr die Himmel neige" makes use of a very simple D major melody, with octave leaps showing that it could not date from before the nineteenth century. Perhaps Honegger invented it himself. The return of the Hosanna is introduced by a lovely orchestral phrase at the words "See, I am with you each day, until the end of time."

The funeral music for Jairus's daughter, which is written for orchestra alone and precedes her raising by Jesus, is built on a somber, Oriental theme in B-flat minor, and we may be reminded of *Le Roi David* and *Judith*. This section continues with the famous "O sacred head sore wounded," given with Bach's own harmonization but surrounded by new, agile contrapuntal lines on the orchestra. This page of the manuscript is also beautiful to look at. The section finally closes with the antiphonal dialogue between angels (Agnus Dei in a Lydian A-flat) and humans (Miserere in a darkly chromatic C minor).

D. "Job"

The whole of the beginning of this part consists of a paraphrase in German of Psalm 150 ("Praise the Lord"), in three sections. The first one, following eighteen measures of orchestral introduction, brings in the voices of the chorus one after the other in a magnificent progression. The second, for solo tenor, is unfortunately incomplete. Even if the lack of words is not serious (the melodic line is present in full), the accompaniment too is missing, apart from a few indications of rhythm. The third section finally allots the whole of the psalm text to the choir in vigorous music with continuously changing measure lengths.

Then follows what is undoubtedly the most amazing passage in all this unpublished music, the extraordinary Oriental lamentation of the "Mimaamaquim." In character, certainly, it is close to the *Mimaamaquim* published six years later in 1946, but the notes are quite different. It would be worth orchestrating this passage, if only to be able to compare it with its successor. The procession in 2/4 of the "Procession of the sick and beggars" is obviously closely wedded to its dramatic context, but the music accompanying Job's recitation ("Who am I to complain against God?") is a sorrow-laden adagio of profound beauty.

E. "THE NATIVITY"

The music for "The Nativity" was entirely reused, in modified form, in sections B, D, F, and G of *Une Cantate de Noël*.

212. *Une Cantate de Noël* (A Christmas Cantata)

Composed between December 1952 and 25 January 1953, almost entirely from fragments of the *Selzach Passion* (see H177 above), which date back to 25 December 1944 (section A) and to 24 January 1941 (the remainder); orchestration completed 16 October 1953 in cantonal hospital in Zurich
"For the 25th anniversary of the Basel Chamber Choir and for its founder Paul Sacher" (who commissioned it)
Liturgical and popular texts (German version by Fred Goldbeck; English version by Rollo H. Myers)
First performance: 18 December 1953, Derrik Olsen (baritone), Basel Chamber Choir and Orchestra, conducted by Paul Sacher, Basel
Performing forces: baritone, mixed choir, children's choir; orchestra: 2.2.2.2.– 4.3.3.0.–harp, organ–strings
Duration: 24 minutes 25 seconds
Salabert

After Honegger's final orchestral testament, the *Monopartita*, illness led to a greatly slower rate in his composing output. At the same time, he maintained its quality, as we can hear from the music for the Claudel documentary, the last incidental music for *Oedipe-Roi*, or the delightful little *Romance for flute and piano*. The composition of *Une Cantate de Noël* provided his last moments of creative happiness and, although the work was based on much older material, it carries nonetheless a symbolic significance in bringing his life to an end on a note of hope—that hope "which is the strongest."

Its structure is symmetrical, simple, and effective. Of the seven main linked sections, C and E on the one hand and D and G on the other correspond with one another, and the epilogue for solo organ corresponds with the opening measures. But it is possible to take a still more "concentric" view of things, with

D (the first carol *quodlibet*) standing as a central pillar, flanked on either side by the two intermezzos with baritone (C and E), and with those in turn surrounded by the main choral episodes (A/B and F)—the first somber in its anxious expectancy, the second radiating vigorous joy.

A. Introduction and De profundis (measures 1–127)

The organ begins without preamble on a thirty-two-foot low pedal C, over which we hear two groups of mysterious, nontonal chords, punctuated by a sinuous line on lower strings. At measure 14 begins a slow, melancholy procession that recalls the *Symphonie liturgique*. Over a two-measure ostinato bass the chorus laments in vocalise, supported by broken sighs on cellos. At the entry of the soprano eighth-note vocalise, the tonality settles on E-flat minor, before the start of the basses' antiphonal De profundis. This was one of the composer's favorite texts, which he set in a number of guises: in French, in Latin, in Hebrew, from *Le Roi David* to *Mimaamaquim*, passing through the *Three Psalms* and the *Symphonie liturgique*.

A new chromatic ostinato in contrary motion on the violins heightens the tension in an E minor full of sharp dissonances—looking back to the opening of *Judith*. Suddenly, at measure 92, the rhythm quickens in exasperation and the orchestra launches into a kind of revolutionary march with marked, aggressive accents and rapid figurations. These culminate in large blocks of dissonant chords on wind instruments and wordless chorus. Again, we are reminded of the *Symphonie liturgique*, this time of the climax before the coda.

B. O Come! (measures 128–174)

A tumultuous crescendo (strepitoso) on strings introduces the chorus's great cry "O come!" on a seven-note chord (comprising the scale of G major with D-sharp in place of D-natural). Then comes a new assault from the strings, leading this time to a complete chorale. Even though the eight-part writing here is dissonant, highly chromatic, and rich in altered chords, it is basically tonal. It is supported by dotted figuration in the strings at the words "O come, O come, Emmanuel!" The children's chorus replies with a delicate arabesque in A-flat major, a sort of popular song, full of a naive confidence (Example 136). This alternation between the two choruses then occurs a second time.

Joie et paix sur   toi___   Is - ra - el voi -   ci   ve - nir   Em   - ma - nu - el

Example 136

C. FIRST INTERLUDE WITH BARITONE (MEASURES 175–191)

This is the first appearance of the baritone, representing the angel who announces the birth of the Savior. It is a kind of arioso, with beautiful, undulating modulations on the organ and discreet comments from the trumpets. The violins' eighth-notes in contrary motion, grouped in pairs, suggest the beating of wings.

D. *QUODLIBET* OF CAROLS (MEASURES 192–294)

The children's chorus begin with the old German carol *Es ist ein Reis entsprungen* (A Child Is Born), setting in train the long central *quodlibet*, which consists of three successive tonal sections. The first, in E major, alternates the phrases of this carol with the combination, on mixed chorus, of *Il est né le divin enfant* (He Is Born, the Divine Child) and a Gloria made up of exuberant vocalises (Example 137). The second section (più vivace in 6/8, in A-flat major) constructs a transparent polyphony from different elements of the German carol *Vom Himmel hoch* (From Highest Heaven). This peeling carillon is linked enharmonically with the dominant of B major, the key of the third and longest section (larghetto in 6/4). Here Honegger superimposes no less than six carols, French, German, Austrian, and English (the newcomers are *O du fröhliche*, or "O Happy One," and the universally popular *Stille Nacht*, "Silent Night"), each one sung in its original language. This astonishing display of polyphonic and polymetric skill (combining 6/4 and 18/8) is nonetheless full of tenderness, conjuring up the childhood of the whole of Europe, while the orchestra adds its own halo of light. The children's chorus here doubles the two-part sopranos of the mixed chorus.

Glo - ri - a   in__ ex - cel - sis

Example 137

Alleluias and vocalized cries of "eia!" are now added to the ensemble. Even if fragmented, all these tunes remain recognizable as they swirl around in a jungle of harmony. Around them, strings form a halo of rapid notes in eleven real parts, illuminating the crib (or the church) with the mystic radiance of thousands of candles, twinkling in the equivalent of a cold, starry night. The vision slowly fades and the music leads on to the next episode.

E. SECOND INTERLUDE WITH BARITONE (MEASURES 295–330)

In the peace of the night, the baritone sings the Gloria in excelsis. A lone child's voice replies with the Gregorian Laudate Dominum—the melody used

by Bach in the well-known chorale "Sleepers Wake" from his Cantata BWV
140. The baritone returns with the words "Et in terra pax," the chorus continues the plainsong, and then suddenly an orchestral crescendo, built on solid
chords in contrary motion, leads to a broken cadence taking us into the C major
of the Laudate Dominum.

F. LAUDATE DOMINUM (MEASURES 331–434)

This allegro in 3/4 is based on Psalm 117, a brief act in praise of God by all
the peoples. It is propelled by massive orchestral chords and, in its virile
strength, the choral writing is worthy of Bach or of the Alleluias of Handel
(Example 138). Some critics have found a resemblance between this piece and
Stravinsky's *Symphony of Psalms*, but I do not share this view, despite the fact that
in both works the harmony is based on the whole diatonic scale. Children's
voices and trumpets superimpose the Gregorian cantus firmus in long values,
exactly as in any Bach cantata. After the doxology in the relative A minor, there
is a repeat of the opening Laudate, still with its Gregorian counterpoint. This
is followed by two splendid Amens in an ascending and descending curve from
the chorus, complete with orchestral echoes, and then by four further, shorter
Amens in energetic quarter-notes.

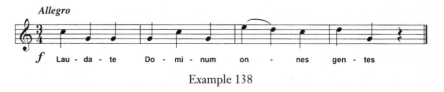

Example 138

G. ORCHESTRAL EPILOGUE (SECOND CAROL *QUODLIBET*)

The orchestra begins this peroration *fortissimo*. Underpinned by a low
pedal C, this Largo proceeds through a long, continuous decrescendo. It is a
miraculous conclusion to the work, bringing together almost all its themes, as
in the earlier *quodlibet*, but this time without voices. Now the graceful ensemble of carols, with the addition of the Gregorian theme, is heard on instruments
alone, like a nostalgic but ever-fading memory. Honegger has recourse to keys
distant from C major, but that tonality remains in control, and the others sound
like ever-growing shadows in the lonely night. Increasingly, they crowd in upon
each other with shorter entries, except for the last.

Gradually the darkness reasserts itself, while the initial pattern of organ
chords sinks down onto the primordial thirty-two-foot C. The final dispersal of
the carol fragments is reminiscent of a peal of bells, which cease sounding, one
after another, depending upon their weight and rhythm. The gentle vision fades
into darkness and silence. A lofty soul, feeling how close it is to its final journey,
takes leave on tiptoe of its fellow men, congregated in fervent desire of that
peace which it had always held most dear.

Category 11: Operas

I.   *Philippa*
II.   *Sigismond*
III. *La Esmeralda*
20.   *La Mort de Sainte Alméenne*
57B. *Judith*
65.   *Antigone*
108. *L'Aiglon*

I have already discussed, in the introduction to this chapter on theater and musical frescoes, the unhappy love affair between Honegger and opera. In this section on operas, I have deliberately included Honegger's three early attempts at the genre in order to underline the fact that, for the young Honegger, opera more than any other medium symbolized the soul of music, and the fact that he discovered the romantic operatic repertory even before he discovered Bach or Beethoven.

After those three early attempts, the list is disappointingly small: there is the uncompleted *La Mort de Sainte Alméenne*, which he never orchestrated; the patchwork of *Judith*, leading, it is true, to that problematic work's most complete and satisfying shape; and then the most complete expression of his operatic ideals, the masterly *Antigone* (although it was too individual and too radical to serve as a launching-pad for other works). After that there is nothing, except the three acts of the five-act *L'Aiglon*, which the composer wrote deliberately in the popular style of traditional grand opera, albeit with total effectiveness and integrity. The fact is that we do not have from Honegger's pen a single full-length opera. Among the great composers of the first half of the century, only Dmitri Shostakovich gives rise to comparable frustration, with an operatic career cut short at the age of thirty (after *The Nose* and *Katerina Ismailova*) thanks to Stalin's tyrannical edicts.

In France, his country of adoption, Honegger was faced with an impossible situation, and sheer love of art was not motive enough for him to persist in pointless endeavor. No creative artist, as we have seen, was further than he was from subscribing to an ivory tower mentality: he needed the stimulus of performance and an audience. As soon as a project ran aground, he would abandon it, as shown by the, happily few, stillborn projects that stud his career, from *La Mort de Sainte Alméenne* to the *Selzach Passion*. He no longer believed in opera as a medium that could attract vast audiences as it had in the past, except for works belonging to that past, and even if the very unfavorable climate for new operatic works in France tended to exaggerate his reaction, we cannot say that he was totally wrong.

Of the composers of successful operas whom Honegger cites—Jules Massenet, Giacomo Puccini, and Richard Strauss—none of them has had successors. But Puccini did not die until 1924, and at the time of *Antigone* Strauss still had half of his operatic output ahead of him. Among Honegger's Swiss contemporaries and juniors, neither Othmar Schoeck nor Heinrich Suter-meister has ever considered abandoning opera. There is therefore a more seri-ous reason, namely that Honegger had lost faith in the genre. As he said, "In the opera house, passionate love means *Tristan* and delicate love *Pelléas*." And he went on: "Three forbidding composers guard the operatic domain: Wagner, Debussy—and Strauss. In avoiding Debussy you fall into Massenet, and in avoiding Strauss into Puccini, which is worse." And how could he not be aware that Fauré's *Penelope* (which he adored to the extent that at the end of his life he rated it higher than *Pelléas*) had no appeal for the great operatic public?

In any case, this large popular audience had, some time before, already turned to a genre that came much closer to fulfilling his aspirations. Honegger was among the first to realize that the twentieth century was the age of the cin-ema, and it was to this opportunity for reconquering the masses that he devoted himself body and soul from the beginning of the 1930s. By this time the partial failure of *Antigone* and of *Judith* in its operatic version had led to his abandon-ing his ambitions in this field. However bitter this renunciation of a genre must have been, a genre that, perhaps more than any other, corresponded to Honeg-ger's specific gifts, his position is coherent and impregnable, and in his view entirely logical. We are left, then, with a truncated operatic career, but one that has to its credit a work that is undeniably a masterpiece, *Antigone*, and in *Judith* a fascinating rescue operation.

I. *Philippa*

Opera in three acts and four scenes, "Opus 1"
May–July 1903
Libretto by the composer based on a story in the journal *La Jeunesse illustrée*
Four main roles: contralto, light tenor, tenor, lyric bass (no soprano!); three
    secondary roles: mezzo-soprano, light tenor, heroic baritone
Fourteen numbers, plus an overture and an introduction for each of the three acts
The work was never orchestrated
Unpublished

II. *Sigismond*

Opera in three or four scenes
c. 1904
Lost

III. *La Esmeralda*

Opera (unfinished)
1907
Based on Victor Hugo's *Notre-Dame de Paris*, on a libretto previously used by Mlle
    Bertin
Only the Overture and the first two scenes of Act I were composed, in a reduction
    for voice and piano: the "Chorus of Vagrants" and "Esmeralda's Aria," the latter
    unfinished.

Even if the naiveté of these three childhood attempts demonstrates a complete lack of professional skill, the works do at least testify to Honegger's early operatic propensities. No other score of his is known to us from before 1907.

20. *La Mort de Sainte Alméenne* (The Death of Saint Alméenne)

Opera in one act (two tableaux)
Late 1918 (reduction for voice and piano completed in December); orchestration unfinished and undated. For the *Interlude*, see H20A (Category 7A, in Chapter 11)
Mystery play by Max Jacob
Only the *Interlude* was ever performed (30 October 1920)
Characters: Saint Alméenne (soprano), the Angel (soprano), the Sister (mezzo-soprano), the Young Man (baritone)
Performing forces: 1.1.1.1.–1.1.0.0.–strings (in the *Interlude*, a second clarinet, a second bassoon, and a second horn are all added)
Duration: 36 minutes 55 seconds
First tableau: "A Flowery Garden in a Cloister" (19 minutes 35 seconds)
Prelude, Scene 1 (Saint Alméenne, the Angel), Scene 2 (Saint Alméenne, the Sister), Scene 3 (the Young Man), Scene 4 (Saint Alméenne)
Second tableau: "The Cell" (12 minutes 55 seconds)
Scene 1 (Saint Alméenne, the Young Man), Scene 2 (the Sister)
Unpublished

I have related in the biographical section of this book (see Chapter 3) how Honegger began this work at the suggestion of Jane Bathori, but then abandoned it when Bathori found she did not have the money to put it on at her Théâtre du Vieux-Colombier. Contrary to what has been claimed in the Honegger literature thus far, *La Mort de Sainte Alméenne* was not incidental music but a real chamber opera, very much under the influence of Debussy (the Debussy of *La Damoiselle élue* but also of *The Martyrdom of Saint Sebastian*). This suited the subject, certainly, but it was still a deliberate choice on Honegger's part. The fundamental difference, though, is that here the writing is essentially contrapuntal, with the Debussy influence manifesting itself on the melodic, harmonic, and rhythmic levels as well as in the delicate instrumental coloring. Honegger orchestrated only 208 measures out of a total of 694, but it would be worthwhile, and far from impossible, to orchestrate the remainder, since the vocal score is complete in the smallest details.

In the first tableau, Max Jacob's mystery play brings before us the mystic dialogue between the Saint and the Well-Beloved, in whose name the Angel replies. The Saint has taken a vow of silence, which is protected by the sisters of the convent. Before leaving, the Angel warns her against a young man whose visit she is expecting. After a brief dialogue between the Saint and a Sister who is worried by her feverish look, the stage is left empty. Enter the Young Man, who unveils his evil design to destroy the Saint at any cost. He leaves and the Saint reappears, troubled by scents that do not remind her of her Well-Beloved. At this point between the two tableaux, the curtain falls for an orchestral Interlude, which was performed in 1920 (see H20A, Category 7A).

In "The Cell" there is a confrontation between the Saint and the Young Man. He pretends to be a holy confessor and tries to get her to leave the clois-

ter by urging her to come and purge the countryside of the plague that is beset-
ting it. Then, when she resists, he reveals to her that her brother has already
died of it and that her mother is seriously ill—she alone can save her. Suddenly,
the Virgin appears and transforms the Young Man into an animal. The Angel
announces to the young girl that her trials are over and that the Virgin herself
is coming to lead her to God. The vision fades and the Sister, penetrating the
gloom of the cell, finds Alméenne's lifeless body. She asks the rest of the community to join her in prayer ("Saint Alméenne, pray for us"), as the curtain falls.

The overall atmosphere, as indicated above, is reflective and meditative.
The music is generally homogeneous, with the exception of the Young Man's
monologue, which is a lively scherzo in 6/8. Alternating with a languid slow
section, this is ironic music, with dry, spiky phrasing, and it provides an indispensable contrast within the context of the whole work. In her dialogue with the
Sister (scene 2), the Saint evokes the sufferings of her Well-Beloved on Calvary.
The passionate declamation over a chromatic, polyphonic accompaniment
already announces *Pâques à New York*. The climax of the score, however, is
undoubtedly the final appearance of the Angel. It is a passage of calm and nobility in which the slightly "Parsifalesque" coloring is underlined by a four-note
countersubject, a barely disguised quotation from *Parsifal*'s bells.

57B. *Judith*—serious opera

November–December 1925 (see H57, Category 10)
"To Claire Croiza." Commissioned by Raoul Gunsbourg for the Monte Carlo Opera
Libretto by René Morax (German version by Leo Melitz)
First performance: 13 February 1926, Mme Bonavia (Judith), Tikin, Gervais
    (Holofernes), Chorus and Orchestra of Monte Carlo Opera, conducted by
    Arthur Honegger, Monte Carlo
Performing forces: same as original dramatic version (H57), discussed under
    Category 10, with the addition of a baritone (Holofernes), a bass (Ozias), and a
    tenor (Bagoas, a Soldier, a Sentinel, an offstage Voice), but without a narrator
Duration: 55 minutes (16:00 + 24:30 + 14:30); in this version, the music of each act is
    continuous, but there are pauses between the acts
New music added to the first, "biblical drama" version: Act I: 4 minutes 35 seconds;
    Act II: 15 minutes 20 seconds; Act III: 4 minutes 20 seconds; Total: 24 minutes
    15 seconds, in all 426 measures of new music (for details, see commentary
    following). From the 576 measures of the first version, the score grew to 711 for
    the third, and to 1002 for this version
Salabert

The additions to Act I are four in number, all fairly unimportant:

a) between Nos. 1 and 2: ten measures of recitative for Ozias (the general of the
Jewish army). This is a spoken role in the first version and does not appear in the
third;

b) the extension of No. 2, discussed under Category 10;

c) the three new measures at the start of No. 4, discussed under Category 10;

d) replacing the spoken recitation between Nos. 4 and 5, thirty-five measures of
a chorus, followed by a confrontation between Judith and Ozias trying to dis-
suade her.

Most of the modifications come in Act II, which is split into two scenes. The first consists of the "Fanfare" (No. 6) and the "Scene by the Spring" (No. 8), with the addition of sung parts for Judith and the Servant. The second begins with the "Incantation" (No. 7) and continues with the "Festive Music" (No. 9). Then comes a new dialogue of forty-one measures, in which Holofernes asks his courtier Bagoas to read the omens of the forthcoming battle. They are ambiguous and Bagoas is insulted as a "clumsy eunuch." Now follows the long scene of 175 measures that is the main addition in this new version. It has to be said that the absence, from both the stage and the music, of the great confrontation between Judith and Holofernes, which is the very kernel of the drama, was obviously an inexcusable omission in the previous version. This new music includes a repeat of the "Festive Music" with words added, and there are frequent thematic links with the pre-existing score.

We hear Holofernes, first invoking the Assyrian gods in a vigorously rhythmic passage, then ordering Bagoas to go and find Judith. Their first dialogue takes place over the repeat of the "Festive Music." She refuses to touch the wine, which is not consecrated, but finally gives in. Holofernes now sends his warriors away and remains alone with Judith for their duet, which is the best of the music Honegger added. It is a slow, sensual passage in 3/4 with an English horn cantilena that we shall hear again at the very end of the last act. There is a sudden break in the mood when Holofernes tells Judith of his intention to destroy her people, and trumpets play the leitmotif shown in Example 111. The lyrical tone gathers force, punctuated by violent iambic accents in the orchestra, but finally settles: Holofernes has gone to sleep. Judith offers a short prayer to God to give her the courage to do her terrible deed, and this leads directly on to No. 9a, which concludes the act, and which is discussed in the analysis of the oratorio version.

In the third act, Honegger added the dramatic "Return of Judith" (No. 10a in the oratorio version), and then a dozen measures of brief and violent interlude link No. 10a and No. 11. The Interlude (No. 11a) is also new, and at the beginning of No. 13 ("Canticle of Victory") Honegger substituted for the spoken recitation a dialogue in which Judith tells the Serving Girl of her sadness, and this is a preparation for the epilogue. In fact, the opera culminates in twenty-seven measures of new music, which totally alters the sense of this ending. The chorus's victorious conclusion is here followed by twelve measures of decrescendo leading to a moving monologue from Judith, who is overcome by remorse ("I see his eyes looking at me, his eyes full of sadness and reproach. I give my life to God in order to forget"). We hear again the English horn cantilena that accompanied the second-act duet, as well as reminiscences in the woodwinds of the motifs that introduced "Judith's Prayer" (No. 3). The music slowly fades in A minor, in an ending that is certainly less spectacular than that of the oratorio version, and is also a further element distancing *Judith* from *Le Roi David*. Honegger described this new version to Georges Auric (in *Le Ménestrel*, 5 March 1926): "It is above all a simple, condensed, dramatic story. At a time when a number of young composers are deliberately returning to the old opera buffa, I decided to attempt a revival of the old form of Italian opera seria."

As I have already said of the oratorio version, *Judith* is undoubtedly a problem work, and Honegger must have realized it, as there are three versions and none of them is perfect. When treated as an oratorio with separate numbers and a narrator, like *Le Roi David*, *Judith* can only suffer from the comparison, having fewer memorable themes and being less direct in expression, more dissonant and complex in language. In its original form, it is on the way to being an opera—a semi-opera that dares not speak its name. Because the music is constructed on a few short, striking musical cells, it tends toward the symphonic and the developmental, an approach foreign to that of *Le Roi David* and, truth be told, to the spirit of the Jorat. At least, that is one of the reasons behind its semi-failure. But the work did not become completely successful as an opera either, even though this is undoubtedly the form that suits it best, both through the inclinations of the story-line and through the presence of new and excellent musical material.

Passages like the first chorus, the "Fanfare," or the "Canticle of the Virgins" are reminiscent of the period of *Le Roi David* and do not fit comfortably into the context. It must be said too that Morax was less inspired this time—trying to repeat a success is always tempting the devil and rarely works. Within its problematic form, *Judith* is full of magnificent music, which we should perhaps just be happy to enjoy.

65. *Antigone*—musical tragedy in three acts

January 1924–February 1927; orchestrated: June to September 1927; preface dated
  September 1927
"To Vaura" (Andrée Vaurabourg)
Libretto by Jean Cocteau, based on Sophocles (German version by Gian Bundi)
First performance: 28 December 1927, E. Colonne (Creon), S. Ballard (Antigone),
  E. Deulin (Ismène), M. Gerday (Eurydice), M. Yovanovitch (Tiresias), P. Gilson
  (Haemon), J. Sales (the Messenger), Chorus and Orchestra of the Théâtre Royal
  de la Monnaie, conducted by Corneil de Thoran, Théâtre de la Monnaie,
  Brussels
Performing forces: mezzo (Antigone), soprano (Ismène), contralto (Eurydice), tenor
  (Creon), baritones (Haemon, the Guard), basses (Tiresias, the Messenger), four
  chorus leaders (soprano, alto, tenor, bass), mixed chorus; orchestra: 3.3.3.3.–
  saxophone–4.3.3.1.–timpani, percussion (bass drum, cymbals, side drum, tam-
  tam)–saw, celesta, harp–strings. N.B. These days the saw is generally replaced
  by the ondes Martenot.
Duration: 44 minutes 10 seconds (11:40 + 26:40 + 5:50)
Salabert

Antigone is a crucial work in Honegger's output and the most radical together with *Horace victorieux*, the experiments of which are here taken to still greater lengths. Even if some details of the harmony and rhythm recall Stravinsky's *The Rite of Spring* and even if the "cannibal" savagery and the expressionist grittiness go back to *Elektra*, Honegger clearly goes much further. In a tense work like the *String Quartet No. 1*, we can still detect a certain "Frenchness," especially in the Adagio, but *Horace* no longer has anything French about it, and *Antigone* still less (not even in the diction and articulation). G. K. Spratt identifies more than thirty "themes," but these are not readily perceptible in performance, if only because there is considerable incompatibility between themes and atonality. True, the six initial cells provide material for the entire orchestral texture and, in numerous metamorphoses, give rise to what Spratt calls "themes." But few of them return frequently and many have only a narrow existence. More than that, because they are swept along by the furious flood of the music and its frantic speed, few of them stick in the listener's memory. The impression is not so much of themes and developments as of a nonthematic texture that suggests a third model: Schoenberg's *Erwartung* (although I have not managed to establish whether Honegger knew this work or not). In fact, apart from a clearly outlined theme like "Brotherly Love" (see Example 142), the most memorable melodies are those I would categorize as "incidental," such as choruses, interludes, or "Love That Strikest All Mankind" (see Example 144), no doubt because they are more "tonal" than the rest, or identifiable through their regular rhythm ("Hymn to Bacchus").

Otherwise, *Antigone* is a model of rhythmic and syllabic declamation. It does not last much longer than the spoken text—forty-four minutes as against about twenty-six. Although there is only one brief passage of spoken declamation—the chorus leader's dialogue with Antigone in scene 8—recitative is the primary means of expression, with the rare "incidental" exceptions just mentioned. "Love That Strikest" is practically the only passage of lyrical singing, and this lasts a mere seven measures. The absence of easily recognizable melodic outlines, closed forms, repetitions, cadence points, or tonal moments where one can catch one's breath, together with the abjuration of lyricism, and a wild speed of utterance that leads to an exceptional density of information— all these elements make *Antigone* the most arduous and least accessible of Honegger's works.

The difficulties of *Horace victorieux* are multiplied by the length of the score and by the presence of voices treated in an unaccustomed way. More than singers with outstanding voices, *Antigone* demands actors with perfect diction. Honegger's prosody, which has been the subject of so much discussion, is here not an optional choice: it is an absolute necessity, given his whole approach. For all its long stretches of pure atonality, *Antigone* is no less colorful than other works by the composer. It is just that he is using a different palette, as we can see from the orchestral texture. In the midst of these blacks, sepias, browns, ochres, steely grays, and glaucous greens, the "incidental" moments of near-tonality present patches of brighter colors, aggressive splashes of red and vivid green, all the more effective for being few in number and widely separated. What is almost entirely lacking is the color white, as well as long notes. The long, colorless chord on harmonics at the end of scene 10, expressing "glacial numbness" and the suspense preceding the final, tragic, consummatory explosion, is the clear exception that proves the rule.

We may have doubts about the very project of *Antigone* and the attitude it implies, but we cannot deny the absolute technical mastery Honegger brought to it, and the infallible instinct of both composer and librettist in their handling of a dramatic and musical time-scale that remains not merely unusual but unique in its genre. A wager maybe, but one that came off, even if *Antigone* will always be a work more admired than loved, appealing more to the intellect than to the emotions, and one that does not reach the depths of our souls as do *Jeanne d'Arc au bûcher*, *La Danse des morts*, or the *Symphonie liturgique*. In any case, Cocteau is not Claudel. It was one of the facets of Honegger's genius that he never repeated himself, and that he was able to make a success of a work such as *Les Aventures du roi Pausole* as well as of an *Antigone*. That would remain a unique experience in which he said all he had to say, with no room for more. *Antigone* contains enough musical material for three hours and may be regarded as the ultimate supernova of opera.

Furthermore, the evolution in Honegger's ethical and aesthetic outlook was such that another *Antigone* was unthinkable after the crisis of 1931–1933. After that, the need to communicate dominated every other and, in his freely chosen mission to be a "composer in the city of men," he felt the preservation of an esoteric, avant-garde language to be a self-regarding luxury that ran counter to his humanist desires (even if it left the "art for art's sake" aesthetes looking glum and disapproving). In *L'Aiglon*, his only later attempt at opera, Honegger would aim to appeal immediately to a wide public (with all the risks of short-term success that implied) and not to a distant and hypothetical elite. Anyway, one cannot imagine an *Antigone* written in collaboration, as *L'Aiglon* was with Jacques Ibert.

Before beginning an analysis of the work, I should like to take up G. K. Spratt's thesis that *Antigone* is in sonata form. According to Spratt's thesis, Act I would be the exposition, with scene 1 ("Antagonists," featuring Antigone and Ismène) forming the "first group of themes," and scene 3 ("Protagonists," with Creon and the Guard) the "second group." Scenes 4/5 and 6/7 of Act II form a two-part development, and scenes 8/9 (Act II) and 10 (Act III) constitute the recapitulation, with scene 11 as a coda. While this analysis is very tempting on paper, it seems to me to be more academic than real, either musically or dramatically—a remark that I would apply to Spratt's work on *Antigone* in general. *Antigone* may be one of Honegger's most solid and perfect structures, but it still works in dramatic and psychological, rather than symphonic, terms. The ambiguous role of themes, the absence of tonality for long periods, and the lack of any tonal plan should warn us not to try to force the work on to a Procustes's bed that does not fit its true nature.

Act I
Scene 1 *(measures 1–121)*
Exposition of the Drama: the two sisters (Antigone, Ismène)

A. ORCHESTRAL INTRODUCTION (MEASURES 1–16)

The short orchestral introduction immediately creates an atmosphere of savage, powerful tension. The pitiless dissonance of this "cannibal" music matches the ferocity of the ancient tragedy (now "desanctified" by Cocteau's brutal vernacular). The first four measures (Example 139) present four of the six main motifs (the other two motifs will follow in measures 10 and 16). The motifs occur in pairs, *a* and *b* in the treble, *c* and *d* in the bass symbolizing the family curse and the shame it brings on the two sisters. Motif *a*, in the shape of a spreading fan, is by far the most important. It is in 4/4 against the prevailing 3/4 and uses only dissonant, nontonal intervals—minor second, augmented fifth, major seventh, and minor ninth. The four motifs differ in their articulation and rhythm, with *a* distinguished from the abrupt, Stravinskyan character of *b*, *c*, and *d*. The fabric they add up to suggests a Phrygian F minor, but with a Lydian sharpened fourth, one of Honegger's favorite modal colorings. The fifth motif, *e*, is always associated with a rasping chord on bassoons, horns, and trombones (D minor with added second and leading note) and has the same fierce rhythmic character (Example 140).

Example 139

Example 140

As the curtain rises, rapidly and violently descending triplets outline the sixth and last motif, which is, like the first, a very important one (Example 141). The minor thirds that form the basis of this motif are the main interval in the opera and the one that will unleash the final catastrophe. The motif symbolizes Creon and his arbitrary, unjust rule.

Example 141

B. Dialogue of the Two Sisters (measures 17–85)

The dialogue is supported by the motifs just mentioned. Antigone announces that further tragedy and shame lie in wait for them. Ismène says that after the mutual fratricide of Eteocles and Polynices she cannot bear anything more. But Antigone explains that the issue is Polynices's unburied body, as motif *f* everywhere in the orchestra indicates that Creon is responsible for this abomination. In reply to her sister's terrified questions, Antigone announces passionately that she intends to bury her brother, despite Creon's edict forbidding such an act. Ismène, whose music is more lyrical than her sister's and so inclines more to tonality, reminds her of their parents' tragic end and emphasizes the total solitude and certain death that await them if they persist in this plan. Antigone is inflexible and says she will therefore have to act alone.

C. Brotherly Love (measures 86–93)

In the only brief moment of calm in this scene, Antigone explains in a kind of trance that her fidelity to her brother is based on respect for the laws of the gods—laws that are far more important than the arbitrary ones of the mortal Creon. She is accompanied by a beautiful theme on alto saxophone (Example 142), which Willy Tappolet justifiably links with "Brotherly Love."[7] This broad, floating melody—the longest in the score—is anchored on a readily heard dominant of F.

Example 142

D. Continuation of the Altercation (measures 94–110)

This section is a return to the frantic principal tempo. For Antigone, Ismène's attitude only adds to the shame and will increase the anger of the gods.

E. Orchestral Epilogue (measures 111–121)

The orchestral epilogue accompanies the successive exits of the two sisters and acts as a symmetrical mirror of the introduction.

Scene 2 (measures 122–163)
Glorification of the Thebans' Victory (chorus)

This chorus of the people serves to introduce Creon. It is a fast, savage, powerful, and brassy movement, in a sweeping style that is closer to the style of *Judith* than to that of *Le Roi David*. Throughout the work, the role of the chorus remains similar to the one it fulfilled in ancient tragedy—that of commenting on the action. It also has two more important interventions, the present one and especially the "Hymn to Bacchus," which serves as an interlude between scenes 9 and 10. The direct, tonal character of these interludes is in deliberate contrast to the fierce atonality of the main drama. But even here the tragedy and its implications remain present, thanks to the organic links uniting *a* with the chorus's three successive themes, which are then heard in combination. But the chorus's themes have still stronger links with *f*, confirming that they are Creon's loyal subjects. A fourth theme leads us without a break into the following scene, the entry of Creon.

Scene 3 (measures 164–254)
The Beginnings of Conflict (Creon, the Guard, bass chorus leader)

A. Creon Supported by the Sycophantic Chorus Leaders (measures 164–195)

The incisive Honeggerian iambuses in Creon's descending minor thirds accompany his speech, culminating in the proclamation of his "ukase" ("That is why I delivered the decree").

B. The Guard's Story (measures 196–225)

A crawling theme in the double basses illustrates the fear of the Guard, who in his terror dares to reveal to Creon only very gradually that his order has been flouted, and that Polynices has been buried. The transparent, pointillist texture is interrupted by Creon's sudden shout of rage as he learns the news, punctuated by a vivid orchestral gesture, a quickly rising run followed by violently hammered rhythms.

C. Creon's Anger (measures 226–247)

One of the male chorus leaders timidly suggests that the burial may be the work of the gods and Creon replies with the famous "*Assez de sottises, vieil-*

lesse!" (Enough nonsense, old man!), with its celebrated emphases. His diatribe is accompanied by two new ideas in the orchestra: an accelerated network of imitations of *a*, symbolizing the trap set by destiny for the future, and an almost visible stamping of rage, going beyond any articulate expression, describing his obsession with treason. This fury ends with the desperate flight of the Guard, while the texture of the sixteenth-notes has turned into a veritable toccata.

D. ORCHESTRAL TRANSITION TO THE INTERLUDE (MEASURES 248–254)

Creon remains alone on the steps of the palace. In the orchestra the theme of Treachery tells us of his obsessive thoughts. It grows dark.

Interlude (unison chorus) (measures 255–297)

This interlude passage is famous for Honegger's very specific prosody (Example 143). The basic interval is the descending third, because it is Creon's people that are singing. It is a paraphrase by Cocteau of Sophocles's famous "Polla ta dhina" (Many are the strange things), later set to music by Xenakis in 1962. An orchestral tutti then presents a long, lyrical melody, after which there is a return to the initial mood, with alternating trumpets replacing the voices. The stage suddenly grows lighter and we are at once in Act II.

Example 143

Act II
Scene 4 (measures 298–440)
The First Conflict: Creon and Antigone
(Creon, Antigone, the Guard, tenor chorus leader, chorus)

Scene 4 forms an entity with the following one; the same is true of scenes 6 and 7.

A. INTRODUCTION (MEASURES 298–302)

A brief comment from the chorus ("God, what a strange omen!") precedes the entry of the Guard.

B. The Guard's Story (measures 303–363)

The Guard enters, dragging Antigone, in a 6/8 presto that limps and staggers; the start, at least, is very close to the Finale of the *First Symphony*. The music for this narrative is entirely atonal, marked by a return of the theme of Treachery and by a string figure realistically evoking the "storm of dust." But Creon brutally interrupts the Guard and addresses Antigone.

C. Antigone's Monologue (measures 364–391)

Antigone calmly states: "I did it, I admit." Then, after a furious Creon has sent the Guard roughly away, Antigone's song blossoms into a magnificently lyrical passage that is almost tonal, with its successions of dominants. At the climax we hear the theme of Brotherly Love (Example 142) on the English horn. The tenor chorus leader comments: "By her inflexible authority we recognize the daughter of Oedipus."

D. Altercation Between Creon and Antigone (measures 392–440)

Creon's anger continues to grow, as does Antigone's serenity. Psychologically, they move ever further from each other and are no longer speaking the same language. She shows by her contempt that he will no longer be able to control her. Somber cello chords underline her words "Who knows if our boundaries have any meaning for the dead?" But when Creon insists on venting his hatred ("Never does a dead enemy become a friend"), she replies nobly "I was born to share love," and the theme of Brotherly Love (Example 142) is heard on the flute, brutally cut short by Creon's shout of "While I am alive, no woman shall make the law!" At this point Ismène enters.

Scene 5 *(measures 441–504)*
Continuation and Development of the Conflict
(Ismène, Antigone, Creon, soprano and tenor chorus leaders)

A. Creon Interrogates Ismène (measures 441–447)

"Ah, there you are, viper!"

B. Ismène Tries to Take Antigone's Side (measures 448–460)

Antigone refuses to accept her sister's sacrifice. The two sisters' dialogue, culminating in the return of the theme of Brotherly Love on the clarinet, is violently interrupted by Creon. His outburst "These two girls are completely mad!" underlines a new trait in his character: vulgarity.

C. Dialogue Between Creon and Ismène (measures 461–478)

In the course of this dialogue, Creon's vulgarity is confirmed. When Ismène mentions Creon's son Haemon, Antigone's fiancé, Creon reacts with unpardonable crudity ("He'll find other wombs") and adds in a spoken shout: "You are starting to bore me, you and your wedding!" As the orchestral texture grows wilder and fiercer, he orders the guards to take the two sisters away. He then leaves in his turn.

D. Orchestral Interlude (measures 479–488)

An orchestral interlude is heard with the stage empty. Its brutal accents are borrowed from the theme *c* and it has an overall Stravinskyan feel.

E. The Soprano Chorus Leader (measures 489–504)

This moving, lyrical interlude is again tonal, starting in F-sharp minor and then modulating. Over a new theme in the orchestra, the chorus leader tells of the terrible tragedy that, as yet unknown, the gods are about to unleash. The uneasy descending thirds in the violas make clear to us who will be at once the cause and the principal victim.

Scene 6 (measures 505–595)
The Second Conflict: Creon and Haemon
(Creon, Haemon, the bass chorus leader)

A. Creon Tries to Convince Haemon (measures 505–526)

Haemon's entry is accompanied by unison chords that are entirely diatonic. They spread out to become his theme, which is merely a diatonic version of *a*, outlining a dominant of A major. Creon mawkishly attempts to get his son on his side. Haemon's immediate response is submissive and suggests that Creon will succeed, while the chorus leader meekly gives his approval. Creon's harangue, a kind of hopping scherzo, is deliberately undistinguished.

B. Haemon's Speech (measures 527–542)

Calmly and with dignity, Haemon reveals to his father that the people are terrorized by his rule. They swallow their words, but do not dare say that they too are on Antigone's side. The orchestral texture here has the delicacy of chamber music. The chorus leader gives his approval to the son as meekly as he did to the father.

C. ALTERCATION BETWEEN CREON AND HAEMON (MEASURES 543–595)

Creon's anger breaks out again, and the tension grows to a point of extreme savagery. The orchestral texture contains ideas derived from *a* and *b*, treated in toccata fashion. The two sides of the dialogue are like clashing swords, and follow so fast on each other that neither participant can any longer listen to the other. Haemon finally leaves the stage in indignation ("Indulge your anger in the presence of courtiers who will tolerate it!") and a link based on the triplets of *b* leads to the next scene.

Scene 7 (measures 596–627)
The Sentence (Creon, soprano, contralto, and tenor chorus leaders)

Scene 7 is a brief one, divided into two sharply contrasting parts.

A. CREON'S SENTENCE (MEASURES 596–617)

While the imitations of *b* continue, the tenor chorus leader tries in vain to get Creon to rescind his decision. Unmoved, Creon utters his condemnation, but agrees to pardon Ismène "who did not touch the carcass." The sentence "I shall wall her up alive in a cave in the desert" is pronounced over five measures of music that come close to paroxysm. Here motif *e* (Example 140), symbolizing the family curse, obviously finds a part. Two measures of horn solo prepare what follows.

B. INTERLUDE WITH THE CONTRALTO CHORUS LEADER (MEASURES 618–627)

At the words "Love that strikest all mankind" Honegger gives us seven measures of sublime lyricism in E major (Example 144). Then, through successions of dominants, we are given a foretaste of what will come in *Amphion*, in *Jeanne d'Arc au bûcher*, in *La Danse des morts*, and in the great symphonies. This is yet another tonal interlude as a welcome and superbly calculated break in the tension, and this is extended by two measures of compassion from the tenor chorus leader for Antigone, whom we now see on the way to her death. The dissolve leading into the following scene is the finest such passage Honegger ever wrote. It consists of a prodigiously long melody ("both sweet and sorrowful," in the words of Willy Tappolet) for saxophone in unison with the musical saw (the ondes Martenot used nowadays did not exist at the time). This tune lasts at its full intensity for sixteen measures and is then taken over by the bass clarinet. Its unbroken curve is the earliest prefiguring of the miracle that would happen twenty years later in the De profundis of the *Symphonie liturgique*, although there it shall appear in a wholly tonal context.

Example 144

Scene 8 (measures 628–742)
Antigone's Farewell (Antigone, Creon, soprano chorus leader, then all four chorus leaders)

A. ORCHESTRAL INTRODUCTION (MEASURES 628–635)

Although the polyphonic context disguises the fact, the long melody is continued, now polarized around the tonic A, even if it is a Phrygian A minor with a Lydian fourth, in Honegger's favorite manner. It is punctuated by short rhythmic motifs derived from *a* (the curse, the cause of Antigone's fate) and from *f* (Creon, who is implicated in Antigone's death).

B. HER WALK TOWARD DEATH, LEVEL 1 (MEASURES 636–666)

Antigone's long lament is superimposed over the preceding music in a free, three-part counterpoint. It is harsh and poignant, and devoid of any tonal attachment. Its intensely beautiful lyricism makes the greatest possible contrast with the dry, sarcastic spoken comments of the soprano chorus leader. These interrupt it four times with heavy, triple-stopped chords on strings with a ferocious, Stravinskyan stubbornness.

C. HER WALK TOWARD DEATH, LEVEL 2 (MEASURES 667–673)

A new level of tension is reached with Antigone's first brief access of despair ("Nothing, nothing, no one, I go to my death entirely alone"). Increasingly, this scene comes to resemble Christ's climb through insults to Calvary. Creon does not hold back with his own insults. His brutal order to take the victim away leads us on to the next level.

D. HER WALK TOWARD DEATH, LEVEL 3 (MEASURES 674–698)

This level is marked by an increase in speed (agitato), which reaches a breathless pace at the words "Farewell, my share in life is stolen from me," while violas play an ostinato of descending figures. At the mention of Eteocles, whom she will see again, we hear the theme of Brotherly Love (Example 142) one last time, soaring in all its purity on the violins. Proudly and with dignity, Antigone once again justifies her action.

E. Her Walk Toward Death, Level 4 (measures 699–709)

On Creon's orders, the drama hastens. Antigone rebels once against her impending death ("O Thebes, my native city, it is finished, I am being taken away") to the sound of the saw (or ondes Martenot). It is the emotional climax of the whole work. A few brazen chords on brass seal her fate.

F. Quartet of Chorus Leaders (measures 710–742)

With his unerring dramatic instinct, Honegger breaks the tension at its highest point with this fast-moving quartet ("Danae was also buried") on an "uncaring, garrulous" motif, as Willy Tappolet calls it, in a sprightly 3/8. It serves as an interlude before the next scene.

Scene 9 (measures 743–828)
Tiresias's Warning to Creon (Tiresias, Creon, tenor chorus leader)

A. Conversation Between Creon and Tiresias (measures 743–791)

1) The old, blind seer enters to a nobly archaic processional theme, which will underline his interventions and his exit. Music of a more slender kind evokes his blindness and the small child who leads him.

2) The music changes character and expresses the horror of Tiresias's speech, describing the bits of Polynices's body taken away by wild animals and desecrating the altars of the Gods.

3) Creon replies angrily. He has no intention of listening to reason and accuses Tiresias of being bribed (the theme of Treachery). The thirds of f underline his obstinacy and the orchestra quivers with rage. But even the warnings of fate embodied in the textural development of a, as heard in section C of scene 3, cannot get him to change his mind.

4) Tiresias is indignant and warns Creon that he will pay for his crime with the death of his son. He then makes a dignified exit to the music of his entrance.

B. Creon Is Distraught and Consults the Chorus Leaders (measures 792–828)

1) For a moment Creon remains indecisive (f is heard softly on the saxophone), as the tenor chorus leader urges him to make haste and free Antigone. His pride rebels against the idea, but reluctantly he yields and rushes off ("Hurry, the vengeance of the gods gallops onward!").

2) The music too breaks into a gallop, liberating the tension that has built up during the preceding immobility. An atonal toccata on unison strings (presto in eighth-notes) is heard with the stage empty, and leads on to the Interlude in the same tempo.

Interlude (chorus) (measures 829–924)

A. Hymn to Bacchus (measures 829–909)

The "Hymn to Bacchus" is the song of triumph sung by the people of Thebes (the home of the Bacchantes) to celebrate Antigone's impending deliverance. In its vehemence and joyfulness it looks forward to the direct, popular style embraced by Honegger in the choruses of *Jeanne d'Arc au bûcher*. It also recalls the essentially physical energy of the toccata and fugue in the fight of the Horatii in *Horace victorieux*, with its simple tune with repeated notes in C major (Example 145).

Example 145

But even here, motif *f* (Creon's thirds) is constantly present, because Creon's subjects will not be exempt from the horrors to come. The orchestral introduction is dominated by boisterous ostinato trumpet calls. The chorus takes over with long tonal phrases interspersed with fierce polytonal interruptions. Example 145 obviously lends itself to the imitative style. Gradually the music works itself up into a state of Bacchic intoxication. It is one of Honegger's great choruses, seemingly unstoppable in its unbridled progression. But the climax is followed by a long, horrified silence.

B. Orchestral Interlude (measures 910–924)

These desperately intense measures depicting the as-yet-invisible and untold catastrophe mark the height of Honegger's expressionism, and they are even more powerful than "The Murder of Camilla," which they recall. Behind the scenes, Creon has discovered the horrible spectacle of Antigone's death and of Haemon's despair, as Haemon spits in his father's face and threatens him with a dagger that he then turns against himself. The antiphony between the strings and the abrupt ostinatos of the brass ensemble will recur, in a more disembodied form, at the start of *Monopartita*.

From measure 915, these ostinatos give way to more violent, dislocated rhythms, on motifs *f*, *e*, and *c*. The absolute climax (as at the moment of Lulu's death cry in Berg's opera) is the orchestral cry at measure 920. This is followed by a gasping decrescendo, as of a heart that has beaten too fast, and this introduces the very short third act.

Act III
Scene 10 (measures 925–972)
Appearance of Queen Eurydice
(The Messenger, Eurydice, bass chorus leader, chorus)

A. The Messenger Announces the Deaths of Antigone and Haemon (measures 925–936)

The music of the orchestra is dominated by motif *f*, transformed now into a funereal idea for horns, and shorn of its biting arrogance. The news of Haemon's suicide provokes the chorus to groaning lamentation.

B. Queen Eurydice's Brief and Only Intervention (measures 937–945)

After a hesitant start, Queen Eurydice gathers strength to make a noble affirmation ("But I am strong, I have some experience of unhappiness").

C. The Messenger's Story (measures 946–965)

From measure 952, "The Messenger's Story" unfolds over the muted repetition of the orchestral interlude of measures 910–924. This repetition is a stroke of genius. Its effect is all the stronger because what had been to some extent no more than an "abstract" orchestral nightmare has, with the addition of words, become an unbearable reality. The absolute climax now coincides with the climax of the horror ("and his heart's blood pours over Antigone"), and the gasping decrescendo with the words "there they become man and wife, in death and a pool of blood."

D. Dialogue of the Messenger and the Bass Chorus Leader (measures 966–972)

The queen has left the stage without saying a word. The dialogue takes place over a long chord in harmonics on divided strings, superimposing A minor, E-flat major, and F-sharp minor. The suspense, in anticipation of Creon's return, is unbearable, like the "glacial numbness" that marks the end of *Horace victorieux*.

Scene 11 (measures 973–1012)
The Final Tragedy of Creon (Creon, the Messenger, bass chorus leader)

A. Creon Carries His Dead Son (measures 973–995)

The king enters staggering, with Haemon in his arms. His despair is rendered by a funereal theme derived from *a*, which dominates this section together with *f*, in insistent pairs of sixteenth-notes, a realistic image of his stumbling gait. His opening words are introduced by a lugubrious countersubject on the saxophone. But there is worse in store for him: the Messenger tells him that Eurydice is dead.

B. Creon's Despair (measures 995–1008)

The music surrounding Creon becomes tender as, brokenhearted and stripped of all aggression, he mourns his wife. Then he abandons himself to wild, convulsive grief ("Help me, someone lead me away"), and we hear short snatches of motif *c* and of the obsessive thirds of *f*. As he collapses on his son's dead body, his final words ("I am falling into a bottomless pit") are echoed by the bass clarinet.

C. Conclusion (measures 1009–1012)

A further four measures are enough to bring the drama to an end. It is the bass chorus leader who has the final word ("Too late, Creon, too late"). The descending thirds E-flat–C of *f* are echoed as a knell by brass and harp in a C minor of Honegger's favorite Phrygio-Lydian variety. The opera ends with three chords, the first two halting, the last a brutal *fortissimo* on full orchestra. Once again, we are reminded of *Horace victorieux*, which also ends in C minor.

Antigone has had the awkward career of all operatic works that last less than a full evening. For preference, Honegger liked it to be paired with another Greek tragedy rewritten by Jean Cocteau: Stravinsky's *Oedipus Rex*. But it could also be coupled with *Judith*, the only other complete opera Honegger wrote—although no one has attempted this, so far as I know. In any case, *Antigone* is certainly a major work in operatic history, and far more than a "small monument," as the composer too modestly described it. It can be directly compared with a Greek tragedy on a much larger scale, and a masterpiece that Honegger unreservedly admired: Georges Enesco's *Oedipus*.

108. *L'Aiglon*—musical drama in five acts

In collaboration with Jacques Ibert. Acts II, III, and IV are by Honegger. Ibert wrote Acts I and V, as well as the ballet waltzes added to Act III for the revival at the Paris Opera (in order to compensate for the large cut made in the duet between the Duke and Thérèse in scene 2). The version discussed here is the final version and the one found in the published vocal score.
Honegger worked on *L'Aiglon* from July 1936 to January 1937
Act II: "almost completed" 14 August 1936; orchestrated December 1936
Act III: exact date of composition unknown; orchestration completed 27 January 1937, Paris
Act IV: "completed" 29 July 1936; orchestrated January 1937, Paris
"To Raoul Gunsbourg"
Libretto by Edmond Rostand, adapted by Henri Cain

First performance: 10 March 1937, Fanny Heldy (the Duke), Vanni Marcoux
    (Flambeau), Endrèze (Metternich), Mlle Schirman (Fanny Elssler), Mlle
    Branèze (Thérèse), Mlle Gadsen (Marie-Louise), Germaine Chellet (the
    Countess), Ceresol (Prokesch), Pujol (the Attaché), Marvini (Marmont), Fraikin
    (Gentz), Monte Carlo Opera Chorus and Orchestra, conducted by Félix Wolfes,
    Monte Carlo Opera
First performance of final version: 1 September 1937, the same performers for the
    roles of the Duke, Flambeau, and Metternich, Paris Opera Ballet,
    choreographed by Serge Lifar, produced by Pierre Chereau, Paris Opera
    Chorus and Orchestra, conducted by François Ruhlmann, Paris Opera
Performing forces: sopranos (the Duke, Thérèse, Marie-Louise, the Countess),
    mezzo (Fanny Elssler), tenors (Gentz, the Attaché), baritones (Flambeau,
    Metternich, Prokesch), bass (Marmont), male chorus; orchestra: 2.2.2.2.–
    4.3.3.1.–timpani, percussion–harp–strings
Duration: 84 to 90 minutes, depending on the version (Act I: 24 minutes; Act II: 15
    minutes; Act III: 18 or 24 minutes; Act IV: 12 minutes 30 seconds; Act V: 14
    minutes 30 seconds); Honegger's contribution amounts to 44 minutes 30
    seconds or 45 minutes 30 seconds
Heugel

In calling *L'Aiglon* a traditional "grand opera," we must accept that the
word "grand" is relative: the work lasts no more than an hour and half in all, so
that it can be played either with a single interval after Act II or with no interval
at all. Its musical language is deliberately direct, without experiments or intellectual fripperies, but aimed simply at making an impact on a popular audience.
Despite that, every detail is carefully crafted. Honegger was writing for the
wider public of 1937, not for posterity, and perhaps the work will no longer be
heard except in certain provincial theaters. But it served its purpose perfectly.

Curiously, Jacques Ibert made fewer concessions than Honegger did, not
only because there was less distance between his contribution to *L'Aiglon* and
his usual style, but because at times his music is the more dissonant of the two.
These concessions, needless to say, are found on the level of language and aesthetics and not on that of technique—in that respect, Honegger's perfectionism
is a match for Ibert's. It has to be said that a work like *L'Aiglon* could only have
been written after several years of intense work for the cinema. For example,
Mayerling is a preparation for a certain Viennese atmosphere, and the whole of
the dramatic end of Act IV, in which the *Marseillaise* and the *Song of Departure*
are superimposed (measures 268–301), is taken from No. 8 ("Les Mendiants de
la gloire") of the music for Abel Gance's film *Napoléon*. Honegger contributed
slightly more than half of the total score.

Chronologically, *L'Aiglon* comes between *Jeanne d'Arc au bûcher* and *La
Danse des morts* and is contemporary both with a great deal of film music and
with the *Second* and *Third String Quartets*. Honegger was responsible for the
two most dramatic acts of *L'Aiglon*: the second, with Metternich's extraordinary
nocturnal monologue, his confrontation with Flambeau, and then his pitiless
destruction of the Duke; and the fourth, with the epic vision of the battlefield
of Wagram. The subject of the opera, and its music likewise, do not call for
detailed analysis, so I shall confine myself to a brief summary of the story and a
description of the most outstanding moments in the music. The libretto is an
ingenious montage/précis of Rostand's play.

The first act, "Opening Wings," composed by Ibert, takes place in 1831 in the lacquer drawing-room in the Schönbrunn Palace during a ball (hence an abundance of Viennese waltzes). It is an opportunity to introduce the various characters (including Marie-Louise, the Duke's mother, who does not appear in the acts composed by Honegger) and to set the scene. We see Metternich, anxious, embittered, and obsessed by his desire to preserve the Duke of Reichstadt from all "evil" influences. The Duke, though, has remained secretly faithful to his father's memory and, despite everything, still regards himself as his heir. With the help of the young French girl Thérèse, his confidante, and especially of Flambeau, one of his father's veterans (who is disguised as a valet), he decides to escape and return to Paris.

The second act, "Beating Wings," is set in the same place, but at night. Flambeau is at the rendezvous and recognizes the signal agreed on by the Duke: the "Little Corporal's" two-peaked hat. Metternich, doing his nightly rounds, sees the hat and the silhouette of Flambeau, who has donned his old uniform, and is terrified, thinking the Emperor has returned. But the illusion is soon broken by the appearance of the Duke's frail figure. As soon as Flambeau has escaped, Metternich cruelly and sadistically destroys the Duke's confidence, citing the bad blood of generations of Hapsburgs, which he has inherited and which obliterates any resemblance to his father.

The music of Act II is marvelously effective, and its length and articulation are judged with an infallible ear. Flambeau's furtive entrance is accompanied by a gently bantering bassoon. Metternich's long monologue in front of the hat rises slowly, turning from chaff to fanatical hatred. But the climax of the act is the terrible scene in which the Machiavellian Austrian minister sets out to destroy the poor adolescent, with Mephistophelian music worthy of Verdi's Iago. The young man is terrified and finally loses his head, calling for help and finally collapsing at the feet of his triumphant persecutor.

The third act, "Bruised Wings," is less hectic and intense. It takes place in the park of Schönbrunn, during a masked ball, and it is the act that gave the two composers the most trouble—hence the reworking I have already mentioned. After the new ballet (with waltzes added by Ibert), we come to the intensely sentimental duet between the Duke and Thérèse, which both composers found so "kitschy" and "sugary" after the first performance that Honegger cut it considerably.

While the accomplices in the escape try to rebuild the Duke's morale, so brutally attacked in the previous scene, his Corsican cousin, the Countess Camerata (who is in the plot) exchanges clothes with the Duke so that he can escape unnoticed. As the maskers return, the Austrian courtier Gentz insults the Emperor's memory and refers to him as a coward. But the French military attaché, even though he is a royalist, takes the Emperor's part because the insult touches the honor of France. The act ends with the triumphant sounds of the "March of Marengo." The music follows the stage action closely throughout. It moves from a gentle, languorous duet to a sad waltz, and then to the delightful pastiche of Haydn and Mozart that accompanies the plotters' deliberations before the exchange of clothes. The pastiche is written for six instruments (flute, oboe, horn, and string trio) playing on stage. This *ancien régime* atmosphere is a direct contrast with the heroic, passionate, and "revolutionary" tone of the act's conclusion.

Although the fourth act, "Broken Wings," is the shortest of the five, it is here that the work incontestably reaches its dramatic and musical climax. The scene is the plain of Wagram at night, where the conspirators meet before their journey to Paris. The brief enthusiasm of the Duke and Flambeau is interrupted by the arrival of the Countess, out of breath. They have been betrayed and their pursuers are approaching. Flambeau, about to be arrested, commits suicide in order to avoid being shot by the Austrians. The Duke demands to be left alone for a moment. He is waiting for his regiment.

Now follows the great visionary scene that is the high point of the work. In order to ease Flambeau's death throes, the Duke gets him to believe that he is dying at the real battle of Wagram, and so realistic is his description that he comes to believe it himself. We hear the chorus of the wounded and dying. At the climax of the vision, as the Duke is preparing to fire on his own regiment, the officer blocks his gesture and the illusion is over. The curtain falls after a tragic conclusion of a mere nine measures.

Honegger here was able to give full rein to his epic genius. The musical language is entirely personal and its harsh grandeur impresses itself on the listener right from the rise of the curtain. The wild chromatic swell of the orchestra, with syncopations and blurred tonal harmonies, evokes the vast plain swept by the wind, and the sense of history too. The Duke is carried away by the thought of his future reign and launches with Flambeau into a passionate, heroic duet based on a memorable theme (Example 146).

Example 146

The tone of Example 146—powerful, direct, peremptory—informs the whole act, with the vision of the dead on the battlefield kindling the sense of illusion. In this music Honegger joins the Mahler of the great songs from *Das Knaben Wunderhorn* or the Mussorgsky of *The General*. The tone continues through the music from *Napoléon*, in which the *Marseillaise* and the *Song of Departure* are superimposed, but with the further addition of the Duke's monologue, as he realizes that he is the victim destined to expiate the deaths of all these men. Then, as the vision abruptly fades, we come to the short, icy epilogue. The Duke gives orders to his regiment with the voice of a robot, and the act ends with a dismissive chord, strangely reminiscent of the last moments of Mahler's *Sixth Symphony*.

Like *Otello* and *Pelléas*, *L'Aiglon* ends with a short, slow act ("Closed Wings," with music by Ibert) in which we see the ultimate moments before a death—that of the Duke, surrounded by officialdom. To comfort him in his final moments, Thérèse sings him gentle French folk songs, but he dies to the reading of the story of his glorious birth. Metternich has the last, unfeeling word: "Put back on his white uniform!" We may feel some regret over the last three measures, fast and loud, and be surprised that a composer of Ibert's stamp should have committed such an error of dramaturgy.

As I have already said, the very nature of a work such as *L'Aiglon* means that its future must be problematic. But certainly the second act and, above all, the fourth deserve a place at least in the concert hall.

Category 13: Ballets

19. *Le Dit des jeux du monde* (see Category 7A, in Chapter 11)
34. *Vérité? Mensonge?*
38. *Horace victorieux* (see Category 7A, in Chapter 11)
40. *Skating Rink*
46. *Fantasio*
58. *Sous-marine*
66. *Roses de métal*
68. *Les Noces d'Amour et de Psyché*
71. *Amphion*
85. *Sémiramis*
96. *Icare*
113. *Un Oiseau blanc s'est envolé*
123. *Le Cantique des cantiques*
142. *La Naissance des couleurs*
154. *Le Mangeur de rêves*
174. *L'Appel de la montagne*
180. *Chota Roustaveli*
189. *Sortilèges*
200. *De la musique*

Honegger's ballets are certainly the least-known of his works, and more than one reader will be surprised, reading the list just offered, to find that there are nearly twenty of them, varying considerably in size and importance. Some of them were written for famous choreographers and for prestigious stages, such as the Paris Opera, while others appeared briefly and almost secretly and called for extremely modest choreographic and scenic resources. It is from this genre too, together with Honegger's incidental music, that the largest number of his scores are lost. Three of them have totally disappeared, and three others survive only in a very fragmentary state.

Since many of the ballets are unpublished, and since only a portion of them are likely to be heard in the concert hall after their ephemeral stage existence, an exhaustive examination in this volume would clearly be out of place. So only the most important of them will be treated in detail. Two of these, *Le Dit des jeux du monde* and *Horace victorieux*, have been played almost always in the concert hall and thus have been analyzed in greater depth in Chapter 11 under Category 7A, Orchestral Works from Stage and Screen—both works being landmarks in Honegger's output. From this point of view, only the two great collaborative efforts with Paul Valéry, *Amphion* and *Sémiramis*, can be put on the same level, followed at some distance by *Skating Rink, Le Cantique des cantiques, La Naissance des couleurs*, and, in a special category of its own, by *L'Appel de la montagne*.

The great opportunity that never came Honegger's way was working for Diaghilev's Ballets Russes. Diaghilev had his own favorites, and it was difficult, if not impossible, to persuade him to change his mind once he had rejected someone. So it was that, despite the influence Cocteau had over him, Diaghilev never used Honegger as a collaborator in the way he did other members of Les Six, like Milhaud, Auric, and Poulenc. When Diaghilev turned down the idea of *Horace victorieux*, Honegger took it instead to Diaghilev's new postwar rival, Rolf de Maré and his Ballets Suédois. De Maré did not accept *Horace victorieux* either, but he did commission another ballet, *Skating Rink*, which, although barely remembered today, was a real success at its premiere. Unfortunately, this success was not followed up, because of the premature dissolution of the Ballets Suédois.

Honegger's second great ballet opportunity was getting to know Ida Rubinstein, who was the instigator of six works, three of them ballets: *Les Noces d'Amour et de Psyché, Amphion*, and *Sémiramis*. If ever there had been the slightest chance of Honegger working with Diaghilev, it was scotched by this collaboration with Rubinstein, which began in 1925–1926 with extensive incidental music (*L'Impératrice aux rochers* and *Phaedra*) and culminated, after the three ballets, in *Jeanne d'Arc au bûcher*.

His collaborations with Rubinstein came to an end due to the interminable back-and-forths over the premiere of *Jeanne d'Arc* and because Rubinstein then retired for reasons of age. After that, his career as a ballet composer was essentially linked to Serge Lifar and the Paris Opera. The only exception was his composition of *Chota Roustaveli* for Monte Carlo, when Lifar had been temporarily removed from the Opera for his collaborationist tendencies during the war. It was with Lifar that Honegger made the highly interesting experiments of *Icare* and *Le Cantique des cantiques*, for which Lifar furnished him with entirely predetermined rhythmic structures as a basis for his music. This does not seem to have worried the composer, and he dealt with these structures as fluently as he did with the extremely precise scenarios laid down by Claudel for his two oratorios. *Le Cantique des cantiques*, in particular, shows not the slightest trace of constraint.

34. *Vérité? Mensonge?* (Truth? Lies?)

Marionette ballet in fourteen scenes by André Hellé
October–November 1920
First performance: 25 November 1920, Salon d'Automne, Paris
Performing forces: flute, clarinet, bassoon, 2 violins, viola, cello, double bass
Duration: impossible to determine (see commentary)
Unpublished (though the "Danse des enfants" became No. 3 of the music for the
    film *Napoléon*)
Only short fragments of the music survive

The music being mostly lost, reconstructing *Vérité? Mensonge?* is highly
problematic. The scenario by André Hellé (the author of *La Boîte à joujoux*, set
by Debussy) has come down to us in the form of a manuscript illustrated with
numerous drawings. The story is as follows: Pierrot, who was given an over-
tender heart at birth by the fairy Carabosse, steals the mirror of Truth, which
reveals men to him as they really are (horrible) and multiplies his miseries and
tribulations. He saves Colombine from a fire, and is first decorated, then left to
die of starvation. He goes to prison for stealing a loaf of bread, and Colombine, who had married him, goes off with Harlequin. In despair, Pierrot throws
the mirror into the well of Truth, and immediately everything comes right.
There is sunshine everywhere, everyone looks good and kind, and Pierrot is
happy once again.

There exist two accounts of the premiere on 25 November 1920, one by
Raymond Charpentier and one by Darius Milhaud. According to these accounts, only four of the fourteen scenes were given—Nos. 1, 4, 8, and 9, corresponding to Nos. 2, 7 (or 9), 12, and 13 in Hellé's scenario. It is quite possible
that Honegger never composed the remainder. Milhaud's account gives details
of the orchestration and describes the music of the Prologue; from this I could
identify it, even though the manuscript has no title. Milhaud also mentions a
blues and a waltz, but these have not survived. The fragmentary piano reduction
that we have identifies the Prologue and scenes 1 and 2, but the stage indications of the Prologue in fact correspond to scene 2, while that of scene 1 corresponds to scene 3 (the score of scene 2 does not contain any stage indications).
The "Danse des enfants," used with the same title in *Napoléon*, was probably
part of scene 12. This charming movement is the longest fragment of the surviving music, and the remaining items share its light and airy character.

40. *Skating Rink*—choreographic symphony

Ballet by Ricciotto Canudo for roller skates
Mid-November 1921–15 January 1922
First performance: 20 January 1922, Rolf de Maré's Ballets Suédois, choreography by
    Jean Borlin, design by Fernand Léger, conducted by D. E. Inghelbrecht,
    Théâtre des Champs-Élysées, Paris
Performing forces: 2.2.2.2.–alto saxophone–4.2.3.0.–cymbals, bass drum–harp–
    strings
Duration: 18 minutes 35 seconds
Universal

Marcel Landowski is severe with regard this work, even though he probably never saw it or heard the music: "The skaters revolving round the rink were intended to convey the monotony of life . . . . The score could not do other than follow suit."[8] José Bruyr provides more detail:

> The Rink—a merry-go-round of grubs in slow motion—was, according to the program, the symbol of sexual frustration that pushes people together and hence, the symbol of the shocks, the disputes, and all the harmony and disharmony of love and hatred. One man alone (Jean Borlin) on his skates—a crazy poet and the Corybant of this frenzy—was the victim of this feeble, cruel game, until the moment came when three words of Canudo's appeared in letters of fire on a screen, like Nebuchadnezzar's vision: "He turns, he turns, he turns." The music kneads three leitmotifs: one weak, one strong, one attractive—seduction, vengeance, triumph. In the balance the music held between love and drama, it was almost as far removed from the Freudian intentions of the scenario as Fernand Léger's "Apacho-cubist" designs.[9]

Certainly, Honegger was not the man for Freudian anguish. Bruyr goes on to quote the amusing review that appeared in the journal *Comoedia*: "*Skating Rink*: English title, Swedish dancers, Italian scenario, Swiss music" (and, one might add, French theater!). The correspondence between Honegger and Rolf de Maré shows that the composer went to a lot of trouble over this work. Canudo's scenario is vaguely reminiscent of that of Debussy's *Jeux*: from the ceaselessly whirling mass of skaters, a woman and two men (the opposite of *Jeux*) break free, and here, as there, sport serves as a pretext for cruel erotic games.

Although *Skating Rink*, a choreographic symphony, was written barely a year after the mimed symphony *Horace victorieux*, it differs from its predecessor in its extraordinary unity (some might call it uniformity, but the subject calls for such treatment). There is no escape from the inexorably whirling 6/4 and, surprisingly, its structure is both the largest sonata form movement Honegger ever wrote and one of the strictest. But between the development and the recapitulation, just after the Golden Section point (measure 322), there is an episode (measures 327–371) that is in strong contrast with everything else. The language is highly chromatic and largely atonal, even though it is possible to hear D as the underlying tonality, as the ending in D minor makes clear.

The introduction (measures 1–41) is athematic, establishing a sense of movement and the basic gyration of the groups of six ascending or descending eighth-notes. This is gray, somber music, recalling *Khamma* rather than *Jeux*. The exposition (measures 42–202) presents three themes in succession, representing the Crowd, the Fool (on English horn and saxophone), and last of all, most memorably, the chromatic, lyrical theme of the Woman (Example 147).

The development (measures 203–326) introduces the Man, the third main character, represented not by a new theme but by Honegger's favorite energetic iambic rhythms. The preceding elements are combined in a complex ensemble. This is in total contrast with the following episode (measures 327–381). Here

(Va. solo)   (Vns.)

Example 147

humanity is described in weightier music, with abrupt, dissonant, Stravinskyan accents in the brass alternating with a sinuous, syncopated theme on lower strings. The recapitulation (measures 372–491) begins with what is perhaps the finest passage in the score, the varied return of the theme of the crowd ("Men and Women") in a richly polyphonic texture. After the fall of Woman (the shape of this, going from piccolo to bassoon, again recalls *Jeux*), we hear the themes of the Fool and the Woman in combination ("Fool's Dance"). The jerky iambics on the brass, representing Man, recur one last time. The return of the music of the Crowd marks the beginning of the coda (measures 492–521) and the work ends abruptly after a forceful, double return of the theme of the Fool.

46. *Fantasio*—sketch in three scenes

Ballet-pantomime by Georges Wague
July–October 1922; orchestrated December 1922
Seems not to have been staged or played until 1992, even though the state of the
    manuscript would suggest the contrary
Performing forces: 1.1.1.1.–1.1.1.0.–timpani, bass drum, cymbals–strings
Duration: 11 minutes 30 seconds
Salabert

    Georges Wague was a great mime who renewed the dramatic potential of his art and exerted a considerable influence. The work was written for one of his young American pupils who apparently looked like Fantasio; according to José Bruyr, she took the score off to the United States. The autograph gives no indication of a scenario. *Fantasio* is good but unpretentious light music, perfectly unified in its atmosphere, rhythm, themes, and D minor tonality.

58. *Sous-marine*—mimed scene

Ballet for Carina Ari
September 1924; orchestrated May 1925
"To Carina Ari"
First performance: 27 June 1925, Carina Ari, Opéra-Comique, Paris
First concert performance: 8 December 1929, conducted by Robert Siohan, Théâtre
    de la Gaîté-Lyrique, Paris
Performing forces: 2.2.2.2.–4.0.0.0.–cymbals, harp, celesta–strings
Duration: 9 minutes
Salabert

Sous-marine and not *Sous-marin* (submariner)! José Bruyr says that thanks to this misunderstanding, the Soviet Russians were always asking for what they thought was an aquatic cousin of *Pacific 2.3.1*. In fact, the subject is that of the mysteries of submarine flora and fauna. It is a highly impressionistic, Debussyan study in sound—a last farewell to the world of *Aglavaine et Sélysette* and *La Mort de Sainte Alméenne*, and as such Honegger never included it in his programs. Even so, it is a very interesting piece. Its fifty-eight broad, slow measures are split up into as many as ten sections, with very strange metrical complexities that are rare in Honegger's work. The tonality is deliberately vague, the wood-wind figuration especially evocative, and the harmonic language refined and unstable. It is curious indeed to come across a piece like this after *Pacific*, and from the same period as *Judith* and *Antigone*.

66. *Roses de métal* (or *Roses en métal*)

Ballet in one act, scenario by the Countess Élisabeth de Gramont
1928 (before June), Paris
First performance: 3 June 1928, "La Petite Scène," produced by Xavier de Courville, Salle Oedenkoven, Paris
Performing forces: 3 Bertrand dynaphones, piano, percussion
The music is lost; all that survives is a transcription of the *Blues* for chamber orchestra (H66A, Category 7A)

It might be entertaining to read the scenario of this early "leftist" ballet. It was dreamed up by "revolutionary" aristocratic ladies and produced with sets and costumes by Madame Shumansky, with choreography by Madame Boutkovsky. The dancers were dressed as oversized dolls in paper cutouts.

Scene 1: A fat millionaire banker is sitting in his office, with gold spilling out of his coffers. Groups of jointed dolls come and greet him, the mob admires him. Gold passes a necklace round his neck—it is his apotheosis.

Scene 2: The banker is asleep. His dreams are acted out by the dolls. He is a gold miner, he is poor, he enjoys life, he discovers a vein of gold, he kills his two companions, he is rich. He wakes up.

Scene 3: Delicious food is brought to the banker. The dance of the food; he may not touch it. He is brought the finest wines in quantity; he may not drink them. He is on a diet. A splendid courtesan comes, offering herself to him with lascivious dances. He cannot respond. He is on a diet. Gold finds it ridiculous and takes off his gold necklace. Immediately, the gold ceases to pour out of his coffers and he himself promptly deflates.

This little piece was the first in which Honegger used electronic instruments. It was revived at the Palais des Beaux-Arts in Brussels on 28 November 1928. It is a pity that the score is lost.

68. *Les Noces d'Amour et de Psyché* (The Wedding of Cupid and Psyche)

Ballet for Ida Rubinstein. The music consists of an orchestration by Honegger of harpsichord and organ works by J. S. Bach
Summer–fall 1928 (perhaps begun late 1927)
First performance: 22 November 1928, Ida Rubinstein Ballet Company, Paris Opera
Performing forces: 3.3.3.3.–2 saxophones–4.3.3.1.–timpani, bass drum–harp, celesta–strings
Duration: 45 minutes
1. Prelude (*Prelude for organ*, BWV 545, transposed from C into D major); 2. Entrance of Mercury (Anglaise from *French Suite No. 3 in B minor*, BWV 814); 3. Entrance of Apollo (Sarabande from *French Suite No. 6 in E major*, BWV 817); 4. Entrance of Diana (Gigue from *French Suite No. 5 in G major*, BWV 816); 5. Entrance of Minerva (Second Minuet from *French Suite No. 1 in D minor*, BWV 812); 6. Entrance of Neptune (second half of *Fantasia in C minor*, BWV 906); 7. Entrance of Venus (Gavotte from *French Suite No. 5 in G major*, BWV 816); 8. Entrance of Mars and Vulcan (Fugue No. 5 in D major from *The Well-Tempered Clavier*, Book 1, BWV 850/2); 9. Entrance of Pluto and Proserpina (*Prelude in G major*, BWV 968, based on Prelude from *Sonata for solo violin in C major*, BWV 1005); 10. Entrance of Bacchus (Fugue No. 21 in B-flat major from *The Well-Tempered Clavier*, Book 1, BWV 866/2); 11. Entrance of Flora (Prelude No. 21 to Fugue No. 21 in B-flat major, BWV 866/1); 12. Entrance of Jupiter (first 110 measures of *Toccata for organ in F major*, BWV 540); 13. Entrance of Psyche (a. Adagio from *Sonata for violin and harpsichord No. 3 in E major*, BWV 1016; b. Polonaise from *French Suite No. 6 in E major*, BWV 817; c. Allegro [first movement] from *Sonata for violin and basso continuo in E minor*, BWV 1023; d. Prelude No. 3 in C-sharp major from *The Well-Tempered Clavier*, Book 2, BWV 872/1; e. continuation and conclusion of a.); 14. General Dance (a. Vivace [first movement] from *Trio Sonata No. 6 for organ in G major*, BWV 530; b. Gavotte from *Partita for solo violin in E major*, BWV 1006; c. Second Minuet from *Partita No. 1 for harpsichord in B-flat major*, BWV 825, transposed into F-sharp major; d. continuation and conclusion of a.); 15. Apotheosis (a. *Prelude for organ in G major*, BWV 568, transposed into C major; b. *Fugue for organ in C major*, BWV 545)
Unpublished. Universal Edition of Vienna has published both the *Suite After J. S. Bach* (H68A, consisting, in order, of Nos. 2, 3, 7, 5, and 4) and the *Prelude and Fugue in C Major by J. S. Bach* (H68B, consisting of Nos. 1 and 15b); see Category 7A, in Chapter 11.

Each piece in *Les Noces d'Amour et de Psyché* is scored for a different ensemble. For example: No. 8, "Entrée de Mars et de Vulcain" (Entrance of Mars and Vulcan), is for trumpets, trombones, tuba, and strings; No. 9, "Entrée de Pluton et de Proserpine" (Entrance of Pluto and Proserpina), is without violins; No. 11, "Entrée de Flore" (Entrance of Flora), uses just a chamber group of flute, clarinet, bass clarinet, bassoon, horn, harp, a desk of violas, and a desk of cellos. The same applies in No. 13a, Adagio of "Entrée de Psyché," which is scored for two flutes, two oboes, two saxophones, trumpet, trombone, tuba, harp, and solo violin; in No. 13b, Polonaise, scored for flute, clarinet, muted horn, harp, and muted string quartet; and in No. 14c, Minuet of "Danse générale," which is scored for two flutes, bass clarinet, bassoon, two saxophones, and two horns. Elsewhere, Honegger uses the full orchestra but, one or two transpositions apart, he remains scrupulously faithful to the original. This is generous payment of a debt toward the composer whom Honegger, from his childhood onward, had admired and loved more than any other.

71. Amphion

Melodrama by Paul Valéry
August 1929
"To Madame Ida Rubinstein"
First performance: 23 June 1931, Ida Rubinstein (Amphion), Charles Panzéra
(Apollo), Chorus and Orchestra of the Paris Opera, conducted by Gustave
Cloëz, designs by Alexandre Benois, choreography by Léonide Massine, Paris
Opera
First concert performance: 14 January 1932, Ida Rubinstein, Henri Fabert,
conducted by Robert Siohan, Université des Annales, Paris
Performing forces: narrator, baritone, four women's voices (the Muses), mixed
chorus; orchestra: 3.3.3.3.–alto saxophone–4.3.3.3.–timpani, percussion–harp,
celesta–strings
Duration: 37 minutes
I: Introduction, Entrance of Amphion, The Dreams, Entrance of the Muses,
Struggle Between the Muses and the Dreams, The Enchantment, Liturgical
Scene, Narrative of Apollo, Amphion Awakes, Dance of Amphion; II:
Amphion's Narrative; III: Prelude, Amphion Invents Scales, Construction of
Thebes (fugue), Chorus of Muse-Columns, Hymn to the Sun, Postlude
Salabert
In 1948 Honegger extracted from *Amphion* the triptych *Prelude, Fugue, Postlude* for
orchestra (see H71A, Category 7A, in Chapter 11)

Amphion is at once one of the most unjustly neglected of Honegger's major
works and the hardest to classify. It is not a ballet, nor an oratorio, nor an opera,
nor a melodrama, but rather a little of each. Valéry's own title of "melodrama"
has not helped the work, because in music it refers to the delivery of a spoken
text over an orchestral background—a hybrid form that has never been popular. Here, this is true only of a single passage of no more than four minutes. In
Sémiramis, on the other hand, it takes up considerably more time (some fifteen
minutes), with less time being given to the chorus and a considerable amount of
time given to dancing, so that in that case one can speak more in terms of a ballet with speech and singing.

So my inclusion of *Amphion* among the ballets is to some extent arbitrary.
A similar case is Stravinsky's *Persephone*, written a few years later: that too is a
setting of neoclassical words (by André Gide), dealing with ancient Greek leg-
end, and intended to be declaimed by Ida Rubinstein. Both these works, with
their dignified and slightly old-fashioned texts, are out of favor today—which
is, in both cases, unfair to the music. It is true that Honegger's collaboration
with Valéry could not be expected to yield such rich results as that with Claudel,
but even so the score of *Amphion* is for the most part admirable. In 1948 Honegger saved the most highly developed music (the last part) for the concert hall, in
the form of the triptych *Prelude, Fugue, Postlude*.

Valéry's scenario is as follows. Apollo chooses Amphion, a primitive man
without culture, and gives him the present of a lyre. With the help of this gift,
Amphion invents scales, then, gradually, music itself. At the sound of his instrument, the stones, of their own volition, come together to make a temple to
Apollo. Music creates architecture—a favorite idea of Valéry's, who followed
Goethe and others in regarding these two arts as indissolubly linked. Amphion,
his work accomplished, is on the point of enjoying his triumph when the muses

turn away from him to seek a new master. A veiled figure, representing love or death, invites him to follow her.

The moral of this story is that once the artist has completed his work he is no longer of interest to mankind. He must disappear, because if he chooses to "live" (to enjoy life), he must give up creative work—which, for him, is the same as death. The grim, stoical conclusion of this is that he, and he alone, is refused the enjoyment of what he has created. It must have stirred deep and as yet unexpressed feelings in the composer. The great crisis and the rethinking of his role, embodied in *Cris du monde*, was only a little more than a year away.

Valéry's idea was an old one. As long ago as 1891, when he was twenty, he had spoken about it to Debussy. What he had in mind was a spectacle that would include everything, but differ from the Wagnerian *Gesamtkunstwerk* in the sense that, although the various artistic disciplines would coexist, they would preserve their autonomy (notably in space and time), and hence their independence.

The scenario of *Amphion* confronted the composer with fearsome difficulties, to which Valéry was the first to admit. He had to use music to express the state of humanity before music existed and then, in the briefest manner, suggest the art's complete evolution from the invention of scales to the most complex double fugue. Honegger succeeded ("I needed a great composer, and I had one," Valéry said), but even so it seems doubtful whether the work is really satisfactory away from the stage. Some critics have been very severe on its neoclassical language, seeing in it a serious regression after the radical atonality of *Antigone*. We need only look at a work like the *First Symphony*—written just after *Amphion*—to realize that this so-called retreat (which I don't in any case accept as such) was dictated entirely by the nature of the subject. This was a criterion Honegger always set great store by, as evidenced by *Les Aventures du roi Pausole*—a work that Honegger was already sketching at the time of *Amphion*.

As G. K. Spratt has shown, *Amphion* is split into three main sections that are very unequal in length. The first, which necessarily contains the least amount of musical material, is the longest. It contains seven paragraphs and begins with an Introduction. After initial confused and inconclusive rumors, this settles on a mysterious pentatonic chord on E (the ancient *doristi* mode of the Greeks, which was one of Honegger's favorites). A pentatonic ostinato on xylophone evokes Amphion, the savage man who is prevented from killing his prey by a woman's voice. After "The Dreams" comes "Entrance of the Muses" (four solo women's voices), who then fight with the Dreams. Here, for the first time, we hear the first threads of the magnificent theme of the future Postlude, on fine modulating harmonies (Example 148).

"The Enchantment" is marked by a theme climbing in fourths, and directly prefiguring the theme of Hope in *Jeanne d'Arc au bûcher*. In the "Liturgical Scene" we hear a slow procession in 3/4 in dotted rhythms, in a noble, classical style very close to that of Stravinsky's recent ballet *Apollon musagète*. Soon the first complete appearance of the chordal theme symbolizing Apollo signals his entry, greeted by the Muses in homophonic psalmodies. Then the full mixed chorus is used for the first time, in music that is fast-moving and full of rough

Example 148

accents. There follows the long "Narrative of Apollo" addressing Amphion ("I have chosen you . . . as a peak is chosen by the lightning") in a noble style, but bereft of all emphasis. He gives Amphion the sacred instrument, with the instruction: "Let my lyre give birth to my temple," while the orchestra begins to outline the elements of the future Prelude (the invention of music).

"Amphion's Sleep and Awakening" makes up the work's most harmonious and consonant section, with the chorus's great chordal pillars and the Muses' serene dialogue. The primitive music of the xylophone and other percussion signals Amphion's awakening, and his brutal dance, for an ensemble of percussion and double basses, follows immediately after it. Suddenly, Amphion sees the lyre (there is a silence over a pedal point). He touches it and unleashes a welter of dissonant brass that terrifies everyone. But a second, more gentle approach produces an enchanting diatonic melody on the flute, accompanied by the harp. The Muses tenderly call to Amphion. His role, as we know, is a spoken one and his first words ("Who calls me?") provoke the response: "You yourself." Then comes the brief Melodrama (measures 364–421) constituting the turning point of the score, and the beginning of which (measures 365–383) will make up the start of *Prelude, Fugue, Postlude*.

The third and final section (measures 422–647) was reused to form the essential material of the 1948 orchestral triptych (see H71A, Category 7A, in Chapter 11). It will suffice here to mention a few of the choral interventions, which of course are absent from *Prelude, Fugue, Postlude*. The first of these (measures 507–518, or, that is to say, measures 122–133 of H71A) is a closely imitative four-voice chorus ("O *mir*acle, O *mar*vel"), totally independent of the simultaneous stretto in the orchestra. The second (measures 534–549, or 149–164 in H71A) is the unison chorus of the Muse-columns, the melody of which will be taken over in H71A by oboes and second violins, then by the trumpet. Finally, the third and most important chorus (measures 571–606), the "Hymn to the Sun" ("O Sun, holy *pres*ence"), corresponds to music that was partly recomposed in 1948, notably at measures 187 to 193 of H71A (the majestic brass stretto recalling Sibelius's *Fifth Symphony*). After that, with rare exceptions, the vocal line is always doubled by instruments. The final intervention of the four-voice chorus ("Admirable Amphion") corresponds to six measures (measures 609–614) removed in H71A. It is just after this that the atmosphere suddenly changes, becoming mistier and darker. The Muses turn away from Amphion and we reach the shadows of the Postlude. In the course of this, the fine melody (Example 148) passes from saxophone to English horn, then to bass clarinet. The music slowly expires, like light at the end of the day.

85. Sémiramis

Ballet-melodrama in three acts (The Chariot, The Bed, The Tower) and two
    interludes by Paul Valéry
May 1933, Paris; orchestrated February 1934, Paris
"For Madame Ida Rubinstein"
First performance: 11 May 1934, Ida Rubinstein, Keith Lester, designs and costumes
    by Alexandre Jakovleff, Chorus and Orchestra of the Paris Opera, conducted by
    Gustavé Cloëz, Paris Opera
First concert performance: 23 February 1936, Concerts Pasdeloup, Paris
Performing forces: female narrator, soprano, two tenors, two basses, five-part mixed
    chorus; orchestra: 3.3.4. (including one double bass clarinet) 3.–saxophone–4.3.
    (including one piccolo).3.1.–timpani, side drum, woodblock, suspended cymbal,
    tam-tam, bass drum–two ondes Martenot, two harps, two pianos, celesta–strings
    (six violins, six violas, six cellos, six double basses)—58 instrumentalists in all
Duration: 54 minutes 30 seconds or 54 minutes 55 seconds (Act I: 16 minutes 35
    seconds; First Interlude: 5 minutes 20 seconds or 4 minutes 55 seconds; Act II: 8
    minutes 30 seconds; Second Interlude: 3 minutes 50 seconds; Act III: 20
    minutes 40 seconds)
Salabert
N.B. The second version (Vivace in 2/4) of the First Interlude (Nocturne) is used
    again in the central part of the Nocturne for orchestra (H102, Category 7); see also
    the use of certain passages (Act I, scenes 3 and 4; First Interlude, first version) in
    the Partita for two pianos (H139, Category 1A)

Semiramis occupies a special place in Honegger's gallery of "strong women." She stands alone in her superb inhumanity, heartlessness, and pride. And yet Antigone too was proud, just as Judith was a voluptuous, hotblooded Oriental, and Joan of Arc, like Semiramis (though the latter of her own accord) would die by fire. Above all, Semiramis is a character that Valéry made to measure, so to speak, for Ida Rubinstein. Unfortunately, that quarter of an hour of recitation at the end of the work would seal its destiny.

Of Honegger's four large ballets with chorus (Amphion, Sémiramis, Le Cantique des cantiques, and La Naissance des couleurs), Sémiramis is at once the longest, at fifty-five minutes, and the one in which there is the least amount of singing. Like Le Cantique des cantiques, it calls forth by its very subject the composer's luxuriant, sensual, Orientalizing vein. In both works Honegger is particularly concerned with refinement of sonority and timbre, and in both cases this results in an orchestral ensemble with relatively few strings: Sémiramis has only four groups of six, and Le Cantique des cantiques has no violins or violas. In Sémiramis the strings are extremely discreet all through the first act and the violins are totally silent. Woodwinds and brass, on the other hand, are very well represented (with even a double bass clarinet, which I cannot find in any other Honegger work, and a high trumpet in D). It is also the only work of his using two ondes Martenot, two pianos, and two harps.

The characters are Semiramis (danced and spoken role), the Captive (danced only), the four Astrologers (two tenors and two basses), and a large supporting cast (five-part mixed chorus, dancers, and so on). In Act I, we hear only the male chorus (briefly, in scene 4), and in Act II only the female chorus. A solo soprano is also heard here and will reappear briefly at the end of Act III—the only act that includes the quartet of Astrologers and Semiramis as narrator. The chorus is thus never heard as a whole body.

Valéry has committed a serious error here (an error that Claudel "the musician" would never have made) in putting the spoken melodrama at the end of the work—and a spoken section that is, moreover, four times as long as that of *Amphion*. This deprives the score of a natural climax and leads, from the musical point of view, to a long decrease in tension. This was largely responsible for the work's failure at its premiere, and the work has never recovered. Indeed, Andrée Vaurabourg forbade any revival, presumably for reasons that had nothing to do with the music; certainly this embargo did not emanate from the composer.

If anyone today wanted to revive this rich and original work, they would have to brave the fury of Valéry's ghost and either reduce or remove this long quarter of an hour of declamation, in which the musical substance is too slender to stand on it own. Valéry said casually to Honegger: "Just stick a little tremolo underneath for me!" Together, the writer and the proud diva played an unkind trick on the composer, who was too modest to take a stand. Kind as ever, he would only say: "*Sémiramis*'s lack of success was amply compensated for by the joy of bringing a work to completion with Valéry as a collaborator. He was not only a great poet, but also a charming man."[10] But, thanks to this "charming man," the composer was not even called onstage after the fifteen-minute fiasco of Rubinstein's "whimpering meows"! And it is significant that G. K. Spratt, who spends more than twenty pages on *Amphion*, has nothing at all to say about *Sémiramis*.

After studying the question carefully, however, I think there is a perfectly reasonable solution. One could go straight from the grandiose second interlude to the sublime coda, which represents Honegger at his best and looks forward to the coda of the *Symphonie liturgique*. That is, one could go from the second measure of figure 76 (measure 744) to figure 101 (measure 1030, "vague trumpets of awakening"). The work would then last thirty-eight minutes, like *Amphion*; there would be no serious loss musically; and we would be spared the four Astrologers.

Even so, it must be said that Valéry recognized his mistake and came to think that his long monologue should be entirely sung, like the final scene of an opera. Unfortunately, such a revision was never made. José Bruyr reminds us that the half-historical, half-legendary figure of the terrible queen of the Assyrians and Babylonians (whose name, Schamiram, means "dove" in Syriac), has been the subject of some fifty musical works, including what is arguably Rossini's most beautiful opera seria (*Semiramide*, 1823). As Marcel Delannoy pertinently remarks:

> This is no longer the passion of *Phaedra*, but Assyrian lasciviousness. In the choruses, a heavy fragrance rises from the famous hanging gardens. In

place of Florent Schmitt's musical eroticism, Honegger prefers a kind of
somber enchantment. On the other hand, when the action justifies the
massive use of brass, there is real substance in the roughness![11]

In fact, we realize from the opening measures that the music is at one with its
subject in being much harsher and more atonal than that of *Amphion*.

ACT I: "THE CHARIOT"

Into the great hall of the palace come prisoners, brutally pushed by servants and soldiers. They tumble down before the throne. The Queen appears
in her chariot, drawn by eight captive kings. They are unharnessed, so that she
can tread on them to reach her throne. Then she orders that the idols of the
vanquished be smashed. Horrified, one of the captives gets up, but the Queen
is overcome by his beauty. She unbinds him and falls down amorously at his
feet. At first the prisoner is stupefied, but then he gains courage and begins
gently to stroke Semiramis's hair. This is the scenario of the first act—the most
active and rapid of the three.

The short, brutal Introduction (lasting fifteen seconds, as Valéry requested)
presents the first of the three themes linked to Semiramis (Example 149). This
rising "staircase-like" theme describes her proud, untamable character, but it
will undergo a number of transformations before its final one, where it comes
close to resembling the bird theme from the *Symphonie liturgique*.

Example 149

The "Entrance of the Captives" takes place to sounds of what Willy Tappolet calls a "barbarous, chaotic tumult." But Semiramis enters to harsh polyphony on winds, dominated by high trumpet and first trombone. This is the fearsome Queen's second theme, that which depicts her royal majesty—hard,
brilliant, pitiless music in a highly dissonant E major (Example 150).

As José Bruyr rightly says: "It is in the mass of brass that Honegger will,
with a chisel tempered by atonality, carve the high relief of his first act." An
inverted form of this theme will pass successively from the tuba and low ondes
Martenot to flute and alto saxophone, and then to E-flat clarinet with saxophone
and ondes—a simple example of Honegger's amazing inventiveness in this work
in the matter of timbre. The graceful procession accompanying the "Toilette of
the Queen" is Ravelian in its refinement and would be reused as the slow movement of the *Partita for two pianos* in 1940. The fierce, dislocated hammering of

Example 150

the destruction of the captives' idols would become its first movement (though, of course, without the male chorus's chromatic, Oriental wailing).

But then the Queen is suddenly seized by the captive's beauty. She gazes on him at length, while the ondes Martenot play her third theme, the theme of love (Example 151), so well described by José Bruyr: "Among the wreathing smoke of incense and myrrh, we hear the voice of two ondes Martenot.... And suddenly the melody takes on the pathetic, heartbreaking tone of an animal wounded by love." As the Queen lies at the feet of her prisoner, the curtain falls on elements of the first theme (Example 149), originally ferocious, now tamed.

Example 151

First Interlude ("Nocturne")

After a tender, lyrical first section (reused in the third movement of the *Partita for two pianos* of 1940), there are two different variants. The first, and longer of the two, is a Vivace in 2/4, reused in its entirety in the central section of the orchestral *Nocturne* of 1936 (H102), with only the occasional change to the orchestration to take account of the absence of the two ondes. The second variant, on the other hand, develops the love music through an ever-more-ardent and passionate crescendo. This culminates in a Largamente dominated by the ondes, way up in the treble. It is certainly a more effective introduction to the act that follows.

Act II: "The Bed"

A pavilion in the middle of the hanging gardens serves as the setting for the burning night of love. The Queen, like a slave, waits on her prisoner. But his returning courage leads him to overstep the mark and he raises his hand to her.

Immediately, Semiramis comes to her senses, calls her amazons, has her passing lover seized, and herself runs him through with her javelin. Bruyr recalls: "The sumptuously barbarian materialism of Jakovleff's decor and costumes was somewhat in opposition to the essential spirituality of Valéry's scenario." Musically, this act consists of a twofold opposition between two sections. The first is a Lento, surrounded by the voluptuous vocalises of a female chorus, with an additional passage for solo soprano the second time. In the orchestra we hear figurations on the ondes deriving from Semiramis's themes (Examples 149 and 151) and the calls of nocturnal birds. The other section is a brief, dance-like Allegretto scherzando.

Then comes an extremely evocative Largo describing the struggle between the two lovers, during which Semiramis is depicted by a solo violin whose increasingly savage recitative-cadenza contains deformed fragments of her love music. The breaking point is reached to a stroke on the tam-tam, through which she summons her amazons, who immediately come running from every side. A fierce Presto, with glissando cries from female voices and ondes, ends with the murderous javelin, and a short decrescendo leads to the Second Interlude.

Second Interlude ("The Climb to the Tower")

Bruyr observes that the Second Interlude "could, from its rhythm, be called a Funeral March." This grandiose procession is built over a dotted, rhythmic, two-measure ostinato, in the style of a passacaglia bass; it is very reminiscent of the Adagio of the *First Symphony*, but here each variation comes in a different key. After the theme of royal majesty (Example 150) a second ostinato is added, a short figure that is none other than the famous opening of the "Abschied" (Farewell) from Mahler's *The Song of the Earth*. In fact, this whole movement, in which Bruyr rightly recognizes "not only the high point of the work, but one of the high points of Honegger's whole output," is a hugely magnified recapitulation of the third scene of Act I ("Entrance of Semiramis"). The music's mighty progress is weighed down by Honegger's favorite iambuses and scalic figures on piano and woodwinds, and at the end of the section the cry of the ondes dominates the whole orchestra. A slow diminuendo leads to the final rise of the curtain.

Act III: "The Tower"

At the top of the tower, four Astrologers chant their prophecies. But Semiramis knows her horoscope. She has loved a man, she must die, and, as dawn breaks, she offers herself to the Sun that will consume her. She lays herself on the marble altar. A light vapor rises, a dove flies off, the altar stands empty in the brilliant light.

In an atmosphere suddenly rarefied we hear the Astrologers (but not in canon, as Valéry had suggested). A strident reminder of the first theme (Example 149) on the two pianos announces the arrival of Semiramis, breathlessly issuing from the staircase of the tower. The "Astral Dance" begins on mysterious string harmonics, punctuated by metal percussion and the cantillation of the Astrologers. This is immediately followed by the Queen's long spoken monologue, in which she gives vent to her mad pride, her desire for transcendence, for "the power to be unique," "great beyond conception," "unbelievable, and through that divine." It is a pity that for two hundred measures the music should be reduced to a minimum—if only Honegger had realized his plan to turn this passage into a long, sung *scena!*

After the monologue is over and Semiramis lies down on the altar, this music takes over for sixty truly sublime measures of pure, diatonic, consonant polyphony in C major. The opening theme (Example 149) is now pacified and combined with memories of other themes, in the peaceful, idealized atmosphere of the end of the *Symphonie liturgique*, but with the final surprise of a chord of A major. For the sake of this epilogue, for the "Climb to the Tower," and for many other beautiful passages, it is imperative to rescue this magnificent work, which remains a prisoner to its unusual and expensive line-up of performing forces and its impossible final melodrama. As to the latter, at least, I have suggested a possible solution.

96. *Icare* (Icarus)

Ballet on rhythms by Serge Lifar
15 June 1935
First performance: 9 July 1935, Ballet of Paris Opera, choreography by Serge Lifar, Paris Opera
Performing forces: percussion orchestra (eighteen players) and double basses; metal instruments: triangle, anvil, antique cymbals, suspended cymbals, small cymbals, large cymbals, gong, tam-tam; wooden instruments: castanets, woodblock, xylophone, maracas, whip, small rattle, large rattle; skin instruments: tambourines (with and without jingles), side drum, snare drum, tenor drum, bass drum, four timpani; wind machine, thunder machine
Duration: 21 minutes
Overture; No. 1: Young Girls; Entrance of the Boys; No. 2: Entrance of Daedalus; No. 3: Icarus (with Adage); No. 4: Boys; No. 5; No. 6: Variation; No. 7: Death of Icarus
Unpublished. For contractual reasons binding Honegger to Ida Rubinstein at the time, the score was signed by J. E. Szyfer. He also wrote the manuscript score held by the Paris Opera. There is no trace of an autograph by Honegger. For further details, see Chapter 6.

For *Icare*, the first of his collaborations with Serge Lifar, Honegger was punctilious in respecting the rhythmic structures imposed on him. Lifar described the process in detail in connection with their second ballet, *Le Cantique des cantiques*. The main musical interest of *Icare* lies in its scoring for a real percussion orchestra, together with various effects and noises produced by the dancers themselves. Jacques Feschotte wrote that the score was an early example of *musique concrète*.

113. *Un Oiseau blanc s'est envolé* (A White Bird Has Flown Away)

Ballet by Sacha Guitry, written for the gala of the HEC (École des Hautes Études commerciale) as part of the Universal Exhibition of 1937
20 May 1937, Paris
First performance: 24 May 1937, corps de ballet of Paris Opera, choreography by Serge Lifar, conducted by Arthur Honegger, Théâtre des Champs-Élysées, Paris (Exhibition of Arts and Techniques)
Performing forces: 1.1.1.1.–saxophone–0.2.(including small trumpet in C) 1.0.–suspended cymbal–piano–strings
Duration: 11 minutes
Unpublished
Music used again almost in its entirety in *Mermoz*

This story about an airman is told in a spoken commentary in octosyllabic verse by Sacha Guitry. It is not surprising that Honegger used it again in *Mermoz*. The different stages of the flight (obstacles, etc.) are very close to those found in Brecht and Weill's *Lindbergh's Flight*, which Sacha Guitry must have known. Except for the first nineteen measures, all the music of the ballet appears in the *Two Suites* from *Mermoz* (H167A, Category 7A, in Chapter 11). The cross-references between the two works are as follows:

Un Oiseau blanc s'est envolé	*Mermoz*
Introduction	Measures 1–19 of No. 4
	(Departure of the Mail)
The Airplane	Measures 4–48 of No. 1 (Title Music)
Entrance of the Wind/	No. 11 (The Wind Rises)
Entrance of the Fog	
Entrance of the Rain/Entrance of Sleep/	Measures 84–155 of No. 14
Entrance of Fear/Struggle/Victory	(Crossing the Atlantic)

123. *Le Cantique des cantiques* (The Song of Songs)

End of 1936–19 January 1937; orchestrated October–November 1937
"To Francis and Andrée [Winter], affectionately"
Scenario in two acts by Gabriel Boissy. Music on rhythms by Serge Lifar
First performance: 2 February 1938, Carina Ari (the Shulamite), Serge Lifar (the Shepherd), Paul Goube (Solomon), Ballet of Paris Opera, choreography by Serge Lifar, designs by Paul Colin, soloists, Chorus and Orchestra of Paris Opera, conducted by Philippe Gaubert, Paris Opera
Performing forces: contralto (the Shulamite), tenor (the Shepherd), baritone (Solomon); mixed chorus; orchestra (about forty players): 3.1.(English horn only) 3.2.–two saxophones–0.4.(including one piccolo trumpet) 4.1.–timpani, percussion (side drum, tambourine [with and without jingles] tenor drum, bass drum, woodblock, triangle, suspended cymbal, cymbals, iron cymbals, three gongs, tam-tam, bouteillophone), piano, celesta, ondes Martenot–cellos, double basses
Duration: 43 minutes 30 seconds (14:00 + 29:30)
Act I: Prelude; 1. The Winegrowers; 2. The Shulamite; 3. The Shepherd; 4. The Shulamite and the Shepherd; 5. Solomon; 6. The Shulamite, the Shepherd, and Solomon; 7. Departure of the Shulamite and Solomon
Act II: 8. Solitude in the Palace; 9. Solomon; 10. The Shulamite and Solomon; 11. The Entertainment; 12. Dream of the Shulamite; 13. The Shepherd; 14. The Shulamite and the Shepherd; 15. The Shepherd and Solomon; 16. Liberation
Heugel

After their first collaboration on *Icare*, Serge Lifar and Honegger worked together again according to the same principles, but now on a much larger scale. The music for *Le Cantique des cantiques* lasts nearly three quarters of an hour, bringing together vocal soloists, mixed chorus, and an orchestra of a particularly original color. Shortly after the premiere, Lifar published in the *La Revue musicale* of March 1938 a significant manifesto entitled "La Danse et la Musique," in which he made his position clear. He maintained that, in a ballet, the authority lay not with the writer of the scenario, nor with the composer, but with the dancer and the choreographer. This seems merely common sense. Lifar wrote: "The dancer must himself lay out a musical scheme for the work, containing indications of rhythm and tempo down to the smallest details. The composer's job is to link the rhythms together." And he insisted on the necessity for a special orchestra, including a large role for the percussion, and in which the chorus would also contribute to the rhythmic and musical realization. The score of *Le Cantique des cantiques*, according to Lifar, fulfilled this ideal and constituted the model for any future collaboration between composer and what he called the "choreauthor."

The response of the music critics was strangely muted. Marcel Delannoy maintains that Honegger was shackled by Lifar's constraints and that his inspiration breaks free only in the final apotheosis (No. 16, "Liberation"). Even Darius Milhaud feels the same sense of repression. Personally, I take an entirely opposite view and find *Le Cantique des cantiques* one of the finest and most rewarding scores Honegger wrote for dancing, and also well able to hold its own in the concert hall. At no point do I feel the constraint of the predetermined rhythms. As for Honegger himself, like any great artist he always knew how to utilize the many constraints to which he voluntarily submitted as so many stimulants to his imagination, from Claudel's scenarios to the very precise demands of radio and cinema. Creative liberty is defined exactly in relation to constraints, as long as they stem from the artist's free will. Fugal writing, sonata form, serial technique—these are all predetermined frames within which the composer's inspiration can blossom.

On the subject of his collaboration with Lifar, Honegger expressed himself unambiguously in a text entitled "About the Choreauthor," published in an issue of the Collection *Comoedia-Charpentier* of 1943, devoted to contemporary ballet:

> In principle, the composer who intends to write a ballet hopes a poet or literary man will give him a point of departure; an idea that will form the dramatic basis of the action. Once he has been given this subject, he will write a symphony on which the choreographer will set himself the task of inventing steps and new poses suitable for getting across the spirit of the subject. Often that turns into mime pure and simple, which makes it boring. The writer contents himself with indicating "General dance," "Graceful divertimento," or "Lysander expresses his love to Cunégonde," and he leaves it to the choreographer to find the gestures that will transmit these profound thoughts to the spectator.
>
> The music the choreographer has at his disposal does not always fit the

way he sees the situation. Once, the dancer and the composer used to agree on an accented rhythm, a waltz, or a rigaudon. More recently, the symphonic pretensions of composers have discredited this way of working. I think it is rational, even so, and I accepted with real gratitude the rhythms which Serge Lifar suggested for the different movements of *Le Cantique des cantiques*. This basis leaves the composer quite free, since he can always enrich the given outline by polyphony. But in this way he has a solid, well-defined scaffolding that will ensure that his music is interpreted rightly, so long as the dancer is faithful to his instructions).

In my opinion, then, the choreauthor is an indispensable partner for the composer and the designer. The writer of the scenario is no more than a graceful ornament to the collaboration. He suggests the titles. The others write the chapters beneath them.

The exemplary good sense and modesty of that text speak volumes for the total lack of narcissism or pretension that characterized Honegger's whole attitude, in both his personal and his artistic life. It was also a wholly professional attitude that ensured Honegger was never betrayed by his collaborators.

The participation of three vocal soloists and a mixed chorus in *Le Cantique des cantiques*, with only a third of the music being for orchestra alone, means that this third long choral ballet is therefore the nearest of the four to being a staged oratorio. This point was made by José Bruyr, who was the only commentator so far to have described the score in any detail. The story is a simple one. The first act takes place in the vineyards of En Gaddi, at the edge of an olive wood. To the despair of the Shepherd who loves her, the Shulamite, the "Rose of Sharon," is taken away by King Solomon, who leads her off to his palace. This is the setting for the second act, in which the most elaborate spectacle and dancing cannot prevent the young girl from remembering her Shepherd. He reappears, she will be returned to him, and all nature will smile upon their happiness.

The choice of performing forces is very individual and to some extent reminiscent of that in *Sémiramis* in the predominance of winds over strings (reduced to cellos and double basses) and in the richness of the brass section (four trumpets, including a small one in C, and four trombones). Horns, however, are replaced by saxophones, as in *Jeanne d'Arc au bûcher*, and there is no oboe, only an English horn. There are important parts for ondes Martenot, piano, and celesta (but no part for harp). There is a wide variety of percussion instruments, as Lifar requested, including iron cymbals and our old friend the bouteillophone. To this relatively small orchestra of some forty players are added vocal soloists and chorus.

The structure of the work in separate numbers looks back to *Le Roi David* rather than to the symphonic ballets like *Amphion* or *Sémiramis*. The thematic material is succinct and the themes are split into two main families. The first is derived from the Shulamite's passionate theme, given to the ondes Martenot in scene 2 (Example 152), and is characterized by its wide melodic leaps and a chromaticism verging on atonality. The second is modal, diatonic, even pentatonic, and more rhythmic and danceable in character. At times it sounds like

Middle Eastern folk music and is astonishingly close to the Israeli folk music of today. Example 153 is a good illustration of this. It is at these points that *Le Cantique des cantiques* recalls *Le Roi David*—for example, the emphatic dactyls of the chorus in scene 3 on the words "La voici, la voici, bondissant comme un faon" (Here she is, here she is, leaping like a fawn), which are so close to the "Éternel, Éternel, viens bénir Israël" (Eternal One, Eternal One, come and bless Israel) from "Festive Canticle," No. 15 of *Le Roi David*.

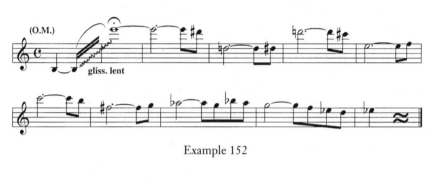

Example 152

Example 153

There is no need here to analyze the seventeen individual pieces, none of which lasts as long as five minutes. They are just little colored pictures, in which Honegger's genius for finding concise and striking images is evident, all the way from the tiny Prelude, written on an incantatory Oriental theme for soprano saxophone. After the happy procession of "The Winegrowers" comes the passionate cry of "The Shulamite," "with the tender blandishments of the ondes Martenot," in José Bruyr's words. This is the most striking leitmotif of the whole work, a line that embraces the range of an eleventh (Example 152). An energetic 5/4 rhythm depicts the Shepherd and a moderate waltz the duet of "The Shulamite and the Shepherd," interrupted by the chorus imitating the rhythm of the horsemen who precede the arrival of Solomon. A long, purely instrumental movement accompanies the first confrontation of the three protagonists, and a short, vigorous section in 3/4 with chorus marks the departure of the King, taking the Shulamite away. This is the end of Act I.

Act II begins with the evocation of the young girl, alone in the palace, dreaming sadly of her absent beloved. Then comes the King's passionate declaration of love, followed by his dialogue with the Shulamite (this movement, No. 10, is the longest in the score). Here the sensuality becomes headier and more insistent, with especially exotic sounds from the orchestra—glissandos from cellos and saxophones, flutter-tonguing on the flute, and a rapid dialogue between clarinet and ondes. But the end is heavy and violent, with percussion well to the fore. "The Entertainment" (No. 11) is a show Solomon puts on for his prisoner. The sinuous melody for male chorus is, according to José Bruyr, an authentic Tibetan theme, as is the rapid dance that follows it. Both are supported by brightly colored percussion in which iron cymbals and bouteillophone play prime roles. The dance ends with an ostinato bass on ondes Martenot and double basses that accelerates through whole-notes, half-notes, and quarter-notes and stops abruptly in a paroxysm.

In the "Dream of the Shulamite" (No. 12), we hear her whispering ("I seek but do not find him") and surrounded by her obsessive theme (Example 152). Then "The Shepherd" appears (No. 13), and we hear his tenor voice for the first time, recalling the dance from scene 4. "The Shulamite and the Shepherd" (No. 14) is the only vocal duet in the score, and through it the Shepherd's song alternates with the ondes motif in all its passionate languor. The confrontation of scene 15, like that of scene 6, is purely orchestral and to some extent a developmental crossroads for the work's principal ideas. If scene 6 engendered the conflict, this scene resolves it. The work ends with No. 16 ("Liberation"), a broad choral finale in three sections: a rhythmic choral dialogue ("Love is strong as death, and jealousy cruel as the grave"), a last passionate recall of Example 152 in canon, and finally a majestic conclusion ("Thou art the rose of Sharon, thou art the lily of the valley"), concluding in a burst of A major. It is easy to hear in this splendid finale the composer of Le Roi David. The entire work deserves to be heard in the concert hall.

142. *La Naissance des couleurs* (The Birth of Colors)

12 May 1940, Paris; orchestrated 15 May–7 June 1948, Bagnoles-de-l'Orne
Ballet by Ernst Klausz (scenario and projections) and René Morax (text)
First performance: 22 June 1949, Ballet of Paris Opera, choreography by Serge Lifar, direction of ballet ensemble by Irène Popard; Legrand, Sauvageot, Decarli, pupils of the École Popard; chorus and orchestra of the Paris Opera, conducted by Robert Blot, Paris Opera
Performing forces: solo soprano, mixed chorus; orchestra: 2.2.2.2.–4.3.3.1.–timpani, anvil, bass drum, cymbals, side drum, tenor drum, tam-tam, triangle, woodblock, castanets, whip–strings
Duration: 32 minutes 45 seconds
Chaos, Nothingness; The Blacks; The Strongest; Discipline; Coronation; Cortege of Gold; Dance of the Child; The Blues; Angelic Choir; The Red; Revolt; Crimson Hymn; Plot of the Blacks; The Rainbow; White Hymn
Unpublished

La Naissance des couleurs is the least familiar of the Honegger/Morax collaborations, possibly because it was not linked to the Théâtre du Jorat. Because of Honegger's exodus and the Occupation, this final choral ballet was left unorchestrated for eight years and has never been revived after its two unsuccessful performances. This failure was in no way due to Honegger's music, but rather to the low standard of the choreography and staging. Apparently the colored projections vital to the work did not function as they should have done.

A review by René Colas in the review *Spectacles* of 1 July 1949 gives a brief summary of the scenario:

> The appearance of Gold in the middle of the primitive dances of black peoples (no allusion to the black peoples of Africa). Yellow is supported, then abandoned, by Blue: he blossoms into Crimson, then is assaulted by Red. Finally, the Rainbow unites all the colors, giving birth to White, who conquers Black.

The poor critic is visibly shaken by the music, which he describes as "strident, intense, rarely tuneful, using and abusing the percussive instruments of the orchestra to produce thunder noises and aggressive rhythms, in Honegger's most extreme manner."

True, this is not the music of Léo Delibes, but, despite a few rough passages, it is predominantly simple and direct, with tunes and motifs that are easy to remember and written in the composer's "public" manner. There is much use of the chorus, but the solo soprano of the "Dance of the Child" is unique and creates a sharp contrast at the center of the work. As the story suggests, the music has a negative pole, of violence and brutality, and a positive one of hymns, sunshine, diatonicism, and tonality.

Among the most striking moments of this highly contrasted score, we may note, after the somber, mysterious introduction, the male chorus's Hindu invocation, accompanied by a wide-ranging theme on muted trombones ("The Strongest"), which will serve to some extent as the leitmotif of the negative forces (Example 154). Then comes the weighty procession of the "Coronation of Gold." The "Dance of the Child," with its solo soprano expressing a little girl's pride and joy in being free, as she dances in springtime, provides a contrast of brightness and love, symbolizing the positive forces of peace. The "Angelic Choir" sings a gentle and joyous tenth-century Latin canticle by Alphanus of Salerno to a very simple tune in A major in the style of *Le Roi David* (Example 155). There is also the rhythmically spoken chorus of "Revolt," the rhythmically complex polyphony, supported by percussion, rising from whispering to shouting.

Example 154

Example 155

The "Crimson Hymn," a straightforward melody typical of its composer, is the first of the mixed chorus's two full-scale appearances, on a rhythmic variant of Example 155. After one last offensive by the forces of Evil and the fairy apparition of "The Rainbow," the work ends with the broad "White Hymn," and its D major will remain predominant until the final apotheosis. One wonders what Honegger's thoughts were when, on 12 May 1940, he ruled a double measure after the words: "Unite, O peoples of the world / Become brothers in the shining light. . . . / And may your brotherly voices unite / In this peace that justice provides."

154. *Le Mangeur de rêves* (The Dream Eater)

Ballet on a scenario by René Lenormand
December 1941
First performance: 21 June 1942, Salle Pleyel, Paris
Lost

174. *L'Appel de la montagne* (The Call of the Mountain)

Ballet on a scenario by R. Favre le Bret
Summer–20 October 1943; orchestrated June–July 1945
First performance: 9 July 1945, Ballet of the Paris Opera (the name of the
    choreographer, who was apparently not outstanding, has been forgotten),
    conducted by Louis Fourestier, Paris Opera
Performing forces: 3.3.2.3.–4.3.3.1.–timpani, percussion–celesta, piano–strings
Duration: 49 minutes 25 seconds (27:15 + 22:10)
First tableau: 1. Introduction and Ensemble; 2. Dance of the Girls of the Cantons; 3.
    Entrance of MacGuire; 4. Entrance of Haecky and the Shepherds; 5. General
    Dance; 6. MacGuire's Variation; 7. Saesli's Variation; 8. Summons to Games; 9.
    The Stone-throwing; 10. Wrestling; 11. Distribution of Prizes and Departure;
    12. Alpeglüe (Sunset)
Second tableau: 13. Introduction, Climb and Fall of MacGuire (passacaglia); 14.
    Appearance of the Goddesses; 15. Round of the Goddesses; 16. Entrance of the
    Malevolent Gods; 17. Appearance of the Jungfrau; 18. Tuba on the Stage
Unpublished (except for *Schwyzer Fäschttag*, H174A, published by Salabert)
Honegger extracted a Suite from the ballet called *Schwyzer Fäschttag* (H174A,
    Category 7A), consisting of numbers 1, 2, 4, 7, 8/9, and 11/12. Number 2
    ("Dance of the Girls of the Cantons") comes from the film *Rapt* (H86, Category
    16)

In France, *L'Appel de la montagne* is the most reviled of Honegger's works. The Parisians did not understand its point, which was to season an outrageously romantic argument by a robust folkloric grain of salt not devoid of certain irony. It can be told in a few lines. We are at Interlaken, in sight of the Jungfrau, in 1815. The shepherds' festival is at its height. A Scottish tourist, MacGuire, falls in love with the pretty peasant girl Saesli, but she prefers her robust compatriot Haecky. "The foreigner gets a fit of Alpine blues: he goes missing in avalanche country," as José Bruyr puts it. Surprised by the fog, he falls into a crevice and faints. He is saved by the Ice Maiden who takes him to her white Venusberg. He resists all temptation and comes back to consciousness, while far away resound the bugles of the guides who have gone off to look for him. He is taken back down to the valley "where," as Bruyr further notes, "one must hope that he will find a less hardhearted native."

The subject of a city-dweller who falls in love with a shepherdess and goes off to ease his heartache on the top of a mountain is one that appears often, with variations. It is the theme of the mountain that is at once a bringer of comfort and a killer, and always an enchanter (we may think of *Manfred, The Fairy's Kiss,* and *Bergkristall*). The subject and the setting here do slightly recall *The Fairy's Kiss,* but whereas Stravinsky treated his story in the melancholy, nostalgic, "pastel" colors of Tchaikovsky, his admitted model, and indeed borrowed his themes, Honegger turned his into a boisterous evocation of traditional Switzerland. *Schwyzer Fäschttag* (H174A) contains the kernel of the music for the first and longer of the two tableaux—that is to say, all the "Swiss" music.

The two "Scottish" movements of the first tableau are No. 3 and No. 6 (No. 5, which does not appear in the Suite, is merely a repeat of No. 1). The "Entrance of MacGuire" introduces two authentic Scottish tunes: "The MacGuire March," in which the English horn imitates a bagpipe, and "Solomon's Temple," a sentimental horn solo that soon turns into the powerful passacaglia theme for MacGuire's climb up the mountain (Example 156). The dance "MacGuire's Variation" (No. 6) brings in a new theme that sounds Scottish but is, in fact, of Honegger's own invention.

(Horn, 8va bassa)

Example 156

The second tableau leads directly to the "Alpeglüe" and, after a short introduction, to the powerful passacaglia of Example 156. This sixteen-measure theme in G major is the subject of four variations (in C major, A-flat major, E major, and C minor)—all of which are rich in contrapuntal devices such as canons and diminutions, and in extra decoration. The final, modulating paragraph is interrupted by the spectacular "Fall of MacGuire." This is followed by the mysterious fairy music of the "Appearance of the Goddesses," by the delightful "Round of the Goddesses," and finally by the strident, menacing music of the "Malevolent Gods," who engulf the theme of the preceding round. Happily, the Jungfrau appears to the sounds of a pastoral woodwind dialogue in C major, and this tonality remains in force until the end. The atmosphere looks forward to the more lyrical passages of the *Fourth Symphony.* The epilogue finally swells to a majestic tutti, before gently settling back again.

180. *Chota Roustaveli*

Georgian choreographic epic in four acts by Nicolas Evreinoff and Serge Lifar
July 1945 (Acts I and IV)
The music of Act II is by Alexander Tcherepnin, that of Act III by Tibor Harsanyi
Inspired by a poem of Chota Roustaveli entitled *The Hero in the Leopard Skin*
First performance: 14 May 1946, New Ballet of Monte Carlo, choreography by
  Serge Lifar, designs and costumes by Prince A. Schervachidze and G.
  Nepokoichitzky, with Serge Lifar (Chota Roustaveli), Olga Adabache (The Bird
  Tzetzkly), Boris Trailine (The Leopard), Youly Algaroff (Tariel), Sirène
  Adjemova (Thamar), Yvette Chauviré (Nestan Daredjan), Janine Charrat
  (Tinatine), Vladimir Skouratov (Avtandil), Monte Carlo
Performing forces: the orchestral score has since become inaccessible—the owner of
  the private collection in which it is housed refuses to have his name made
  public. All that is available is the piano reduction
Duration of the two acts written by Honegger: 45 minutes (22:30 + 22:30)
Act I: Prelude; 1. Birds; 2. Entrance of the Leopard; 3. Passage of the Birds; 4.
  Entrance and Dance of Chota; 5. Passage of the Birds; 6. Combat with the
  Leopard; 7. Appearance and Dance of Tzetzkly; 8. Recitation of Poem (spoken);
  9. Appearance of Thamar
Act II: 1. Chota and Tzetzkly; 2. Birds; 3. War Dance of Chota; 4. Dance of
  Tzetzkly; 5. Chota, Tzetzkly, and Thamar; 6. Finale and Appearance of Saint
  George
Unpublished

This full-length work was obviously an important event in the history of
ballet, even though it does not seem to have been revived after the tours that
immediately followed the premiere (notably in London). Delannoy speaks of
Honegger's contribution as being a "somewhat hasty collaboration" in this
"giant ballet," even though it consisted of forty-five minutes of music for large
orchestra. Bruyr, once again, is the only writer to discuss it in detail and gives a
large amount of interesting information on the poem, its author, and the history
of Georgia. But these clearly go beyond the remit of the present volume. Also,
he has nothing to say about the music and makes the mistake of attributing to
Honegger Acts II and III instead of Acts I and IV.

The scenario is inspired by the Georgian national epic, Chota Roustaveli's
The Hero in the Leopard Skin, a poem in 1,553 stanzas. Roustaveli lived at the
beginning of the thirteenth century in the court of the legendary queen
Thamar, the subject of Mily Balakirev's tone poem. After spending one night
with her lovers, the Queen would then have them thrown into the stormy
waters of the river Terek. Her castle stands on the banks of the river at the bottom of a rugged gorge (an Oriental version of the tower of Nesle). Chota was
madly in love with the Queen and dedicated his poem to her, but she repelled
his advances. As a result, he lived on. Here is a summary of the story:

Act I: "The Hunt" (set in the forest)

Chota's muse is the little bird Tzetzkly, but his main inspiration comes
from the Queen. He transforms himself into his hero, Tariel, who kills the
Leopard and puts on its skin, the symbol of strength, courage, and love. He
can no longer remain separated from his beloved, the Princess Nestan Daredjan, and returns to her.

ACT II: "THE FESTIVAL" (SET IN THE PALACE OF NESTAN DAREDJAN).
MUSIC BY TCHEREPNIN

The princess, to whom the poet attributes all of Thamar's virtues, is waiting for Tariel in the company of Avtandil and his fiancée, the Princess Tinatine. To amuse themselves, the young princesses learn the Davlouri, the dance of the mountain warriors. Tariel arrives and reads them his poem. Suddenly, Thamar appears and announces that the enemy is at the gates of the palace.

ACT III: "AT WAR" (SET AT THE FOOT OF THE WALLS). MUSIC BY
HARSANYI

The princesses observe the battle, during which Tariel saves Avtandil and repels the Turkish enemy. Thamar renders homage to her people's bravery. The princesses celebrate the victory, but the Turks succeed in capturing Nestan Daredjan, and Tariel rushes off to save her.

ACT IV: "IN PRISON" (SET IN THE FOREST)

Tariel, guided by his muse Tzetzkly, returns to the place where Chota Roustaveli created him, and he rescues his beloved. The poet is glorified by the people of Georgia, to whom Saint George promises his eternal protection.

Serge Lifar's rhythmic constraints are compounded here by those of local Oriental color and Georgian folk songs. Honegger, with his usual professional, chameleonlike adaptability, wrote music that was simple and functional, luxuriantly orchestrated (according to the critics of the time), and tonal and melodic throughout. In short, he followed the pattern of his other collective work premiered in Monte Carlo, *L'Aiglon*.

The Prelude to Act I immediately presents Chota's resolute, leaping theme, then Thamar's long, lyrical melody. The "Dance of Chota" is built on a graceful folk tune in repeated notes with tambourine accompaniment. Thamar's appearance at the end of the act conjures up an atmosphere of Caucasian sensuality worthy of Balakirev, Borodin, or indeed Khachaturian. The dreamlike andante that opens Act IV likewise recalls the atmosphere of the "Polovtsian Dances" from *Prince Igor*, and we may easily imagine the spirited "Dance of Tzetzkly" (No. 4) in a brilliant orchestral garb of piccolos and tambourines, in the style of Rimsky-Korsakov's Russian ballets. Number 5 is the traditional long set piece (lasting nine and a quarter minutes), which develops the themes of the three main characters in a particularly lyrical manner. This is followed by a majestic Finale in F-sharp major, with an apotheosis on the brass at the triumphant appearance of Saint George.

189. Sortilèges (Magic Spells)

Spring 1946
"To Lélia Bederkhan"
First performance: summer 1946, Lélia Bederkhan and her company of eight
dancers, Comédie des Champs-Élysées, Paris
Lost

The music for *Sortilèges*, written for four ondes Martenot, has disappeared.

200. De la musique

Ballet on a scenario by R. Wild ("Little ballet for the Thompson [sic]—Houston
company," according to the composer's manuscript catalog)
First half of 1950
There is no trace of a performance
Lost

THIRTEEN

Incidental Music

One particular aspect of Honegger's genius has been highlighted several times during the preceding discussion of his music: namely, his illustrative gift, of describing a character, a situation, or a mood with great economy, but at the same time with an astonishing vigor and accuracy. And he does this with means that are purely musical, indeed abstract, owing nothing to facile, naturalist imitation or to the program music techniques typical of the romantic symphonic poem. *Le Chant de Nigamon*, which is practically the only Honegger work that belongs to the older genre, keeps its distance from the procedures of someone like Richard Strauss and is formally so rigorous that, were it not for the three American Indian melodies he quotes, one would have a job to know what the source of his inspiration had been. Indeed, its essentially symphonic construction precludes it from the present discussion, which concentrates on the art of the medieval illuminator and the miniaturist.

This gift of the concise, striking image predestined Honegger to a fruitful career as a cinema composer, but we can see that it was an innate element in his creative genius, manifesting itself in *Le Roi David* at the latest, and perhaps even as early as *Le Dit des jeux du monde*. Even so, his intense activity in films from 1933–1934 onward could only have sharpened this rare faculty, which shows itself even more clearly in his works for radio, where the music has to suggest the image, than in his stage or film music, where the image already exists. For the sake of convenience, I have grouped the works into three sections: incidental music for the stage, music for radio, and music for film. In fact, there are no firm barriers between this group of chapters and those that surround it. The titles quoted above prove it. *Le Roi David* may be a grand "fresco," but it is also a succession of short tableaux illustrating the painter's art, and one could say the same of *Nicolas de Flue* and even of the first version of *Judith* (although not of the following ones). In the same way, part of his film music—the numerous popular songs, as well as the tangos, fox trots, and waltzes that accompany them—demonstrates an ability denied by and large to composers of so-called serious music and has undoubted links with the "light music" that will conclude our inventory of the composer's output.

A large part of the music under discussion is functional, written in general at high speed for contexts and circumstances that had no durable existence. In general, these pieces make no claim to an autonomous life outside the conditions that produced them and so have remained unpublished. The losses are greater than in any other area of Honegger's creative work. The composer saved for the concert hall the music he thought worthy of survival in the form of suites, and these have been examined in detail in Category 7A in Chapter 11 (or 4A in those fewer cases where the music is for a chamber group). That is why I have restricted myself here to considering pieces of remarkable quality, those worthy of appearing on disc or in the concert hall beside those chosen by the composer.

Category 14: Music for the Stage

21. *La Danse macabre*
35. *Les Mariés de la tour Eiffel* (see Category 7A)
39. *Danse de la chèvre* (see Category 4A)
41. *Saül*
45. *Antigone* (see Category 4A)
48. *The Tempest*
49. *Liluli*
60. *L'Impératrice aux rochers*
61. *Phaedra*
62. *Pour le cantique de Salomon* (see Category 4A)
63. *Three Songs of the Little Siren* (see Category 8A)
104. *14 Juillet* (see Category 7A)
111. *Liberté* (see Category 7A)
119. *La Construction d'une cité* (see Category 9A)
146. *Mandragora*
147. *L'Ombre de la ravine*
149. *Les Suppliantes*
150. *Huit Cent Mètres*
151. *La Ligne d'horizon*
165. *Le Soulier de satin*
172. *Sodome et Gomorrhe*
175. *Charles le Téméraire*
187. *Prométhée*
190. *Hamlet*
194. *Oedipus* (André Obey)
195. *L'État de siège*
208. *On ne badine pas avec l'amour*
210. *Oedipe-Roi* (Thierry Maulnier)

The most important of these scores are *The Tempest*, *L'Impératrice aux rochers*, *Phaedra*, the Greek tragedies (*Les Suppliantes*, *Prométhée*, and the two versions of *Oedipus*), *Le Soulier de satin*, and *Hamlet*. Only the first three call for a symphony orchestra, but choruses are a favorite resource. These scores are very unequal in length, ranging from a few minutes to more than an hour.

21. *La Danse macabre*

Incidental music for a play by Carlos Larronde
March 1919, Paris
First performance: 28 March 1919, decor by Fauconnet, Théâtre de l'Odéon, Paris
Two pieces: "Dance in the Charnel-Houses"; "Fair in the Market-Square"
Lost

41. *Saül*

Incidental music for the play by André Gide
February–March 1922
First performance: 16 June 1922, Théâtre du Vieux-Colombier, Paris
Performing forces: trumpet, cello, percussion (side drum, cymbals, bass drum), piano
Six pieces, the third of which is partially missing
Unpublished

The instrumental colors are unusual and original. But even if the score were complete, this music would not work away from the stage.

48. *The Tempest*

Incidental music for Shakespeare's play, in the French adaptation by Guy de Pourtalès
February 1923–end of 1929 (*Prelude*: February 1923; *Two Songs for Ariel*: April 1923; the rest by stages until the end of 1929)
First performance: 26 December 1929, conducted by Albert Wolff, Monte Carlo Opera; at the revival at the Théâtre de l'Odéon in Paris, on 2 April 1930, the music was filled out with borrowings from other Honegger works, notably *Napoléon* and *L'Impératrice aux rochers*
Performing forces: a) *Prelude*: 2.2.2.2.–4.2.3.1.–percussion–strings; b) what survives of the remaining music: solo soprano; 2.2.2.2.–2.2.0.0.–suspended cymbal–harp, celesta–strings
Duration (of surviving music): 23 minutes (including 6 minutes for the Prelude)
Surviving music: 1. Prelude; 2. The Magic Cape; 3. Entrance Motif (Ariel's Motif); 4. Ritornello of Caliban; 5. Song of Ariel ("Come unto these yellow sands"); 6. Enchantment; 7. Finale (End); 8. Ritornello of Stefano; 9. Ariel Plays His Pipe; 10. Ariel as Hag (Scherzo); 11. Prospero's Cell; 12. Act IV Dance; 13. Song of Ariel ("Where the bee sucks")
N.B. 1: No. 11 (Prospero's Cell) is in A-B-A form, in which the A sections repeat No. 2 (The Magic Cape) and the B section No. 7 (Finale); these A sections also recur in the A sections of No. 20 (The Rock) in *L'Impératrice aux rochers* (see H60). Number 3 (Ritornello of Ariel) is an amplified repeat of the introduction and conclusion of No. 6 (first Song of Ariel)
N.B. 2: It would be possible to make a concert suite for soprano and small orchestra consisting of Nos. 2, 12, 3 leading to 5, 11, 13, 10, and 7, in that order (duration: 14 minutes)
Only the *Prelude* (see H48A, Category 7A) and the *Two Songs for Ariel* (see H48B, Category 8A) have been published, by Salabert

The reconstitution of this music has been extremely laborious, and some parts of it seem definitely to be lost. It is difficult to establish the extent of these losses, especially as some movements are perhaps to be found in other works (notably in *Napoléon*, in the "Calme" and the "Children's Dance"). Only the *Prelude*, which was composed first and which has been published and recorded several times, uses a large orchestra. Apart from the *Prelude* and the *Two Songs for Ariel*, which have already been discussed in their proper place, the most remarkable pieces are the two scherzos and especially "Prospero's Cell"—a long, slow, somber, and mysterious 6/4 movement in C-sharp minor, with a fine lyrical flowering in the central section. Of the two scherzos, "Ariel as Hag" is a short, brilliantly orchestrated piece of fairy music in a lively 2/4. The delightful "Act IV Dance" is longer. It has a grace about it that is reminiscent of Fauré, and is almost a homage to the famous "Sicilienne" from *Pelléas et Mélisande*, with its diaphanous texture of harp and string harmonics.

49. *Liluli*

Incidental music for the play by Romain Rolland
March 1923
First performance: 31 March 1923, Salle des Fêtes de Suresnes
Performing forces: piccolo, cello, piano; soprano, two-part chorus (high and low)
Duration: 2 minutes 30 seconds
1. Chorus of Workers; 2. Laïra
Unpublished

Two tiny pieces, the first of which combines two old popular songs in counterpoint: "Ah Joseph dites-nous" (Ah, Joseph, tell us) and "Darrié chez nous y a't'un vert bocaige" (Behind our house there's a green wood).

60. *L'Impératrice aux rochers* (The Empress of the Rocks)

Incidental music for the play in five acts and a prologue by Saint-George de
    Bouhélier, *Un Miracle de Notre-Dame* (*L'Impératrice aux rochers*)
6 August–13 November 1925
"To Ida Rubinstein"
First performance: 18 February 1927, Ida Rubinstein, Suzanne Després, Jean Hervé,
    Desjardins, Grétillat, soloists, chorus, and orchestra of Paris Opera, conducted
    by Philippe Gaubert, Paris Opera
Performing forces: solo soprano, mixed chorus, numerous spoken roles; orchestra:
    3.3.3.3.–4.3.3.1.–timpani, bass drum, cymbals, bells, side drum, tam-tam–harp,
    celesta–strings
Total music duration: 65 minutes
1. Prologue (with narrator)
Act I: 2. Introduction (Prelude); 2a. The Hunt of the Emperor (hunting fanfares
    onstage); 3. Interlude; 4. Interlude (The Council Chamber); 5. Entrance of the
    Pope; 6. Departure of the Emperor (with chorus)
Act II: 7. Prelude (Snow in Rome); 8. Interlude; 9. Interlude (The Tower); 10.
    Postlude;
Act III: 11. Prelude (The Gardens of the Palace); 12. Open-air Music; 13. Postlude;
    14. Interlude (The Return of the Emperor); 15. Procession of the Empress; 16.
    Interlude (The Storm);

Act IV: 17. Introduction (Prelude: The Orgy in the Palace); 18. Festive Music; 19. Vocalise (solo soprano); 20. Interlude (The Rock); 21. Apparition; 22. no title; 23. Finale (with chorus of sopranos)
Act V: 24. Introduction (Prelude: The Ruins of the Temple); 25. Interlude (The Square in Front of the Cathedral); 26. Final Chorus
N.B. 1: No. 14 became the Finale of the *Partita for two pianos* (H139)
N.B. 2: Honegger extracted from his score an *Orchestral Suite* (H60A, Category 7A), consisting of Nos. 2/3, 7, 16, 11, and 17/18 (without 18D), in that order. Number 7 ("La Neige sur Rome") also exists in a transcription for solo piano (H60B, Category 1A)
N.B. 3: One could make an excellent second suite for the concert hall using Nos. 4/5, 9, 12, 20, 24/25, and 14, in that order (duration: 22 minutes 30 seconds)
N.B. 4: No. 20, except for the middle section, is identical with "Prospero's Cell" from *The Tempest* (H48)
N.B. 5: Nos. 3, 5, 6, 10, 12, 13, 21, 22, and 23 have indications (cues) for Ida Rubinstein's spoken contributions
Salabert

L'Impératrice aux rochers is one of Honegger's most massive scores, and far and away his longest piece of incidental music. It lasts over an hour, and is scored for large orchestra, in part with chorus. It is a vast "portfolio of pictures" in which the music, while creating atmosphere, has no pretensions to symphonic development, nor to the psychological study of characters. It is not highly complex and requires no detailed analysis.

Willy Tappolet sums up the story as follows[1]:

The Empress Victoria is ruling in Rome. While her husband, the Emperor Aurelius, is out hunting, he is wounded by an arrow fired by an unknown hand. It is Otho, a pretender to the throne, who has tried to commit this murder.

After the Emperor's departure for the Holy Land, Otho tries to gain the Empress's favors. But none of his ploys succeeds in winning her over. Then, on the Emperor's return, she finds herself slandered and even rejected. She is condemned to die on a rock.

But the Holy Virgin intervenes. She has taken pity on the innocent woman, grants her life, and gives her a miraculous flower. A drop of the dew distilled from it cures Otho, who is infected with the plague. And he, once cured, takes Victoria back to her husband Aurelius.

The long prologue with narrator seems not to have been given at the premiere. The narrator is a "ringmaster" whose patter interrupts the music to explain the story and introduce the various characters. This is very close to the technique used later in *Christopher Columbus* and in *Saint François d'Assise*, both written with William Aguet for the radio. Logically enough, the music is a kind of gallery, showing several of the score's main themes. Music plays its largest role in Acts III and IV. The chorus is heard briefly in Act I, then more substantially in Act IV and the last finale. I will content myself here with saying a little about the pieces that might go to make up a second suite, since the already existing one has been discussed in Category 7A.

Number 4 ("The Council Chamber") is a fine, broad, well-developed movement in B-flat minor, which could very well open such a suite, and which reaches its climax in No. 5 ("Entrance of the Pope"), based on the same material. Number 9 ("The Tower") is a dark, dramatic movement in F-sharp minor, and is based on Prince Otho's sinister motif and two other striking ideas. It rises to a pitch of considerable rhythmic violence, before sinking back into guarded menace. Number 12 ("Open-air Music") is a charming intermezzo for a small orchestra of two flutes, English horn, clarinet, two horns, celesta, harp, violins, and violas, in B major; again, the theme has a Fauréan gracefulness. Number 14 ("The Return of the Emperor"), already reused as the Finale of the *Partita for two pianos*, would make an excellent ending for a second suite. This could also include No. 20 ("The Rock"), the outer sections of which are a repeat of "The Magic Cape" from *The Tempest* (it is unclear, in fact, which was the repeat and which the original, but *The Tempest* was certainly put on after *L'Impératrice aux rochers*), and Nos. 24 and 25 run together.

Number 24 ("The Ruins of the Temple") is in a gentle 9/8 rhythm and its tone is set by the nostalgic, ascending theme in F minor on the English horn, contrasting with the sudden animation of No. 25 ("The Square in Front of the Cathedral"). Here a decisive ostinato in sixteenth-notes on the bassoon gives way in the middle section to the tender theme of the Empress, on the English horn. This itself is framed by the ceremonious chorale on brass in D major that will dominate the choral Finale. This Finale will lead to a peaceful apotheosis and thence to a gentle coda, a final homage to Fauré. The vocalises in this superb polyphonic passage are strongly reminiscent of the Fauréan ones in No. 24 of *Le Roi David* ("I shall love the Lord with a tender love").

61. *Phaedra*

Incidental music for the tragedy by Gabriele d'Annunzio (French translation by
   André Doderet)
March–April 1926 (probably completed around 10 April)
"To André George." Commissioned by Ida Rubinstein
First performance: 19 April 1926, Ida Rubinstein, decor by A. Bakst, conducted by
   Arthur Honegger, Teatro Costanzi, Rome
Performing forces: 2.2.2.2.-2.2.3.1.–timpani, cymbals–strings–eight contraltos
   (unison chorus)
Duration of music: 26 minutes 30 seconds (22 minutes of this are taken over into the
   Suite, H61A)
Act I: 1. Prelude; 2. Procession of the Suppliants
Act II: 3. Prelude; 4. The Kiss; 5. Curse of Theseus
Act III: 6. Prelude; 7. Lamentations of Aethra; 8. Chorus of the Priestesses of
   Aphrodite (in the list of contents in the autograph this is given as "Song of the
   Young Men"); 9. Death of Phaedra
N.B. 1: The eight contraltos sing in Nos. 3, 7, and 8
N.B. 2: The *Orchestral Suite* (H61A, Category 7A) contains Nos. 1, 2, 3, 5, 6, and 9
Only the *Orchestral Suite* (H61A) has been published, by Salabert

Although the score of *Phaedra* is much shorter than that of *L'Impératrice aux rochers*, it is very much more significant. Only three very short pieces, lasting four and a half minutes in all, are omitted from the *Orchestral Suite* (H61A): "The Kiss," full of plaintive languor; the highly Oriental "Lamentations of Aethra"; and the twinging 5/4 "Chorus of the Priestesses of Aphrodite."

146. *Mandragora*

Incidental music for the play by Niccolò Machiavelli
11 March 1941 (date of completion)
First performance: 2 April 1941, Troupe of Le Jeune Colombier, produced by Jean-Jacques Aubier, Théâtre Monceau, Paris (on the same bill: *L'Ombre de la ravine*, H147)
Performing forces: flute, alto saxophone, harp, piano duet, side drum, string quartet (ten players)
Duration of music: 21 minutes
Nine numbers
Unpublished

This is delicate chamber music for a very particular instrumental grouping, with numerous harp and piano solos. It is very simple, tonal music, often with a popular feel, but too closely tied to the stage action to stand on its own.

147. *L'Ombre de la ravine* (The Shadow of the Ravine)

Incidental music for the play by J. M. Synge
March 1941 (Prelude: 18 March; Postlude: 19 March)
First performance: 2 April 1941, Troupe of Le Jeune Colombier, produced by Jean-Jacques Aubier, Théâtre Monceau, Paris (on the same bill: *Mandragora*, H146)
Performing forces: flute, harp, and string quartet
Duration of music: 4 minutes 45 seconds
Salabert

The incidental music for *L'Ombre de la ravine*, too, is chamber music, in two thematically linked sections. It could well be played in the concert hall, where it would create a misty, neoimpressionist atmosphere. Delightful, for all its brevity.

The quantity of Honegger's incidental music in 1941, after many years of silence on this front, stems from the temporary closure of cinema studios because of the war and the Occupation, which deprived Honegger of his basic livelihood. This situation would be repeated in 1943–1944, but in the meantime the composer returned to the film world.

149. *Les Suppliantes*

Incidental music for the tragedy by Aeschylus, in the translation by André Bonnard
May–June 1941, Paris (Chorus I: 11 May 1941; score completed: 7 June 1941)
First performance: 5 July 1941, Yvonne Gouverné Chorale, Conservatory Concert Society, conducted by Charles Münch, Roland-Garros Stadium, Paris (on the same bill: *Huit Cent Mètres*, H150)
Performing forces: female chorus (plus solo tenor and male chorus in Chorus III); two clarinets, two bassoons, three trumpets, four trombones, ondes Martenot, timpani, percussion (bass drum, cymbals, rattle, side drum, tam-tam, tambourine, triangle)—fourteen instrumentalists in all
Duration of music: 31 minutes 15 seconds
1. Prelude; 2. Melodrama I; (unnumbered) Fanfare for the Suppliants; 3. Chorus I (with Panic Dance); 4. Greeting to the Gods; 5. Chorus II; 6. Chorus III; 7. Melodrama II; 8. Chorus IV; 9. Entrance of the Egyptians; 10. Chorus V; 11. Chorus VI; 12. Melodrama III; 13. Chorus VII
Unpublished

Les Suppliantes is the earliest and longest of Honegger's four sets of inci-
dental music for Greek tragedies. Unlike the two versions of *Oedipus*, both *Les
Suppliantes* and *Prométhée* (in excellent French translations by the great Swiss
Hellenist André Bonnard) were intended for performance in the open air.
These two scores also use similar resources, even though their musical language differs. Honegger explained the options he chose for *Prométhée* (see
H187, where his text is reproduced), and it is extraordinary to see to what extent
it corresponds with that adopted later by Xenakis, even to the musical result:
unison or two-part chorus, predominance of wind and percussion, and modal
and diatonic language. The only clear difference is in Xenakis's use of the original Greek text as a further aid to authenticity.

José Bruyr is, once again, the only commentator to discuss *Les Suppliantes*.
He makes a few mistakes over the forces involved, but speaks rightly of the
"sultry howling" of the ondes Martenot, and of the decorative final procession,
which he compares with that of *Judith*. The score consists mainly of a long
orchestral Prelude (with shouts from the chorus) and seven great choruses. The
Prelude is based on the solemn theme heard first in the trombones (Example
157), symbolizing the majesty of Zeus. It shows a tendency found throughout
the score, to use both the major and minor third, corresponding to the Greek
"chromatic" mode (replacing the interval of a second by the minor third).

Example 157

Chorus I is the longest of the seven. It introduces the 12/8 meter which will
recur frequently because it is best fitted to the trochees (long-short) of ancient
prosody. The line of these modal monodies is spare and strong, with the mobile
third degree, and every now and again we find Honegger's typical accentuation:
"Je me plais à *gémir*" (I take pleasure in my groans). A violent accelerando leads
to the "Panic Dance," where the orchestra takes a far more active part; and we
may be surprised to discover the music of the 3/4 Vivace marcato section of
the future *Monopartita*, in the same key of B minor. The movement ends with
an extremely violent tutti, with flutter-tonguing, furious glissandos on ondes
Martenot, and cross-accents.

The beginning of Chorus II is an exception in being in two parts, while
the male chorus's only appearance in Chorus III, barbarous in its ferocity, is in
four parts (but heterophonic rather than polyphonic). Chorus V is the most
dramatic of all, as the words dictate ("A terrible fear takes hold of me"). From
its disturbed, convulsive beginning, it moves on, at the height of the sacred
horror, to shouting pure and simple, the final cry of panic, which leads directly
into Chorus VI. This is a brief, flashing battle scene. There is no singing here,
and the climactic paroxysm of shouting abruptly fades at the liberating entrance

of the Greeks, with the brass roughly hammering away at C major. The catharsis comes with the majestic procession of Chorus VII, which can be compared (on a smaller scale) with the one that crowns Milhaud's *Eumenides*. The music now abandons the modality that has prevailed so far and becomes resplendently tonal, culminating in an A major of great orchestral splendor. The score of *Les Suppliantes* is both grandiose and concise, and would be perfectly viable in the concert hall in the form of the Prelude and the seven Choruses. Its direct impact realizes the ideal Honegger expressed of music that would be "straightforward, simple, and impressive."[2]

150. *Huit Cent Mètres* (800 Meters)

Incidental music for André Obey's "sporting drama"
June 1941
First performance: 5 July 1941, Roland-Garros Stadium, Paris (on the same bill: *Les Suppliantes*, H149)
Lost. The performing forces and duration are unknown

Paul le Flem's review (*Paris-Midi*, 8 July 1941) gives an idea of what the music of *Huit Cent Mètres* was like:

> Honegger proceeds mostly by brief touches of sound. Like the interjections of the crowd and the jokes of the speaker, the music contributes to the whole in a sporadic, dissipated manner, in line with the scenario. It melts into the ensemble, rather than risking a voice of its own. It has an episodic character, underlining rhythms, disappearing suddenly, and reappearing to vanish once more.

151. *La Ligne d'horizon*

Incidental music for the play "in two acts and nine ports of call" by Serge Roux
September 1941
First performance: 25 October 1941, Théâtre des Bouffes-Parisiens, Paris
Performing forces: 1.1.1.1.–alto saxophone–1.2.2.0.–percussion (cymbals, tam-tam, tenor drum, triangle, woodblock), xylophone, piano, Hawaiian guitar–strings; solo tenor and unison male chorus
Duration of music: 18 minutes 50 seconds
Act I: 1. The Port of Cannes (The Departure); 2. On the Sea (Destination Unknown); 3. In Sight of Syracuse (News Items, with solo tenor); 4. Samos (One Minute); 5. Pondichéry (The Bets Are Laid, with solo tenor)
Act II: 6. Shanghai (The Prison of Habit); 7. Hiva Hoha (Request Stop); 8. Honolulu (A Retreat); 9. Tomorrow (Life Begins Again, with unison male chorus)
Unpublished

These nine pieces are written for a small chamber orchestra, of the kind then found in the cinema pit, and make up an entertaining collection of musical images in which Honegger treats us to his own version of his friend Ibert's *Escales* (Ports of Call). It would go well on radio with a linking narrative acting as a summary of Serge Roux's play. These simple, delicate watercolors do not call for analysis.

165. *Le Soulier de satin* (The Satin Slipper)

Incidental music for Paul Claudel's play
March 1943
First performance: 27 November 1943, conducted by André Jolivet, Comédie-
    Française, Paris
Performing forces: soprano, baritone, chorus–clarinet, trumpet–percussion (bass
    drum, cymbals, maracas, side drum, tam-tam, triangle; one performer)–ondes
    Martenot, piano–strings
Duration of music: very hard to estimate, because the pieces are very short and not
    musically autonomous, with only two of them (Nos. 15 and 16) lasting more
    than two minutes
In all, twenty-three pieces, of which the longest are: 1. Overture; 5. Rumba of
    Jobarbara (with soprano); 10. Chorus of the Trial (with soprano, baritone, and
    chorus); 15. The Double Shadow (with soprano and baritone); 16. The Moon;
    21. Death of Prouhèze; 23. Final Scene
Salabert

From the stage point of view, *Le Soulier de satin* is certainly one of Honegger's most important pieces of incidental music, and Claudel put this collaboration on the same level as that in *Jeanne d'Arc au bûcher* and *La Danse des morts*.
But from the musical point of view, Honegger's contribution amounts to no
more than a large number of short pieces, which certainly work in the theater
but not on their own. The lovely "Rumba of Jobarbara" (1 minute 45 seconds
of music) and "The Double Shadow" (3 minutes)—which suggested to Pierre
Boulez the title of one of his recent works—are almost the only pieces that
might be played outside their original context.

Honegger behaved, in fact, with his usual excessive modesty in putting
himself at the service of Claudel and following his indications, very precise as
always, to the letter. As he wrote to the poet: "I'm very proud, rather like the flea
in the lion's mane." The very real abnegation implied by the task of the illuminator (which could very well have made for an appropriate title for this chapter),
means that the best incidental music is one that succeeds totally in effacing
itself, but that one would sorely miss if it were not there.

172. *Sodome et Gomorrhe* (Sodom and Gomorrah)

Incidental music for the play by Jean Giraudoux
September or October 1943
First performance: 10 October 1943, Théâtre Hébertot
Performing forces: six trombones, two timpani, cymbals, tam-tam
Duration: seven very short pieces
Unpublished

These scraps of music would be of interest chiefly to trombonists, because
of the very strange effects (flutter-tonguing, mutes, and so on).

175. *Charles le Téméraire* (Charles the Bold)

Incidental music for the play in four acts and six tableaux (with prologue) by René
    Morax
January–24 February 1944

First performance: 27 May 1944, Leopold Biberti (Charles), female chorus, Choral
 Union of Vevey, brass band, conducted by Carlo Hemmerling, Théâtre du
 Jorat, Mézières (Vaud)
Performing forces: numerous spoken roles; mixed chorus; two trumpets, two
 trombones–percussion (timpani, side drum, bass drum, tam-tam, bells, muffled
 drum)
Duration of music: 16 minutes
Eight choruses, two fanfares, one march
Editions Papillon, Geneva

The music for this final and more modest collaboration with René Morax
needs little commentary. Morax's play is long and complicated and suffers from
dramaturgical weaknesses: the battle of Morat is an almost identical repeat of
the battle of Grandson and, even if Charles's profound neurosis is penetrat-
ingly observed, there are too many secondary plots which tend to distract the
spectator from the main action. There is also the extra invention of a young
girl from the Vaud who is in love with the Duke and who rejoins the Burgun-
dian ranks and pays for her loyalty with her life.

As money was short, Honegger this time had only an amateur chorus and
a small brass band, and one can only admire his skill in making so much of so little. The only choruses that are remotely substantial are Nos. 1, 2, 4, 7, and 8
(Nos. 3, 4, 5, and 6 are unaccompanied). Some of the choruses return to the
atmosphere of *Nicolas de Flue*, which shares some of the same story, but in a
sparer, more austere style. These simple, straightforward pieces would certainly be a blessing for amateur choral societies if they were easily obtainable in
print, which is not the case at the moment. The violence of Chorus III, in which
the Swiss sing of their victory and hatred in a brutal hymn, is in complete contrast with both the gentle charm of Chorus IV, in which the full chorus accompanies the soloist in a truly orchestral way, and with Chorus VI, for female chorus only, with its supple counterpoint around the Gregorian plainchant "Salva
nos, Domine."

Choruses VII and VIII, however, are the finest and longest. The last, in
particular, ends in a short but impressive Requiem aeternam for six voices—
only twelve measures long, but of an authentic grandeur that makes us regret
that Honegger never wrote a complete Requiem. The brief "Military March,"
no doubt intended for the end of Act III, between Choruses VI and VII, is
notable for its very strange modulations and for its striking fanfares.

187. *Prométhée* (Prometheus)

Incidental music for the tragedy by Aeschylus, in the French translation by André
 Bonnard
January–May 1946 (No. 10: 30 January 1946; Choruses: completed before March;
 Prelude: March; Finale: 19 May 1946)
First performance: 5 June 1946, Avenches Open-Air Theater (Vaud)
Performing forces: female chorus; three clarinets, three bassoons, three trumpets,
 three trombones–percussion (bass drum, cymbals, suspended cymbal, tam-tam,
 tenor drum, triangle, antique cymbal in E, timpani in C and E)
Duration of music: 24 minutes
1. Prelude; 2. Entrance of the Oceanides; 3. Interlude; 4. Entrance of the Chariot of

the Ocean; 5. Chorus of the Oceanides; 6. Chorus of the Oceanides; 7. Repeat of No. 3; 8. Chorus of the Oceanides; 9. Departure of Io; 10. Chorus of Oceanides; 11. Finale
Unpublished

Prométhée was Honegger's second and, unfortunately, last setting of Aeschylus, for which he had the benefit of André Bonnard's exemplary translation. The performing forces he chose are very similar to those in *Les Suppliantes*, with the one important difference that here there are no ondes Martenot—no doubt they were impossible to find in Switzerland in the spring of 1946. The setting this time was far more impressive than Roland-Garros stadium: the play was staged in the Roman theater of Avenches (Aventicum), the capital of Roman Helvetia. The place lies not far from Morat and its lake, in the fertile valley of the river Broye which, upstream, waters Moudon.

There are only four choruses, as against the seven in *Les Suppliantes*, but the instrumental sections are decidedly longer (No. 2 in particular). The music itself is quite different from that in the earlier work, being much harsher and more complex, and often atonal (in short more "modern"). In this sense, *Prométhée* is to *Les Suppliantes* what *Judith* was to *Le Roi David*. From the opening measures of the Prelude, the terrible Aeschylean stridency of this music seizes us by the throat. These hard blocks of brass and these shrieking clarinets belong to a mineral, unbreathable universe.

Soon the sound expands into a rough chorale that looks forward to the beginning of the *Fifth Symphony*, though here it is atonal. Only the compassionate Oceanides will bring some touches of human warmth to these icy wastes of the Caucasus, from their appearance in No. 2 to the sound of music that is extraordinarily fluid and luminous. Their choruses are more complex and chromatic than those in *Les Suppliantes* and are surrounded by a much richer orchestral texture, which also tends to obscure the sense of tonality. But their monody obeys the same principles of scansion—a synthesis of Greek prosody and Honegger's own style of accentuation. The second chorus in particular is a model of exact declamation, of true choral recitative. In the Finale's last thirteen measures of grandiose coda, the music returns to the brazen sonorities and savage atmosphere of the beginning.

I think it is interesting to read at this point what Honegger himself wrote, explaining the principles that guided him in writing *Les Suppliantes* and *Prométhée*.[3]

We know very little in detail about the part music played in Greek tragedy. Scholars such as Paul Mazon, Henri Berguin, and Paul Masqueray agree in considering the melodramas as a psalmlike declamation, articulated by a flute accompaniment from which it stood out. Following this conception, I thought I could enlarge the scope of this accompaniment and make it polyphonic, without infringing upon its style, because it is possible that there were several flutes playing their own parts. Most translators, taking their cue from the different meters employed and from what Mazon calls "the evidence for the character of each of them," have accompanied the text with musical indications which I thought it prudent to bear in mind.

The choruses are set almost wholly as monody, firstly to aid compre-
hension of the text, and secondly because, as G. Urbain says, "the singers
confined themselves to the unison." In the musical language proper, I have
deliberately stayed well away from anything that might recall the classical
tonal system, which in any case does not seem to me to have anything to do
with the evocation of archaic Greece.

190. *Hamlet*

Incidental music for Shakespeare's play, in the translation by André Gide
August–September 1946
First performance: 17 October 1946, produced by Jean-Louis Barrault, Théâtre
   Marigny, Paris
Performing forces: soprano (Ophelia), men's voices; three trumpets, three
   trombones–timpani, three percussionists (bass drum, cymbals, side drum,
   triangle, woodblock)–ondes Martenot
Duration of music: consists of very short fragments
The music includes eight fanfares, seven pieces for ondes Martenot and percussion,
   and four pieces for unaccompanied singers
Salabert

Of the fanfares, only the last, a proud "Funeral March," is at all substantial.
From the movements for ondes and percussion, one could pick out the "Interlude" and "Pantomime," two charming miniatures that would be performable
out of context. Of the sung pieces, the third, for Ophelia ("If he has not already
returned") proves, surprisingly, to have been the origin of the theme of the
Andante from the *Concerto da camera* (see Example 74).

194. *Oedipus*

Incidental music for the play by Sophocles, in the translation by André Obey
June 1947
First performance: 19 December 1947, Théâtre des Champs-Élysées, Paris
Performing forces: unison chorus, two ondes Martenot, bass drum, cymbals,
   xylophone
Duration of music: about 20 minutes (17 of them for chorus)
1. Prelude; 2. Fanfares; 3. Chorus I; 4. Chorus II; 5. Chorus IIa; 6. Chorus III; 7.
   Entrance of Jocasta; 8. Chorus IV; 9. Chorus V; 10. Interlude; 11. Melodrama;
   12. Exit of Oedipus; 13. Final curtain
Unpublished. Held by Salabert

The unison choruses are quite extended and return to the simple modal
style of those in *Les Suppliantes*. They are thus quite different from the more
complex ones in *Prométhée*. The ondes Martenot mainly give cues to the voices,
but sometimes they enter into dialogue with them. The vocal writing is highly
varied: straight speech, rhythmic speech, homophonic passages for two or three
voices, alternation between a solo voice and the ensemble, and so forth. Of the
very short instrumental fragments, four (Nos. 1, 7, 10, and 12) could well be
performed in the concert hall.

195. L'État de siège

Incidental music for the play by Albert Camus
October 1948
First performance: 27 October 1948, produced by Jean-Louis Barrault, Théâtre
    Marigny, Paris
Lost

The score has disappeared—it was destroyed during the riots of May 1968 at the Théâtre de l'Odéon—but there exists a recording of a performance in the archives of INA in Paris.

208. On ne badine pas avec l'amour (Do Not Trifle With Love)

Incidental music for the play by Alfred de Musset
November 1951
First performance: 13 December 1951, produced by Jean-Louis Barrault, Théâtre
    Marigny, Paris
Lost

The score of *On ne badine pas avec l'amour* was also destroyed during the riots of May 1968 at the Théâtre de l'Odéon.

210. Oedipe-Roi (Oedipus Rex)

Incidental music for the tragedy by Sophocles, in the translation by Thierry
    Maulnier
March–3 April 1952
First performance: 14 May 1952, Comédie-Française, Paris
Performing forces: spoken chorus; 1.1.1.1.–0.1.1.0.–percussion (bass drum,
    bouteillophone, cymbals, high drum, low drum, tam-tam)–ondes Martenot—
    nine performers in all
Duration of music: around 15 minutes (consists of very short fragments)
1. Overture and Scene 1; 2. Entrance of Creon; 3. Exit of Oedipus; 4. Entrance of
    the People, and Ritornello during Chorus I; 5. Entrance of Tiresias; 6.
    Ritornello during Chorus II; 7. Ritornello during Chorus III; 8. Entrance of
    Jocasta; 8a. Cries of Jocasta; 9. Ritornello during Chorus IV; 10. Ritornello
    during Chorus V; 11. Melodrama (Oedipus and the Chorus); 12. Finale
Unpublished

This is Honegger's last set of incidental music, and also the last original music he wrote (unless we count the little *Romance for flute and piano*, H211). It is a remarkably unified and concentrated score. Although the Overture lasts only three minutes, it is an unusually powerful piece and certainly more than a mere prelude. It immediately presents us with Oedipus's strident theme, a veritable cry in which we can recognize the hand that wrote the beginning of the *Fifth Symphony* (Example 158). The somber, syncopated procession recalls the slow Trios in the second movement of that symphony. All through the score, one is struck by the highly original use made of the ondes Martenot, as well as of the bouteillophone, first employed in *Le Dit des jeux du monde* over thirty years earlier.

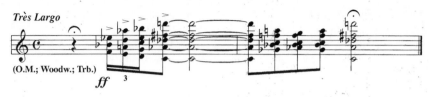

Example 158

Category 15: Music for Radio

84. *Les Douze Coups de minuit*
92. *Radio-Panoramique* (see Category 7)
140. *Christopher Columbus*
163. *Pasiphaé* (see Category 4A)
176. *Battements du monde*
197. *Saint François d'Assise*
198. *Marche contre la Mort*
199. *Tête d'Or*
209. *La Rédemption de François Villon*

As I have already said, it is surely here, in his music for radio, in the absence of any visual support, that Honegger's "image-making" genius declares itself most strikingly. By far the greatest contribution to this area of his output was made by the three collaborations with William Aguet, which count among the most important works ever written for radio. A version of *Don Quixote* was intended to form a trilogy with *Christopher Columbus* and *Saint François d'Assise*, but the project was never realized and was in the event replaced by *Battements du monde*.

84. *Les Douze Coups de minuit* (The Twelve Strokes of Midnight)

Radio mystery by Carlos Larronde
End of 1933
First broadcast: 27 December 1933, Groupe Art et Action, produced by Mme
    Autant-Lara, Colonial Radio Service
First concert performance: 10 May 1935, Conservatory Concert Hall, Paris
Performing forces: mixed chorus; harp, piano duet, organ–timpani, percussion
Duration: eleven very short fragments
Unpublished

Carlos Larronde's radio mystery is set in the year 1040—a year in which numerous plagues threatened the end of the world—and describes the building of a cathedral. But the manuscript contains only a dozen brief fragments, more like "sound objects." No recording has survived and, as there are no indications of production or of the spoken text, we can no longer get any idea of how all these elements came together. All we know is that the result was substantial enough to warrant a concert revival.

140. *Christopher Columbus*

Radio play by William Aguet
January–21 February 1940
Commissioned by Lausanne Radio
First broadcast: 15 April 1940, William Aguet (narrator), François Porché Chorus, Suisse Romande Orchestra, conducted by Ernest Ansermet, Studio of Lausanne Radio (La Sallaz)
Performing forces: spoken roles: Narrator (The Magician), Christopher Columbus, King Ferdinand, Queen Isabella, several small roles; solo tenor; mixed chorus; orchestra: 1.1.2.1.–2.3.2.0.–timpani, two percussionists (bass drum, cymbals, bells, rattle, side drum, tam-tam, woodblock)–harp–strings
Duration: 63 minutes 20 seconds (38 minutes of music)
First tableau: 1. Prologue
Second tableau (The Alhambra Palace): 2. Evocation; 3. Burlesque Coronation; 4. Exit of the King
Third tableau (The Rabida Chapel): 5. End of Mass; 6. Procession (Chorus of sailors)
Fourth tableau (Palos): 7. Lamentations of the Women of Palos; 8. Departure of Christopher Columbus
Fifth tableau (The Crossing): 9. Rhythm of Time; 10. Prayer of the Ships' Boys; 11. Miracle of the Wind; 12. Chant; 13. Prayer of Christopher Columbus; 14. Te Deum
Sixth tableau (The Return): no music
Seventh tableau (The Death of Queen Isabella): 15. Prayer of the Dead; 16. no title, leads into 17. Finale
N.B. Number 12, "Chant," became the second of the *Four Songs for Low Voice*, "Derrière Murcie en fleurs" (see H184, Category 8, in Chapter 10)
Salabert

William Aguet, a Swiss of French origin, was a writer, actor, and above all a man of radio. After René Morax, he was Honegger's second major collaborator in French-speaking Switzerland. *Christopher Columbus*, in particular, was hailed at the time by the critic Émile Vuillermoz as one of the composer's "most perfect achievements," which indicates a work of no secondary importance, but one which, like the future *Saint François d'Assise*, is a true oratorio for radio, and as such able to be performed in the concert hall.

Christopher Columbus contains some of Honegger's most moving and memorable ideas, and certain choruses especially are at least as good as the more famous ones in *Le Roi David*. Honegger is here at his most inventive and spontaneous, and understands perfectly the particular demands of radio—notably the difficulty of having music and speech sounding simultaneously. In the Prologue for example, a succession of images of a medieval perfection, a "neutral" ritornello sets the scene for the introduction of each of the characters. In the movement "Rhythm of Time" (No. 9), which is repeated several times under spoken words and which, as it has to, evokes the monotony of the interminable crossing, Honegger manages never to tire the ear, thanks to tiny details of rhythm, harmony, and timbre. There is only one soloist—the tenor in No.

12—but there are a number of splendid choruses (Nos. 5, 6, 7, 8, 10, 13, 14, 15, and 17) that bring the work close to the great oratorios.

The seventeen numbers in the score of *Christopher Columbus* are spread over six of the seven tableaux of Aguet's play (the sixth does not contain any music). The Prologue sets the scene with a few energetic measures: an ascending pentatonic theme of a heroic character, symbolizing the celebrated *descubridor*, and a threefold call from the chorus. All this lasts exactly ten seconds. Then the Narrator appears. He is a true master of ceremonies, in this case a Magician, trying to capture Columbus's face in his mirror. His long search forms the subject of the Prologue. It is an evocation of a whole epoch, because the mirror shows successively the last battle of The Hundred Years' War, King Louis XI astride his mule, the burning of Savonarola, Leonardo da Vinci painting *The Last Supper*, François Villon in a field of gibbets, and many others. Every time, Honegger creates the exact image in just a few measures.

Finally, a peddler puts the Magician on the right track, and the second tableau takes us to the court of the Catholic Kings at Grenada. Here, Columbus is the subject of jests and snubs, except from Isabella, who manages to persuade her royal husband to finance the expedition. Most notable in this tableau is the suggestive orchestral "Evocation" (No. 2) of the fabulous world of Columbus's imagining. With the expedition decided upon, the third tableau takes us to the Rabida Chapel. Here we find the splendid "Procession" (No. 6)—the first great climax of the score, with the alternation between the chorus of sailors and their fine theme in the tenors (Example 159) and the monks' solemn "Ave maris stella" in the basses. Finally, the women join the sailors, who are about to depart.

Example 159

In the fourth tableau, we are in the port of Palos for the embarkation. After a brief chorus of lamentation from the women, we come to the second high point, the chorus No. 8 accompanying the "Departure of Christopher Columbus." The women's theme (Example 160) is splendidly rhythmical with a marine swing to it, and its Lydian fourth recalls the "great unassuaged departures" of Fauré's song cycle *L'Horizon chimérique*—Columbus, after all, has his own horizons. In the fifth and longest tableau ("The Crossing"), the musical insertions are more numerous, but shorter. The most notable of them are the delightful "Prayer of the Ships' Boys" (No. 10), which is on the same level as the canticles in *Le Roi David* with its alternating major and minor thirds; the astonishing descriptive music in the "Miracle of the Wind" (No. 11) with its glissandos in harmonics; the nostalgically Spanish solo tenor's "Chant" (No. 12);

the tenderly reflective "Prayer of Christopher Columbus" (No. 13); and finally the Te Deum that greets the sighting of the American soil—this last insertion is only a minute long, but represents a tremendous explosion of joy.

A - dieu, Chris-tophe Co - lomb   A - dieu, des - cu - bri - dor

Example 160

The sixth tableau tells of Columbus's miserable return to Europe, a bitter and broken man, and does not contain any music. The third high point of the score is reached in the final tableau, telling of the death of Queen Isabella; poetic license enables Christopher Columbus to attend her in her final moments. Here the music is practically continuous, with first of all the "Prayer of the Dead" (No. 15), consisting of an impressively austere De profundis in the Phrygian mode on E, later combined with the plainchant of the women's Libera me, Domine, sung on a single pitch (*recto tono*).

The final meeting of the *descubridor* and the dying queen is accompanied by a very beautiful Adagio in E major on muted strings (No. 16)—tender, ethereal music which fades into eternity. Aguet's text is of the highest quality ("It is my turn now," says the Queen, "to discover a world still greater than that which you have given us"). The brief Finale (No. 17), spare yet grand, returns once more to the material of the "Prayer of the Dead," with the support of the full orchestra.

176. *Battements du monde* (Heartbeats of the World)

Radio play by William Aguet
January 1944; orchestrated March 1944
Commissioned by Lausanne Radio
First broadcast: 18 May 1944, William Aguet (narrator), Suisse Romande Chorus and Orchestra, conducted by Ernest Ansermet, Studio of Radio Lausanne (La Sallaz)
Performing forces: spoken roles: the Narrator, the Devil; solo soprano, solo children's voices, female chorus; orchestra: 2.2.2.2.–2.2.2.0.–timpani, percussion (bass drum, cymbals, side drum, tenor drum, tambourine, triangle) harp, piano–strings
Duration of music: 27 minutes 20 seconds, in fifty very short sections, some of which are repeats and several of which run into each other; the longest lasts no more than thirty-four measures. Duration of total program: 46 minutes 30 seconds
Salabert

If *Christopher Columbus* and *Saint François d'Assise* are practically radio oratorios, the same is not true of *Battements du monde*. Deeply moving as it is, there is an intimate osmosis between text and music, with the latter being broken up into tiny sections. Even where they run into each other, the longest stretch of continuous music (which comes twice) is no longer than three minutes.

This commission from Radio Lausanne came at the instigation of the International Union for Children's Aid, and it is a protest against the barbarism that war inflicts upon them. The man covered with sin, but wanting to regain the path of his lost childhood, is led by a child made mute by the horrors of war. The Devil reveals himself as a formidable protagonist, representing the total powerlessness to love that is the absolute evil. Even the polluted elements abandon man (the destruction of the environment now takes care of this in peacetime!) and the starving children beg to be fed: "Have some grenades!" says the Devil. (In French, the word *grenade* means both grenade and pomegranate.) They implore to be allowed to remain small, and pray "for these wretched little ones who pretend to be big." At the end, the pilgrim meets Eros and is horrified to discover that he has the face of a leper, because mankind has spat in his face. At the moment when the Devil seems to be triumphant, there arrives the ultimate salvation: the Child Jesus in the cradle—child, man, and God—in whom each of us can reconcile the child and the adult. With this vision the work reaches a peaceful conclusion.

Apart from the two crucial spoken roles of the Man and the Devil, there is also a large part for the spoken children's chorus, which sings only in No. 44, the canticle "Ô doux Seigneur" (O Sweet Lord). This has been published separately, and even recorded. As in *Christopher Columbus* and *Saint François d'Assise*, there is only a single solo number, but it is one of the pinnacles of the work, a moving lullaby for mezzo-soprano and chorus dedicated to the children who as yet exist only in their mothers' imaginations. But everything in this score demands to be quoted, up to the serene polyphony of the conclusion, which looks forward to *Une Cantate de Noël*.

At the extreme opposite is the Devil's leitmotif, a sneering clarinet solo, and the eerily barbarous "March of the Ogres" (No. 46), the Herods of yesterday and today. And how can one dispel from one's mind the intolerable vision of the Nazi SS troops throwing Jewish children alive into the fires of their crematoria, or smashing their skulls against walls before their mothers' eyes? No doubt William Aguet, in safety in Switzerland, was unaware of such horrors at the beginning of 1944. *Battements du monde* remains one of those works of protest which, one hopes against hope, will no longer be needed at some future time.

197. *Saint François d'Assise* (Saint Francis of Assisi)

Radio play by William Aguet
Date of composition uncertain; most likely end of 1948–early 1949, certainly completed before 11 June 1949, the date of the recording by Lausanne Radio (see letter from Honegger to Paul Sacher, 12 June 1949)
Commissioned by Lausanne Radio
First broadcast: 3 June 1949, William Aguet (narrator), Hugues Cuenod (tenor), Chorus of La Tour-de-Peilz, conducted by Carlo Boller, Suisse Romande Orchestra, conducted by Ernest Ansermet, Radio Lausanne Studio (La Sallaz). The work was awarded the Swiss Radio Prize
Performing forces: narrator, solo tenor, mixed chorus; orchestra: 2.2.2.2.–0.3.3.0.– timpani, percussion (cymbals, tambourine, rattle, bells)–piano–strings; plus an

ensemble of ancient instruments for Nos. 4 and 5 (two recorders, quintet of viols, spinet)
Duration: 70 minutes 45 seconds (including 38 minutes of music)
Twenty-seven pieces, the longest of which are: 1. Orchestral Prelude (Allegretto); 4. Music for the Banquet (ancient instruments); 5. Song of the Troubadour (tenor and ancient instruments); 10. Reconstruction of the Church; 14. Foundation of the Clarissas; 16. Preaching to the Birds; 18. The Stigmata; 20. The Fire; 24. Canticle of the Sun; 25. Agony and Death of Francis; 26 and 27. Finale
Salabert

Of the three collaborations between Honegger and William Aguet, *Saint François d'Assise* is without doubt the most spiritual in feeling, both because of its subject and because of its chronological position. We can sense here the Honegger of his late style, with its pure, refined modal language. In their joint preface to the score, the two collaborators explained: "*Saint François d'Assise* is not a radio play, but the pious homage of a composer and a writer to a man for whom the language of God, man, and beasts held no secrets."

All twenty-seven movements are short—apart from the "Song of the Troubadour," No. 5, none is longer than three minutes—and in their concision we find the final synthesis of all the riches of his inspiration. There are no less than nine movements for wordless, unaccompanied chorus. Here, the Magician of *Christopher Columbus* has become the Juggler, which explains why the merry and lively Overture sounds like fairground music. In any case, it is soon joined by the broad, simple theme, like a cantus firmus, depicting the character of Francis.

Two movements (No. 4, "Music for the Banquet," and No. 5, "Song of the Troubadour" for tenor, the only movement involving a solo singer) call for a group of ancient instruments (recorders, viols, and a spinet) for a highly successful pastiche, although in reality it is more renaissance than medieval. This is the only use in the whole of Honegger's output of such instruments, which were not to be found everywhere in 1949!

The reconstruction of the church of Saint Damien is described in a robust and joyful choral piece (No. 10), full of emphatic dotted rhythms. Whereas the Palm Sunday procession (No. 12), in which Saint Claire takes part, includes the Gregorian plainchant *Pueri hebraeorum* in counterpoint with a sober, diatonic line on violins, the Magnificat greeting the foundation of the Clarissas (No. 14) is plainchant of Honegger's own invention. The preaching to the birds calls forth a charming descriptive symphony (No. 16) in which strings in rapidly crossing figurations imitate the beating of wings, while woodwinds and piano exchange brief "ornithological" replies. We are here halfway between *Mother Goose* and Messiaen, but Aguet specifies that tropical birds are not included, whereas Messiaen certainly included them in his opera on the same subject!

The movement describing the Stigmata (No. 18) is full of mute anguish and the least tonal in the work, with its chromatic falling triplets and an atmosphere recalling, at certain moments, that of Debussy's *The Martyrdom of Saint Sebastian*. Since I cannot cite every movement, I shall move on to the "Canticle of the Sun" (No. 24), which is one of the great moments in the score. The canticle is given as a spoken recitation, and beneath it the varied orchestral texture is articulated by a marvelous phrase that recurs like a refrain, each time a semitone higher: "Blessed be Thou, Lord my God, for our sister Death"(Example 161).

Example 161

The word "Death" is the only one that is harmonized, and always a minor third down (for example, in G-sharp minor when, as it is the first time, the phrase is in B). But there is a wonderful detail on the last repeat of this refrain when the phrase, in E, is harmonized not in the C-sharp minor we were expecting, but in C major. The phrase "for our sister Death" is immediately repeated, this time with a unison on the word "Death" in a moving spirit of acceptance, followed by a roll on timpani and a swelling tremolo low in the piano. The same theme (but this time given to the noble, sepulchral tones of the trombone) is found buried in the string polyphony of No. 25, accompanying the "Agony and Death of Francis."

The work ends in grandiose fashion with a double Finale (Nos. 26 and 27). We begin with a funeral procession (No. 26). The chromatic lament is articulated by low voices, like a litany, and harmonized in bare, infinitely desolate parallel fifths ("God has taken you from us, Francis, we shall never more hear your voice"). This alternates with the chant of the high voices, accompanied on the orchestra by diminutions of the litany. The sad procession fades, while a celestial voice encourages the crowd to sing something more cheerful to please the departed.

Then, without a break, comes the Finale proper (No. 27), one of Honegger's most complex movements, even though its thirty-four measures last a mere two minutes. Rarely has his polyphonic writing been as rich as in this A-A'-B form. The first two sections are based on a four-measure ostinato bass (F-sharp-E-C-D), transposed first into F, then G. The whole cycle is then repeated as A'. Above it rings out one of the most lovely Alleluia themes Honegger ever invented—an arabesque of pure vocal joy (Example 162).

Violins play a lighthearted, rhythmic theme against enormous bell-like chords on pianos. This all unrolls like a complex, festive piece of clockwork, from which the transpositions of the ostinato bass remove all risk of monotony. Honegger surpassed himself here and, as with Bach, the second cycle (A') adds

Example 162

further supplementary voices to the ensemble. The third cycle (B) is a coda based on the same material, which seems about to embark on a third series of variations, but after a surprise move to B-flat major settles in F-sharp major. The chorus has been silent during these three measures, but now it sings its Alleluias in pure homophony after all the polyphonic complexities. In my opinion, this finale surpasses the famous one in *Le Roi David* and constitutes on its own a justification for putting on the magnificent work it brings to an end.

198. *Marche contre la Mort* (March Against Death)

Radio score on a text by Antoine de Saint-Exupéry in memory of the aviator Henri
    Guillaumet, "The Eagle of the Andes"
Summer 1949, Paris
Commissioned by Experimental Studio of French Radio
Lost

If Honegger had not mentioned the work in a letter of 3 July 1949 to Ernest Ansermet, and if it did not appear in his manuscript catalog, we might question its existence.

199. *Tête d'Or* (Head of Gold)

Music for a radio version of the play by Paul Claudel
December 1949–January 1950
First broadcast: sometime in 1950, French Radio. The recording was made on 16
    January 1950
Performing forces: 1.1.1.1.–0.3.3.0.–timpani, percussion (bass drum, suspended
    cymbal, side drum, tam-tam, rattle, muted drum)–strings
Duration of music: very hard to estimate, perhaps some twenty minutes; the play and
    music together last 106 minutes in all
Twenty-one movements, the longest of which is forty-two measures
Unpublished

Version by Pierre Boulez
Made at the request of Andrée Vaurabourg for the performances of Claudel's *Tête
    d'Or* at the Odéon-Théâtre de France
First performance: 21 October 1959, Alain Cuny in the title role, produced by Jean-
    Louis Barrault, decor and costumes by André Masson, Odéon-Théâtre de
    France, Paris
Performing forces: 1.1.1.1.–1.2.1.0.–timpani, percussion, harp–strings
Duration: Boulez extended some of Honegger's pieces and composed new ones,
    more than doubling the length of the score (676 measures instead of 291)
Salabert has a photocopy of the autograph manuscript

The music for *Tête d'Or* is unique in existing in two versions by two different composers. It began as a radio score, because Claudel's play, at his own insistence, was not given on the stage in his lifetime. In 1959, four years after the deaths of both Claudel and Honegger, Pierre Boulez made a new version for the production by Jean-Louis Barrault. By that time Boulez was no longer Barrault's house composer.

He adapted the performing forces to those available at the Odéon, but his work amounts really to a recomposition and contains a quantity of new music.

The main instrumental problem Boulez had to resolve was the presence in the original of three trumpets and three trombones, which he had to replace by only one horn, two trumpets, and one trombone. He also added a harp and considerably filled out the percussion section—no surprise, coming from him. Overall his version is, as we might expect, more complex, more refined, more "modern." This is not to say that it necessarily equals the harsh, "primitive" power of the original, which is spare and grandiose, in Honegger's late manner, in short paragraphs, in an austere, diatonic, modal style, but not afraid to indulge in fairly abrupt dissonances. The tempos are in general slow or moderate, often in 3/4, with the usual proliferation of dotted rhythms. It is music quite close to that for the final film documentaries on Bourdelle (H201) and Claudel (H206). A comparison of one of the two flute solos entitled "The Nightingale" gives a good example of Boulez's work: we recognize straightaway the hand of the composer of *Le Marteau sans maître* (Examples 163*a* and 163*b*).

Example 163a

Example 163b

209. *La Rédemption de François Villon*

Music for a radio "evocation" by José Bruyr
November–December 1951 (before 12 December)
First broadcast: 30 December 1951, French Radio (Paris). The recording was made
    on 12 December 1951
Performing forces: two men's voices; orchestra: 1.1.1.1.–1.2.0.0.–cymbals–strings
    (4.4.4.3.2.)—twenty-five instrumentalists in all
Duration: 43 minutes 10 seconds (including about 14 minutes 40 seconds of music,
    with repeats; the two orchestral movements last 4 minutes 50 seconds)
Three very short movements and two movements for orchestra: 1. Snow (slow and
    heavy); 2. Rain and Wind (violent and animated, slower)
Salabert

This final radio work is an evocation of the poet Villon as hungry, cold, and in a state of material and moral destitution. Honegger's music consists essentially of two short movements for orchestra, which are the final testimony to his image-making genius. What more striking picture could there be of a snowy evening than these harshly chromatic, dissonant undulations in eighth-notes on divided violins and violas, combined with somber melodies in the low woodwinds? Likewise, "Rain and Wind," with its violence and astringent sonorities, evokes a nature hostile to mankind: it makes one shiver, despite the slow, more melodic, less strident coda that concludes it at its second appearance, at the end of the second tableau. These two totally unknown pages are concentrates of the essential Honegger. Unfortunately, there is no obvious way of rescuing them, since they are too short and fragile to lead an independent life in the concert hall.

Category 16: Music for Film

Readers of this book, and especially of its biographical section, will have realized that the meeting between Honegger and the cinema was predestined in every way. He possessed in the highest degree all the qualities that were required: both musical qualities—concision, clarity, a sharp sense of the image and its relationship with the sound, and a technical certainty that allowed him to adapt instantly to any language whatsoever—and human qualities—rapidity, precision, a methodical mind, and above all modesty, a capacity to adapt, and psychological subtlety. These were the virtues that made Honegger an ideal partner for filmmakers, and the virtues for which he was immediately valued at his true worth. The complete absence of misplaced pride meant that he was philosophical in the face of the sort of thing that happened over *Pygmalion*, when he was surprised to find at the first showing that his title music had been replaced by a Strauss waltz.

If we discount those composers who specialized in cinema—such as Georges Auric, who had no fewer than sixty-two film scores to his credit— Honegger was more prolific in this field than any of his "serious" musical colleagues: his friends Ibert and Milhaud produced "only" thirty and twenty-five scores, respectively. His first two films, both prestigious projects, were alone in being silent: *La Roue* and *Napoléon*. Both films were by Abel Gance, through whom Honegger came into the film world and for whom he was later to write one of his most elaborate film scores, *Le Capitaine Fracasse*. In the days of silent film, the role of the composer was very different from what it was to become later. It consisted for the most part in arranging and adapting music of the most diverse and, alas, heteroclite origins, which explains the small amount of music Honegger wrote for the two films in question. From the time of the first extended, original score—Saint-Saëns's score for *The Assassination of the Duc de Guise* in 1908—original scores had been very few in number. One particularly luxuriant score was by Florent Schmitt for the 1925 version of *Salammbô*, a film in no way worthy of such musical magnificence.

With the advent of the talkies, everything changed. It was in November 1933 that Honegger's career in this genre began, with his work on Raymond Bernard's trilogy *Les Misérables*. He would write no fewer than forty scores between 1933 and 1951, with only three interruptions. The first two (July 1939–April 1942 and September 1943–July 1945) were due to the closure of the film studios following the outbreak of war and the Occupation, and the third (June 1946–March 1950) was due to illness. We may note too that the first two gaps were filled by a revival of incidental music.

The sometimes frantic pace of his activity (nine films in 1937, six in 1942) was clearly prompted by financial necessity. Honegger began it at the end of 1933, in a time of recession and economic crisis. At the same time, his music was being played less often and the revenue accruing from the success of *Les Aventures du roi Pausole* was unfortunately lost in an unwise investment. Even so, as the composer wrote in his autobiographical notes, this new activity was set in train for several reasons, "not all of them financial." We know, in fact, that in his case the choice of the cinema corresponded with an urgent need to re-establish contact with the public, a contact that had been somewhat weakened since *Antigone* and *Cris du monde*. The concessions implied by such a choice varied considerably from one film to another, but they were carefully calculated and never affected the technical quality of Honegger's work. We also know that the string quartets and the oratorios undertaken with Claudel were written simultaneously with this film music, as were the symphonies.

The quality of the scores varies a good deal, but it is always linked with the quality of the film concerned. With his seismographic sensibility, Honegger reacted instantly to stimulation, just as every great opera composer had always done—Mozart, for instance, three of whose miracles were aided by the genius of da Ponte. In Honegger's case, too, the inspiration fluctuates in the course of a single film for precisely these reasons. His best film scores are those written for the best films on which he worked. There is, though, one exception that proves the rule—*Mermoz*. For one thing, a great deal of Honegger's music for *Mermoz* was based on his earlier ballet *Un Oiseau blanc s'est envolé*, but it was the subject he responded to, not Louis Cuny's mediocre direction.

The list of Honegger's film music shows the variety and extent of his collaborations, which included some of the great names of the cinema, such as Gance, G. W. Pabst, Marcel Pagnol, Anthony Asquith, Yves Allégret, Christian-Jaque, beside one or two solid but unappreciated talents such as Dimitri Kirsanov, Raymond Bernard, and Pierre Chenal. As well as clearly commercial films, dealing with war (aviation, in particular) and spying, we also find adaptations of great popular classics by Victor Hugo, Théophile Gautier, Balzac, Dostoyevsky, and Turgenev, or, more rarely, works of an experimental character, such as *L'Idée*. But the music is always perfectly adapted to the subject, as well as to the intellectual and aesthetic level of the film. It is absolutely functional, but at the same time, of the quality we should expect from such a composer. In this respect, Honegger's music is fairly unusual in the history of film.

On almost half his films, Honegger worked in collaboration with other composers. This was a common practice of the times and allowed him to save precious time. The most faithful and devoted of these "accessories" was Arthur Hoérée who, from *Rapt* to *La Tour de Babel*, collaborated with Honegger on no fewer than nine films. Together with Maurice Jaubert, who unfortunately worked only once with Honegger, Hoérée was probably the most knowledgeable practitioner of film sound techniques between the wars, and the success of *Rapt*, the first joint effort between him and Honegger, owed much to Hoérée's skill as well as to the fact that the director, Dimitri Kirsanov, was himself a musician. Hoérée and Honegger were also the joint authors of a basic text, "Details of the Music for the Film *Rapt*," published in the special December issue of *La Revue musicale* in 1934. This was Honegger's second important pronouncement on the subject of film music, the first ("From the Cinema of Sound to Real Music") having appeared in January 1931 in the review *Plans*. We can see that the first of these texts dates from before the start of Honegger's film career, the second from its earliest phase. It is therefore worthwhile to take a brief look at both of them before turning to the music itself.

In the article of January 1931, written right at the beginning of the period of the talkies, Honegger is curiously reticent about them, and he makes a distinction between them and the cinema of sound, about which he is enthusiastic:

> It is possible that the talking film will not manage to go beyond the limits of a theater on a screen. It seems, at first sight, to commit an error against the very essence of the cinema, which is to be, above all, an art of *sensitivity*, acting directly on the individual without the mediation of understanding. As soon as you appeal to perception, as soon as *seeing* and *hearing* give way to *understanding*, the meaning of everything changes, the dream is at an end, the sensual spell of the cinema is broken. If there is any useful way in which the human voice can intervene and move us, it is in crying and lamenting, in every means that needs not to be *understood*, but *felt*. It is the *tone* of the voice that touches us. In this case it occurs only as *sound*, and so the film is rather one with sound than a spoken one.

There is no doubt that, with the arrival of the talkies, a certain conception of cinema, linked with the currents of expressionism, died the death. We may regret that fact, as we may also regret the way in which the dominance of color over black and white would later impoverish the image of some of its expressive possibilities. Such a mixture of improvement and impoverishment is the price paid for all technical progress. On the other hand, Honegger's article contains extremely clear and sensible views when it comes to the crucial problem of the relationships between image and sound at the moment of editing:

> Cinema editing operates on an entirely different principle from musical composition. Composition is about *continuity* and demands a logical development. Cinema editing is about *contrasts and oppositions*. . . . *It is a question of bringing together two "montages" that are different in nature and do not have the same rules*. . . . As things are, we can say that the rules of cinema editing are, and will remain, more flexible than those of music. *The filmmaker and*

*the composer will, then, first have to agree on a preliminary cutting of the film,
but, in the final editing, it is the filmmaker who will have to be the more flexible
of the two and adapt his cuts to the necessary development of the melodic line.*

This is a utopian vision, as Honegger was soon to learn, to his loss, once he
was on the treadmill of the commercial cinema. In an article dated 1941, which
is included in his *Notes sur la musique*, Milhaud mentions in half-irritated, half-
amused tones some of the disappointments in store for the film composer, who
has to work at frantic speed on elements that will not in the end be used, or else
will be deformed so that their meaning is lost. In *Cavalcade d'amour*, a film on
which Milhaud and Honegger in fact worked together, the idea was to link the
three episodes of the film (the same love story taking place successively in the
Middle Ages, in 1830, and in 1939) with a sung ballad, which would serve as a
leitmotif after it had been sung in the title music. But, for reasons that had nothing to do with art, this title music disappeared and the whole musical point was
lost. "That's the cinema for you!" was Milhaud's comment.

But to return to Honegger and the very interesting ideas he expresses in his
article:

The cinema of sound will not reach maturity until it has realized *such a
close union between simultaneous visual and musical expression that they explain
and complete one another on an equal footing.* This synthesis will mark the
birth of a curious art, *addressing itself at the same time and with the same
intensity to two senses.* So far we have had no more than a few glimpses of it,
in King Vidor's *Hallelujah*, and especially films by Ruttmann and the
Mickey Mouse films. It is clear that in *Mickey Mouse, it is the musical rhythm
itself which gives rise to the images.* There already, music has become as
important as film.

Honegger was talking of Walt Disney's first animated pictures, called indeed *Silly Symphonies*, and we can certainly say that it was in Honegger's all-too-
rare animated features (*L'Idée* of 1934, significantly the first project he accepted,
and then *Callisto* in 1943) that he could come closest to his ideal.

Continuing his reasoning, he arrives at its logical conclusion:

One day, no doubt, music will inspire films, which would, after all, be less
illogical than having films inspired by books, given that films and music
have more in common than films and books do. . . . We can go further.
*Sound film is quite capable of filling out music, of completing it by giving it real
meaning.* Because music is in fact the art that has the least *real* meaning. . . .
*It does not have a real, concrete representation that is perceptible in an identical
way by every listener. Perhaps the sound film will provide it with one. . . . The*
same artistic feeling is expressed differently, depending on the nature of
the artist's talent. Whether it is music or speech, graphic art or choreography, it is a question of the same *reality* expressed in one of its aspects.
*There exist, there must exist, exact relationships between these different expres-
sions of something identical, and ones that are reversible so that, if we understood
them, we could translate one by another. . . .* Music can cease to be misunder-

stood or massacred and become itself, can enter into reality and be, like the cinema and with it, a real, unanimous, collective force, no longer subject to the anarchic alterations of individuals, but acting with all its strength on a crowd transported with enthusiasm.

We may find the conclusion of this crucial text shattering, with its aura of quasi-totalitarian collectivism (we should remember it was written in 1931), a tone that seems to contradict Honegger's increasing tendency toward an ardent, even anarchic individualism. In fact, it both reminds us and informs us of a number of things. The first of these is the profoundly concrete nature of the composer's musical imagination, which seized more readily on images than on words or gestures. When he speaks of music as "the art that has the least real meaning," we would today translate this as "the art that is to the least extent a bearer of signification." Honegger is trying here to revive the old myth of the synthesis or synergy of the arts, in a sense that is no doubt closer to that of Scriabin's synesthesia than of Wagner's *Gesamtkunstwerk*.

And what is the driving force behind all this? It is the desperate need to communicate, if possible through all five senses and beyond—a need that, as we have seen, outweighs even the rights of individual liberty so fiercely defended at the very time that Honegger was writing *Cris du monde*. It is a paradox and an unmistakable sign of emotional crisis that this article, defending, even encouraging an immersion in a bath of sight and sound, "a real, unanimous, collective force," in opposition to the "anarchic alterations of individuals," and acting with all its strength on a "crowd transported with enthusiasm," should appear at the very moment that *Cris du monde* was mobilizing the energy of despair to defend a diametrically opposite position. Was it, perhaps, this insoluble conflict of dialectic that tried to find escape in the horrific explosion of the Second World War? As for Honegger himself, his solution was to climb upward to the final measures of *Jeanne d'Arc au bûcher* and the Dona nobis pacem of the *Third Symphony*, before he finally admitted defeat in the *Fifth*, an echo twenty years later of that in *Cris du monde*: two impasses, two heads banging against a wall.

To return once again to this text, which underlines all the "elective affinities" joining Honegger to the "seventh art" of the cinema, we may note that his vision of music inspiring films was realized in that same year of 1931 in the Soviet Union, where the filmmaker Tsekhanuski worked on *Pacific 2.3.1*. Jean Mitry's marvelous version would appear later, in 1950.

Honegger's second text turned away from theory toward practice, and specifically toward the music for the film *Rapt*, which he wrote jointly with his musical collaborator Arthur Hoérée.

As an introduction, the authors complain that in sound films

the composer's role is reduced more and more to the bare minimum. Usually he finds himself treated like a carpet maker who comes to measure surfaces for which disposition he has not been responsible, but who is graciously allowed to cover them with some material or other.

Happily this was not the situation with Dimitri Kirsanov, who was a professional musician and who even went to the lengths of suggesting several sound combinations. As a result, the soundtrack treated noises on a level with music. There are several exciting equivalences between the score and the screen images, such as the two-part fugue with stretto written by Hoérée to illustrate the goat being chased by the shepherd's dog. Hoérée also explains how one of the most successful musical sequences was improvised:

> At the end of the recording, someone realized that the "Procession Leaving the Church" had not yet been set to music. No problem. Honegger took over the tubular bells, I improvised at the harmonium on the theme of the *Chanson de Ronsard*, one of Honegger's most beautiful pieces, and Régine de Lormoy-Hoérée sang the tune from memory. Kirsanov sang a second part for the final cadence and . . . the result was excellent.

The article goes on to describe processes of editing, of dissolves, of filtering and deforming the sound, all of which are standard nowadays but were totally new at the time. Among the most striking moments was the passage in reverse in Elsi's song, intended to express a mysterious dream atmosphere. This was five years earlier than the much more famous passage included in Maurice Jaubert's "Waltz" in Julien Duvivier's *Carnet de bal*—music that is better known because the film is too. Here the effect is particularly subtle:

> The music was transcribed in retrograde, recorded like that, but then inscribed on the tape backward. The order of the notes was thus re-established, but the resonance of each of them preceded its attack, giving a very effective kind of halo. The mixing in this scene allowed us to superimpose three sounds, recorded separately: the music, a whispered text that was dictated by the hero's conscience as he dreamt with his eyes open, and finally the ticktock of a clock, which got louder like a hallucination (thanks to the potentiometer controlling the electric current) and hammered pitilessly on the hero's temples.

The article gives various other examples of this sort and also underlines the composers' intention of avoiding natural noises and replacing them with musical equivalents. For example:

> the glug-glug of the basin was imitated by string trills and fast scales on the piano. The peddler announces himself by blowing on a horn, and the echo of his call is heard on string harmonics, sounding far away. . . . To describe the storm, we asked the orchestra to improvise set pieces, according to our instructions: distant storm, medium-sized storm, violent storm, thunder, rain. With these ten meters of film we were able to parallel the action with a complete storm (more than one hundred meters), reproducing this effect, cutting that one, bringing up the thunder either as recorded or backward, so that it either approached or moved away. . . . The links between these various fragments were made by means of synthetic sound, that is to say by drawing on the film itself the vibrations needed to link different sonorities.

If all that sounds like rather a rag-bag now, we would do well to think of the inventive genius required over sixty years ago to make such sounds with primitive technology. In any case, *Rapt* is exceptional, and after that Honegger never again had the opportunity to work with film men who went along with experimental research, not only in principle, but accepting the time and money it involved.

The limits of this book preclude the detailed analysis of the fifteen or so hours of music that Honegger wrote for the screen. A list of these forty-two film scores is accompanied here by a few succinct remarks on the most important of them. As has been done for the incidental music, the suites and various extracts arranged by the composer for concert use have already been discussed under Category 7A. But some of the other music that deserves similar treatment is here examined at greater length.

First, a few words are in order concerning the orchestral forces used by Honegger. The standard small band for most of these scores consists of flute, oboe, clarinet, bassoon, saxophone (almost always alto), trumpets and trombones generally in pairs (more rarely single), piano, percussion (one player), and strings. The latter do not normally include double basses until 1937, but rarely dispense with them after *La Citadelle du silence* and *Regain*. Their absence until then was dictated by the limitations of the recording equipment of the time, with the risks of overload and distortion. These limitations also dictated the use of a single woodwind, but Prokofiev took advantage of them, in *Alexander Nevsky*, for example. Honegger's favorite ondes Martenot appear in nine films, and to great effect in *Rapt*, *L'Idée*, *The Demon of the Himalayas*, and *Crime and Punishment*. The horn (rarely doubled) is also used in nine films, the harp only in six. After *Napoléon*, the large symphony orchestra becomes the exception, as few producers were willing to accept the expense. It is found, even with chorus as well, in *The Demon of the Himalayas*, the only German film on which Honegger collaborated, in *Mayerling*, and in *Le Capitaine Fracasse*, although this last score has to be judged by the tape since the orchestral score is lost. Even such powerful music as *Mermoz* contents itself with the usual performing forces, except that the string section is a little larger than usual. Let us now turn to a swift overview of this huge body of work.

Table 13-1. Honegger's Film Music

Opus No.	Title	Director	Musical Collaborator	Date of Composition	Duration of Surviving Music by Honneger	Status	Edition	Popular Songs
44.	*La Roue* (S)	Abel Gance		Nov. 1922	3:50	B	Salabert	
64.	*Napoléon* (S)	Abel Gance		late 1926–early 1927	21:15	B	Salabert	
86.	*Rapt*	Dimitri Kirsanov (from C. F. Ramuz)	A. Hoérée	Feb. 1934	12:10	C		
87.	*L'Idée* (CS)	Bertold Bartosch (from Frans Masereel)		May 1934	24:00	B		
88.	*Les Misérables*	Raymond Bernard (from Victor Hugo)		Nov. 1933–summer 1934	60:25	B	Salabert	
90.	*Cessez le feu*	Jacques de Baroncelli (from Joseph Kessel)		fall 1934	12:00–15:00	CF	Coda	2
91.	*Le Roi de la Camargue*	Jacques de Baroncelli (from Jean Aicard)	Roland-Manuel	Oct. 1934	2:00	AC		
93.	*The Demon of the Himalayas*	Andrew Marton and G. O. Dyhrenfurth		Oct. 1934–Feb. 1935	35:00–40:00	ACF		3
94.	*Crime and Punishment*	Pierre Chenal (from Feodor Dostoyevsky)		April 1935	27:30	B		
98.	*L'Équipage* (or *Celle que j'aime*)	Anatole Litvak (from Joseph Kessel)	M. Thiriet	end 1935	14:00	B	Echo	1
100.	*Les Mutinés de l'Elseneur*	Pierre Chenal (from Jack London)		Jan. 1936	21:15	BE	Coda	1
101.	*Mayerling*	Anatole Litvak (from Claude Anet)	M. Jaubert	Feb. 1936	13:20	B	Echo	

Opus No.	Title	Director	Musical Collaborator	Date of Composition	Duration of Surviving Music by Honneger	Status	Edition	Popular Songs
106.	*Nitchevo (L'Agonie du sous-marin)*	Jacques de Baroncelli	Oberfeld	Nov. 1936	20:00–25:00	CF	Ray Ventura	2
109.	*Mademoiselle Docteur (Salonique, nid d'espions)*	G. W. Pabst (from Georges Neveux)		Dec. 1936–Feb. 1937	35:00–40:00	B (apart from a blues)		
110.	*Marthe Richard au service de la France*	Raymond Bernard (from Bernard Zimmer)		late Feb.–early Mar. 1937	35:00–40:00	CF	Choudens	
112.	*Liberté*	Jean Kemm	A. Hoérée	1937	completely lost	ADG		
116.	*La Citadelle du silence*	Marcel L'Herbier	D. Milhaud	24–29 July 1937	17:30	B (apart from one piece)		
117.	*Regain*	Marcel Pagnol (from Jean Giono)		4–28 Sept. 1937	35:00	C (small portion missing)		
121.	*Visages de la France* (DS)	A. Vigneau, Paul Nizan, André Wurmser		Oct. 1937	20:00	AC		
124.	*Miarka ou la fille à l'Ourse*	Jean Choux (from Jean Richepin)	T. Harsanyi	Nov. 1937	c. 15:00	DE	Salabert	2
125.	*Passeurs d'hommes*	René Jayet (from Martial Lekeux)	A. Hoérée	Nov. 1937	8:10	DG		
126.	*Les Bâtisseurs* (DS)	Jean Epstein	A. Hoérée	Nov. 1937	4:00	AC		
129.	*Pygmalion*	Anthony Asquith and Leslie Howard (from G. B. Shaw)	W. Axt	June 1938	3:25	C		1

Table 13-1 (continued)

Opus No.	Title	Director	Musical Collaborator	Date of Composition	Duration of Surviving Music by Honneger	Status	Edition	Popular Songs
130.	L'Or dans la montagne (Faux Monnayeurs)	Max Haufler (from C. F. Ramuz)	A. Hoérée	Oct. 1938	8:30	B		
134.	Le Déserteur (Je t'attendrai)	Léonide Moguy	H. Verdun, etc.	Mar. 1939	39:00	C	Salabert	
136.	Cavalcade d'amour	Raymond Bernard and R. Désormière	D. Milhaud	July 1939	1:40	DF (the rest lost)	Heugel	O Salutaris
156.	Le Journal tombe à 5 heures	Georges Lacombe (from O. P. Gilbert)		late April–mid-May 1942	27:40	CE	Choudens	
157.	Huit hommes dans un château	Richard Pottier	A. Hoérée	July 1942	c. 8:00–10:00	DE	Éditions Royales	
158.	Les Antiquités de l'Asie occidentale (DS)	Henri Membrin		Aug. 1942	16:35	AB		
159.	Musiques pour France-Actualités			Sept. 1942?		ADG		
160.	La Boxe en France (DS)	Lucien Gasnier-Raymond	A. Jolivet	2 Oct. 1942	3:20	ADE	Choudens	1
161.	Secrets	Pierre Blanchar (from Ivan Turgenev)		Oct. 1942	39:00	AB		
164.	Callisto, ou la petite nymphe de Diane (CS)	André Marty	Roland-Manuel	Feb. 1943	21:00	DE	Pierre Noël	
166.	Le Capitaine Fracasse	Abel Gance (from Théophile Gautier)		April 1943 (songs: Sept. 1942)	45:00–50:00	DE	Josette France	5 (1 lost)

Opus No.	Title	Director	Musical Collaborator	Date of Composition	Duration of Surviving Music by Honneger	Status	Edition	Popular Songs
167.	*Mermoz*	Louis Cuny		Mar.–May 1943	50:00	CE	Choudens	
170.	*La Nativité* (DS)	André Marty (unrealized project)		Aug. 1943	9:00	E (unfinished)		
171.	*Un Seul amour*	Pierre Blanchar (from Balzac)		June–22 Sept. 1943	44:00	ACE	Salabert (the two Romances)	2
183.	*Un Ami viendra ce soir*	Raymond Bernard		July–Nov. 1945 (*Chant de la Délivrance*: 27 May 1945)	21:40	DE	Choudens	1
185.	*Les Démons de l'aube*	Yves Allégret	A. Hoérée	Dec. 1945–early Jan. 1946	c. 12:00	CE	Choudens	
188.	*Un Revenant*	Christian-Jaque	A. Hoérée (orchestration)	June 1946	28:30	CE	Choudens	
201.	*Bourdelle* (DS)	René Lucot		Mar.–May 1950	21:30	B		
205.	*La Tour de Babel*	Georges Rony	T. Harsanyi and A. Hoérée	late May–early June 1951	19:15	AB		
206.	*Paul Claudel* (DS)	André Gillet		July 1951 (completed: 18 July)	13:15	B		

Key: CS = Cartoon Short; DS = Documentary Short; S = Silent Film; A = Film no longer exists; B = Orchestral score survives complete; C = Orchestral score survives incomplete; D = Orchestral score is lost; E = Piano score is complete; F = Piano score is incomplete; G = Piano score is lost

44. *La Roue* (see Category 7A)

64. *Napoléon* (see Category 7A)

86. *Rapt*

I have already stressed the innovative character of the music for *Rapt*, Honegger's first collaboration with Arthur Hoérée. It is an adaptation of a novel by C. F. Ramuz, *La Séparation des races*. A young man from the mountains of the Valais, a French-speaking Roman Catholic, falls in love with a young Bernese Protestant, German-speaking girl from the opposite side of the mountain, and carries her off. The two communities, opposed in so many ways and physically separated for at least six or seven months every year, break out into violent conflict.

The film suffers, unfortunately, from the old-fashioned, artificial acting of the stars—it is impossible to forget for a moment that they are city-dwellers. From this point of view, the other film inspired by Ramuz for which Honegger and Hoérée wrote the music, *L'Or dans la montagne*, shows considerable progress. Although the actors (Jean-Louis Barrault, Suzy Prim, Alexandre Rignault, and Alerme) in *L'Or dans la montagne* are again Parisians, they make a great effort to adapt to the milieu of the Valais. In *Rapt*, Honegger's contribution comes especially in the country scenes and the ball (the first of the "Peasant Dances" will reappear in the ballet *L'Appel de la montagne*) and occurs mainly in the second half of the film. As film music it is perfect, but its very symbiosis between image and sound means that it is quite ineligible for the concert hall—the best compliment one could pay it.

87. *L'Idée* (The Idea)

This short, twenty-four-minute film is an animation of engravings photographed using a technique of several superimposed viewpoints. It is a superb satirical short protesting against the repression of popular political uprisings and arguing in favor of the emergence of democratic ideas. The collaboration between Bertold Bartosch and Honegger was first proposed in the summer of 1933, even before that of *Les Misérables*, but it came to fruition only in May 1934. The music of *L'Idée* is among the most remarkable Honegger ever wrote for the cinema. It is continuous and uses twelve instrumental soloists, with a significant part for the ondes Martenot, which symbolize the young girl representing "The Idea"—of liberty, justice, and brotherly love. Honegger wrote this score with particular care and it could be successful in the concert hall. A long, lyrical melody (lasting thirty-eight measures) on the ondes Martenot depicts "The Idea" and, throughout the film, is opposed, either whole or in part, to hostile, sarcastic music with square rhythms.

The story must have had resonances for Honegger at that time, as its message finally comes to be that of *Cris du monde* (though reached by different routes). "The Idea," represented by the silhouette of a young, slim, naked girl, is everything within us that rises up against the slavery that weighs on laborers and young idealists, and more generally on individuals thirsty for liberty, whether they are poets or scholars. She and her adorers are hunted down by the tribunal, which condemns her. Policemen and soldiers repress protest meetings and strikes; they are all in the service of the capitalists, who appear at the end in all their hideousness. The Popular Front was not far off. But at the end "The Idea" reappears, because she is immortal, and a luminous tutti brings the music to a conclusion in E major. Unlike the pessimistic message in *Cris du monde*, we find here for the first time, in this little, unknown work, that "there is Hope, which is the strongest." A few months later, Honegger would begin *Jeanne d'Arc au bûcher*.

88. Les Misérables

The *Orchestral Suite* of *Les Misérables* (H88A) is discussed under Category 7A in Chapter 11. There exists a complete recording of the full hour of music by the Bratislava Radio Symphony Orchestra, conducted by Adriano. This recording even includes the end of the twelfth sequence, "The Convicts' Chain," a grandiose, terrifying vision that has already been heard in the opening title music. This is the only part of the score still lost, but it has been recon- stituted by ear and collated with the title music. Honegger's musical language here is the most openly popular of all his films, but without concessions or banalities. It remains permanently wedded in our memory to the hero of Hugo's great drama, the powerful atmosphere of which Honegger captures without apparent effort.

Among the pieces that do not figure in the Suite, I may mention No. 8 ("Cosette and Marius"), the title music of the second of the three films, which brings in their intensely Schumannesque love theme and follows it with a waltz in which *Les Aventures du roi Pausole* seems to have been rewritten by Tchai- kovsky. The "Festivities at Montfermeil" (No. 9) presents a succession of rather clumsy peasant waltzes more reminiscent of the ländler of German-speaking Switzerland than of the valse-musettes of the Paris suburbs. The touching mel- ody accompanying the "Death of Éponine" on the barricade (No. 17) is curi- ously prophetic of the theme of the *Monopartita* (Example 94). But one could go on quoting examples interminably.

90. Cessez le feu (Cease-fire)

It was from the fall of 1934, just after his terrible car crash in Spain, that Honegger's "years in the galley" on the film front really began. During those years, he wrote numerous film scores, some purely commercial (*Cessez le feu* is the first of these), some on a higher artistic level. Many of these scores survive in a more or less fragmentary state, and Honegger did not hesitate to reuse some pieces: for example, an excellent tango from the film under discussion would appear again in *Le Journal tombe à 5 heures*. His more commercial films are full of songs, and sometimes excellent ones. In *Cessez le feu*, the "Song of the Squadron," with words by Joseph Kessel, the scriptwriter on the film, sets off a series of march-like songs in 6/8, mostly in the minor. We find something similar in the song "Companions of Follevie" from *Nicolas de Flue*.

91. *Le Roi de la Camargue*

The film itself has disappeared. Only a brief passage of the music survives, and even that cannot be attributed to the film with certainty.

93. *The Demon of the Himalayas* (Der Dämon des Himalayas)

Here, too, the film has disappeared, but the score survives. It was one of Honegger's largest and most exciting scores, as the Berlin UFA put huge forces at his disposal: a symphony orchestra, a chorus, and a trautonium (the German equivalent of the ondes Martenot). Honegger was never again to have such performing forces in the cinema. It was to be a mammoth, spectacular production, retracing Günther Oskar Dyhrenfurth's expedition to Kanchenjunga, the third-highest peak in the world.

As in *Jeanne d'Arc au bûcher*, Honegger used saxophones instead of horns. The two main pieces, each lasting about thirteen minutes, are "Snow Storm" and the final sequence "Ascent and Fall," and they would make a superb diptych in the concert hall, superior even to the *Two Suites* from *Mermoz*. The long F minor "Snow Storm," consisting of 273 measures, is based on three highly visual ideas, and has come down to us in two versions. Apart from the autograph, there is a copy in which the music is written in retrograde. Honegger was obviously using here on a huge scale the reversing process that had been tried out for the first time in *Rapt*, and which in the present film must have produced an overwhelming effect.

"Ascent and Fall" is of similar dimensions (233 measures). It is a powerful passacaglia on an eight-measure theme in D minor. (MacGuire's ascent of the Jungfrau in *L'Appel de la montagne* will also take the form of a passacaglia, which is appropriate to the evocation of this kind of effort.) But here the theme is occasionally interrupted or obscured by lack of breath at high altitude (symbolized by gasping syncopation) or by the unleashing of wind and snow. The appearance of the trautonium, sailing upward from its lowest bass note, ends in the catastrophe of the Fall. This is followed, after a suspenseful pause, by the appearance of the Demon, the *fortissimo marcatissimo* of the "Collapse," and finally the blinding "Flash of Lightning." Then comes the giddy descent through seven octaves of the orchestra. The final credits, entitled "Vision," add a serene D major epilogue, with unison chorus. This is undoubtedly one of the greatest film scores of that period.

94. *Crime and Punishment* (Crime et Châtiment)

This fine film version of Dostoyevsky's *Crime and Punishment* by Pierre Chenal shows, together with Harry Baur, the very young Pierre Blanchar as Raskolnikov. It remains remarkably faithful to Dostoyevsky, and the acting, surprisingly, has not become dated. The music is some of Honegger's best, and this too is able to survive (at least on disc). The score is in thirteen sections, but is highly unified, being based on six leitmotifs. The most important of these are Raskolnikov's, an abrupt, uneasy theme on bass clarinet, and Sonia's, passionate and gasping, on ondes Martenot. The two longest and most interesting sections are No. 4 ("Setting Out for the Crime") and No. 8 ("Nocturnal Visit"). Honegger's ability to conjure up a Russian atmosphere is astonishing, especially in the short *Traktir* sequence ("Cabaret," No. 7).

98. *L'Équipage*, or *Celle que j'aime* (The Crew, or The Girl I Love)

This fairly successful commercial film was based on a very popular book of the period. It is of interest in being the first musical contact Honegger had with the subject of aviation, and the score is a modest precursor of that for *Mermoz*, whose theme is hinted at in the title music.

100. *Les Mutinés de l'Elseneur*

The score for *Les Mutinés de l'Elseneur* is efficient, functional music of a certain nautical color, and there is a good deal of brass writing (especially for the horn, which is rare in Honegger's film scores). The title music is a stirring storm piece, which was taken over six years later as No. 7 of *Le Journal tombe à 5 heures*. The violent horn call is marked "stopped and brassy, very close to the microphone," and obviously the intention was to overload the recording.

101. *Mayerling*

For *Mayerling*, Honegger's only collaboration with Maurice Jaubert, Honegger (unusually) had a large symphony orchestra at his disposal. His score, which is quite short, possesses a romantic/Viennese color perfectly suited to its subject, and from this point of view it certainly served as a trial run for *L'Aiglon*, especially for its third act. The principal theme, which opens the title music, is a semi-quotation from the first movement of Tchaikovsky's *Fifth Symphony*. But the most important section, in which this theme reappears, is the long final scene: the double suicide of the unfortunate heroes. This is music of intense pathos, in a desperately post-romantic harmonic style. This is another score that would be viable both in the concert hall and on disc.

106. *Nitchevo (L'Agonie du sous-marin)* (Nitchevo, or The Agony of the Submarine)

This is commercial music for a film of the same type. It includes several pastiches of Oriental music, a fox trot, a waltz, an excellent sung tango, and another song, "De l'Atlantique au Pacifique" (From the Atlantic to the Pacific), which was a real success in its day, being recorded by Damia.

109. *Mademoiselle Docteur (Salonique, nid d'espions)*

Mademoiselle Docteur, or *Salonique, nid d'espions* (Salonica, Nest of Spies), is a spy film by G. W. Pabst, with Dita Parlo in the title role. Honegger wrote nineteen short movements for the score, samples of his extraordinary expertise but no more than that. We come across a cancan, cheap Oriental nightclub music, nasal oboes, and the inevitable blues, waltz, and tango—this latter one excellent as always. Someone should make an anthology of Honegger's tangos.

110. *Marthe Richard au service de la France*

In this spy story, very much of its time, Erich von Stroheim, with extraordinary naiveté, allows himself to be led by the nose by the beautiful spy Edwige Feuillère. Honegger wrote twenty-two numbers of every kind, only three of which are at all substantial. Two of them, "Attack of the Airplanes" and "Finale of the Armistice," would be reused in their entirety some fifteen years later, in *La Tour de Babel*. This "Finale" is a collage in which the cheerful din makes one think surprisingly of Charles Ives, as it superimposes the *Madelon, Ah y fallait pas qu'il y aille, It's a Long Way to Tipperary*, the *Ça ira*, and the *Chant du départ*, before culminating in the *Marseillaise*. The score contains two more tangos, as successful as usual, and for No. 10 rescues a piece from the composer's extreme youth, *Orgue dans l'église* (see H110A, Category 1A).

116. *La Citadelle du silence*

For this, his only collaboration with Marcel L'Herbier, Honegger was joined by Darius Milhaud. L'Herbier gave Honegger the opportunity for a second Russian subject after *Crime and Punishment* with this romantic story of Nihilist conspirators at the end of the nineteenth century. Milhaud looked after the ball sequences (in which he could not resist writing a South American section, rather incongruously in this context!), while Honegger took charge of processions, marches, hymns, and choruses, as well as the title music. The best music comes in the long "Scene in the Chapel" for unaccompanied male chorus in pure Russian liturgical style (including humming), and especially the moving "Hymn to Liberty," also unaccompanied, on words by Jean Anouilh. This is on the same level as the *Chant de la Délivrance* from *Un Ami viendra ce soir*, although they differ in tone. Both of them suggest what we may have lost in the famous *Chant de Libération* (H155), first performed by Charles Münch.

117. *Regain* (Aftermath)

For the *Orchestral Suite* from the film *Regain* (H117A), see Category 7A. In discussing the *Suite*, I underlined the whole score's exceptional quality, and it deserves to be known and recorded in its entirety. Only the section of the "Fair at Manosque" seems to be lost. The title music, broad and majestic, like the vast horizons of the countryside, sets the scene for the whole. Its huge string chords ring out like bells, and from them emerges a pastoral theme on the saxophone, which reappears in "Hiver" (Winter), a piece included in the *Orchestral Suite*.

Among the pieces not included, apart from the unforgettable "Song of Aubignane" (No. 2), one should mention the wonderful "Summer" ("Panturle in the Sun," No. 8), a tender woodwind dialogue evoking the early morning, a "missing link" between the *Pastorale d'été* and the *Fourth Symphony*. Then comes "Night in the Barn" (No. 9) with its chromaticisms and uneasy shudders, the Nocturne ("Panturle and Arsule near the Stream," No. 11) with its long, lyrical tune on violins, and finally "The Plowshare" (No. 12), a powerful piece with dotted rhythms like a French overture. The epithet "French" could indeed be used to describe the whole of this fine score.

121. *Visages de la France*

This short film was a typical product of the Popular Front. It was dedicated to the Soviet Union for the twentieth anniversary of the October Revolution, and it reviews the whole of French history from a Marxist perspective. No copy exists in a fit condition to be shown. Eight of the eleven sequences Honegger wrote have survived. The most remarkable of these is the last, which superimposes in counterpoint the *Internationale* (complete) and the *Marseillaise* (not quite complete).

124. *Miarka ou la fille à l'Ourse*

This story of a little gypsy girl adopted by the noble inhabitants of a provincial château gave Honegger the opportunity to explore an unusual area of expression, but he left most of the work to Tibor Harsanyi. There is, indeed, an amusing contrast between Honegger's Spanish gypsy music and Harsanyi's Hungarian *tzigane* and *czardas*. Of the two songs, "Song of the Road" reverts to the composer's favorite style of marching song in 6/8.

125. *Passeurs d'hommes*

Honegger wrote four pieces for *Passeurs d'hommes*, a story of Belgian resistance fighters on the Dutch border in 1915, with Hoérée composing the rest. The score is lost. The "Cabaret" sequence repeats, in slightly modified form, the melodic line of the "Peasant Dance" from *Rapt*, which will find its final destination in *L'Appel de la montagne* (H174).

126. *Les Bâtisseurs* (The Builders)

Honegger's contribution to *Les Bâtisseurs*, a documentary retracing the whole history of architecture, was limited to the *Hymne du Bâtiment* (H126A, Category 9A). The film is lost.

129. *Pygmalion*

Pygmalion was the only English film Honegger ever worked on. It was not a lucky choice for him, since most of what he composed was replaced by commercial music. The score of two very interesting sequences in the film has disappeared; and the title music, which is all that survives in score, was not used.

130. *L'Or dans la montagne (Faux Monnayeurs)* (Gold in the Mountain, or Counterfeiters)

L'Or dans la montagne was Honegger's second and final contact with C. F. Ramuz and the Valais, and once again Hoérée was involved. It is an excellent screen adaptation of *Farinet ou la fausse monnaie*. Honegger wrote only three sequences for the film, but they are very good and deserve to be heard both in the concert hall and on disc. After vigorous title music in the earthy style of *Regain*, there is a poetic evocation of a misty dawn and the dramatic, breathless final pursuit. This leads to a slow epilogue and to the return of the opening title music.

134. *Le Déserteur (Je t'attendrai)* (The Deserter, or I'll Wait for You)

This is another commercial war film and, as usual, the quality of Honegger's long, functional score reflects that of the film. But there is one interesting sequence, "Train in the Fog" (No. 2), which divides the orchestra into two groups. One of these plays only when the film shows the outside of the train and falls silent when we turn to the conversations in the compartment—a kind of "masking" of the sound.

136. *Cavalcade d'amour*

The film *Cavalcade d'amour*, on which Honegger collaborated with Milhaud, was the last he worked on before the outbreak of war. Milhaud took from his music the popular *La Cheminée du roi René*, while Honegger extracted from his own contribution the *O Salutaris* (H136A, Category 8A). The rest of the score has disappeared. One of its best movements was an unaccompanied Kyrie with solo soprano.

156. Le Journal tombe à 5 heures

Le Journal tombe à 5 heures marked Honegger's return to the studios after a break of nearly three years due to the war and the Occupation. It is a professional, efficient adaptation (the same might be said of the music) of a novel that had its moment of success. It takes us into the offices and corridors of a large daily newspaper, with a young woman devoured by ambition (Marie Déa), the owner of the paper played masterfully by Pierre Renoir, and a colleague who begins as a contemptuous rival but later falls in love (Pierre Fresnay). It is very much an actors' film, and Honegger endowed it with some excellent "mechanistic" title music depicting the grinding of the presses and a delicious waltz ("Villa Rambaud," No. 6) in the style of the "Variation of Saesli" in *L'Appel de la montagne*. Other pieces were taken from earlier films: the tango from *Cessez le feu*, and "In Distress" (No. 7) from the dramatic title music to *Les Mutinés de l'Elseneur*.

157. Huit hommes dans un château (Eight Men in a Castle)

Huit hommes dans un château is an entertaining story of an old castle whose ghost prevents the ruined nobles that own it from selling up. But all ends well. Most of the music is by the faithful Arthur Hoérée, who had got the measure of his friend's style so well that one can easily be fooled, in the title music, for example. Honegger's music goes all out for horror effects, and the ghost is depicted with ondes Martenot, string harmonics, and a certain amount of "hou-houing."

158. Les Antiquités de l'Asie occidentale

The film, which was produced by the French Office for Art and Historical Films and dedicated to the collections of the Louvre, has disappeared. But the score survives intact and is worth hearing on its own. Its fourteen sequences are grouped into the title music and four sections, all firmly unified. In the orchestra, violins and violas are, unusually, missing, but important parts are played by the xylophone, celesta, harp, and piano. But what is the well-known statue of the "Woman of Elche" doing in Asia Minor at the end?

159. Musiques pour France-Actualités

This appears in Honegger's manuscript catalog, but it is impossible to identify. It is probably lost.

160. La Boxe en France (Boxing in France)

The documentary itself has disappeared. Honegger's only contribution was a charming but conventional *Hymne au sport* (H160A, Category 9A), on words by José Bruyr ("Chests out, all together . . .").

161. *Secrets*

It is a great pity that the catastrophic fire in the archives of Bois-d'Arcy destroyed both of the films on which Honegger worked with Pierre Blanchar, who was better known as an actor than as a director and who was, we may recall, the chief coordinator of the Resistance cinema in his capacity as President of the Liberation Cinema Committee. Both films were based on good, classical subjects, and the composer lavished every care on his two opulent scores. They have survived almost complete, and run to forty and forty-five minutes.

Secrets takes its inspiration from Turgenev's *A Month in the Country* (in a well-off Provençal family, a young boy's tutor sows discord in female hearts). The music is generally romantic in style, like its subject. It favors luminous keys, and there are some Russian elements.

164. *Callisto, ou la petite nymphe de Diane*

Callisto, ou la petite nymphe de Diane was Honegger's first collaboration with André Marty, one of the few Frenchmen of the time to devote himself to cartoons. A second joint project (*La Nativité*) would be interrupted by events during the Second World War and would not come to anything. Callisto, a nymph of Diana, is seduced and deceived by Jupiter, who takes on the appearance of Diana. Diana guesses what has happened because the nymph refuses to undress to bathe, like her companions. She banishes her. Callisto lives on her own, but Juno's vindictiveness catches up with her and transforms her into a bear, and her baby as well; and the two become the familiar celestial constellations (Ursa major and Ursa minor).

The film is a delight, but as the music survives only in the form of a printed piano reduction and the autograph has disappeared, it is impossible to determine either the make-up of the orchestra or the respective parts played in the collaboration between Honegger and Roland-Manuel. It was a unique attempt at a filmed cantata for narrator and small ensemble. The French cinema would not provide any more examples of films sung in their entirety until the, quite different, musical comedies of Jacques Demy. It is a pretty, neoclassical score featuring impressionist orchestration in the danced passages.

166. *Le Capitaine Fracasse*

The loss of the orchestral score of *Le Capitaine Fracasse* is one of the most serious in Honegger's output, and certainly the most serious in the field of the cinema. It is one of his great pieces of film music and, with his usual prodigality, Abel Gance did not stint on the resources: chorus and large orchestra, in this case the Yvonne Gouverné Chorale and the Conservatory Concert Society (conducted by the composer himself with enormous gusto). Together with *The Demon of the Himalayas*, it is the only film score for large orchestra written entirely by Honegger. The film itself has always been underestimated and is virtually unknown. True, it is one of baroque luxuriance, but it gave Honegger the opportunity for the first time in his film career to explore a quite new expressive area, that of a picaresque heroism full of panache. It is not surprising therefore that one thinks from time to time of *Don Juan* or *Till Eulenspiegel*, even though the next moment we may be in the purest French, seventeenth-century classical tradition—especially in the songs, which are possibly the most beautiful Honegger ever wrote for the cinema and which deserve to be heard in their own right. The heroic, leaping theme depicting Sigognac, one of the composer's most memorable, is heard both in the minor and the major, on horn and then trumpet (Example 164). The two tunes (couplet and refrain) of the "Song of Thespis's Chariot" together form another of the film's leitmotifs, and they combine epic grandeur with popular spontaneity and stick in the memory. There are many other good things in the music, and we must hope that one day the orchestral score will be found.

Example 164

167. *Mermoz*

For a discussion of the two orchestral suites from the film *Mermoz* (H167A), see Category 7A. There is little to add to what has been said about the *Two Suites*, which contain almost all the best music of the score. It is, at fifty minutes, one of the longest and most consistently inspired of Honegger's film scores.

170. *La Nativité*

The film *La Nativité* was never made, and all that remains of the music for this unfinished project are some nine minutes of music in a piano reduction. But it is certainly worthwhile publishing the delightful little Gloria in excelsis for mixed chorus and piano (No. 5), lasting just over two minutes (Example 165). This passage lies halfway between the Alleluias of *Le Roi David* and *Une Cantate de Noël*, for which it can be seen as a preparation.

Glo - ri - a in ex - cel - sis De - o

Example 165

171. Un Seul amour

The story for *Un Seul amour* is taken from Balzac and is set in 1814. A nobleman has taken a ballet dancer to his castle and married her, but the dancer's previous lover follows her and tries to exert pressure on her. The husband deals with the blackmailer and dies shortly afterward. The film has vanished, like Pierre Blanchar's other production, *Secrets*. The score is a long one and includes two sequences in the purest romantic ballet style; unfortunately, their orchestration has not survived. There are also two sentimental sung Romances that live up to their title. The longest sequences are the last ("Hope") and the great expressive Adagio of the "Vengeance of Clergue" (No. 16).

183. Un Ami viendra ce soir (A Friend Will Arrive This Evening)

Honegger returned to the studios of his friend Raymond Bernard, after two years of forced interruption, for this story of Resistance fighters in the Vercors who are disguised as mental patients in a nursing home run by a doctor who is himself a member of the *maquis*.

The film is above all a showpiece for individual actors. One of the protagonists is a pianist, hence the presence of three piano pieces in the score (see H183A, Category 1A), including the well-known "Souvenir de Chopin." But the best piece is undoubtedly *Chant de la Délivrance*, with words by José Bruyr. This is one of the finest songs ever inspired by the Resistance, in a style very close to the militant songs of Eisler or Kurt Weill on words by Bertolt Brecht. It had been written independently of the film some weeks earlier.

185. Les Démons de l'aube (Demons of Dawn)

This war story shows the Foreign Legion harassing the Germans in Tunisia and ending up in Provence. It was Honegger's only collaboration with Yves Allégret. This is certainly not Allégret's best film, and the music is likewise of secondary importance.

188. Un Revenant (A Ghost)

This excellent film by Christian-Jaque is the only one of his films for which Honegger wrote the music, as Hoérée had confined himself to orchestrating the ballet *Andromède et Persée*. *Un Revenant* is a sharp satire on the moneyed bourgeoisie of Lyons and can still be viewed with pleasure. Christian-Jaque was marvelous at directing actors, and here the "sacred monsters"—Louis Jouvet as a choreographer, Ludmila Tcherina as a ballerina, François Périer as a young, bashful, bourgeois lover, Louis Seigner and Gaby Morlay as his parents, not to mention Marguerite Moreno who does an amazing "number"—all give of their best. Honegger himself even makes a brief appearance in his own role of Composer, saying just one word ("Certainement!"), surrounded by clouds of pipe smoke—as it was June 1946, they had to scour the whole of Lyons to find a plug of tobacco needed for just one shot—and Hoérée plays the Conductor. As always when inspired by a film of quality, Honegger produced a fine score for this, his last long fiction film. The music lasts about half an hour, but not all the orchestration has come down to us. The broad title music, describing gray Lyons and its rivers, sounds all of a piece. The "Promenade through Lyons" (No. 7) is prettily bucolic, while No. 12, accompanying Jouvet as he describes the young son of the family, is an excellent example of imitation in sound: fluid, whimsical, with a change at each new adjective.

201. *Bourdelle*

Apart from his collaboration on *La Tour de Babel*—for which he did not hesitate to empty out his bottom drawer—Honegger's film career ended on a high note with two documentaries about artists he loved: the sculptor Bourdelle and Paul Claudel. In both cases, Honegger composed scores of great beauty that deserve to be played in the concert hall and on disc. They are examples of his last manner: serious, noble, and sparse. Bourdelle himself had been a great admirer of Honegger's, and it was his widow who asked the composer to take part. The title music introduces on the trumpet the majestic theme that will serve as a leitmotif and which, according to Honegger, symbolizes Bourdelle's genius. It is a magnificent idea, carrying real sculptural force (Example 166). Among the most striking sequences, I would cite the powerful 6/4 passage of "Hercules the Archer" (No. 6), which could have been the basis for a symphonic development; the central allegro "Bourdelle's Studio" (No. 8), the longest section in the score; and especially the evocation of the "Busts of Beethoven" (No. 10). This homage to that much-loved Titan takes the form of a short, but flashing allegro in D minor, which is an authentic stylistic copy, without any blunders or literal quotations.

Example 166

205. *La Tour de Babel* (The Tower of Babel)

This montage of uncut, live footage from the two world wars was rapidly taken out of circulation because of its unauthorized showing of secret documents. No copy survives that is fit to be given in public.

Honegger took the sequences called "Airplanes" and "Armistice" from his music for *Marthe Richard au service de la France*, but he also wrote some short new pieces, including a little cycle of four military marches without strings, in which he gave vent to all his hatred of war. If the fourth deserves its subtitle "Heavy March," the second, with its weighty trombone solo, is still more oppressive: this is the enemy against which the procession marches in revolt in the Dona nobis pacem of the *Third Symphony*. What a contrast with the peaceful, sunny marches (*Grad us*, *Nicolas de Flue*) written for Switzerland before the war!

206. *Paul Claudel*

Paul Claudel, a final, magnificent homage to the poet's genius, is a worthy epilogue to *Jeanne d'Arc au bûcher*, *La Danse des morts*, the *Three Poems of Claudel*, *Le Soulier de satin*, and *Tête d'Or*. In André Gillet's film, Claudel's words are read by Jean-Louis Barrault and the poet himself takes part. It is a model of sobriety and respect (but without falling into the trap of official eloquence), and the music is on the same level.

The style is that of Honegger's final manner, and we may be reminded of the *Suite archaïque* because of the diatonic, modal language, and of the *Concerto da camera* because of the transparency of the orchestration, without brass or even double basses. The music is so clearly modal that we can no longer call it tonal. I see it as a secret homage to Fauré, whose music runs like a thread through the whole of Honegger's creative career—at the end of his life, he admitted preferring *Penelope* to *Pelléas et Mélisande*. It is indeed Fauré's influence that is felt in this predilection for moderate 3/4 movement with dotted rhythms, and for these peaceful melodic motifs, so simple in their conjunct motion. This is music of wisdom and serenity.

FOURTEEN

Light Music

If we exclude noncommercial jazz, then so-called light music (popular song, dance music, operetta, musical comedy, and so on) is really a quite different domain from that of so-called serious music. It is exceptional for a composer to be active in both fields, at least in Europe where light music was, and still is, a closed shop, reserved for specialists, with quite separate economic rules and distribution networks, and a budget far higher than that for serious music. Honegger, with his solid successes in the differing fields of oratorio, symphony, and sonata, is a very remarkable exception.

No doubt his long, hard apprenticeship lay at the root of his ability to move with equal ease in every musical genre, even those that are not taught in conservatories. We may add to that his marvelous adaptability and his imitative skill—"chameleonesque," in the best sense of the word. Honegger's own personality is always present, even when he seems to be performing with elegance and nonchalance (the public does not need to know that these characteristics are the result of hard work). A popular song or an operetta by him bear his hallmark as inescapably as any of his string quartets or symphonies. That immediately implies a complete lack of pretension and an acceptance that every form of expression is valid, both aesthetically and ethically, so long as the quality of inspiration does not suffer and it is approached with professional conscientiousness. We may, indeed, find it hard to imagine Messiaen or Boulez indulging in popular songwriting. They have never been moved by that sense of social solidarity, that love and respect for simple people that make Honegger worthy to be called "a composer in the city of mankind."

Other composers, some of note, have tried to cover as wide a range, but none has done so with such ease and naturalness. We only have to compare *Les Aventures du roi Pausole* and the only slightly later *Le Testament de tante Caroline* by Roussel. Roussel's piece has the air of an enjoyable holiday task, an ironic, refined divertimento by a great musical and philosophical master, but there is still a touch of stiffness about it, and its stylistic borrowings lack freshness. We find nothing of the sort with Honegger. He lowers his sights without resorting to affectation or vulgarity. And *Les Aventures du roi Pausole* was written around the same time as such serious and different works as *Amphion*, the *First Symphony*, and *Cris du monde*.

If we start looking for parallel cases, we come across the significant fact that neither Milhaud nor Poulenc wrote an operetta. And when the composer of *Les Mamelles de Tirésias* tackles a subject that any other composer, and Honegger first among them, would have treated as an operetta, he remains true to his habitual style and language. In the same way, many of the texts on which he wrote delightful light songs have never prompted him to turn them into *chansons*. Among foreign composers, we might mention Kurt Weill. But with him the relationship works the other way: it is rather his rare concert works that have crossed over from his normal field, that of the theater and songs. As a result, the only composer with whom Honegger could be compared in this respect is his friend Jacques Ibert, with whom, after all, he collaborated on *Les Petites Cardinal* (H128).

This final chapter therefore basically examines two categories of works: songs (many of which were written for films and have already been discussed in that context) and operettas.

Category 9: Popular Songs (Chansons)

50.   *Chanson de Fagus*
82.   *Le Grand Étang*
97.   *Fièvre jaune*
118. *Tuet's weh?*
120. *Jeunesse*
122. *Armistice*
127. *Three Songs by René Kerdyk*
133. *Hommage au travail*

Category 9A: Popular Songs for Film

Refer to the table in Chapter 13 for more details on the films.

90A. From the film *Cessez le feu*: "Chanson de l'escadrille" (Song of the Squadron); "Chanson du cul-de-jatte" (Song of the Legless Cripple); "Valse (Rengaine) de Lagasse"
91A. From the film *Le Roi de la Camargue*: "Ma plaine finit vers l'occident" (My Plain Ends in the West); "En Camargue les filles sont belles" (lost)
93A. From the film *The Demon of the Himalayas*: "Chant de la caravane"; "Les trois petits moutons"; "Le Cocu du désert" (The Cuckold of the Desert). It is not entirely certain that these were written by Honegger.
98A. From the film *L'Équipage*: "Chanson du lapin" (lost); "Quand par hasard le noir cafard" (When Those Blues Come Along)

100A. From the film *Les Mutinés de l'Elseneur*: "L'Elseneur est un voilier à vaches" (The Elseneur Is a Pig of a Sailboat)

106A. From the film *Nitchevo (L'Agonie du sous-marin)*: "De l'Atlantique au Pacifique"; "Triste est mon coeur" (tango)

119A. From the incidental music for the film *La Construction d'une cité*: "Chanson des quatre"; "Chanson de l'émigrant"

124A. From the film *Miarka ou la fille à l'Ourse*: "Chanson de la route" (Song of the Road); "Chanson de l'eau"

126A. From the film *Les Bâtisseurs*: *Hymne du Bâtiment*

160A. From the film *La Boxe en France*: *Hymne au sport*

166A. From the film *Le Capitaine Fracasse*: "Sérénade de Scapin" (lost); Arietta "Si mon coeur parlait, Lysandre" (If my heart spoke, Lysander); "Chanson du chariot de Thespis" (two versions, the first unpublished); "Chanson pour Isabelle"

171A. From the film *Un Seul amour*: *Deux Romances sentimentales*: "Quand tu verras les hirondelles" (When You See the Swallows) and "Si le mal d'amour"

183B. From the film *Un Ami viendra ce soir*: *Chant de la Délivrance* (Song of Deliverance): "Nous sommes cent. . . ." (There are a hundred of us)

Of the three dozen or so popular songs Honegger has left us, three quarters of them belong to his film music, and some have disappeared. They can be split into three types. The first, and by far the most common, is the march in 6/8, and in this genre Honegger is at his most successful and seductive. Into this category come *Le Grand Étang*, *Jeunesse*, "Chanson de la route" (No. 2 of the *Three Songs by René Kerdyk*, H127), "Chanson de l'escadrille," "Quand passe la caravane," "L'Elseneur est un voilier à vaches," "De l'Atlantique au Pacifique," "Chanson de l'émigrant," *Hymne du Bâtiment*, *Hymne au sport*, and the first version of the "Chanson du chariot de Thespis."

The second type adopts the rhythm of a waltz or java: "On est heureux" and "Le Naturaliste" (Nos. 1 and 3 of *Three Songs by René Kerdyk*), "Valse (Rengaine) de Lagasse," "Chanson des quatre," and the second version of the "Chanson du chariot de Thespis." The third type imitates the tango or fox trot: *Fièvre jaune*, "Quand par hasard le noir cafard," and "Triste est mon coeur." These songs are almost always of the strophic variety with couplets and refrains, and clearly in a simple, tonal, popular style. They are often excellent and some were sung and recorded at the time by well-known stars (Marianne Oswald, Lys Gauty, Damia, and Agnès Capri, among others). Some of them deserve a closer look.

50. *Chanson de Fagus*

May 1923 (?). The autograph bears only the dates 1923–1924
"To Paul Pélissier, with great sympathy"
Poem by Fagus
First performance: 24 March 1926, Gabrielle Gills, Le groupe Nivard, Andrée Vaurabourg, Salle Gaveau, Paris (*Revue musicale* concert)

Performing forces: soprano, mixed chorus (SATB), piano
Duration: 1 minute 30 seconds
Salabert

The song *Chanson de Fagus* predates all Honegger's others by at least ten years. (His period of greatest activity in this field was from around 1932 to 1945.) It is also quite different from them in being much more complex and sophisticated. The text and its setting suggest the folklore of the French countryside. The soprano takes the lead and the chorus (which can be simply one to a part) replies, although the two roles are briefly reversed. The piano part is a brilliant one, with chords and arpeggios, and these, together with the many striking modulations, give this piece a special character. But it is hard to place in the repertory, and one wonders who would sing it nowadays.

82. *Le Grand Étang* (The Great Pool)—Song of the Fifteenth Century

1932 (no further details are given)
"For Marianne Oswald"
Poem by Jean Tranchant
Performing forces: voice and piano (or small orchestra)
Duration: 1 minute 45 seconds
Unpublished

The story is set in the fifteenth century, at the time of the poet François Villon and the gibbet of Montfaucon. The pacifist, anarchistic character of the words and the personality of the dedicatee, who made an unforgettable disc of it, make this Honegger's first genuine popular song. It is the closest of them all to the work of Kurt Weill, and it is on the score of this song (and not that of *Fièvre jaune*) that Honegger should have written his inscription to the composer of *The Threepenny Opera*: "You see how far your influence is spreading!" It is a marvelous little piece and, as we might imagine, Honegger the resolute pacifist responded readily to the words. The film *L'Idée* would follow shortly.

97. *Fièvre jaune* (Yellow Fever)

Paris, September or October 1935
Poem by Nino
Duration: 2 minutes 30 seconds
Max Eschig

An excellent variety song in the style of the times.

118. *Tuet's weh?* (Did That Hurt?)

5 October 1937
"For my dear Hegi, affectionately"
Cabaret song after W. Lesch
Duration: 1 minute 30 seconds
Unpublished

Tuet's weh? is a satirical song composed for Honegger's brother-in-law, the singer Emil Hegetschweiler, who ran a cabaret in Zurich. The words are in Zurich dialect and, like the military march *Grad us* (H141), they illustrate the composer's lifelong attachment to German-speaking Switzerland. He had spoken the dialect from boyhood.

120. *Jeunesse* (Youth)

1937 (very likely October)
Written for the FMP (Fédération musicale populaire)
Words by Paul Vaillant-Couturier
Performing forces: voice and piano (or orchestra); harmonized for four mixed voices
    by Louis Durey in 1959
Duration: 3 minutes 45 seconds (all five verses)
Chant du Monde (who also published Durey's harmonization)

The song *Jeunesse* was very well-known in its day, and it turned up again in the fifth sequence of the film *Visages de la France* (H121), written immediately afterward. It gave expression to the feeling behind the Popular Front and its refrain remains its symbol sixty years later (Example 167).

En a - vant   jeu - nes - se de France, fai - sons se le - ver   le   jour

Example 167

122. *Armistice*

1 November 1937
Poem by René Kerdyk
Performing forces: voice (unison chorus) and piano
Duration: 7 minutes
Unpublished

This fairly long work is another appeal for peace. It obviously refers back to 11 November 1918 (the end of the First World War) and to the sacrifice of millions of lives that would, it was hoped, ensure that war would never break out again. But less than two years later . . .

127. *Three Songs by René Kerdyk*

1935–1937 (no more precise details survive)
No. 1: "To Marcelle Gerar"
Performing forces: voice and piano
Duration: 9 minutes (3:45 + 2:30 + 2:45)
1. On est heureux; 2. Chanson de la route; 3. Le Naturaliste
Les Oeuvres françaises, Paris, 1937 (Nos. 1 and 2 only; No. 3 was unpublished and
    has disappeared. We have only the disc recorded at the time by Agnès Capri.)

"Chanson de la route" is another appeal for peace. The two outer songs are attractive waltzes, the second being a graceful pastiche of the style of 1900.

133. *Hommage au travail* (Homage to Work)

31 December 1938, Paris
Words by Maurice Sénart
Duration: 2 minutes
Max Eschig

Hommage au travail was no doubt written by Honegger out of friendship for his publisher, who was the author of the highly edifying words. It is a deliberately banal piece and should be taken with a pinch of salt.

119A. Two Songs from the incidental music for *La Construction d'une cité*

September–October 1937
Production by Jean-Richard Bloch
Words by J.-R. Bloch (according to José Bruyr, in collaboration with Jean Villard-
    Gilles)
Other collaborators on the music were Darius Milhaud, Jean Wiéner, and Roger
    Désormière
First performance: 18 October 1937, decor by Fernand Léger, conducted by Roger
    Désormière, Vel' d'Hiv', Paris
Performing forces: voice and piano (the orchestration has disappeared)
Duration: 4 minutes 30 seconds (3:00 + 1:30)
1. Chanson des quatre; 2. Chanson de l'émigrant
R. Deiss

These two splendid songs (a waltz and a march) were, it seems, Honegger's only contribution to the production *La Construction d'une cité*.

Category 12: Operettas

76. *Les Aventures du roi Pausole*
78. *La Belle de Moudon*
128. *Les Petites Cardinal*

Honegger's three contributions to the world of operetta can be summed up as a real masterpiece that had a deserved success, a racy comedy set in the district and atmosphere of the canton Vaud, and a collaborative work harshly treated by fate.

76. Les Aventures du roi Pausole (The Adventures of King Pausolus)

Operetta in three acts
May 1929–18 November 1930
"To the composer of *Choucoune*, Fernand Ochsé"
Libretto by Albert Willemetz from the novel by Pierre Louÿs
Premiere: 12 December 1930, Dorville (Pausole), Koval (Taxis), Jacqueline Francell (La blanche Aline), Pasquali (Giglio), Meg Lemonnier (Mirabelle), Blanche (Le Fermier), Germaine Duclos (Diane), Claude de Sivry (Dame Perchuque), Régine Paris (Thierrette), produced by Louis Blanche, conducted by Arthur Honegger, Théâtre des Bouffes-Parisiens, Paris
Performing forces: twenty-two singing roles (nine principals), ballet, chorus; orchestra: 1.1.1.1.–saxophone–1.1.1.0.–two percussion (bass drum, triangle, tenor drum, cymbals, suspended cymbal, timpani in E-flat, hand bells, gong, castanets, woodblock)–piano, celesta–strings (6.6.4.4.2.)—thirty-four players in all
Duration of music: 73 minutes 35 seconds (28:50 + 27:40 + 17:05). The entire production lasts about 2 hours 40 minutes.
Act I: Overture; 1. Chorus of the Siesta (The Queens); 2. Exit of the Queens; 3. Aria of Taxis ("I've done, why not admit it"); 4. Aria of Aline ("Papa always insists I entertain myself alone"); 5. Ballet; 6. Entrance Into the Woods of Justice (Pausole and Chorus); 7. Aria of Giglio ("I have the honor to be your page"); 8. Septet of Seven Different Opinions (The Queens); 9. Finale (The Queens, Taxis, Pausole, Giglio, chorus)
Act II: Prelude; 10. Chorus of Farmers' Wives (with the Sharecropper); 11. Travesti Duet (Aline, Mirabelle); 12. Ritornello of the Mule (same music as for the Prelude); 13. Cantata (the Sharecropper, Thierrette, the Farmers' Wives); 14. Aria of the Cup of Thule (Pausole); 15. American Exit of the King; 16. Trio (Aline, Mirabelle, Giglio); 17. Aria of Aline ("Forgive me, darling daddy"); 18. Aria of Diane; 19. Duet of Revolt (Taxis, Perchuque, chorus); 20. Finale (Pausole, Giglio, Taxis, Diane, the Sharecropper, the Sergeant, chorus, and soloists)
Act III: 21. Chorus of Soubrettes; 22. Dream Duet (Diane, Giglio); 23. Entrance of the Spanish Chocolate (Thierrette, chorus); 24. Aria of Taxis ("Ah, dear God, what have I seen!"); 25. Telephone Duet (Aline, Pausole); 26. Aria of Giglio ("Love is like music"); 27. Pausole's Farewells (Pausole, with Aline at the end); 28. Finale (all except Pausole)
Salabert

"An opéra-comique with elaborate underclothing" was what Chabrier called his *Le Roi malgré lui*. It is a perfect description also of *Les Aventures du roi Pausole*, which gave Honegger his biggest theatrical triumph—four hundred performances in Paris and almost as many in the provinces and abroad. Paradoxically, it is the longest of all his works, with an hour and a quarter of music.

The composer recognized three models for the work: Mozart, Chabrier, and Messager, and *Pausole* is clearly a descendant of Chabrier's *L'Étoile*. There are even similarities between the characters (between Ouf the First and Pausole, and between Lazuli and Giglio). Honegger was aiming at a Mozartian perfection, and the score shows his refusal to go along with a hierarchy of genres. Here we find the teasing high spirits of a man who tended to be taken either for an austere Protestant psalmist or a rugged sports lover. The *Six Poems of Jean Cocteau*, the *Concertino for piano and orchestra*, the *Chanson de Fagus*, and several other "trifles" ought to have provided due warning, to the experts as well as to the general public, but it is true that *Les Aventures du roi Pausole* gave a freer rein than hitherto to this side of Honegger's temperament.

He always loved operetta, as we can see from his support for Louis Beydts (whose works, such as *Moineau* and *Les Canards mandarins*) are now forgotten. With *Pausole*, Honegger fulfilled the dream of Debussy, who, at the end of his life, had had enough of austerity and intellectual pretension, and exclaimed "Now, let's write operetta!" Pierre Louÿs had brought to life again the exquisite wantonness of the eighteenth century in the terms of 1900, and Honegger, with the help of his excellent librettist, enjoyed himself reinterpreting 1900 in the terms of 1930, incorporating jazz and music hall. A revival in Lausanne on 31 December 1990 went on to transpose the work into our own times, and there is no reason why this little game of mirrors should not continue. *Les Aventures du roi Pausole* is now too far from us in time to become obsolete or dated. It is outside time: it is "ageless and will always remain so," as Saint-Saëns once said of the music of Fauré's last period.

Before we pluck from between the staffs of Honegger's score some of the tasty fruits of the cherry tree beneath which the debonair king of Tryphème dispenses justice, we should note that Honegger's famous style of wordsetting finds no place here, except in very special circumstances. On the contrary: like Chabrier and Offenbach, Honegger draws on the pitfalls of traditional prosody for some of his most hilarious comic effects. Each number uses a different instrumental ensemble and Honegger is wonderfully subtle in the way he treats his orchestra of some thirty players. His favorite saxophone has important contributions to make in Nos. 4, 5, 11, 15, 19, 20, 22, and 28.

ACT I

Right from the Overture, the freshness of the counterpoint, the impertinence of the trumpet, and the harmonic progressions all reveal Honegger's unmistakable fingerprints. The cheerful opening theme will recur in the "Ritornello of the Mule" in Act II, while a second, more sensual and flexible idea foreshadows the second of the three movements of the Ballet (No. 5). The 3/4 middle section of the Overture has a Fauréan gracefulness about it and contains the most memorable tune of the Trio in Act II, full of delightful harmonic progressions (Example 168). Apart from this diversion, and despite its brevity, the Overture is in Honeggerian sonata form with reversed recapitulation. It culminates in a triumphant coda on the "Hymn of Tryphème" (Finale of Act II), followed by a final return of the opening theme. Altogether it is an entrancing movement.

As the curtain goes up, we find ourselves in the harem of King Pausole's 365 wives. The seven queens of the week are lazily getting themselves ready in a "Chorus of the Siesta" that suggests a mood of exquisite idleness, with its

Example 168

undulating chromatic thirds, which recall "Sous bois" from Chabrier's *Pièces pittoresques*, seasoned occasionally with a sharpened Lydian fourth. Diane, the queen of the day, is happy at the thought of performing her annual duty in the royal bed. Enter the great eunuch Taxis, who is in charge of the harem. He announces himself in the style of the best songs in 6/8 that Honegger would later write ("I've done, why not admit it") before inspecting these lighthearted ladies and handing out reprimands and punishments.

This is followed by the arrival of Dame Perchuque, the duenna and governess of the fair Aline, the king's daughter. Although he is liberal with his subjects, the king treats her with a tender severity and allows her no freedom whatever. This is what she explains to Mirabelle, a dancer *en travesti* who has come to organize and dance the ballet demanded by Pausole. If Mirabelle's ambiguous behavior shocks Taxis and Perchuque to the point that they leave the stage, it has a dramatic effect on the naive Aline, who takes Mirabelle for a young man. Her first aria ("Papa always insists I entertain myself alone") is a fresh, delicately sensual number, reminding us less of Fauré than of Messager. And Messager seems also to be the inspiration behind the Ballet that follows.

The Ballet consists of a theme and five characteristic variations (of these, "the Melancholy one" and "the Voluptuous one" are gently reminiscent of Fauré), an intermezzo very much in the harmonic style of 1900 and based on the second theme of the Overture, and a skittish gallop. Then it is time for Pausole to dispense justice, stretched out under his cherry tree, which he does to the sounds of a cheerful but rhythmically somewhat gawky march. The young page Giglio is accused of having insulted a minister, but he wins the king over in a brief, charming aria worthy of Chabrier, but including Honegger's distinctive style of wordsetting ("J'ai l'*hon*neur d'être votre page"). Pausole is exhausted and wants to go to bed with Diane, but then Dame Perchuque drops a bombshell: the fair Aline has run off with Mirabelle.

What is to be done? The queens are consulted and each one is of a different opinion. This ensemble (No. 8) is a stunning vocal toccata in which the occasional use of two eighth-notes tied across the measure gives the impression of a samba. When this is repeated, Diane superimposes on it a cantus firmus in half-notes, in a technique unexpectedly borrowed from *Le Roi David*. Pausole decides to take Giglio's advice, follow his daughter at his leisure, and enjoy the journey. The main part of the Finale is a bright, spirited passage in 6/8, and its memorable refrain ("We shall do just as we like") concludes the act in a spirit of unpretentious good humor. This is already the atmosphere of the Popular Front and the beginning of paid holidays, as immortalized by René Clair and Jean Renoir (it is indeed a pity that Honegger never collaborated with either of these two).

Act II

By way of an overture we hear the evocative "Ritornello of the Mule," the easy trot of which carries the king along. We are at the Golden Cockerel, a model farm where Pausole is breaking his journey, but which for the moment is also where the two fugitives are hiding. The busy "Chorus of Farmers' Wives" is an example of Chabrieresque humor, entirely verbal in origin with its fast repeated syllables, sometimes sung, sometimes spoken. Mirabelle finally owns up to the Princess that she is in fact a girl, and this "Travesti Duet" is among the most charming and best-known numbers in the score, with its delightfully naughty wit, its elements of ragtime and 1930s jazz, as well as the displaced accents on "*mas*culin" and "*fé*minin."

Pausole arrives to the sound of his trotting mule, and the farmers greet him in the brief Cantata, which is an amusing parody of official, academic music based on an absurd subject in repeated notes and descending scales. This is treated to a fugal exposition with voluble countersubjects—the whole passage is extremely funny. A vocal cadenza by the Sharecropper ends falsetto in an "ecclesiastical" cadence over a pedal point. The king is thirsty and holds up an old, embossed cup whose sad history he recounts in the "Aria of the Cup of Thule," parodying Gounod's *Faust* (*not* Berlioz's). But it is hard to take this seriously when the fanfares proclaiming "the king drinks" are in the style of a brisk, 1900s cabaret dance. The mock-pathetic ending is utterly hilarious and contains one of the best of Willemetz's many puns: "Et voilà comme il s'en alla/Du vin d'ici dans l'eau de là" (And that's how he escaped from the wine here to the water beyond). These words are then repeated over the brisk ritornello, which will make a timely return at the beginning of the Act III Finale. Here, the king's "American" exit is only temporary, to the highly entertaining sound of forty seconds of real jazz.

Meanwhile the plot thickens. Giglio is pestering the young farmer's daughter Thierrette and she tells him that Aline and Mirabelle are on the farm. He puts on Thierrette's clothes and threatens the two fugitives with denunciation if they do not allow him to share in their goings-on. Aline is confused and prefers the kisses of the false peasant girl to those of Mirabelle. The witty, even risqué Trio, with Mirabelle dressed as a boy and Giglio as a girl, is one of the high points of the score, and we may wonder how the critic Henry Prunières could possible say that *Pausole* lacked sensuality. There is plenty of it here, drawing on Chabrier for the A sections of this A-B-A-B form, and on Fauré for the B sections. These repeat the bewitching tune already heard in the Overture (Example 168), now reworked as a trio in modulating polyphony. This may be operetta, but supported by the most sumptuous "underclothing"!

Immediately after this trio, Giglio admits to Mirabelle that he is a man, and agrees to help the two girls to run away and hide. Mirabelle now puts on Thierrette's clothes in order to escape Taxis's prying eyes. The king, after a visit to the farm, dozes off. Aline is moved at finding him there and sings him a tender lullaby ("Forgive me, darling daddy"). Sensuality here gives way to true feeling. The style is Honegger's own, full of lovely modulations, counterthemes, and imitations in the orchestra. It is a small masterpiece and deserves to take its place among the character items in recitals of French song.

Aline leaves, the king wakes up, and Thierrette tries to get him to marry her. But Diane furiously puts her in her place. The extended intervals of her aria (No. 18), which go way beyond what one normally finds in operetta and which are accompanied in the orchestra by ideas that are almost atonal, give it a strange, troubled atmosphere. This is the world of the 1930s nightclub in the small hours, telling of a woman's unrequited passion (it is possible, indeed, that it was not sung at the early performances). Taxis and Dame Perchuque arrive to tell the king that his harem is in revolt—a long, noisy orchestral introduction leads to their breathless duet.

The king is unhappy and exhausted, but Giglio tells him some good news about Aline and, in the Finale, Pausole accedes to the demands of his people. Everything ends in triumph as the "Hymn of Tryphème" (already heard at the end of the Overture) sums up this happy nation's slightly subversive code of conduct: never upset your neighbor but, that aside, do anything you like. Here, Honegger jokingly concurs with the view ("We ask to be left alone"), which, in all seriousness, would continue to obsess the composer until his death.

ACT III

We are in the Hotel of the White Breast and Westphalia, where the king is resting. His sleep must be fairly deep to withstand the busy, noisy "Chorus of Soubrettes" with its trombone syncopations. Giglio takes the place of the sleeping Pausole and he and Diane enjoy a night of love. This is the pretext for a duet (No. 22) that, like the Trio in the previous act (No. 16), is a delight, pitched in Honegger's favorite pearly E major. The enchanting A major refrain is a slow waltz of the Boston variety with languorous harmonies. It will recur to conclude the whole work (Example 169).

Example 169

Then comes the irresistible "Entrance of the Spanish Chocolate" (which, in the Lausanne performances, was placed before Pausole's abdication). This is the score's great bravura number, calling for an encore. With its castanets, it is authentically Spanish in the extreme. Honegger called it a "fast bolero," but it is nearer to being a *paso doble* (Example 170). The Trio of the middle section is a fast *jaleo* in 3/8.

Example 170

Giglio goes off to look for Aline and Mirabelle, not knowing that they are in the hotel. At this point they enter, Mirabelle complaining because Aline pronounced Giglio's name during their night of love. Taxis has spied on their activities and expresses his horror at such behavior in a parody of a well-known popular song of 1900 (Example 171). Aline has learned from the newspaper that her father is in Tryphème. She telephones him, not knowing he is in the next room, and we have the charming "Telephone Duet" in the style of Chabrier. Suddenly, she finds herself face to face with Giglio, who takes the opportunity of declaring his passion and persuading her of the technical superiority of the masculine sex when it comes to making love to women. His aria ("Love is like music") is a 1900 waltz, with attractive flute decorations.

Example 171

There is no music during the complicated, Feydeauesque imbroglio that follows. Diane tries once more to seduce Giglio, but Mirabelle has taken his place. Aline makes love with Giglio, Mirabelle with Taxis, and Diane with Mirabelle. The king finally discovers that his daughter is in the hotel and Giglio uses the king's own loose morals to trap him into agreeing to let him marry Aline.

It only remains to bring matters to a conclusion. Pausole is utterly exhausted by everything that has happened and decides to abdicate and enjoy a quiet life. He does this in a spoken passage accompanied by the orchestra playing quiet, slow reminiscences of the "Hymn of Tryphème." These are followed by some of the preceding motifs, which pass by like a dream, and the passage ends with pure sounds of Aline's aria from Act II (No. 17), at the point where she sings "Hush! He's asleep." Then comes the brief finale. We hear first the brisk tune ("That's how he went off") from the "Cup of Thule" aria, then a repeat of Example 169—relevant from the point of view of both words and music. So, Honegger's final masterstroke, *Les Aventures du roi Pausole* ends on tiptoe, in a dreamy, poetic atmosphere. It is certainly not a common operetta!

78. *La Belle de Moudon*

Operetta in five acts
January (No. 2 is dated 24 January)–31 March 1931
Libretto by René Morax
Premiere: 30 May 1931, Lucy Berthrand (Isabelle), Jacques Servières (Albert
    Praroman), Jean Mauclair (the Chevalier), Jacques Béranger (Praroman), Renée
    Dubois (La Criblette), Suzanne André-Weith (Gizèle de Gisors), Hélène Rieder
    and Alice Ecoffey (pianos), the Moudon brass band, conducted by Charles
    Pasche, Théâtre du Jorat, Mézières (Vaud)
Performing forces: actors (spoken roles); solo soprano and contralto, children's

chorus, mixed chorus–two pianos–brass band (three saxophones, two cornets, two trumpets, three trombones, three bugles, five saxhorns, tenor drum, bass drum, cymbals)
Duration: a whole evening, about 42 minutes 15 seconds of music
Act I: 1. Overture; 2. Romance of the Daisy (Isabelle); 3. Chorus of Washerwomen ("With the beetle"); 4. Chorus of Washerwomen ("It will soon be midday"); 5. Chorus of the Stagecoach
Act II: 6. Chorus ("It is the hour when all is at peace"); 7. Waltz; 8. Song of Petit-Jean (Gizèle)
Act III: Introduction; 9. Chorus ("Shade and silence"); 10. Voices of the Forest (children's chorus and mixed chorus)
Act IV: 11. Introduction; 12. Aria of Isabelle ("You flee, ungrateful one"); 13. Barcarolle (Pastiche); 14. Entrance of the Brass Band; 15. Polka
Act V: 16. Chorus ("A year has passed"); 17. Final Couplet (Isabelle and chorus)
Unpublished, but available for rental from Foetisch Frères, Lausanne
Nos. 9 and 10 published by Editions Papillon, Geneva

No cheerful comedy had ever been given at the Théâtre du Jorat. René Morax wanted to provide one, so he wrote this witty story set in the canton Vaud. And, thanks to his libretto and Honegger's music's being perfectly fitted to the milieu and the performers, the work was a great success. Moudon, we should note, is a small town some six miles north of Mézières. Some years later, an abortive adaptation of the work for a Paris audience attempted to transform the heroine into the "Belle of Meudon"! (Meudon is a suburb of Paris.) The work is not really an operetta—there is not enough music for that and, apart from two solos for Isabelle and one for Gizèle, all the roles are spoken, including those two. It would be fairer to call it a Vaudois peasant comedy "with songs." Honegger himself spoke of it as a vaudeville.

The score includes nine choruses (six of them unison, two unaccompanied, and one a children's chorus), six instrumental pieces for brass band, and four solo arias (including the choral finale). Only the arias call for professionals, even though the unaccompanied choruses are not easy for amateurs.

The story, full of twists and turns, takes place between 1836 and 1840, in the era of stagecoaches. Albert Praroman, a conservative aristocrat and son of the Moudon notary, is in love with Isabelle, the daughter of the left-wing cafe-owner Braillard. Praroman *père* is furious at the idea of this mésalliance and sends his son abroad. An Italian called Farinelli comes through Moudon. He is enthusiastic about Isabelle's voice and decides to turn her into an opera star. But her first Paris concert also includes the well-known singer Gizèle de Gisors and is a disaster. Albert meets his beloved in the capital, marries her, and takes her back to Moudon. There he finds his father ruined, beaten by Braillard in the elections, and forced to leave the area. He leaves Isabelle in a forest near the town and, on his own, goes to see his parents to ask their forgiveness. While he is away, Isabelle is so tired she goes to sleep. The spirits of the forest appear to her in a dream—an opportunity for a sung and danced divertimento. When she wakes, she finds herself in the presence of Farinelli. He takes her to Venice, finds better teachers for her and, after much hard work, she finally becomes a great singer. Now famous, she returns to Moudon a year later, calling herself Belinda. She just manages to buy back the lawyer's house, which is being auctioned, and falls into the arms of father and son. All is well that ends well.

The Overture wittily combines the severe style of passing notes, dissonant counterpoint, and chorale-type harmonies, with romantic fripperies. It sets the tone for the work: fresh, simple, unfussy, but as always superbly fashioned. The "Romance of the Daisy" is a perfect pastiche of an 1830s romance, complete with vocalises, cadenzas, and a high B-flat. The first "Chorus of Washer-women" is straightforward, in the style of Jaques-Dalcroze, the second more lively, including a saxophone solo—for this entertaining, exuberant piece of jazz they had to bring in a player from outside Moudon. While the "Chorus of the Stagecoach" goes back to the style of Jaques-Dalcroze, the delightfully relaxed 12/8 chorus number "It is the hour when all is at peace" sounds a little like Fauré. After the Waltz in turn-of-the-century peasant style, the "Song of Petit-Jean" is another pastiche, of an 1880s *café-concert* song in polka rhythm with solo violin.

Then comes a complete change of atmosphere, introduced by a few mysterious measures of impressionist harmonies on the two pianos, ushering in the chorus "Shade and silence" before the danced divertimento that accompanies Isabelle's dream. This is a very beautiful piece of unaccompanied choral writing, full of chromaticisms that are hard to pitch, and it makes one sorry that Honegger did not compose more in this genre. The divertimento itself, "Voices of the Forest," is by far the longest number in the score, lasting nine minutes and thirty-five seconds. Its form is the concentric A-B-C-D-E-D-C-B-A. Section A repeats the two-piano introduction with hardly any changes; B is a slow humming chorus; C a unison children's chorus over a lively piano accompaniment that could have belonged to *Le Cahier romand*, with its grating dissonances evoking crickets and grasshoppers; D is a peaceful unaccompanied lullaby; and E a soprano solo ("Life is a song that never ends") over a restless piano accompaniment. This is the only point at which Honegger resorts to his own particular brand of accentuation. The reversed recapitulation mixes sections A and B.

Isabelle's aria "You flee, ungrateful one" is a spirited parody of a big romantic Italian aria, complete with its virtuosity, while the "Barcarolle (Pastiche)" is a loving homage to Fauré—the piano accompaniment, especially, might almost be taken for the real thing. The final numbers for brass band, entirely Swiss in inspiration, are alternately clumsy and sprightly. They lead to the real vaudeville of the Finale, where for the first time Isabelle, with her high Bs, joins forces with the chorus and the brass band. The final words, "If this entertainment had the honor of pleasing you," recall the end of Stravinsky's and Ramuz's *Renard* ("And if the story has pleased you"). But really the last words belong to the repeat of the blues section from the second "Chorus of Washerwomen," with the exuberantly swung saxophone solo adding the final touch.

Numbers 9 and 10 together, preceded by the brief Introduction, deserve to be published and played (and indeed danced) independently of the rest of the work. It would make up a divertimento-cantata for a grouping of soprano, chorus, and two pianos, for which the only other Honegger work is the short *Chanson de Fagus*. The music is of the highest quality.

128. *Les Petites Cardinal*

Operetta in two acts and ten tableaux, in collaboration with Jacques Ibert
October–26 December 1937 (according to a letter from Ibert, Honegger was already
at work on No. 13 on 12 October; Nos. 2, 4, and 15 were completed in
November, Nos. 14a and 15 in December, and No. 13 on 26 December)
Libretto by Albert Willemetz and Paul Brach, from the novel by Ludovic Halévy
Premiere: 13 February 1938, Saturnin Fabre (Monsieur Cardinal), Marguerite Pierry
(Madame Cardinal), Yvette Lebon (Virginie), Monique Rolland (Pauline),
Claude Lehmann (Jacques), Enrico Bertolasso (Mario), Robert Pisani (the
Marquis), Henri Fabert (Monsieur Durand/Rebuffat), decor and costumes by
Fernand Ochsé, conducted by Marcel Cariven, Théâtre des Bouffes-Parisiens,
Paris
Performing forces (sung and spoken roles): sopranos (Pauline, Virginie,
Marguerite—from Gounod's *Faust*—the Female Crony, and seven other small
soprano roles); mezzo (Madame Cardinal); tenors (Monsieur Cardinal,
Monsieur Pluque, Jacques, the Marquis of Cavalcanti, the Producer, Gounod's
Faust, Monsieur Durand/Rebuffat, the Male Crony); bass (Mephisto); chorus,
orchestra: 1.1.1.–saxophone–1.1.1.0.–percussion–piano–strings
Duration of Honegger's music: 35 minutes (25:00 + 10:00); the full production lasts a
whole evening
Act I: 1. Introduction; 2. Scene of the Shepherd; 4. Entrance of the Little Cardinal
Girls; 9. From the Madeleine to the Opera; 10. Interlude; 12. Couplets (Advice)
of the Good Fellow; 13. Finale
Act II: 14. Entr'acte; 14a. Chorus of Little Bridges; 15. Migraine Trio; 21. Calumny
Aria; 22 and 23. Interludes. The rest of the score, which consists of twenty-eight
numbers altogether, is by Jacques Ibert.
Choudens et Royalty

Why was *Pausole*'s success not repeated? Certainly not because this was a
collaboration between Honegger and Ibert (*L'Aiglon* had been a popular triumph), nor because it was any less carefully put together—far from it. But it is
difficult to succeed twice in the same area, as we have seen with *Le Roi David* and
Judith. Coming second is itself a handicap, and here doubly so in that it was a
second operetta and a second collaboration with Ibert. The story of *Les Petites
Cardinal* is also less interesting, the characters less sharply drawn because they
are too numerous, and there are too many extra bits and diversions. They may
be good in themselves, but they interrupt the story, and this in any case was
framed in too prescribed a setting: 1880s Paris had been done to death. Also,
although the dialogue had its excellent moments, it was less successful and could
not match *Pausole*'s display of fireworks, with puns exploding every minute; and
while the actors at the premiere were first-class, their singing was not up to the
same standard.

Finally, the circumstances were quite different. In February 1938, it was
harder to give in to laughter, with dark clouds gathering over Europe, and only
a month to go between the premiere and the *Anschluss*. The illusions of the
Popular Front had been dissipated to give way to bitter reality, and Fascism, triumphant in Spain after the horrors of Guernica thanks to German and Italian
support, was showing signs of vigor in France. In short, audiences had no heart
for this kind of entertainment. As for the music, it must be said that the style is
less highly seasoned than in *Les Aventures du roi Pausole*: it is nearer to Lecocq
than to Chabrier or Offenbach, and there are fewer memorable tunes or harmonic refinements. As well as witty glances at Mendelssohn, Gounod, and Ros-

sini, there is also what José Bruyr (who is one of the few commentators to mention the work) calls "the folklore of the sidewalk."

The story tells of the Cardinals, a respectable bourgeois couple who have sent their two daughters, Pauline and Virginie, to join the Opera ballet, in the hope that they may one day make the transition from the Opera to the Madeleine, where all the best weddings are held. But, of course, the two young ladies—one lively, witty, and a realist with her eye on material things, the other a dreamy romantic—intend to follow their own ideas.

Honegger wrote rather less than half of the music overall, and most of that belongs to Act I. But Ibert's contribution is equally good and includes some successful numbers, such as the well-known waltz "It is the charm of Florence." Honegger composed the whole of the splendid Finale of Act I, except for the very beginning. Ibert produced some of his best music for the Finaletto-Revue Sketches of Act II, but this is exactly the kind of passage already mentioned that, for all its intrinsic qualities, holds up the action. But let us look now at the music written by Honegger.

The "Scene of the Shepherd" shows us a dancing class that turns into a flirtation with the poor fireman who is standing in for the crowd. This little ballet scene on point is a perfect pastiche of the kind of music written by Delibes or Minkus between 1860 and 1880. One of the most charming numbers is the "Entrance of the Little Cardinal Girls," in which the two heroines, preceded by their theme, introduce themselves and complacently spell out the differences in their characters and aims. The parents' duet, "From the Madeleine to the Opera," understandably includes a sly reference to Mendelssohn's *Wedding March*. In the "Couplets of the Good Fellow," Mephisto, who has been appointed as the protector of virtue and conjugal legitimacy, lightly moralizes, with the odd quotation from Gounod ("Chaste and holy dwelling," then "Charming in the arbor").

Honegger's largest contribution is the episodic Finale of Act I; he wrote the last nine minutes of this ten-minute number. Although the vocal writing is polyphonic, it retains the lightness of a Mozart finale. There is another hit at Gounod when Mephisto even offers to sing the Ave Maria "according to custom" at the marriage announced by Virginie, and then to bless the happy couple. After an animated conversational ensemble of good wishes, the old Marquis, who is to be the bridegroom, announces to the sound of one of the leitmotifs of the score that "We're leaving for Florence."

But the other sister, Pauline, has disappeared—not, however, without leaving a letter, which Virginie now reads out loud, saying that she has eloped with her lover. Her father promptly curses her, in the great tradition of grand opera. This genre also makes an unexpected appearance at the end of the act, when the Producer reminds the crowd of guests that they are in the foyer of the Opera and that their hubbub is disturbing the performance of *Faust* in the nearby auditorium. Mephisto (who is playing his own role) and the tenor Mario Rossi (who is playing Faust) hurry back onstage. The Finale ends with a display of virtuosity in which the repeat of the previous ensemble is now heard with Marguerite's apotheosis ("Pure, radiant angels") in long notes as a cantus firmus over the top. The act ends in a great burst of laughter at this contrapuntal prowess, which we have come to expect from the composer of *Le Roi David*.

In the "Migraine Trio" in Act II, Honegger once again surpassed himself in writing dense but airy polyphony. After a falsely tragic introductory recitative, he gives us one of his best tangos, which deserves to be in any anthology of operetta. It is no surprise that the "Calumny Aria" is a parody of Rossini's *The Barber of Seville*. Here, in response to the words *"piano, piano,"* Monsieur Cardinal suddenly retorts: "No, calumny does not lead you to the piano. The piano? Come, come! It leads you to the violin!" (The French word for violin, *violon*, is also slang for prison.)

Category 17: Various Unclassifiable Works

27. Orchestration of a Mussorgsky song
132. *L'Alarme*
141. *Grad us*
155. *Chant de Libération*
Orchestration of Fernand Ochsé's *Choucoune* (c. 1922)
Orchestration of Maurice Jaubert's *L'Eau vive* (1945?)
Arrangements for soloists, chorus, and orchestra of two popular songs (1936 or 1937):
    a) *La Femme du marin* (Aunis)
    b) *Les Trois Princesses au pommier doux* (Franche-Comté)
Unidentified fragments

27. Orchestration of a Mussorgsky song

This work was mentioned by Honegger in a letter to his parents of 23 January 1920. It has not been found.

132. *L'Alarme*

December 1938
Work for voice, chorus, and orchestra

Mentioned by Honegger in his manuscript catalog, *L'Alarme* has not been found.

141. *Grad us* (Forward March)

March 1940
Arranged for military band by H. Hofmann. Commissioned by Basel Radio
Performing forces: piccolo, two flutes, two oboes, clarinet in E-flat, three clarinets, two bassoons, two trumpets, cornet in E-flat, flugelhorn, two alto bugles, two

tenor bugles, baritone bugle, bass bugles in E-flat and B-flat, three trombones, bass drum
Duration: 4 minutes
Hug, Zurich

This piece was commissioned by Basel Radio for "the year of the March," 1940. A strict translation of the title would be "Straight Ahead" rather than "Forward March." It is a typical example of the functional piece for which Honegger the artisan could be relied upon to deliver, and it has the advantage over similar pieces of being well written and containing attractive tunes. It is a light, fast-moving little piece in 6/8 and in B-flat, of the "quick-march" variety.

155. *Chant de Libération* (Song of Liberation)

April 1942 (in the composer's manuscript catalog, it is referred to as "song by Bernard Zimmer for the film"; this film has not been identified)
Text by Bernard Zimmer
Performing forces: baritone, chorus, and orchestra
First performance: 22 October 1944, Jacques Rousseau (baritone), Conservatory Concert Society Chorus and Orchestra, conducted by Charles Münch, Conservatory Concerts, Paris
The score is lost, even though it figured briefly in Salabert's catalog

The review by Maurice Brillant in the journal *L'Aube* of 28 October 1944 suggests that the loss of this score is cause for profound regret:

A short, powerful piece that starts with a bang, and is based on a poem by Bernard Zimmer. The baritone sings virile, yet poignant verses, to which the chorus responds with two martial refrains. The orchestration is rich and sober and, far from trying to impress on its own account, is concerned simply with supporting and serving the vocal parts. There is no padding or rhetoric, the argument is presented frankly and openly. It is a work in which total clarity, density, nervosity, passion, and power combine to make a complete success. Reluctant as I am to mix up the arts, it reminds me of Rude's sculpture *La Marseillaise*, which has the same clear, dense, nervous style, full of movement, and which really sings. The best compliment I can pay Honegger is that Rude's masterpiece seems made to illustrate his own—which is fine music and popular in the best sense of the word. And to its other merits is added that of having been written in 1942. We rejoice and are honored that Honegger was a composer of the Resistance. An enthusiastic audience asked for this *Chant de Libération* to be encored, and Münch was happy to comply.

Unidentified Fragments

These are all autographs in the possession of Pascale Honegger in Lausanne. They may be fragments of works that are lost. They consist of the following: a short piece for organ or harmonium, two piano reductions (the second of which, despite being the longer of the two, is incomplete), and thirteen measures of a piece—also incomplete—for cinema orchestra.

Part Three
GATHERING THE THREADS

It is inevitable that when you spend more than a year and a half in the company of a man and his work you begin to identify closely with him. I hardly knew Arthur Honegger, having met him for only a dozen or so sessions of a course he taught in the first half of 1953—it was the last one he was able to give—but I still have the memory of a great spiritual presence in the fall of its life. It was, though, more the daily contact with hundreds of letters and personal documents and with hundreds of scores—usually autograph scores, which made them seem closer in some real manner—not to mention innumerable talks with Pascale Honegger about her father, whom she resembles in so many ways, that made Honegger seem like an intensely living presence with whom I could almost hold a conversation.

So I have deliberately left until the end of the book this portrait sketch of Honegger as man and composer. Just as it is only normal for me to want to sum up at the end of my research, so the reader too, after having read the facts of Honegger's biography and examined his output, will want to think about what sort of man Honegger was. As to defining Honegger's musical style and language, many facets of these have been covered in the course of analyzing individual works, and so I have refrained from repeating myself and simply referred the reader to the passages in question.

The publication of *Écrits* (Paris, 1992), the large volume comprising all Honegger's writings, is a great complement to this book. That volume contains, among other things, the well-known collection of interviews with Bernard Gavoty that was published under the title *Je suis compositeur* (I Am a Composer), which, though long out of print, is still an indispensable document for anyone seeking to trace Honegger's creative processes, his working methods, or his aesthetic orientation. In preparing this portrait I have also had recourse as often as possible to unpublished documents, especially the small school notebooks in which, particularly at the end of his life, Honegger noted down thoughts and reflections, together with quotations and newspaper cuttings that caught his eye.

This third portion of the book is presented in the form of a triptych. The first part of it describes Honegger's physical appearance and his character; the second synthesizes the details of his musical language; and the third attempts to evaluate, albeit provisionally, the composer's place in the music of the twentieth century and in the overall history of the art.

FIFTEEN

Honegger's Physique and Character

Apart from his outstanding musical gifts, Honegger was also blessed by Nature with physical beauty and charm, not to mention a robust constitution (at least until the catastrophe of summer 1947). Countless private and public photographs attest to these physical attributes, taking us on a journey from the chubby little boy in Le Havre to the tragic figure of his last years. He was not tall, only about five feet six inches, but he was vigorous and well-proportioned, with a rather thick neck, broad shoulders, and a powerful torso.

This "sporty" outline gradually spread with age to a certain portliness that was encouraged by an active appetite. The well-known riposte, recorded by Arthur Hoérée, made to a friend who was shocked at the manner in which Honegger was putting away chocolate cake—"Don't worry, with me it all gets turned into music!"—was unfortunately not entirely true. Certainly Juliette Pary's description (in her memoirs *L'Amour des camarades*) of Honegger's "three ample chins" in 1936 or 1937 is distinctly exaggerated, as the photographs show, but a family snapshot taken a little later, at the Thévenet's in Montquin, does reveal "spare tires" that are somewhat short of athletic. They made a healthy departure during the war and the Occupation, only to return with a vengeance in peacetime and would have an undoubted part to play in his first heart attack. As we know, even this event had no immediate effect on his silhouette, since he was determined, in the face of common sense, to return to his earlier frantic pace of living, and it is only in the photographs of the last three or four years of his life that we see the haggard body of someone seriously ill.

The photographs of him as a baby, especially the one showing him prophetically clutching a locomotive, show a singularly determined mouth under the dark gaze and darker curls. At nineteen, Turly the student has a rebellious quiff, or tuft of hair, over his left eye, which is colder and more analytical than its dreamier counterpart. The nose is well-formed, a little long perhaps (it would curve down as the years went by), and his expression is one of concentrated energy with a touch of stiffness, no doubt a result of his shyness and emphasized by his floppy bow tie.

In the photographs of the following years, however, this adolescent "skinny cat" look would gradually change as the curve of the face became fuller and more pronounced, and his expression becomes dreamy and gentle, if slightly clouded, with a hint of sensuality. We see him at Mézières with the two Morax brothers, still a very young man with his hands behind his back, solidly set on rather short legs that are slightly apart. But in the famous photo of 1925, showing Les Six standing around Jean Cocteau seated at the piano, Honegger is looking us straight in the eyes with a rather cool, fixed frankness, very different from the numerous snapshots, both from that period and later, in which we see that warm, cordial smile supported more often than not by the indispensable pipe. Perhaps the finest photo of these years shows him at the time of Rugby, wearing his driving outfit—here we see all the virile yet gentle brilliance of his early maturity. Then we pass through the "classic" portraits of him in overalls on the footplate of a stationary Pacific locomotive, and come to Honegger as the happy husband and father. Here we see him looking with protective tenderness at the baby Pascale on his knee, as she puffs conscientiously on her father's pipe, or laughing uproariously as he upends the sledge in the snow, listening, apparently, to his daughter's childish screams.

But then there is the portrait taken of him at Le Grand-Mesnil in 1936, leaning on a lawnmower, in which we can sense the peasant robustness of Panturle in Regain. In the wartime photos we see an unmistakably democratic, even proletarian Honegger, with a beret and shopping basket, pushing a bicycle. After the Liberation come the years of fame, with biographers and reporters bearing cameras, providing us with pictures of the master at work, his spectacles pushed up high on his massive forehead and the expression of concentration as he studies the manuscript of some emerging masterpiece. As for those showing Honegger on the conductor's rostrum, like the one taken of him with the Czech Philharmonic, they strike us with their seriousness and simplicity, absolutely devoid of starry posturing. Then there is the brutal shock as we turn to the portraits of the final years, charting the inexorable decline of this once godlike figure into precocious frailty. He still has most of his hair, but now it is gray, and his imperious nose stands out ever more clearly from the thinning cheeks. Finally, we come to the terrible, heartrending beauty of the final portrait, taken from Georges Rouquier's 1954 film: a look of tragic intensity from those huge eyes that have eaten away the emaciated face, the flame of the soul that has consumed the ruined body. The abundance of this visual documentation, which includes in addition to these photographs the numerous painted or sculpted portraits of Honegger, are a rare godsend for a biographer.

We also have a number of recordings of his voice. He expresses himself in a remarkably elegant French, and the voice is gentle, but not deep. On the contrary, it is a slightly veiled "baryton Martin," about which he complained in some manuscript notes: "I have a very quiet voice and I can't shout. That's why I always lose arguments and why I've got out of the habit of finishing my sentences, because someone always interrupts me before I've got to the end." In the latest recordings, the effects of his illness are apparent in the gasps and the shallow, whistling breath.

Before his 1947 attack, Honegger enjoyed excellent health and seems never to have suffered any serious illness. Some of his letters to his parents mention exhaustion, but that is entirely understandable, given the intensity of his work schedule. All his life he seems to have had slight allergy problems affecting his breathing, notably the fairly frequent attacks of sinusitis. Honegger kept up his health and strength as long as he could through vigorous sport and exercise. As a boy, he had "invented" bicycle polo and had instinctively kept a balance between physical exuberance and mental activity. One curious fact is that, coming from a Zurich family but being born in Le Havre, Honegger was more attracted by the sea than by mountains, and all through his life he swam but did not climb. This is what he had to say about himself at the end of his life:

Attracted as I was by every kind of sport, I always took intellectual pursuits seriously. Even when I was no longer young, I was proud of my legs, which were those of a runner rather than an intellectual, and of a torso that was not that of a bookworm. Today, thanks to regrettable whims on the part of my myocardium, whims that affect the state of my coronary arteries, the one-time rugby player is practically immobile.[1]

To conclude, here is a mosaic portrait of the composer at the height of his early maturity, recorded by the journalist Jean Barreyre. Barreyre had asked for an interview, so Honegger took him in his Bugatti for a hair-raising ride through Paris and its suburbs. The following description appeared in the daily paper *L'Intransigeant* on 20 July 1930:

The composer of *Le Roi David* has a high, nobly curving forehead, hazel-brown eyes, a delicately shaped nose, curly hair, bronzed skin, a mouth with a mischievous smile, and the hand he holds out is fleshy, sensitive, and tapering like Victor Hugo's.

After that sketch of Honegger's physical appearance, we come to a brief summary of his character, many details of which we have already touched on. The fact that he was treated, at least during his lifetime, with respect and usually with admiration by his colleagues is in itself fairly rare, as was pointed out with a touch of envy by his old comrade in arms Darius Milhaud, whose own career was more contentious. But there is something even more exceptional: as a man, Honegger seems not to have had any enemies. What follows are some tributes from those who knew him.

In a speech given at Honegger's funeral service in Paris on 2 December 1955, Fritz Münch, Charles's brother, had this to say:

We were all profoundly struck by the humanity emanating from this man, by the goodness that formed the ground of his being, and by the complete absence of all ill-nature, jealousy, or pettiness. As a result, even though he could be categorical in making a stand, he was never negative and never wounded anyone unnecessarily—he always brought a positive approach to everything he said and did, and he always loved the young, and not only the young. We never met him without coming away the richer for it, precisely because of his attitude toward people and things. Unintentionally he helped us to become better beings, simply because this humanity was the essence of his nature.

From Jean Cocteau, at Honegger's graveside: "Arthur, you have been a wonderful friend. Today is the first time you have caused us pain!"
From Olivier Messiaen:

Honegger was not only one of the greatest composers of his time, he was also a true man: a man of strength and willpower, a tremendous worker, kind toward everyone and especially toward his younger colleagues: all his life he protested against injustice and defended order and truth, like Judith, like Joan of Arc, like Antigone.

From Darius Milhaud:

He was always like a brother to me. . . . Arthur Honegger was a marvelous example to others in the life he led of relentless hard work, in his simplicity, his good nature, and modesty: rare qualities in a creative artist also visited by success and genius.

From Francis Poulenc: "To begin with, Honegger intimidated me despite the jovial smile of greeting he always sported, but it didn't take me long to get to know him and everything went splendidly."
And from the composer Maurice Thiriet: "Like his music, he was a man of greatness and simplicity: welcoming and infinitely—almost intimidatingly—kind to his younger colleagues"
One could continue like this for some time. I can say that I have not come across one discordant note in this hymn of praise, even from those who are less in sympathy with his music. He had the rare gift of making friends, and not only the gift but the need. Once his friendship was given, it remained unalterable throughout his life. But it was not only musical colleagues he befriended, such as Jacques Ibert, to whom he was especially close, Arthur Hoérée, Roland-Manuel, and many others. There were also Fernand Ochsé, Francis and Toné Winter, Jacques and Paule Thévenet, Albert Willemetz, as well as literary collaborators such as René Morax and Paul Claudel. We must also find a special place for two benefactors, Werner Reinhart and Paul Sacher, the second of whom provided far more than material support. As the years went by, Paul and Maya Sacher undoubtedly became the best friends Honegger and his family had, as we can tell from their splendid correspondence from which this book has quoted at length and which really should be published one day. The name Paul Sacher also brings to mind interpreters of Honegger's music, and among those, Charles Münch was also a dear friend.
Honegger had the knack of breaking the ice instantly and putting the person he was talking to at ease. This intense need to communicate was the main motivating force behind his music, and it extended also to his personal relationships. He liked playing the part of the affectionate elder brother who could be relied upon for good advice, and directed this kind of open friendliness toward women too, not always without danger, as his magnetic charm tended to push matters rather quickly beyond the limits of pure friendship. I found in one of the little notebooks previously mentioned an interesting reflection on his

Protestant education: "This Puritan side has stayed with me despite my interest in all the problems of sexual psychopathology and my reading of Havelock Ellis and Freud, all of which have led me to view the relationships between men and women with a certain freedom." There was, however, an invisible yet insurmountable barrier separating this marvelous cordiality from the enclosed space of his fiercely guarded privacy. His whole life was organized in order to preserve this space in which his creativity could flourish, free from prying eyes and, more especially, ears. Hence his "elephantine discretion" (his own phrase), which meant that he could never go on composing the moment he felt himself being observed or spied upon. That is why he always felt the need to live on his own, "like a bear," separated from his family by several apartment blocks and leaving his lair only when the day's work had been done. And he would go back to it immediately after the end of the free time he devoted to his family and friends, or to the simple pleasures of daily existence, whether in the areas of art, food, or sport.

His temperament was certainly more sanguine than choleric. Even so, he was a "grump," a "grouch" who could be roused to exasperation by the inconveniences of daily life. This tendency grew more noticeable with age. He developed a profound, and ultimately obsessional, hatred of certain constraints, as is shown by his incessant diatribes against the tax and customs authorities, whom he elevated into major oppressors of humanity. It was always this fiercely individual libertarianism that shone through, and it was this almost animal instinct for defending his own property that prompted reflections like the following, taken from one of the notebooks he used toward the end of his life: "In all good faith, no woman will ever believe that one might prefer solitude to her presence."[2] His own wife was aware of this, to her loss, and everyone who knew and loved him felt a "lack"—that of never seeing enough of him. We may remember his son Jean-Claude during the war, praying that an air-raid warning would prolong his father's weekly visit and force him to stay overnight. And then there is Poulenc's testimony:

> If I am not so close to Honegger as I am to Auric or Milhaud, it is, quite prosaically, a simple matter of the telephone: Arthur never answers the telephone, never opens the door if you ring the bell of his studio, and hardly ever checks his mail. You must admit, that makes intimacy difficult. When I meet him at the theater or at a concert, with his wife, I say to myself with some feeling: "How sad that we see so little of each other!"

We have, then, this permanent, necessary contrast. On the one hand, there are the famous "recitals" on the doorbell of the studio on the boulevard de Clichy, which were met with the unyielding silence of the composer at work. On the other hand, there is the cheerful companion who enjoyed the pleasures of the world and who could, for example, write to his friend Aloys Mooser (the severe, much-feared Geneva critic) the following lighthearted letter—it was sent on 4 February 1924 with the well-known program note for *Pacific 2.3.1*:

Dear Father Aloys,
   So you've come a cropper fooling about in places best left to the backs of postcards! [Mooser was a keen mountaineer.] That's what comes of wanting to ski at unsuitable heights. . . . You know that if you come to Paris your sofa awaits you and you can have as much cheap tobacco as you can get through. See you soon, dear Father Aloys. . . . your respectful son.

Further evidence comes from Juliette Pary in her description of a workers' meeting at the time of the Popular Front. In the middle of the meeting, an old street sweeper addressed this *cri du coeur* to the composer: "Mr. Honegger, all I can say is, in the seventeenth district you're a real popular guy!" We know that for Honegger the acceptance of the people was as important as the respect of music professionals.

   The result was that his popularity was on a level unthinkable these days for a composer of "serious" music. It came, too, from writing such works as *Les Aventures du roi Pausole*, *Jeunesse*, and the film music, in addition to his symphonies and quartets. How delighted he was to discover a picture of himself included in a tin of a popular brand of French cocoa as a promotional gift! And how he must have relished the long article published in *Point de vue* shortly after his return from the United States in 1947, with a photograph showing him smiling broadly with his "three large chins" (alas) and sitting in his study (even though the caption claims he is monitoring a rehearsal at the Théâtre des Champs-Élysées). The caption alone would have given him pleasure: "Arthur Honegger, an eclectic composer, has two audiences: the music-lovers of the Salle Pleyel, and the working girls who patronize cheap cinemas." The article tells us, among other choice tidbits, that the king of trumpeters, Louis Armstrong, the great "Satchmo," was presented with a Sevres vase by the French President, but still had one regret as he left to go back to the United States, "that of not meeting Arthur Honegger, as he'd hoped." The article continues: "'He's the greatest contemporary French composer,' Armstrong told his friends, and he's secretly thinking of playing the famous *Deliciae basilienses* with his Hot Five. The result would certainly be interesting." The journalist goes on to mention Honegger as the composer of a *Pastorale des fées* (!) and describes him as a great French composer, correcting himself a few lines later by saying "Honegger isn't French, but Swiss." He goes on to tell us that "people hint that Vaura writes the pieces that appear under her husband's name. It's not true. There are some parts of Honegger's output that Vaura has never even heard." That is really popular fame.

   From the jealously guarded solitude of his studio came both the "Lamento" from *La Danse des morts* and the tango from *Mata-Hari*. As Bernard Gavoty says so rightly of Honegger at the end of *Je suis compositeur*:

   You're neither an angel nor a beast, because you have your feet on the ground and, sometimes, your head among the stars! In the midst of all the false angels of music who are beasts without knowing it, it is comforting to find, in the front rank of contemporary artists, a man like the rest—a man who, quite simply, has at times the wings and the smile of an angel!

SIXTEEN

Two Countries, Three Cultures

In 1911, when the nineteen-year-old Honegger had to make the choice, he opted for the Swiss nationality of his forebears. But he always lived in Paris, and the French cultural environment was absolutely vital for him. He may have been a Swiss plant, but he drew his sap from the nourishing compost of France. When I say "Swiss," I should specify "German-speaking Swiss," which makes his case rarer and more interesting.

Honegger's relationship with Switzerland was always both close and ambiguous. As he said to Bernard Gavoty:

> Although I was born in Le Havre of Swiss parents, I've spent most of my life in France and learned my craft there, as though I were a Frenchman. But, deep inside, I have kept a kernel of something Swiss—what Milhaud used to call my "Helvetic sensitivity."
>
> What do I owe to Switzerland? No doubt, the Protestant tradition, a great difficulty in fooling myself over the value of what I do, a naive sense of honesty, and a familiarity with the Bible. That's a very disparate group of things.[1]

Honegger always thought of Switzerland as a place for holidays, as the place where his family lived, and later, immediately after the Second World War when living conditions in France were very difficult, as a place of refuge. But he never envisaged settling there. He even held it against his parents that they went back there for their retirement. He found the Swiss cultural and intellectual climate too narrow and provincial in its outlook, and the oxygen of Paris was indispensable to him as a permanent stimulant. He knew that in Switzerland his creative genius would wither for lack of nourishment. Truth be told, one sometimes has the feeling that, possibly without realizing it, he was ungrateful to Switzerland. Certainly his hometown of Zurich took a long time to recognize his worth, and he never forgot the insult when they refused his *String Quartet No. 1* on the grounds that it was immature and imperfectly crafted. Zurich also waited until the last moment (1951) before giving Honegger his last commission, for *Monopartita*. But of Honegger's two great patrons, one came from Winterthur and the other from Basel.

Honegger grumbled about his months of military service "without danger but without glory" during the First World War. One wonders what he would have said, had he opted for French citizenship, of four years in the trenches, during which he might perhaps have been killed. And when, in 1946, he says how happy he is to have found a haven of tranquillity and, to some extent, of material prosperity in his native land, when he vehemently and continuously denounces the politicians for visiting their peoples (or "subjects," as he puts it) with a disastrous war and consequences that are no less so, he does perhaps forget to make a brief bow in the direction of the politicians of Switzerland, who were the only ones to spare their citizens these calamities.

But what exactly does being Swiss mean, especially for someone from the German-speaking part who has been, as it were, French-ified? We may be struck by the fact that this completely bilingual composer, having persuaded his parents not to send him to complete his studies in Germany, never thereafter set any German text to music, apart from one tiny piece, a cabaret song written in the Zurich-German dialect. (The *Selzach Passion*, which he never finished because of the death of the librettist Caesar von Arx, would have been the exception that proves the rule.) Frank Martin, on the other hand, who was born in Geneva of partially French parentage and who spoke no other language, successfully set, with the help of his German-speaking wife, works of Rilke and Hofmannsthal, as well as of Shakespeare (*The Tempest*) in Schlegel's German translation. And when Martin too left Switzerland, it was not to go to Paris but to the Netherlands, where his wife came from.

The fact is that, even if there does exist a Swiss people, there is no Swiss nation, in the definite, long-standing sense in which there is a French nation or the no less definite, if more recent sense in which there is a German nation. Even so, beyond cultural differences, there is clearly a specific Swiss identity. The river Sarine separates two cultures and two languages (German-Swiss and French-Swiss), but the Jura and the Rhine separate two models of social intercourse, two civic and political traditions, and that is perhaps more significant. Because on either side of the Sarine, people live according to similar communal structures and according to the same definition of democracy, and it is significant that Catholics and Protestants are spread variously on either side of this frontier. The dichotomy we find in Honegger between his fierce need of independence, even of solitude, and his no less passionate striving for communication with the body of mankind is echoed in the decentralized individualism of the Swiss, coexisting with their highly developed sense of communal structures. If Honegger had been wholly French, he would surely not have been the "composer in the city of men" to the same extent.

A comparison between *Jeanne d'Arc au bûcher* and *Nicolas de Flue*—two large-scale works relatively close in time—will illustrate, better than any long theoretical discourse, the profound differences between the political and ideological attitudes of France and Switzerland. Switzerland's habitual tendency to close up on itself in a self-satisfied way is symbolized by the well-known Swiss expression "There's nobody like us." Only Switzerland could have provided the background for a patriotic, religious work like *Nicolas de Flue*, intended to be performed by a whole community pooling its amateur choral and instrumental resources, including brass and wind bands. If we leave aside all value judgments about the work's text or music, it has to be said that Denis de Rougemont's libretto would appear impossible, grotesque, even improper in France, where too many bloody wars and too much abuse by a centralizing state have devalued the word "fatherland" and degraded patriotism into chauvinism. In Switzerland, the pride in being *Vaudois* or *Valaisan* is combined with a more general but no less powerful feeling that they share certain fundamental ethical values with those in other cantons—values that are the very raison d'être of the Swiss Confederation. From the time of that agreement onward, the concept of patriotism has not been spattered with blood, nor has it been cheapened by any hint of a boastful superiority. In *Jeanne d'Arc*, Claudel and Honegger avoided any reference to current events in order to rise above them, as it were, through a vision that was both nationalist and universal. Whereas the link between past and present is permanent in *Nicolas de Flue*, in *Jeanne d'Arc au bûcher* it operates, again at a more abstract spiritual level, only in the Prologue added after the tragic events of the Second World War. And *Jeanne d'Arc au bûcher*, unlike *Nicolas*, is a work intended for professional performers of the highest caliber, and a work of a decidedly more "elitist" quality, for all the universality and broad outreach of its music. One final detail is very telling: in *Jeanne d'Arc au bûcher*, the words "Faith," "Hope," and "Love" are much in evidence, but the word "Peace," which is the keystone of *Nicolas de Flue*, is never mentioned.

The situations of French-speaking and German-speaking Switzerland are very far from being parallel. The French-speaking community is small (a million and a half people), and the area it inhabits is too small to be able to nourish its creative artists on any permanent basis; furthermore, it is exposed to the constant danger of becoming a satellite of Paris, with that city's colossal powers of attraction. C. F. Ramuz, the greatest of all French-speaking Swiss writers, felt these problems deeply, and he described them in masterly fashion, while underlining both the specific character of his area—in *Une Province qui n'en est pas une* (A Province That Is Not a Province)—and its limitations—in *Besoin de grandeur* (An Urge to Greatness).

German-speaking Switzerland, on the other hand, possesses Basel, a city with an old humanist culture, as well as Zurich, an economic and financial metropolis. With a population of more than four million, German-speaking Switzerland can sustain its own cultural life and is not menaced by any center like Paris, since Germany is, like Switzerland, by tradition decentralized. Paradoxically, though, this leads to a certain provincialism, emphasized by the presence of numerous dialects, whereas in French-speaking Switzerland people speak and write the French of France, with barely broader nuances than are to be found in any province in France. As Switzerland's German-speaking artists have no need to leave the country in order to survive, they run the danger of becoming prisoners of their own territory. Even if Henri-Frédéric Amiel, C. F. Ramuz, and Étienne Barilier are as distinct from their French-speaking colleagues in France as Gottfried Keller, Friedrich Dürrenmatt, and Max Frisch are from their colleagues in Germany, the differences are still plain to see.

What would have happened to Honegger had he been born in Zurich and stayed there? This is hard, if not impossible, to imagine. But let us simply take the case of his younger contemporary Willy Burkhard, whose *The Vision of Isaiah* is the equal of Honegger's great oratorios and, with many other works, supplies ample evidence of genius. Burkhard's reputation is confined to German-speaking Switzerland and his music is relatively unknown in Germany and in French-speaking Switzerland. As for the German-speaking Klaus Huber, the greatest Swiss composer of today, it was only when he was past sixty that he really achieved international fame. The Swiss model was for years considered by the rest of the world as an anomaly not to be imitated, as an archaic survival. Now it is in the process of becoming unexpectedly relevant with the fading of the Jacobin, centralizing concept of the nation-state and the emergence of a regional Europe, whose spiritual father quite naturally turns out to be the Swiss Denis de Rougemont. The example of Belgium or, more recently, of the former Yugoslavia, shows that you cannot make different peoples live together against their will under a single state government.

It is in fact Denis de Rougemont, in his book *La Suisse, ou l'histoire d'un peuple heureux* (Switzerland, or the History of a Contented People), who in talking about *Nicolas de Flue* gives us valuable testimony as to Honegger's "Helvetic" nature:

> Over the two months during which I worked with Honegger practically every day, I was highly entertained to discover the German-Swiss traits in his strong, sensitive character: his exclamations in *schwyzerdütsch*, which sounded so curious coming from a man who spoke exquisite French, his intimate knowledge of the customs, responses, and feelings of the people who were going to hear the work, and his cheerful, friendly simplicity.

Honegger's music belongs, then, to two countries and three cultures, and provides a perfect example of cultural symbiosis. His literary sources were exclusively French, or at least used the French language, as did his Swiss collaborators René Morax, Denis de Rougemont, and William Aguet (who, although he came from a family from Lutry near Lausanne, had been born in Paris). But we must also put into the balance Honegger's exceptional ability to adapt. This genius I have referred to, entirely approvingly, as "chameleonlike," and it enabled him to write works with different cultural orientations, just as the great masters of the past such as Handel, Gluck, and Mozart did, without ever losing one iota of his own personality. Is there anything more specifically Parisian than Honegger's songs on words by Apollinaire and Cocteau, the sonatinas, the *Seven Short Pieces*, *Les Aventures du roi Pausole*, and the numerous popular songs? And how much closer can one get to the real heart of France than *Jeanne d'Arc au bûcher*, the music for the film *Regain*, or the *Concerto da camera*?

But then there are the splendid works that belong to the French-speaking Swiss heritage: *Le Roi David*, *Judith*, the inimitable Vaudois operetta *La Belle de Moudon*, not to mention *Le Cahier romand*, the *Three Psalms*, or the two films based on works by Ramuz (*Rapt* and *L'Or dans la montagne*). A work as plainly "federal" as *Nicolas de Flue* belongs to French-speaking Switzerland in its librettist and its chosen interpreters, but it belongs to the German-speaking part in its subject and the place intended for its premiere. In this respect it bridges the Sarine, as it were, to the German-speaking areas, to which belong the symphony *Deliciae basilienses* and *L'Appel de la montagne* certainly, but also, and perhaps more closely still, those harsher passages in which Honegger's Alemannic inheritance declares itself most obviously: the quartets, *Le Chant de Nigamon*, *Horace victorieux*, the *First Symphony*, the *Symphonic Movement No. 3*, *Monopartita*, and even *Antigone*. And this despite the fact that the most profound and lasting influence on Honegger's musical language, even though it is certainly not the most immediately noticeable, is that of Gabriel Fauré, the most intimately French of all composers.

French culture was therefore the nurse of Honegger's genius, and he repaid the debt more than generously. His works could certainly never have emerged elsewhere. And yet, we may ask whether France was always appreciative of this adopted son who made her such magnificent offerings, and whether the Switzerland he pretended sometimes to look down on slightly was not finally a more faithful supporter. The table listing where Honegger's works were commissioned and first performed answers such questions better than any prolonged speculation.

We can see from the table that all the large oratorios were commissioned and premiered in Switzerland, with the single exception of *Jeanne d'Arc au bûcher* (although its premiere was in Switzerland, it was the result of a French commission). Three of the symphonies were commissioned or first performed in Switzerland, the other two in the United States. Apart from *Le Dit des jeux du monde* (Jane Bathori for the Vieux-Colombier) and *Le Cantique des cantiques* (Serge Lifar for the Paris Opera), all the large French commissions came from Ida Rubinstein. None of the large premieres after 1938 took place in France, except *L'Appel de la montagne*. And *Antigone*, the most crucial work of all, was premiered in Brussels, not reaching Paris until sixteen years later. In all, twenty-three major first performances took place in Switzerland, as against twelve in France and twelve elsewhere.

If it was Paris that gave Honegger rapid and lasting fame, it is clear that it was Switzerland that brought this initial groundwork to fulfillment. The imbalance is just as great with respect to commissions. There were seven in France as against seventeen in Switzerland, and even if one takes into account the years of war and the Occupation, during which France could hardly concern itself with the Arts, the balance is scarcely redressed.

From the chronological point of view, it is interesting to note that France was supportive of Honegger particularly at the beginning of his career, even if it then played his music regularly thereafter. Switzerland, mistrustful as ever of novelty, paused after the two early commissions from René Morax and began to commission Honegger again only around 1930 with *Cris du monde*, then with the arrival on the scene of Paul Sacher. France may have been more energetic in loudly proclaiming Honegger as *its* finest contemporary composer, but Switzerland was actually more useful in issuing commissions and giving first performances, and it never ceased to regard as one of its own this prodigal son who made his career on the banks of the Seine.

Table 16-1

Work	Commission	First Performance
String Quartet No. 1		France
Le Dit des jeux du monde	France	France
Horace victorieux		Switzerland
Le Roi David	Switzerland	Switzerland
Chant de joie		Switzerland
Pacific 2.3.1		France
Concertino for piano and orchestra		France
Judith (oratorio)	Switzerland	Switzerland
Judith (opera)	Monaco	Monaco
L'Impératrice aux rochers	France	France
Phaedra	France	Italy
Antigone		Belgium
Rugby		France
Amphion	France	France
Cello Concerto		United States
First Symphony	United States	United States
Les Aventures du roi Pausole		France
Cris du monde	Switzerland	Switzerland
La Belle de Moudon	Switzerland	Switzerland
Symphonic Movement No. 3	Germany	Germany
Sémiramis	France	France
Radio-Panoramique	Switzerland	Switzerland
Jeanne d'Arc au bûcher	France	Switzerland
Nocturne for orchestra		Belgium
String Quartet No. 2		Italy
L'Aiglon	Monaco	Monaco
String Quartet No. 3	United States	Switzerland
Le Cantique des cantiques	France	France
Les Petites Cardinal		France
La Danse des morts	Switzerland	Switzerland
Nicolas de Flue	Switzerland	Switzerland
Partita for two pianos		Switzerland
Christopher Columbus	Switzerland	Switzerland
Second Symphony	Switzerland	Switzerland
L'Appel de la montagne		France
Charles le Téméraire	Switzerland	Switzerland
Battements du monde	Switzerland	Switzerland
Chota Roustaveli	Monaco	Monaco
Sérénade à Angélique	Switzerland	Switzerland
Third Symphony	Switzerland	Switzerland
Fourth Symphony	Switzerland	Switzerland
Concerto da camera	United States	Switzerland

Work	Commission	First Performance
Saint François d'Assise	Switzerland	Switzerland
Fifth Symphony	United States	United States
Suite archaïque	United States	United States
Monopartita	Switzerland	Switzerland
Une Cantate de Noël	Switzerland	Switzerland

The composer's own choice was to retain a Swiss passport but to live permanently in Paris. This was an accurate reflection of the "double nationality" he spoke of in his interviews with Bernard Gavoty. The unity and diversity of Honegger's work confirms this dual status, but Switzerland can legitimately lay claim to this famous son whose career France enabled to flourish.[2]

SEVENTEEN

Political and Social Ideas; The Role of the Composer

No trace of any political or social preoccupations can be found in Arthur Honegger's writings or his music before 1930. From this point of view, *Cris du monde* marks the great turning point, as the first ideologically inspired work marking the beginning of a decade, at least, of "committed" compositions. This turning point coincided both with the grave world crisis that followed the Wall Street crash of October 1929 (a crisis that shattered the illusory prosperity of a dormant Europe now at the mercy of the appetites of totalitarian ideologies) and with Honegger's profound personal crisis. Honegger had been severely shaken by the semi-failures with the public of such central works as *Judith*, *Antigone*, and that same *Cris du monde*, and he turned his attention inward, asking himself questions about his function in society and the usefulness of his creative work. We shall see, in the following chapter, that this phase corresponded with a decade during which religious inspiration disappeared totally from his output.

Cris du monde warns against the danger of the enslavement of the individual by a continually encroaching collectivization, aggravated by the burden of state institutions and by the growing deterioration in what is now called the "quality of life," especially in the matter of noise pollution. This increasing restriction on the space reserved for individual freedom would continue to haunt the composer until his death, leading him gradually to a real hatred of all coercive political structures, a hatred that came close to anarchy. That hatred stemmed from the failure of a democratic ideal trampled by the triumphant march of Nazism and of Stalinism—although, because the latter force held out for so long, the composer would die before he could see the end of it. War was the incarnation of absolute evil and of bestiality triumphant. Its denunciation does find a place in *Cris du monde*, but it would develop enormously in the works that followed, to the point where it became the other great leitmotif of a creative artist who had assumed the role of a Cassandra. Honegger's untiring pacifist crusade began in a lighthearted manner in the "Hymn of Tryphème" so popular with King Pausole's subjects, and then rose to heights of tragic expression in *Battements du monde* and in the "Liturgical" Symphony (*Symphonie liturgique*), which could equally well have been called the "Symphony for Peace."

This imperious need for personal freedom and for a protected private space, this phobia about being jostled by the crowd—a phobia that we might regard as egoism—comes into open conflict with the even stronger necessity of communicating, especially during these crisis years. And communication is the indispensable breath of life for every creative artist who refuses to live in an ivory tower. Texts like "Pour prendre congé"[1] and "Du cinéma sonore à la musique réelle"[2] eloquently reflect this terrible dilemma, and show that Honegger, in his anxiety at having lost his audience, had chosen, for the moment at least, to make communication his absolute priority. This led to declarations that we may find bewildering, especially in the political context of the years 1930–1933. They are in any case opposed to the tenets of *Cris du monde*, although they do show the composer as a true humanist (one no longer dares to say a "progressive").

In order to escape his isolation, Honegger was therefore prepared to sacrifice the pleasure of indulging in certain experiments with musical language, which he now came to consider a narcissistic brand of intellectual luxury. This is shown by his well-known remark to Marcel Delannoy: "One can, one must speak to the wider public without making concessions, but also without being obscure. . . . Music must change character, become straightforward, simple, impressive. The masses can't be bothered with technique and fussy perfectionism."[3] "Without making concessions"—that says it all. It is relevant here to quote a wise remark Paul Collaer made to Éveline Hurard about Les Six:

> The composers did not write for the people, they expressed what the people were feeling. . . . Honegger tried to write for the public, while the others, when they wrote, say, *Le Boeuf sur le toit* or *Cocardes*, expressed themselves as the people would have done.

That Honegger had long been aware of the exact nature of the problem is clear from an article in *Chantecler* of 15 May 1926, in which he expresses his amazement at the stormy reception of *Phaedra* (even though he understood the extra-musical ingredients involved):

> In general there are two things the public do not like: continuous dissonant harmonies and the use of special effects (low instruments in a high register or muted brass). The worst dissonances used in a piece that is in essence purely rhythmic do not normally upset listeners.

Much later, in the talk he gave for UNESCO in Venice in September 1952 (see Chapter 9), Honegger returned to this theme of the composer's responsibility for his loss of contact with the public:

> For me, what has distanced the music-lover from the composer is the latter's somewhat childish whim of writing and expressing himself in a manner that is deliberately complicated. Reading music is already such a difficult business that it is pointless to confuse it unnecessarily. It is harder these days to find a score that is clear than to find one that is super-subtle, and too often one yields to the attractions of a notation that gives players the shakes. It is a cheap way of giving an impression of transcendent mas-

tery, with changes of time signature, cataracts of notes, and chords piled up like skyscrapers. It's childish, . . . and now only naive people are impressed by this kind of writing. It is an infallible sign of clumsiness.

This passage illustrates Honegger's dislike of the deliberately obscure and his "naive sense of honesty" that he refers to as part of his Swiss inheritance.[4] In a manuscript note in one of the little notebooks he used during the final years of his life, Honegger expresses the same idea more forcefully and succinctly: "*Difficult music*. Let's be clear about what we mean. There is a kind of music that is difficult to write and easy for the listener. There is also a kind that is difficult for the listener, but easy to write."

At heart, Honegger's position is similar to that of Martinů, the contemporary composer to whom he is closest, even though they hardly knew each other. In reply to a questionnaire sent by Bernard Gavoty, Martinů said simply: "When the composer cuts himself off, so does the public."[5] It is certainly a choice that every artist is free to make. But not all embrace the anchorite-like vocation of a Webern.

The attitudes we have just described might seem to suggest that Honegger could be classed as a "progressive" composer, wedded to the notorious "social realism." Needless to say, he was nothing of the sort, and we have seen how little he had to say about his one trip to the Soviet Union—and that trip was in 1928, even before the great kulak purge inaugurated the era of Stalin's bloody tyranny, and before the aesthetic rectification that was just one of its less murderous consequences. Honegger never belonged to any party (the very idea has us shrugging our shoulders), but, if he was never involved in politics, he was political in the sense that he belonged wholly and actively to the *polis*, to the "city of men."

His sympathies were with the Left (during his lifetime this term still meant something), and never so strongly as during the 1930s. In fact, the 1928 ballet *Roses de métal*, which has unfortunately been lost, was an anticapitalist work—in a lighthearted sense, but no less scathing for that. The great cry of anarchist revolt in *Le Grand Étang*, then the collaboration on Bertold Bartosch's extraordinary film *L'Idée*, are forewarnings of Honegger's unavoidable involvement in the cultural politics of the Popular Front. He was at one with the whole of the intellectual and artistic elite of France in the brief moment of splendor of that "great illusion," from 1936 to 1937. Important elder figures, such as Albert Roussel and then Charles Koechlin, agreed to be presidents of the Popular Federation of Music, and Honegger, along with many others such as Milhaud, Auric, Ibert, Roland-Manuel, Marcel Landowski, and more, contributed to those great collective enterprises that were landmarks of the Popular Front: *14 Juillet*, *Liberté*, and *La Construction d'une cité*. Then there was the celebrated *Jeunesse*, which remains the Popular Front's living symbol, and the film *Visages de la France*, dedicated to the Soviet Union to mark the twentieth anniversary of the October Revolution, in which Honegger combines the *Marseillaise* and the *Internationale* in counterpoint. But two later testimonies show that he always knew how to keep his distance from any partisan involvement.

The composer Max d'Ollone wrote to him: "Like you, I am a socialist (not in the political sense) and an enemy of false elites." And Honegger himself wrote to Milhaud in January 1953: "When it comes to it, we are the 'progressive composers' far more than our friend Durey or Serge Nigg."

As the political dangers forced themselves into the public consciousness during the winter of 1937–1938, Honegger began to make the denunciation of war his absolute and lasting priority, and we have come across this denunciation in many guises in examining his life and works. He knew that, apart from the suffering and destruction it brings with it, war is responsible for the increasing disappearance of that space for individual freedom which he held to be the most valuable thing of all. This hatred of war lay at the root of another increasingly ferocious hatred, of governments, accused of imposing wars on the people whom they control and hurl into poverty and death, at the same time as they have the presumptuousness to make them pay the costs. This was to misunderstand the very real death wish that, for example, drove the German people to give themselves of their own free will to Hitler and greet war with those well-documented shouts of hysterical joy. Here is yet another thought in one of those little notebooks from his final years: "Wars are always fought for Right and Liberty. By which is meant: imposing the right of the stronger, the liberty to massacre the weaker. After every war, the world loses a little more of the little liberty left to it."

After the war especially, all illusions had been brutally dissipated and Honegger's enthusiasm gave way to bitterness and disenchantment. But he remained until his last breath the intransigent, resolute democrat so loudly proclaimed by his denunciation of the Fascist peril in 1939 (see Chapter 7). With this went a warning against repeating the mistakes of Munich (the Munich Agreement of 1938), which shows that his pacifism was lucid and within the bounds of reason. The *Chant de Libération* of 1942, unfortunately lost, and the passionate *Chant de la Délivrance* from the film *Un Ami viendra ce soir* prove that his position did not change, as does the expression, in the article "Music and Liberation" (in *Labyrinthe*, 15 February 1945), of his wish to see "names such as Mendelssohn, Milhaud, and Dukas, proscribed by the Nazi madness" appearing as soon as possible on concert programs.[6]

This is a good moment to remind ourselves that we would search all Honegger's writings and sayings in vain to find the smallest trace of racial or religious discrimination: it was a concept completely foreign to his free and honest spirit. In this he recalls Albéric Magnard, the composer of the *Hymn to Justice* written, we may remember, under the impact of the Dreyfus Affair. Magnard is mentioned in the article just mentioned, and the two composers have many features in common: Jean Matter, indeed, sees in Magnard "the link between Franck and Honegger." Magnard's generosity and inflexible sense of justice had led him, too, to embrace the ideals of the Left, to the point of entrusting the printing of his works in 1902 to a unionized communist press. He too had suffered a painful disillusionment after experiencing a similar conflict between a fierce need for independence and the feeling that a creative artist had a duty to humanity. In fact, both composers followed in the path of Beethoven, who was the first composer to see his art as a moral mission addressed to all his fellow beings.

If the tax and customs authorities ended up being scapegoats in Honegger's eyes, obsessive *bêtes noires* whom he turned on with regularity and who were cited by him as partly responsible for the climax of furious indignation in the Dona nobis pacem of the *Symphonie liturgique*, they were harmless supernumeraries compared with the horsemen of the nuclear apocalypse upon whom he constantly brooded, particularly after his heart attack. Here are two examples, from among many others found in the same notebooks, of his anti-tax stance:

> A Finance Minister is a man who regularly puts up the price of stamps, gas, and tobacco. His job is to make the victims of the government's incompetence pay for it.
>
> The tax authorities demand ten million francs from André Gide's daughter as inheritance tax *in advance*, plus ten million as a penalty. Nobody bats an eyelid. A man contributes to his country's glory and gives it a body of work that will, in any case, cease to profit his heirs in fifty years' time when it enters the public domain. That is his reward. I have read, though, that it sometimes happens that thieves go to prison. And when I see how our civilization is vanishing, I am the one accused of pessimism and of seeing the black side of things. Frankly, all one can do is laugh!

This pessimism, plainly evident in the book *Je suis compositeur*, has been attributed by some people to his failing health. No doubt this played a part, but it was not the only reason. The interviews in question took place in 1950 and Honegger died five years later, from all points of view at the worst possible moment. I shall describe in a later chapter the situation in which music found itself at the beginning of the 1950s when "serial terrorism" was at its height. Happily, its reign did not last long, but while it did its protagonists denied all validity to anything that did not come from them, in the name of a historical determinism based on the dialectical notion of progress codified by Theodor Adorno, whose writings took on the powers of Holy Writ. The alternatives—*musique concrète*, still at the stage of basic babbling; Stalinist "progressivism"; or official, post-Fauréan academicism—were hardly more enticing. It seemed like a real impasse. Honegger died too soon to see the escape from the darkness of some years later, and to see the resultant gradual restoration of his true place in the scheme of things.

But there were more serious matters. The 1950s was also the period when the Cold War was at its height and when people realized that, after the United States, the Soviet Union also possessed a nuclear capability. Belief in an imminent apocalypse was very widespread and was one of the ingredients in Honegger's pessimism, to the point that aesthetic questions, however pressing, were relegated to second place.

The tone of *Je suis compositeur* is set by passages such as the following, unhappily notorious at the time:

I sincerely believe that, in a few years from now, the art of music as we conceive it will no longer exist. It will disappear, as indeed will the other arts, but music will do so more quickly.

Every action is converging toward a single outcome: a final war that will destroy everything.

Our first task will be to avoid dying of hunger or cold. That is how the future seems to me—and it won't be long in coming.

I have the very clear impression that we are at the end of a civilization. Decadence lies in wait for us, it already has us in its power. . . . Our artistic life is on the way out. . . . I'm afraid music will be the first to go.

The end of our musical civilization will lead shortly to the end of our civilization overall, and we must have the courage to face it with lucidity, as one waits for death. To deny it would be merely a lack of clairvoyance. There's no point in rebelling against it. One must judge the situation calmly.

Forty years later, humanity has become accustomed to living with the nuclear sword of Damocles permanently hanging over it, even if the threat has recently receded somewhat. In the meantime another menace has surfaced—one already foreseen in *Cris du monde*—that of the destruction of the environment, which threatens the survival of life on the planet. It is likely that those who pontificate today on the subject in predicting the apocalypse are as wrong as Honegger was in 1950, not because the danger is nonexistent—far from it—but because one must hope that mankind will find a way of surmounting the problem, before the next problem shows its head. Survival, and human survival in particular, is thus the precarious, ever-disputed victory that the life instinct wins by a whisker over the death instinct. To believe in survival one must have a little trust in Divine Providence. It seems that Honegger, like so many others, lacked this, as we shall see in the following chapter.

The undeceived views he expressed about the specific problem of the composer's usefulness and his work in contemporary society were really altruistic since he, unlike so many of his colleagues, had his music played regularly. On this front, things seem to have improved. More new music is played now than forty or even twenty years ago, and with the arrival of the compact disc, that music is more widely heard than ever before. So although Honegger's complaints were to some extent justified in their time, they are not so any longer. They have anyway never prevented anyone from composing, simply because here too the life instinct wins through and a composer cannot behave otherwise.

When Honegger writes, "The composer is an idealist and therefore, in our era, a lunatic, but not dangerous, . . . a sort of intruder who absolutely insists on sitting down at a table he has not been invited to," he is expressing a point of view that applies to all eras.[7] He proves the point himself by going on to quote the example of his beloved Gabriel Fauré:

As for the royalties we composers get from our symphonies, quartets, sonatas, songs, and other bits and bobs, we know that Gabriel Fauré—

Director of the Conservatory, Commander of the Legion of Honor, the composer who opened secret doors to undreamed-of horizons—was, for all his celebrity, unable to raise the requisite sum of money to qualify as a permanent member of the Society of Authors, Composers, and Publishers of Music.

In this same speech he also suggests useful ways of developing the public's taste for new music:

What we must do is get music to be heard in concerts, on disc, and especially on radio, beginning with contemporary composers and then going progressively back to the classics. First must come the living language, the language of the listener's own time. Then comes the study of the languages that gave rise to it. The essential thing is to produce listeners, consumers of music, and people who are curious about the art of music, and not budding professionals like the ones turned out by conservatories.

Let's create readers of music who will, for their own pleasure, spend their evenings sight-reading a Schubert sonata or a Poulenc impromptu, and perhaps even a sonata with a cellist friend. But let's not do anything to encourage the champion virtuoso. There are simply too many of them and they do music more harm than good.

As to this last point, the situation has not changed, unfortunately, and conservatories still turn out thousands of people on to the dole. Honegger's suggestion is exactly the same one made by Heitor Villa-Lobos around the same time, that we should see "conservatories of musicalization."

The public must be offered works of quality that do not automatically turn it off contemporary music. Honegger asked the crucial question:

One should not forget the problem of the work's quality. If it is at all viable and deserving support, then it has to be imposed several times and not just once. It is necessary to give up combinations of comradeship, intrigue, and pressure, and have the guts to discourage non-values in order to promote those authors who have a chance of catching the audience's ear. Who shall take care of this? The critics, the musicians, or the People's Commissaries?

The answer can exist, as shown through the example given by Honegger himself.

There are orchestras that are supported only by music-lovers, without recourse to public bodies, such as the Basel Chamber Orchestra, for example, which has just celebrated its twenty-fifth anniversary. During this time it has played not one Beethoven symphony, because all the other orchestras have put them into their programs continuously. This group played only classical works ignored by everyone else, or modern works. Of course, the early days were difficult, but then it attracted an ever-larger public, which learned to take an interest in scores that were new to it, and to listen to the music rather than compare vagaries of interpretation. It is an example of artistic education.

An example, indeed, since forty years later, despite the recent disbanding of the Basel Chamber Orchestra, the good seed sown over sixty years by Paul Sacher has produced a rich harvest. Basel, which is a city of no more than medium size, now boasts a cultivated musical public not afraid to listen to new works.

Honegger spent his last years in a France, whose government was totally uninterested in music. The almost complete absence of state commissions drew from him caustic remarks like the following:

> They glorify the massacres of the war by heroic statues with lists of names beneath them, but not by cantatas. And if they did, the cantata commissions would go to officials and not to the young. It would be difficult to decide fairly between the dodecaphonists and the progressives.

Here too the situation has entirely changed since the first Director of Music, Marcel Landowski, provided a stimulus that remains active.

So everything is far from being as catastrophic as Honegger feared. Perhaps he had an inkling of this all the same, since he said to Bernard Gavoty at the end of the first chapter, "Pessimism Without Paradoxes," of *Je suis compositeur*:

> When my over-sour reasoning seems to you to go too far . . . your perspicacity will suggest arguments to you that I shall be only too happy to go along with, as I have children who can reasonably expect to be still alive in the year 2000![8]

"Because . . . there is Hope, which is the strongest."

EIGHTEEN

The Problem of Faith

Honegger is, with Olivier Messiaen, undoubtedly the greatest religious composer of the twentieth century. From the childhood *Oratorio du Calvaire* to the final *Cantate de Noël*, religious inspiration is certainly the longest and strongest string in Honegger's creative bow. This continuing impulse is evidenced by some thirty works of every form and size, from simple songs to vast oratorios. But beyond that, Honegger's whole approach belongs to an inescapably spiritual conception. His words and his writings confirm the fact explicitly, while his contemporaries and commentators are unanimous on the subject. Following are some relevant testimonies.

Fritz Münch, in his funeral oration of 2 December 1955, said of Honegger:

> Of this too I am certain: in his soul he was profoundly religious. In his private life, the great reserve that was one of his distinguishing marks often hid the depth of his character, but it comes out in his music. . . . A great thinker has said that, in music alone, it is impossible to tell lies. The tone Honegger brings to psalms of trust, hope, and penitence are of such total sincerity and of such expressive power that they must come from a deeply religious nature. . . . And the older he became and the more experience he gained of life, the more he felt the need to give his great works religious endings. They came quite naturally to him, as a sign of his inner life, which was expressed in his music without his having to think about it.

The composer Tony Aubin said: "His inspiration was of the highest quality. This inspiration seems to me to tend toward an absolute of a religious kind." The critic Jacques Feschotte wrote in his biography of the composer:

> He was certainly very far from demonstrating any superficial or exterior devotion. But who, among the men of our time, has felt and expressed more profoundly the miraculous power of the superhuman voice of Christ, who showed our souls an everlasting hope, than the great composer of *Pâques à New York, La Danse des morts*, the *Symphonie liturgique*, and *Une Cantate de Noël*? . . . I am convinced that it is essentially at the foot of the Cross that he achieves his true greatness. And, in the silence, I hear his voice, that raucous low voice of his last years, emphatically repeating: "There is Hope, which is the strongest. . . ." That is the brief but passion-

ate profession of faith that he has expressed musically, in a language that will never die.

Denis de Rougemont introduces a further dimension, which I think is important.

If Honegger's style in most of his works that have a "religious subject" should be described as essentially Christian, it is not because of the subjects or the words and situations he has set to music, nor even of the man's beliefs, whatever they were. His music is Christian because it is a prayer, if prayer is the act of someone who is open and directed toward love: that is to say, to God as He presents himself to the "heart" of man. His music is Christian in the sense that it signifies, by its very emotionality, "the physical adequation (of man) with the world," to use one of Ansermet's phrases, or "the common foundation of the world and of my own existence" (of my conscience), or possibly "the foundation of *being* in the world, in knowing God."[1]

Marcel Landowski puts the same point of view more concisely in his biography of Honegger, saying "If Arthur Honegger was not religious in the dogmatic sense of the word, he was profoundly spiritual."

The composer had been turned away from this "dogmatic sense" by the individualist, analytical tradition of his Protestant inheritance. This was the main source of his close knowledge of the Bible, which he himself attributed to his Swiss birth, although only half of Switzerland belongs to the reformed church. We may recall the words in which he told of his acceptance of the *Le Roi David* commission: "I accepted with pleasure because the subject suited my 'Bible-loving' tendencies." But the Bible is the common property of Christians of all faiths and, in the case of the Old Testament, of Jews as well. The absence of dogmatism in Honegger's religious sensibility shows itself in an ecumenism in which the broad, tolerant spirit extends to his whole mental attitude:

> I seem to be particularly drawn to religious music. Being a Protestant, I have always loved the art of the chorale as practiced by Bach, but that has not prevented me from appreciating the intensity of Jewish chant, and I have had the great joy of collaborating several times with the greatest Catholic poet, Paul Claudel.[2]

This is confirmed and amplified by a manuscript note:

> Although I am a Protestant, since there was talk at one point of making me a priest, I have now and have had in the past as very dear friends both Jews and free-thinkers, and I became the collaborator of the greatest Catholic poet of our age.

As for his more generally spiritual conception of his art, he has emphasized it many times:

Music, in my opinion, belongs much more to magic than to painting or
sculpture, and even to poetry, or architecture, which is merely music
frozen in space. It has nothing to do with the concrete values that are the
basis of the other fine arts. It is far above them, intangible.[3]

After the early but significant *Oratorio du Calvaire*, conceived when the
composer was but fifteen years old, Honegger's religious sensibility continued
to express itself in some of his finest songs (Jules Laforgue's "Petite chapelle,"
Francis Jammes's "Prière," Paul Fort's "Cloche du soir"). Soon after that came
a fragment of an unfinished mystery play, the *Cantique de Pâques*, then *La Mort
de Sainte Alméenne*, and the wonderful *Pâques à New York*. This first phase comes
to an end with the two great Biblical oratorios written with René Morax, *Le
Roi David* and *Judith*, and with *Pour le cantique de Salomon* and *L'Impératrice aux
rochers* in 1926.

Then there was nothing more in this field until *Jeanne d'Arc au bûcher* in
1935. This was the beginning of a new series of religiously inspired works,
which would extend up to his death: *Le Cantique des cantiques, La Danse des morts,
Nicolas de Flue, Three Psalms, Battements du monde*, the *Symphonie liturgique, Mimaamaquim, Saint François d'Assise*, and finally *Une Cantate de Noël*. And that is
without including unfinished projects such as the film *La Nativité* and especially the immense *Selzach Passion*.

Such consistency calls for no further comment. As we know, the interme-
diate period from 1926 to 1934 was that of Honegger's great spiritual and artistic crisis, leading to a tragic creative impasse. And it was indeed "the greatest
Catholic poet of our age" who enabled Honegger to emerge from it victorious.

There is a striking parallel here between the creative lives of Honegger
and of Messiaen, who also experienced a serious crisis and an impasse at the
beginning of the 1950s. He was turned away from his religious path in the
direction of the great "Tristan" trilogy of the *Turangalîla Symphony, Harawi*,
and the *Cinq rechants*, in which sacred love for the moment made way for pro-
fane love. He needed to pass through the cleansing fire of birdsong before finding his path once more in *Chronochromie*—by which time Honegger had been
dead for five years. In both cases, this temporary interruption of the ascending
creative curve caused by a momentary absence of the Spirit (Holy or creative,
they are the same) reminds me strongly of the fearful, sarcastic remark made by
Branchu, the devil/cobbler in Ramuz's *Règne de l'Esprit malin*: "What it is to be
no longer supported!"

Was Honegger always supported? No doubt he was—otherwise his music
would not exist—but perhaps he never realized it. We may be shocked, indeed,
at reading some of his intimate thoughts, even though Pascale Honegger's
irrefutable testimony may have prepared us for them. Certainly the question of
whether or not he had faith is not determined by the fact that he never was a
believer, that he never went to any church, that he never went through a religious marriage ceremony with his wife (who was born a Catholic), nor that he
did not have his daughter baptized.[4] However, as is confirmed by other things
his daughter has said, the composer of *Jeanne d'Arc au bûcher* was on his own

admission an agnostic, or at the least a tormented spirit aspiring to a faith that, in the last resort, he could not find.

Of course, not all of us have the privilege of being "born a believer," like Olivier Messiaen, or of experiencing a shattering revelation, like that of the teenage Paul Claudel by a pillar in Notre-Dame cathedral or that of Saul of Tarsus on the road to Damascus. There is perhaps no more disconcerting and unfathomable mystery than this distribution of grace. But the most important thing is to have the thirst and desire for it, as we are told by "God speaking through the mouth of Blaise Pascal," as Messiaen described it: "You would not be searching for me if you had not already found me." We may remember too another great tormented believer, Arnold Schoenberg, whose last written notes were for an unfinished *Psalm*, proclaiming an invincible hope: "And despite everything, I pray." This is very delicate, painful ground, and in treading it and uncovering the secret corners of a soul one must observe the most extreme discretion and reserve. But in the case of a great religious composer like Honegger it is not, I think, a question we can simply evade.

It must be said, however, that the written evidence that follows belongs to Honegger's last years, when he was suffering from an increasingly distressing illness. There is, for example, a terrible pessimism in the following:

> So many churches, cathedral domes, so many masterpieces by the greatest artists of every age, so many massacres, deaths, tortures, persecutions, and so much suffering, all to glorify the doctrine of that little Jew, "Love one another," which is the most startling failure in the world.

And this state of moral dereliction prompted Honegger to quote, on another page of the notebooks, the terrible saying attributed to Stendhal: "The excuse for God is that He does not exist." Nothing, anyway, could be clearer than the following statement made to Bernard Gavoty in 1950 and recalled by him in an article that appeared in the 10 December 1955 issue of *Le Figaro littéraire*, entitled "A Friend's View of Honegger":

> I can't take an interest in something it is impossible for me to imagine. It is impossible to imagine eternity. I can conceive that there may perhaps exist a hidden force, a supreme power that totally escapes my intelligence, but the very fact that it escapes me prevents me from adhering to it.

And he defines himself as being "a believer and irreligious." Jean Matter believes that the other way round would be nearer the mark, and I think he may well be right.

Honegger's numerous commentaries on the *Symphonie liturgique* confirm what has just been said and also underline the immense nostalgia he felt for that happy certainty that persisted in eluding him. He speaks in those commentaries of the "feeling of a divine refuge," and then, in the De profundis clamavi, of the "sorrowful meditation of mankind abandoned by the divinity—a meditation that is already a prayer," and elsewhere of "God, perhaps." We are surely close here to the entreaty of the father of the wild epileptic, begging

Jesus: "I believe! Help thou mine unbelief!" (Mark 9, 24). A great Bible reader such as Honegger could not, surely, have been unaware of this.

It is worth noting to what extent the text of the De profundis, combining the depths of misery with an inextinguishable hope, haunted him, whether in French, Latin, Hebrew, or as an instrumental paraphrase. Over his whole output we find ten times or more the expression of this great thirst, this lack, this upward aspiration, "so that I may be ONE in You and You be ONE in me," as Claudel says in "Espérance dans la Croix" (Hope in the Cross), which is perhaps the spiritual high point of *La Danse des morts*. If God did not give Honegger the grace of an undoubting belief, he gave him that of expressing it in his music, and of consoling and strengthening the many thousands of human beings who, like him, might be in denial. Honegger must, in some profound part of himself, have been aware of the burden, but also of the privilege, of this mission.

NINETEEN

Tastes and Influences

There is an old saying: "Tell me what you're reading and I'll tell you who you are." Let us make our way up to the large studio on the boulevard de Clichy and cast an eye over the bookcase (or rather the bookcases, since, to our surprise, we find there is not one but seven). True, some of them are for music (we shall look at these in a moment), including one whole case containing his bound "complete works," a gift from Mica Salabert—although it would in fact take more than one case to house his entire output of sixty or so hours of music.

Apart from that, Honegger was a voracious, indeed compulsive reader, and the extent of his interests and culture leaves one breathless. Here are works of philosophy, psychology, and theology, reflecting a continual process of thought and questioning. As we should expect from someone so preoccupied with his fellow human beings, history occupies a privileged place. Also, the past helps in the understanding of a present that is not rejected, but mercilessly examined and criticized and so actively and lucidly absorbed. The pessimistic Honegger of his last years was more than ever an avid newspaper reader, preferring to "know what sort of meal they're going to make out of me." Hence the mass of clippings carefully pasted into the little notebooks, glossed with biting remarks. There are very few scientific or technical works, but we do find all the great novels, both classic and modern. This predilection marries with Honegger the symphonist and stage composer, and with a narrative sense that was very unusual for a creative musician. Honegger himself explained the link to Bernard Gavoty.[1]

> I really think a symphony or a sonata can be compared to a novel, with its themes being characters. We get to know them and then follow them through their evolution and psychological development. We come face to face with their physical appearance. Some arouse our sympathy, others cause us repulsion. They oppose each other or combine; they like each other, form alliances, or engage in conflict.

Olivier Messiaen would speak in not very different terms of his "rhythmic characters," though placing them on a stage rather than in a novel. Looking through Honegger's library, we also discover his passion for detective stories: they take up a complete cupboard, with a large number by Georges Simenon. What he admired in Simenon, the creator of Maigret, was both his technical skill and his extraordinary fertility, qualities Honegger himself possessed in the highest degree. He did not, however, disguise his envy of the advantage that was enjoyed by the novelist, whose fertility was welcomed and encouraged, whereas that of composers was regarded as a calamity.

There is a good deal of poetry on the shelves, too, not only for disinterested reasons but of course also for the use he intended to make of it. In 1925, in an article that appears in *Dissonances*, he explained:

> Very selfishly, I admit, what I ask above all of a poem is that it furnish me with the pretext and materials for a musical construction that parallels its literary construction. If, in addition to that, the poet's words touch some sensitive spot within me, then I've found what I'm looking for.

The list of his poets and collaborators, both dead and contemporary and including the cinema, contains well over eighty names. I have mentioned the poets in my discussion of the songs. Some of his collaborators were friends, sometimes close friends, who inspired several works over long periods of time. Guillaume Apollinaire, Blaise Cendrars, Max Jacob, Jean Giraudoux, Gabriele d'Annunzio, René Bizet, and Denis de Rougemont were used only once, but he turned several times to works by Jean Cocteau (*Les Mariés de la tour Eiffel, Six Poems, Antigone*), by Paul Valéry (*Amphion, Sémiramis*), by René Morax, and by William Aguet. But his most important collaboration, the one he himself placed above all the others, was that with Claudel—a rare and exceptional union, on much the same level as that between Richard Strauss and Hugo von Hofmannsthal.

In *Je suis compositeur*, Honegger goes into some detail about this collaboration, which was stimulated by a shared aspiration toward spirituality and by a common feeling for verbal and musical rhythm (he had no difficulty getting Claudel to understand and accept his reform of prosody, which was, whatever has been said, so well in tune with the spirit of the French language that we find it even in the speeches of General de Gaulle). It was also animated by the poet's outstanding musicianship. As we know, Claudel gave Honegger such precise indications that they amounted to a veritable sound scenario. I have discussed this aspect with reference to *Jeanne d'Arc au bûcher* and *La Danse des morts*, but here is another particularly eloquent example quoted by Honegger, concerning the final scene of *Le Soulier de satin*:[2]

> 1) Wind instruments (various flutes), extremely raw and acid, hold the same note on and on till the end of the scene; from time to time, one of the instruments stops, uncovering the underlying lines, which continue their progress;
> 2) three plucked notes on strings, rising in scales;
> 3) one note with the bow;
> 4) dry roll with sticks on a small flat drum;
> 5) two small metal gongs;
> 6) ventral and, in the middle, explosions on an enormous drum

The slender musical resources available at the Comédie-Française meant that Honegger could not follow these indications to the letter, and he admitted with a smile that Claudel "was less easy to follow when he wrote things like: 'The music imitates the noise of someone beating a carpet.'"[3] A few years later, the advent of *musique concrète* would have made that possible.

When evening came, Honegger emerged from his productive lair and became once more the most cheerful of companions. He had a real taste for conviviality and social life, and divided his time between his friends and family, on the one hand, and plays and concerts on the other. A composer with such a pronounced visual sense needed to refresh his eyes as well as his ears. It is no surprise to find that the prolific composer of so much incidental and film music was an aficionado of the theater and the cinema. In both cases, he kept a close watch on the contemporary scene; and if his library does not contain very many theatrical works, it is because he preferred the experience of live performance to that of merely reading the text. But the composer of *Les Aventures du roi Pausole* was also keen on operetta. Far from regarding it with snobbish disdain, he took a lively interest in it and in the output of all his colleagues.

This brings us to an activity that he considered as far more than a way of earning his living, namely music criticism. His many reviews for *Comoedia* have at last been collected into a single volume[4] and they provide us with invaluable information about his musical tastes. For example, we find here confirmation of his love-hate relationship with opera, the result of his ill-fated and frustrated passion for that genre. But when he felt a performance was going to bore him, he would happily go instead to some sporting occasion. A good game was also a show, and perhaps, too, an experience shared with a cross section of humanity.

It was probably the absence of a public, and especially of any direct human contact or movement, that made Honegger less responsive to the plastic arts, such as painting or sculpture, than he was to spectacle. Anyway, he seems to have spent less time at exhibitions than in theaters and cinemas, and he certainly did not have that passion for painting which prompted his friend Poulenc to devote one of his finest song cycles to "the work of the painter" (*Le Travail du peintre*). This passage from the notebooks is eloquent on the subject:

> I've come to the conclusion that there's a hierarchy in the arts, wholly arbitrary perhaps, and I feel that for many years in France the fine arts did not include music. That seems to me perfectly acceptable, because music floats above architecture, painting, engraving, and literature. It belongs to a domain that is more mysterious, esoteric, partaking of magic.

We shall have occasion to discuss this attitude in detail in the following chapter.

Before we embark on Honegger's tastes in music and look at his favorite composers, as well as those he admired less, a word of warning may be appropriate. We should not be guided solely by his critical articles, nor even by the things he said. We should at the same time look at his own music and try to find there the influence of his great ancestors and elder colleagues, as well as the less frequent influence of his contemporaries.

Honegger as a critic set out on a precise mission, as he informs us unequivocally in the preface to the volume *Incantation aux fossiles*, which was published in his lifetime and contained a first selection from his critical writings for *Comoedia*.[5] That mission was to denounce the fearful routine of musical life, the increasing narrowness of the repertory, and the extravagant cult of the star performer, while on the other hand defending works, and especially French works, that were undervalued, and, in particular, living and young composers. This explains the sometimes acid remarks he made about the great classics—remarks that should be considered in this context.

As we know, the impressions gained during childhood are always the deepest and most enduring. For Honegger, these were opera, Beethoven, and J. S. Bach. As far as opera was concerned, it is understandable that he did not stop with his earliest discoveries in Le Havre, and that he soon moved on from Gounod and Meyerbeer to Wagner. But he remained true to Bach and Beethoven all his life, and his music reflects their profound influence. Together with Wagner, they make up Honegger's premodern trinity of composers. We may notice, though, that Mozart is not included—a point I shall return to. It is a totally German trinity, a fact that cannot be explained by Honegger's German-speaking Swiss ancestry alone and that underlines the anomaly of his position at the heart of Les Six. An admiration for J. S. Bach was all very well, but there was a problem with a member of the group who unambiguously proclaimed his allegiance to Beethoven and preached by example in writing quartets, sonatas, and then symphonies—not to mention one who (horror of horrors) was an ardent Wagnerian and who tried in vain to counteract his friend Milhaud's visceral hatred for "the ogre of Bayreuth who gobbles up everything."

Honegger never repented of his admiration for Wagner, and it is worth quoting from Jacques Feschotte the letter Honegger sent to Wieland Wagner in July 1953:

> Unlike most composers of my generation, I've remained a fervent admirer of Wagner's works. For me, he is the dominant personality of the nineteenth century, and not only in the strictly musical field but in that of art in general. His influence has made itself felt on all artists, both on his admirers and on those who have tried to react against his ascendancy. I can quite understand the kind of hatred that some people feel for him. He fixed, so to speak, an ultimate limit in the development of opera and, after him, it has never risen to the same heights again. I'm not denying the value of some of the works that came after him: *Boris Godunov*, *Pelléas et Mélisande*, *Penelope*, and the operas of Richard Strauss. . . . But none of them has been able to supplant *Tristan*, or *Die Meistersinger*, or *Parsifal*.

Messiaen agreed with Honegger in his passionate admiration for Wagner, and especially for *The Ring*, which Honegger does not mention. But for Honegger, the giant shadow of the Master of Bayreuth seems to have blotted out the rest of the nineteenth century. In his 1950 radio interviews with Bernard Gavoty, he admitted: "Schubert, Mozart, Schumann, and Chopin don't move me that much. In any case, I've heard them too often." Not a very good excuse, since he never heard Bach, Beethoven, or Wagner "too often," nor Fauré or Debussy, as we shall see. Coming from an essentially romantic artist, and one who rejoiced in the fact, this blank over some of the great names of musical romanticism is a considerable surprise. Then there is the question of Mozart. Certainly, Mozart is quoted as one of the admitted models for *Les Aventures du roi Pausole*, along with Chabrier and Messager. But that is rather to play down the extent of Mozart's genius, for which Honegger does not seem to have had any particular affinity, at least until the end of his life. There are from that period some excellent critical articles on Mozart, and Honegger refers explicitly to both him and Haydn in connection with the *Fourth Symphony*. But the main point of these articles is to contrast the spirit of that symphony with the spirit of the *Third*. In fact, we can never hear Mozart behind Honegger in the way that he is always present in the music of Poulenc—mainly in the phrasing, the anacrusis, and especially the feminine endings, and we find the same thing in Prokofiev. D'Indy was certainly not one to give Honegger a taste for Mozart (nor for Schubert, for that matter), as he lumped them all together as being simply "songbirds." All in all, Honegger's predilections for Bach, Beethoven, and Wagner are fairly close to those of the Schola Cantorum (to which the juvenile 1912 sonata also bears witness). Nowadays we are at last able to make a distinction between the creative work of the Schola, which consists of some great and beautiful works, and its proclamations of doctrine. We can now smile at the latter—although they were cause for anxiety in their time—and, with the passage of the years, the same will no doubt be true for those of Boulez and his disciples.

Bach was always for Honegger the absolute reference point, the ultimate resort. It was not merely chance that led him back to Bach in a series of almost literal tributes (*Sonata for solo violin*, *Three Psalms*, the chorale "O sacred head sore wounded" in the *Selzach Passion*) at the time of his great distress after returning from his exodus at the end of 1940. But Bach's profound influence was visible in *Le Roi David* at the latest, especially in No. 3, "Praised be the Lord, full of glory." In a more general and fundamental manner, it was Bach who provided the grounding for Honegger's counterpoint, with all its incomparable solidity and powers of expression. From Beethoven, Honegger inherited a virile energy of discourse and a vigor in his thematic outlines, together with a blend of ardently romantic subjectivity and an architecture that is both amazingly concise and solid enough to withstand any pressures. There are many passages in Honegger's music to which one could apply Romain Rolland's striking remark about the Appassionata: "A torrent of lava in a bed of granite!"

As for Wagner, his presence is felt, as is only to be expected, in Honegger's dramatic music, his oratorios, operas, and stage and film scores. Thus it is not so much the direct references to Wagner, such as the introduction and conclusion of the Adagio of *String Quartet No. 1*, that catch the eye. Rather, one is struck by Honegger's acute understanding of the Wagnerian concept of *time* and of the procedures he uses to give it body: the timely slowing down of tonal and modulatory rhythm and, especially, the twofold repetition of the same harmonic progression. The analytical section of this book has given some typical examples.

Honegger was luckily too young to feel the full force of Wagner's influence, and so did not have to free himself from it in order to survive. Similarly, the youngest contemporary composers no longer have to take sides over the "serial" question. Even so, Honegger's passion for Wagner could sometimes make him deaf to the genius of some other mid-nineteenth-century composers. This deafness could reach monstrously unjust proportions, such as toward Verdi, about whom he wrote: "Is it really true that the Java called 'La donna è mobile,' the vulgarity of which would choke an accordion on the rue de Lappe, is sufficient to confer nobility on this story of a packaging error?"

Furthermore, Honegger's enormous admiration for Fauré prevented him from appreciating Berlioz's incontestable genius: "There's more *real* music in two pages of a Fauré quartet than in the whole of Berlioz's extrovert, theatrical *Requiem.*" In this, Honegger was certainly not followed by Messiaen, nor indeed by Milhaud, who named Berlioz as one of his favorite composers together with Couperin, Rameau, and Bizet. These are composers who do not figure in Honegger's French-ified, German-speaking Swiss inheritance. He said to Bernard Gavoty about Claudel: "Maybe his opinions could strike a composer as disconcerting: like his inexplicable love of Berlioz, which counterbalances a whole-hearted animosity toward Wagner."[6]

As our discussion approaches the twentieth century, we should remember that in Le Havre the young Honegger heard no new music, and that he spent a further two years in Zurich before he finally made contact with avant-garde music in Paris. For him, "modern" music consisted of Richard Strauss and Max Reger, and even Brahms, all then unknown in France. Honegger admitted that "Richard Strauss was an important influence in the matter of orchestration," but if we listen closely to *Le Chant de Nigamon*, to *Horace victorieux*, and indeed to *Antigone*, we can hear that there was perhaps more to it than that, since the last of the three was influenced at least indirectly by *Elektra*. As for Reger, his chromatic counterpoint, rich in harmonic tension, his curious synthesis of Bach-like polyphony and post-*Tristan* harmony, and even certain of his subtle and unexpected modal nuances are all to be found in a work like Honegger's *String Quartet No. 1*.

But then he arrived in Paris at the age of nineteen. His words to Bernard Gavoty leave no room for doubt: "As for France, I owe her everything else: an intellectual flowering, and my musical and spiritual maturation."[7] Debussy was, without doubt, "the great adventure of my youth," he said. Significantly, it was *The Martyrdom of Saint Sebastian* that had an overwhelming impact on him because, as always, what he was seeking was novelty at the service of emotion, not novelty as an end in itself. Debussy's influence would be very powerful, but brief and localized: especially in some of Honegger's songs (those of the *Four Poems for Voice and Piano* and the *Six Poems of Apollinaire*), in *Aglavaine et Sélysette*, then in *La Mort de Sainte Alméenne*, and finally in *Sous-marine*. As he told Gavoty, "no one wanted to copy Debussy any more because there was no more that could be done in that way. He had exhausted the seam."

We shall see, in Chapter 21, the underlying reasons why I feel Fauré's influence was more decisive and lasting than Debussy's. That influence was also slower to take hold: "It took me a long time to come to terms with Fauré's personality. For a long time I thought of him as a salon composer. Once I emerged from this, I took enormous pleasure in submitting myself to his example."[8] But as early as 1925, he had admitted in the journal *Dissonances*: "I owe a great deal to Fauré. It was he who provided me with a counterbalance to Wagner. Debussy was no less useful to me. He taught me to beware of overemphasis and false pathos."

In fact, if Debussy's more immediate impact showed itself in the area of aesthetics, in the choice of sonority, and in certain temporary borrowings of vocabulary, the influence of Fauré was much more fundamental. This was especially true with regard to the long, flexible, but gently unfolding melodic line, and still more with regard to the harmonic structures, the ease of modulation, the subtly ambiguous balance between tonality and modality, and indeed the modal interpretation of chromaticism over a substratum that is basically diatonic. Fauré's presence is felt especially in Honegger's last works, the *Suite archaïque*, the music for the films on Bourdelle and Claudel, the incidental music for *Oedipe-Roi*, and so on. We may recall that although Fauré and Honegger were born almost half a century apart, they became good friends—thanks to their mutual admiration and the time they spent together at Annecy-le-Vieux in the summer of 1923. Honegger venerated Fauré, while Fauré, like d'Indy, considered Honegger to be the most gifted composer of the younger generation.

Unlike Debussy or Fauré, Ravel played only a very episodic role in the formation of Honegger's musical language, even if his *Hommage à Ravel*, written when he was twenty-three, is a very clever pastiche of the older composer's style. Much later, in his 1950 radio conversations with Gavoty, Honegger made the penetrating remark that "Ravel is a little like Utrillo, who used to paint pictures from postcards." Albert Roussel, on the other hand, was for Honegger (as for almost all his young contemporaries after the First World War) the great respected elder, as being the closest to the young in his music and in his ideas. During the same period in which Honegger was beginning his career as a symphonist, Roussel's symphonies were without question the most important then being written, and not only in France.

Roussel's great predecessor in this field was Albéric Magnard, killed in 1914 at the age of only forty-nine. Honegger discovered his music, as he did that of de Séverac, through Milhaud, who admired them both passionately. The Scherzo of Honegger's *First Violin Sonata* is highly reminiscent of Magnard, but the mood of his symphonies shows a wider application of Magnard's influence. As for Milhaud himself, although he was a few months younger than Honegger, he had some influence on him during their years at the Paris Conservatory, being more precocious, and less shy and provincial. We find a little of Milhaud in some of the *Seven Short Pieces*, in some of the movements of the sonatinas, in the "Canticle of the Virgins" in *Judith*, and even in some of the noisier brass passages in the Finale of the *First Symphony*. But I shall explain, in Chapter 21, why Honegger exerted barely any influence on Milhaud.

For the young composers of this generation, the two great revolutionary masters of musical thought after Debussy were quite clearly Stravinsky and

Schoenberg. Stravinsky's influence on Honegger has often been stressed and, in my opinion, greatly exaggerated. Like all his colleagues, Honegger had reeled under the impact of *The Rite of Spring*, but it seems to me that the expressionist violence of *Horace victorieux* and *Antigone* owe far more to Vienna. Honegger used to bring his Paris colleagues the latest Schoenberg scores from Switzerland—they were unobtainable in France—and Schoenberg left a considerable mark on Honegger's music, even if this influence, too, was limited in time and extent. I have mentioned it in connection with the *String Quartet No. 1* (where, significantly, it coexists with the directly opposite influence of Fauré), and especially in connection with *Le Dit des jeux du monde*. In the slow, lyrical movements, Schoenberg's influence is far more significant than Stravinsky's, and although some have detected Stravinsky's influence in the movements for percussion, these movements are in fact closer to Milhaud.

Honegger seems to have been one of the first people in France to give due credit to Bartók. This was during the First World War, and he would always remain a great Bartók admirer. We can see Bartók's influence in the recitatives of the third movement (Ritornello and Serenade) of the *Suite archaïque*. In his preface to Serge Moreux's 1949 book on the Hungarian composer,[9] Honegger wrote:

> In my opinion, it is Bartók far more than [Erik Satie] who, with Schoenberg and Stravinsky, is the true representative of this generation's musical revolution. He is less direct and sparkling than Stravinsky, less dogmatic than Schoenberg, but he is perhaps the most profoundly musical of the three. He is also perhaps the one whose development has been the result of the most constant and well-organized efforts.

Those last two sentences apply wholeheartedly to Honegger, who was not "sparkling" nor "dogmatic," but above all "profoundly musical" and "constant and well-organized" in his own creative endeavors. In fact, Honegger was bound to distance himself increasingly from Stravinsky as the latter took up with the charms of neoclassicism and as his prodigious technique (which Honegger would always admire) battled with ever smaller success against a withering of the heart and the lack of inspiration that came with it.

Honegger did not live to see Stravinsky's final volte-face toward serialism, but we can be in no doubt as to what he would have thought of it. In fact, twelve-tone Schoenberg soon ceased to interest him. About Schoenberg, whom he described elsewhere as a "grammarian of genius," Honegger said to Marcel Delannoy:

> Schoenberg is perhaps the greatest genius among present-day composers. But in following his ideas to their ultimate conclusion he has ended up in a blind alley, in an art of abstraction. He has lost contact with the public. Personally, I cannot follow his music just by listening to it.[10]

And there we touch on the fundamental problem of the realities of acoustics, which is one of the main topics of Chapter 21.

Among his contemporaries, Honegger particularly admired the music of Prokofiev and Martinů, who both reciprocated his feelings. We have seen how he was moved to tears by the first performance of Martinů's *Double Concerto*, conducted by Paul Sacher on 9 February 1940. As for Prokofiev, it was he who, exasperated during the 1920s by the great fashion of "going back" to this and that (which was, in its way, an early manifestation of a certain retrospective spirit), said to Honegger one day: "Soon you and I will be the only ones not going back to something."

Another great composer for whom Honegger had nothing but total admiration was Georges Enesco. Having become acquainted with one another in 1913, the two remained close friends all their lives. In the article Honegger wrote when Enesco's *Souvenirs* was published in 1955, he showed his true fraternal feelings.[11] "He is a great man," he writes, "his life is both pure and busy, his output is magnificent." He calls Enesco's *Third Violin Sonata* "a crucial work in the violin repertory of the last thirty years," and describes *Oedipus* as "the outstanding work of one of the greatest masters, a work that can bear comparison with any of the operatic masterpieces. . . . It is absolutely original, and of a dramatic power that is simply overwhelming." He then goes on:

> I also like the fact that when Enesco was just about to start writing *Oedipus*, he set himself these three rules:
> 1) It must move along! No pathos, no repetitions, no pointless speeches, the action must unfold rapidly.
> 2) The audience must not be bored. This is, in any case, a logical consequence of No. 1.
> 3) The audience must understand the words. I'm convinced that people don't go to the Opera *just* to hear the music.
> A successful opera must have a plot and a libretto that are intelligible. There you have it!

Every word of that passage could be applied to *Antigone* and, no doubt, to all the operas of the period, but *Oedipus* must have been the closest to Honegger's tastes and ideals. He goes on to quote other sections of Enesco's *Souvenirs*, and they come so near to his own convictions and preoccupations that it is worth repeating them as well:

> I'm happy that, in the middle of the anarchy in which we live, a man of Enesco's stature should get up and say to our young composers: "Be yourselves. Don't live in fear of being more or less than your neighbor. If you have something to say, say it, in your own way—that's fine. If you have nothing to say, be silent—that won't be bad either! Don't be haunted by the notion of artistic progress. In art, one progresses only by going very slowly. Don't look for a new language: look for 'your' language—that is to say, the means of expressing exactly what is in you. Originality comes to those who don't look for it."
> Don't you find it wonderful that a violinist who was one of the greatest of the great dares to write: "Our age is the age of the traveling star—a sure sign of decadence. When people pay more attention to the performer than

to the composer, when they get more enthusiastic about the way someone plays a trill or brings off an arpeggio than about the genius required to write a sonata or an opera, that means our time is near!"

As a critic, Honegger ceaselessly defended his colleagues, more particularly those who were French, as well as those of his seniors who were undervalued. These included Guy Ropartz (the two men were close friends and mutual admirers), and some who were already dead, like Magnard, Maurice Emmanuel, and Roussel. Witness his simple joy in recounting the reaction of a young reader who had been encouraged by an article of his to go and hear a Roussel symphony: "That guy Honegger was right, that Mr. Roussel is a real knockout!"

Most of Honegger's efforts obviously went into supporting his contemporaries (with a special place being reserved for his comrades in Les Six) and his juniors. He was quick to appreciate the worth of Jolivet, Landowski, and Dutilleux, but he gave pride of place to Messiaen, in whom he recognized the most important creative artist of the generation immediately after his own. And I add, Messiaen was Honegger's true successor at the head of musical creativity in France and of an essentially religious and spiritual conception of the art. I shall take the opportunity in the following chapters, as I have already in previous ones, to underline the many affinities between these two composers, apart from their obvious differences.

Illness forced Honegger to give up his career at the moment when the musical world was turned upside down by the arrival in force of serial and electronic music. Honegger wrote no articles on these subjects, but he did express his opinions in conversations, interviews, and even speeches. These opinions were, at the time, necessarily regarded as reactionary. It has taken forty years for people to judge them more fairly and to realize, more often than not, that they were well founded; they will be examined in detail in Chapter 22.

TWENTY

Ethics, Aesthetics, and Craft:
The Mission of the Creative Artist and
the Mystery of Creativity

Max Reger, with his usual rough Bavarian humor, liked to ask the riddle "Question: Why is a composer like a pig? Answer: Both are appreciated only after they're dead." He also used to tell the story of what happened one evening when he went to visit some friends. The little country servant girl had asked her mistress what this guest did for a living. The lady of the house drew herself up proudly and said: "He's a composer!" "Wow!" said the girl in astonishment, "a living composer! Do they exist?" Honegger, like the dynamic ex-rugby player he was, did not beat around the bush in talking to Bernard Gavoty, but charged straight in with: "The most important thing about a composer is that he should be dead."

We know that things were not always so, and that under the *ancien régime* the composer had a very precise social role that ended with his death. After the French Revolution of 1789, however, the composer, freed from the constraints laid on him by an employer, began to write for a hypothetical posterity without worrying about being understood immediately. So it was that Beethoven, with an eye on the future, was the first "posthumous" composer.

Since for Honegger the need to communicate with people directly was always the absolute priority, he could not be happy with this state of affairs. Which is not to say that he too did not nourish the secret hope of the Roman poet Horace: "Non omnis moriar" (I shall not wholly die). *To be* and *to have been*—an existential dilemma, and indeed a dilemma we cannot formulate as precisely as we might wish because of the significant lack of a future infinitive tense in our language. Although Honegger was acclaimed and understood in his lifetime, immediately after his death he seemed to be losing his bold wager. With the passage of time, we now know that he won it.

A sentence of his that perfectly defines his position, and the means employed to achieve it, has often been quoted: "My efforts have always been directed toward the ideal of writing music that is understandable by the great mass of listeners but sufficiently free of banality to interest music-lovers."[1] His interviewer Bernard Gavoty commented: "An art that is both popular and personal." But Honegger went on:

If your melodic and rhythmic shapes are precise and stick in the mind, the listener will never be frightened by the accompanying dissonances. What puts him off is swimming around in a sound-swamp from which he cannot see dry land and in which he rapidly sinks. Then he gets bored and stops listening.

Detractors of this sensible, humane attitude tend to forget the essential caveat "without concessions." But it mirrors exactly what Mozart wrote to his father in 1782, with reference to his three new piano concertos (K. 413–415):

> These concertos tread exactly a middle way between being too difficult and too easy. They're very brilliant, agreeable to the ear, and natural, without being vapid. Here and there are passages from which connoisseurs alone can derive satisfaction, but they're written so as to please the less learned as well, though they won't know why.

The composer therefore must renounce laboratory researches as an end in themselves and must distance himself from the fetishism of matter by pursuing the cult of the Spirit: in short, he must give priority to the content, not to the container. We have seen that Honegger described his *Symphonie liturgique* as a "direct reaction against the fashion for so-called objective music." This clearly expressed attitude ran totally counter to the ideas prevalent at the time of his death and prompted a journalist to ask him: "Do you consider yourself to be a neoromantic?" His blunt reply was: "No, a romantic pure and simple!" And Jacques Feschotte, who tells this story, received Honegger's approval of this definition he gave of romanticism: "the superiority of feeling over reason, the primacy of imagination over logic."[2]

That is all very well, but it devalues the demands of the architect, as Honegger wrote:

> For me, a symphonic work must be constructed logically, without the possibility of inserting the smallest anecdotal element between the different sections. I repeat: one must give the impression of a speech in which everything follows on from something else; one must create the image of a thought-out construction.[3]

This ties in with what Honegger stated in his interview with Paul Landormy in 1920 (as discussed in Chapters 3 and 10): "I attach a great importance to musical architecture and would never willingly sacrifice it to literary or pictorial requirements."[4] Note that he says "literary or pictorial," and not "expressive." But the stature of Honegger's romanticism and its profound affinity with that of Beethoven stems from the fact that he knew how any tendency toward sentimentality (not to be confused with expression) leads both to the message being engulfed in subjectivity and to a consequent weakening of its impact on the listener. Because if the composer identifies with his emotions instead of distancing himself from them, he prevents any identification on the part of the listener. That is the real meaning of Berlioz's splendid advice: "One must try to write burning things coldly."

Another misunderstanding was touched on by Gavoty: "In your opinion, the question of musical vocabulary is a secondary one; the only things that matter are the thoughts the composer wishes to express." Honegger: "I'm still convinced of that today."

Another extract from *Je suis compositeur* confirms this point of view:

> I cannot imagine music constructed according to rules that have been laid down in advance. I am neither a polytonal, nor an atonal, nor a twelve-tone composer. It's true, the musical material of today is based on the scale of twelve chromatic notes, but it is employed with the same freedom the poet enjoys with regard to the letters of the alphabet, or the painter with regard to the colors of the spectrum.[5]

The meaning is clear: not only is vocabulary not a secondary matter, but the *choice* one makes from it is crucial. Honegger knew perfectly well that it needs to be different depending on whether you are writing a string quartet or film music, just as the text of a popular song does not use the same words as a philosophical treatise. What counts is the degree to which the music fits the context, and here, over Honegger's forty years of creativity, the unifying element is his distinct *style*—that ultimate reward for having been faithful to oneself. Rare indeed are the composers (I think firstly of Messiaen) who have matched Honegger in this respect during this fickle century.

All his life, Honegger remained faithful to a belief in the "magic" properties of music—those properties that, in his view, essentially distinguish music from the other arts and place it above them. At the end of his life, he was afraid these properties would disappear. As he said in *Je suis compositeur*,

> The longer I live, the more I see music drifting away from its vocation: magic, incantation, that sense of ceremony that should surround manifestations of art. . . . Once, a concert was a form of celebration, a meeting at which this magic manifested itself in the presence of men assembled for a religious ceremony.[6]

He also said of the cinema (though his remark is true in a general sense too): "Music possesses a rare power of evocation, and there are any number of words that could be suppressed and replaced by a paragraph of music that everybody would respond to and understand."

This takes us a long way from the Stravinsky of *The Poetics of Music*, where he claimed that music was incapable of expressing anything and confined music's role to that of being a "construction in time." Stravinsky thus also ties in with Hanslick's reactionary aesthetic ideas, which have, unexpectedly, been restored to favor by the proponents of Boulez's aesthetics, including Boulez himself.

Honegger's reply: "My essential aim is not to astonish or even to charm: it is to move people." This was a declaration made in 1942 that, two and a half centuries later, recalls François Couperin's famous remark: "I confess freely that I prefer what touches me to what surprises me." Two other remarks that Honegger liked to quote were "My heart is called *Even so*" (spoken by Hercules in the epic *Olympian Spring*, written by the great German-speaking Swiss poet and Nobel prizewinner Carl Spitteler) and "There is a need for musical bread!" (Jean Cocteau in *The Cock and the Harlequin*). Honegger ground plenty of flour for that particular bread! This humanly committed stance, of which we have seen many examples, meant that this great master of abstract forms—such as the symphony, the string quartet, and the sonata—mistrusted, to some extent, the concept of "pure music": "My music is not in any sense pure music, any more than the Bible is a pure book. I prefer its impurity and mine to neo-classical innocence, which often borders on emptiness." We may take that as a dig at Satie and his acolytes, and we may wonder what Honegger would have said of their present-day successors, the advocates of minimalism and of "new simplicity"?

In *Je suis compositeur*, Gavoty's awkward, probing questions, gradually cutting the composer's ground from under him, brought Honegger to the point where he had to tackle the mysteries of the creative process. Clearly, and understandably, Honegger found this task perplexing. In one of his little notebooks, he noted down this remark from Salvador Dali: "A publisher asked me to write a book about technique in painting. I wrote it. In rereading it, I learned how to paint." No doubt this was not an altogether serious comment, but Honegger never did write any treatise. For him, the composer's job, at least when working in "abstract" forms, was much harder than the painter's or the sculptor's because there was no model. Hence the following well-known image he invoked in *Je suis compositeur*:

> Writing music is like putting up a ladder without being able to lean it against a wall. No scaffolding: the edifice under construction maintains its balance only by the miracle of a sort of inner logic, an innate sense of proportion. I am at the same time the architect and the spectator of my work: I write and I appraise. . . . In music there is a large element of magic, of the inexplicable.[7]

But these problems are considerably reduced beyond the domain of what Honegger refused to call pure music: "In my own case, symphonic works give me a great deal of trouble. On the other hand, as soon as I can refer to a literary or visual stimulus, [as with a sculptor's model], work becomes much easier."[8] And his technique ensured that when he was working for the theater or the cinema it was not only easier, but also extremely fast. There, the visual imagination with which Nature had endowed Honegger took over. But it was of no help when he was writing symphonies or quartets: "I'm like a steam engine: I need to be warmed up, it takes me a long time to get ready for real work."[9]

There then follows an attempt to describe the slow, painful labor of composition, groping about in the twilight, in the dark even, broken by sudden, brief rays of inspiration. And this description is almost as embarrassed as the work it describes. Compared with *Je suis compositeur*, the notebooks contain remarks that may be less finely honed, but are sometimes more revealing:

Find the little group of notes that makes up what is called a theme, a melody, and that will nearly always be the germ of the work. It may be a fine melodic line that you are proud to have found and which, the next day, turns out to be horribly dull. It may be the insignificant little motif that suddenly becomes so important that it imposes its sovereignty on everything else—the theme that you carry with you for years, and that you suddenly find to be the one you're looking for.

This is Beethoven's method, and that passage could be a commentary on the famous notebooks that Honegger also used; he had learned the habit from Gédalge, and they still survive. Honegger goes on:

And then, at the last minute, everything crumbles: the form doesn't correspond to the material, or perhaps the material, through its own energy, effortlessly creates a form quite different from the one you had envisaged. The joy at that moment of having brought to fruition what you had in mind. Or at least, that's what you think. The sadness at leaving beings, entities that have become like living friends with whom you have had an intense relationship.

Elsewhere, in *Je suis compositeur*, he wrote: "I often start off on the wrong track. Then, like a ragpicker, I refill my basket and set off in quest of more relevant material." But the object of this quest was always the melodic idea, the most important element for this profoundly vocal composer, for whom making music was above all *singing*, whether on the violin or on the trombone.[10]

Again in *Je suis compositeur*, he says:

I imagine the highest form of melody as being like a rainbow, rising and falling without there being any moment when you could say "There, you see, he's repeated fragment B, there fragment A"—all of which are things that belong to the world of musical craft and that are of interest only to students.[11]

To this we may add this fragment from the notebooks: "The melodic line, the only emanation of the spirit that is completely detached from all material references, even from the words."

He took the trouble of copying into the same little book this reflection by Thomas Mann on Schopenhauer:

He glorified music as no thinker had done before him. He assigned it a quite special place, not beside the other arts, but above them, because music is not, like them, a representation of the external world, but much rather a representation of will itself, and including, together with the physicality of the world, the metaphysical representation of the "object-in-itself."

But, in the last resort, the mystery of music defies all verbal explanation, as Honegger agreed in one of the introductions he wrote for Paul Sacher to accompany the *Symphony for Strings*:

I've always thought it was difficult to write about music, which is precisely the expression of what it is impossible to express in words. Telling the story of a symphony or a sonata is as impossible as describing a good wine or a tasty dish. The problem is even greater when it comes to describing one of your own works, because there you are inhibited by a certain discretion in the enthusiasm it inspires in you.

Here we see that extraordinary modesty that we have come across many times already in the course of this volume. It goes as far as making him speak, in one of the notebooks, of "various clumsy efforts that some kind friends call 'my works.'" But we have seen that he judged himself with great lucidity, establishing among these "clumsy attempts" a hierarchy of quality. He may, like Magnard, have been perpetually dissatisfied with his music, feeling that he "lived in the suburbs of his ideal," but he was also absolutely objective in recognizing his successes, especially when it was a question of technique—an area in which he was even more scrupulous and demanding with regard to himself than to other people.

With his Swiss "naive sense of honesty," he hated deception and trickery, denouncing for example "external deformity masking the absence of any real invention, any real daring." Hence some of his best-known remarks, such as the following, in which Honegger is speaking of the process of the composer hearing his work for the first time in rehearsal:

> The most appropriate comparison seems to me to be that of the shipbuilder who, at the very moment his ship is launched, runs the risk of the horrifying experience of seeing it capsize. In music, luckily, such an accident is not so blatantly obvious. Many modern scores float upside down. Very few people notice the fact.[12]

And again: "If certain composers built their own houses or cars, they would have been reduced to rubble long ago!"[13]

The same horror of trickery, the same intransigent honesty characterized his teaching. Honegger never lost his belief in the virtues of the sort of traditional technique he had learned from Gédalge and Widor. This led to a breakdown in communication one day when a young foreigner, just arrived in Paris, came to show him his compositions. Honegger immediately removed forbidden fifths and octaves, and that was the end of the meeting. No doubt there was more to be seen than that in those sketches by Xenakis (the name of the foreigner in question). Messiaen, on the other hand, dissuaded Xenakis from attending the normal Conservatory classes, feeling that he had no need of them. Honegger must have thought that by submitting himself to that discipline Xenakis would be spared long years of trial and effort and would reach his goal sooner. From his point of view, he was certainly right. But would Xenakis have become what he is without following his own path, even if it was undoubtedly harder and longer? In any case, Xenakis has built a number of constructions, both architectural and musical, that show no sign of falling down.

Honegger's concern for practical efficiency is also illustrated by his tireless campaign to simplify and rationalize musical notation. With Schoenberg and Prokofiev, he was one of the first to give up the usual transpositions in orchestral scores (for clarinets, saxophones, horns, trumpets, etc.) and to write his scores "in C"—a practice that has been widely followed since, to the extent that those composers who have not done so are now in the minority. He showed a similar concern over the notation of rhythms and phrasing, and over the practice, still current in his day, of having a key signature that led continual modulation to produce a mass of accidentals.

All of this was done in the name of his slogan, "simplification, logic, economy." Applied to his own scores, it makes his manuscripts models of clarity and efficiency, and a joy to both the eye and the spirit. We should note here one important point: if Honegger's metronome markings are almost all a little on the slow side (unlike those of most composers), the reason was, according to his daughter, that all his life he used an old clockwork metronome that he inherited from his parents and which was a little "tired" (whereas Beethoven's metronome obviously suffered from tachycardia)!

This chapter began in a lighthearted vein, before skirting the sublime with Schopenhauer. Now, as it concludes with a bump, like a good Honeggerian sonata form with reversed recapitulation, I cannot resist the pleasure of ending with this quotation: "We are coffee filters: you pour boiling water on us and our music is the result of the infusion."[14]

TWENTY-ONE

The Musical Language

The key to Honegger's musical language, and to his overall attitudes, both positive and negative, lies in a short phrase I heard from his own lips (although he said it to others too): "For me, an isolated sound is a dominant." This expresses Honegger's perception of an acoustical reality, as modified by the tempered scale. This acoustical reality is that of the "sphericity" of sound, to use the composer Giacinto Scelsi's term: that is to say, of sound endowed with volume and depth, of complex sound complete with its halo of harmonics. Since it is in absolute opposition to the concept of a combination of points, it is therefore incompatible with serial theory, a fact that explains Honegger's implacable rejection of the latter—in which he is joined by composers as varied as Messiaen, Scelsi, Ohana, Xenakis, and all the young, so-called spectral school of Murail, Grisey, Radulescu, and others.

Honegger's antiserialism is therefore in no sense the manifestation of a reactionary outlook, as the serialists have tried to make us believe. As the evolution of musical language since his death has shown, this rejection is based on the very nature of music. But in his case it was emphasized by his refusal to consider any material other than the tempered scale of twelve semitones. It was this refusal (shared, I may say, by Messiaen) that engendered Honegger's pessimism as to the possibilities of musical language evolving or being enriched. He dwelt on the subject in *Je suis compositeur*:

> It seems to me there are two categories of composer: those who have had the audacity to bring new stones to the edifice; and those who have shaped them, set them in place, and used them to build cottages or cathedrals. For the first, the task is finished until someone uses new intervals—quarter-tones, thirds of tones, tenths of tones. For the others, research can go on for as long as anyone has anything to say. Because there is no longer the potential for new harmonies, nor are there any melodic lines that have not already been employed, but there is always an original use one can make of harmonies both old and recent. . . . The same is true of chords containing all twelve chromatic tones. They've been used regularly by composers for the last thirty years. But today it's impossible to add an extra thirteenth tone. The stock is complete.[1]

It is, indeed, unless one crosses the border of the thirteenth tone, and Honegger did not envisage such a thing: "I have absolutely no faith in the success of such hazardous enterprises. I repeat: the human ear is being continually blunted, for the very simple reason that it is subjected to the wear and tear of noises that our fathers never knew."

This is debatable. For a start, the wear and tear in question—if it really exists in this environment of ours, ever more forcefully invaded by decibels—is concerned, from the physiological point of view, with our perception of *dynamics*, not of *pitch*. It is still serious enough, even so, and Honegger sounded a cry of warning in his UNESCO talk in Venice in September 1952:

> Our existence is dominated more and more by the noise that surrounds us. Living in this noise, we shall all be deaf before very long. The radio belonging to your concierge or your next-door neighbor emits a flood of noises from dawn till midnight. It may be the B minor Mass or the mad bellowing of accordions. You come across this noise everywhere: in the street, in shops, cafes, restaurants, even taxis. It's even laid on in factories. Do you really think that someone who, during the day, has perhaps heard Beethoven's *Fifth* half a dozen times, is going to rush to a concert hall that evening and pay a relatively large sum of money to hear it a seventh time? Any number of schoolchildren and students do their mathematics homework with the radio on. They get into the habit of thinking of music as "background noise" to which their minds pay no more attention than they do to the paint on the walls.

Not only does this metastatic proliferation of sound pollution exist, it has become considerably worse, and Honegger could not foresee the arrival of the Walkman or of the sound-junkies in streets and public places, with their headphones clamped over their ears. All the same, concert halls are not empty and the compact disc has spread music more widely than ever—including the good music Honegger was defending.

Honegger becomes even more apocalyptic in *Je suis compositeur*:

> Noise hardens our ears, and I really think that in a few years from now we shall be able to distinguish only between very large intervals. We shall be unable to appreciate the semitone, and will be able to hear only the third, then the fourth, and finally the fifth. . . . At the rate we're going, we shall by the end of the century have a music that shall be very primitive and barbaric and will fit a rudimentary tune to brutally articulated rhythms. That will be just the thing for the atrophied ears of the music-lovers of the year 2000![2]

This sounds very like an all-too-accurate premonition of "hard rock" and its sins, not to mention "minimalist" and "process" music. Even so, these forms are not the whole story—far from it. If millions of music-lovers still have enough hearing left to appreciate Honegger and even to savor the refinements of his harmony, there is also an audience (small, certainly, but growing) for the new music of micro-intervals. Honegger foresaw the truth, certainly, but not the *whole* truth, and that is the important thing.

New music today has not only reached a state of unprecedented refinement in the choice of pitches and their combinations, it also deals with the finest nuances of *pianissimo* in such a way as to give a definite lie to Honegger's predictions. The reasons for his refusal to consider microtones must be sought, and perhaps found, elsewhere, such as in the well-known statement that began this chapter. That statement shows that Honegger had a very fine, discriminating ear for harmony, a tonal ear because it had been conditioned by the cultural atavism of the tempered scale. But by giving a fairly favorable reception to the earliest essays in *musique concrète* (there was as yet no talk of electroacoustic music), he subverted his own argument and implicitly accepted that temperament had been overtaken.

In giving priority to the parameter of pitch, I am only placing Honegger in a Western musical tradition for which that same priority has been established fact for at least the last six centuries. But one cannot envisage this parameter without the others—especially the organization of durations, which depends closely on it. There is a particular sense of movement, an articulation, an accentuation, and a phrasing that are tied to the concept of tonality, or at least to an argument dominated by the presence of the harmonic cadence, and this cadence informs Honegger's writing, even if in a very extended sense.

The dissociation of parameters is one of the most serious errors in serial theory and it has led, for example, to aberrations: aesthetic monstrosities such as Schoenberg's *Fourth String Quartet* or his two concertos. These works are dodecaphonic in their organization of pitch, but are clearly tonal in their rhythmic articulation—the argument depends on anacrusis, inflections, and the accentuation of appoggiaturas that are obviously not part of the melodic-harmonic material. Hence the unbearable impression of it being Schumann or Brahms with "wrong notes." With Alban Berg the case is clearly different: his choice of series implies coexistence with the tonal harmonic system, albeit highly chromaticized, to the point that the series is more of a superstructure ensuring the enrichment of the harmonic field. As for Webern, his rhythmic organization takes full account of the abandonment of tonal functions.

To return to our departure point: for Honegger, a single pitch is, for all intents and purposes, a dominant. A dominant demands cadential resolution and forms the hypothesis of a musical discourse, of a dynamic of phrasing and form founded on the age-old notion of tension and relaxation, of systole and diastole. Honegger's music, far from denying tonality, enriches and energizes it by adding elements that increase and renew its resources—hence my choice of the word "metatonality." The function of the dominant depends, with adaptations due to the tempered scale, on the harmonic spectrum, at least in its lower partials, dominated by the powerful seventh over the still stronger foundation of the fifth. The fifth is significantly absent from the whole-tone scale used by Debussy to undermine tonality. That is why this scale appears rarely with Honegger, on whom Debussy's harmonic influence was no more than temporary. "Drowning the key" was not Honegger's priority. In fact, there is a total incompatibility between the whole-tone scale and tonality, because of this absence of the fifth from the former.

Harmony based on the whole-tone scale, which can amount to the chord of the augmented fifth enriched with added notes, is static, nonresolving harmony. It thus neutralizes the notion of dissonance and "freezes" the harmonic movement. In any case, in Debussy's music this harmony coexists with long stretches of tonal harmony (based, that is, on dominant functions) as well as with others that rest on superimposed fourths. The powerfully antitonal properties of this interval, together with those of the tritone, were also recognized, in the first decade of the twentieth century, by Bartók, Schoenberg, and Scriabin. The static, nonresolving properties of an aggregate of fourths are most strikingly illustrated in Honegger's work in "Hope in the Cross" in *La Danse des morts* ("so that I may be ONE in you"). The other undermining force, deriving from *Tristan*, is chromaticism. Obviously a synthetic composer like Honegger will choose to make an ensemble of all these treasures in order to enrich his inherited language rather than destroy it.

A dominant resolves, as I have said. That is why Honegger's concluding triads often include added seconds, sixths, leading tones, and even augmented fourths, but never the seventh or the diatonic fourth (the seventh of the dominant key). We find these in both Stravinsky and Milhaud, and in fact their presence, suggesting an unresolved dominant, signifies that this unresolved dominant is to be heard simultaneously with the tonic—in other words, it signifies that the passage is bitonal. In Honegger, as in Roussel (whom he resembles in this respect), bitonality and polytonality are never more than passing, and they remain within the orbit of a predominant tonality. On the rare occasions when a dominant seventh in Honegger's work does not resolve, it is because the argument remains suspended, exactly like a sentence ending in ellipsis points. The best example is the inconclusive conclusion of the *Pastorale d'été*, which prolongs beyond silence the enchantment of the dominant established in the very first measure.

Honegger's essentially dynamic conception of musical argument therefore led him very soon to look for solutions other than those suggested by Debussy. And it was here that Fauré's example was crucial and his influence long-lasting. According to the view that prevailed until recently, among both composers and music theorists, to go from Debussy to Fauré was a signal step backward. Well, it all depends what you are looking for. What Honegger found in Fauré was a model of how to enlarge tonal and cadential syntax through recourse to scales other than the major and minor of tonal music—in short, through recourse to the *modes*.

Perhaps the most radical and complete example of this original approach, of treating modes like keys, is to be found in Sibelius's *Sixth Symphony* of 1923. It is to be distinguished from the approach that consists of deducing an appropriate syntax either from already existing scales, as with Maurice Emmanuel, or from specially invented scales, as with Messiaen. With Fauré, as with Sibelius, the presence of a flattened seventh can signify a borrowing either from the subdominant or from the *G* mode (Mixolydian), just as an augmented fourth can signify one either from the dominant or from the *F* mode (Lydian). Honegger had no intention of ignoring this lesson. The fundamental difference between tonal and modal approaches offers rich possibilities, underlined by the fact that tonally the flattened seventh leads to the fourth degree, while modally it is part of the scale in which the tonic is the fifth. The difference is also underlined by the fact that the augmented fourth provides a precisely inverse, symmetrical alternative modulating toward either the fifth degree or the mode on the fourth. But for Honegger, who wanted to avail himself of all the resources of the chromatic scale, that was not enough.

Altering the notes of a mode deprives it of its character, its true color—as Messiaen was well aware. But without alteration there can be no modulation, hence the harmonically static character of modal music which, in its pure state, excludes modulation. Fauré gave his modes harmonic energy by making them function as keys, and Honegger took this approach much further.

How to reconcile modality with chromaticism? The answer was to invent synthetic modes in which chromatic notes are in no sense alterations or borrowings from elsewhere but rather elements of the mode in their own right. One of Honegger's favorite modes (*Antigone* is based on it) is the Phrygian minor (mode on E, also called the "superminor" because all its changing degrees are minor), but with an augmented fourth that grafts on to it its antithetical Lydian or "supermajor" mode. The scale thus created (if we take C as the tonic, to make things clearer) therefore contains both F-sharp and B-flat, the augmented fourth, and the flattened seventh, the essential degrees in the acoustic scale. It is also called the "Bartók scale," because Bartók used it frequently and it appears often in folk music, where he undoubtedly found it. It owes its name of acoustic scale to the fact that it is closer to natural resonance than the tempered scale. The only reason that the latter has prevailed over the acoustic scale is that the cadential, tonal harmonic system demands one leading tone (hence the raising of the seventh degree) and only one (hence the lowering of the fourth). In the early period of the cadence's life, we still see the cadence with "twin leading tones," found in Machaut.

But nothing could be further from Honegger's musical ecumenism and his desire to incorporate new ideas than adherence to a system, however attractive. His music is successively tonal, modal in the sense I have just described, polytonal (in passing), and even atonal. Similarly, purely diatonic stretches are found next to those that are totally chromatic. I should reiterate here a warning that is too often ignored, but which is relevant throughout Honegger's music: diatonicism is not a synonym for tonality (nor, in Honegger, for modality) any more than chromaticism is a synonym for atonality. In Honegger's music, chromatic notes often assume the function of passing notes or appoggiaturas (whether resolved or not). This fact is emphasized by the frequent presence of perfect fifths, which support the harmonic edifice. Thanks to the help of natural resonance, these fifths function far more often as dominants than as tonics— which brings us back to the first sentence of the present chapter.

The succession of dominants is one of the great discoveries of romantic harmony. The first composer to use this technique consciously and systematically was Robert Schumann (a fact too often ignored), whose progressions for the most part move in a conjunct and diatonic manner. Liszt and Wagner would expand the process to include chromatic successions and successions that move by thirds or even tritones, thanks to the help of enharmony. Honegger agreed that he was always quick to absorb every tradition and take over whatever could be of use to him, and from his predecessors' discoveries he fashioned his own style by taking them a good way further. His attitude was always evolutionary rather than revolutionary.

In the works of those turn-of-the-century composers who subscribed to modal habits, such as Debussy, Sibelius, and Scriabin, the stretches of music that avoid a cadential syntax and attraction are generally hexatonic—that is to say, based on the whole-tone scale. But with those who followed in the path of *Tristan*, especially the Schoenberg of the early years, these stretches are chromatic, even clearly atonal. It was to this movement that Honegger's music attached itself as soon as it chose to leave the functional harmony that corresponded to its enriched metatonal vocabulary. These atonal passages, which are the most dissonant in his music—from the *String Quartet No. 1* and *Horace victorieux* to *Antigone* and the Dies irae of the *Symphonie liturgique*—are always carefully gauged in length and prompted by expressive needs. They are characterized by their wide intervals, with enormous, "expressionist" leaps recalling those of the Second Viennese School, and they represent the Germanic element in Honegger's music at the other extreme from the predominantly diatonic, conjunct movement of his "French" music.

So, whether tonal, modal, polytonal, or atonal, Honegger's harmony is rarely in a state of repose. The magnetism of its dominant resonances continually, and in a manner very reminiscent of Fauré, fuels his nostalgia for "great unassuaged departures" toward the "unknown horizon" of illusory tonics, which are no sooner reached than turned into new dominants. The state of repose is either an ending, a psychological resolution at the end of a work, or else a strangely hypnotic passage, like the midday siesta that suspends all harmonic movement at the center of the first movement of the *Fourth Symphony*.

As evidenced in statements I have already quoted, Honegger regarded the state of saturation by all twelve chromatic notes as an impasse. This saturation "freezes" the harmonic flow as surely as the six notes of the whole-tone scale, and it was so contrary to his instinct for energetic argument that he was careful to avoid it, all the more so because he knew that, provided the intervals and timbres were judiciously chosen, a chord of seven or eight tones, or even only four or five, can carry a charge of dissonant tension higher than that of a twelve-tone chord, in which mixing all the colors together produces a deadly gray, as Messiaen also noted.

There remains the question of the very rare twelve-tone themes. The best-known of these comes in the second movement of the *Fifth Symphony*. Whereas Alban Berg before him had chosen series in such a way that they contained tonal melodic outlines (and therefore the resonances that came from these), Honegger puts them into a context that is tonal at least by implication and, in the aforementioned work, is careful to alternate them with passages that are not serial, but tonal or modal. And he relies on striking melodic and rhythmic shapes to seize the listener's attention and counteract the graying effect of using all twelve tones.

The reason I began this chapter on the totality of Honegger's musical language by looking at length at its harmonic and tonal aspects is because those aspects constitute the most direct application of his belief that an isolated sound is a virtual dominant. My brief allusion to the twelve-tone theme of the Scherzo from the *Fifth Symphony* can lead us conveniently to an examination of the melodic element. This was crucial for a composer for whom melody remained the basis of invention and of expression—we have seen in what exalted, even mystical terms he spoke of it. It was the veritable touchstone of his inspiration, because song is the prime mover of music and, with him, that was where invention began. It is rare for any of his original ideas to be rhythmic rather than melodic and, where that is the case, it is never long before a tune arrives to "clothe" the rhythmic structures. We shall see that, with Honegger, rhythm is conditioned by melody, which is itself conditioned by speech.

In praising Honegger as one of the great harmonists of his time, I have dealt with what must be called a very *French* aspect of his genius, particularly in the suppleness with which he reconciles tonality and modality. This places him in a direct line of succession that ended, from his point of view, not with Debussy or Ravel, but with Fauré. It is true nonetheless that an equal place in his language and thought is taken by counterpoint. And we could attribute his innate feeling for counterpoint to his German-speaking ancestry, were it not again for the example of Fauré. It was Fauré who, like their great common fore-bear J. S. Bach, possessed the secret of reconciling the needs of harmony and counterpoint in a synthesis. That synthesis remains unsurpassed and is the most lively and convincing response to the quarrel between horizontalists and verticalists that occupied French musical minds at the beginning of the twentieth century, and that today strikes us as so fatuous.

We can see the speed with which Gédalge developed his pupil's gift for polyphony by looking at the works he wrote between 1914 and 1917. But Honegger stated unequivocally that his great model was J. S. Bach, whose chorales in particular remain unsurpassed as examples of harmonic counterpoint. It is in Bach and Bach alone that we can find the counterparts of those contrapuntal marvels of his music. The Finale to *Le Roi David* is the earliest and perhaps the best-known of these marvels, but it is quite modest beside the great *quodlibets* of the coronation scene in *Jeanne d'Arc au bûcher*, of *La Danse des morts*, and of *Une Cantate de Noël*, not to mention the astonishing clockwork mechanisms of the recapitulation/stretto in the Finale of the *Fourth Symphony* or of the final chorus of *Saint François d'Assise*. Nor should we forget the didactic tour de force of the Scherzo from the *Fifth Symphony*. This is exceptional, though, in that it is perhaps the only such passage in Honegger's output in which art does not seek to conceal art.

The numerous music examples in the second part of this book make up an extraordinary anthology of the richest and most varied melodic outlines, and they could have been multiplied three or four times. In this field, Honegger's inspiration seems to have been truly inexhaustible, and it is a gift he shared with very few of his contemporaries: one thinks at once of Milhaud and Prokofiev. But it seems to me he surpasses them both in that he is not only a prodigious inventor of *melodies*, but also of *themes*, in the sense that Beethoven was. For that, it is of course essential that the musical idea be striking, memorable, and clearly and strongly defined, but it must also lend itself to development: that is to say, even when it is expanded and its intervals changed, it must still be immediately identifiable.

It may, according to the needs of its context, be condensed and concise, or it may spread itself with a surprising breadth. The exceptional power and amplitude that characterize it are complemented by the firmness of its periodic structure. It may be purely vocal in essence, and not only in the case of music that is sung: we may think of the two principal themes of the first movement of the *Fourth Symphony* (Examples 51 and 55), or of the immense arch of the *Pastorale d'été*, of which Example 80 gives only the beginning. Or it may present a less smooth, more rugged contour, more specifically instrumental in origin, like the athletic, vigorous themes of the *Symphony for Strings* (Examples 38 and 40).

A Honegger theme will often contain such a profusion of motifs that it could serve as the basis for a whole piece. Its structure remains purely classical, both on the level of the phrases (we can easily recognize antecedent, consequent, and conclusion) and on that of their individual articulation (anacrusis, accent, inflection). This is, once again, because they are based on the physiological rhythm of singing, conditioned by human breathing. For all these themes are singable, not just those written for the voice, and this is a basic reason why they stick in our memory like a physical experience. Finally, in cases that the composer himself recognized as exceptional, we find a sublime, apparently unlimited flight transcending totally the very notion of a theme. The first of these was the great central climax of the Adagio of the *String Quartet No. 1*, followed by the link between scenes 7 and 8 in *Antigone*, the "Lamento" of *La Danse des morts*, and the De profundis of the *Symphonie liturgique*. It is moments like these that remove any last doubts one might have about classing Honegger among the greatest composers of all time.

Many of these themes occur in a clearly tonal harmonic context, one that is frequently mobile, modulating, and more usually based on a dominant than on a tonic. But the atonal themes, which are no less common, etch themselves on the memory just as firmly, as much by the choice of intervals, even when these are hard to sing, as by their rhythms.

Rhythm is vital to Honegger's music and, as with the Beethoven of the *Fifth* and *Seventh Symphonies*, we find with Honegger a number of themes that strike us by their rhythm before their melody. Examples immediately come to mind from the first movements of the *First* and *Third Symphonies* (Example 30 in particular). This rhythmic variety occurs, too, in the context of a largely invariable tempo and of a measure-length that is also extremely stable. Honegger knew that the details of a varied articulation, including a number of irrational values, will stand out more clearly the more perceptible the underlying pulse, just as, in matters of pitch, "foreign notes" make their greatest impact in a harmony framework that is strictly organized, whether tonal or not. Compared with the iridescence and infinite nuances of Debussy's language, Honegger's may seem almost rough, but that was the choice of a whole generation that was alarmed by the symptoms of a language collapsing at the end of its course. What frightened Honegger more than anything, as we shall see in his rejection of serialism, was a grayness brought on by uniformity of material.

I have already said that Honegger's rhythm was essentially vocal and, more precisely, that it was based on the accentuation of the language—the French language that was his own, but that he violated in such a surprising way by putting accents on the first syllables of words and, more generally, on consonants. There are languages in which this kind of accentuation occurs naturally and affects the rhythmic style of composers who speak them: the Hungarian Bartók or the Czech Janáček. Honegger took his reform of prosody extremely seriously, and the length of his explanations in *Je suis compositeur* bears witness to the fact that he had seen it bitterly criticized and misunderstood:

> What I had to discover at all costs was a way of making the sung text *comprehensible*. . . . I therefore tried to find the right stress, especially on initial consonants, and discovered that on this point I was in clear opposition to traditional principles. Here I was glad to have the approval of Claudel, whose doctrine I did not know of at the time. The important thing in the word is not the vowel, but the consonant. This plays the role of a locomotive, dragging the complete word behind it. . . . In our time, and for dramatic declamation, the consonants project the word into the hall and make it strike. . . . My personal rule is to respect the shape of the word so as to give it its full power. . . . This system of prosody is pushed to extremes in *Antigone*. . . . In a phrase, if two or three key words are given their full value, the general sense becomes clear at once. It was a great comfort to find that I was in total agreement with Claudel on this point. The support Claudel gave me was invaluable: the thesis I was proposing was no longer a private obsession, the technique of a single composer, but the studied conviction of the greatest poet of our age. I may also call on the testimony of Paul Valéry, who also supported me. In applying my principles, I sought merely to restore to French singing its natural quality.[3]

As I have already said, Honegger must have been further confirmed in his point of view listening to the speeches of General de Gaulle, who also believed in the impact of key words. In accordance with this accentuation, the fundamental rhythm of all Honegger's music is the iambus (short-long, with the accent on the short). This characteristic goes back a long way, too: in early childhood (see Chapter 1) he had already sensed that the anacrusis did not exist, and so moved the initial accented short note to the other side of the bar line, on to the strong beat. It is curious that Beethoven came close to this procedure in his later works by his paradoxical harmonization of anacrusis, and it is significant that this did not escape the notice of Honegger, who mentions it in his conversations. The general frequency in his music of dotted rhythms and feminine endings (these last often corresponding to an appoggiatura followed by its resolution) shows the extent to which his rhythmic syntax remained conditioned by tonality. Dotted rhythms and feminine endings have, significantly, disappeared from contemporary music, or very nearly.

We may, on the other hand, be surprised to find him adopting a wholly skeptical attitude with regard to the validity of a tonal plan in the architecture of a work. It is true that in doing so in his youth he was reacting against the position of Vincent d'Indy and the Schola, for whom this tonal plan was a necessary preliminary to the composition of a work.

> I used to say to him that the dogma of tonality seemed to me an absolutely outdated notion. You might as well force a contemporary playwright to observe the unity of place found in classical tragedy: plenty of masterpieces do without it! What gives a piece of music unity is the ensemble of melodic and rhythmic correspondences, all elements that act far more powerfully on the listener than references to tonality. Not everybody has perfect pitch.[4]

In fact, unlike Vaura, Honegger himself did not have perfect pitch. The fact remains that, as our analyses have shown, most of Honegger's works, and especially those in abstract forms, follow a very definite tonal plan, whether or not he respects the classical hierarchy of tonalities. Like Bartók, he often substitutes the augmented fourth for the classical dominant. But whatever he may say, the solidity of a highly logical tonal plan contributes to the parallel solidity of his large forms—not that such plans were necessarily predetermined, the point which was no doubt the grounds for his quarrel with d'Indy.

This brings us to a consideration of Honegger's treatment of form. He was fundamentally a tonal composer, even if in the widely extended sense I have already described, and he remained faithful to the large forms based on the notion of theme and development, although usually treating them in an unusually concise fashion. What he said about the *Symphony for Strings*, in the introduction he wrote for its first performance under Paul Sacher, remains valid for his entire instrumental output:

> My general concerns with regard to this symphony also governed all my other orchestral works:
> 1) Formal rigor, suppression of the recapitulation as found in classical works, where it always produces a feeling of undue length.
> 2) Search for themes with strong enough outlines to catch the listener's attention and allow him to follow the development of the whole story.
> 3) I have not tried to find any program, any literary or philosophical basis. If this work expresses or provokes emotions, the reason for this is that they presented themselves quite naturally, since I express my thoughts only in music, and perhaps without being entirely conscious of the fact.

So we find in Honegger's music the standard forms he inherited from the classical composers: sonata form, rondo, lied, scherzo, simple *da capo*, and theme and variations (this last often in the form of a passacaglia or chaconne). The most striking and best-known modification he brought to sonata form was, of course, the reversed recapitulation, beginning with the second subject. He justified it on grounds of architectural symmetry, but this is open to several objections. First of all, since temporal and spatial perception are essentially different, visual symmetry is not necessarily experienced in the same way as acoustical symmetry. Second, a sonata exposition constitutes an entity, just as the development and recapitulation constitute others. This is vitally important for the tonal plan, but it is true that Honegger did not regard that as a priority. The fact remains that the recapitulation of the main theme (in the tonic in classical works) is a crucial psychological moment in sonata form and is felt as such. It also often coincides with the Golden Section point in the movement.

In most of Honegger's sonata movements, the second group of themes is not dealt with in the central development section, which seems to move the sonata form in the direction of a lied in five sections:

Exposition		Development (1st Group)	Reversed Recapitulation	
A	B	A	B	A

Because the recapitulation of the first group (A) comes so late and is often shortened, it gives the impression of being a coda. The result may also remind us of a preclassical binary form, and that is the case in the Finales of the last three symphonies, where the exposition is followed by a "developing recapitulation" and nothing else.

After examining pitch and rhythm, we may be considerably surprised when we turn to the two other traditional parameters of sound. In the field of dynamic nuances, Honegger sets himself apart from almost all his contemporaries by a Spartan sobriety bordering on asceticism. His dynamic indications are sparse and, in orchestral works, are often restricted to a general indication applying to the ensemble as a whole. Such abstinence takes us back to the baroque era, and in fact dynamics, apart from basic contrasts between *piano* and *forte*, are no more important in his music than they are, for example, in that of J. S. Bach.

In the same way, timbre for its own sake did not interest him any more than it did Beethoven or Magnard. He always remained faithful to the traditional practice, abandoned by most contemporary composers, of not orchestrating a work until it had been composed and worked out in the smallest detail—a self-contained stage in the creative process that was normally short and achieved without difficulty. His feeling for sound-color was certainly as refined as that of many of his contemporaries, and works such as *Sémiramis*, *Le Cantique des cantiques*, or *La Naissance des couleurs* demonstrate that a seductive orchestral sensuality was by no means beyond his powers. His habitual sobriety in this respect was therefore the result of choice, made by a composer who gave expression of feeling priority over the senses. His predilection for timbres that had been little used before, such as the saxophone, or that were entirely new, such as the ondes Martenot that he used before any of his contemporaries, shows that he was not without a sense of color. He also crusaded in his writings and conversations on behalf of enlarging the orchestra to include the above instruments, as well as saxhorns, which were normally relegated to brass bands. And he underlined his demands with a request that is the very opposite of reactionary: "Let us fight courageously against stupid routine and a false respect for traditions that are on their last legs."[5]

TWENTY-TWO

Honegger's Place in the Twentieth Century

In 1971, in the liner notes for a recording of *Le Roi David*,[1] I wrote:

> On 27 November 1955, after a long illness, Arthur Honegger died at the age of sixty-three, at the height of his fame. This fame was founded upon the enthusiasm of the general public as well as on the admiration of his colleagues, and it spread over the entire world. An abundant discography reflected this happy situation, which at that time seemed unassailable. . . . Honegger certainly had not been part of the avant-garde for many years, but the path chosen by the composers of the avant-garde was so far removed from his own that no conflict seemed possible. Pierre Boulez himself paid his respects to the older composer who had encouraged his early career, and numerous pupils seemed destined to capitalize on his legacy.
>
> Then, almost immediately after his death, a thick veil of obscurity descended upon his music, and it gradually disappeared from concerts and record catalogues. Switzerland and the Eastern bloc, it is true, remained faithful to him (Czechoslovakia especially), but in France his reputation underwent a brutal eclipse. . . . Since we are talking here of a creative artist of the first rank, it is relevant to look at the many and complex reasons for this lamentable situation, which I, for my part, am sure is no more than temporary.
>
> Was the decline in Honegger's popularity a fierce reaction against his success, stirred up by less fortunate rivals? But those rivals did not profit by the change in the situation. Was it a result of the deaths of the great interpreters of his music? But the decline in popularity had begun before the deaths of the most eminent of these, Charles Münch and Ernest Ansermet, and their followers are still alive today. Was it a change in public taste? That is easy to say, but those who organize musical life do not often consult with this public; they are, to a large extent, the opinion formers. But even so, the public shows an undimmed enthusiasm for *Le Roi David* and *Jeanne d'Arc* on the occasions, all too rare, when it is permitted to hear them. The younger generation of listeners is delighted to be discovering treasures that it has been deprived of by a very narrowly prescriptive musical establishment.
>
> It has to be said that some tiresome acolytes have done Honegger's cause considerable harm by setting him up in opposition to the avant-garde, in the name of respect for tradition. His name therefore came to symbolize some dubious positions, even certain backward-looking, aca-

621

demic tendencies that in fact have nothing to do with his music. The resulting situation is paradoxical in more than one respect. He is reproached for remaining loyal to the tonal system, whereas he often makes bold forays away from it—and no one thinks of leveling similar criticisms at Poulenc's infinitely more traditional music.

People make these charges while at the same time remaining systematically ignorant of Honegger's most advanced works. When *Horace victorieux* and *Antigone* were first written, they were in the forefront of the avant-garde of their time—together with the contemporary works of Bartók (*The Miraculous Mandarin*) and Prokofiev (the *Second Symphony* and *The Fiery Angel*). No one reproaches those two composers with having subsequently diluted their own musical styles; Honegger, on the other hand, is reproached for that very same thing—even though his counterpoint in fact remained decidedly astringent in his quartets and symphonies. In any case, he always employed the language that exactly suited the expression of the moment.

Many years have passed since I wrote those words, and as one might have expected, the situation has changed. Honegger has crossed the desert, so to speak, and emerged from this absurd state of purgatory; he has recovered the position, both in the concert hall and on disc, that he should never have lost, and which is naturally his—that is to say, a position among the very greatest composers.

As I have already said, Honegger died at one of the worst moments in musical history, and in history as a whole: at the height of both the Cold War and the serial "Ice Age." It was Marcel Landowski who first established a link between the two, and I am sure that he is right. The apostles of pure serialism shamefully averted the legacy of Schoenberg, that great spiritual and religious idealist, and turned his idea of twelve-tone music into an arbitrary system, entirely cerebral and stripped of all expressive necessity. It was presented by an intolerant, totalitarian ideology as the only possible path, legitimized by the laws of historical determinism and by the dogma of the dialectical notion of progress, as preached by the great prophet Adorno. The Stalinist communists likewise averted the legacy of Karl Marx—a philosopher and sociologist who was also impelled by indisputably humanist motives—and after his death set up the most fearful and bloody system of repressive government in human history. The *homo dodecaphonicus* and *homo sovieticus* that Landowski speaks of are parallel, aberrant products of a system "hostile to mankind" (as its former victims in the East themselves call it, now that they are free to say so). They are the wretched robots, happily stillborn, resulting from an exclusively materialist conception, deprived of the light of the Spirit: "What it is to be no longer supported!" (in the words of C. F. Ramuz).

Both systems showed a destructive hostility toward all that was different from themselves, and both ended by imploding and collapsing, to reveal, in the words of Claudel, their "worthless, empty" nature.

It is true that "real socialism" had a slightly longer, more tenacious hold on life than serial music. But then the latter did not have an army and a repressive police force at its disposal, only the pressure expertly organized by the self-proclaimed avant-garde turned Mafia.

By a traditional swing of the pendulum, the hard-line communist Old Guard has been exposed for what it really was: a reactionary group of the extreme right. Similarly, recent evolution in music—an evolution that Honegger would have greeted with joy, would have seen as compatible with his own aims, and would have been part of—has relegated the so-called sacred monsters of serial dogmatism to the status of dinosaurs. In any case, an institutionalized, empowered avant-garde is a contradiction in terms, and forfeits its avant-garde status by the very fact of giving itself that title. From the aesthetic viewpoint, Pierre Boulez—a creative artist of genius recognized unequivocally as such by Honegger and by Vaura (whose prize pupil he was)—was intelligent enough to see the situation plainly, and he opted, musically speaking, to be a Gorbachev rather than a Georges Marchais.[2] The same cannot be said of the pack of fawning dogs barking round him.

If serial music had been the subject of purely aesthetic debate (and we shall be looking at Honegger's specifically musical arguments on that question), then the consequences would not have been so devastating. Obviously, at the beginning of the 1950s it was imperative that one play the Second Viennese School, Varèse, and Messiaen. But in order to do that was it necessary to boycott Honegger, Tippett, Shostakovich, Xenakis, and Ohana? It was certainly not Honegger who politicized the debate, but rather those who succeeded in casting him, and all those who did not fall in with Adorno's Marxist pronouncements, into the dungeons.

It took seventy years for the world to convince itself that a system that forced its victims to stand in line for hours in the snow for a miserable bag of potatoes, and that also had the presumption to deprive them of their freedom in the name of some hypothetical future Golden Age, was not viable and did not work.

It took much less time for the world to convince itself that a musical system based on an abstract combination of sounding dots on a sheet of music paper, a system of "paper music" that ignored the acoustic realities of natural resonance and gave priority to the way music looked over how it sounded, was not viable and did not work. It took less time, yes, but meanwhile Honegger, who had foreseen and prophesied this demise before most other people, was dead.

Honegger's own denunciation in *Je suis compositeur* of the emptiness of the serial system rests on arguments that are in no way reactionary and in no sense bespeak a conservative or backward-looking spirit.

> This serial system prides itself on a very narrow set of rules. The dodecaphonists seem to me like convicts who, in an effort to run faster after having broken their chains, promptly attach huge iron balls to themselves. Their dogma is exactly comparable with that of academic counterpoint, but with the difference that, whereas the aim of counterpoint is to make your writing flexible and to stimulate invention by means of disciplined exercises, the principles of serialism are presented not as a means, but as an end.

> I do not believe that serialism offers the composer any possibility of self-expression, because his melodic invention is subjected to intransigent laws which shackle the free expression of his ideas. I am not in any way opposed to discipline when it is freely agreed to, or even sought out, for artistic reasons. But this discipline must make sense, and must not be arbitrary and implacable. Furthermore, the anarchic freedom of the harmony that results from the superimposed lines opens the way to the most dangerous false ideas. . . . It must not be forgotten that the listener hears music vertically, and that the most complex contrapuntal combinations lose all interest and become child's play when they can bypass any sort of discipline.[3]

Honegger goes on to denounce the suppression of modulation (which, he says, reduces musical discourse to an amorphous, undifferentiated, static gray) as well as the poverty of form. This poverty of form was in fact the reef on which serial music was finally shipwrecked. The problem of form is eluded, both in the music and in the theoretical works of this school (which sacrifices form to make room for the discussion of *material*). In fact, serial combinations produce a discourse that is unintelligible to the ear since it is incapable of recognizing the *function* of a given sound—this function is discernible at best to the eye only after a process of long and complex analysis. The ear cannot interpret a musical argument without reference to a harmonic system, whether tonal, modal, spectral, or whatever, so long as it is based on a hierarchy and a certain polarization. This is not the case with serial music, in which the weightlessness not only generates an acoustical chaos by combining and juxtaposing sounds without bothering with whether or not their harmonic ranges are compatible, but is also a factor in limiting the number of available pitch classes by suppressing enharmony.

They say you never really recognize a blind alley until you walk right to the end of it and bang your head against the wall. It is necessary then, at least for those honest and intelligent enough to recognize the situation, to retrace your steps before setting out in a new direction. There is no point regretting the fact that, in this respect as in many others, Honegger was clairvoyant, before his time, and therefore played the melancholy role of a Cassandra.

Words like the following, from *Je suis compositeur*, cannot have given pleasure to the enlightened leftists of the time, but they do confirm, forty years earlier, the frightening parallel drawn by Marcel Landowski:

> The aim of a conquest is to create more space and to abolish frontiers, not to close them more tightly still. The efforts of creative artists have always been directed at a liberation from formulas and conventions. But what contrary examples there are all round us! Demagogies evolve into an imperialism more autocratic than the one they destroyed, while dictatorships return to demagogy![4]

And one cannot think of words more prophetic than these:

I'm very much afraid that the impetus of twelve-tone music will trigger a movement toward music that is oversimple and overrudimentary. People will attempt to heal the damage done from swallowing sulfuric acid by drinking syrup. Their ears, exhausted by intervals of the ninth and seventh, will welcome accordion music and sentimental songs as the most blessed relief![5]

The promotion of Boulez's *Structures* and Stockhausen's *Zeitmasse*, to the detriment of the *Symphonie liturgique*, has led directly to Steve Reich, Philip Glass, and to the so-called new simplicity imported from Germany and Russia. Just as Honegger never turned his back on the future, he also sought to counter the destructive sterility of permanent revolution with the fruitful common sense of evolution. We can see this from the following words, again taken from *Je suis compositeur*, which in the 1950s necessarily branded Honegger as a reactionary:

The surprise factor in any discovery is soon dissipated, and one soon discerns, behind the great innovators, the masters who inspired them. . . . "There is no spontaneous generation in art," someone once said. I think that's true. A long chain links the old traditionalists to the most daring innovators. The latter noisily proclaim their contempt for the old masters in order to raise a bit of dust and cover up the shackles that are bruising their ankles.[6]

This is an echo, thirty years on, of the famous remark (cited elsewhere in this book): "It is pointless to break down doors that one can open." Among those virtues that Honegger felt he owed to Switzerland, perhaps he forgot the most important: common sense. At any rate, this passage is a direct refutation of Boulez's famous claims for "cultural amnesia," which are, as it happens, signally disproved by the entire range of Boulez's music and ideas. At Honegger's death, Boulez was not slow to offer a heartfelt homage to the older man:

While he was disturbed by the questions raised by a new generation, he bent his mind to blending this disquiet with his own experience. His goodwill, what is more, did not allow him to let himself be rebuffed by the new discoveries. . . . Honegger deserves our thanks for having given us the taste for adventure.

We can hardly be surprised that, of all Honegger's works, Boulez singled out *Horace victorieux* and *Antigone*. These, as we know, were the secret preferences of the composer himself, and of Milhaud (who also cited *Jeanne d'Arc au bûcher*). In the final analysis, Honegger was badly served, as I have already suggested, by the support of those who were too fervent in his cause. This was especially true of Bernard Gavoty, who instituted a veritable Honegger cult of the most public kind, but who was also known as a critic with no time for the avant-garde.

We can now see, with hindsight, how lucid and clairvoyant Honegger was in denouncing the inanity of serialism as well as the "simplistic cretinism" of the adherents of Zhdanov's socialist realism, while being sympathetic toward the first tentative steps of *musique concrète*. We have seen how, at the time of his death, the outlook was not very hopeful, and how there seemed almost to be no future at all for anyone who did not believe in music beyond the tempered scale of twelve semitones.

Honegger was one of the first, if not the very first, to denounce the stupid irrelevance of identifying the level of dissonance with the level of modernity, and he realized that the twelve-tone cluster was the ultimate limit of harmonic saturation. If he had lived ten years longer, he would have witnessed the barrier of the thirteenth tone broken, and beyond the barrier, he would have seen the vast reaches of a new harmony that is universally consonant in the celebration of the range of natural harmonics and in which the conventional concept of dissonance is exceeded and neutralized because the chromatic semitone is no longer the smallest interval available. Honegger's poor health may reasonably be taken as an excuse for his pessimism, but a little faith in the future might have brought to his mind the story of the young Mahler and the old Brahms strolling together in the countryside. Brahms was holding forth gloomily about the end of music, saying he was "the last of the Caesars." As they crossed a small stream, Mahler pointed to the clear, swift-flowing ripples of the water and replied: "There goes the last wave."

Epilogue

We have now reached the end of this long exploration of a man and his work: a great and lovable man, and a magnificent body of work that posterity cherishes and will continue to cherish. His music has achieved the rare miracle of speaking to the listeners of its own time and to us today, and to our children. And, as we saw in the course of the last chapter, it has regained in the liberated context of the end of this century a relevance that it seemed to have lost during the "Ice Age" that has just come to an end. What will be the position history finally accords Arthur Honegger and his music? Perhaps it is too early to tell, or perhaps the answer is not that important. He himself, with his typically Swiss, no-nonsense sense of humor, would have responded to such a question with a great guffaw of laughter. That he belongs among the "greats" of the twentieth century seems plain enough to me. But also that he was neither a Bach nor a Beethoven: as I have already said, there is no Bach or Beethoven in the twentieth century. That said, however. . . .

Once upon a time there was a great composer, well endowed with talents and good looks, whose parents were well off and encouraged him in his vocation. Thanks to a prodigious technique, he mastered every style with disconcerting ease, without ever ceasing to be himself or to have a recognizable style. Despite his success, he was always hard on himself, being conscious of both his limitations and his abilities. Spiritually, he came from the tradition of Protestantism and the chorale, and he was the great reviver of the oratorio, which had fallen on hard times. He also applied his genius to the cultivation of chamber and orchestral music. He had a feeling and a taste for works that were successful on every front, without weak patches or *longueurs*, and also for elegance, as one can see both from his manuscripts and from his dress and deportment.

His generosity and tolerance made him universally loved. He was neither a revolutionary nor a fossil, but he knew how to maintain the happy medium in a period characterized by excess and hysteria. His contemporaries saw in him the reincarnation of Johann Sebastian Bach, whom he adored and whose greatest continuator he was. But immediately after his early death, he was the target of a denigration and an ill-will that drove him into disfavor, indeed semi-oblivion, from which he did not emerge for some time. He has now emerged, however, and he is once again placed beside the greatest. His name was Felix Mendelssohn. His name was Arthur Honegger.

627

It is a striking fact that, a mere twenty years ago, such a comparison would not have been in the least flattering to Honegger, but would have amounted to classing him as a second-rate composer, almost a *petit maître*. But Mendelssohn too has recently regained the high position he ought never to have lost. It is just a question of time bringing perspective.

Sometimes, when you are at the foot of a high mountain, you are overwhelmed by its vastness. As you leave the mountain via the narrow valley that descends toward the plain, the great summit is hidden, because of the twists of the gorge, by smaller peaks that suddenly seem to be higher than the great summit. But as soon as you get down on to the plain, the summit reappears, and the farther away you go, the higher up the horizon it climbs, until finally it takes its rightful place among the family of great snow-capped peaks.

That is how I see Honegger's posthumous reputation. He was a man, with his weaknesses and his genius, with his joys and sorrows, who, like all of us, passed from the De profundis to the Alleluia, strengthening our hope and faith and helping us secure the indispensable link between the created and the Creator, the umbilical cord of our salvation,

"Because ONE is necessary."
(Paul Claudel/Arthur Honegger: *La Danse des morts*)

Brussels–Paris–Arolla, January 1990–25 July 1991
Revised and updated for the present translation, Fall 1997
S.D.G.

Chronological List of Works

After each number in the chronological order ("opus number"), which is normally preceded by an "H" for Honegger or for Halbreich, the number of the category of the work, as defined in the body of the book in Part Two, is found in parentheses. To facilitate cross-reference with the text, the works are also grouped according to the nine biographical chapters of Part One. Chronological order for the present list was determined by the final completion date of each piece or group of pieces, including the orchestration. For example, *Horace victorieux*, which was composed before *Le Roi David* but orchestrated after it, is here listed afterward. I have had to make certain exceptions to this rule, as in the case of the incidental music to *The Tempest*, for example. Honegger worked on this between 1923 and the end of 1929, but the *Prelude* and *Two Songs for Ariel*, which are its best-known parts and the only ones so far published, go back at least to 1923. There is also the case of the ballet *La Naissance des couleurs*, which was written in 1940 but not orchestrated until 1948. To have held rigidly to the general principles would have led to some absurd situations.

CHAPTER ONE

Childhood Attempts

I. (11)	*Philippa*, May–July 1903
IA. (4A)	*Overture* to *Philippa*, August 1907
II. (11)	*Sigismond*, c. 1904—Lost
III. (11)	*La Esmeralda*, 1907—Unfinished
IIIA. (4A)	*Overture* to *La Esmeralda*, 1907
IV. (10)	*Oratorio du Calvaire* (Calvary Oratorio), 1907—Lost
V. (8)	Three Early Songs, 1906–1908?—Lost
VI. (3)	*Six Early Sonatas for violin and piano*, March–July 1908

1. (1)	*Three Pieces for piano* (*Scherzo, Humoresque, Adagio*), 1909–1910
2. (4)	*Adagio for violin and piano*, c. 1910—Lost

CHAPTER TWO

3. (3)   *Sonata for violin and piano in D minor*, February–October 1912
4. (3)   *Sonata for cello and piano*, c. 1912 or 1913—Lost
5. (8)   *Two Songs* (including *Barcarolle*), 1913–1914?—Lost
6. (4)   *Trio for violin, cello, and piano in F minor* (first movement only),
              August–October 1914
7. (8)   *Four Poems for Voice and Piano*, November 1914–May 1916
8. (1)   *Toccata and Variations* for piano, May–September 1916
9. (8)   *Three Poems of Paul Fort*, August–November 1916
10. (7)   *Prelude* for *Aglavaine et Sélysette*, November–December 1916
11. (8)   *Nature morte* (Still Life), February 1917
12. (8)   *Six Poems of Apollinaire*, August 1915–March 1917
13. (4)   *Rhapsody for two flutes, clarinet, and piano in F*, April 1917
14. (1)   *Fugue and Chorale for organ*, September 1917
15. (2)   *String Quartet No. 1* in C minor, June 1913–October 1917
16. (7)   *Le Chant de Nigamon* (The Song of Nigamon), September–
              December 1917
17. (3)   *First Sonata for violin and piano in C-sharp minor* (*First Violin
              Sonata*), July 1916–February 1918

CHAPTER THREE

18. (10)   *Cantique de Pâques* (Easter Canticle), July 1918; orchestrated
              November 1922
19. (7A/13)   *Le Dit des jeux du monde*, May–November 1918
20. (11)   *La Mort de Sainte Alméenne* (The Death of Saint Alméenne),
              completed December 1918—Not orchestrated
20A. (7A)   *Interlude* from *La Mort de Sainte Alméenne*, October 1920?
21. (14)   *La Danse macabre*, March 1919—Lost
22. (4)   *Furniture Music* (Musique [Pièces] d'ameublement), March
              1919
23. (1)   *Three Pieces for piano*, November 1915 (*Hommage à Ravel*) and
              May 1919 (*Prélude* and *Danse*)
24. (3)   *Second Sonata for violin and piano in B* (*Second Violin Sonata*),
              April–November 1919
25. (1)   *Seven Short Pieces*, October 1919–January 1920
26. (1)   *Sarabande*, from the *Album des Six*, January 1920?
27. (17)   Orchestration of a Mussorgsky song, January 1920—Lost
28. (3)   *Sonata for viola and piano* (*Viola Sonata*), January–March 1920
29. (3)   *Sonatina for two violins in G major*, March–June 1920
30. (8)   *Pâques à New York* (Easter in New York), March–July 1920
31. (7)   *Pastorale d'été* (Summer Pastorale), August 1920
32. (3)   *Sonata for cello and piano in D minor* (*Cello Sonata*), June–Sep-
              tember 1920
33. (4)   *Hymne pour Dixtuor à cordes* (Hymn for Ten String Instruments
              in B minor), October 1920
34. (13)   *Vérité? Mensonge?* (Truth? Lies?), October–November 1920—
              Partly lost

35. (7A/14)	*La Noce massacrée* from *Les Mariés de la tour Eiffel*, February 1921
36. (4)	*Cadenza* (for violin solo) for the *Cinéma-Fantaisie* based on Milhaud's *Le Boeuf sur le toit*, 1920 (or before May 1921)
37. (10)	*Le Roi David* (King David), February–May 1921; reorchestrated July–August 1923
38. (7A/13)	*Horace victorieux* (Horace Triumphant), November 1920–August 1921
39. (4A/14)	*Danse de la chèvre* (The Goat Dance), November 1921?
40. (13)	*Skating Rink*, November 1921–January 1922
41. (14)	*Saül*, February–March 1922—A fragment of this is lost
42. (3)	*Sonatina for clarinet and piano* (*Clarinet Sonatina*), October 1921–July 1922

CHAPTER FOUR

43. (4)	*Three Counterpoints*, October–November 1922
43A. (1)	*Suite* from *Three Counterpoints* for piano duet, date of transcription unknown
44. (7A/16)	*Overture* from the film *La Roue* (The Wheel), November or December 1922
45. (4A/14)	*Antigone* (incidental music), December 1922
46. (13)	*Fantasio*, July–October 1922; orchestrated December 1922
47. (7)	*Chant de joie* (Song of Joy), November 1922–January 1923
48. (14)	*The Tempest* (incidental music), February 1923–end of 1929—Partly lost
48A. (7A)	*Prelude* from *The Tempest*, February 1923
48B. (8A)	*Two Songs for Ariel*, from *The Tempest*, April 1923
49. (14)	*Liluli*, March 1923
50. (9)	*Chanson de Fagus*, May 1923? (manuscript 1923–1924)
51. (8)	*Six Poems of Jean Cocteau*, May 1920–June 1923
52. (1)	*Le Cahier romand*, July 1921–July 1923
53. (7)	*Pacific 2.3.1* (*Symphonic Movement No. 1*), March–December 1923
54. (8)	*Chanson de Ronsard*, February 1924
55. (6)	*Concertino for piano and orchestra*, September–November 1924
56. (4A)	*Prelude and Blues for four chromatic harps*, 1925?—Lost
57A. (10)	*Judith* (biblical drama), December 1924–April 1925
57B. (11)	*Judith* (opera seria), November–December 1925
57C. (10)	*Judith* ("action musicale," i.e., oratorio), early 1927
58. (13)	*Sous-marine*, September 1924; orchestrated May 1925
59. (4)	*Hommage du trombone exprimant la tristesse de l'auteur absent*, June 1925
60. (14)	*L'Impératrice aux rochers* (The Empress of the Rocks), August–November 1925
60A. (7A)	*Orchestral Suite* from *L'Impératrice aux rochers*
60B. (1A)	*La Neige sur Rome* (Snow in Rome), for piano, from *L'Impératrice aux rochers*
60C. (1A)	*Suite* (*Partita*) *for two pianos*, adapted from *L'Impératrice aux rochers*, late 1928 or early 1929

61. (14)   *Phaedra*, March–April 1926
61A. (7A)   *Orchestral Suite* from *Phaedra*
62. (4A/14) *Pour le cantique de Salomon* (For the Song of Solomon), May 1926
63. (8A/14) *Three Songs of the Little Siren*, end of 1926
64. (7A/16) *Suite* from the film *Napoléon*, late 1926–early 1927
65. (11)   *Antigone*, January 1924–September 1927
66. (13)   *Roses de métal* (or *Roses en métal*), 1928 (before June)—Lost
66A. (7A)   *Blues* from *Roses de métal*, 1928?
67. (7)   *Rugby* (*Symphonic Movement No. 2*), August–September 1928
68. (13)   *Les Noces d'Amour et de Psyché* (The Wedding of Cupid and Psyche), summer–fall 1928 (perhaps dating back to late 1927)
68A. (7A)   *Suite After J. S. Bach*, from *Les Noces d'Amour et de Psyché*
68B. (7A)   *Prelude and Fugue in C Major by J. S. Bach*, from *Les Noces d'Amour et de Psyché*
69. (1)   *Hommage à Albert Roussel*, December 1928
70. (8)   *Vocalise-Étude*, 1929 (before June)
71. (13)   *Amphion*, August 1929 (probably begun earlier)
71A. (7A)   *Prelude, Fugue, Postlude* from *Amphion*, spring 1948 (before mid-May)
72. (6)   *Concerto for cello and orchestra in C major* (*Cello Concerto*), August 1929; orchestration completed November 1929
73. (4A/16) *Berceuses for Bobcisco*, December 1929
74. (4A/16) *J'avais un fidèle amant* (I Had a Faithful Lover), December 1929
75. (5)   *First Symphony*, December 1929–May 1930
76. (12)   *Les Aventures du roi Pausole* (The Adventures of King Pausolus), May 1929–November 1930
76A. (1A)   *Suite for piano*, adapted from *Les Aventures du roi Pausole*, late 1930 or early 1931
77. (10)   *Cris du monde* (Cries of the World), November or December 1930–March 1931
78. (12)   *La Belle de Moudon*, January–March 1931

CHAPTER FIVE

79. (4)   *Prelude for sub-bass and piano in C major*, February 1932
80. (3)   *Sonatina for violin and cello in E minor*, September 1932
81. (1)   *Prelude, Arioso, and Fughetta on the name BACH*, October 1932
81A. (7)   *Prelude, Arioso, and Fughetta* (transcription for string orchestra, by Arthur Hoérée), 1936?
82. (9)   *Le Grand Étang* (The Great Pool), 1932
83. (7)   *Symphonic Movement No. 3*, October 1932–January 1933

CHAPTER SIX

84. (15)   *Les Douze Coups de minuit* (The Twelve Strokes of Midnight), end of 1933
85. (13)   *Sémiramis*, May 1933; orchestrated February 1934
86. (16)   *Rapt*, February 1934

87. (16)	*L'Idée*, May 1934
88. (16)	*Les Misérables*, November 1933–summer 1934
88A. (7A)	*Orchestral Suite* from the film *Les Misérables*, 1934
89. (4)	*Petite Suite for two instruments and piano*, August 1934
90. (16)	*Cessez le feu* (Cease-fire), October 1934—Music partly lost
90A. (9A)	*Three Songs* from the film *Cessez le feu*—One song is lost
91. (16)	*Le Roi de la Camargue*, October 1934—Lost except for one piece, which is of uncertain attribution
91A. (9A)	*Two Songs* from the film *Le Roi de la Camargue*—Lost
92. (7/15)	*Radio-Panoramique*, January 1935
93. (16)	*The Demon of the Himalayas* (Der Dämon des Himalayas), October 1934–February 1935—A small fragment of this is lost
93A. (9A)	*Three Songs* from the film *The Demon of the Himalayas*, probably April 1935
94. (16)	*Crime and Punishment* (Crime et Châtiment), April 1935
95.(1)	*Berceuse* for *Le Bal des Petits Lits blancs*, June 1935
96. (13)	*Icare*, June 1935
97. (9)	*Fièvre jaune* (Yellow Fever), September or October 1935— Identical to "The Road to Mandalay" (different words)
98. (16)	*L'Équipage (Celle que j'aime)* (The Crew, or The Girl I Love), end of 1935
98A. (9A)	*Two Songs* from the film *L'Équipage (Celle que j'aime)*—One song is lost
99. (10)	*Jeanne d'Arc au bûcher* (Joan of Arc at the Stake), January–December 1935 (Prologue completed November 1944)
100. (16)	*Les Mutinés de l'Elseneur*, January 1936
100A. (9A)	*Two Songs* from the film *Les Mutinés de l'Elseneur*—One song is lost
101. (16)	*Mayerling*, February 1936
102. (7)	*Nocturne for orchestra*, March 1936
103. (2)	*String Quartet No. 2 in D*, 1934–June 1936
104. (7A/14)	*La Marche sur la Bastille* (March on the Bastille), from the show *14 Juillet*, June 1936
105. (7)	*Largo for string orchestra*, September 1936
106. (16)	*Nitchevo (L'Agonie du sous-marin)* (Nitchevo, or The Agony of the Submarine), November 1936—Orchestral score partly lost
106A. (9A)	*Two Songs* from the film *Nitchevo (L'Agonie du sous-marin)*
107. (7/14)	*Les Mille et Une Nuits* (The Thousand and One Nights), December 1936–January 1937
108. (11)	*L'Aiglon* (Acts II, III, and IV; the rest by Jacques Ibert), July 1936–January 1937
109. (16)	*Mademoiselle Docteur (Salonique, nid d'espions)*, December 1936–February 1937—A blues is missing
110. (16)	*Marthe Richard au service de la France*, February–March 1937— A very small part is lost
110A. (1A)	*Orgue dans l'église* (The Organ in the Church), from the film *Marthe Richard au service de la France*, 1910 or 1911
111. (7A/14)	*Prélude à la Mort de Jaurès*, from the show *Liberté*, April 1937— Lost
112. (16)	*Liberté* (film by J. Kemm), 1937—Lost

113. (13)   *Un Oiseau blanc s'est envolé* (A White Bird Has Flown Away), May 1937
114. (2)   *String Quartet No. 3* in E, September 1936–June 1937
115. (1)   *Scenic Railway*, summer 1937
116. (16)   *La Citadelle du silence*, July 1937—One movement is missing from the orchestral score
117. (16)   *Regain* (Aftermath), September 1937—A small portion is lost
117A. (7A)   *Orchestral Suite* from the film *Regain*
118. (9)   *Tuet's web?* (Did That Hurt?), October 1937
119. (14)   *La Construction d'une cité*, September–October 1937—Only 119A is by Honegger
119A. (9A)   *Two Songs* from *La Construction d'une cité* ("Chanson des quatre" and "Chanson de l'émigrant")
120. (9)   *Jeunesse* (Youth), October 1937
121. (16)   *Visages de la France*, October 1937—Partly lost
122. (9)   *Armistice*, November 1937
123. (13)   *Le Cantique des cantiques* (The Song of Songs), end of 1936–January 1937; orchestrated October–November 1937
124. (16)   *Miarka ou la fille à l'Ourse*, November 1937—Orchestral score lost
124A. (9A)   *Two Songs* from the film *Miarka ou la fille à l'Ourse*
125. (16)   *Passeurs d'hommes*, November 1937—Orchestral score is lost and piano reduction is partly lost
126. (16)   *Les Bâtisseurs* (The Builders), November 1937—Only 126A is by Honegger
126A. (9A)   *Hymne du Bâtiment*, from the film *Les Bâtisseurs*
127. (9)   *Three Songs by René Kerdyk*, 1935–1937—Third song is lost
128. (12)   *Les Petites Cardinal* (in collaboration with Jacques Ibert), October–December 1937
129. (16)   *Pygmalion*, June 1938—Partly lost
130. (16)   *L'Or dans la montagne (Faux Monnayeurs)* (Gold in the Mountain, or Counterfeiters), October 1938
131. (10)   *La Danse des morts* (The Dance of the Dead), July–November 1938
132. (17)   *L'Alarme*, December 1938—Lost
133. (9)   *Hommage au travail* (Homage to Work), December 1938
134. (16)   *Le Déserteur (Je t'attendrai)* (The Deserter, or I'll Wait for You), March 1939—Partly lost
135. (10)   *Nicolas de Flue*, December 1938–May 1939; reorchestrated December 1939
136. (16)   *Cavalcade d'amour*, July 1939—Lost, except for 136A
136A. (8A)   *O Salutaris*, from the film *Cavalcade d'amour*
137. (8)   *Possèdes-tu, pauvre pécheur* (Do You Possess, Poor Sinner), July 1939
138. (8)   *Three Poems of Claudel*, March 1939–January 1940
139. (1A)   *Partita for two pianos* (based on H60 and H85), January 1940
140. (15)   *Christopher Columbus*, January–February 1940
141. (17)   *Grad us* (Forward March), March 1940
142. (13)   *La Naissance des couleurs* (The Birth of Colors), May 1940; orchestrated May–June 1948

CHAPTER SEVEN

173. (1)   *Two Sketches for Piano*, April 1942 (No. 2) and October 1943 (No. 1)

174. (13)   *L'Appel de la montagne* (The Call of the Mountain), summer–October 1943; orchestrated June–July 1945

174A. (7A)   *Schwyzer Fäschttag* (Swiss Holiday), Orchestral Suite from *L'Appel de la montagne*

175. (14)   *Charles le Téméraire* (Charles the Bold), January–February 1944

176. (15)   *Battements du monde* (Heartbeats of the World), January–March 1944

177. (10)   *Selzach Passion*, sketches dated June 1938, then intermittent work from November 1940 to December 1944—Unfinished and not orchestrated; large sections reused in *Une Cantate de Noël* (H212)

178. (8)   *O Temps suspends ton vol* (O Time, halt your flight), January 1945

179. (4)   *Morceau de concours pour violon et piano* (Competition Piece for violin and piano), June 1945

180. (13)   *Chota Roustaveli* (Acts I and IV), July 1945—Orchestral score is inaccessible, in a private collection

181. (4)   *Paduana for solo cello in G major*, July 1945

182. (7)   *Sérénade à Angélique*, October 1945

183. (16)   *Un Ami viendra ce soir* (A Friend Will Arrive This Evening), July–November 1945—Orchestral score is lost

183A. (1A)   *Three Pieces* for piano from the film *Un Ami viendra ce soir*

183B. (9A)   *Chant de la Délivrance* (Song of Deliverance), from the film *Un Ami viendra ce soir*, May 1945

184. (8)   *Four Songs for Low Voice*, February 1940 (No. 2, from H140), February–March 1944 (Nos. 3 and 4), and December 1945 (No. 1)

185. (16)   *Les Démons de l'aube* (Demons of Dawn), December 1945–January 1946—Orchestral score mostly lost

186. (5)   *Third Symphony* (*Symphonie liturgique*), January 1945–April 1946

187. (14)   *Prométhée* (Prometheus), January–May 1946

188. (16)   *Un Revenant* (A Ghost), June 1946—Orchestral score partly lost

189. (13)   *Sortilèges* (Magic Spells), spring 1946—Lost

190. (14)   *Hamlet*, August–September 1946

191. (5)   *Fourth Symphony in A* (*Deliciae basilienses*), June–October 1946

192. (8)   *Mimaamaquim*, December 1946; orchestrated June 1947

193. (4)   *Intrada for trumpet and piano in B-flat major*, April 1947

194. (14)   *Oedipus* (André Obey), June 1947

CHAPTER EIGHT

195. (14)   *L'État de siège*, October 1948—Lost

196. (6)   *Concerto da camera* for flute, English horn, and strings, August–October 1948

197. (15)   *Saint François d'Assise*, end of 1948 or beginning of 1949 (before June)

198. (15)	*Marche contre la Mort* (March Against Death), summer 1949— Lost
199. (15)	*Tête d'Or* (Head of Gold), December 1949–January 1950
200. (13)	*De la musique*, first half of 1950—Lost
201. (16)	*Bourdelle*, March–May 1950
202. (5)	*Fifth Symphony* (*Di Tre Re*), August–December 1950
203. (7)	*Suite archaïque* (Archaic Suite), December 1950–January 1951
204. (7)	*Monopartita*, February–March 1951
205. (16)	*La Tour de Babel* (The Tower of Babel), May–June 1951
206. (16)	*Paul Claudel*, July 1951
207. (7)	*Toccata on a Theme of Campra*, November 1951
208. (14)	*On ne badine pas avec l'amour* (Do Not Trifle With Love), November 1951—Lost
209. (15)	*La Rédemption de François Villon*, November–December 1951
210. (14)	*Oedipe-Roi* (Thierry Maulnier), March–April 1952

CHAPTER NINE

| 211. (4) | *Romance for flute and piano*, 1952 or 1953 |
| 212. (10) | *Une Cantate de Noël* (A Christmas Cantata) (based on H177), December 1952–January 1953; orchestrated October 1953 |

UNDATABLE WORKS

213. (1)	*Très modéré* for piano
214. (4)	*Arioso for violin and piano* (late 1920s?)
215. (4A/16)	*Andante for four ondes Martenot* (early 1943?)
216. (4A/16)	*Colloque* (Conversation) for four instruments
217. (4A/14 or 16)	*Introduction and Dance for flute, harp, and string trio*
218. (7/16)	*Chevauchée*
219. (7/16)	*Pathétique*
220. (7)	*Vivace (Dance)*
221. (7/14?)	*Allegretto*
222. (8)	*La Nuit est si profonde* (The Night Is So Profound)

LOST ORCHESTRATIONS AND ARRANGEMENTS

Orchestration of Fernand Ochsé's operetta *Choucoune* (c. 1922)
Orchestration of Maurice Jaubert's *L'Eau vive* (1945?)
Arrangements for soloists, chorus, and orchestra of two popular songs: *La Femme du marin* (Aunis) and *Les Trois Princesses au pommier doux* (Franche-Comté). Recorded 1936–1937.

APPENDIX TWO

Note on Recordings

By agreement between the author and Librairie Arthème Fayard, publisher of the original French edition of this volume, in order to ensure that this book would conform with the other books in the same series, it was decided to not provide a discography. It is no doubt true that nothing becomes dated quite as quickly as a discography, and this is particularly so in the case Honegger, especially since the arrival of the compact disc. Recently there has been a heartening increase in the number of published recordings of his music—clearly a sign that his reputation is healthy, given that recording companies generally bring out music they expect to be able to sell.

Honegger's discography has always been large—some works, like *Pacific 2.3.1* and the *Symphony for Strings*, have even been recorded more than twenty times in all—but it became much sparser during the "barren" years of the 1960s and 1970s, and many older recordings have indeed never been reissued. The large number of new recordings has only partially compensated for these gaps, and some large Honegger works that used to be available are not so any longer. Others have never had the honor of being recorded. It is to be hoped that such gaps will soon be filled.

Meanwhile, most of Honegger's major works are well represented in the catalogs. His chamber music is there complete, and his best-known oratorios, his symphonies, and his other large pieces of orchestral music are, with rare exceptions, even available in several excellent versions. Recent interpretations aside, important classic versions by artists such as Charles Münch, Ernest Ansermet, and Herbert von Karajan have sensibly been brought out on compact disc, with an improvement in quality that is sometimes startling.

The same has been done with some of the all-too-few recordings of the composer conducting his own music. These recordings are revelations in terms of the quite amazing energy they display, and it is to be hoped that we shall soon have access to everything that survives in this field. This hope applies equally to the rare recordings of Claire Croiza's exceptional voice, both as singer and actress. They are a lesson in vocal technique, in diction, in beauty, in nobility, and in emotion. Then there is the long conversation between Honegger, Paul Claudel, and Bernard Gavoty on *Jeanne d'Arc au bûcher*. This is a fabulous document (what beautiful French they all speak!) and it should be reissued. There are other recordings of the same kind, which should also be brought out.

Notes

The correspondence and diaries of Arthur Honegger and his wife Andrée Vaurabourg are unpublished and are held at the Paul Sacher Foundation in Basel. Honegger's notebooks are also unpublished, and they are held at the Bibliothèque nationale in Paris (MS. 17690). It has therefore generally not been possible to provide references for these sources in the notes. The author provides a detailed discussion of his use of sources in the bibliography.

Honegger's important autobiographical work, *Je suis compositeur*, to which the author frequently refers throughout this book, is no longer in print. The following notes refer to the pagination of Honegger's collected writings, *Écrits* (1992), in which the full text of *Je suis compositeur* is included.

A complete English translation of *Je suis compositeur* was published in 1966 under the title *I Am a Composer* (London: Faber). In the present work, however, all translations of quoted passages from *Je suis compositeur* are by Roger Nichols.

Many of the remarks attributed to Paul Claudel are reproduced courtesy of the Société Paul Claudel in Paris and the Paul Sacher Foundation. Letters written by Arthur Honegger to Darius Milhaud are quoted courtesy of the Paul Sacher Foundation and Madeleine Milhaud.

—Ed.

Part One: Chronicle of a Life

CHAPTER 1

1. Apart from the subject of the present volume, several Honeggers have made names for themselves in the musical life of the twentieth century, including the cellist Henry, a longtime member of the Suisse Romande Orchestra; the violinist Blanche, wife of the flutist Marcel Moyse; and the eminent musicologist Marc, author of one of the best French musical encyclopedias. None, however, is related to the composer.

Curiously, the name Honegger is an exact synonym for the name of another composer, from a rather different time and place, Roland de Lassus (1532–1594). The Walloons of Lassus's native Belgian province of Hainaut do not pronounce the final *s* of the name Lassus. His name, therefore, sounds very similar to the Italian *di lassù*, which literally means "from up there"; however, the Italians committed a serious mistake in calling him di Lasso, rather than di Lassù!

2. Hélène Jourdan-Morhange 1955, *Mes amis musiciens* (Paris: Les Éditeurs français réunis).
3. Honegger 1966, 125.
4. Honegger 1992.
5. Fifteen years later, Caplet's masterpiece, *Le Miroir de Jésus*, would be a vibrant, if sadly unacknowledged, link between *The Martyrdom of Saint Sebastian* of Debussy, whose disciple and assistant he was, and Messiaen's *Trois Petites Liturgies de la Présence Divine*.
6. Joseph Delteil 1990, *Le Musée de Marine*, 2nd ed. (Collot/Le Temps qui Passe).
7. Honegger 1992, 689.
8. Quoted in Bruyr 1947.
9. Honegger 1992, 636.
10. *Ibid.*

CHAPTER 2

1. Honegger 1992, 691.
2. Darius Milhaud interviewed in *Le Figaro*, 4 May 1962.
3. *Ibid.*
4. Quoted in George 1926.
5. Milhaud interviewed in *Le Figaro*, 4 May 1962.
6. Letter from Arthur Honegger to Arthur and Julie Honegger, 25 February 1915.
7. Arthur Honegger to Arthur and Julie Honegger, 17 March 1915.
8. Éveline Hurard-Viltard 1987, *Le Groupe des Six, ou le matin d'un jour de fête* (Paris: Méridiens/Klincksieck).
9. Jourdan-Morhange, *op cit.*, 1955.
10. Milhaud interviewed in *Le Figaro*, 4 May 1962.
11. *Ibid.*
12. Arthur Honegger to Arthur and Julie Honegger, undated (probably October 1915).
13. Illian Alvarez de Toledo, Marquis of Casa Fuerte, was a Spanish nobleman well-known in Parisian artistic and social circles, and a great lover of music.
14. Arthur Honegger 1951, "Souvenirs sur la classe de Vincent d'Indy au Conservatoire," *La Revue internationale de musique* 10 (Spring/Summer): 345.
15. Quoted by Lucienne Delforge in *La France Socialiste*, 31 August 1942.
16. Delannoy 1986.
17. Milhaud interviewed in *Le Figaro*, 4 May 1962.
18. Delannoy 1986.
19. Arthur Honegger to Arthur and Julie Honegger, 6 November 1916.
20. Arthur Honegger to Arthur and Julie Honegger, 30 October 1916.
21. Arthur Honegger to Arthur and Julie Honegger, undated (probably November 1916).
22. Arthur Honegger to Arthur and Julie Honegger, 23 December 1916.
23. Quoted in Delannoy 1986.

24. Arthur Honegger to Arthur and Julie Honegger, undated.
25. Francis Poulenc 1978, *My Friends and Myself*, trans. James Harding (London: Dobson); originally published in 1963 in French as *Moi et mes Amis*, ed. Stéphane Audel (Paris: La Palatine).
26. Arthur Honegger to Arthur and Julie Honegger, June 1917.
27. *Ibid.*
28. Hurard-Viltard, *op. cit.*, 1987.
29. Jean Cocteau 1920, *Carte blanche* (Paris: Éditions de la Sirène).
30. Quoted in Hurard-Viltard, *op. cit.*, 1987.
31. Jourdan-Morhange, *op. cit.*, 1955.
32. Hurard-Viltard, *op. cit.*, 1987.
33. Delannoy 1986.
34. Honegger 1992, 692.
35. Arthur Honegger to Arthur and Julie Honegger, 19 December 1917.
36. Arthur Honegger to Arthur and Julie Honegger, arrived 30 December 1917.
37. Quoted in Delannoy 1986.
38. Hurard-Viltard, *op. cit.*, 1987.
39. Arthur Honegger to Arthur and Julie Honegger, 27 January 1918.
40. Arthur Honegger to Arthur and Julie Honegger, 13 June 1918.

CHAPTER 3

1. Arthur Honegger to Arthur and Julie Honegger, 24 December 1918.
2. Arthur Honegger to Arthur and Julie Honegger, 29 March 1919.
3. This work is mentioned under the title of *Entrée, Nocturne et Berceuse* in a typed catalog of Honegger's works that ends with the year 1941.
4. Hurard-Viltard, *op. cit.*, 1987.
5. Arthur Honegger to Arthur and Julie Honegger, 23 January 1920.
6. Arthur Honegger to Arthur and Julie Honegger, 27 October 1920.
7. Éveline Hurard-Viltard (1987) states that "Souvenir d'enfance," the third of the Cocteau poems, was sung for the first time at this concert. I have, however, been unable to verify this.
8. Arthur Honegger to Arthur and Julie Honegger, 11 December 1920.
9. Notably in Meylan 1970, in interviews with Gavoty in the *Journal musical français*, and by numerous other biographers of Honegger, including Bruyr 1947, Delannoy 1986, and W. Tappolet 1957.
10. Bruyr 1947.
11. Georges Duplain 1988, *L'Homme aux mains d'or* (Lausanne: Éditions 24 Heures).
12. Quoted in Claude Tappolet 1989, *Lettres de compositeurs suisses à Ernest Ansermet* (Geneva: Georg).
13. Honegger 1992, 704.
14. Honegger 1992, 150.
15. Bernard Gavoty has suggested that it was 27 March, but it was probably at least a week later.
16. Arthur Honegger to Julie Honegger, 8 May 1921.
17. Honegger 1992, 704.
18. Arthur Honegger to Arthur and Julie Honegger, 4 October 1921.
19. Arthur Honegger to Arthur and Julie Honegger, 27 October 1921.

20. Quoted in Bruyr 1947.
21. Paul Sacher has told me he thinks this must be none other than Paul Collaer, but Collaer's profound admiration for Milhaud, to whom he would devote a huge monograph, makes that difficult to believe.
22. Arthur Honegger to his father, Arthur Honegger, 12 March 1922.

CHAPTER 4

1. Henri Hell 1978, *Francis Poulenc* (Paris: Fayard).
2. Delannoy 1986.
3. *Ibid.*
4. Quoted in C. Tappolet, *op. cit.*, 1989.
5. Paul Sacher Foundation, Basel.
6. Delannoy 1986.
7. Arthur Honegger to Aloys Mooser, undated. Courtesy Bibliothèque publique et universitaire, Geneva.
8. One of these portraits shows the composer sitting in a chaise longue. It is now in Paul Claudel's study at his summer house at Brangues, in the Isère department of southeastern France.
9. Spratt (1987) incorrectly dates this performance as 6 February 1926.
10. *Voix de son Maître* GL 668.
11. Pierre Meylan 1966, *René Morax et Arthur Honegger au Théâtre du Jorat* (Lausanne: Éditions du cervin); 2nd. ed. 1993 (Geneva: Éditions Slatkine).
12. *Ibid.*
13. W. Tappolet 1957.
14. Paul Bertrand 1925, review of *Judith* in *Le Ménestrel* 34: 121.
15. René Morax to Werner Reinhart, 31 December 1925.
16. Arthur Honegger to Ernest Ansermet, 12 January 1926.
17. Fiume, the Italian name for the port of Rijeka, was long disputed by Italy and Yugoslavia. In 1919, a band of volunteers, led by d'Annunzio, captured the town for Italy.
18. Delannoy 1986.
19. This score was long thought lost, but I managed to find a copy in the music library of Radio-France.
20. Honegger 1992, 705.
21. Werner Reinhart to René Morax, 10 June 1927.
22. In fact, Essen was not able to put on *Antigone* until the beginning of February, just after the Brussels performance.
23. Arthur Honegger to René Morax, undated.
24. Arthur Honegger interviewed in *Paris-Soir* by Carol Bérard, 20 April 1928.
25. According to Meylan 1993, Honegger that evening conducted a performance of *Judith*, featuring Claire Croiza in the title role and Ida Rubinstein as narrator. I have been unable to find any trace of this. Vaura's diary does, however, mention that the composer was present that evening at a concert given by the Caecilia Chorale of Antwerp, conducted by Louis de Vocht, which included Milhaud's *Les Choéphores* and the "Processional" from his *Eumenides*, and in which Claire Croiza took part. Clearly, there is some confusion here.
26. This concert hall, which has since disappeared, was located at 15 avenue Hoche. The ballet was repeated on 5 and 6 June.

27. Paul Sacher's role in cultural diffusion has been similarly beneficial and effective. Over more than sixty years since 1926, his Basel Chamber Orchestra (BKO) has created a loyal audience very different from that which attends traditional concerts, and Sacher has turned that audience into one of the best educated anywhere, especially with regard to the music of the twentieth century. It is true that he has had an infallible instinct for choosing "his" composers from among the greatest. If today Basel is one of the cities most receptive to modern music in the whole world, with proportionately far larger audiences than Paris (Basel is, after all, a city of barely 200,000 inhabitants), the reason is that the good seed sown with such perseverance by Paul Sacher has yielded a superb harvest. His activity continues today, thanks to a foundation, superbly located next to Basel Cathedral overlooking the Rhine, that houses one of the richest collections in the world of musical manuscripts, letters, and other documents relating to the music of the twentieth century.

28. Only since December, according to Madeleine Potier's article in *Comoedia*, 27 May 1931.

29. Honegger 1992, 707.

30. According to Pierre Meylan (1993), Honegger was in a thoroughly bad temper, wanting apparently to give the part of the "Belle" to Claire Croiza. It is hard to imagine her in such a character role.

CHAPTER 5

1. Arthur Honegger, unpublished autobiographical sketch, undated. Courtesy of Pascale Honegger.

CHAPTER 6

1. Peter Sulzer 1980, *Zehn Komponisten um Werner Reinhart*, vol. 2 (Winterthur: Stadtbibliothek).

2. Pascal Lecroart and Huguette Calmel 1993, *Jeanne d'Arc au bûcher de Paul Claudel et Arthur Honegger* (Paris: Publimuses).

3. Honegger 1992, 332.

4. Richard Wagner to Franz Liszt, cited in the introduction to the score of Hector Berlioz's *Romeo and Juliet* (Breitkopf).

5. Paul Sacher to Arthur Honegger, 31 October 1936.

6. G. K. Spratt (1987) seems to be in error in mentioning, for the date 1 May in the same theater, the first performance of an interlude from music Honegger composed for a film by Jean Kemm, also called *Liberté*, which tells the life story of the sculptor Bartholdi, whose work included the Belfort Lion and the Statue of Liberty. Even if this music is mentioned in the list drawn up by Arthur Hoérée of his collaborations with Honegger, it does not appear in the list made by the composer himself, which is in other respects very complete. No trace of the score can now be found and the film no longer exists, so the whole business remains something of a mystery. The *Prélude à la Mort de Jaurès* has also disappeared.

7. Denis de Rougemont interviewed on Radio-Cité, Geneva, 2 December 1984.

8. Arthur Honegger to Paul Sacher, 26 December 1939.

CHAPTER 7

1. Quoted in Maillard and Nahoum 1974, 55.
2. Fritz Piersig, who was the Paris music officer for the Department of Propaganda, and who held the rank of non-commissioned officer.
3. Spratt (1987) incorrectly gives the date of 18 September.
4. Lecroart and Calmel, *op. cit.*, 1993.
5. Fred K. Prieberg 1982, *Musik im NS Staat* (Music Under the Nazi Regime) (Frankfurt: Fischer Taschenbuch Verlag).
6. René Morax to Werner Reinhart, 9 June 1942.
7. Pascale Honegger, from a conversation with the author.
8. Delannoy 1986.
9. Contrary to the claim by Claude Tappolet, Honegger did not begin teaching at the École normale until November 1946.
10. Arthur Honegger 1948, "La symphonie liturgique d'Arthur Honegger," *La Revue des jeunesses musicales de France* 4: 2–10, quoted in Honegger 1992, 254.
11. Jean-Louis Barrault to Arthur Honegger, 10 February 1946.
12. Arthur Honegger to Paul Sacher, postcards sent on 22 February 1946.
13. *Ibid.*
14. The premiere took place on 14 May. It would be given in London for the first time on 1 July.
15. A recording of the performance of 12 December is in the archives of the National Audiovisual Institute (INA) in Paris.
16. Quoted in Delannoy 1986.

CHAPTER 8

1. Arthur Hoérée 1979, "Latinisme et Germanisme chez Arthur Honegger," *Bulletin de la Classe des Beaux-Arts* 5, vol. 16: 92–93. Hoérée recalls Honegger's famous reply to a journalist who was concerned at his prodigious consumption of chocolate cakes: "Don't worry! With me they're entirely transformed into music!"
2. The premiere took place on 28 October 1948. The score cannot now be found, although there is a recording in the archives of the National Audiovisual Institute (INA) in Paris.
3. Arthur Honegger to Paul Sacher, 18 November 1948.
4. INA archives.
5. Arthur Honegger to Paul Sacher, 7 April 1950.
6. Delannoy 1986.
7. Koussevitzky would not, in fact, do so; he died on 4 June at the age of seventy-seven. Münch conducted in his place.
8. Paul Sacher to Arthur Honegger, 4 May 1951.
9. Ernest Ansermet to Arthur Honegger, 5 October 1951.
10. Paul Sacher to Arthur Honegger, 23 October 1951.
11. We may note in passing that the excellent baritone Diego Ochsenbein shortly afterward changed his name to the somewhat less edible one of Derrik Olsen!
12. Arthur Honegger to Paul Sacher, 27 December 1951.

CHAPTER 9

1. *Birchermüesli*, a mixture of cereal, dried fruit, and yogurt, was invented by Dr. Bircher as a curative meal for his patients. Nowadays it is a popular meal throughout Switzerland and elsewhere.
2. Feschotte 1966.

Part Two: Inventory of Works

INTRODUCTION

1. Halbreich 1994.

CHAPTER 10

1. Frédéric Robert 1968, *Louis Durey l'aîné des six* (Paris: Les Éditeurs Français Réunis).
2. W. Tappolet 1957.
3. Spratt 1987.
4. Arthur Honegger interviewed in *La Victoire* by Paul Landormy, 20 September 1920.
5. W. Tappolet 1957.
6. Arthur Honegger interviewed in *La Victoire* by Paul Landormy, 20 September 1920.
7. Honegger 1948. See also Honegger 1992.
8. Bruyr 1947.
9. Delannoy 1986.
10. Bruyr 1947.
11. *Ibid.*
12. W. Tappolet 1957.
13. Bruyr 1947.
14. *Ibid.*

CHAPTER 11

1. Arthur Honegger 1948, "La symphonie liturgique d'Arthur Honegger," *La Revue des jeunesses musicales de France* 4 (15 February): 2–10, quoted in Honegger 1992, 254.
2. Honegger 1992, 250–252.
3. Arthur Honegger 1947, "Symphony No. 4: Deliciae basilienses," *Newsletter of the Basel Chamber Orchestra (BKO)* 18 (10 January), quoted in Honegger 1992, 235–236.
4. Honegger 1992, 727.
5. Arthur Honegger 1952, "Fifth Symphony: Di Tre Re," *Newsletter of the Basel Chamber Orchestra (BKO)* 44 (8 March), quoted in Honegger 1992, 280–281.

6. Honegger 1992, 724.
7. Delannoy 1986.
8. Arthur Honegger to Aloys Mooser, undated. Courtesy of Bibliothèque publique et universitaire, Geneva. Also cited in Arthur Hoérée 1927, "Arthur Honegger et les locomotives," *La Revue Pleyel* (August): 349.
9. Arthur Honegger to Aloys Mooser, undated. Courtesy of Bibliothèque publique et universitaire, Geneva.
10. Honegger 1992, 700.
11. *Ibid.*
12. Exact original source uncertain, but see Arthur Honegger 1931, "Pour prendre congé," *Plans* 7 (July): 43–46, and Honegger 1992, 111–116.
13. W. Tappolet 1957.
14. *Ibid.*

CHAPTER 12

1. Honegger 1992, 680–681.
2. Honegger 1992, 699.
3. W. Tappolet 1957.
4. Lecroart and Calmel, *op. cit.*, 1993.
5. Honegger 1992, 331 and 699.
6. For Claudel sources, see the introduction to the Notes; see also Honegger 1992, 331–334.
7. W. Tappolet 1957.
8. Landowski 1978.
9. Bruyr 1947.
10. Honegger 1992, 708.
11. Delannoy 1986.

CHAPTER 13

1. W. Tappolet 1957.
2. Honegger 1992, 203.
3. Honegger 1992, 209.

Part Three: Gathering the Threads

CHAPTER 15

1. Honegger 1992, 165.
2. Honegger notebook, courtesy the Paul Sacher Foundation, Basel.

CHAPTER 16

1. Honegger 1992, 688–689.
2. As a final gloss I should add that while it was Switzerland that gave me the opportunity to write the present volume by giving me the commission, it was France that published it.

CHAPTER 17

1. Arthur Honegger 1931, "Pour prendre congé," *Plans* 7 (July): 43–46, quoted in Honegger 1992, 111–116.
2. Arthur Honegger 1931, "Du cinéma sonore à la musique réelle," *Plans* 1 (January): 74–79, quoted in Honegger 1992, 105–111.
3. Quoted in Delannoy 1986.
4. Honegger 1992, 688.
5. Bohuslav Martinů, quoted in Bernard Gavoty's *For or Against Modern Music* (Paris: Flammarion, 1957).
6. Arthur Honegger 1945, "Music and Liberation," *Labyrinthe* (15 February).
7. Arthur Honegger, September 1952, speech to UNESCO in Venice.
8. Honegger 1992, 620.

CHAPTER 18

1. Denis de Rougemont interviewed on Radio-Cité, Geneva, 2 December 1984.
2. From a 1950 recording entitled "Arthur Honegger vous parle," Series *Disque Festival: Leur oeuvre et leur voix* (Their Works and Their Voices), quoted in Honegger 1992, 275–278.
3. Honegger 1992, 275.
4. Pascale Honegger was in fact eventually baptized, but not out of any ideological principles. The baptism took place when she was already a schoolgirl and at her own request—so that she could wear a pretty communion dress like her friends at the religious school (to which her parents had sent her, both for convenience and because it was a good school).

CHAPTER 19

1. Honegger 1992, 674.
2. Arthur Honegger 1946, "Paul Claudel Créateur musical," *XXème Siècle* 26 (11 April): 1, 7, quoted in Honegger 1992, 203–207, 710.
3. Honegger 1992, 710.
4. See Honegger 1992.
5. These writings are also now available in Honegger 1992.
6. Honegger 1992, 204.
7. Honegger 1992, 691.
8. *Ibid.*
9. Serge Moreux 1949, *Belá Bartók: sa vie, ses oeuvres, son langage*, with preface by Arthur Honegger (Paris: Richard Masse Éditeurs); 2nd ed. 1955.

10. Quoted in Delannoy 1986.
11. Arthur Honegger 1955, "En lisant les *Souvenirs* de Georges Enesco," *Le Figaro littéraire* (19 March), quoted in Honegger 1992, 323–326.

CHAPTER 20

1. Honegger 1992, 692.
2. Feschotte 1966.
3. Honegger 1992, 678–679.
4. Arthur Honegger interviewed in *La Victoire* by Paul Landormy, 20 September 1920.
5. Honegger 1992, 683.
6. Honegger 1992, 722.
7. Honegger 1992, 674.
8. Honegger 1992, 680.
9. Honegger 1992, 684.
10. Honegger 1992, 682.
11. Honegger 1992, 670.
12. Honegger 1992, 675.
13. Honegger 1992, 679.
14. Arthur Honegger 1931, "Pour prendre congé," *Plans* 7 (July): 43–46, quoted in Honegger 1992, 111–116.

CHAPTER 21

1. Honegger 1992, 712.
2. Honegger 1992.
3. *Ibid.*
4. Honegger 1992, 682.
5. Honegger 1992, 659.

CHAPTER 22

1. Arthur Honegger, *Le Roi David*, Instrumental Ensemble and Soloists, Charles Dutoit, Erato 2292-45800-2.
2. Georges Marchais was the leader of the French Communist Party (PCF) from 1972 to 1994. Under his leadership, the party took an increasingly hard, pro-Moscow line.
3. Honegger 1992, 716.
4. Honegger 1992, 717.
5. *Ibid.*
6. Honegger 1992, 722.

Selected Bibliography

A complete bibliography of all writings devoted to Arthur Honegger lies far beyond the scope of the present volume, as it would have to include countless articles and studies from newspapers, journals, and reviews, not to mention thousands of critiques, notices, and interviews. A comprehensive list, updated to late 1986, can be found in the large work by Geoffrey K. Spratt, *The Music of Arthur Honegger*. The following bibliography includes only works devoted entirely to Honegger or written by Honegger himself.

WORKS DEVOTED ENTIRELY TO HONEGGER

Bruyr, José. 1947. *Arthur Honegger et son oeuvre*. Paris: Corréa.

Delannoy, Marcel. 1986. *Arthur Honegger*. 2nd ed. (including catalog of Honegger's works by Spratt). Geneva: Éditions Slatkine. Original edition, Paris: Pierre Horay, 1953.

Feschotte, Jacques. 1966. *Arthur Honegger*. Paris: Seghers.

von Fischer, Kurt. 1978. Arthur Honegger. In *Neujahrsblatt der Allgemeinen Musikgesellschaft, auf das Jahr 1978*. Zurich: Hug.

Gauthier, André. 1957. *Arthur Honegger*. Lyons: EISE.

George, André. 1926. *Arthur Honegger*. Paris: Aveline.

Gérard, Claude. 1945. Arthur Honegger. In *Nouvelle Revue de Belgique*. Brussels.

Guilbert, Yves. 1959. *Arthur Honegger*. Paris: Apostolat de la Presse.

Halbreich, Harry. 1992. *Arthur Honegger: Un musicien dans la cité des hommes*. Paris: Librairie Arthème Fayard.

———. 1994. *L'Oeuvre d'Arthur Honegger, Chronologie, Catalogue raisonné, Analyse complète, Étude du langage et du style, Discographie critiques*. Paris: Honoré Champion.

———. 1995. *Honegger. Les Grands Suisses* Series. Geneva: Éditions Slatkine.

Landowski, Marcel. 1978. *Arthur Honegger*. 2nd ed. Paris: Éditions du Seuil. Original edition, 1957.

Maillard, Jean, and J. Nahoum. 1974. *Les Symphonies d'Arthur Honegger*. Paris: Leduc.

Matter, Jean. 1956. *Arthur Honegger, ou la quête de joie*. Lausanne: Foetisch.

Meylan, Pierre. 1993. *René Morax et Arthur Honegger au Théâtre du Jorat*. 2nd ed. Geneva: Slatkine Reprints. Original edition, Lausanne: Éditions du Cervin, 1957.

———. 1970. *Arthur Honegger, Humanitäre Botschaft der Musik*. Frauenfeld-Stuttgart: Huber.

Pavcinsky, Sergej. 1972. *The Symphonies of Arthur Honegger*. Moscow: Sovietsky Kompozitor (in Russian).

Rappoport, Lidya. 1967. *Arthur Honegger*. St. Petersburg: Muzyka (in Russian).

Roland-Manuel. 1925. *Arthur Honegger*. Paris: Éditions Maurice Senart.

Spratt, Geoffrey K. 1987. *The Music of Arthur Honegger*. Cork, Republic of Ireland: University Press.

Sysoeva, Elena. 1975. *Simfonii A. Honeggara*. Moscow: Muzyka (in Russian).

Szöllösy, Andras. 1980. *Arthur Honegger*. 2nd ed. Budapest: Gondolat (in Hungarian).

Tappolet, Willy. 1938. *Arthur Honegger*. Translated into French by Hélène Breuleux. Neuchâtel, France: La Baconnière. Original German edition, Zurich: Hug, 1933.

———. 1957. *Arthur Honegger*. Translated into French by Claude Tappolet. Neuchâtel, France: La Baconnière. Original German edition, Zurich: Atlantis, 1954.

Voss, Hans-Dieter. 1983. *Arthur Honegger: Le Roi David*. Munich/Salzburg: Katzbichler.

WRITINGS BY ARTHUR HONEGGER

1948. *Incantation aux fossiles*. Lausanne: Éditions d'Ouchy. Published in a German translation under the title *Beschwörungen*, Bern: Scherz, 1955.

1957. *Arthur Honegger, Nachklang, Schriften, Photos, Dokumente*. Edited by Willi Reich. Zurich: Arche.

1966. *I Am a Composer*. Translated by Wilson O. Clough. London: Faber. Original French edition, *Je suis compositeur*, Series *Mon métier* (My Profession), Paris: Éditions du Conquistador, 1951.

1975. *Liste des oeuvres* (List of Works). Zurich: Archives Musicales Suisses.

1979. *O muzykal'nom iskusstve*. St. Petersburg: Muzyka.

1980. *Beruf und Handwerk des Komponisten: Illusionslose Gespräche, Kritiken, Aufsätze*. Translated by Eberhardt Klemm. Leipzig: Reclam. (This is a German translation of *Incantation aux fossiles* and *Je suis compositeur*.)

1992. *Écrits*. Edited by Huguette Calmel. Paris: Honoré Champion.

As can be seen from the above list, the present volume follows on the heels of some two dozen other works, most of which have long been out of print. After the early studies by Roland-Manuel and André George, and the first of the two books by Willy Tappolet, the first book of real value is that written by José Bruyr. Despite quite a few inaccuracies and unwarranted statements, it is nonetheless valuable for its brisk, lively, poetic style and for the mass of information it contains on rare works, such as the ballets, incidental music, and so on, which are not mentioned by any other author. Marcel Delannoy's book, which was recently reissued, is more reliable but less complete, and interesting mainly as the personal, and sometimes highly subjective, record of someone who knew Honegger well. It may still be highly recommended.

Willy Tappolet's second book, although well-meaning and very German in its seriousness and thoroughness, roused Honegger to fury, both because of its numerous errors and because of Tappolet's ignorance of the period and the milieu, especially the period of Les Six. Even though the French translation is not always very happy, it remained the most complete study until the appearance of the monumental work by Geoffrey K. Spratt. Within the limits imposed by the format of their respective series, the little monographs by Marcel Landowski and by Jacques Feschotte (the latter unfortunately now out of print) are excellent introductory works, showing great enthusiasm and understanding of the subject.

Among more specialized volumes, I must mention the masterly analysis by Jean Maillard and Jacques Nahoum of the symphonies, the fascinating book by Pierre Meylan on Morax and the Théâtre du Jorat (a work that is full of vital information unavailable elsewhere), and the very detailed monograph on *Le Roi David* by Hans-Dieter Voss, which deserves to be translated.

Which brings me to the enormous work by Geoffrey K. Spratt. This is the largest volume on the subject before the present one, for which it has frequently served as a research base, especially for the catalog of works. The catalog included in the present book can be thought of as "a Spratt revised, corrected, and amplified," while Spratt's second version of his Honegger catalog is already very much more complete than the one included in the reissue of Delannoy's book. I have done no more than continue along the same road, without imagining that my own work is definitive. As for the body of Spratt's long book (650 pages, including a large number of musical examples), it retains its original character of a university thesis. There is no biographical section, but the analyses are very detailed (if extremely abstract and theoretical) and concern mainly the oratorios and stage works that were the initial subject of his thesis. There are, however, surprising omissions—for instance, there is nothing on *Horace victorieux*. It is therefore more than anything a book for specialists, but I freely acknowledge that it has never left my table during the writing of the present work.

Finally, I would like to mention a publication of primary importance: the *Écrits*. A collection of all Honegger's writings, brought together and edited by Huguette Calmel, it includes, among other things, the two books *Incantation aux fossiles* and *Je suis compositeur*, which, though well-known, have been out of print for a long time. But these make up a good deal less than half of this fascinating and indispensable volume. A task for the future must be the publication of Honegger's huge body of correspondence, of which a foretaste has been given through the many quotations in the biographical section of this book. But that would be a mammoth undertaking indeed.

Index of Names

The names Arthur Honegger and Andrée Vaurabourg do not appear in this index.